a handbook
of
comparative
librarianship

a handbook of comparative librarianship

THIRD EDITION REVISED AND ENLARGED

M MACKEE LèsL ALA

CLIVE BINGLEY LONDON

First published 1970
Second edition published 1975
This third, revised and enlarged edition published 1983 by Clive Bingley Limited, 16 Pembridge Road, London W11 3HL and printed in England by Redwood Burn Limited, Trowbridge, Wiltshire.

British Library Cataloguing in Publication Data

MacKee, Monique
A handbook of comparative librarianship — 3rd ed.
1. Comparative librarianship — Bibliography
I. Title II. Simsova, Sylva. Handbook of comparative librarianship
020 Z665

ISBN 0-85157-348-7

Typeset by Bookmag, Henderson Road, Inverness, in 9 on 10 point Times

CONTENTS

INTRODUCTION TO THE THIRD EDITION

A handbook of comparative librarianship first appeared in 1970, with a second edition in 1975. It included two parts: 'Comparative librarianship and comparative method' by S Simsova, and 'Guide to sources' by M MacKee

Since then, comparative librarianship has become accepted as a teaching method and a research approach. The two parts of the handbook were geared to those complementary but different needs. For that reason and because of the considerable increase of the literature dealing with the subject, it was felt that it would now be more useful to publish the two parts as separate works. The first part has already appeared as *A primer of comparative librarianship* by S Simsova (Bingley, 1982), and this volume is the second part of the earlier editions, revised and updated.

It seems useful to emphasize once more that this handbook is not meant in any way to fulfil the functions of a comprehensive directory of librarianship around the world. It is intended primarily as a research guide. As such it aims at facilitating the initial identification of the sources available at the international, regional or national level; at introducing a country's librarianship in its historical, geographical and social perspectives; at presenting it in a light as objective as possible by balancing international sources against local ones and offering a variety of viewpoints. It is hoped that this guide will offer its users enough incentive for further research without suppressing the need for exploration and personal achievement.

The preparation of this edition, with the extensive revisions necessary in order not only to update it but at the same time to keep it within manageable limits, has involved considerable time spent in consulting and sifting sources, restructuring the literature on every country and preparing the manuscript. The compiler is therefore most grateful for the help received from Patricia MacKee in gathering sources and from Margaret Blackburn in preparing the typescript. It goes without saying that any deficiency or error remains the sole responsibility of the compiler.

Monique MacKee
August 1982

HOW TO USE THIS GUIDE

Scope and coverage
The aim behind the selection of sources has been to give an idea of the general structure and of the particular features of librarianship in a given country, to show the events and conditions which have contributed to its present condition, and to indicate the direction in which it might develop.

The revisions for this edition have been extensive in the cases of the better documented countries. Only a few main landmarks of the literature have been kept and the other references replaced by similar ones more recently published. It has been very difficult at times to select amongst equally interesting works, but the bibliographical sources should alleviate these necessary omissions. In the case of less well documented countries, new entries have been added to existing ones, in order to build up a body of documents on that particular country.

As far as possible, references in the English language have been complemented by sources in other languages in order to broaden the accessibility of the literature.

Some changes have been introduced in this edition. More entries have been briefly annotated, when the title does not reflect all the points useful to comparative studies. The main change has been the disappearance of the symbols and numbers used to identify the bibliographical references.

Form of entries
Entries include as much detail as needed to trace them. Titles are given in most cases in the original language for Latin scripts. Transliterated titles have been left as found; there will therefore be some discrepancies due to the various systems of transliteration used in the sources. A [ ] indicates that the given title is either a translation or an interpretation of the contents.

Periodical titles are abbreviated mainly in accordance with the lists published in *Library literature* or in *LISA*; titles of periodicals outside the field of librarianship are given in full.

The names of most organizations are now represented by international acronyms. These are given with the name of the organization when it is first mentioned and used exclusively in further references within the same area. A list of international acronyms with their explanation regularly appears in *Unesco journal* (see p 22).

Organization of sources
Here again a few changes have been introduced in order to rationalize further the categories of entries. (See Section 1 in particular.)

Listed below are the headings used and their contents. The user should expect a few variations on points of details caused by the nature of the material found.

For the convenience of the user, this key to entries is also printed on the front and rear end pages.

1 Libraries and information centres with national or similar status and scope of functions within the network of libraries. Other libraries able to supply information on bibliography, librarianship or documentation have been included as necessary.

2a Official or semi-official bodies with organizing functions in the fields of bibliography, librarianship or documentation. These may include regional or international bodies with a supportive role.

2b Professional organizations whose aim is to promote librarianship and related fields exclusively or as part of their overall purpose.

2c Professional activities: Professional education and research; Professional issues, seen through the literature.

3a Reference sources: dictionaries, encyclopaedias, directories and yearbooks, guides and surveys (but for these see also under 3d or 3f). Not included: the yearbooks of library associations or similar bodies, which can be easily traced.

3b Bibliographical services, bibliographies; abstracts and other recurrent sources; special bibliographies.

3c Librarianship periodicals and serials.

3d Statistical sources: publishing bodies, printed sources; surveys (see also under 3a or 3f).

3e Legislation, including copyright, censorship, lending rights; standards for libraries.

3f Further readings, in the following sequence:

- — General background of the region or country: history, culture, education.
- — Librarianship: History, philosophy, sociology, trends.
Organization, management, cooperation, assistance.
- — Public libraries: Structure and functions, services.
Provision to special groups: minority groups, hospitals, prisons, etc.
- — School and children's libraries.
- — Academic and research libraries, special libraries.
- — Documentation, information.
- — Automation, networks, etc.
- — Architecture and design (only if it has a specific interest).

Geographical organization

As in previous editions, it was thought that a hierarchical listing of regions and countries would provide a more logical and economical use of the material available. The broad regions correspond to recognized geographical entities. In addition, some subsections have been created on the basis of existing material (see for instance areas designated as 'English-speaking . . .' or 'French-speaking . . .') or of some affinity of interests.

This plan therefore gives the user the facility of complementing the literature dealing with a given country with that of the region it belongs to. The names of the countries are those in current use and found in general international sources (see General, 3a). The index to this volume provides points of entry for individual countries.

- Zambia
- Zimbabwe

Southern Africa
South Africa, Republic of
Botswana
Lesotho
Namibia
Swaziland
Mauritius
Seychelles
St Helena and Tristan da Cunha

French associated Eastern Africa
Comoro
Djibouti
Madagascar
Reunion

Western Africa
English-speaking West Africa
- Gambia
- Ghana
- Liberia
- Nigeria
- Sierra Leone

French-speaking West Africa
- Benin
- Guinea
- Ivory Coast
- Mali
- Mauritania
- Niger
- Senegal
- Togo
- Upper Volta

French-speaking Central Africa
Burundi
Cameroon
Central African Republic
Chad
Congo
Gabon
Rwanda
Zaire

Portuguese associated Africa
Angola
Cape Verde
Guinea-Bissau
Mozambique
Sao Tome e Principe

Spanish associated Africa
Guinea Ecuatorial

Section five

THE MIDDLE EAST AND NORTHERN AFRICA

Asian region
Afghanistan
Iran
Iraq
Israel
Jordan
Lebanon
Syria
Turkey

Arabian Peninsula and Gulf region
Saudi Arabia
Yemen
Gulf States: Oman, UAE
Bahrain
Kuwait
Qatar

African region
Egypt
Libya
Sudan
North Africa
- Algeria
- Morocco
- Tunisia

Section six

ASIA AND THE PACIFIC

Southern Asia: general
South Asia (Indo-Pak subcontinent)
- Bangladesh
- India
- Nepal
- Pakistan
- Sri Lanka

Eastern Asia: general
North East Asia
- China, People's Republic of
- China, Republic of (Taiwan)
- Hong Kong
- Japan
- Korea, Republic of
- Korea, People's Democratic Republic of
- Mongolia

South East Asia
- Burma
- Thailand

SECTION 1

GENERAL AND INTERNATIONAL

GENERAL AND INTERNATIONAL

1 National Libraries.

'Current trends in national libraries' *Lib Trends* 1955 4(1). Whole issue.

'Bibliothèques nationales et scientifiques' in International congress on libraries and documentation centres, Brussels, 1955 *Proceedings* Nijhoff, 1958, Vol 3, 112-5.

Esdaile A *National libraries of the world: their history, administration and public services* 2nd ed LA, 1957, 413p.

Mumford L Q 'The role of national libraries in science and technology' in *Regional seminar on the development of national libraries in Asia and the Pacific area. Paper* Unesco, 1963, 16p.

Burston G 'National libraries: an analysis' *Int Lib Rev* 1973 5(2) 183-94, refs.

'Meetings of Directors of National Libraries: second meeting, Oslo, 12-13 August 1975' *Int Lib Rev* 1976 8(3) 233-5.

'The role of national libraries in national and international information systems': Theme of the meeting of Directors of National Libraries, Oslo, 1975. *Draft paper* prepared for further discussion. Mainly on NATIS.

'The role of national libraries in national and international information systems: a policy statement approved by directors of national libraries meeting in Lausanne, 20-21 August 1976' *Unesco Bull Lib* 1977 31(1) 7-25. Amended statement prepared at the Oslo meeting for this conference.

'Directors of national libraries: summary report of the 4th meeting, Brussels, 7-9 September, 1977' *IFLA J* 1978 4(1) 55-6.

Line M B 'The role of national libraries: a reassessment' *Libri* 1980 30(1) 1-16.

Thompson A ed *National library buildings: proceedings of the colloquium held in Rome, September 1973* Verlag Dokumentation, 1975, 144p. (IFLA Publications, 2).

1 International libraries and documentation centres.

- United Nations.

Field N S 'The United Nations library in Geneva' *Unesco Bull Lib* 1969 23(6) 320-2.

Dale D G *The United Nations Library: its origin and development* ALA, 1970, 236p.

- World Health Organization (WHO) Library.

Weitzel R 'Die Bibliothek der WHO' *Med Biblioth Dok* 1977 1(1) 30.

- Educational Resources Information Center (ERIC), Bethesda, MD. See details under:USA.

- International Youth Library, Munich.

Churward S M 'Twenty years of the International Youth Library' *Lib Ass Rec* 1968 70 280.

Scherf W 'Zur Entwicklung der Internationalen Jugendbibliothek in München' *Buch Biblioth* 1971 23(6) 567-76, refs.

— 'International Youth Library: achievements and projects within a multicultural context' *Unesco J* 1979 1(1) 23-8.

- International Children's Library, Amsterdam. See under: Netherlands.

- Pratt Institute for International Librarianship Studies, New York.

Aman M M 'Pratt Institute Center for International Librarianship Studies: a review of functions, services and collections' *Int Lib Rev* 1969 1(4) 479-86.

2a International organizations.

- Union of International Organizations, Brussels.

Murra K O *International scientific organizations: a guide to their library, documentation and information services* Library of Congress, 1962, 805p.

United Nations Educational, Scientific and Cultural Agency (Unesco), and its departments and programmes.

In the mind of men Unesco, 1972, 318p. History of Unesco, its contributions to development.

Meyriat J *Rapport à Mr le Directeur Général de l'Unesco sur l'ensemble des services de documentation de l'organisation* Unesco, 1978, 17p.

Unesco programmes and realizations are recorded every year in *Unesco Journal of Information Science, Librarianship and Archives Administration* (before that in *Unesco Bulletin for Libraries*). The *Journal* is part of the activities of Unesco's General Information Programme.

Pobukovsky M 'Unesco's integrated documentation network: the CDS/ISIS system' *Unesco J* 1980 2(3) 195- . CDS:Computerized Documentation System; ISIS: Integrated Science Information Systems (of ILO).

Tocatlian J 'Training information users: programmes, problems, prospects' *Unesco Bull Lib* 1978 32(6) 355-62, refs.

Keresztesi M 'Diffusion of modern library thought and practice by means of Unesco Fellowships for travel and study abroad' *Libri* 1979 29(3) 193-206, refs.

- Unesco International Advisory Committee on Documentation, Libraries and Archives (IACOD).

- Unesco Department of Documentation, Libraries and Archives (LAD).

Cain J 'Structures and functions of the Unesco Department of Documentation, Libraries and Archives' *Unesco Bull Lib* 1971 25(6) 311-7, 331.

Unesco *Development of national and regional information systems and services: summary of the activities of the Department of Documentation, Libraries and Archives, 1967-1974* Unesco, 1975, 47p (COM.75/WS/11 Apr 1975).

- Unesco International Copyright Information Centre.

Dock M-C 'The Unesco International Copyright Information Centre' *Information: News and Sources* 1975 7(3) 93-5.

The Centre publishes: *Information Bulletin.*

- Unesco/International Bureau of Education. The Bureau (IBE) was created in Geneva in 1925. In 1929 became in intergovernmental agency, and in 1965 was integrated to Unesco.

Furtado A 'International cooperation in the field of educational information: the role of the International Bureau of Education (IBE)' *Unesco Bull Lib* 1975 29(5) 249-54.

Unesco (IBE) Secretariat 'The problem of information at the national and international levels which is posed by the improvement of educational systems' *Unesco Bull Lib* 1978 32(4) 216-36. Paper at the 36th session of the International Conference on Education, Geneva, 1977.

Unesco (IBE) Secretariat 'International information networks and their role in the transfer of educational experience' *Unesco Bull Lib* 1978 32(4) 237-51.

Unesco/IBE publishes:

Studies and surveys in comparative education.

Educational Documentation and information. Quarterly.

4 *Country education profiles.*

IBEDOC Information quarterly.

- Unesco. NATIS concept.

Tel B *The design and planning of national information systems (NATIS).*

Sewell P et al *Establishing a legislative framework for the implementation of NATIS.* See other documents in section 3f.

- Unesco. UNISIST concept. International System for Scientific and Technical Information. Programme for international cooperation.

Unesco ICSU *UNISIST: study report on the feasibility of a world science information system* Unesco, 1971, 161p.

UNISIST information policy objectives (UNISIST proposals) Unesco, 1974. (SC/74/WS/3).

UNISIST guidelines, studies and publications Unesco Document SC-76/WS/73.

For other documents see under 3f.

International Board on Books for Young People (IBBY).

British Council.

Saunders W L and Broome E M *Library and information services of the British Council: a review* British Council, 1977, 89p.

2b General.

- International Council of Scientific Unions (ICSU).

Baker F W G *The International Council of Scientific Unions: a brief survey* Unesco, 1977, reissued 1979.

— 'Science information and information science: the role of ICSU' *Unesco J* 1979 1(4) 233-41.

- International Associaton for Mass Communication Research (IAMCR), Lausanne.

- International Reading Association (IRA). Based in the USA. Publishes:

Journal of reading (for teachers).

Reading research quarterly.

2b Librarianship.

IFLA *Répertoire des associations de bibliothécaires* 6th ed Nijhoff, 1961; *Suppléments*, to 1967.

Fang J R and Songe A H *International guide to library, archival and information science associations* 2nd ed Bowker, 1980, 448p.

Fang J R and Vagianos L 'Library and information associations in the international arena' *Int Lib Rev* 1974 6 241-51.

Fang J R and Songe A H 'Professional associations at the national level: a survey of their major interests' *IFLA J* 1976 2(4) 237-41. Comments on the above guide.

— 'A survey of professional associations at the international level: their characteristics and major interests' *IFLA J* 1978 4(1) 40-5.

Scott E 'IFLA and FID: history and programs' *Lib Q* 1962 32(1) 1-18.

Rayward W B 'IFLA and FID — Is it time for federation' *IFLA J* 1977 3 80-1.

- International Federation of Library Associations and Institutions/Fédération Internationale des Associations de Bibliothécaires (IFLA/FIAB). 1929- . Restructured in 1976.

Cambio E P *The International Federation of Library Associations and Institutions: a selected list of references* 2nd rev ed Verlag Dokumentation (for IFLA) 1977, 52p. (IFLA Publications, 11).

'International Federation of Library Associations (IFLA) in *Encyclopedia* 12 (1974) 403-18.

Rayward W B 'Great expectations: a personal report and critique of goings on in 5

Lausanne at the 1976 restructuring of the International Federation of Library Associations' *Amer Lib* 1976 7(10) 634-8, 656. On new statutes, new name, etc.

Wijnstroom M 'The new constitution of IFLA' *IFLA J* 1976 2(4) 224-8.

IFLA: statutes. Rules of procedure IFLA, 1979, 48p.

Carroll F L 'IFLA and other international library associations, institutions and organizations' *Int Lib Rev* 1978 10(3) 217-29, refs. On IFLA's new statutes.

IFLA: 50 years of international librarianship IFLA, 1977.

Koops W R H and Wieder J eds *IFLA's first 50 years: achievements and challenge in international librarianship* Saur Verlag, 1977, 158p. (IFLA Publications, 10).

On this 50th anniversary see also:

Unesco Bull Lib 1977 31(4) 203-9.

Ass Biblioth Fr Bull Info 1977 (94) 9-47.

Herald Lib Sci 1978 17(2/3) 184-94.

IFLA sections, programmes, activities:

'The IFLA medium-term programme: a summary' *IFLA J* 1976 2 87-92.

Pomassl G 'IFLA and international bibliographical activities (1966-1976)' *Herald Lib Sci* 1978 17 172-81.

IFLA Journal 1979 5(3) 215-38. Series of papers on IFLA's Division of Collections and Services.

Gombocz I 'The forty years of the Committee on the Exchange of Publications' *IFLA J* 1975 1(1) 9-20.

IFLA's Universal Bibliographic Control (UBC). See under 3b .

[IFLA and contemporary library problems] *IFLA J* 1977 3(3) 221-99. Whole issue.

Van Swigchem P J 'IFLA and the public libraries' *Unesco J* 1979 1(4) 256-9.

'IFLA. Subsection on Library work with Children — report on activities 1955-1970' *Int Lib Rev* 1971 3(1) 35-49.

Carroll F L 'The raison d'être of IFLA's School Library Section *J Lib Hist* 1977 12(4) 364-76.

Berkeley U 'International development in school librarianship — the contribution of IFLA's Section on School Libraries' *Educ Lib Bull* 1979 22(3) 35-41.

Kaden V 'IFLA work in progress: directory of art libraries' *Art Lib J* 1979 4(4) 23-5. IFLA project.

IFLA publishes a *Directory* giving details of members, sections, officers, statutes, etc; an *Annual*: reports, proceedings of council meetings, etc.; *Publications*, series of monographs.

For the meetings see:

Abudulahi I *A bibliography of IFLA conference papers 1968-1978* Copenhagen, IFLA Clearinghouse, Royal School of Librarianship, 1979, 86p.

Theme of recent conferences:

Liverpool, 1971: The organisation of the library profession.

Budapest, 1972: Reading in a changing world.

Grenoble, 1973: Le Contrôle Bibliographique Universel (UBC).

Washington, 1974: National and international library planning.

Lausanne, 1976: New statutes and reorganisation.

Brussels, 1977: 50th anniversay.

Strbské Pleso (Czechoslovakia), 1978: Universal availability of publications (UAP). With a pre-session seminar in Potsdam on 'Development, management and planning of national library systems in developing countries'.

Copenhagen, 1979: Legislation for libraries.

Manila, 1980: Development of libraries and information systems: global information exchange for greater international understanding.

6 - Fédération Internationale de Documentation (FID)/International Federation

for documentation. 1938- .

Arntz H 'International Federation for Documentation (FID)' in *Encyclopedia* 12 (1974) 377-402.

— '80 éves a Namzetkôzi Dokumentációs Szôvetség' *Tudom Musz Tajek* 1975 22(9) 621-31.

Judge P J 'FID — past and present' in Russell H M ed *Information for agriculture* Melbourne, Standing Committee on Agriculture and FID, 1979, 15-8.

Svidorov F A 'Role and activities of the International Federation for Documentation' *Unesco Bull Lib* 1967 21(4) 196-9, 206. Hill M 'The Fédération Internationale de Documentation (FID) and the UK' *State Libn* 1979 27(3) 33-4.

FID/ET (Education and Training) Clearinghouse, University of Maryland, 1980- . The material covers both librarianship and information.

The recurrent publications of the FID are:

FID Yearbook.

FID Directory. The latest edition 1979/80 (FID 575).

FID: R & D projects in Documentation and librarianship 1971- . Current awareness publication.

FID Newsletter on education and training programmes for specialized information personnel. Experimental issue November 1977.

Recent conferences:

Brussels, 1975: Information systems design for socio-economic development: retrospect and prospect.

Mexico, 1976: Information and development.

Edinburgh, 1978: New trends in documentation and information. (Published by Aslib, 1980, 521p.)

- Commonwealth Library Association (COMLA), Kingston, Jamaica. 1972- .

- Association of International Libraries/Association des Bibliothéques Internationales (AIL/ABI), Geneva. 1963- .

Dimitrov T D 'Organization profile: Association of International Libraries' *Info: News Sources* 1975 7(1) 30-1.

- International Association of National Libraries.

Hookway H T 'An International Association of National Libraries (1) An International Association of National Libraries: a review of existing related association' *Int Lib Rev* 1975 7(3) 381-405. Unesco, etc., SCAUL, IFLA, Archives, Music associations, etc. A proposal.

- Association Internationale des Ecoles des Sciences de l'Information (AIESI), Montreal. 1977- . French-speaking countries.

Cartier G 'Fondation de l'Association Internationale des Ecoles des Sciences de l'Information' *Doc Biblioth* 1977 23 161-4.

'Un sigle nouveau: l'AIESI' *Bull Biblioth Fr* 1977 22 461-5.

See also *Unesco Bull Lib* 1978 32 304-6; *Leads* 1978 20 8-10.

See also under: General: French-speaking countries.

- Library Association (London) International and Comparative Librarianship Group. Publishes *Focus on International and Comparative Librarianship; Handbook.*

- International Association of Metropolitan Libraries (INTAMEL) 1968- .

Campbell H C 'International Association of Metropolitan City Libraries (INTAMEL)' in *Encyclopedia* 12 (1974) 247-53.

- International Association of School Librarianship (IASL) 1971-.

Owens W W 'The IASL first annual conference, London, 29-31 July 1972' *School Libn* 1972 20(4) 294-7.

Nilson M 'Ziel und Aufgaben der International Association of School Librarianship' *Schulbibliothek Aktuell* 1975 (3) 5-6.

Cooke M J 'An international view of school librarianship' *School Libn* 1979 27(4) 322-5, Work of the IASL.

- International Association of Technological University Libraries (IATUL) 1955- . Hold triennial conferences.

Schmidmaier D 'The history of the International Association of Technological University Libraries (IATUL)' *IATUL Proc* 1976 8 42-5. Translated from *Zentrbl Biblioth* 1976 90(1) 21-3.

- Association Internationale des Documentalistes et Techniciens de l'Information (AID)/International Association of Documentalists and Information Officers. Paris. 1962- .

- International Federation for Information Processing.

- International Association of Agriculture Librarians and Documentalists (AID-BA). 1955- .

Fusionie Y Moran A and L *International agricultural librarianship: continuity and change* Greenwood, 1979.

Viaux J 'La création d'une association internationale de bibliothèques d'art et son rattachement éventuel à l'IFLA' *Inspel* 1976 11(4) 144-6. Proposal.

- International Association of Law Librarians (IALL). 1959- .

- Medical Library Associations.

Directory of Medical Library Associations Chicago, Medical Library Association, 1968.

- International Association of Music Libraries. 1957- . Publishes *Fontes Artis.*

Wood T E 'International Association of Music Libraries' in *Encylopedia* 12 (1974) 254-7.

- International Federation of Record Libraries/Fédération Internationale des Phonothèques (FIP).

2c Education. General. Principles and trends.

Bramley G *A history of library education* 2nd ed Bingley/Saur, 1980.

— *World trends in library education* London, Bingley, 1975, 234p.

Shera J H *The foundations of education for librarianship* Becker & Hayes/Wiley, 1972, 54p.

Kurshid A 'Intellectual foundations of library education' *Int Lib Rev* 1976 8(1) 3-21.

Schur R H *Education and training of information specialists of the 1970's* OECD, 1972 (OECD/DAS/STINFO/72-9) and also Sheffield Postgraduate School of Library and Information Science, 1972.

Dailey J E 'Crisis available on the hire-purchase plan: the changing nature of education for librarianship' *Libri* 1972 22(2) 120-9.

Sabor J E 'International cooperation in the training of librarians' *Unesco Bull Lib* 1965 19(6) 285-90, 296.

International Institute of Intellectual Co-operation *Rôle et formation du bibliothécaire. Étude comparative sur la formation professionelle du bibliothécaire* Paris, The Institute, 1935, bibl.

Reid-Smith E R *Resource sharing in professional education for librarianship: an international approach* ERIC, 1977, 11p. (ERIC report ED-176 761).

FID/TD *Training of documentalists* Report of the meeting, Warsaw, May 1964 FID, 1964, 46p.

Symposium on education for librarianship Warrenton 7-10 September 1965 Spartan Books/Macmillan, 1965, 175p.

International Conference on Education for Scientific Information Work.
8 *Proceedings* (London 3-7 April 1967) FID, 1967, 270p. (FID 422).

Bone L E 'International conference on education for librarianship' *Int Lib Rev* 1969 1(2) 173-82.

International Conference on Training for Information Work, Rome November 1971 *Proceedings* Italian National Information Institute, 1972, 511p. (FID 486).

Carroll F L 'Internationalism in education for librarianship' *Int Lib Rev* 1972 4 103-26. See also *Int Lib Rev* 1970 2(1) 19-39.

Simsova S 'Comparative librarianship as an academic subject' *J Libp* 1974 6(2) 115-25, refs.

Dailey J E 'International and comparative library education' in *Encyclopedia* 12(1974) 320-5.

Enright B J *New media and the library education* Bingley, 1972; Linnet, 1972, 162p.

Borko H *Targets for research in library education* ALA, 1973, 239p.

2c Education. Courses: surveys, curricula, standards, needs.

Neelameghan A and Tocatlian J 'UNISIST activities in education, training and manpower development in the information field' *Int Forum Inf Doc* 1977 2(2) 28-32.

FID News Bull Supplement: Newsletter on education and training programmes for specialized information personnel FID/ET 1979- . Quarterly.

Rovelstad M V 'IFLA and library education' *J Educ Libp* 1975 16(2) 105-18.

Kecskeméti C *La formation professionnelle des archivistes: liste des écoles et des cours* Unesco, Conseil International des Archives, 1966, 94p.

FID *Training facilities in documentation and information work* 2nd ed rev 1969, 294p. (FID 461). First published 1965, 218p. (FID 373).

World guide to library schools and training courses in documentation 2nd ed Bingley, 1981, 549 p. (Previous edition Unesco, 1972).

Foskett D J 'Survey of training programmes in information and library science' *Unesco Bull Lib* 1975 29(1) 23- .

— *NATIS: preliminary survey of education and training programmes at university level in information and library science* Unesco, 1976, 149p.

AIESI *Repertory of library schools* 1975. In French, for schools in French-speaking countries.

Velez Mediz R 'La formación profesional de los bibliotecarios en algunos paises extranjeros' *Bol Bibliot Nacion* (Mexico) 1955 6(1) 29-37.

'Education for librarianship abroad in selected countries' *Lib Trends* 1963 12(3) 121-355, whole issue. Individual articles are not entered in the section concerned.

Journal of Education for Librarianship 1966 6(4) 231-317, whole issue.

Whatley H A *Comparative study of education for librarianship in twenty five countries* MA Thesis, Strathclyde U, 1968.

Bone L E *Library education: an international survey* U of Illinois Graduate School of Library Science, 1968, 388p. Americas and Europe.

Hanz B 'Library school histories' *Int Lib Rev* 1971 3(1). Selected from *Liber amicorum (G 340)*. Denmark, Great Britain, Yugoslavia, Pakistan, South Africa, USA.

'Standards for library schools, 1976' *IFLA J* 1976 2(4) 209-23.

Revell D H 'Terminal behaviour and the criterion measure in education with particular reference to education for librarianship' *Vocational aspect of secondary and further education* 1969 21(48) 47-51.

Goldhor H *Education for librarianship: the design of the curriculum of library schools* U of Illinois Graduate School Library Science, 1971.

Parr E A and Wainwright E J eds *Curriculum design in librarianship: an international approach* Proceedings of the Colloquium of Education for Librarianship held at the Western Australian Institute of Technology, August 1973. Perth, WAIT Aid, 1974, 162p. Papers on general principles and on selected countries: USA, UK, Malaysia, Australia, Papua New Guinea.

Van der Brugghen W *Syllabus for a documentation course* The Hague, FID, 1975, 72p.

Asheim L E 'Specialized education and training of qualified public librarians in an industrial and computerized society' *Libri* 1968 18(3/4) 270-82.

Unesco course for teachers of librarianship August-November 1968, Copenhagen. See *Unesco Bull Lib* 1969 23(4) 178-82.

UNISIST/FID *International school and workshop for teachers and workers in the information field* 4th series, May 1979, Graz and Vienna.

Ochs M 'A taxonomy of qualifications for music librarianship: the cognitive domain' *Notes* 1976 33(1) 27-44.

Brodman E 'Education for medical librarians around the world' *Med Lib Ass Bull* 1964 52 99-116.

Mikhailov A I and Giljarevskij R S *An introduction course on informatics/documentation* (Unesco FID 1971) Spanish translation:

— *Curso introductorio de informatica/documentación* Caracas, Fundaciòn Instituto Venezolano de Productividad, 1974, 238p. (FID 481).

Saracevic T 'Information science education and development' *Unesco Bull Lib* 1977 31(3) 134-43.

2c Research: Methodology: International and comparative approach: Delphi method.

Wynar B S *Research methods in library science: a bibliographic guide with topical outlines* Libraries Unlimited, 1971, 153p. (Research studies in library science, 4).

Bundy M L and Wasserman P *Reader in research methods for librarianship* NCR Microcard Editions, 1970, 363p.

Goldhor H *An introduction to scientific research in librarianship* U of Illinois, 1972, 201p. (1969: Bureau of Education).

Beal C 'Studying the public's information needs' *J Libp* 1979 11(2) 130-51, refs.

Busha C H and Harter S P *Research methods in librarianship: techniques and interpretation* Academic P, 1980 417p.

Busha C H ed *A library science research reader and bibliographic guide* Libraries Unlimited, 1980.

Delanette M *Informatique. Méthodes et techniques numériques* Paris, Delagrave, 1967, 191p.

Romerio G F and Cavara L 'Assessment studies of documentation systems' *Inf Stor Retrieval* 1968 4 309-25.

Fairthorne R A 'Progress in documentation: empirical hyperbolic distributions for bibliometric description and prediction' *J Doc* 1969 25(4) 319-43, 62 refs.

King D W and Bryant E C *The evaluation of information services and products* Information Resources P, 1971, 306p.

Monk D *The use of survey research organizations and the costing of survey research* SSRC, 1972, 51p.

Slamecka V and Borko, H eds 'Planning and organization of national research programs of information science' *Inf Proc Manag* (1980 16(4/5) 177-251. Round table on National Research Programs in Information Science, Georgia Institute of Technology, September 1979. Papers on general issues and on some selected countries: USA, USSR, Japan, UK, France, West Germany.

Simsova S et al 'Comparative librarianship; the next ten years: an exercise in the Delphi technique' in *Proceedings of the ICLG Conference Scotland 1974* (A. Wheatley ed). LA/ICLG 1974, 75-97.

— A Delphi survey of comparative librarianship *Int Lib Rev* 1975 7(4) 417-26.

Fisher R G 'The Delphi method: a description, review and criticism' *J Acad Libp* 1978 4(2) 64-70, refs.

Cook S A 'The Delphi connection or, public library know thyself' *Wilson Lib Bull* 1978 52(9) 703-6.

Dane C 'The benefits of comparative librarianship' *Austr Lib J* 1954 3(7) 295-6.

Jefferson G 'Comparative librarianship' in *Public library administration* Bingley, 1965, 18-28.

Foskett D J 'Comparative librarianship' in *Progress in library science* 1965 125-46.

Shores L *Around the library world in 76 days: an essay in comparative librarianship* Peacock P, 1967, 28p.

Jackson M M *Comparative and international librarianship: essays on themes and problems* Bingley/Greenwood, 1970, 307p.

Collings D G 'Comparative librarianship' in *Encyclopedia* 5(1971) 492-502.

Greenaway E 'Progress in international librarianship' *Amer Lib* 1972 3(7) 803-7.

Danton J Periam *The dimensions of comparative librarianship* ALA, 1973, 184p.

Burnett A D et al *Studies in comparative librarianship: three essays presented for the Sevensma Prize* ***1971*** LA, (for IFLA), 1973, 95p. Essays by A D Burnett, R K Gupta and S **Simsova.**

Sable M H *International and area studies in librarianship: case studies* Scarecrow, 1973, 166p.

Setty Unapathy K 'International and comparative librarianship' *Ann Lib Sci Docum* 1973 20(1-4) 75-80.

Parker J S 'International librarianship: a reconnaissance' *J Libp* 1974 6 219-32.

Krzys R 'International and comparative study in librarianship, research methodology' in *Encyclopedia* 12(1974) 325-43.

Williamson W L ed *A search for new insights in librarianship: a day of comparative studies* U of Wisconsin, Library School, 1976, 106p (Sri Lanka, Pakistan, Germanies compared, Latin America, Puerto Rico/Jamaica).

Foskett D J ed *Reader in comparative librarianship* Information Handling Services, 1976, 333p. (Readers in Librarianship and Information Science, 23).

Harvey J F ed *Comparative and international library science* Scarecrow, 1977, 286p.

Rovelstad M V 'New international librarianship: a challenge to the profession' *Unesco Bull Lib* 1978 32(3) 436-43.

Burnett D and Cumming E E eds *International library and information programmes* LA, 1979, 102p. Proceedings of 10th anniversary of the LA Comparative and International Librarianship Group. See also in *IFLA J* 1978 4 60-2.

Foskett D J *Introduction to comparative librarianship* Bangalore, S Ranganathan Endowment, 1979.

Qureshi N 'Comparative and international librarianship: an analytical approach' *Unesco J* 1980 2(1) 22-8, refs.

Simsova S *A primer of comparative librarianship* Bingley, 1981, 96p.

2c Professional issues.

FID *Manpower in the field of documentation and library services* Unesco, 1973, 197p. (COM/WS/332). Covers 50 countries.

Planning information manpower Unesco, 1974, 70p. (COM-74/NATIS/ Ref 5). Two papers given at Unesco Intergovernmental Conference on the Planning of National Documentation, Library and Archives Infrastructures, Paris Septem- 11

ber 1974; Harvard-Williams P 'Library and documentation: manpower planning, professional structures and educational training'. Franz E G 'Archives: manpower planning, training facilities and the preparation of curricula for regional training centres'.

Volmer H M and Mills D L *Professionalization* Prentice-Hall, 1966.

Chaplin A H 'The organization of the library profession. Final report of two plenary sessions of the IFLA General Council, Liverpool, 1971' *Unesco Bull Lib* 1972 26(4) 178-83. Includes the list of papers related to the theme.

— ed *The organization of the library profession: a symposium based on contributions to the 37th session of the IFLA General Council, Liverpool 1971* 2nd ed Verlag Dokumentation Saur, 1976, 132p. (IFLA Publ., 6).

Hanks G and Schmidt C J 'An alternative model of a profession for librarians' *Coll Res Lib* 1975 36(3) 175-87.

Stone E W *Factors related to the professional development of librarians* Scarecrow, 1969, 281p.

Khan H A 'Human relations in library service' *Timeless Fellowship* 1974 75(9) 77-87.

Smith N M and Fitt S D 'Vertical-horizontal relationships: their application for librarians' *Spec Lib* 1975 66(11) 528-31.

Dehart F E *The librarian's psychological commitments: human relations in librarianship* Greenwood, 1979. (Contributions in librarianship and information science, 27).

Baum W K 'The expanding role of the librarian in oral history' in *Louisiana State University Library Lectures: numbers 29 through 35 September 1974-April 1976*, 33-43.

Meri S L 'Kirjastonhoitajan amattietiikasta' *Kirjastolehti* 1969 62(2) 48-50. Professional ethics.

Weeraperuma S *Staff exchanges in librarianship* Poets and Painters P, 1970, 71p.

Shera J H 'Librarians against machines' *Wilson Lib Bull* 1967 Sep 65-73, 27 refs.

Varennes R de 'Bibliothèques et bibliothécaires d'aujourd'hui et de demain à l'ère électronique' *Ass Canad Biblioth Langue Fr Bull* 1969 15(2) 59-66, 27 refs.

Warren G G *The handicapped librarian: a study in barriers* Scarecrow, 1979, 147p.

[LfSC Feminist Group] *Librarians for Social Change* 1974 (5) 3-23 Special issue. Includes papers on Cuba, Australia.

3a Dictionaries — Acronyms.

Brewer A M ed *Dictionaries, encyclopedias and other word related books* 3rd ed Gale Research, 1982, 3 vols.

Fachwörterbücher und Lexika: ein internationales Verzeichnis/International bibliography of dictionaries 5th ed Verlag Dokumentation, 1972, 511p. (Handbuch der technischen Dokumentation und Bibliographie, 4). Classified.

Spillner P *Internationale Wörterbuch der Abkürzungen von Organizationen* 2 Aufl Verlag Dokumentation, 1970-72, 3 vols.

Lennox-Kay A R P and J L comps *Bailey's catalogue of dictionaries and grammars in the languages of the Orient, Africa, the Americas and Oceania* Folkstone, Bailey and Swinfen, 1980, 123p.

Lewanski R C 'Bibliography of dictionaries in the field of library science and related subjects' *Unesco Bull Lib* 1964 18(6) 277-84.

Thompson A *Vocabularium bibliothecarii* 2nd ed Unesco, 1962, 627p. English/French/German/Spanish/Russian, with local editions.

Rolland-Thomas P et al *Vocabulaire technique de la bibliothéconomie et de la bibliographie — suivi d'un lexique anglais/francais* Association Canadienne des

Bibliothèques de Langue Française, 1969, 187p.

Pipics Z *Dictionarium bibliothecarii practicum ad usum internationalem in XXII linguis/The librarian's practical dictionary in 22 languages/Wörterbuch des Bibliothekare in 22 Sprachen* 6th rev enlarged ed Verlag Dokumentation, 1974, 385p.

Kunze H and Ruckl G eds *Lexikon des Bibliothekswesens* 2. neubearbeite Aufl Leipzig, Verlag fur Buch- und Bibliothekswesen, 1974-75, 2 vols.

Dictionary of library science, information and documentation in six languages Elsevier, 1975.

Allen C G ed *A manual of foreign languages for librarians* Bowker, 1975, 803p.

Harrod L M *The librarians' glossary of terms used in librarianship, documentation and the book crafts, and reference book* 4th ed West View P/Deutsch, 1977, 903p.

Stolk H A *Glossary of documentation terms* NATO, 1970, 43p.

Wersig G and Neveling U comp *Terminology of documentation: a selection of 1,200 basic terms published in English, French, German, Russian and Spanish* Unesco P, 1976, 274p. Sequel to Thompson's *Vocabularium bibliothecarii.*

Camille C and Dehaine A *Dictionary of data processing/Dictionnaire de l'informatique* Harrap, 1970. 278p.

Dubuc R et al *Dictionnaire anglais-français, français-anglais de l'informatique* Dunod, 1971, 214p.

Gingnay M *Dictionnaire d'informatique anglais/français* 2e ed Masson, 1971, 140p.

Weik, M H *Standard dictionary of computers and information processing* Hayden Books, 1970, 326p. A bibliography includes 150 previously published dictionaries on the subject.

Mongomery A C comp and ed *Acronyms and abbreviations in library and information work: a reference handbook of British usage* LA, 1975, 97p. Expansion of a list in *Library and Information Bulletin* 1973 (22).

Judje P J 'Alphabet soup unscrambled: the information programmes behind the acronyms' *Aust Acad Res Libr* 1976 7(2) 77-92.

Tayyeb R and Chandna K comps *A dictionary of acronyms and abbreviations in library and information science* Canadian Library Association, 1979, 146p.

Vaillancourt P M *International directory of acronyms in library, information and computer sciences* Bowker, 1980, 518p.

3a Encyclopaedias: General: Librarianship.

Encyclopedia Americana Encycl Amer Corp, 1977, 30 vols. (Published title varies 1829-).

Encyclopedia Britannica 15th ed Encycl Brit Inc, 1974, 19 vols. In sections: Macropedia, etc.

Encyclopédie française 1935-. See in Vol 8: La civilisation écrite', for libraries. Updated by loose leaves.

Handbuch der Bibliothekswissenschaft 2nd ed Harrassowitz, 1952-65. 4 vols. Ed. F Milkau. (First ed 1931-42 ed by G Leyh).

Great Soviet encyclopedia Macmillan/Collier Macmillan, 1973. Translation of *Bol'shaia sovetskaia entsiklopediia* 3rd ed (See under USSR 3a). General, special, regional information.

Banks A S ed *Political handbook of the world: government, regional issues and intergovernmental organizations as of Jan 1* McGraw Hill [for Center for Social Analysis of the State U of New York at Binghamton and for the Council on Foreign Relations] 1979, 630p.

Kunze H and Ruckl G *Lexikon des Bibliothekswesen* 2nd rev ed. 13

Kluth R *Grundriss der Bibliotheklehre* Harrassowitz, 1970, 372p. Textbook, but includes a comparative librarianship section, mostly on Europe and USA; bibliography of 848 international items.

Saur K G *Die internationale wissenschaftliche Dokumentation und Information* 4th ed Verlag Dokumentation, 1969, 663p. (*Handbuch der technischen Dokumentation,* vol 1). Standards, state of the art in various countries, directory: associations, dictionaries, encyclopaedias, bibliographies, etc.

Landau T *Encylopaedia of librarianship* 3rd ed Hafner/Bowes, 1966, 484p.

Kent A et al, eds *Encyclopedia of library and information science* Dekker, 1968- (vol 32 1982). See relevant articles with the countries or subjects.

Kruzas A T and Sullivan L V *Encyclopedia of information systems and services* 3rd ed Gale Research, 1978, 1035p.

3a Directories.

Internationale Bibliographie des Fachadressbücher/International bibliography of directories 5th ed Verlag Dokumentation, 1973, 536p.

Europa yearbook London, Europa Pub, 1959- . Now in two volumes. Political and economic.

World of learning London, Europa Pub, (32nd ed 1982). Research and cultural organizations, universities and libraries.

World of learning London, Europa Pub, 1947- . Academic world.

OECD *Handbook of information, computer, and communications activities of major international organizations* Paris, OECD, 1980, 233p.

Directory of United Nations information systems and services UN, Inter-Organization Board for Information Systems, 1978, 267p.

World communications: a 200-country survey of press, radio, television and film 5th ed Unipub, 1975, 533p.

Bowker annual of library and booktrade information 25th ed 1980.

International literary market place 1980- (ILMP) 5th ed Bowker. By country. Includes Library Association — main libraries and library journals.

Taubert S ed *The book trade of the world* Verlag für Buckmarkt-Forschung/ A Deutsch/ Bowker, 1972-6, 3 vols. I Europe and international section; II Americas, Australia, New Zealand; III Africa, Asia.

Directory of universities and institutes offering literacy training programmes Tehran, IIALM, 1977, 78p.

Directory of organizations offering literacy training courses Tehran, IIALM, 1977, 211p. (International Institute for Adult Literacy Methods).

Unesco *World survey of education. Handbook of educational organisations and statistics* 1959 [1955], 946p.

— Vols II-IV, 1958-66. Surveys of every aspect of education: primary, secondary, higher. Also in French.

Unesco *Directory: educational documentation and information services/Répertoire: services de documentation et d'information pédagogiques* Unesco, International Bureau of Education, 1975, 60p. Then updated every two years. (Cf 1979, 76p).

Nitecki J Z *Directory of library reprographic services: a world guide* 6th ed Microform Review for ALA, 1976, 178p.

IFLA *A brief guide to centres of international lending and photocopying* 2nd ed BLLD/IFLA, 1979, 21 [161] p.

FID *Bibliography of directories of sources of information* 1960, 22p. (FID 328).

Intergovernment Bureau for Informatics, Rome *International directory of computer and information systems services* 2nd ed Europa, 1971, 475p.

World guide to science information and documentation services Unesco, 1965.

FID *World guide to technical information and documentation services/Guide mondial des centres de documentation et d'information techniques* 2nd ed rev and enlarged Unesco, 1975, 515p. Partial update of *World guide to science information and documentation services.*

National Technical Information Services *Worldwide directory* 3rd ed FID, 1970, 61p. (FID 464).

Unesco — ISORID *International directory of institutions active in the field of research in information, libraries and archives* Unesco/PGI, 1979.

— *International directory of specialists active in the field of research in information, libraries and archives* Unesco/PGI, 1979.

Lewanski RC *Library directories. A bibliography of library directories* 1967 ed, (with a bibliography of library science dictionaries) American Bibliographical Center, 1967, 49p. (Bibliography and reference series, 4).

Bowker *Library resources market place* 1980, latest edition.

Wedgeworth R et al, eds *ALA World encyclopedia of library and information services* ALA, 1980, 616p.

Jackson M M ed *International handbook of contemporary development in librarianship* Greenwood P, 1981.

Wales A P *International library directory: a world directory of libraries* 3rd ed for 1969-70 London, Wales, 1968, 1221p.

Chandler G *International and national library and information services* Pergamon, 1982. (Recent advances in library and information services, 2).

World guide to libraries/Internationales Bibliotheks-Handbuch 5th ed Saur, 1980, 1030p. By regions and countries.

Steele C *Major libraries of the world: a selective guide* Bowker, 1976, 479p.

Simmler O *World directory of administrative libraries: a guide to libraries serving national, state, provincial and landerbodies* Verlag Dokumentation, 1976, 475p. (IFLA Publication, 7).

Becker C A *Community information service: a directory of public library involvement* U of Maryland Library Service, 1974. (Student contribution series, 5).

International Co-operative Alliance *Directory of co-operative libraries and documentation services/ Répertoire des bibliothèques et services de documentation des coopératives/ Verzeichnis Genussenschaftlicher Bibliotheken und Dokumentationsdienste* London, The Alliance, 1974, 69p.

Ray C ed *Library services to children: an international survey* 2nd ed Verlag Dokumentation, 1978, 158p.

Boalch D R *World directory of agriculture libraries and documentation centres* IAALD, 1960.

Buntrock H *Survey of the world agricultural documentation services* FAO, 1970, 55p.

Pacey P ed *Art library manual: a guide to resources and practice* London & New York, Bowker, 423p.

Ristow W W ed *World directory of map collections* Verlag Dokumentation, 1976, 326p.

Directory of major medical libraries worldwide US Directory Service, 1980, 171p.

Benton R ed [For International Association of Music Libraries — Commission of Research Libraries] *Directory of music research libraries/ Répertoire international des sources musicales — Preliminary edition* Part I:USA, Canada (1967); Part II: Great Britain, Scandinavia, Switzerland (1969); Part III: Spain, France, Italy, Portugal (1972) U of Iowa P (In progress).

CNRS *Performing arts libraries and museums of the world* 1967, 801p.

Ruoss G M *A world directory of theological libraries* Scarecrow, 1968, 22p.

Duchein M 'International directory of archives/Annuaire international des ar- 15

chives' in *Archivum* (Paris PUF) 1975 22 and 23.

Bakewell K G B *Industrial libraries throughout the world* Pergamon, 1969, 184p.

3b Bibliographic control: UBC, MARC, UAP.

Davinson D *Bibliographic control* 2nd ed Bingley, 1981, 164p.

Anderson D *Universal bibliographic control* Unesco, 1974. (COM.74/NATIS/Ref 3). Part of the conference referred to in 3f: Unesco Intergovernmental Conference on Planning of National Documentation, Library and Archives Infrastructures. Published in an extended version as:

— *Universal bibliographic control: a long term policy — a plan for action* Verlag Dokumentation, 1974, 87p. Originally a working document from IFLA for the conference.

Inspel 1974 9(1/2). Issue on reviews of the implications for special libraries of UBC.

Anderson D 'Universal Bibliographic Control and the information scientist' *Info Sci* 1976 10(1) 11-22, refs.

— 'IFLA's programme for UBC: the background and the basis' *IFLA J* 1975 1 4-8.

Soper M E and Page B F 'Trends in bibliographic control: international issues' *Lib Trends* 1977 25(3) 561-721.

Library of Congress MARC Development Office *Information on the MARC system* 2nd ed 1972, 31p.

International seminar on the MARC format and the exchange of bibliographic data in machine readable form, Berlin 1971. *Proceedings* Verlag Dokumentation, 1972, 196p.

IFLA. International Office for UBC *International MARC network: bibliographic study; preparation for the International MARC network Study Steering Committee* London, The Office, 1977, 28p. (Occasional papers, 4).

Jabben R and Strohl-Goebel H eds *Informationsnetze: Auswahlbibliographie* Dokumentationszentrum für Informationswissenschaften, 1976, 14p.

Van der Wolk J 'The nature and bibliographical control of re-recorded information' *Unesco Bull Lib* 1971 25(6) 332-7, 343. On microfiches, etc.

Kanevsky B P and Vanwijngaerden F L J *Echanges internationaux de publications: bibliographie 1960-1970* Commission Belge de Bibliographie, 1974, 63p. (Bibliographia belgica, 127).

Line M B 'Universal availability of publications (UAP)' *Unesco Bull Lib* 1977 31(3) 142-51.

'Universal availability of publications (UAP), 44th IFLA meeting Strbké Pleso, 1978 Preliminary account' *IFLA J* 1978 4(2) 117-65. Full proceedings in *IFLA Annual* 1978.

Towards a common bibliographic exchange format? Proceedings of an International Symposium on bibliographic exhange formats, Taormina, April 1978 London, UNIBID/Budapest, OMKDK-Technoinform, 1978, 214p.

Cathro W S 'The upheaval in bibliographic exchange standards 1974-1984' *Cataloguing Australia* 1979 5(3) 14-28, refs.

3b National and international bibliographic services.

Unesco and Library of Congress *Bibliographic services: their present state and possibilities of improvement* Library of Congress, 1950.

Larsen K *National bibliographical services: their creation and operation* Unesco, 1955, 142p. Also in French.

Murty A T 'Literature explosion and bibliographic services' *Herald Lib Sci* 1976 15(2) 132-8.

Anderson D 'The role of a national bibliographic centre' *Lib Trends* 1977 25(3) 645-63.

Massil S *Resource sharing for national bibliographic services* Unesco, 1977, 21p.

Libri 1974 24(3) 209-28, 60 refs on the International Institute of Bibliography, Brussels, 1895-? . Created by Besterman, it was a landmark in the development of international cooperation in bibliography.

Cohen D B 'Unesco's bibliographic services' *Int Lib Rev* 1977 9(2) 127-60.

Beaudiquez M *Les services bibliographiques dans le monde, 1970-1974* Unesco, 1976, 391p.

— *Bibliographical services throughout the world, 1970-74* Unesco, 1977, 419p. English edition of the above.

This directory is the latest edition of a Unesco publication. See:

Collison R L *Bibliographical services throughout the world, 1950-1959* Unesco, 1961, 228p. Also in French.

Avicenne P *Les services bibliographiques dans le monde, 1960-1964* Unesco, 1967, 231p. English edition, 1969.

— *Les services bibliographiques dans le monde, 1965-1969* Unesco, 1972, 303p. Also in English.

3b National bibliographies.

Peddie R A *National bibliographies: a descriptive catalogue of the works which register the books published in each country* Grafton, 1912.

Heyl L *Current national bibliographies: a list of sources of information concerning current books of all countries* Rev ed ALA, 1942, 34p.

Conover H F *Current national bibliographies* Library of Congress, 1955, 132p. (Reprinted: Greenwood, 1968).

Pomassl G *Comparative survey of existing national bibliographies* Unesco, 1975, 127p. Also published as:

— *Synoptic tables concerning the current national bibliographies* Bibliotheksverband DDR/Deutsche Bücherei, 1975.

Cheffin R H *A Study of national bibliographies: a survey of their contents* Unesco, 1977, 52p. (PGI/77/UBC/10).

Commonwealth Secretariat *Commonwealth national bibliographies: an annotated directory* The Secretariat, 1977, 98p.

Unesco/IFLA International Office for UBC *The national bibliography: present role and future developments — International Congress on National Bibliographies, Paris, 1977. Working documents* Unesco. PGI, 97p. (PGI/77/UBC/2).

IFLA International Office for UBC 'International Congress on National Bibliographies, Paris 12-17 September 1977: report and recommendations' *IFLA J* 1978 4(1) 10-20.

The congress was also reported in:

International Cataloguing 1977 6(4) 42-4.

New Zealand Libraries 1978 41(3) 79-82.

Unesco Bulletin for Libraries 1977 31(4) and 1978 32 202-4.

Sicco M 'Bibliografie nazionali e cataloghi collettivi: esperienze all 'estero' *AIB Boll* 1978 18(2) 106-15, refs. Review of the situation in 13 selected countries from all regions.

3b Bibliographies of Bibliographies — Reference works.

Carter E J 'Theodore Besterman: a personal memoir' *J Doc* 1977 33(1) 79-87.

Cave R 'Besterman and bibliography: an assessment' *J Libp* 1978 10(3) 149-61, refs.

Besterman T *A world bibliography of bibliographies and of bibliographic cata-* 17

logues, calendars, abstracts, digests, indexes and the like 4th ed Lausanne, Societas Bibliographica, 1965, 5 vols. Classified.

Toomey A F *A world bibliography of bibliographies 1964-1974* (from the Library of Congress card catalogue) — *a decennial supplement to T Besterman World bibliography of bibliographies* Rowman and Littlefield Saur/SVK, 1977, 2 vols.

Bohatta H and Hodes F *Internationale Bibliographie der Bibliographien* Klostermann, 1950. Section III: Buch und Bibliothekswesen.

FID *Index bibliographicus: directory of current periodical abstracts and bibliography* 4th ed, 1959-64, 2 vols.

Totok W et al *Hanbuch der bibliographischen Nachschlagewerke* 3rd ed Klostermann, 1966, 362p.

Gudovshchikova I V *Obshchaja mezdunarodnaja bibliografija bibliografii* Leningrad, Institute Krupskaja, 1969, 104p.

Sawoniak H *Rozwój i metodyka powszechnych i narodowych bibliografii bibliografii* Warsaw, National Library, 1971, 496p. Includes a list of 300 national bibliographies of bibliographies.

Bibliographic index: a cumulative bibliography of bibliographies 1937- . Wilson, 1938- .

Childs J B 'Reference guides' in *Encyclopedia* 25 1978 202-10. Lists main guides to reference material, in regions and countries.

Higgens G *Printed reference material* Library Association, 1980.

Winchell C M *Guide to reference books* 8th ed ALA, 1967.

Sheehy E P *Guide to reference books* 9th ed (Revised and updated version of the 8th edition by C M Winchell) ALA, 1982, 283p.

Cheney F N *Fundamental reference sources* ALA, 1971, 318p.

Walford A J *Walford's guide to reference material* 4th ed LA, 1980- , 3 vols. Vol 1: *Science and technology* ed by Harvey A P and Drubba H, 1980, 750p; Vol 2: *Social and historical sciences, philosophy, and religion* ed by Harvey A P and Taylor L J, 1982, 800p.

Walford A J ed *Walford's concise guide to reference material* LA, 1981, 434p.

Widener Library shelflist 7: bibliography and bibliography periodicals Harvard U P, 1966, 1066p.

See also for general information:

International books in print.

Cumulative book index 1898- .

Books in print and *British books in print* and equivalent records in other languages.

3b Bibliographies of special materials and special topics.

New York Public Library *Guide to Festschriften* G K Hall, 1977, 2 vols.

Reynolds M M *A guide to theses and dissertations: an annotated internationl bibliography of bibliographies* Gale Research Co, 1975, 599p.

Sinnassamy F *Survey of the present state of bibliographic recording in freely available printed form of government publications and those of intergovernmental organisations* Unesco, 1977, 160p.

Collison R *Published library catalogues: an introduction to their contents and use* Mansell Info, 1973, 184p.

Nelson B R *A guide to published library catalogs* Scarecrow, 1982.

Unesco *Bibliography of publications issued by Unesco or under its auspices — the first 25 years: 1946 to 1971* Unesco, 1973, 385p.

Unesco list of documents and publications (ULDP) 1972- . Quarterly record in English only. Supersedes *ARC List* 1949-1971.

Unesco *Annual catalogue.*

Winckler P A *History of books and printing: an annotated bibliography* Gale Research Co, 1979. (Books, publishing and libraries information guide series, 2).

Danielson W A and Wilhoit G C *A computerized bibliography of mass communication research, 1944-1964* Magazine Publishers Ass, 1967, 399p.

Internationale Bibliographie zur Soziologie und Psychologie des Lesens/International bibliography to the sociology and psychology of reading Verlag Dokumentation, 1971, 230p.

Hall J L comp *On-line information retrieval 1965-1976: a bibliography with a guide to on-line data bases and systems* Aslib, 1977, 125p. (Aslib Bibliographies, 8).

Hawkins D T 'On-line information retrieval bibliography, 1965-1976' *On-line Rev*, 1977 1(1), 55p. Will be updated regularly in *On-line.*

Hall J L and Brown M J *Online bibliographic data bases: an international directory* 2nd ed Aslib, 1981, 213p.

3b Sources on librarianship and information science. General.

Schutze G *Documentation sources book* Scarecrow, 1965, 554p.

— *Information and library science source book, a supplement* Scarecrow, 1972, 483p. 1964-1969.

New reference tools for libraries 1966-67 with a bibliography of new books on the library sciences Maxwell, 1969, 243p.

Die Fachliteratur zum Buch- und Bibliothekswesen/International bibliography of the booktrade and librarianship Verlag Dokumentation/Bowker 1973-75, 2 vols. Revised 1976, 704p. (11th ed.)

Thornton J L and Tully R I J *Scientific books, libraries and collectors: a study of bibliography and the book trade in relation to science* 3rd rev ed LA, 1971, 508p.

Library/Information science: bibliographies, guides, reviews, survey 1973-1975 Aslib, 1976, 104p; (Aslib bibliography series, 3).

Library bibliographies and indexes Gale Research, 1975- . Irregular.

For older material see:

Cannon H G T *Bibliography of library economy, 1876-1920* ALA, 1927, 680p. Reprinted 1968. Continued by *Library Literature.*

Jordan A H and Jordan M *Canon's Bibliography of library economy 1876-1920: an author index with citations* Scarecrow, 1976, 473p.

Glogoff S J 'Cannons' Bibliography of library economy and its role in the development of bibliographic tools in librarianship' *J Lib Hist* 1977 12(1) 57-63.

Burton M and Vosburgh M E *Bibliography of librarianship* LA, 1934, 176p.

FID Publications: an 80 years bibliography, 1895-1975 FID, 1975, 94p. (FID 531).

3b Sources on librarianship and information science. Special materials and topics.

Danton J Periam and Pulis J F *Index to Festschriften in librarianship, 1967-1975* K G Saur, 1979, 438p. Previous edition: 1970, 461p.

Lieberman I *A working bibliography of commercially available audiovisual materials for the teaching of library science* U of Illinois, Graduate School of Library Science, 1968, 77p.

Schachter G A and Thomison D *The library science dissertations, 1925-1972: an annotated bibliography* Libraries Unlimited, 1974, 293p.

Magnotti S *Master's theses in library science, 1970-1974* Whitston Pub, 1976, 198p.

FID *R & D projects in documentation and librarianship.* 1971- .

Harrison H P 'Progress in documentation: non-book materials: a decade of development' *J Doc* 1979 35(3) 207-48, 328 refs.

Diaz A J ed *Microforms and library catalogs: a reader* Microform Review, 1977.

McNally P T *Non-book materials in libraries: an annotated bibliography* 19

Toowoomba, Queensland, Darling Down Institute P, 1979, 147p.
Di Felice C 'Film and public libraries: a survey of the literature' *Film Lib Q* 1978 11(4) 26-8.
Vervliet H D L *ABAB: Annual bibliography of the history of the printed book and libraries* Nijhoff for IFLA, 1971- .
Shirley S 'An annotated bibliography of education for medical librarianship, 1940-1968' *Bull Med Lib Ass* 1969 57(4) 391-8.
Pritschard A ed *Bibliometrics: a bibliography and index.* Vol 1 1874-1959 Watford, The Author?, 1981.
Hunter N R *Library management bibliography* 2nd ed MCB Pub Ltd, 1978, 153p.
Aman M M 'The year's work in international librarianship: 1970' *Int Lib Rev* 1972 4(2) 235-50.
— *International librarianship: a guide to literature 1960-1970* Seminar P, [1975?].
Davey J 'Interlibrary lending around the world — a review of recent papers' *BLL Rev* 1975 3(3) 77-9.
Briquet de Lemos A A *Descriptions of interlibrary lending in various countries and a bibliography of interlibrary lending* BLLD for IFLA Office for International Lending, 1980, 136p.
Adeyami N M 'A selected review of the literature on library cooperation' *Int Lib Rev* 1976 8(3) 283-97.
Albright J B 'A bibliography of community analyses for libraries' *Lib Trends* 1976 24(3) 619-43. 1970-75 in English.
Mann M *The reading habits of adults: a select annotated bibliography* British Library, 1977, 72p. 609 refs, 1930- .
Horns V D 'Remedial reading: a guide to selecting materials dealing with remedial reading' *Choice* 1972 9 180-90.
Harris C G S and Taylor P J *Educating users of library and information services, 1926-1976: an international bibliography* Aslib, 1978.
Lockwood D L *Library instruction: a bibliography* Greenwood P, 1979, 166p.
White A G *Metropolitan libraries: a selected bibliography* Council of Planning Librarians, 1976, 7p.
Basler B K and Basler T G *Health sciences and librarianship: a guide to information sources* Gale Research Co, 1977, 186p.
Hynes A 'Bibliography of bibliotherapy reference material 1970-1975' *Health and Rehabilitation Library Services* 1975 1(2) 22-5.
Cummings E E *Hospital and welfare library services: an international bibliography* LA, 1977, 174p. 1863-1972.
Pool J *Library services for the blind and physically handicapped: a bibliography 1968-1978* IFLA, 1978, 73p.
IFLA. Committee on Work with Children *Professional literature of library work with children* The Hague, Central Association of Public Libraries, Bureau Boek en Jeudg, 1966.
Zell H M and Machesney R J *An international bibliography of non-periodical literature on documentation and information* Maxwell, 1965.
Elias A W *Key papers in information science* ASIS, 1971, 223p.
Dewey B E and Howard R *Media and instructional technology in the library: a bibliography of readings* New York, Center for Instructional Communications, 1971, 25p.
Davison P S 'A selective bibliography on information retieval' *SDC Bull* 1969 (1) 1-32.
Woods E W *Computer application to library technical processes: a bibliographical essay* Catholic U of America, 1967. Thesis.
20 Cayless C F and Potts H *Bibliography of library automation 1964-1967* BNB

Council, 1968, 107p.

Tinker L *An annotated bibliography of library automation 1968-1972* Aslib, 1973, 85p.

McCafferty M *An annotated bibliography of automation in libraries and information systems, 1972-75* Aslib, 1976, 147p.

Dewe A *An annotated bibliography of automation in libraries, 1975-1978* Aslib, 1979, 76p.

Library Automation Research and Consulting (LARC) *A bibliography of literature on planned or implemented automated library projects* Parts I and II, 1973, 66 and 67p. (World Survey Series, Vols 9 and 10).

Kremeneckaja A V and Polubinskaja V K *Bibliotečnye zdanija Arhitektura, stoitel'stvo, oborudovanie i techniskoe osnaščenie — Bibliografičeskij ukazatel', 1960-1970* Moskva, Strojizdat, 1973, 343p.

3b Abstracts — Indexes — Annual surveys.

Skolnik H 'Historical development of abstracting' *J Chem Info Comp Sci* 1979 19(4) 215-8, refs.

Goldstein S 'The table of contents approach to library literature: 1914 to the present' *CALL* 1972 1(1) 3-5.

FID *Abstracting services in science, technology . . . and humanities* 2nd ed 1969, 2 vols.

Whatley H A *A survey of the major indexing and abstracting services for library science and documentation* LA, 1966, 78p.

Dansey P 'A bibliometric survey of primary and secondary information science literature' *Aslib Proc* 1973 25(7) 252-63.

De Vries I 'Referaat — en registertijdschriften in bibliotheek- en documentatiewezen' *Open* 1974 6(11) 562-72.

Edwards T *A comparative analysis of the major abstracting and indexing services for library and information sciences* Unesco, 1975, 202p. (COM.75/WS/25,Sep 1975).

— *Unesco Bull Lib* 1976 30(1) 18-25.

Keen M A 'A retrieval comparison of six published indexes in the field of library and information science' *Unesco Bull Lib* 1976 30(1) 26-36.

Manzer B M *The abstract journal, 1790-1920: origin, development and diffusion* Scarecrow, 1977.

CNRS *Bulletin signalétique* 1956- . (1947-55 as Bulletin analytique). Librarianship in Section 101.

Internationale Bibliographie der Zeitschriftenliteratur aus allen Gebeiten des Wissens (IBZ) 1965- . Dictionary sequence.

Current contents — Education. Includes library science.

Advances in librarianship, New York and London, 1970- . Some volumes on a theme.

Annual review of information science and technology, ASIS 1966- .

'Bulletin de documentation bibliographique' in *Bulletin des Bibliothèques de France.* On librarianship and related fields.

Current awareness — Library Literature (CALL) 1972- .

Indian Library Science Abstracts.

Indices de revistas de bibliotecología (IREBI), Madrid, 1973- . Published by the Instituto Bibliográfico Hispanico, Madrid, with the Centro de Documentación Bibliotecológoica (U Nacional del Sur) and the Oficina de Educación Iberoamericana.

Documentation abstracts 1966-68. Continued as:

Information science abstracts.

Library science abstracts 1950-68. Continued as:

Library and information science abstracts (LISA). In classified order.

Edwards T 'LISA: a traditional abstracting service?' *Int Forum Info Doc* 1976 1(2) 25-34.

Library and information services today (LIST) Science Associates International, 1971- . Annual international index.

Library literature 1933- . Dictionary sequence.

Nauchno-technicheskaja informatsija 1963- . In two sections since 1967. See details under: USSR, 3b.

Progress in library science, 1965-1967.

Bibliographia anastatica. Now *Bulletin of reprints* Verlag Dokumentation.

World transindex 1978- . Delft, International Translation Centre. Merger of several translation index services.

3c

Duprat G et al *Bibliographie des repertoires nationaux de périodiques en cours* Unesco/IFLA, 1969, 141p.

Ulrich's international periodicals directory Bowker, Annual, with supplements.

Irregular serials and annuals Bowker. Latest edition: 1981.

Winckler P A *Library periodicals directory* 2nd ed Long Island U, Graduate Library School, 1967, 76p.

Periodičeskie i prodolžajuščiesja izdonija po informatik. Spravočnik Mezdanarodnyj Centr Naučnoj i Techničeskoj Informacii, 1974, 188p.

Janzing G comp and Brown K R ed *Library, documentation and archives serials* 4th ed FID, 1975, 203p. (FID Publ, 532).

International Serials Data System (Paris) *Bulletin de l'ISDS/ISDS Bulletin* 1974- . Annual cumulations. World recording of periodicals with ISSN, amendments, etc.

De Prospero E R and Mott T H eds *International series in library and information studies* Saur Verlag, 1979- .

CALL (Current awareness-library literature) 1972- . See for comments on library periodicals, changes in scope, in titles, etc.

Jones D Graham 'This incredible stream of garbage, the library journals, 1876-1975' *Indexer* 1976 10 9-14.

Short list of periodicals with an international interest:

Library Research: an international journal Norwood, Ablex. 1979- . Quarterly.

Journal of Education for Librarianship, Urbana 1960- .

International Library Review 1969- .

Libraries in International Development ALA, International Relations Office 1968- .

Leads: a fact sheet issued by the ALA's International Relations Round Table.

Association of International Libraries *Journal* Anglet (France), AIL, 1976- .

— *Newsletter*. English and French text.

Journal of Library History and Comparative Librarianship 1966- .

Library History Review: a quarterly journal devoted to the history and bibliography of libraries and related subjects Calcutta, K. K. Roy, 1974- .

Unesco Bulletin for Libraries 1947-1978.

Bansah S *Bibliographie, dépouillement du Bulletin de l'Unesco à l'Intention des Bibliothèques, 1947-1967* Dakar, IFAN, 1969, 72p.

'*Unesco Bulletin for Libraries:* thirtieth anniversary' *Unesco Bull Lib* 1977 31(3) 127.

Unesco Journal of Information Science, Librarianship and Archives Administration 1979- . Supersedes *Unesco Bulletin for Libraries.*

Unesco *Cultures* 1977- . Quarterly.

Unesco *PGI* 1977- . Replaces: *NATIS Newsletter* 1975-77 and *UNISIST Newsletter* 1973-76. Notes and news on the General Information Programme and other Unesco programmes.

Unesco/IBE *IBEDOC Information:* quarterly newsletter 1975- .

IFLA Journal 1975- . Supersedes *IFLA News Bulletin.*

IFLA *Libri* 1950- .

LA *Journal of Librarianship* 1969- .

Library and Information Science 1963- . Mita Society, Japan.

Library Quarterly 1931- .

Library Trends 1952- .

Library World 1898- . Now: *New Library World.*

Wilson Library Bulletin 1914- .

Public Library Quarterly New Yord 1979- .

Journal of Academic Librarianship Boulder, Col 1975- .

Outlook on Research Libraries Lausanne 1978- . News, trends.

International Association of Agricultural Librarians and Documentalists *Review AIBDA/Revista AIBDA* 1980- . Supersedes *Quarterly Bulletin/Boletin Informativo.*

Arts Libraries Society (ARLIS) *Arts Library Journal* 1976- . Supersedes *ARLIS Newsletter.*

International Journal of Law Libraries 1973- . Supersedes: *IALL Bulletin*, 1960-1972.

Behavioral and Social Sciences Librarian New York 1979- .

Fontes Artis Musicae 1954- . International Association of Music Libraries.

IATUL Proceedings 1966- .

Library Acquisitions: practice and theory (LAPT) 1977- .

International Classification Verlag Dokumentation 1974- .

The Serials Librarian New York 1976- . Includes news on serials.

Library Security Newsletter New York 1975- .

Annual Review of Information Science and Technology New York 1966- . Cumulative index 1966-1975.

International Forum on Information and Documentation FID/VINITI 1975- . English/Russian.

FID Newsbulletin 1951- .

Newsletter on Education and Training Programmes for Specialized Information Personnel FID/ET with Unesco 1979- . Supplement to *FID Newsbulletin.*

EUROMICRO Journal: international journal of microprocessing and microprogramming 1975- .

Information on Tools and Equipment for Library and Information Activity Budapest, National Szechenyi Library, 1977- .

Journal of Information Science: principles and practices 1979- . Supersedes *Information Scientist* 1960-78.

Journal of Research Communication Studies Elsevier 1979- .

Network: international communications in library automation LARC 1974- .

Scientific and Technical Informatin Processing 1974- . Translations into English of papers from *Nauchno-technicheskaja Informatsija,* Series 1.

International Council for Archives *Archivum.*

3d

US Library of Congress. Census Library Project *Statistical yearbooks: an annotated bibliography of the general statistical yearbooks of major political subdivisions of the world* Library of Congress, 1953 (Reprinted Greenwood, 1978, 23
123p.)

Lancaster H O *Bibliography of statistical bibliographies* Oliver and Boyd, 1968, 103p.

Cormier R *Les sources des statistiques actuelles: guide de documentation* Gauthier-Villars, 1969, 287p. In three parts: world, Europe, France, giving in each the organizations and libraries dealing with statistics, research and bibliographies, results.

Wasserman P et al *Statistical sources* Gale research, 1965, 387p.

Koops W R H 'A center for statistical data on national libraries' *Libri* 1972 22(2) 153-4.

Department of Trade *National statistical offices of overseas countries* London, Dept of Trade, 1978, 33p.

World broadcasting: a statistical analysis Temple U, Radio-Television-Film Dept, 1975 (Communications research reports, 6).

UN *Compendium of social statistics*

UN statistical yearbook 1949- . Section on: Education, culture.

Unesco statistical reports and studies Topical monographs.

Unesco *Basic facts and figures* 1952-61. Then :

Unesco statistical yearbook 1963- . E/F to 1976 (for 1975); E/F/S 1977- . 'Libraries and Museums' are included.

Unesco *Statistiques internationales concernant les bibliothèques et la production des livres* 1955, 48p.

'International library statistics' *Unesco Bull Lib* 1955 9(2/3) 53-5. Recommendations for methodology.

Stock K F *Entwicklung und Stand der Bibliotheksstatistik. Überblick, Einzelprobleme und Anwendungs Möglichkeiten* Graz, K F Stock, 1968, 212p, 294 refs (Thesis).

Mallaber K A et al *International standardization of library statistics: a progress report* Oceana (for IFLA and ISO), 1968, 216p. (IFLA international manuals, 4).

International standardization of library statistics. Final report Unesco 1969, 46p. Prepared for the intergovernment conference on the subject, May 1970, See:

Schick F L 'The international standardization of library statistics' *Unesco Bull Lib* 1971 25(1) 2-11.

— 'International statistics programs' *Am Lib* 1972 3(1) 73-5.

'Recommendation concernant la normalisation internationale des statistiques relatives aux bibliothèques' *Bull Biblioth Fr* 1971 16 81-92. See also: 1967 12(4) 125-44.

IFLA 1974 Conference Committee on Statistics and Standards presented a programme session on the conference theme 'National and international library planning'. Several papers on statistics.

Williams J *Library statistics: a handbook of concepts, definitions and terminology* ALA, 1966, 160p. Part of a project on international standardization. Since 1968 Unesco and other international organizations have been working on new standards for library statistics and on encouraging countries to report their published statistics. The latter is done regularly in the *Unesco bulletin for libraries*. There is also an annual international statistical study in *Bowker's annual of libraries and book trade information,* contributed by F Schick.

Stock K F *Grundlagen und Praxis der Bibliotheksstatistik* Verlag Dokumentation, 1974, 397p. (Bibliotheksstudien, 2).

Eyssen J 'INTAMEL — Statistik 1974' *Buch u Bibliog* 1975 27 1140-4.

— 'INTAMEL (2) International statistics of city libraries 1974' *Int Lib Rev* 1976 8(2) 141-9.

3e

Meyriat J *A study of current bibliographies of national official publications* Unesco, 1958.

Boast C and Foster L 'Current subject compilations of state laws: research guide and annotated bibliography' *Law Lib J* 1979 72 209-21.

Fang J R 'National library associations and their impact on library legislation: an international survey' *IFLA J* 1979 5(4) 276-81, bibl.

'Legal deposit libraries' in *Encyclopedia* 14 (1975) 140-81. Mainly on deposit laws.

Patterson L R *Copyright in historical perspective* Vanderbilt U P, 1968, 264p.

Clark A J *The movement for international copyright in 19th century America* Greenwood P, 1973 (Thesis, Catholic U of America, 1960).

Unesco and United International Bureaux for the Protection of Intellectual Property *Copyright laws and treaties of the world* 1956. French edition: 1960; Spanish edition: 1962. *Supplements* updating the original compilation.

Copyright bulletin Unesco, 1948- . For current awareness. And:

Revue internationale du droit d'auteur 1953- .

Barker R E *International copyright: the search for a formula in the '70s* London, Publishers Associaton, 1969, 22p. And:

'Copyright' in *Encyclopedia* 6(1971) 33-154.

Lunn J *Working document for joint meeting of Section on Bibliography and National Libraries, IFLA, Manila, Aug 22 1980. Study on a model law for legal deposit. 3rd draft.* Ottawa, n.d., 101p.

Pomassl G *Surveys of existing legal deposit laws* Unesco, 1977, 91p.

Unesco *A guide to the operation of the agreement on the importation of educational, scientific and cultural material* (Florence agreement) 4th ed 1969, 36p. Also in French.

— *A guide to the operation of the agreement for facilitating the international circulation of visual and auditory materials of an educational, scientific and cultural character* (Beirut agreement) 2nd ed 1969, 31p. Also in French.

Sewell P H et al *Establishing a legislative framework for the implementation of NATIS* Unesco, 1977, 60p. (CC-76/NATIS/8).

Chartrand G-A 'Le droit de prêt au public' *Doc et Biblioth* 1977 23(4) 181-5.

Boaz M 'Censorship' in *Encyclopedia* 4 (1970) 328-38.

Daily J E 'Censorship, contemporary and controversial aspects of' in *Encyclopedia* 4 (1970) 338-81, 141 refs.

Haight A L *Banned books 387 BC — 1978 AD* Bowker, 1978, 196p.

Anderson A J *Problems of intellectual freedom and censorship* Bowker, 1974, 195p.

Berninghausen D J *The flight from reason: essays on intellectual freedom in the Academy, the press and the library* ALA, 1975, 175p.

Carbone S *Draft model law on archives: description and text* Unesco, 1971, 243p.

Duchein M 'La législation archivistique' in *Archivum* 1972 20.

Baldina I V 'O bibliotechnom zakonodatel'stve kapitalisticheskikh stran' (Library legislation in capitalist countries) *Bibl Bibliog Rubezhom* 1969 (28) 23-44, 26 refs.

Mittal R L *Public library law: an international survey* Delhi, Metropolitan Book Co, 1971, 622p.

Gardner F M *Public library legslation: a comparative study* 2nd ed rev and updated by H C Campbell, Unesco, 1978, 181p. (PGI/WS/30).

Unesco 'Recommendations relating to school, public, national, university and special libraries. Extract from working document (COM/CS/190/3)' *Int Lib Rev* 1969 1(3) 317-32. 25

Unesco *International standardization of library and documentation techniques* 1972, 282p., 275 refs.

IFLA, Section on Public Libraries *Standards for public libraries* Verlag Dokumentation, 1973, 53p. Unesco Manifesto as revised in 1972. Full text.

Withers F N *Standards for library service: an international survey* Unesco, 1974, 421p. (Documentation, libraries, archives: studies and research, 6). Expansion and revision of document issued in 1970, including extensive sources on public libraries in general and in 20 countries including Belgium, France, Federal Republic of Germany and the Netherlands.

Koops W R H and Harvard-Williams P eds *Standards for public libraries* 2nd ed IFLA, 1977, 53p. (IFLA publication, 9).

3f General.

Meyer J W and Hannan M T eds *National development and the world system: educational, economic and political change, 1950-1970* U Chicago P, 1979, 334p.

Sternberg B and Sullerot E *Aspects sociaux de la radio et de la télévision. Revue des recherches significatives 1950-64.* Mouton, 1966, 138p. Bibl pp 51-119.

Walther K K 'Kommunikationstheoretische Aspekte der Flugschriftenliteratur des 17. Jahrhunderts' *Zentbl Biblioth* 1978 92(5) 215-21.

Armand L et al *Premier festival international du livre de Nice. Colloques 1969* Nice, Ciais & Cie, 1970, 125p. See details of the symposia in *Bull Bilioth Fr* August 1970, 669-70.

'International book scene 1973: an introduction' *Publishers Weekly* 1973 204(13) 29, 96-159. Series of articles on book production and distribution in connection with the second book fair, Frankfurt, 1973. The Frankfurt Book Fair now is an annual event. See reports in *Bowkers Annual.*

Meeting of experts on book promotion, Unesco May 1973. *Report* Unesco, 1973. (COM-73/CONF-606/4).

Vervliet H D L *The book through five thousand years: a survey* Phaidon, 1972, 496p. Translation of:

Liber librorum: cinq mille ans d'art du livre, un panorama historique Bruxelles, Arcade, 1972, 511p. Also in Dutch, German and Italian.

Johnson E D *Communication: an introduction to the history of writing, printing, books and libraries* 4th ed Scarecrow, 1973, 322p.

Loi S 'La produzione libraria nel mondo' *Accademie e Biblioteche d'Italia* 1975 43(1-2) 45-9.

Hasan A *The book in multilingual countries* (Reports and papers on Mass Communication, 82) Unesco, 1978, 40p.

Hills P ed *The future of the printed word: the impact and the implications of the new communications technology* Pinter, 1980, 172p.

3f History of Librarianship. Development.

Roy K K 'Problems of defining and organising library history' *Lib Hist Rev* 1974 1(1) 9-36.

Kelly T 'Thoughts on the writing of library history' *Lib Hist* 1975 3(5) 161-9.

Vortius J *Grundzüge der Bibliotheksgeschichte* 6th ed Harrassowitz, 1969, 128p.

Masson A and Salvan P *Les bibliothèques* 3rd ed PUF, 1970, 128p.

Weimann K H *Bibliotheksgeschichte* Verlag Dokumentation, 1975, 254p.

Olle J G H *Library history: an examination guide book* Bingley, 1979.

Thornton J L *Selected readings in the history of librarianship* 2nd ed LA, 1966, 408p. Supersedes:

A mirror for librarians: selected readings in the history of librarianship Grafton, 1948, 207p. And:
Classics of librarianship: further readings . . . 1957, 203p
Dunlap L W *Readings in library history* Bowker, 1972, 137p.
Smith J M *A chronology of libraries* Scarecrow, 1968, 263p. Bibl pp 190-210.
Rider A D *A story of books and libraries* Scarecrow, 1976, 173p.
Johnson E D and Harris M H *History of libraries in the Western World* 3rd ed, completely rev Scarecrow, 1976, 354p.
Richardson E C *The beginning of libraries* Princeton U P, 1914; Archon, 1963, 176p.
— *Biblical libraries: a sketch of library history from 3400 BC to AD 150* Princeton U P, 1914, 252p.
Thompson J W *Ancient libraries* Archon, 1962.
Haider S S 'Libraries in ancient and medieval towns' *Pakistan Lib Bull* 1977 8(3-4) 26-40.
O'Connor J '[An analysis of the Alexandrian Library within its environment, and a critical evaluation of how well it was able to function in its social system]' *Lib Papers* 1979 4(2) 2-13, refs.
Cagnat R L V 'Les bibliothèques municipales dans l'Europe romaine' *Mémoires de l'Institut National de France Académie Inscriptions et Belles Lettres* 1909 38(1) 1-26.
Johnson D R 'The library of Celsus, an Ephesian phoenix' *Wilson Lib Bull* 1980 54(10) 651-3.
Runciman S 'The ancient Christian libraries of the East' *Bulletin of the Association of British Theological and Philosophical Libraries* 1978 (11) 6-14.
Tanner I 'A history of early Christian libraries from Jesus to Jerome' *J Lib Hist* 1979 4(4) 407-35, refs.
Hobson A *Great Libraries* Putnam, 1970, 320p.
Chandler G *Libraries in the modern world* Pergamon, 1965, 172p.
Penna C V 'Thirty years of action by Unesco for the development of documentation, library and archives services in its member states' *Unesco Bull Lib* 1976 30(6) 311-9.
Jackson M M ed *International handbook of contemporary developments in librarianship* Greenwood, 1981, 619p. Since 1945.

3f Philosophy and sociology of librarianship. Libraries in society.

Thompson J *A history of the principles of librarianship* Bingley/Linnet Books, 1977, 236p.
Broadfield M A *A philosophy of librarianship* Grafton, 1950, 120p.
Mukherjee A K *Librarianship: its philosophy and history* Asia Pub House, 1967, 220p.
Thompson J *Library power: a new philosophy of librarianship* Bingley, 1974, 111p.
Kemp D A *The nature of knowledge: an introduction for librarians* Bingley/Linnet Books 1976, 199p. Based on systems theory.
Nitecki J Z 'Metaphors of librarianship: a suggestion for a metaphysical model' *J Lib Hist* 1979 14(1) 21-42, refs.
Bundy M L and Aronson R *Social and political aspects of librarianship* State U of New York, School of Library Science, 1965, 99p.
Eberling B V 'The sociology of libraries and librarianship' *Libri* 1966 16(1) 87-111.
Escarpit R *La révolution du livre* 2nd ed Unesco, 1969. English edition: *Book revolution* Harrap, 1966. Other translations.

Shera J H *Sociological foundations of librarianship* Asia Pub House, 1970, 195p.
Onozawa N '[Growth of civil society and development of libraries]' (In Japanese) *Annals of Japan Society of Library Science* 1974 20(1) 14-30.
Carter E 'Literacy, libraries and liberty. The Arundel Esdaile Memorial Lecture, 1968' *J Libp* 1969 1(2) 73-87.
Benge R C *Libraries and cultural change* Bingley, 1970; Linnet, 1970, 278p.
IFLA 36th session in Moscow, August 1970, on the theme: *Libraries as a force in education* Papers in:
Libri 1970 20(4) 283-329; 1971 21(4) 336-86.
IFLA conference 1971 in Liverpool. Papers in:
INSPEL July/Oct 1971 and Jan 1972: *Libri* 1972 22(2) 155-62.
Unesco symposium, Moscow 1972 on the theme: *Books in the service of peace, humanism and progress*. Published?
Unesco International Book Year programmes on the theme: *Books for all.* See in:
Unesco Bull Lib 1971 25(3) 131- . In:
Bowker Annual 16th ed, 1971, and:
Newsletter of the International Book Year Unit of Unesco, Summer 1971-?
Liebaers H 'Le bibliothécaire international' *Unesco Bull Lib* 1967 21(2) 93-7.
— 'Librarian as the artisan of reading' *Unesco Bull Lib* 1972 26(3) 122-8.
Lindsay J 'On liberalism and librarianship' *Libns for Soc Change* 1974/75 7 4-6.
Schuman P Glass *Social responsibilities and libraries* Bowker, 1976.
Bonn G S and Faibisoff S eds *Changing times, changing libraries* Allerton Park Institute, 1976.
Gerard D ed *Libraries in society: a reader* Bingley, 1978, 163p.

3f Planning — Management — Effectiveness

Penna C V *The planning of library and documentation services* 2nd ed rev and enlarged by P H Sewell and H Liebaers, Unesco, 1970, 158p. (2nd imp: 1972). Originally published: 1967, 37p. and in *Unesco Bull Lib 1967* 21(2) 60-92.
Stockham K A *The government and control of libraries* Deutsch, 1969, 110p.
Lowell M H *The management of libraries and information centers* Scarecrow, 1968-1971, 4 vols.
Kemper R E 'Library planning: the challenge of change' *Adv Libp* 1970 1 207-39.
— *Library management: behavior-based personnel systems (BBPS): a framework for analysis* Libraries Unlimited, 1971, 104p.
Vol 1 ed by Redfern B; *Studies in library management* Bingley/Linnet Books. Vols 2-4 ed by Holroyd G; Vols 5-7 ed by Vaughan A.
Vosper R and Newkirk L I eds *National and international library planning. Key papers at the 40th Session of the IFLA General Council, Washington 1974* Verlag Dokumentation, 1976, 168p. (IFLA Publ., 4)
Kehr W et al, eds *Zur Theorie und Praxis des modernen Bibliothekswesens: Band 1 — Gesellschaftliche Aspekte; 2 — Technologische Aspekete; 3 — Betriebswirtschaftliche Aspekte* Verlag Dokumentation, 1976, 3v.
Wilson P *Public knowlege, private ignorance: towards a library and information policy* Greenwood, 1977 (Contributions in librarianship and information science, 10).
Morse P H *Library effectiveness: a systems approach* MIT P, 1968, 217p.
Chapman E A et al, *Library systems analysis guidelines* Wiley, 1970, 226p.
Thomas P A *Task analysis of library operations* Aslib, 1971, 72p.
Lancaster F W and Cleverdon C W eds *Evaluation and scientific management of libraries and information centres, Bristol 17-29 August 1975* Leyden, Noordhoff, 1977, 184p. (NATO Advanced Institute Series E, 18).

Penna C V et al *National library and information services: a handbook for planners* Butterworth, 1977, 231p.

3f Cooperation: General. Schemes.

Lewis S *Principles of cultural cooperation* Unesco, 1970.

Rudomino M I 'K istorii mezhdunarodnykh bibliotechnykh svyazel: predystoria IFLA 1853-1926' *Bibliot Biliog za Rubezhom* 1977 (63) 18-43. Prehistory of IFLA international meetings in the 19th century.

Jefferson G *Library cooperation* Deutsch, 1966.

Grove P S ed 'Library cooperation' *Lib Trends* 1975 24(2) 157-423. Whole issue.

Kumar P S G 'Centenary of international librarianship' *Her Lib Sci* 1978 17(2/3) 117-22.

[International studies] Special issue of *Int Lib Rev* 1974 6(4) 371-504.

Parker J S 'The overseas library consultant' *Lib Rev* 1979 28 214-25.

Clark D 'Helping librarians to help their users' *Unesco Bull Lib* 1978 32(6) 363-74.

Dargent J L *Echanges internationaux de publications: bibliographie 1817-1960* Brussels, Commission Belge de Bibliographie, 1962, 2 vols. IFLA has recently recommended that a supplement be prepared (B P Kanevsky in cooperation with the Royal Library in Brussels).

Kanevsky B P 'International exchange of publications and the free flow of books' *Unesco Bull Lib* 1972 26(3) 141-9.

Lofquist W S 'Exportation and importation of books and periodicals' in *Encyclopedia* 8(1972) 316-29.

Gombocz I 'Economic aspects of the international exchange of publications' *Unesco Bull Lib* 1971 25(5) 267-81.

INTAMEL 'Review of the 3 years research and exchange programme approved at the 4th annual meeting in Baltimore in 1971' *Int Lib Rev* 1972 4(2) 251-62.

Nattrass G R 'Interlibrary lending around the world — a review of recent papers' *BLL Rev* 1976 4(1) 11-16, refs.

Clark R L *Archive-library relations* Bowker, 1976, 218p.

Malclès L-N 'L'entr'aide des bibliothèques par les catalogues collectifs. Actes du congrès international des bibliothèques, Madrid, 1935' *Revue du Livre* 1935 87-94.

'International implications of the shared cataloging program: four papers; IFLA, 33rd session, Toronto 1967' *Libri* 1967 17 270-313.

Birket-Smith K *Local applicability of the Library of Congress classification: a survey with special reference to non-Anglo-American libraries* Danish Centre for Documentation, 1970, 72p. (FID 405).

Liebaers H 'Shared cataloguing' *Unesco Bull Lib* 1970 24(3) 126-38, bibl.

Maltby A *Classification in the 1970s: a discussion of development and prospects for the major schemes* Bingley, 1972, 269p. Indicates trends towards a compatible general system.

For networks: NATIS, etc., see below 'Networks' and 'Automation' sections.

3f Users education — Information services

Lubans J ed *Educating the library user* Bowker, 1974, 435p.

Bamberger R *Promoting the reading habit* (Reports and papers on mass communication, no. 72) Unesco, 1975.

Fjällbrant N 'Teaching methods for the education of the library user' *Libri* 1976 26(4) 252-67.

Lubans J ed *Progress in educating the library user* Bowker, 1978, 230p.

Lester R 'Why educate the library user?' *Aslib Proc* 1979 31(8) 366-80.

Kochen M ed *Information for action: from knowledge to wisdom* London, 29

Academic P, 1975, 248p.

Whittaker K 'Towards a theory for reference and information service' *J Libp* 1977 9(1) 49-63.

Budal M 'The readers' advisory situation in the public library: the significance of non-verbal communication' *J Libp* 1977 9(1) 29-37.

For users' needs see also with specific types of libraries.

3f Public libraries

Murison W J *Public library: its origin, purpose and significance* 2nd rev ed Harrap, 1971, 244p.

'Unesco public library manifesto' *Unesco Bull Lib* 1972 26(3) 129-31. IFLA revision of the 1949 manifesto.

Pellisson M *Les bibliothèques populaires à l'étranger et en France* Paris, Imprimerie Nationale, 1906, 220p.

Bostwick A E *Popular libraries of the world* ALA, 1933, 316p.

McColvin L *The chance to read: public libraries in the world today* Phoenix House, 1957, 284p.

Morel E *Bibliothèques; essai sur le developpement des bibliothèques publiques et de la librairie dans les deux mondes* Mercure de France, 1908, 2 vols.

Hassenforder J 'Trois pionniers des bibliothèques publiques: E Edwards, M Dewey, E Morel. Etude biographique comparée' *Educ Biblioth* 1964 (11) 11-40.

— 'Comparative studies and the development of public libraries' *Unesco Bull Lib* 1968 22(1) 13-9.

Houle C O *Libraries in adult fundamental education: the report of the Malmö seminar* Unesco, 1951, 103-49.

Monroe M E *Library-adult education: the biography of an idea* Scarecrow, 1963.

Vollans R F *Libraries for the people: international studies in librarianship in honour of Lionel McColvin* LA, 1968, 265p.

Chandler G 'Public libraries in development' *Int Lib Rev* 1974 6 231-5.

Penland P R 'Counselor librarianship' in *Encyclopedia* 6(1971) 240-54, 61, refs.

'[Special section on the Division of Libraries serving the general public]' *IFLA J* 1978 4(3) 226-61.

'Metropolitan public library problems around the world' *Lib Trends* 1965 14(1) 1-116.

Campbell H C *Metropolitan public library planning throughout the world* Pergamon, 1967, 168p.

— *Public libraries in the urban metropolitan setting* Bingley/Linnet, 1973, 298p. Comparative study.

[INTAMEL International Meeting, Gothenburg, 1969] *Int Lib Rev* 1969 1(4). Several articles.

INTAMEL 'Recommended international guide lines: metropolitan libraries' *Int Lib Rev* 1972 4 254-62.

[INTAMEL Working party, Italy, 1972. Research studies] *Int Lib Rev* 1973 5(1) 63-136. Series of papers, by countries or comparative.

Irmler J 'Rural libraries: a comparative international study' *Int Lib Rev* 1970 2(1) 49-55.

3f Services to special groups

Simsova S 'The marginal man' *J Libp* 1974 6(1) 46-53.

Bloomquist H et al *Library practice in hospitals: a basic guide* Case Western U P, 1972, 361p.

30 IFLA. Libraries in Hospitals Section 'Hospitals library studies, 1967-71' *Int Lib*

Rev 1972 4(3) 351-91. Series of articles on a number of countries.
Zaccaria J S and Moses H A *Facilitating human development through reading: the use of bibliotherapy in teaching and counseling* Champaign, Stipes Pub, 1968, 270p.
Monroe M E *Reading guidance and bibliotherapy in public, hospital and institution libraries* U of Wisconsin Library School, 1971, 76p.
Moody M L and Limper H K *Bibliotherapy: methods and materials* ALA, 1971, 161p.
Ta'avoni S 'Libraries for the blind' *Iranian Lib Ass Bull* 1975 8(2) 10p.
Schauder D E and Cram M D *Libraries for the blind: an international study of policies and practices* Stevenage, Peregrinus, 1977, 152p. (Library and information studies, 4).
Cylke F K ed *Library services for the blind and physically handicapped: an international approach.* Key papers presented at the IFLA Conference 1978 Verlag Dokumentation/Saur, 1979, 400p. (IFLA publication, 16).
— *Library services for blind and physically handicapped individuals* L of C National Library Service of the Blind and Physically Handicapped, 1979, 30, 20p.
— 'International co-ordination of library services for blind and physically handicapped individuals: an overview of IFLA activities' *Unesco J* 1979 1(4) 242-8.
See also a bibliography under 3b.

3f Children's and School Libraries.

Saunders H E *The modern school library: its administration as a material center* Scarecrow, 1968, 215p.
Davies R A *The school library: a force for educational excellence* Bowker, 1969, 386p.
Lowrie J E *School libraries: international development* Scarecrow, 1972, 247p.
Waite C A *School libraries in the 1970s: a symposium* U of London, Institute of Education Library 1972, 70p.
'Unesco and school library development' *Unesco Bull Lib* 1969 23(6) 286-319.
IFLA *Library service to young adults* Bibliotekscentralen, 1968, 166p.
Könyves-Töth L 'Youth library services in public libraries: an international survey' *Int Lib Rev* 1972 4(3) 303-11.
IFLA *Library service to children* [1] Ed: E. Colwell 1963, 2nd ed: 1965, 125p. *Library service to children* 2. 1966, 92p. (Bibliotekstjänst). 3: *Training* Bibliotekscentralen, 1970, 100p.
IFLA *Library services to children: an international survey* Biblioteksjänst, 1969.
Van Dyke F Z 'International activities in the field of children's libraries' *Int Lib Rev* 1971 3(4) 469-84, 51 refs.
IFLA. Subsection on library work with children 'Report on activities 1955-70' *Int Lib Rev* 1971 3(1) 35-49. See also under 3b.
Bolt J 'School library services: a world view' *Ill Lib* 1972 54(7) 476-644.
'International Association of School Librarianship: first annual conference, London, 1972' *School Libn* 1972 20(4) 294-7.
'School library services as components in national library systems within the framework of NATIS' Presession seminar IFLA/Unesco, Oslo 1975.
Delannoy J P *Guide for the conversion of school libraries into media centres* Unesco, 1977, 62p.
Wilson Lib Bull 1979 54(2) 92-114. Special issue on 'The Year of the Child'.
[Children and libraries] *Unesco J* 1979 1(1) Whole issue.
Ray C comp 'Services for the handicapped, submitted by C. Ray [IFLA studies]' *Int Lib Rev* 1977 9(2) 183-207, refs.

3f Academic and research libraries

Thompson J ed *University library history: an international review* Bingley, 1980, 330p.

— *An introduction to university library administration* Bingley/Linnet, 1970, 136p.

Booz, Allan & Hamilton Inc *Problems in university library management* Association of Research Libraries, 1970.

Rogers R D and Weber D C *University library administration* Wilson, 1971, 454p.

Saunders W L *University and research library studies* Pergamon, 1968, 221p.

Moys E M 'Problems involved in the creation of new university libraries' *Unesco Bull Lib* 1966 20(1) 54-63.

Palmer R P *Computerizing the card catalog in the university library: a survey of user requirement* Libraries Unlimited, 1972, 141p.

White L W 'Departmental libraries' in *Encyclopedia* 6(1971) 596-603, bibl.

Symposium on libraries in the university, Geneva AUPFEL, 1965 AUPFEL, 1966, 335p.

International Seminar on University Libraries SCONUL and Unesco, 1968.

Saunders W L 'Humanistic institutions or information factory?' *J Libp* 1969 1(4) 195-210, 16 refs.

Lincoln C M *University libraries as information centres: proceedings of the 6th meeting of IATUL, Zurich, 26-30 May 1975* Loughborough U of Technology Library, 1976, 92p.

Fjallbrant N and McCarthy K eds *Developing library effectiveness for the next decade. Proceedings of the 7th Meeting of IATUL, Louvain, 1977* Gothenburg, IATUL/Chalmers U of Technology Library, 1978, 235p.

Poole H ed *Academic libraries by the year 2000: essays honoring Jerrold Orne* Bowker, 1977.

3f Special libraries — Documentation centres

Batten W E ed *Handbook of special librarianship and information work* 4th ed Aslib, 1975, 430p.

Saunders W L *The provision and use of library and documentation services* Pergamon, 1966.

Johns A W *Special libraries: development of the concept, their organization and their services* Scarecrow, 1968, 245p.

Silva M *Special libraries* Deutsch, 1970, 96p.

Reichardt G ed *Special libraries — worldwide* Verlag Dokumentation (for IFLA), 1974, 360p. Role of IFLA's Special Libraries Section. Activities of special libraries in 23 countries.

Congrès international des bibliothèques et des centres de documentation, Bruxelles 1955 Nijhoff, 3 vols.

1976 Brussels Special Libraries Conference (with the Lausanne Conference) 'The international role of special libraries' Reported in *Inspel* 1976 11(4) 131-40.

1st Worldwide Conference on Special Libraries, Honolulu, June 1979 Theme: 'Politics and economics: their impact on library information services'.

Halm J van *The development of special libraries as an international phenomenon* New York, Special Libraries Association, 1978, 626p. 100 countries reviewed.

Kujoth J *Readings in nonbook librarianship* Scarecrow, 1968, 463p.

Harrison H P *Film library techniques* Focal P, 1973, 272p.

Teague S J *Microform librarianship* Butterworths, 1977, 117p.

Evans H *Picture librarianship* Bingley, 1980, 133p.

IAALD *Primer for agricultural libraries* 1967, 72p.

32 Harada K 'The world-wide network of agricultural libraries' *IAALD Q Bull* 1972

17(2) 68-77. See the whole issue for international aspects of agricultural documentation.
Fusonie A and Moran L eds *International agricultural librarianship: continuing and change: proceedings of an international symposium held at the National Agriculture Library 4th November 1977* Greenwood, 1979, 127p.
Annan G L and Falter J W *Handbook of medical library practice* 3rd ed MLA, 1970, 411p.
Sewell W *Reader in medical librarianship* NCR Microcard Editions, 1973, 382p.
Taines S I et al, eds *International Congress on Medical Librarianship. Second conference Washington 1963* (Abstracts of papers submitted) Excerpta Medica, 1963, 128p.
Davis K E and Sweeney W D eds *International Congress on Medical Librarianship, Third Conference, Amsterdam, May 1969. Proceedings* Excerpta Medica, 1970, 541p.
Brodman E 'Medical libraries around the world' *Med Lib Ass Bull* 1971 59(2) 223-8.
Recent practices in map libraries. Proceedings of a map panel . . . Montreal 1969 Special Library Association, 1971, 36p. Includes sources of information on maps and atlases.
Ristow W W *The emergence of maps in libraries* Linnet; Mansell, 1980 [352p].
Freitag W M 'Art libraries and collections' in *Encyclopedia* 1(1968) 511-621.
'Acts of the 9th international congress of libraries and museums of the performing arts, Genoa 1970' *Boll Museo Bibliot dell'Attore del Teatro Stabile di Genoa* 1970 (3) 145p.
Comptes rendus du premier congrès international des phonothèques, Paris, 1967 Paris, Phonothèque Nationale, 1970, 266p. (Cahiers de la FIP, No. special, 1).
Jones M *Music librarianship* Bingley, 1979.
Benton R ed [11th International Congress of Music Libraries] *Fontes Artis Musicae* 1978 (1) 1-105.
Blunt A *Law Librarianship* Bingley, 1980, 120p.
IALL [IALL Roundtable at Lausanne, Switzerland, August 24 & 25, 1976] *Int J Law Lib* 1976 4(2) 78-119.
Centres de documentation scientific et technique. Contribution de l'Unesco à leur développement Unesco, 1965, 40p. English edition out of print.
Strauss L J et al *Scientific and technical libraries: their organization and administration* 2nd ed Wiley, 1972, 450p, bibl.
Mount E *Scientific and technical libraries in the seventies* Gale Research, 1981 (Books, publishing and libraries information guide series, 4).
Mason D 'PPBS [Planning Programme Budgeting Systems]: applications to an industrial information and library service' *J Libp* 1972 4(2) 91-105.
Bakewell K G B *Industrial libraries throughout the world* Pergamon, [1980].
Laundy P *Parliamentary librarianship in the English-speaking world* LA, 1980, 154p.

3f Documentation — Information

Majewski Z 'Dokumentacja-informacja naukowa-informatologia' *Akt Probl Inf Dokum* 1976 21(3) 6-7.
Uniejewska H 'W sprawie nazwy dyscypliny zajmujacej sie teoria i prakyka informacji naukowej' *Akt Probl Inf Dokum* 1976 21(4) 8-9.
Farradane J 'Towards a true information science' *Info Scientist* 1976 10(3) 91-101.
Leupolt M 'Some considerations on the nature of information' *Int Forum Info Doc* 1978 3(3) 29-34, refs.

Schultz C K *H P Luhn: pioneer of information science, selected works* Spartan/Macmillan, 1968, 320p.

Rayward B W *The universe of information: the work of Paul Otlet for documentation and international organisation* VINITI (for FID), 1975, 390p. (FID publication 520).

Schwartz S and Willers U *Knowledge and development. Reshaping library and information services for the world of tomorrow. A festschrift for Bjorn Tell* Stockholm, Rapel Institute of Technology Library, 1978, 307p.

Meadow C T *The analysis of information systems* Wiley, 1966, 301p.

Lancaster F W 'Evaluating and testing of information retrieval systems' in *Encyclopedia* 8(1972) 234-59, 62 refs.

Kochen M *The growth of knowledge: readings in organization and retrieval of information* Wiley, 1967, 368p.

Passman S *Scientific and technological communication* Pergamon, 1969, 161p.

VINITI *Mezdunarodnij forum po informatike. Sbornik statej* 1969, 2 vols. Sponsored by FID. In English:

FID/RI *Problems of information science. Collected papers* VINITI, 1972, 240p. (FID 478). Shorter version.

Saracevic T *Introduction to information science* Bowker, 1970, 776p.

Hanson C W *Introduction to science-information work* Aslib, 1971, 199p.

Unesco *National issues for policy-makers: the consolidation of information* Unesco, 1974.

Aines A A and Day M S eds 'National planning of information services' in *Annual Review of Info-Science and Technology* 1975 10 3-42.

OECD Ad Hoc Group on Scientific and Technical Information. *Information for a changing society: some policy decisions* OECD, 1971, 50p.

CEDOC (Argentine) *Users of documentation: proceedings of the 35th FID Congress* CEDOC, 1972.

Rozsa G *Scientific information and society* Mouton, 1973, 159p.

Deutsche Stiftung fur Internationale Entwicklung *International expert meeting on the ways and means to an international information system for economic and social development, Dec. 1975,* Berlin Bonn, Die Stiftung, 114p.

Information systems design for socio-economic development: retrospect and prospect. FID symposium, Brussels, 1975. (80th anniversay of the FID). FID, 1976, 145p. (FID publication 542).

Wessel A E *The social use of information* Wiley, 1976.

Rich R F ed 'Knowledge production and utilization: the use of scientific information in decision making' *American Behavioral Scientist* 1979 22(3) Whole issue (6 papers).

Information policy for the 1980's: proceedings of the EUSIDIC Conference, Copthorne, U.K., 3-5 October 1978 Learned Information, 1979, 123p.

Anderla G *Information in 1985: a forecasting study of information needs and resources* OECD, 1973, 131p.

Vilentchuck L ISLIC International Conference on Information Science, Tel Aviv, 1971 *Proceedings* ISLIC, 1972, 803p.

Debone A ed *Information science: search for identity: proceedings of the 1972 NATO Advanced Study Institute in Information Science held at Seven Springs, Champion, Pennsylvania, August 12-20, 1972* New York, Marcel Dekker Inc, 1974, 491p. (Books in library and information science, 7).

Horsnell V ed *Informatics 2; proceedings of a conference held by the Aslib Coordinate Indexing Group, March 1974, Oxford* Aslib, 1975, 100p.

Information systems: their interconnections and compatability; proceedings of a Symposium on Information Systems: Connection and Compatibility organized

by the International Atomic Energy Agency and co-sponsored by the Food and Agriculture Organization of the United Nations and Unesco, held in Varna, Bulgaria, 30 Sept. - 3 Oct. 1974 Vienna, International Atomic Energy Agency, 1975, 470p.

Vickery B C et al *Final report on International Research Forum in Information Science* (BLRDD report 5262) British Library Research and Development Department, 1975.

Information science and education 2nd IFIP International Conference, Sept. 1975, Marseilles. International Federation for Information Processing.

3f Networks — NATIS concept, etc.

Swedish Cabinet Office. Secretariat for Future Studies. *Man in the communication system of the future* The Secretariat, 1974.

Girard A and Moreau M 'L'utilisateur face à 10 millions de références: "les problèmes d'interrogation"' *Information et Documentation* (Association Nationale de la Recherche Technique) 1976 (3) 43-60.

Elman S A 'The humanization of information science' *Spec Lib* 1976 67(9) 421-7, refs.

Nora S and Minc A *L'informatisation de la société* (Rapport au Président de la Republique Française) Documentation Francaise, 1978, 163p + Appendices 4 vols. Translated as:

— *Computerization of society* MIT, 1980, 186p.

Miller F and Tighe R L 'Library and information networks' in *Annual Review of Information Science and Technology* 1974 9.

Guilloux R ed *Réseaux et systèmes de documentation* Gauthier-Villars, 1975.

Schwarz S ed *The interactive library: computerized processes in library and information networks: proceedings of a seminar held in Stockholm, Nov 25-28 1974* Swedish Society for Technical Documentation, 1975, 286p.

Bullard S R et al, eds 'Multitype library networking: a symposium (special section)' *Library Acquisitions: Practice and Theory* 1978 2(3/4) 159-91.

'Information systems and networks' *Unesco J* 1980 2(2). Whole issue.

Rouse W B and S H *Management of library networks: policy analysis, implementation and control* Wiley, 1980, 288p.

AGARD *National and international networks of libraries, documentation and information centres: papers presented at the Technical Information Panel Specialists' Meeting held in Brussels, Belgium, 2-3 Oct. 1974* AGARD, 1975, 84p.

Kraus D H et al *National science information systems* MIT, 1972.

National Information Systems (NATIS): objectives for national and international action Paris, Unesco, 1974, 32p. (COM-74/NATIS/Ref 5); and ERIC Report ED-167 094.

Unesco Intergovernmental Conference on the Planning of National Documentation Library and Archives Infrastructures, Paris, September 1974. Main documents:

- *Final report* Unesco, 1975, 65p. (COM/MD/30).
- *National Information Systems* (NATIS) Unesco, 1974 (COM.74/NATIS/3), and revised edition, 1975 (COM-74/NATIS/3 Rev).
- *Working document* Unesco, 1974 (COM.74/NATIS/4).
- Arntz H *Planning of national documentation, library and archives infrastructures* Unesco, 1974, 44p. (COM.74/NATIS/2).

(See also two papers on manpower in section 2c, Professional issues).

Reports of the conference in:

- *IFLA J* 1975 1(2) 139-45.
- *Unesco Bull Lib* 1975 29(1) 2-15.

Olier J H d' and Delmas B *Planning national infrastructures for documentation, libraries and archives: outline of a general policy* Paris, Unesco, 1975 (COM.74/24-1-4/A).
Report of this conference in:
- *Unesco Bull Lib* 1975 29(6) 355/6.
Mohrhardt F E and Penna C V 'National planning for library and information services' *Adv Libp* 1975 5 62-122.
Design and planning of national information systems (NATIS): a policy paper for government planners Unesco, 1976, 26p.
Goodman H J A 'Planning and plans for national library and information services' in *Encyclopedia* 22(1977) 338-481.
Penna C V et al, eds *National library and information services: a handbook for planners* Butterworths, 1977, 230p.
UNISIST International Symposium on Information Systems and Services in Ongoing Research in Science, Paris, October 1975. Proceedings Hungarian Central Technical Library and Documentation Centre, 1976, 496p; *Final report* Unesco/UNISIST, 1971, 60p.
UNISIST II Intergovernmental Conference on Scientific and Technological Information for Development Paris, 1979. Final report Unesco, 1979, 23p.
Chandler G 'Proposed development of resource sharing networks (UNISIST, NATIS, ALBIS)' *Int Lib Rev* 1976 8(3) 237-64.

3f Automation

Artandi S *An introduction to computers in information science* Scarecrow, 1968, 153p.
Kimber R T *Automation in libraries* Pergamon, 1968, 140p.
LARC *A survey of automated activities in the libraries of the world* 1971-73, 12 vols.
Library Trends 1970 18(4). Issue on 'Issues and problems in designing a national program of library automation'. USA, Canada, Western Europe, Australia, New Zealand, South Africa.
Unesco Bull Lib 1969 23(1). Issue on the impact of computers on libraries.
Becker J and Burchinal L G *Planning for information technology* Paris, Unesco, 1974, 34p.
Marshall D B 'User criteria for selection of commercial on-line computer-based bibliographic services: an industrial practical case study' *Spec Lib* 1975 66(11) 501-8, refs.
First international on-line information meeting, London, 13-15 Dec. 1977, organised by Online Review Learned Information, [1977], 238p.
Tedd L A *An introduction to computer-based library systems* Heyden, 1977, 222p. (Heyden international topics in science, 5).
Kent A and Galvin T J eds *On-line revolution in libraries* Proceedings of 1977 Conference in Pittsburgh M Dekker, 1978, 303p.
White M S 'Conference report: First International Online Information Meeting' *On-Line Rev* 1978 2(1) 31-40.
Second International On-Line Information Meeting, London, 5-7 Dec. 1978 Learned Information, 1978, 286p.
Lancaster F W *Towards paperless information systems* Academic P, 1978, 179p.
Inhaber H and Alvo M 'World science as an input-output system' *Scientometrics* 1978 1(1) 43-64.

3f Architecture — Design

Bleton J 'Pour un Centre international de documentation et d'information sur la construction et l'equipment des bibliothèques' *IFLA J* 1978 4(1) 34-9. In 1961 an IFLA Committee on Library Buildings was created. International documentation 1969-70 was collected by the Direction des Biblothèques. Lack of funds stopped these activities. Suggests reactivating the Centre with IFLA's aid.

Thompson D E 'History of library architecture: a bibliographical essay' *J Lib Hist* 1969 4(2) 133-41.

Clark J W *The care of books: an essay on the development of libraries and their fittings from the earliest times to the end of the 18th century* CUP, 1901 (Reprinted: Folcroft, 1973).

Bauforum: Fachzeitschrift fur Architectur. . . (Vienna) 1970 3(17). Issue on 'Bibliotheksbauten' 72p.

Brawne M *Libraries: architecture and equipment* Pall Mall P, 1970, 188p.

Mason E *Mason on library buildings* Scarecrow, 1980, 333p.

Nordgarden A and Salonen K 'International conference in Finland on library buildings' *Scand Publ Lib Q* 1975 8(4) 115-20.

Nikas M 'Function first in library design' *Contract* (New York) 1968 Nov.

Orr J M *Designing library buildings for activity* Deutsch, 1972, 152p.

Thompson G *Planning and design of library buildings* London Architectural P Ltd and New York, Nichols Publ Comp, 1977, 189p.

Cohen A and E *Designing and space planning for libraries: a behavioral guide* Bowker, 1979, 250p.

Brown H F *Planning the academic library: Metcalf and Ellsworth at York* Oriel P, 1971, 97p. Course held at York Institute of Advanced Architectural Studies, 1966.

Ellsworth R E *Academic library buildings: a guide to architectural issues and solutions* Colorado Ass't U P, 1973, 530p.

Humphreys K W ed *Colloque sur le construction des bibliothèques universitaires, Lausanne 29 June - 2 July 1971* Birmingham/Lausanne, 1972, 154p. (LIBER, suppl., 1).

Pierce W S *Furnishing the library interior* M Dekker, 1980, 288p. (Books in library and information science, 29).

Metcalf K D *Library lighting* Ass Res Libraries, 1970, 99p.

1

Aje S B 'National libraries in developing countries' in *Advances in Librarianship* 1977 7 105-43.

'National libraries — Section 2: National libraries in developing countries' in Xuereb P *Manual of library economy* Shoestring/Bingley, 1977, 47-60.

Bandara S B 'Can university libraries serve the national library role in developing countries' *Libri* 1979 29(2) 127-43, refs.

Nyeng P 'Danske faglige og videnskabelige biblioteker (5): folkebibliotekernes platoniske forhold til U-landslitteratur og mellemfolkeligt samvirkes bibliotek' *Bibliotek 70* 1977 (20) 562-4. On libraries specializing in India and East Africa (and the Third World in general).

2a

UN General Assembly *Cultural and scientific institutions in non-self governing territories. Report prepared by Unesco* UN, 1959, 34p. (Document A/4144).

Institutions for documentation and research on cultural development Unesco, 1975, 117p. (SHC.75/WS/14).

Spiller D 'International organisations and their effect upon the libraries of developing countries' *Int Lib Rev* 1979 11(3) 341-51, refs. Mainly Unesco, IFLA, FID.

Welch T F 'Information for regional development: an introduction to the information activities of the United Nations Centre for Regional Development (UNCRD)' *Lib Info Sci* 1974 (12) 43-50.

UN Advisory Committee on the Applications of Science and Technology to Development. Mentioned in *Unesco J* 1979 1 276., in connection with the Vienna Colloquium 1979.

The most relevant of the UN agencies is of course Unesco itself. See references in: General, references above, and:

Alam A M N 'Unesco's activities to facilitate access of developing countries to protected works' *Unesco J* 1979 1(3) 191-9, refs.

Amongst other international agencies whose work is of interest here the following may be mentioned:

International Institute for Adult Literacy Methods, Tehran. See activities, publications, etc in sections below.

International Institute for Educational Planning. Library planning is amongst its programmes.

International Bureau for Education (IBE), Geneva. Now attached to Unesco. See under: General, 2a.

Amongst regional or national agencies, see:

- USA (For details see under USA: Directories, etc.)

US Agency for International Development (US AID), with regional agencies.

US Information Agency (USIA) and its regional centres: US Information Services (USIS).

Carnegie Corporation of New York. Library Services.
Ford Foundation.
Franklin Book Programs.
Rockefeller Foundation.
- Europe.
British Council. 1934— . With regional libraries.
Offices de la Recherche d'Outre Mer, Paris.
Deutsche Stiftung für Entwicklungsländer, Bonn.
Institut pour les Pays en Voie de Développement, Antwerp University. 1920- . Formerly: Institut Universitaire des Territoires d'Outre Mer. Library and documentation centre.
Institut d'Etudes des Pays en Développement. Université Catholique de Louvain.
Peace Research Institute, Oslo. Coordinates collections of materials on developing countries for Scandinavia.

2b

Eaton A J 'IFLA and university libraries in developing countries' *Herald Lib Sci* 1978 17 168-72.
FID. Committee on Developing Countries.
Commonwealth Library Association (COMLA). 1971- . HQ in Kingston, Jamaica.
Harrison K C 'The Commonwealth Library Association' *Int Lib Rev* 1971 5(3) 283-7.
Mellemfolgeligt Samvirkes/Association for International Cooperation.
Norwegian Library Association Committee on Developing Countries, 1975- . Keeps contacts with the Norwegian Agency for International Development (NORAD), maintains lists of librarians who have worked in developing countries, etc.
'Bibliotekenes rolle i U-landsinformasjonen' *Bok Bibliot* 1978 45(5) 223-7. From a seminar, Oslo, April 1978.

2c

Palmer B I 'Education and training of librarians in the newly developing British Commonwealth countries' *Lib Trends* 1959 8(2) 229-42.
Lohrer A and Jackson W V 'Education and training of librarians in Asia, the Near East and Latin America' *Lib Trends* 1959 8(3) 243-77, bibl.
Bonn G S *Library education and training in developing countries* Honolulu, East West Center P, 1966, 199p.
Sabor J E *Methods of teaching librarianship* Unesco, 1969, 149p. Editions in English, French, Spanish. Specially adapted to the needs of developing countries.
Dean J *Planning library education programmes: a study of the problems involved in the management and operation of library schools in the developing countries* A Deutsch, 1972, 137p.
Burgess R S 'Education for librarianship — US assistance' *Lib Trends* 1972 20 515-26. Selected schemes.
Bowden R 'Improving library education in developing countries: a Unesco and Loughborough University experiment' *Unesco Bull Lib* 1976 30(5) 255-61, refs.
Education and training: theory and provision with a look at new developments and an example of the challenge confronting information workers. FID pre-congress seminar, Edinburgh, 1978 FID, 1979, 149p, bibl. (FID Publications, 576). 39

Latin America, East Africa, Arab countries.

Benge R 'Library education in the Third World: some personal comparisons' *Lib Rev* 1979 28 226-31. Part of an issue on 'Exporting knowledge'.

Kotei S I A 'Some variables of comparison between developed and developing library systems' in Foskett D J ed *Reader in comparative librarianship* 1976, 149-58. Based largely on African culture.

Soltani p et al 'Sending librarians abroad' *Int Lib Rev* 1971 3(2) 229-37.

Jackson M M 'Culture shock and the black librarian abroad' *Wilson Lib Bull* 1974 49(3) 234-9.

3a

Kurian G T *Enclyclopedia of the Third World* Mansell, 1979, 2 vols. Dictionary arrangement. Includes international and regional organizations.

Pearcy G E and Stoneman E A *Handbook of new nations* Van Nostrand, 1968, 32p.

James L F *Africa, Latin America and the East* Pergamon, 1973, 236p. (Series: Western Man in the Modern World).

Great Britain. Ministry of Overseas Development. Library *Guide to sources of information on developing countries* 1970, 13p. Mimeo. Organizations, their work and services.

- Foreign and Commonwealth Office *A yearbook of the Commonwealth* 1969- . 1951-68 as *Commonwealth Relations Office yearbook.*

- Central Office of Information (COI) publishes series of monographs and reference lists on countries of the Commonwealth.

France. Documentation Française [Official agency] publishes series of informative monographs on foreign countries. To be traced from the index: *Tables de la Documentation Française.*

Directory of organisations offering literacy training courses Tehran, International Institute for Adult Literacy Methods (IIALM), 1977, 211p.

Directory of universities and institutes offering literacy training programmes Tehran, IIALM, 1977, 78p. Personnel training for teaching.

3b

Clarke D A ed *Acquisitions from the Third World: papers of seminar of LIBER, September 1973* Mansell, 1975, 276p. Includes papers on general and regional schemes: SALALM, SCOLMA, Farmington, Scandia, etc and their problems.

Carroll J and Thompson J eds 'Workshop on acquisitions from the Third World: proceedings [Library of Congress, February 1977]' *Lib Acquisitions* 1977 1(2) 117-33. Problems due to the publishing situation in developing countries.

Bossuat M-L et al, eds *Le Contrôle Bibliographique Universel (UBC) dans les pays en développement. Table ronde.. Grenoble août 1973* Verlag Dokumentation/Saur (for IFLA), 1975, 165p. Includes texts of legal deposit laws.

Requa E G and Statham G *The developing nations. A guide to information sources concerning their economic, political, technical and social problems* Gale Research, 1965, 339p.

Hoover Foundation *Guides*. On individual countries.

American Universites. Field Staff *A select bibliography: Asia, Africa, Eastern Europe, Latin America* Hanover, 1960, 534p. Updated by *Supplements*.

Wilson G *A handbook of library holdings of Commonwealth literature in the United Kingdom* Commonwealth Institute Library, 1971, 59p.

Commonwealth Institute *Selected readings lists for advanced studies*. Series of bibliographies on individual countries or on problems.

40 *Catalogue of the Foreign Office Library* G K Hall, 1972, 8 vols.

Catalogue of the Colonial Office Library G K Hall, 1964, 15 vols. Library now incorporated in the Foreign and Commonwealth Office Library.

Livres actualité, Paris. Series of bibliographies on individual countries.

VEB. Bibliographisches Institut, Leipzig *Asien, Afrika, Latinamerika* 1967- .

International Institute for Adult Literacy Methods *Literacy documentation* 1972 .

— *Literacy discussion* 1970- . Quarterly, English and French.

Conover H F 'The bibliography of newly developing areas' *Lib Trends* 1959 8(2) 322-41.

Dutta S 'Abstracting problems in developing countries' *Unesco Bull Lib* 1968 22(5) 247-52.

Kumar G and Kumar K *Bibliography* New Delhi, Vikas Publ House, 1976, 257p.

Umapathy K S *American books for library science programs in developing countries* Tiptur, Sudarshana Prakashana, 1972, 72p. With special reference to India.

Bansah S *Bibliographie, dépouillement du Bulletin de l'Unesco à l'Intention des Bibliothèques, 1947-1967* Daker, IFAN, 1969, 72p.

'Library development: an annoted bibliography' *Lib Int Development* (ALA) 1969 (15) 6p.

3c

Institut pour les Pays en Voie de Développement *Afrika, Latijns Amerika, Azie,* Antwerp, Papers in English and French.

Institut d'Etudes des Pays en Développement *Cultures et Développement,* Louvain.

Unesco *Cultural Development Newsletter* 1975- . 3 a year Contains a current awareness section.

Mellemfolkeligt Samvirkes *M S-Biblioteksnyt.*

FID/DC Occasional publications 1973- . Committee for Developing Countries.

ALA *Libraries in International Development.*

3e

Bruce R K 'Legal problems facing libraries in developing countries' *IATUL Proc* 1967 2(3) 8-13.

3f

Schaffler H G and Prybyla J S *From underdevelopment to affluence : Western, Soviet, Chinese views* Appleton, 1968.

Harrison K C 'Towards regionalization' *Lib Ass Rec* 1977 79(1) 20-1.

Unesco *Mass media and national development. The rôle of information in the developing countries* 1964, 333p.

Van Bol J M and Fakhfakh A *L'emploi des moyens de communication de masse dans les pays en voie de développement/The use of mass media in developing countries* Brussels, Centre International de Documentation Economique et Sociale Africaine, 1971, 2 vols.

Unesco *Cultural policy: a preliminary study* 1969, 51p. See also other monographs in the series on industrial countries.

Commonwealth Secretariat *Education in the developing countries of the Commonwealth: abstracts of current research* 1969, 160p.

Curle A *Educational problems of developing societies, with case studies of Ghana, Pakistan and Nigeria* Expanded and updated ed, Praeger, 1973, 200p.

Sinclair M E *School and community in the third world* Croom Helm, 1980, 188p.

Burnett M *ABC of literacy* Unesco, 1965.

Unesco *World literacy at mid-century* 1957.

— *Literacy 1967-1969: progress achieved throughout the world* 1970, 113p. Also F/S.

Furter P *Possibilities and limitations of functional literacy: the Iranian experiment* Unesco, 1973, 59p.

Final report: International Symposium for literacy, Persepolis, Iran, September 1975 39p. In appendix the 'Declaration of Persepolis' and a list of working documents prepared for the conference.

Spencer J ed *Illiteracy in the developing world. British Committee on Literacy* U of Reading, British Committee on Literacy, 1976, 64p.

Kibirige H M 'Libraries and illiteracy in developing countries: a critical assessment' *Libri* 1977 27(1) 54-67.

Lepage R B *The national language question: linguistic problems of newly independent states* OUP, 1964.

Fishman J A et al *Language problems of developing nations* Wiley, 1968, 521p. (33 papers of a conference).

Milburn S 'The provision of vernacular literature' *Lib Trends* 1959 8(2) 307-21, refs.

Unesco *Books for the developing countries — Asia, Africa* 1962, 31p.

Anderson F *Carnegie Corporation library programs: 1911-1961* Carnegie Corporation, 1963.

Moore B F 'The flow of ideas: a proposal for an international book institute' *ALA Bull* 1968 62(3) 249-54.

Franklin Book Programs *Books for developing countries: a guide for enlisting private industry assistance* US Agency for International Development, 1969, 45p.

Nalhotra D-N 'The book famine in developing countries' *Unesco Bull Lib* 1970 24(4) 211-5.

Aman M M *Books in a starving world: a quest for enrichment; an international book year conference, 6 May 1972. Selected reading for participants* St John's University, Department of Library Science, 1972, 11p.

Altbach P G and Smith K eds 'Publishing in the 3rd world' *Lib Trends* 1978 26(4) 449-599.

Oyeoku K K 'Library and the 3rd world publisher: an inquiry into a lopsided development' *Lib Trends* 1978 26 505-14.

John M 'Libraries in oral-traditional societies' *Int Lib Rev* 1979 11(3) 321-39, refs.

Berninghausen D K 'The American library consultant overseas' *Int Lib Rev* 1969 1(1) 97-105.

Brewster B J *American overseas library technical assistance, 1940-1970* Scarecrow, 1976, 434p.

Needle J 'Peace Corps librarians in the developing world' *Spec Lib* 1977 68(5/6) 206-10.

Williamson W L *Assistance to libraries in developing nations: papers on comparative studies*. Proceedings of a conference held at the Wisconsin Center, Madison, May 14, 1971 U of Wisconsin, Library School, 1971, 68p. Papers on methodology in comparative research, on individual regions. See in relation to developing countries in general: Elmendorf W W 'Cross-cultural aspects of assistance to developing countries'.

Benge R C *Communication and identity* Bingley, 1972; Linnet, 1972. Complex book on the philosophy of assistance to the third world and the respect of cultural identities.

— *Cultural crisis and libraries in the 3rd world* Saur/Bingley, 1979, 255p.

White C M 'Acceleration of library development in developing countries' *Advances in Libp* 1970-1 241-85.

Asheim L *Librarianship in developing countries* Illinois U P, 1966, 95p.
Borchardt D H 'Library services in underdeveloped areas' *J Educ Libp* 1968 9(2) 54-75.
Hutchings F G B *Librarianship, a short manual; with special reference to developing countries* Kuala Lumpur, OUP, 1969, 133p.
Chantal J de 'Bibliothèques et archives du Tiers-Monde: problèmes et perspectives' *Doc et Biblioth* 1975 21(2) 85-95.
Briquet de Lemos A A *The portrait of librarianship in developing societies as sketched by the foreign observer* Loughborough U of Technology, 1977, 123p.
Abdul Huq A M and Aman MM *Librarianship and the Third World* Garland Pub, 1977. (Reference Library of Social Science, 40).
Evans P C C 'Libraries and nationhood' *Lib World* 1962 63(744) 323-8.
Rappaport P 'The rôle of libraries in the developing countries' *Lagos Libn* 1968 3(4) 5-8.
Foskett D J 'Libraries and educational planning: some reflections on a Unesco seminar' *Unesco Bull Lib* 1971 25(2) 67-72.
'Seminar on the role of libraries in information on developing countries' *Bog og Bibliotek* 1978 45(5) 223-34.
FID/DC *Study on national structures for documentation and library services in countries with different levels of development, with particular reference to the needs of developing countries* Unesco, 1973, 200p. (COM/WS/301).
Chandler G *International librarianship: surveys of recent developments in developing countries and in advanced librarianship* (Submitted to the 1971 IFLA pre-session seminar for developing countries, sponsored by Unesco, Liverpool City Libraries, August 24 - September 1, 1971) LA, 1971, 208p. 20 reports from countries of the third world. See a summary in:
Unesco Bull Lib 1972 26(2) 69-72. Another seminar was held at the FID congress, Budapest, 1972.
Harvey J F 'International library report implementation' *Int Lib Rev* 1980 12(2) 115-25, refs.
Nazmutdinov I K 'Seminar bibliotechnykh rabotnikov stran Azii, Afriki i Latinskoi Ameriki' *Sovetskya Bibliografiya* 1975 (154) 32-6.
Fonotov G P 'Seminar of librarians from Asia, Africa and Latin America in the USSR' *Unesco Bull Lib* 1976 30(2) 101-3.
Vervliet H D L ed *Resource sharing of libraries in developing countries.* Proceedings of the 1977 IFLA/Unesco Pre-session Seminar for Librarians from Developing Countries, Antwerp University August 30 - September 4, 1977, K G Saur, 1979, 286p. (IFLA Publ. 14).
Linz W ed *Proceedings of the General Conference on the Planning of Archival Development in the 3rd World, Dakar, 28-31 January 1975* International Council of Archives, Verlag Dokumentation, 1976, 117p. (Archivum, Special vol., 1) English and French.
Unesco *Regional meetings of Experts on the National Planning of Documentation and Library Services (Arab Republic of Egypt, 1974; Uganda, 1970; Sri Lanka, 1967; Ecuador, 1966): summary of the main recommendations* Paris, Unesco, 1974, 13p.
IFLA 'Planning of national library systems; report of the IFLA pre-session seminar for developing countries held in Potsdam (DDR) August 1978' *IFLA J* 1979 5(1) 54-6.
'World-wide task of literature bureaux *Unesco Bull Lib* 1954 8(7) E69-E70.
Hockey S W 'Public library services in the developing commonwealth' Paper in *Librarianship overseas* LA, London and Home Counties Branch week-end conference 1964 19-37.

Anderson D P 'Developing areas: international seminar, Moscow-Tashkent April 1972: The public library and its readers, a comparison of the aims and objectives of the public libraries in developed and developing countries' *Int Lib Rev* 1972 4(3) 433-42. Short report on the seminar in: IFLA *News* 1972 (41) 17-9.

Campbell H C 'Metropolitan public library research in developing countries' *Unesco Bull Lib* 1973 27(1) 18-21. On the INTAMEL conference.

Asheim L E 'University libraries in developing countries' *ALA Bull* 1965 59(10) 795-802.

Gelfand M A *University libraries for developing countries* Unesco, 1968, 157p. (Reprinted: 1971).

Krishan K *Research libraries in developing countries* Delhi, Vikas Pub House, 1973, 464p.

Holdsworth H 'University libraries in developing countries: standards and expectations' *Lib Rev* 1979 28 232-8.

Oyelese, W O 'Acquisition in university libraries: problems in developing countries' Unesco Bull 1978 33(2) 81-6.

Parker D and Carabelli A *Guide for an agricultural library survey for developing countries* Scarecrow, 1970, 59, 182p.

Reynolds C F 'Medical libraries in developing countries' *Int Lib Rev* 1969 1(4) 42-9, 9 refs.

McCarthy C 'Medical libraries in developing countries: an international approach' *Int Lib Rev* 1978 10(4) 435-46, refs.

Institut Ali Bach-Hamba, Tunis *La documentation et l'aide au développement du tiers monde.* Colloque du 11 au 13 novembre 1968 1969, various pagings. 16 papers, international and African aspects. Includes a list of previous meetings and a list of international and national organizations interested in the development of documentation.

Arntz H 'Die Rolle der Dokumentation für die Entwicklung der dritten Welt' *Nachr Dok* 1969 20(1) 3-9. In English:

— 'The role of documentation in developing countries' *Unesco Bull Lib* 1971 25(1) 12-7.

Van Niel E 'Automation of libraries in developing countries' *Int Lib Rev* 1974 6(4) 373-86.

FID/DC Working Group *Function and organization of a national documentation centre in a developing country. FID/DC working group under the direction of Harald Shütz* Unesco, 1975, 218p. (Documentation, Libraries and Archives. Studies and research, 7).

Improving information transfer: workshop in Rabat, May 1976 *Final report* Unesco, 1976.

Tell B 'Regional co-operation in information' *Unesco Bull Lib* 1976 30(3) 130-9, 146. Working paper discussed at the Workshop on the improvement of information transfer, Rabat 1976 (Unesco).

Raizada A S 'The Rabat workshop — a pointer for resource mobilization [May 1976]' *Unesco Bull Lib* 1977 31(1) 35-9, 60.

Robredo J 'Problems involved in setting up and operating information networks in the developing countries' *Unesco Bull Lib* 1976 30(5) 251-4.

Weitzel R 'MEDLINE services to the developing countries' *Med Lib Ass Bull* 1976 64 32-4.

Munn R F 'Appropriate technology and information services in developing countries' *Int Lib Rev* 1978 10(1) 23-8.

Howse F G *Some problems in the management of technical services in libraries in developing countries* Loughborough U of Technology, 1980, 172p. (MLS

dissertation).

'National Academy of Sciences Study Group issues recommendation on technical assistance program for scientific and technological information transfer in developing countries' *Information* 1972 Part I 4(5) 245-9. Full report *Scientific and technical information for developing countries.*

Studies of information technologies in developing countries Harvard U, Program on Information Technologies in Developing Countries, 1976.

DEVSIS Study Team *DEVSIS: the preliminary design of an international information system for the development sciences* Ottawa, Int Development Research Centre, 1976, 258p.

Adimorah E N O 'Problems of scientific information work in developing countries' *Info Scientist* 1976 10(4) 139-48.

FID *Information systems design for socio-economic development : retrospect and prospect* FID, 1976.

Kigongo-Bukenya I M N *Resource sharing of libraries in developing countries: the case for library networking* ERIC, 1977, 22p. (ERIC report ED-176 765).

Lyengar T K S *Developing countries and its information needs and supply: a brief report of an international seminar* ERIC, 1977, 7p. (ERIC report ED-176 757) Summary of 30 papers at the UN/ICSU/COSTED International Seminar on 'Technical Information Services for Developing Countries' Indian Institute of Technology, Madras, 1977.

Samaha E 'Research information in progress: a survey and analysis of systems and services in developing countries' *Unesco Bull Lib* 1978 32(5) 322-32.

McAnany E G ed *Communication in the rural 3rd world: the role of information in development* Praeger, 1979.

Dusoulier R N 'Le marché de l' information. Une analyse des besoins dans les pays en voie de developpement' *Documentaliste* 1979 16(5/6) 191-4.

Tell B V 'The awakening information needs of the developing countries' *J Info Sci* 1980 1(1) 285-9.

Fonseca E N de *Conservação de bibliotecas e arquivos em regioes tropicais: A presentação de Gilberto Freyre* Brasilia, Ed ABDF, 1975, 46p.

Bell L and Faye B *La conception des bâtiments d'archives en pays tropical* Unesco, 1979, 190p.

Seng C T 'Public library buildings for Asia: some preliminary observations' *IFLA J* 1978 4(2) 110-3.

Marshall D N 'University library buildings in tropical regions' *Timeless Fellowship* 1974/75 (9) 101-6.

Hoare P 'Consideration of some planning factors and standards relating to university libraries in tropical developing countries' *Toktok Bilong Haus Buk* 1978 (25/26) 16-27, refs.

APPENDIX: French-speaking countries

2a

Paris. Agence de Coopération Culturelle et Technique. Links French-speaking countries throughout the world.

2b

Association Internationale des Ecoles des Sciences de l'Information (AIESI), Montreal. 1977- . Comes under the more general Association des Universités Partiellement ou Entièrement de Langue Française (AUPELF). See:

Unesco Bull Lib 1978 32 Item 203.

Cartier G 'Fondation de l'Association Internationale des Ecoles des Sciences de l'Information (AIESI)' *Doc Biblioth* 1977 23(3) 161-4. (See also in 3f below).

2c

Lajeunesse M 'Education and training of information specialists in French-speaking countries: a comparative study' *Unesco J* 1979 1(2) 124-37. Includes detailed tables of courses available.

3a

Rebouillet A and Tetu M eds *Guide culturel, civilisations et littératures d'expression française* Hachette, 1977, 380p.

Lajeunesse M *Répertoire des écoles des sciences de l'information* Montreal, AIESI, 1978, 110p.

3b

Francophonie France-Expansion, 1972- . Quarterly. Includes an annual cumulation: 'Douze mois d'edition francophone'.

3c

Documentaliste

3f

Documentaliste. 1971 Special issue, 96p. On documentary activities in French-speaking countries. Mainly automation.

SECTION 2

EUROPE

EUROPE

General and Western Europe. See also Eastern Europe.

1

National libraries: their problems and prospects. Symposium on national libraries in Europe, Vienna 8-27 September 1958 Unesco, 1960, 125p. (2nd impression 1963). *Final report* also available from Unesco as a separate document. For comments on the symposium see:

'Symposium on national libraries in Europe' *Unesco Bull Lib* 1959 13(1) 1-4, 20.

Wormann C D 'National libraries of our time: the Unesco symposium on national libraries in Europe' *Libri* 1959 9(4) 273-307.

Iiams T M 'National libraries of Latin Europe: some observations' *Amer Lib* 1971 2(10) 1081-5. Lisbon, Madrid, Paris, Rome, Vatican.

2a

Majault J *Education documentation centres in Western Europe: a compiled study* Unesco, 1963, 25p.

European Information and Education Organization.

2b

European Association of Research Libraries (LIBER).

Clavel J-P 'European Association of Research Libraries' *Unesco Bull Lib* 1972 26(1) 47-8. Also in *IFLA News* 1972 (40) 13-4.

Humphreys KW 'LIBER's relations with other bodies' *LIBER Bull* 1978 (11) 42-6.

'[Organizations of professional children's librarians]' *Int Lib Rev* 1972 4(3) 285-302. Series of short papers on organizations in various countries.

European Association of Scientific Information and Dissemination Centres (EUSIDIC). See activities under 3f.

2c

Cowley J D 'The development of professional training in librarianship in Europe' *Lib Q* 1937 7(2) 169-95.

'Education for librarianship abroad in selected countries' *Lib Trends* 1963 12(2) 121-355. Czechoslovakia, East Germany, Great Britain, Greece, The Netherlands, Poland, Spain and the USSR.

IFLA Committee on Professional Development 'La Formation des bibliothécaires en Europe' *Libri* 1966 16(4) 282-311, refs.

Library Association 'Library qualifications in the European Community: statement by the Library Association Council' *Lib Ass Rec* 1973 75 53, 56.

Schur H 'The European Communities and the harmonization of educational and professional qualifications' *J Libp* 1975 7(1) 49-65. General, includes documentation.

Davinson D 'Trends in library education — Europe' *Adv Libp* 1976 6 217-52, refs.

Meyriat J 'La formation des professionels de l'information dans les pays membres 49

des Communautés Européennes' *Documentaliste* 1977 14(2) 39-46.
'Journée d'étude à l'ENSB: la formation professionnelle des bibliothécaires en Europe' *Bibliog Fr* 1977 166 (21) 890-2.
Education for librarianship in the European Economic Community and the mutual recognition of qualifications Loughborough U of Technology, 1977, 138p, refs.
See also a Seminar on Library Education in Europe held at Liverpool Polytechnic, Department of Library and Information Studies, September 1974. Published?.
Lajeunesse M 'Education and training of information specialists in French-speaking countries: a comparative study' *Unesco J* 1979 1(2) 124-37, refs. European countries included: France, Belgium, Switzerland.
Thompson A H *MEILLEUR: mobility of employment international for librarians in Europe; professional staff exchanges and secondments between libraries in Western Europe: a survey of opportunities and difficulties* LA, 1977, 68p (Research Publications, 20).

3a

Europa Yearbook. Vol 1 is concerned with Europe.
Council of Europe *Annuaire Européen* Vol 26 (1978) Nijhoff, 1980, 696p.
Allen C G *Manual of European languages for librarians* Bowker, 1975, 496p.
Lewanski R C *European library directory* Olschki, 1968, 774p.
— *Subject collections in European libraries: a directory and bibliographical guide* 2nd ed Bowker, 1978, 495p.
International Association of Law Libraries *European law libraries guide* London, Morgan-Grampian, 1971, 678p.
Round Table of Art Librarians *Directory of art libraries in Europe: a preliminary list* Bristol Polytechnic, Faculty of Art and Design Library, 1979, 62p.
Répertoire européen des organismes de recherche et des chercheurs dans le domaine de l'information Lausanne, International Association for Mass Communication Research, 1968, 93p. Teaching institutions, libraries, etc.
Harvey A P and Pernet A eds *European sources of scientific and technical information* 5th ed Hodgson, 1981, 504p.
Pratt G ed *Data bases in Europe: a directory to machine-readable data bases and data banks in Europe* Aslib and EUSIDIC, 1975, 66p. (European users series, 1).
Tomberg A ed *Ibid* Aslib, 1976, 63p (European users series, 1, 2nd ed).
Tomberg A ed *EUSIDIC database guide* Learned Information (European Bibliographical Centre), 1978, 130p.

3b

Coward R E and Yelland M eds *The interchange of bibliographic information in machine-readable form: papers given at the Western European Seminar on the Interchange of . . ., held at Banbury May 1974*. Sponsored by the British Council, the British Library and the Library Association. Library Association 1975, 100p. (LA Research Publications, 17).
Steele C and Walker G eds *European acquisitions and their bibliographical control: proceedings of an exchange of experience seminar, Oxford March 1974* U of Lancaster Library, 1975, 135p. Seminar on the theme: 'Europe — the neglected continent?'.
Sicco M 'Bibliografie nazionali e cataloghi collettivi: esperienze all 'estero' *AIB Boll* 1978 18(2) 106-115, refs. In Europe: Belgium, France, West Germany, Great Britain, Scandinavia.

Horecky P L *Southeastern Europe: a guide to basic publications* U of Chicago P, 1969.
Hart E 'Music: national provision and activities in libraries of Austria, France, Great Britain and the United States. Part I: National collections' *Brio* 1971 8(1) 3-6; 'Part II: bibliographies and catalogues' *Brio* 1971 8(2) 1-5, refs.
Jesse A comp 'Ausbildung in 'Information und Dokumentation' — eine Auswahlbibliographie' *Nachrichten* 1977 53(6) 377-85. Complement to:
'Bibliographie in Information und Dokumentation' *Nachrichten* 1976 52(6) 345-54.

3c

Ligue des Bibliothèques Européennes de Recherche *LIBER Bulletin* 1972-.
— *LIBER News Sheet* 1978- .

3d

OECD *[Annual surveys of economic conditions of European countries.]* Individual volumes by country, including non-member countries.

3e

Farkas L 'Irányzatok a külföldi könyvtári törveny-hozában' *Könyv Figyelö* 1972 18(1) 23-41, refs. Czechoslovakia, Bulgaria, Denmark, East Germany, Finland, Great Britain, Poland.
Withers F N *Standards for library service: an international survey* Unesco, 1974. Revision and expansion of a document issued in 1970. General and by country. For Europe: Belgium, France, West Germany, The Netherlands.
Dietz A *Copyright law in the European Community: a comparative investigation of national copyright legislation, with special reference to the provisions of the Treaty establishing the European Economic Community* Sijthoff and Noordhoff, 1978, 312p.

3f

Burns E MacNall *Western civilizations: their history and their culture* 8th ed Norton, 1973, 927p.
Joll J *Europe since 1870: an international history* Harper & Row, 1973.
Eisenstein E L 'Some conjectures about the impact of printing on Western society and thought. A preliminary report' *J Modern Hist* 1968 40(1) 1-56.
Johnson E D *A history of libraries in the Western world* 3rd rev ed Scarecrow, 1976.
Irwin R 'Ancient and medieval libraries' in *Encyclopedia* 1 (1968) 339-415.
Wilson N G 'The libraries of the Byzantine world' *Greek, Roman and Byzantine Studies* 1967 8 53-80.
Thompson W J *The medieval library* Hafner, 1957. First published 1939.
Dana J Cotton and Kent H W *Literature of libraries in the 17th and 18th centuries* Scarecrow, 1967, 6 vols in one. Reprint of McClurg edition, 1906-1907.
Jackson S L 'Highlights of continental librarianship, 1680-1789' *J Educ Libp* 1971 11(4) 344-50.
Gudovchtchikova I V *Choix de textes en français sur les livres, les lecteurs, les bibliothèques* Institute of Culture N K Krupskaia, 1967, 334p.
Liebaers H 'Impact of American and European librarianship upon each other' in *Libraries and the life of the mind in America* ALA, 1977, 67-83.
Liebaers H 'Towards a European librarianship: reflexions on the Brussels symposium on library methods' *Libri* 1958 8(1) 67-75.
Unesco *Conference on the international exchange of publications in Europe. Final*

report Unesco, 1960 (Unesco/CUA/104).

[Second European conference of European exchange experts, Vienna, April 1972] *Unesco Bull Lib* 1973 27(1) 54-6.

Razumovsky M 'La collaboration en matière d'acquisition d'ouvrages dans quelques pays d'Europe et aux Etats Unis' *Bull Biblioth Fr* 1963 8(4) 161-74, refs. France, East and West Germany, Great Britain, USSR.

Dewe M *Library supply agencies in Europe* Library Association, 1967, 314p. (FLA thesis, 1967). Scandinavia, West Germany, The Netherlands, Hungary, USSR.

Smith A *Books: East and West* London, Eucorg (European Cooperation Research Group), 1973. Report on the flow of publications between Western and Eastern Europe.

Carnovsky L 'Patterns of library government in European nations' *Lib Q* 1954 24(2) 138-53.

[Symposium on national systems of libraries in Europe, Prague, 1970] *Int Lib Rev* 1970 2(1) 41-7.

Institut International de Cooperation Intellectuelle *La mission sociale et intellectuelle des bibliothèques populaires* 1937, 444p.

Kaufman P 'Some community libraries in 18th century Europe: a reconnaissance' *Libri* 1972 22(1) 1-57, refs.

Parkhill J T *Amsterdam to Westminster: jottings from a library journey through metropolitan Northern Europe, July-August 1967* Canadian Library Association, 1968, 47p. (CLA occasional papers, 75). Scandinavia, France, Germany, Switzerland, The Netherlands.

Gardner F M 'Public libraries in Europe: an overall view of standards and developments' in *Proceedings*, LA Public Libraries Conferences, Eastbourne, September 1975 LA, 1975, 32-40.

Vijnstroom M *De openbare bibliotheek in Europa* Bibliotheek en Lektuur Centrum, 1976, 75p.

Fang J R 'Contemporary [public] libraries in Western Europe' in *Encyclopedia* 24 (1978) 390-422. Includes sections by country with references.

Anglo-Scandinavian Public Library Conference, 8th Brighton 1976 *Service points in sparsely populated areas: papers and discussions . . . with a report of the study tour* LA, 1976, 47p.

Stevenson G T 'Library adult education activities in public libraries in Germany, Denmark and England' *ALA Bull* 1963 57(7) 643-54.

IFLA. Libraries in Hospitals Sub-section comp *Organization, description of work and statistics of library services in hospitals, institutions and for the handicapped in Australia, Belgium, Denmark, FDR, Finland, New Zealand, Poland, Sweden* IFLA, 1977, 116p.

European Conference of Directors of Braille Printing Houses and Braille Libraries, Madrid, April 1978. Sponsored by the World Council for the Welfare of the Blind. Unpublished report to IFLA by H B Paris.

Károlyi A 'Iskolai könyvtarak nyugaton' *Könyvtátari Figyelö* 1975 21(6) 646-59. School libraries in Western European countries from the Hungarian abstract Journal.

Ben-David J *Centers of learning: Britain, France, Germany, USA: an essay* [prepared for the Carnegie Commission on Higher Education] McGraw Hill, 1977, 208p.

LIBER Bulletin 1978 (9/10). Issue on proposal, discussion and organization of a project on 'Academic Book Price'. LIBER meeting in Leiden April 1977. First step: preparation of statistics as a data base.

52 *Les bibliothèques universitaires devant l'explosion démographique et l'accroisse-*

ment de l'édition. [Papers of a congress held at Liège University.] (Congrès et Colloques de l'Université de Liège, 44).

Koops W R H and Stellingwerff J eds *Symposium on Developments in Collection Building in University Libraries in Western Europe, Amsterdam, 1976* Saur Verlag, 1977, 109p. Belgium, Germany, Great Britain, The Netherlands represented.

Humphreys K W 'The crisis for academic libraries in Southern Europe' *Bibliot Univ Coimbra Bol* 1978 34.

Gaskell E 'Library services of the European Communities' *INSPEL* 1978 13(3/4) 173-80. Special libraries.

Fawcett T *The present state of library cooperation in the visual arts in the Federal Republic of Germany, the German Democratic Republic, France and The Netherlands* U of East Anglia, 1977, 53p. (BLRD report 5340).

Villier I F A de 'Staatsdiensbiblioteke in Europa en Suid-Afrika — 'n vergelyking' *South Afr Lib* 1975 42(4) 139-142.

Robine N 'Le chercheur dans la bibliothèque de recherche [LIBER survey]' *LIBER Bull* 1978 (9/10) 2-43. Originally published in *Bull Bibliot Fr* 1977 22(7) 413-48.

Clavel J-P 'Les bibliothèques de recherche dans les années 1980' *LIBER Bull* 1974 (4) 20-48.

Kujath K 'The economic libraries of the European Communities' *INSPEL* 1978 13(3/4) 181-204.

Piróg W 'Training of documentation and information users' *Unesco Bull Lib* 1970 24(5) 266-72, 275. Mostly about Europe.

EURIM: a European conference on Research into the Management of Information Servies and Libraries: presented by Aslib . . . 20-22 November 1973 Unesco/ Aslib, 1974, 192p.

EURIM II: Application of Research in Information Services and Libraries March 1976, Amsterdam Aslib, 1977, 266p. (Ed W E Batten).

Dewe A and Deunette J eds *EURIM III: a European conference on the contribution of users to planning and policy making for information systems and networks* by Aslib/Association Nationale de la Recherche Technique, etc., 25-27 April 1978, Künsterhaus, Munich. *Proceedings* Aslib, 1980, 100p.

EURIM IV: European Conference on Innovation in Primary Publication: Impact of producers and users, Brussels, March 1980. See in *Unesco J* 1979 1 277.

Van Dijk M *Seminar Wholesalers of Documentary Information: proceedings* Brussels, Bureau Marcel Van Dijk, 1974, 385p.

Appleyard R K 'The European connection: international cooperation in the use of information resources' *Aslib Proc* 1975 27(2) 38-47.

[Systems of information and documentation in the social sciences] *Info Proc Manag* 1978 14(3/4). Whole issue.

'The availability and use of business information: proceedings of a two-day conference arranged with cooperation of the Aslib Economic and Business Information Group held at the Geological Society of London on 23-24 June 1975' *Aslib Proc* 1975 27(11-12) 425-79.

Slamecka V and Borko H eds 'Planning and organisation of national research programs of information science' *Info Proc Manag* 1980 16(4/5) 177-251.

Guilloux R comp *Réseaux et systèmes de documentation* Gauthier-Villars, 1975, 340p. Networks in Europe and USSR, and the USA.

Davies G W P 'Information networks in the European Community' *Info Scientist* 1975 9(3) 91-8. Symposium.

First European Congress on Documentation Systems and Networks, Luxembourg, 16-18 May 1973 Commission of the EEC, 1974, 397p.

Second European Congress on Information Systems and Networks, Luxembourg, 27-30 May 1975 Verlag Dokumentation, 1976, 231p.

Third European Congress on Information Systems and Networks: overcoming the language barrier, Luxembourg 3-6 May 1977 Verlag Dokumentation, 1977, 2 vols.

Tomberg A 'European information networks' *Annual Rev Info Sci Tech* 1977 12 219-46.

Battrick B ed *The future of cooperative information processing in Europe: proceedings of EUSIDIC Conference, Frascati, 6-8 December 1973* ESRO Scientific and Technical Information Branch, 1974, 100p.

Pratt G and Harvey S eds *On-line age: plans and needs for on-line information retrieval: proceedings of EUSIDIC Conference, Oslo 4-5 December 1975* Aslib, 1976, 127p. (European Users series, 3).

MacCafferty M ed *User education: towards a better use of information resources. Proceedings of the EUSIDIC Conference, Graz, December 1976* Alsib/EUSIDIC, 1977, 139p.

Carosella M P 'Conferenza dell' EUSIDIC, Berlino 9-11 novembre 1977' *AIB Boll* 1978 18(1) 54.

Tedd L A 'Report on a visit to European computer-based information services' *Program* 1979 13(2) 47-57.

Ungerer H 'EURONET: the EEC on-line information network' *Unesco Bull Lib* 1979 31(3) 128-33.

Dunning A J 'The origins, development and future of EURONET' *Program* 1977 11(4) 145-55.

Hjerppe R '[EUSIREF — European Scientific Information Referral]' (In Swedish) *Tidskr Dok* 1977 33(3) 37-8. Cooperative programme for computerized services initiated by EUSIDIC.

'European Documentation and Information System for Education (EUSIDEC)' *Bibliog Doc Terminol* 1978 18 157.

Cultural Data Bank for Europe. Organized on the basis of recommendations of the Helsinki Conference on Security and Cooperation, Bucharest March 1977 under Unesco Division of Cultural Development's Documentation and Information Department. Held its second meeting in Brussels, June 1978, its first Committee meeting, Liège, December 1979. See:

Dienes G 'Európa Kulturális Adatbank' *Könyvtari Figyelö* 1980 26(4) 363-9.

AUSTRIA

1

Österreichische Nationalbibliothek, Vienna. 1526- .

Stummvoll J 'Die Österreichischen Nationalbibliothek' *Biblos-Schriften* 1964 (39).

— *Geschichte der Österreichishen Nationalbibliothek* Vienna, Prachner, 1968. In the Series *Museion*.

— 'Austria, National Library of' in *Encyclopedia* 2 (1969) 119-27.

Duchkowitsch W 'Beitrage zur Geschichte der ehemaligen Hofbibliothek in Wien' *Biblos* 1977 26(1) 69-81.

Universitätbibliothek Wien.

'200 Jahre UB Wien' *Biblos* 1977 26(1) 1-62.

Österreichische Institut für Bibliotheksforschung, Dokumentation und Information.

2a

Bundesministerium für Unterricht. Beirat für Bibliothekswesen.

Bundesministerium für Wissenschaft und Forschung.

— Arbeitskreis für Bibliothekreform, 1970- .

2b

Vereinigung Österreichischer Bibliothekare (VÖB), Vienna. 1946- .

Verband Österriechischer Volkbüchereien, Vienna, 1948- .

Stickler M 'Der Verband Österreichischer Volksbüchereien 1948-1978' *Biblos* 1978 27(1) 51-60.

Österreichische Gesellschaft für Dokumentation und Information (ÖGDI). 1951-71 as: Österreichische Gesellschaft für Dokumentation und Bibliographie (ÖGDB).

2c

Kammel K 'Bibliothekarausbildung in Öesterreich' *Biblos* 1969 18(1) 6-9.

Stickler M 'Volksbibliothekare in Öesterreich' *Biblos* 1961 10(4) 161-73.

Fischer E 'Ausbildung der Bibliothekare an wissenschaftlichen Bibliotheken in Österreich' *VSB/SVD Nachr* 1976 52(6) 330-4. See also under Switzerland, 2c.

3a

Area handbook for Austria American U, Foreign Area Studies, 1976, 278p.

VÖB *Handbuch österreichischer Bibliotheken. I Bibliotheksverzeichnis*, new ed 1971, 394p; II *Statistik und Personalverzeichnis,* 1961, 139p. III *Rechtsvorschriften und Erlasse zum österreichischen Bibliothekswesen* Öesterreichische Nationalbibliothek, 1963, 202p. (Biblos-Schriften, 30, 31, 34).

ÖGDB *Dokumentation und Information in Öesterreich-Dokumentationsführer für Wissenschaft, Technik und Wirtschaft* 2e, vollstandig überarbeitet Auflage der Schrift Vienna, Kommissionsverlag Brüder, 1970, 100p. Revision of *Dokumentation in Öesterreich,* 1953.

3b

VÖB Kommission für Bibliographie *Bibliographie der österreichischen Bibliographien* 1972?

Silvestri G 'Zur Geschichte der nationalen Bibliographie in Öesterreich' *Zentbl Biblioth* 1969 83(3) 136-45.

VÖB Kommission für Bibliographie *Öesterreichische Bibliographie* 1946- . Now fortnightly, cumulative indexes.

For retrospective bibliographies from the 15th century see in *Bibliography, Documentation, Terminology* 1971 11(3).

Silvestri G 'Auswahlbibliographie zur Geschichte der österreichischen Bibliotheken' *Biblos* 1969 18(4) 239-61.

3c

VÖB *Biblos* 1952- . Quarterly. Contains a current bibliography on librarianship.

— *Biblos-Schriften* 1953- . Reports, proceedings, monographs on current problems, etc.

— *Mitteilungen* 1947- .

ÖGDB Nachrichten 1959-71. Superseded by:

ÖGDI-Mitteilungen 1971- .

Bundesministerium für Unterricht *Neue Volksbildung* 1949- . (1949-53 as: *Buch und Bücherei).*

Erwachsenenbildung in Österreich 1950- .

3d

'Statistik der Österreichischen Bibliotheken' Annual feature in *Biblos* no 4.

Krones F 'Die leistungen öffentliche Büchereien in Österreich im Jahre 1978' *Erwachsenenbildung in Österreich* 1980 31(2) 182-8.

3f

Behmer H 'Funktion und Leistung der Bücherei' *Neue Volksbildung* 1968 20(6).

Müller R 'Buch und Bücherei als Mittel der Erwachsenenbildung' *Erwachsenenbildung in Öesterreich* 1970 21 Dec.

Vetter G 'Bücherei zwischen Kooperation und Spezialisierung' *Erwachsenenbildung in Öesterreich* 1979 30(5) 325-35.

'Struktur- und Finanzierungsprobleme der österreichischen Büchereien' *Erwachsenennbildung in Öesterreich* 1977 28(4) 180-8.

Hegenbarth H 'Der wissenschaftliche Dienst an der Steiermarkischen Landesbibliothek und seine Gefährdung in Vergangenheit und Gegenwart' *Biblos* (Aust) 1974 23(3) 225-41.

'Sonderheft Vorarlberg' *Biblos* 1976 25(3) 221-95.

Koski L N 'Mobil bibliotekjeneste i Wien, Østerrike' *Bog og Bibliot* 1980 47(1) 22-4.

Martin W J ed *Library service to the disadvantaged* Linnet Books/Bingley, 1975, 185p.

Hofinger J 'Developments in Austrian university libraries' *Lib Trends* 1964 12(4) 513-27.

Bundesministerium für Wissenschaft und Forschung *Reform des wissenschaftlichen Bibliothekswesens 1971-1975. Stand und bisherige Ergebnisse (Juni 1975). Zwischenbericht* Bundesministerium, 1975, 71p.

Baumgartner F 'Zur Lage de Universitätsbibliotheken statistisches Material' *Biblos* 1979 28(1) 3-12, refs. Quantitative assessment of the 1975 University reform.

ÖGDI *Erster Österreichischer Dokumentationstag — Manuskripte und Diskussionsbeiträge* The Society, 1973, 168p.

Daten, Dienste, Dokumente: wissenschaftliches Dokumentations- und Informationswesen in Österreich: Zielsetzungen, Beispiele Bundesministerium für Wissenschaft und Forschung, 1975, 206p. (Prepared for UNISIST).

Rauch W 'Scientific information and documentation systems tomorrow: the example of Austria' *J Info Sci* 1979 1(1) 35-41. Delphi study by the Austrian Academy of Sciences.

Stock K F and Lang L *Untersuchungen zur Verwizlichung eines österreichischen Bibliotheksnetzes mit EDV-Einsatz. Forschungsauftrag des Bundesministeriums für Wissenschaft und Forschung*. Österr. Inst. Bibliotheksforschung, Dok. u. Info., 1975, 288p.

BELGIUM

1

Bibliothèque Royale de Belgique/Koninklijke Bibliotheek van België, Brussels, 1837- .

Bibliothèque Royale — Mémorial 1559-1969.

Vanwijngaerden F 'Brussels. La Bibliothèque Royale de Belgique' in *Encyclopedia* 3 (1970) 416-29.

— 'The Royal Library Albert 1: instrument of knowledge and depository of our written and printed patrimony' *IFLA J* 1977 3(1) 12-23.

Reed A 'The Bibliothèque Royale de Belgique as a national library' *J Lib Hist* 1975 10(1) 35-51.

Attached to the library are the following departments:

- Centre National de Documentation Scientifique et Technique (CNDST)/Centrum voor Wetenschappelijke en Technische Documentatie (NCWTD), 1964- .

Jaeger H de 'Centre National de Documentation Scientifique et Technique' in *Encyclopedia* 4 (1970) 399-405.

— 'The National Center for Scientific and Technical Documentation, Brussels: a decade of progress' *IFLA J* 1977 3(1) 24-7.

- Comité National de Bibliothéconomie et de Bibliographie.

2a

Ministère de l'Education Nationale/Ministerie van Nationale Opvoeding, Conseils des Bibliothèques Publiques.

Institut Belge d'Information et de Documentation (INBEL)/Belgisch Instituut voor Voorlichting en Documentatie, Brussels, 1962- .

Conseil National de la Recherche Scientifique. Commission Nationale d'Archives, de Bibliothèques, de Recherche, de Documentation, 1959- .

Commission Belge de Bibliographie (Unesco Sub-committee), 1951- .

Flemish Library Centre, Antwerp, 1976- . Centralizes the technical services to the Dutch speaking region.

2b

Association des Archivistes et Bibliothécaires de Belgique/Vereniging van Archivarissen en Bibliothecarissen van België, Brussels, 1907- .

Association Professionnelle de Bibliothécaires et Documentatlistes (APBD), 1975- . Previously: Association Nationale des Bibliothécaires d'Expression Française, 1964-75.

Vlaamse Vereniging van Bibliotheek-, Archief-en Documentatiepersoneel (VVBAD), Antwerp, 1921- .

Association Belge de Documentation/Belgische Vereniging voor Documentatie.

Association Scientifique et Technique pour la Recherche en Informatique Documentaire (ASTRID), Ghent, 1971- .

2c

Van Bellaiengh G and Van Hove J 'La formation professionnelle' *Bull Biblioth France* 1966 11(1) 29-35.

'Bibliotheekscholen — Écoles de Bibliothécairs' *Arch Biblioth Belg* 1972 43(3/4) 757.

Van Slype G 'Projet de programme d'une licence spéciale en science de l'information à créer en Belgique' *Cah Doc* 1977 31(1) 3-32.

— 'Formation des bibliothécaires — documentalistes en Belgique' *Cah Doc* 1977 31(2/3) 85-92.

'Colloque sur la formation des spécialistes non-universitaires de l'IDST, Bruxelles 1979' *Cah Doc* 1979 33(2/3) 43-135, refs.

3a

INBEL *België: een overzicht* Appendix: Statistics.

CNDST *Inventaire permanent des institutions belges de recherche disposant d'une bibliothèque ou d'un centre de documentation.*

3b

Van Hove J *La bibliographie en Belgique* Commission Belge de Bibliographie 1951- . Annual survey of new bibliographies, sometimes irregular, eg 1968-1972 published in 1974. See other volumes in *Bibliographia belgica.*

Lefevre M 'La Bibliographie de Belgique' *IFLA J* 1977 3(1) 56/61.

Bibliothèque Royale *Bibliographie de Belgique/Belgische bibliografie* 1875- . Based on the acquisitions of the Library (the legal desposit law dates from 1966 only). Monthly with annual index, 1959- .

INBEL *Belgica selecta. Liste trimestrielle choisie et commentée des publications récentes éditées en Belgique* 1969- . Selection by the Royal Library.

Books from Belgium/Le livre belge 1962- . (Trade list).

'Bibliographie de l'histoire du livre en Belgique/Bibliografie van de geschiedenis van het boek in Belgie' in *De Gulden Passer* every year. Also separately reprinted.

'Bibliothèque et livres: bibliographie analytique/Boek en bibliotheekwesen' in *Archives et Bibliotheques de Belgique.*

3c

Répertoire des périodiques paraissant en Belgique 1951.

Répertoire permanent de publications périodiques éditées en français en Belgique Société pour la Diffusion de la Presse. Updated twice a year. A similar list is also published for Flemish periodicals.

Bibliothèque Royale *Bulletin.* Contains lists of bibliographies.

Belgian Commission for Bibliography *Bibliographia Belgica.* Series of bibliographies.

— *Bulletin*

Association des Archivistes et Bibliothécaires *Archives et Bibliothèques de Belgique/Archief-en Bibliotheekwesen in België* 1923- .

VVBAD *Bibliotheekgids* 1922- .

Coninck P de 'De ontwikkeling van (De) Bibliotheekgids van 1946 tot begin 1969: bijdrage tot de naoorlogse geschiedenis van het Vlaams bibliotheekwezen' *Bibliotheekgids* 1976 52 132-50, 185-99.

Association Belge de Documentation *Cahiers de la Documentation/Bladen voor de Documentatie* 1947- .

ASTRID *ASTRID series on information science.*

3d

Institut National de Stastiques *Bulletin de statistique.*
See also under 3a above *België: een overzicht.*

3e

Moniteur belge
Brock J 'Le dépôt légal' *Bull Biblioth France* 1966 11(1) 15-28.
— 'Le dépôt légal, hier et aujourd'hui' *IFLA J* 1977 3(1) 62-9.
Haenens L P 'Belgian standards in documentation and libraries' *Unesco Bull Lib* 1968 22(2) 82-5, 89.

3f

Rock P and Schevenhels L *Adult education and leisure in Flanders* Ministerie van Nationale Opvoeding, 1968.
Collard A 'La bibliothéconomie en Belgique de 1901 a 1925' *Arch Biblioth Belgique* 1925 3 68, 81, 100- .
Liebaers H 'Les bibliothèques et la documentation en Belgique' *Bull Biblioth France* 1966 11(1) 1-8.
Delsemme P 'Belgium, libraries in' in *Encyclopedia* 2(1969) 292-329.
'Libraries and librarianship in Belgium' *IFLA J* 1977 3(1) 9-69 Special section on Belgium.
'Interbibliothecair leenverkeer NVB-Vergadering' [Conference papers] *Open* 1980 12(3) 117-47. 1 paper on Belgium.
Lemaitre H *La lecture publique* Brussels, 1931.
Schevenhels L 'Public library development in Belgium' *Lib Q* 1960 20(1) 39-42.
Charlier J 'La democratisation de l'enseignement et de la lecture publique' *Bibliotheekgids* 1960 36 (2/3) 49-54. Summary of a colloquium.
Ministerie van Nationale Opvoeding *Organisation and functioning of public libraries, French speaking part of Belgium and Brussels* 1966. Also in *Int Lib Rev* 1972 2.
Stenbock-Fermor T 'A "penny library" in Belgium: an evaluation report on an experiment' *Unesco Bull Lib* 1970 24(3) 153-6.
Valgaeren L *Van volksbibliotheek naar openbare bibliotheek in Vlaanderen: schets van de evolutie van volksbibliotheek naar openbare bibliotheek: toekomstperpectiev* VVBAD, 1976, 85p. A shorter version was published in *Bibliotheekgids* 1974 50(2) 50-76.
Munch P 'Kulturhuse — netop nu: spredte belgiske indtryk' *Bogens Verden* 1976 58(9) 398-403.
Verbercht H 'Het beroepsbeeld van de voltijdse bibliothekaris in de middelbare bibliotheek in Vlaanderen' *Bibliotheekgids* 1976 52(4) 219-30.
Heidbuchel E 'Public libraries in the Dutch-speaking part of Belgium' *IFLA J* 1977 3 34-41.
Schittecat F 'Flemish youth and the book' *Bookbird* 1977 15(4) 17-22.
Mertens J 'Schoolbibliotheek en mediatheek: algemere aspekten' *Bibliotheekgids* 1976 52(4) 232-4.
Huys B ed [Music libraries in Belgium] *Fontes Artis Musicae* 1976 23(3) 107-42. Whole issue.
'Les bibliothèques de sciences sociales en Belgique' *Inspel* 1978 13(3/4) 116-33.
'Souhaits en matière d'organisation de la documentation sur le plan national' *Cah Doc* 1971 25(1) 23-30.
Walraet M 'Bibliothèques spécialisées et centres de documentation: regroupment et restructuration' *Arch Biblioth Belgique* 1969 40(1/2) 13-33, bibl.
Jaeger H K de 'Automation at Belgian National Centre for Scientific and Technical Documentation' *Int Business Equipment* 1972 9(4) 36-46.

CYPRUS

1

Ministry of the Interior Library, Legal deposit library which incorporates the former library of the British Government in Cyprus.

Ministry of Education Library, Nicosia. 1962- . Incorporates Cyprus Public Library.

- Library of the Institute of Education, Nicosia. 1972- .

Turkish Public Library, Nicosia. 1955- . Part of the Turkish Education Office.

2a

Kentron Epistemonikōn Erevnōn (Cyprus Research Centre), Nicosia. 1967- . Under the Ministry of Education.

Ministry of Education. Library Inspectorate.

2b

Library Association of Cyprus, Nicosia. 1962- .

2c

Petrides S 'Libraries and library training in Cyprus' in *Unesco course for teachers of librarianship* Copenhagen, 1970, p 4.

3a

Cyprus, a handbook on the island's past and present Nicosia, Greek Communal Chamber, 1964.

'Cyprus' in *Middle East and North Africa* (Europa Yearbooks) Europa Publications.

3b

Stephanou C D *Bibliography of Cyprus* Pedagogical Academy, 1960/61, 1962/65, 1966- .

3c

Ministry of Education *Cyprus today: a quarterly cultural and information review,* 1963- . Includes a bibliographical section.

3d

Cyprus Statistics and Research Department *Statistics of education.*

3e

Official gazette Printing Office. 1960- .

3f

Serghis P 'The cultural service of the Ministry of Education' *Cyprus Today* 1970 8(3/4) 80.

Stephanou C D 'Libraries in Cyprus' *Assistant Libn* 1975 68(3) 42-3, 52.

Altan M H 'Die Bibliotheken in türkisch-zypriotischen Bundestaat' *Biblos* (Austria) 1979 28(4) 306-9.

Harvey J F 'West Asian special libraries and information centres' *Ann Lib Sci Doc* 1973 20(1/4) 26-38. Includes Cyprus.

FRANCE

1

Bibliothèque Nationale (BN), Paris. 1480- . Formerly: Bibliothéque Royale, to 1795. Legal deposit 1537. Administers the Service d'Information Bibliographique and the Bureau pour l'Automatisation des Bibliothèques (BAB), 1971- .

Lethève J 'La Bibliothèque Nationale et son rôle international' *Ass Biblioth Fr Bull Info* 1972 (76) 127-36.

'La Bibliothèque Nationale et ses relations avec les bibliothèques françaises' *Ass Biblioth Fr Bull Info* 1975 (88) 131-41.

'Problèmes et transformations à la Bibliothèque Nationale' *Ass Biblioth Fr Bull Info* 1977 (96) 117-25, 127-9, 132-41. Special feature with seven papers.

Other libraries enjoy legal deposit privilege under the terms of the Réunion des Bibliothèques Nationales:
- The Arsenal, Paris.
- The Opéra library, Paris.
- The Conservatoire National de Musique, Paris.
- Bibliothèque Ste Geneviève, Paris. Public library.

Wintzweiller M *La Bibliothèque Ste Geneviève de jadis à aujourd'hui* The Library, 1972, 36p.

Strasburg University Library.

Sansen J 'Les transformations de la Bibliothèque Nationale et Universitaire de Strasbourg' *Bull Biblioth Fr* 1977 22(1) 25-33.

Centre National de la Recherche Scientifique (CNRS). Centre de Documentation, Paris. 1940- .

2a

Secrétariat d'Etat aux Affaires Culturelles. Direction du Livre. 1975- . For public libraries. Has a research and documentation office.

Secrétariat d'Etat aux Universités. Service des Bibliothèques. 1975- . Cooperation, administration and personnel for all libraries, finances. The two bodies above have replaced, following the 1975 reorganization, the Direction des Bibliothèques, 1945-1975.

'La Direction des Bibliothèques et de la Lecture Publique et les bibliothèques de France' *Bull Biblioth Fr* 1973 18(7) 295-347. Prepared for the 1973 IFLA meeting in Grenoble.

'Le démantèlement de la Direction des Bibliothéques et de la Lecture Publique' *Ass Biblioth Fr Bull Info* 1975 (89) 213-5.

Bouvy M 'Libres propos sur la "crise"' *Lecture Biblioth* 1975 (35) 35-8.

Institut National des Techniques de la Documentation.

Bureau National de l'Information Scientifique et Technique (BNIST). 1973- . Coordination and research. Head of a network of specialized information centres. Training of users and specialists.

'Le Bureau National de l'Information Scientifique et Technique (BNIST)' (In English) *Info Hotline* 1977 9(9) 30-1.

2b

Association des Bibliothécaires Français (ABF), Paris. 1906- . See its *Annuaire* for details of branches, sections, groups, etc.

Association Française des Documentalistes et des Bibliothécaires Spécialisés (ADBS), Paris. 1963- .

Association des Bibliothécaires Pédagogiques.

See *Biblio* 1972 (51). Chronique 1022-24.

Groupe Informatiste des Bibliothécaires Universitaires et Spécialisés (GIBUS).

Association Française des Bibliothèques Publiques. 1971-76 as: Association pour le Développement des Bibliothèques Publiques (ANDBP). 1977- . Association pour la Médiathèque Publique.

Association de l'Institut National des Techniques de la Documentation (AINTD) 1953- .

Association de l'Ecole Normale Supérieure de Bibliothécaires. 1967- . See its *Annuaire* (1978 issue covers 1967-1976).

Association Nationale de la Recherche Technique (ANRT), Paris. 1953- .

Union Française des Organismes de Documentation (UFOD). 1932- .

Club des Banques de Données (Databanks Club). 1970- .

2c

Salvan P 'The National School of Librarianship in Paris' *Unesco Bull Lib* 1965 19(4) 202-6. The School (ENSB) has been transferred to Villeurbanne (Lyons) in 1975.

Gardner R K *Education for librarianship in France: an historical survey* Case Western Reserve U, 1968. PhD Thesis.

'La formation professionnelle' *Ass Biblioth Fr Bull Info* 1975 (89) 195-204.

Frigiolini C 'La formazione dei bibliotecari in Inghilterrra e in Francia' *Accad Bibliot Ital* 1976 44(2) 143-9.

'Le CAFB et ses débouchés; résultats de l'enquête menée par l'ENSB' *Bull Biblioth Fr* 1977 22(7) 470-1. Main diploma in librarianship.

'Direction du Livre: stages de formation continue organisés en 1977' *Bull Biblioth Fr* 1977 22 600-1.

'Initiation aux techniques documentaires. Un an d'enseignement au Centre d'Education Permanente de l'Université de Nice' *Bull Biblioth Fr* 1975 20(4) 163-71.

Sorieul F 'Les stages de documentation en France' *Argus* (Quebec) 1978 7(5) 119-26, bibl.

Poindron P 'L'Institut National des Techniques de la Documentation et la formation des documentalistes en France' *Bull Biblioth Fr* 1963 8(7) 313-25.

Sutter E 'Stages et formation des spécialistes de l'information' *Documentaliste* 1976 13(3) 100-3.

Breton J 'Quelques réflexions sur le rôle futur des professeurs de l'ENSB' *Ass Biblioth Fr Bull Info* 1972 (75) 75-84.

Merland M 'Les travaux de recherche à l'Ecole Nationale Supérieure de Bibliothécaires' *Bull Biblioth Fr* 1977 22(4) 223-30.

Martin H-J 'Les chartistes et les bibliothèques' *Bull Biblioth Fr* 1972 17(12) 525-38.

Boisard G 'Do women hold the reins of power in French libraries?' *Unesco Bull Lib* 1975 29(6) 303-14. Survey with statistics.

3a

Gingnay M *Dictionnaire d'informatique anglais-français* Masson, 1970, 140p.

Serrurier C *Bibliothèques de France: description de leurs fonds et historique de leur formation* Nijhoff, 1946, 346p.

Direction des Bibliothèques *Les bibliothèques de France au service du public* 1969, 20, 22p.

Ollivier M *Répertoire des bibliothèques et organismes de documentation* BN, 1971, 735p. Previous edition as *Répertoire des bibliothèques d'étude et organismes de documentation,* 1963, 3 vols. Originally published by Unesco: *Répertoire des bibliothèques de France,* 1950-51.

'Liste et adresses des bibliothèques centrales de prêt des départements' *Bull Biblioth Fr* 1971 16(5) 288-93.

Newman L M *Libraries in Paris: a student's guide* Scorton, Conder Research, 1971, 175p.

ANRT *Centres français de documentation scientifique et technique, domaines d'activité et liste des responsables* ANRT, 1971.

3b

De la Haye M *The development of bibliographical services in France: a survey* University College London, 1968, 77p. MA Thesis.

Bibliographie de la France Numéro spécial, 1961 for the 150th anniversary of the service. Set of papers.

Honoré S 'L'automatisation de la partie officielle de la *Bibliographie de la France*' *Bull Biblioth Fr* 1975 20(1) 1-5. Automated in 1975, INTERMARC format adopted. From that date onward the bibliography is published as follows:

Bibliographie de la France. Part 1: *Bibliographie officielle* Bibliothèque Nationale. Section: *Livres* weekly. Supplements on serials, musical works, maps. Based on legal deposit.

Bibliographie de la France-Biblio. (Partie: *Annonces*) Cercle de la Librairie. Trade publication issued by the Association of Booksellers. 1972, Vol. 161-. *Biblio* was published separately 1933-1971.

Cercle de la Librairie *Livres de l'année-Biblio.* Annual cumulation.

Retrospective bibliographies:

Journal général de l'imprimerie et de la librairie BN and Cercle de la Librairie, 1811- .

Lorenz O *Catalogue général de la librairie française (1840-1925),* 35 vols.

Livres de l'année 1922-1933.

BN *Catalogue général des livres imprimés* 1924- . Supplements.

Current publications. Cumulated records:

Catalogue de l'édition française CEF.

Répertoire des livres disponibles de langue française France-Expansion 1972- .

Francophonie France-Expansion, 1972- . Quarterly. Cumulated as: *Douze mois d'édition francophone.*

CNRS *Bulletin signalétique.* 1945- . *Information scientifique et technique.* Covers librarianship, documentation, information.

Bulletin des Bibliothèques de France Section 'Bulletin de documentation bibliographique'. 1956- . Analytical index of current publications and book reviews in the field of library science and bibliography.

Baize L 'Les bibliothèques publiques françaises: essai de bibliographie 1965-1972' *Lecture Biblioth* 1974 (31) 15-34; 1974 (32) 5-30; 1975 (33/34) 5-34.

3c

Annuaire de la presse et de la publicité. 1887- .

BN *Répertoire des annuaires français* 1958-68. Supplements.

Bibliographie de la France. Supplément A: Publications en série.

BN *Bulletin des bibliothèques de France.* 1955- .

BN *Bulletin de la Bibliothèque Nationale.* 1976- . Quarterly.

ABF *ABF Bulletin d'information*. 1907- . 1907-25 as *Bulletin de l'ABF;* 1926-36 as *ABF Chroniques*.
ABF *Education et bibliothèques* 1961-65; *Lecture et bibliothèques* 1967-76; *Médiathèques publiques* 1977 (41)- . Current sponsor; Association pour la Médiathèque Publique.
Documentaliste ADBS 1964- .
ANBM *Bulletin*. 1968- .
UFOD *La documentation en France*.
Sciences de l'information. 1972- .
ANRT *ANRT information et documentation*. 1971- .
Club des Banques de Données *Bulletin de liaison*. 1970- .

3d

France: facts and figures Paris, USIS, 1955- . Irregular.
Institut National de la Statistique et des Etudes Economiques *Bulletin*. Weekly.
- *Annuaire*.
Association des Maires de France. Commission des Communes Urbaines *Enquête statistique sur les bibliothèques municipales* 1968, 57 leaves.
'Bibliothèques municipales. Statistiques' in *Bull Biblioth Fr* Annually.
'Bibliothèques centrales de prêt. Fonctionnement et statistiques' in *Bull Biblioth Fr*. Annual.
'Bibliothèques centrales de prêt. Statistiques 1976-1977. Rétrospective 1972-77' *Bull Biblioth Fr* 1979 24(9/10) 446-72.
Bouvy M 'Du coté des statistiques' *Mediathèques Publiques* 1979, (52) 23-35. First part.
Enquête statistique générale auprès des bibliothèques universitaires (ESGBU). Synthèse des résultats obtenus pour 1975' *Bull Biblioth Fr* 1978 23(8).

3c

Journal officiel.
Barber G 'French Royal decrees concerning the book trade, 1700-1789' *Austr J French St* 1966 3(3) 312-30.
Ulysse R *Recueil des lois, décrets. . . concernant les bibliothèques publiques communales, universitaries, scolaires et populaires* Champion, 1883, 258p.
Recueil des textes législatifs concernant les bibliothèques, en vigueur au 1er mars 1954. See also *Bulletin officiel du Ministère de l'Education* 1954 (Chap 51Bi-56Bi).
Richter N 'La législation française des bibliothèques publiques' *Ass Biblioth Fr Bull Info* 1979 (103) 105-9.
Bouvy M 'Examen d'un projet' *Médiathèques Publiques* 1979 (5é) 36-44. Text of a proposed library law and comments.

3f

François M ed *La France et les français* Gallimard 1972, 167p.
Ministère des Affairs Culturelles *Some aspects of French cultural policy* Unesco 1970, 65p.
Le livre français Imprimerie Nationale 1972, 408p.
Spire A and Viala J P *La bataille du livre* Ed Sociales, 1976, 302p.
Lottman H R 'Publishing in France' *Publ Weekly* Apr 1979 215(18) 53-6, 102.
McLaughlin M M *Intellectual freedom and its limitations in the University of Paris in the 13th and 14th centuries* Arno P, 1977, 524p.
Bécourt D *Livres condamnés, livres interdits, régime juridique du livre: liberté ou censure?* Cercle de la Librairie, 1972, 584p.

Martin H-J *Livre, pouvoir et société à Paris au 17e siècle* Droz, 1969, 2 vols.
Bollème G et al *Livre et société dans la France du 18e siècle* Mouton, 1965, 238p.
Werdet E *De la librairie française: son passé, son présent, son avenir* Dentu, 1860, 394p. (Repr Gregg, 1971).
Whitmore H E 'Readers, writers and literary taste in the early 1830s: the cabinet de lecture as focal point' *J Lib Hist* 1978 13 119-30.
— 'The Cabinet de Lecture in France, 1800-1850' *Lib Q* 1978 48 (1) 20-35.
Ferguson J *Libraries in France* Bingley/Archon Books, 1971, 120p.
Trapenard A 'Origines et développement des bibliothèques de la ville de Paris' *Bull Soc Hist Paris* 1970 217-32.
Riberette P *Les bibliothèques françaises pendant la Révolution (1789-1795)* BN, 1970, 157p.
Neveux P and Dacier E *Les richesses des bibliothèques provinciales de France* Paris, 1932, 2 vols.
Clarke J A *Gabriel Naudé, 1600-1653* Archon Books, 1970, 183p.
Dobi A 'Napoleon's great librarians' *Wilson Lib Bull* 1974 49(3) 229-33.
McCrimmon B 'Mérimée as library reformer' *J Lib Hist* 1969 4(4) 297-320.
Hassenforder J 'Un pionnier des bibliothèques: Eugène Morel 1869-1934' *Lecture Biblioth* 1969 (12) 5-13.
Porcher J and Masson A *Humanisme actif: mélanges d'art et de littérature offerts à Julien Cain* Hermann, 1968, 2 vols.
Salvan P 'France, libraries in' in *Encyclopedia* 9 (1973) 37-66.
Welsch E K *Libraries and archives in France: a handbook* Rev ed New York, Council for European Studies, 1979.
Grolier E de 'France, libraries and information science' in *Encyclopedia* 9 (1973) 67-79.
Whitmore H E 'Librarianship in France and the United States: a comparative study with some implication for emerging nations' in Williamson W L *Assistance to libraries in developing nations*, 1971, 57-67. (See under: Developing countries 3f).
'Coordination et coopération des bibliothèques; congrès national de l'ABF, Caen, mai 1976' *Ass Biblioth Fr Bull Info* 1976 (92) 133-70.
Garreta J-C 'Le prêt interbibliothèques' *Ass Biblioth Fr Bull Info* 1976 (92) 150-3. Project for a national lending centre.
Nortier M 'Le Centre National de Prêt' *Ass Biblioth Fr Bull Info* 1977 (96) 120-2.
Chauveinc M 'Pour ou contre le CNP (Centre National de Prêt)' *Ass Biblioth Fr Bull Info* 1979 (104) 169-71.
'Collaboration des bibliothèques entre elles et avec d'autres organismes culturels' *Ass Biblioth Fr Bull Info* 1978 (99) 69-83; 85-92. Two-day school, Troyes, 1978.
[Franco-Soviet seminar, 1976] (In Russian) *Bibliot Bibliog za Rubezhom* 1977 (65) 5-42.
Dobrynina N E 'Nekotorye aspekty sovremennykh issledovanii chteniya vo Frantsii i Velikobritanii' *Bibliot Bibliog za Rubezhom* 1974 (50) 38-62. Research on the sociology of reading.
Bamberger R *Développer l'habitude de la lecture* Unesco, 1975, 55p.
ABF [Conference papers on user education, La Rochelle, 1979] *Ass Biblioth Fr Bull Info* 1979 (105). Bibliography 39-41.
Richter N 'Histoire de la lecture publique en France' *Bull Biblioth Fr* 1977 22(1) 1-24.
Hassenforder J *Développement comparé des bibliothèques publiques en France, en Grande Bretagne et aux Etats Unis dans la seconde moitié du 19e siècle (1850-1914)* Cercle de la Librairie, 1967, 210p.
Richter N 'Aux origines de la lecture publique: naissance des bibliothèques 67

populaires' *Bull Biblioth Fr* 1978 23(4) 221-49.
— 'Aux origines du club de lecture' *Bull Biblioth Fr* 1977 22(4) 207-21.
Jenny J 'Bibliothèque municipale et bibliothèque populaire? Deux choses bien différentes (en 1892)' *Lecture Biblioth* 1974 (32) 34-8.
Gueth F 'L'évolution des bibliothèques publiques' *Ass Biblioth Fr Bull Info* 1976 (90) 5-7.
— 'Pour un plan de développement des bibliothèques publiques françaises' *Ass Biblith Fr Bull Info* 1975 (86) 15-9.
'Propositions de l'Association des Bibliothécaires Français concernant l'organisation de la Direction des Bibliothèques et de la lecture publique' *Ass Biblioth Fr Bull Info* 1975 (86) 33-5.
'La solution française au problème des bibliothèques publiques: la bibliothèque de secteur' *Lecture Biblioth* 1975 (33/34) 35-50. Special section: two papers.
'La médiathèque de secteur' *Médiathèques Publiques* 1979 (49) 7-44, refs.
Garrigoux A 'La lecture publique en France' *Doc Fr* 1972 (Notes et Etudes Documentaires, 3948).
Guérin E 'Les bibliothèques publiques françaises' *Bull Biblioth Fr* 1973 18 298-316.
Lecomte H *Les bibliothèques publiques en France* Lyon, Presses de l'ENSB, 1977.
D'Amore M G 'Il sistema di pubblica lettura in Francia' *AIB Bol* 1978 18(3/4) 245-50, refs.
Ronsin A 'Le choix des livres dans les bibliothèques publiques' *Médiathèques Publiques* 1979 (51) 5-9.
Bouvy M 'Bibliothèques publiques et censure' *Lecture Biblioth* 1976 (37) 17-34.
'Bibliothèques publiques et club de lecture' *Lecture Biblioth* 1973 (28) 5-37. Special issue, 15 papers.
'Bouvy M 'Bibliothèques publiques et culture' *Lecture Biblioth* 1976 (39/40) 57-101. Special section on extension work.
Guitrat C 'A Grenoble: réflexions sur l'animation culturelle dans les bibliothèques publiques' *Lecture Biblioth* 1976 (39/40) 67-81.
Gascuel J and Guiton J 'L' animation et les techniques audiovisuelles dans les bibliothèques: compte rendu du stage organisé à Massy du 16 au 24 janvier 1976' *Bull Biblioth Fr* 1976 21(9/10) 437-42.
Gautier J-C 'Vidéologie-bibliothéconomie' *Lecture Biblioth* 1976 (38) 19-24.
'Un essai des synthèse: le Groupe Animation' de l'ENSB' *Lecture Biblioth* 1976 (39/40) 59-64.
Isaac F L 'La bibliothèque publique d'information: the world's next great library' *J Acad Libp* 1978 3 333-7. Pompidou Centre. For other papers on this library see:
Bogens Verden 1977 59(4).
Kirjastolehti 1978 71(12) 484-6.
Accad Bibliot Ital 1978 46(5) 357-61.
Unesco Bull Lib 1978 33(2) 96-101.
Centre George Pompidou *Bibliothèque publique d'information* 23p. Guide to the library.
Auclair J-C 'La documentation municipale; 1. La nécessité de la documentation municipale' *Documentaliste* 1980 17(2) 47-53; 2. L'organisation de la documentation municipale *Documentaliste* 1980 17(3) 107-16, refs.
Grunberg G 'Immigrés et bibliothèques publiques' *Ass Biblioth Fr Bull Info* 1978 (99) 99-101.
Curzin J 'Les handicappés visuels et la lecture: situation et perspectives d'avenir' *Bibliog Fr Chronique* 1973 (17) 506-16.

Begel M 'Les handicappés physiques et la lecture' *Médiathèques Publiques* 1978 (46) 5-38, bibl.

Guenebaud J 'Relations between hospital libraries and public libraries — France' *Int Lib Rev* 1974 6(4) 403-6.

'Bibliothèques d'hopitaux: journées d'étude de 4 mars 1976' *Lecture Biblioth* 1976 (37) 9-16.

Neuquelman Y 'Les bibliothèques et la lecture en milieu pénitentiaire' *Médiathèques Publiques* 1978 (48) 5-26, bibl.

Baudin G 'Origines et développement des bibliothèques publiques pour la jeunesse' *Médiathèques Publiques* 1977 (42) 5-12.

'Le livre, la bibliothèque et l'enfant' *Lecture Biblioth* 1967 1(3/4) 1-84.

Patte G 'Children's libraries in France' *Int Lib Rev* 1974 6 435-48.

Pointeau H-F 'Les clubs de lecture dans une section enfantine: Caen' *Lecture Biblioth* 1974 (31) 11-14.

Parmegiani C-A 'Les stages de littérature enfantine de la Joie par les Livres' *Bull Biblioth Fr* 1976 21(11) 509-11.

Altmayer O 'Où en est Lecture Jeunesse?' *Ass Biblioth Fr Bull Info* 1978 (99) 97-8.

'Les adolescents dans les bibliothèques' *Ass Biblioth Fr Bull Info* 1979 (103) 79-89, refs. Four papers at a day workshop.

Janod J-M and Soumy J-N 'Aperçus sur la lecture chez les jeunes de 14-16 ans scolarisés en CES et CET en milieu rural et semi-rural: note de synthèse pour le diplôme supérieur de bibliothécaire' *Lecture Biblioth* 1976 (39/40) 13-56.

Makin J L *The history and development of French university libraries* Loughborough U of Technology, 1977, 67p, bibl.

Audet M C 'Les bibliothèques universitaires de France' *Ass Canad Biblioth Langue Fr, Bull* 1968 14 93-197; 1969 15 31-48.

Tessier Y 'Apprendre à s'informer: les fondements et les objectifs d'une politique de formation documentaire en milieu universitaire' *Doc Biblioth* 1977 23(2) 75-84.

'Plan de réorganisation des bibliothèques universitaires' *Ass Biblioth Fr Bull Info* 1975 (88) 151-4.

'S.O.S. B.U.: qui sauvera les bibliothèques universitaires?' *Ass Biblioth Fr Bull Info* 1978 (98) 41-7.

Thirion G 'Situation des bibliothèques universitaires' *Ass Biblioth Fr Bull Info* 1978 (98) 7-31, 34-8. Some comparisons with British and German libraries.

Robine N 'Le chercheur dans la bibliothèque de recherche' *Bull Biblioth Fr* 1977 22 413-48; Reprinted in *LIBER Bull* 1978 (9/10) 2-43.

Thirion G 'La recherche en France et les bibliothèques des universités *LIBER Bull* 1978 (9/10) 46-66.

'Bibliothèques universitaires et spécialisées *Ass Biblioth Fr Bull Info* 1979 (102) 7-9, 11-5, 17-9, 21-3, 25-32. Study day on the documentation role of libraries.

'Bibliothèque interuniversitaire A, Paris: bibliothèque de la Sorbonne. . .' *Bull Biblioth Fr* 1977 22 403-4.

Pelou P 'Les bibliothèques spécialisées en France' *Inspel* 1977 12(2) 7-14.

Germain C M 'France: libraries of law and librarians' *Law Lib J* 1979 72(2) 235-44, refs.

Hunnisett B *History of fine arts libraries in France* University College London, 1971. Thesis.

— 'Fine arts libraries in Paris' *ARLIS Newsletter* 1974 (21) 3-23.

Van Dijk M and Slype G *Le service de documentation face à l'explosion de l'information* Editions d'Organisation, 1969, 266p.

[Documentation problems in France] *Documentaliste* Special issue 1971.

Olier J H d' 'L'organisation en France du réseau d'information scientifique et technique' *ANRT Info Doc* 1972 2 98-104.

Sutter E Types de documents et interconnexion des réseaux: faut-il tout mélanger?' *Documentaliste* 1976 13 151-3.

'Voyage à Paris' *Nachr VSB* 1977 53(1) 26-35. Specialized information centres.

Esplin Y 'Information — French style' *Austr Spec Lib News* 1977 10(4) 139-50.

'Nemzeti tudományok és müszaki információpolitika Franciaorszagban' *Tudom Mus Tajek* 1979 26(7/8) 335-8.

Englefield D J T 'Information services for the French National Assembly' *New Lib World* 1974 75(894) 261-2.

Meyriat J 'L'automisation documentaire en France' *Documentaliste* 1972 9(2) 94-101.

Chauveinc M *Introduction au projet Monocle* Grenoble, Bibliothèque Universitaire, 1970, 160p.

Seguin J-P and Beyssac R 'L'informatique à la bibliothèque des Halles' *Bull Biblioth Fr* 1972 17(9/10) 407-26.

Chauveinc M 'Library automation in France' *Libri* 1975 25(1) 48-74.

Nora S and Minc A *Computerisation of society* MIT, 1980, 186p. From the French *L'informatisation de la société* Documentation Française, 1978.

'Bibliothèques municipales. Construction, équipement' *Bull Biblioth Fr* 1975 20(3) 75-117. Developments since 1968.

Bleton J 'Stroitel'stvo zdenii universitetskikh bibliotek vo Frantsii v 1965-1973 gg' *Bibliot Bibliog za Rubezhom* 1975 (54) 40-50.

Gascuel J 'La pierre. . . et la lecture publique' *Ass Biblioth Fr Bull Info* 1976 (90) 9-19.

GERMANY

General and pre-1945.

1

Deutsche Staatsbibliothek, Berlin. 1661- . Originally Preussiche Staatsbibliothek. In 1945 the collections were shared and part of them were transferred to West Berlin. See: German Federal Republic, section 1.

Deutsche Bücherei, Leipzig. 1912- . For details see German Democratic Republic, section 1.

2b

Verein Deutscher Bibliothekare. 1900- . Now the West Germany Association.

Verein Deutscher Volkbibliothekare. 1922- .

2c

Schmidmaier D *Versuch einer Bibliographie zur bibliothekarischen Wissenschaftspädagogik im deutschsprachigen gebeit 1500-1970* Freiberg, Bergakademie, Bibliothek, 1970, 105p. (Veröffentlichungen, 41). Bibliographical supplement to a thesis, with a summary of the thesis.

3a

Neveling U and Wersig G *Terminologie der Information und Dokumentation* Munich, DGD, 1975.

Minerva Handbücher. Die Bibliotheken, Vol.1: *Deutschland* De Gruyter, 1929-1934.

3b

Cazden R E 'Some developments in 19th century bibliography: Germany' *Libri* 1977 27(2) 116-24.

Moll W 'German national bibliographies' *Lib Res Tech Services* 1961 5(4) 310-4. Historical survey.

Deutsche Nationalbibliographie Deutsche Bücherei. Superseded: *Wöchentliches Verzeichnis* 1842-1930.

Bibliographie der deutschen Zeitschriftenliteratur Leipzig then Osnabruck, 1896- . (IBZ Part I; see in General, under 3b).

Busche J *Bibliographie zum Bibliothek- und Büchereiwesen* (Ed: U von Dietze), Harrassowitz, 1966, 223p; Selective, covers 1900-1964. Continued by *Fachbibliographischer Dienst Bibliothekswesen.* (See in German Federal Republic, 3b).

Vorstius J *Die Erforschung des Büch- und Bibliothekswesen in Deutschland 1933-1945: systematische Bibliographie. . .* Amsterdam, Erasmus, 1969, 235p.

Andrae F *Volkbücherei und Nationalsozialismus: materialen zur Theorie und Politik des öffentlichen Büchereiwesens in Deutschland 1933-1945* Harrassowitz, 1970, 200p.

Deutsche Gesellschaft für Dokumentation *Deutschsprachiges Schriftum zur Dokumentation* DGD, 1969, 32p. Covers 1960-1969. Updated by: *Deutsche Dokumentationsliteratur.* 1968- .

3c

Zentralblatt für Bibliothekswesen. 1886- .
— Supplements: *Beiheft* (nos 1-73, 1888-1942 repr: Kraus, 1968).
Blätter für Volksbibliotheken und Lesehallen Leipzig. 1900-1920.

3e

Lansky R *Bibliographie zum Bibliotheksrecht — . . .ab 1900 zum Recht der öffentlichen Bibliotheken und Büchereien in Deutschland Klostermann, 1970, 227p.*

3f

Mellor R E H *The two Germanies* Harper and Row, 1978, 448p.
'Germany, libraries and information centers in' in *Encylopedia* 9 (1973) 395-532. History and West Germany.
Mehl E and Hannemann K *Deutsche Bibliotheksgeschichte* Berlin, E Schmidt, 1969, 110 cols. Originally published in 1952.
Kolb R "A beautiful, delightful jewel": Cyriakus Spangenberg's plan for the 16th century noble's library' *J Lib Hist* 1979 14(2) 129-59.
Kettig K 'Philipp Buttman (1764-1829) Bibliothekar und Gelehrter' *Biblioth Wissenschaft* 1968 5 103-57.
Diatzko K *Beiträge zur Theorie und Praxis des Buch- und Bibliothekswesens* Leipzig (Halle), 1894-1904, 8 parts, Reprinted 1968 by Harrassowitz, 2 vols.
Ogura C 'Die Formation des Begriffs der Bibliothekswissenschaft in Deutschland und ihre Quellen' (In Japanese) *Tosh Kai* 1971 23(3) 84-100, 104 refs.
Young J D *A short history of German public libraries from the early 19th century to the present day* LA, 1970, 274p. FLA Thesis.
Mühle W *Zur älteren Bücherhallen bewegung als Beginn der deutschen Volkbücherei im Zeitalter des Imperialismus* ZIB, 1968, 139p.
Lüdtke H 'Von der literarischen Suppenbüche zur Bildungsanstalt der Nationsoziale Intentionen des Bücher- und Leserhallen im Wilhelminischen Deutschland' *Buch Biblioth* 1979 31(5) 409-10, 412-4, 416-26, refs.
Eyssen J 'Bildung durch Bücher? Volkbüchereien während der Weimarer Republik' *Buch Biblioth* 1979 31(10) 875-8, 880-2, refs. Paper at the second meeting of the Wolfenbüttel Study Group on history of librarianship.
'Chicago-Leipzig 1931 bis 1933 zu einem amerikanisch-deutschen Kapitel in der beginnenden Leserforschung' *Buch Biblioth* 1979 31(10) 859-73, refs. Creation of the Institut für Leser- und Schriftumskunde in Leipzig, 1927- .
Kupfer W 'Politischer Ursprung und Entwicklung der öffentlichen Bibliothek' *Buch Biblioth* 1979 31(10) 883-8, 890-4, refs.
Süle T *Bücherei und Ideologie: politische Aspekte im 'Richtungstreit' deutscher Volksbibliothekare, 1910-1930* Cologne, Greven, 1972, 87p.
Andrae F comp *Volksbücherei und Nationalsozialismus* [1933-1956] Harrassowitz, 1970, 200p.
Esterquest R T 'A statistical contribution to the study of libraries in contemporary Germany' *Lib Q* 1941 11(1) 1-35. Effects of pre-war politics.
Mühle W 'Zu einigen Entwicklungstendenzer der öffentlichen Bibliotheken in beiden deutschen Staaten' *Bibliothekar* 1968 22 1016-27. Comparative study of public library development in the two German states.
 Thielo H *Grundlagen für die bibliothekarische Regionalplanung* Harrassowitz,

1966. Comparative study of the two German states.

Steinberg H-J 'Workers' libraries in Germany before 1914' *History Workshop* 1976 (1) 168-80.

Wehmer C 'The organisation and origins of German university libraries' *Lib Trends* 1964 12(4) 491-512, bibl.

Hartmann K J 'Das Problem der Institutsbibliotheken' *Zentrl Biblioth* 1939 56(1) 17-37.

Zenner H O *German research libraries before, during and after World War Two* Kent State U, 1958, 253p. Thesis.

Hoffman H H 'Co-operative acquisitions in German research libraries, 1800-1930' *Lib Q* 1964 34(3) 249-57.

For the period 1945 onwards see German Federal Republic, and German Democratic Republic (in the section: Eastern Europe).

GERMAN FEDERAL REPUBLIC

1

Deutsche Bibliothek, Frankfurt. 1946- . Deposit library and bibliographical centre.

Die Deutsche Bibliothek 1945-1965. Festgabe für Hanns W Eppelsheimer zum 75 Geburstag Klostermann, 1966, 192p. (*Z Biblioth Bibliog Sonderheft* 3).

Staatsbibliothek Preussischer Kulturbesitz, Berlin. 1945- .

'Les fonctions de la Staatsbibliothek Preussischer Kulturbesitz, Berlin Quest: tâches suprarégionales et régionales' *Bull Biblioth Fr* 1979 24(11) 527-32.

Orgel-Köhne A and Orgel-Köhne L *Staatsbibliothek Berlin* Arami/Saur, 1980, 152p.

2a

Bibliographische Institut. Leipzig, 1826-45; Mannheim, 1945- . East Germany reorganized their section of it as VEB Leipzig.

Sarkowski H *Das Bibliographische Institut: Verlagsgeschichte und Bibliographie, 1826-1976* The Institute, 1976, 314p.

Arbeitsstelle für Bibliothekstechnik (ABT), Berlin. For its activities see *Buch und Bibliothek* 1974 26(11) 971-4.

Arbeitsstelle für das Bibliothekswesen (AFB), Berlin. 1958- .

In 1978 the above two bodies were incorporated to form:

Deutsches Bibliotheksinstitut (DBI), Berlin, 1978- . Research and training.

Wassner H 'Das Deutsche Bibliotheksinstitut — eine Hoffnung?' *Buch Biblioth* 1977 29 116-8.

Segebrecht D 'Beschlossene Sache: des Deutsche Bibliotheksinstitut in Berlin. Jahrestagung des DBV in Duisburg' *Buch Biblioth* 1977 29(1) 75-8.

Zentralstelle für maschinelle Dokumentation.

Schneider K *Die Zentralstelle für maschinelle Dokumentation in Frankfurt am Main* Beuth-Vertrieb, 1969, 207p.

Wissenschaftsrat (Science Council), Cologne. 1957- .

2b

Borsenverein des Deutschen Buchhandels (Publishers)

Deutsche Forschungsgemeinschaft (German Research Society), Bonn. 1949- . Assistance to research; has a committee on library and publishing.

Schmidt W and Oertel D *Fünfzehn Jahre Bibliotheksarbeit. . 1949-1964* Klostermann, 196l, 196p. Role of the Society.

Young J D 'A short history of library associations in Germany' *Lib Ass Rec* 1967 69(12) 422-6, refs.

Schmidt-Künsemüller F A 'Les associations de bibliothèques et de bibliothécaires en République Fédérale d'Allemagne' *Ass Biblioth Fr Bull* 1971 (73) 201-5.

Verein Deutscher Bibliothekare (VDB), Stuttgart, 1900- . Re-formed in 1948.

Verein der Diplom-Bibliothekare an Wissenschaftlichen Bibliotheken, (VdDB), 1948- .

'VDB, VdDB, Kooperation zwischen beiden Vereinen' *Bibliotheksdienst* 1975 (6) 295-6. Amalgamation not possible but closer cooperation recommended between the two associations.

Verein der Bibliothekare an Öffentlichen Bibliotheken (VBB). 1949-68 as Verein der Deutscher Volkbibliothecare.

Thauer W 'Dreissig Jahre VBB' *Buch Biblioth* 1979 31(7/8) 671-7, refs.

Deutscher Bibliotheksverband (DBV), Berlin. 1949-1973 as Deutscher Büchereiverband. Institutional membership only.

Arbeitsgemeinschaft der Spezialbibliotheken (ASpB), Frankfurt. 1946- .

Arbeitsgemeinschaft der Spezialbibliotheken (ASpB): Bericht über die 15. Tagung in Düsseldorf 18 bis 21st März 1975 Universitätsbibliothek der Technische Universität Berlin, Abteilung Pub, 1976, 260p.

Verband der Bibliotheken des Landes-Nordrhein-Westfalen.

All these associations coordinate their activities since 1967 through the Deutsche Bibliothekskonferenz.

Verband der Deutschen Wissenschaftlichen Bibliotheken der Bundesrepublik und Westberlins. 1971- .

Internationale Vereinigung der Musikbibliotheken (AIBM) — Deutsch Gruppe BRD, Bremen. 1952- .

Dorfmüller K 'Die Arbeitsgemeinschaft der Musikbibliotheken und die deutsche Gruppe der Association Internationale des Bibliothèques Musicales (AIBM)' *Arbeitsgemeinschaft der Spezialbibliotheken (ASpB),* Düsseldorf, 1975, 123-7.

Deutsche Gesellschaft der Dokumentation, Frankfurt, 1948- . (DGD).

Deutsche Gesellschaft für Dokumentation (DGD) *Deutscher Dokumentartag 1974, Bonn-Bad Godesberg, 1974* Verlag Dokumentation 1975, 2 vols.

Verein Deutscher Dokumentare (VDD). 1961- .

2c

Edmunds H 'Zur Neuordnung der bibliothekarischen Ausbildung' *Verband Bibl LNW Mitt* 1968 18 184-99.

Krieg W 'La formation des bibliothècaires en Allemagne Fédérale' *Bull Biblioth Fr* 1969 14 83-94.

Carroll F L 'Library education in West Germany' *Wilson Lib Bull* 1969 43(10) 992-6.

— 'West German library schools 1968-1972' *Int Lib Rev* 1973 5(3) 329-33.

Sinkyavichyus K A 'Bibliothechnoe obrazovanie v Federativnoi Respublike Germanii' *Bibliotekovedenie i Bibliografiya za Rubezhom* 1975 (52) 45-59, 65.

Schoch G and Ringshausen H 'Das Hamberger Modell der Bibliothekarischen Ausbildung' *DFW* 1975 23(2) 29-41.

[Professional education for School Librarians] *Schulbibliothek Aktuell* 1979 (1). Whole issue.

Kostrewski B 'Education in medical documentation in West Germany' *J Info Sci* 1981 3(2) 81-90.

Thun H-P 'Die Koordinierung bibliothekarischer Fortbildungsarbeit in der Bundesrepublik Deutschland: Bericht über acht frustrierende Jahre' *Buch Biblioth* 1977 29(2) 143-7.

Koch H A 'Die Bibliotheksforschung in der Bundesrepublik Deutschland' *Z Biblioth Bibliog* 1976 23 273-300.

— 'Die Bibliotheksforschung in der Bundesrepublik Deutschland seit 1976' *Z Biblioth Bibliog* 1979 26(5) 345-69, refs.

Röhling H 'Von der Bildung des Bibliothekars über seine Weiterbildung zu einer neuen Bildung?' *Mitteilungsblatt* (Verband der Bibl des Landes Nordrhein-Westfalen) 1979 29(3) 294-303, refs.

Breifleb J 'Library management research in the Federal Republic of Germany: a survey' *INSPEL* 1976 11 45-55.

Funk R and Branthin E eds *Personalwirtschaftliche Probleme in öffentlichen und wissenschaftlichen Bibliotheken: Referate und Berichte des Fortbildungsseminars Berlin, Oct. 1974* Deutscher Bibliotheksverband 1975 249

Gen H - P 'Law librarians in the Federal Republic of Germany: their education and prospects' *Int J Law Lib* 1975 3(2) 115-34, refs.

3a

Handbuch der Bibliothekswissenschaft (Milkau) 2 Aufl, Bande bis 3, H Fuchs ed *Verwaltungslehre* Harrassowitz, 1968.

Handbuch der öffentlichen Bibliotheken 1977- , 10th ed Deutschen Bibliotheksverband, 1977, 447p.

DBV *Deutsches Bibliotheksadressbuch: Verzeichnis von Bibliotheken in der Bundesrepublik Deutschland einschliesslich Berlin (West) 1974-* DBV, 1974, 603p.

Meyen F ed *Verzeichnis der Spezialbibliotheken in der Bundesrepublik Deutschland einschliesslich West-Berlin* 2nd rev ed ASpB, 1970, 207p.

3b

Sampath P and Samulski P 'German bibliographical services' *Ann Lib Sci Doc* 1971 18(3) 117-31.

Weitzel R *Die deutschen nationalen Bibliographien* 3 Aufl. Frankfurt, Büchhändler-Vereinigung, 1963, 95p. Supplement 1976, 4p.

Deutsche Bibliothek *Deutsche Bibliographie* 1947- . Weekly. In three series since 1965, including periodicals and official publications. 5-yearly cumulations. Covers East German publications as well as Swiss and Austrian.

Verzeichnis Lieferbarer Bücher (Books in print) Verlag der Büchhändler-Vereinigung und Verlag Dokumentation, 1971, 2 vols. Annual.

DBV *Fachbibliographischer Dienst Bibliothekswesen* 1965- . Continues *Bibliographie zum Bibliothek- u Buchereiwesen.* Harrossowitz, 1966, 223p. Covers 1900-1964.

Zentralinstitut für Bibliothekswesen, Berlin. *25 Jahre publizistische Tätigkeit des Zentalinstituts für Bibliothekswesen und seiner Mitarbeiter 1950-1974 — Auswahbibliographie* Berlin, The Institute, 1975, 106p.

Chandler G 'INTAMEL: Federal Republic of Germany metropolitan city libraries — publication 1966-74' *Int Lib Rev 1975 7(3) 317-59.*

Heidtmann F 'Neue Aufgaben für die öffentlichen Bibliotheken auf den Bereich Lesen für den Beruf?' *Bibliotheksdienst* 1976 (10) 518-24.

Die Fachliteratur zum Buch- und Bibliothekswesen (Vol 2 of *Handbuch der technischen Dokumentation und Bibliographie*) 8th ed Verlag Dokumentation, 1967, 636p. Updated annually.

DGD *German Documentation Literature. Deutsche Dokumentation Literatur* 1968—.

DGD *Deutschsprachiges Schriftum zur Dokumentation* 1969, 32p.

3c

DBV (Through AfB, then DBI) *Bibliotheksdienst* 1961- . (1961-66 as *Büchereidienst*). Supplements: *Bibliotheksdienst. Beiheft.*

VBB *Büch und Bibliothek* 1948-1971 as *Bücherei und Bildung.*

'Aus der Aufangszeit der Zeitschrift BuB: ein Gespräch mit Rudolf Joerden' *Buch Biblioth* 1978 30(11). Series of papers on the journal itself.

76 VDB *Zeitschrift für Bibliothekswesen und Bibliographie* 1954- . Supersedes

Zeitschrift für wissenschaftliche Bibliotheken, 1948-1953.
— *Sonderheft.*
Bibliothek: Forschung und Praxis 1977- . 3 p.a. on a central theme.
DBV *Schulbibliothek Aktuell* 1975- . Quarterly. Edited by Beratungstelle für Schulbibliotheken.
DBV *Musikbibliothek Aktuell* 1975- .
Arbeitsgemeinschaft für Medizinisches Bibliothekswesen *Medizin Bibliothek Dokumentation* 1977- . Quarterly.
Nachrichten für Dokumentation, DGD 1950- .

3d

Statistisches Bundesamt *Statistiches Jahrbuch für die Bundesrepublik Deutschland.*
Liebenow P *'Deutsche Bibliotheksstatistik' Z Biblioth Bibliog* 1971 28(6) 386-8.
— *Die neue 'Deutsche Bibliotheksstatistik': Bedeutung und Problematik für Spezialbibliotheken* Report in 15th Conference (ASpB) Dusseldorf 1975 Universitätsbibliothek der Technische Universität Berlin, Abteilung Publ 1976, p. 79-83.
DBV *Gesamstatistik*, and *Schnellstatistik*. Annual.
— (*Statistik der kommunalen öffentlichen Büchereien der Bundesrepublik* (7th ed, 1970).
— *Schnellstatistik kommunaler öffentlicher Bibliotheken und Büchereien.*
[Library statistics] *Buch Biblioth* 1975 27(5). Several papers.
Fohrbeck K and Wiesband A J *Bibliotheken und Bibliothekstantieme: Materialbericht und Erhebungen zu Bestand, Ausleihe und Entwicklungstendenzen in den Bibliothekssystem der BRD* Verlag Dokumentation, 1974, 1552p.

3e

Lansky R comp *Bibliographie zum Bibliotheksrecht* [from 1900] Klostermann, 1970; Supplements 1972, 1974, 1976.
Beiträge zum Bibliotheksrecht *Bibliotheksdienst — Beiheft 132* DBAB, 1978, 78p.
Rakowski F and Bayer F 'Vorarbeiten für Bibliotheksgesetz-entwurfe' *Büch u Bildung* 1969 21(7) 20-8.
'Grundsätze und Normen für die Büchereigesetzgebung in der Ländern der Bundesrepublik Deutschland' *Büch u Bildung* 1970 22 364-7.
Kaspers H Bibliotheksrecht DBV, 1976, 67p. (Schriftenreihe der Bibliothekar-Lehrinstitute, C1) Law of 1975 for public libraries.
Nitze A *Die Rechtsstellung der wissenschaftlichen Bibliotheken* Berlin, Duncker & Humbolt, 1967, 172p.
Hoffman K - D 'Bibliotheks-Tantieme' *Bibliotheksdienst* 1971 (4) 141-68.
Cyntha H *Beschreibung und Bewertung Arbeitsplätzen und Dienstposten in wissenschaftlichen Bibliotheken* Hannover-Waldhausen, Nordwestverlag., 1975, 64p.
Dorffeldt S 'Der Gesamtvertrag zur Bibliothekstantieme' *Buch Biblioth* 1975 27(7/8) 648-56.

3f

Lottman H R 'German publishing now: stable, profitable — and perhaps less eager for imports' *Publishers Weekly* 1980 217(21) 33-59.
Sauberzweig D 'Kulturpolitische Aspekte der Haushaltskrise' *Buch Biblioth* 1978 30(7/8) 512-7.
Vorstius J *Grundzuge der Bibliotheksgeschichte* 6 Aufl Neubearb. von S Joost Harrassowitz, 1969, 128p.

Brown E 'War damage, 1939-45 and postwar reconstruction in libraries in the Federal German Republic and England: a comparison' *J Libp* 1975 7 288-308.

Busse G von *West German library development since 1945* Library of Congresss, 1962, 82p, bibl.

Busse G von Ernestius H *Das Bibliothekswesen in der Bundesrepublik Deutschland — eine Einführung* Harrassowitz, 1968, 302p.

— *Libraries in the Federal Republic of Germany* Harrassowitz, 1972, 308p. Translation of the above, revised and enlarged.

Büch u Bildung 1968 July/August. Issue for the IFLA Meeting, on all aspects of librarianship.

Betteridge A *The structure of the library system in the Federal Republic of Germany* Leeds Polytechnic, Department of Librarianship, 1971, 83p. (Occasional papers series.)

Krieg W ed *Bibliotheksorganisation — Methoden der Analyse und Gestaltung: Referate des Fortbildungsseminars, Köln, Nov. 1972* Cologne, Greven Verlag, 1973, 304p.

Stupnikova T S 'Nekotorye voprosy organizatsii bibliotechnogo dela v Federativnoi Respublikd Germanii' *Bibliotekovedenie i Bibliografiya za Rubezhom* 1975 (52) 24-44, refs.

'Germany, libraries and information centers in' in *Encyclopedia* 9(1973) 395-532, bibl.

Welsch E K *Libraries and archives in Germany* Pittsburgh, Council for European Studies, 1975, 275p.

Schwerpunktthema Bibliothekswesen *Börsenblatt für den Deutschen Buchhandel* 1978 34(37) 893-908.

Study tours in West Germany see:

Bull Biblioth Fr 1969 14(3) Special issue.

Nachr/Nouv/Notiz 1975 51(6) 225-40.

AIB Boll 1976 16(2) 156-64.

Ass Biblioth Fr Bull Info 1978 (98) 53-60.

PICA Mededelingen 1979 2(10) 6-11.

Bieber H et al, ed *Stadtbibliothek und Regionalbibliographie: Festschrift für Hans Moritz Meyen* Deutsche Bibliotheksverband, 1975, 238p.

Bibliothek und Buch in Geschichte und Gegenwart: Festgabe für Friedrich-Adolph Schmidt-Künsemüller zum 65. Geburtstag am 30 Dez 1975 Verlag Dokumentation, 1976.

Gebhardt W 'George Leyh 1877-1977: Betrachtungen an seinem hundertsten Geburtstag' *Z Biblioth Bibliog* 1977 24(3) 209-23.

Alsheimer R ed *Bestandserschliessung und Bibliotheksstruktur: Rolf Kluth zum 10-2-79* Harrassowitz, 1979.

Klozbücher A *Formen des Integration und Zentralisation der wissenschaftlichen Stadtbibliothek und der öffentlichen Bücherei* Cologne, Greven Verlag, 1969, 123p, bibl.

— Shorter version in *Libri* 1969 19(1) 1-16.

Deutscher Büchereiverband *Bibliothekarische Kooperation* 1971, 41p. (Bibliotheksdienst, Beiheft 56).

Junginger F and Totok W eds *Zentrale und Kooperative Dienstleistungen im Bibliothekswesen: Vortrage, gehalten auf den 65. Deutschen Bibliothekartag vom 20. bis 24. Mai 1975 in Konstanz* Klostermann, 1976, 155p.

Tehnzen J 'Zur Effizienz des Leihverkehrs der deutschen Bibliotheken' *Bibliotheksdienst* 1976 (6) 300-10.

Mauperon A 'La formation des utilisateurs en Grande Bretagne et en République Fédérale d'Allemagne' *Documentaliste* 1976 13(1) 13-6.

Vodosek P 'Arbeiterbibliothek und Öffentliche Bibliothek: zur Geschichte ihrer Beziehung von der esrsten Hälfte des neunzehnten Jahrhunderts bis 1933' *Buch Biblioth* 1975 27(4) 321-8.

Chaplan M A 'American ideas in the German public libraries: three periods' *Lib Q* 1971 41 35-53.

Mirbt K - W *Pionere des öffentlichen Bibliothekswesens* Harrassowitz, 1969, 120p. (Beitrage zum Büchereiwesen, Reihe B. Hefte 2).

'Öffentliche Bibliothek, Bildungsplanung und Gesetzgebung' *Bibliotheksdienst. Beiheft* (62), 1971 47p.

Totok W and Weimann K H 'Regionalbibliotheken in der Bundesrepublik Deutschland' *Z Biblioth Bibliog Sonderheft* 1971 (11) 354p.

Steinberg H *Lesen in öffentlichen Bibliotheken* Berlin, Stapp Verlag, 1974, 69p.

Chiappetti F S 'Decentremento della pubblica lettura nella Repubblica Federale di Germania' *AIB Boll* 1978 18(3/4) 256-62, refs.

Beyersdorff G *Kosten-Leistungs-Analyse in Öffentlichen Bibliotheken des Bundesgebietes* Deutscher Bibliotheksverband, 1974, 255p.

Chandler G 'The German library system: libraries in large cities' *Int Lib Rev* 1969 1(2) 241-62.

Braun B 'Offentliche Bibliothek und kommunale Kulturpolitik in der Bundesrepublik Deutschland' *Bibliothek: Forsch u Praxis* 1978 2(2) 77-111, refs.

Dittrich S 'Kritische Anmerkungen zum Funktionsmodell Mediathek' *Schulbibliothek Aktuell* 1977 (2) 64-8.

Lutz B 'Nahe an Jahr 2000' *Unsere Sammlung* 1980 (1) 4-9.

Lüdkte H 'Bibliotheksarbeit mit ausländischen Mitbürgern' *Buch Biblioth* 1979 31(5) 432-4, 436.

Wassner H et al *Gutachten zum Ausbau und zur Förderung der Bluidenhörbibliotheken in der Bundesrepublik Deutschland und in West Berlin* DBV, 1975, 192p (Materialien der Arbeitsstellen für das Bibliothekswesen, 11).

Die Krankenhausbücherei: Referate des Fortbildungslehrgangs für Bibliothekare an Krankenhausbüchereien, Düsseldorf, 1971 Cologne, Greven Verlag, 1973, 117p.

Kirfel H *Organisation und Integration von Krankenhausbibliotheken* Deutscher Bibliotheksverband & Arbeitsstelle für das Bibliothekswesen, 1975, 153p.

Schmidt H 'Bibliotheksdienste für Behinderte in der Bundesrepublik Deutschland Ergebnisse einer Umfrage' *Bibliotheksdienst* 1977 (11) 562-8.

Hodick E 'Bibliotheksdienst für Behinderte in der Bundesrepublik Deutschland: Ergebnisse aus der Kirchlichen Buchereiarbeit' *Bibliotheksdienst* 1978 (2) 101-14.

Shwetlik C *Dienste der öffentlichen Bucherei für Behinderte* DBV, Arbeitsstelle für das Bibliothekswesen, 1974, 61p. (Schriften der Bibliothekar-Lehrinstitut, Reihe A).

Weimar V *Zur Entwicklung des Truppenbüchereiwesens* Deutscher Bibliotheksverband & Arbeitsstelle fur das Bibliothekswesen, 1975, 40p.

Hundrieser D *Gefängnisbibliotheken: Untersuchungen zur Bibliotheksarbeit in Justizvollzugsanstalten* Berlin, Deutscher Bibliotheksverband & Arbeitsstelle für das Bibliothekswesen, 1976, 86p.

Koch N and Renard R *Pädagogische Bibliothekswesen in Deutschland* Munich, List Verlag, 1965, 328p. History and present problems.

Weinreuter E A 'Die Schulmediothek — Unterrichstechnologie in Dienste der Pädagogik' *Schulbibliothek Aktuell* 1977 (1)3- .

'Schulbibliotheken in Gymnasien (Oberstufe)' *Schulbibliothek Aktuell* 1978 (1). Whole issue.

Hodick E 'BASIS 12: neues Programm zur Grundausbildung von Mitarbeitern in

Katholischen öffentlichen Büchereien' *Unsere Sammlung* 1976 (1) 12-21.
Chronz E 'Strukturen der katolisch-kirchlichen Büchereiarbeit-1' *Unsere Sammlung* 1980 (1) 10-3.
Stoltzenburg J *The relation of the university libraries to their universities in the Federal Republic of Germany. Developments and tendencies* IFLA, 1970, 10p.
Deutsche Forschungsmeinschaft. Bibliotheksausschuss *Emfehlungen für die Zusammenarbeit zwischen Hochschulbibliothek und Institutsbibliotheken* Bad Godenberg, Der Bibliotheksausschuss, 1970.
Koch H-A 'Die Bibliotheksforschung in der Bundesrepublik Deutschland' *Z Biblioth Bibliog* 1976 23 273-300.
Delrieu S 'Visite à quelques bibliothèques allemandes, mars 1976' *Ass Biblioth Fr Bull Info* 1976 (93) 195-211.
Studies in the organisational structure and services in national and university libraries in the Federal Republic of Germany and in the United Kingdom (Meeting, Bristol, 1978) K G Saur/Bingley, 1979, 227p.
Gemeinsame Probleme von Staats- und Hochschulbibiotheken in Grossbritannien und der Bundesrepublik Deutschland . . ./Common themes in academic librarianship in the FGR and in the United Kingdom . . . Deutsches Bibliotheksinstitut/SCONUL, 1981, 285p. Meeting in Constance, May 1981.
Biskup P 'Subject specialists in German learned libraries: impressions from a 1975 visit to the Federal Republic of Germany' *Libri* 1977 27(2) 136-53.
Oho F 'Spezialbibliotheken in Deutschland (presented to IFLA General Council Meeting, Brussels, Sept. 1977, Division of Special Libraries)' *INSPEL* 1977 12(4) 163-90.
Wissenschaftsrat *Empfehlungen des Wissenschaftsrates zum Ausbau der wissenschaftlichen Einrichtungen* Bundesdruckerei, 1964, Vol 2 *Wissenschaftliche Bibliotheken.* Recommendations for reorganization of research institutions and their libraries which led to the legislation of 1970.
Arbeitsstelle für das Büchereiwesen *Bibliotheksplan 1969* Deutscher Büchereiverband, 1969, 71p. (Bibliotheksplan I).
DBV *Bibliotheksplan '73: Entwurf eines unfassenden Bibliotheksnetzes für die Bundesrepublik Deutschland* Bibliothekskonferenz, Deutscher Bucherieverband e.V., Arbeitsstelle für das Büchereiwesen, Berlin, 1973, 176p. (Bibliotheksplan II).
For comments on this plan see:
Libri 1974 24 157-63.
INSPEL 1975 10 48-60.
'Literaturversorgung unter den Aspekt der Planung von Fachinformationssystemen (FIS)' *Nachr Dok* 1975 26(2) 47-9.
Arntz H 'Documentation in the German Federal Republic' *Rivista dell'Informazione* 1973 4(5/6) 71-83.
Interministeriellen Arbeitsgruppe beim Bundesministerium des Innern und die Bundesregierung *Das Informationsbankensystem: Vorschläge für die Planung und den Aufbau eines allgemeinen arbeitsteiligen Informationsbankensystems für die Bundesrepublik Deutschland* (Holder Report) Carl Heymanns Verlag, 1971-1972, 3 vols.
Bundesministerium für Forschung und Technologie *Programm der Bundesregierung zur Förderung der Information und Dokumentation (IuD-Programm) 1974-1977* The Ministry, 1975, 147p.
The programme of the Federal Government for the Promotion of Information and Documentation (I & D-Programme) 1974-77 Institut für Dokumentationswesen, 1976, 125p.

'Programen der Bundesregierung zur Forderung der Information und Doku-

mentation' *Nachr Dok* 1975 26(2) 41-6.

Kenney B 'Die Planung von nationalen Informationssystemen in der Bundesrepublik Deutschland, England und der USA' *Nachr Dok* 1975 26(4/5) 136-42.

Deutsche Forschungsgemeinschaft *Über-regionale Literaturversorgung Denkschrift* 1975, 116p.

OECD *Review of national scientific and technical information policy: Germany* OECD, 1977, 122p.

Neuere Formate für Verarbeitung und Austausch bibliographischer Daten: Bericht eines Symposiums veranstaltet von der Arbeitsstelle für Bibliotekstechnik am 30 April 1974 Verlag Dokumentation 1975, 101p.

Lingenberg W 'Some aspects of library automation in the Federal Republic of Germany' *Program* 1978 12(1) 42-53.

Neubauer K W 'Staatsbibliothek Preussischer Kulturbesitz and the German "CONSER" project' *Leads* 1978 20 1-4.

Schlitt G 'Die Arbeit der Kommission für Baufragen in Verein Deutscher Bibliothekare (VDB)' *Buch Biblioth* 1974 26(10) 895-8.

Philipp F-H ed *Materialien zu neueren Bibliotheksbauten: Ergebnisse einer Erhebung der Kommission für Baufragen des Vereins Deutscher Bibliothekare* Berlin, Deutscher Bibliotheksverband & Arbeitsstelle für das Bibliothekswesen, 1974, 91p.

Philipp F-H ed; Mariscotti de Gorlitz A M comp *Materialien zu neueren Bibliotheksbauten II: Ergebnisse einer Erhebung der Kommission für Baufragen des Vereins Deutscher Bibliothekare* Berlin, Deutscher Bibliotheksverband & Arbeitsstelle für das Bibliothekswesen, 1976, 59p.

GREAT BRITAIN

General and England and Wales. The problems and activities specific to Scotland and to Northern Ireland have been treated separately for the sake of clarity.

1

British Library. Reorganized in 1972 for increased efficiency and rationalization of its services, as a network to which belong a number of existing national libraries and specialized libraries.

Department of Education and Science *Report of the National Libraries Committee* ('Dainton report') HMSO, 1969 (Cmnd 4028).

Line M B 'The developing national library network in Great Britain' *Lib Resources Tech Serv* 1972 16(1) 61-72.

'[The British Library]' *State Libn* 1977 25(1) Whole issue on the services of the British Library.

Hookway H T 'The resources of the British Library' *Aslib Proc* 1975 27(1) 2-7.

Fung M C '[The British Library]' (In Chinese) *Lib Info Sci* 1978 4(2) 171-9, refs.

The libraries included in the network are:

- British Library. Department of Printed Books. Previously British Museum Library.

Esdaille A J K *The British Museum Library, a short history and survey* Greenwood P, 1979 (Reprint of 1948 edition).

- British Library. Reference Division. Previously Patent Office Library then National Reference Library: Science Division and National Reference Library: Life Sciences Section.
- British Library Research and Development Department (BLRD). Previously Office of Technical and Scientific Information (OSTI).

Gray J C 'Information Centre profile: the British Library Research and Development Department (BLRD)' *Info: News and Sources* 1975 7(2) 62-3.

— 'Grundzätze der Forschungsförderung der Abteilung für Forschung und Entwicklung der British Library' *Biblioth Forsch Praxis* 1979 3(2) 106-11.

For the period prior to the reorganization see:

OSTI: the first five years, 1965-1970 HMSO, 1971, 64p.

- British Library Lending Division (BLLD), Boston Spa. Previously, 1962-72, National Lending Library for Science and Technology (NLLST). Now also includes the National Central Library. Their main function is to be the central agency for interlending.

Houghton B *Out of the dinosaurs. The evolution of the NLLST* Bingley, 1972, 127p.

Line M 'The British Library Lending Division and Western Europe' *LIBER Bull* 1974 (5/6) 65-73.

Davey J S and Smith E S 'The overseas services of the British Library Lending Division' *Unesco Bull Lib* 1975 29(5) 259-67.

Laaksomaa P 'BLLD maailman suurin kaukopalvelukirjasto' *Kirjastolehti* 1980
 73(2) 85-7, illus. Includes statistics.

Line M B 'Organisational profile 3: the British Library Lending Division' *J Info Sci* 1980 2(3/4) 173-82.

Plaister J M 'The effect of the British Library Lending Division on inter-library lending' *Aslib Proc* 1976 28(5) 193-203.

Filon S P L *The National Central Library: an experiment in library cooperation* Library Asociation, 1977, 300p.

- Library Association Library, London. 1877- . Acts as a special library in the field of librarianship and cooperates with other large libraries in the field.
- National Library of Scotland. (See details in: Scotland, 1.)
- National Library of Wales, Aberystwyth.

Llyfrgell Genedlaethol Cymru: crynodeb byr o'i hanes a'i gweithgareddau The Library, 1974, 39p.

The National Library of Wales: a brief summary of its history and its activities 4th ed The Library, 1978, 40p.

To assess the overall meaning of the British Library structure within the NATIS concept see:

Hookway H T 'Concept of a national organisation for information: the British Library, achievements and potentials' *Aslib Proc* 1979 31 88-96.

Higham N 'Impact of the British Library on the national and international scene' *Aslib Proc* 1979 31 97-105. Both are papers at the Aslib's 52nd annual conference.

2a

Department of Education and Science (DES), Arts and Libraries Branch.

Library Advisory Councils (for England and Wales). 1964- .

Paulin L 'Review of the work of the Advisory Councils for England and Wales' *J Libp* 1975 7(2) 132-40.

2b

Publishers Association. 1896-.

Kingsford R J L *The Publishers Association, 1896-1946* CUP, 1970, 228p.

Library Association (LA), London. 1877-.

Haslam D D 'The Library Association' in *Encyclopedia* 14 (1975) 312-37.

Munford W A *A history of the Library Association 1877-1977* LA, 1976, 360p.

One hundred years: a collection to celebrate the Library Association Centenary by members of staff at College of Librarianship, Wales The College, 1977, 77p.

Knott J ed *LA 77: essays in librarianship* Newcastle-upon-Tyne Polytechnic, Department of Librarianship, 1977, 74p.

Proceedings of the LA Centenary Conference [London, 1977] LA, 1977, 96p.

For shorter publications on the LA centenary see:

Herald of Library Science 1977 16(4) 283-398, refs.

Library Association Record 1977 79(4) 195, 197.

For a short history see:

Journal of Librarianship 1974 6(3) 137-64.

Amongst the sub-groups of the Library Association the following is of special interest here:

International and Comparative Librarianship Group (ICLG). 1968-.

'International and Comparative Librarianship Group — ten years of precocity' *Lib Ass Rec* 1978 80 15-21.

Dewe M 'The International and Comparative Librarianship Group (ICLG), 1968-' *Unessco J* 1980 2(1) 55-9, refs.

A new group of the LA:

School Libraries Group.
Saunders J 'The formation of the School Libraries Group and the future for school libraries' *Educ Lib Bull* 1980 23(1) 28-33, refs.
Standing Conference of National and University Libraries (SCONUL), London. 1950-.
Association of Assistant Librarians (AAL). 1895-.
Ramsden M T *A history of the Association of Assistant Librarians, 1895-1945* AAL, 1973, 289p.
Circle of State Librarians.
Association of British Library Schools.
Association of British Theological and Philosophical Libraries. (ABTAPL). 1954-.
British and Irish Association of Law Librarians (BIALL). 1969-.
International Association of Music Libraries. UK Branch.
Art Libraries Society (ARLIS), Hull. 1969-.
Phillpot C 'ARLIS: the Art Libraries Society' *Lib Ass Rec* 1972 74(1) 5-6.
Association of Special Libraries and Information Bureaux (Aslib). 1926-.
Taylor P J ed *Essays on Aslib* Aslib, 1978, 90p.
Institute of Information Scientists, Reading. 1958-.

2c

Bramley G *A history of library education* 2nd ed Bingley/Archon 1980. UK and USA, influence on other English-speaking countries.
Schur H and Saunders W L *Education and training for scientific and technological library and information work* HMSO, 1968, 88p.
Library Advisory Councils *Report on the supply and training of librarians* [Chairman F W Jessup] HMSO, 1968, 72p.
LA Education Committee. Sub-Committee of Staff Training in Librarianship *Report on library school field work* LA, 1971, 21p. Summary in *Lib Ass Rec* 1972 74(1).
'What the library schools are doing' *YLG News* 1974 18(3).
'First Scandinavian-British Conference on Education for Librarianship, July 1974' Reported in *Unesco Bull Lib* 197 29(1) 51-3.
Bottle R T 'Education for information and library work' *Aslib Proc* 1976 28(1) 22-9.
Frigiolini C 'La formazione dei bibliotecari in Inghilterra e in Francia' *Acad Bibliot Ital* 1976 44(2) 143-9.
Slatter M *Assessing the need for short courses in library/information work* Aslib, 1976, 88p. (Occasional publications, 19).
'The work of a large multi-role library school [Leeds Polytechnic] *Unesco Bull Lib* 1976 30(3) 140-6.
'The Library Association working party on 'The future of professional qualifications: recommendations and implementation' (Chairman: L V Paulin), *Lib Ass Rec* 1977 79(9), Supplement, 8p.
Curriculum development in librarianship and information science: proceedings of a workshop held at the College of Librarianship Wales [July 1977] British Library, 1978, 142p?
Kohn P 'What the students think: education for librarianship' *Assist Libn* 1977 70(4) 62-7.
Needham C D 'La formazione professionale dei bibliotecari in Gran Britagna' *AIB Boll* 1979 19(1) 11-9.
Revill D H 'Examination and assessment within education for librarianship' *J Libp* 1979 11(2) 107-25, refs.

Benešová D 'Vzdělaváni knihovníku ve velké Británii' *Ctenar* 1979 31(10) 330-34; 31(11) 365-6.

Evans D W 'African studies and British library schools' *Afr Res Doc* 1978 (16/17) 12-7.

Wallis H 'The training of map curators in Great Britain' *Inspel* 1975 10(1/2) 28-33.

Dow J *Education for British school librarians — dilemmas of dual qualifications* Loughborough U of Technology, 1979, 167p, refs.

DES *Directory of short courses in librarianship and information work* 1967-.

Edwards R J *In-service training in British libraries: its development and present practice* LA, 1977, 232p.

Training in libraries: report of the Library Association Working Party on training LA, 1977, 26p.

Jones K H *Teaching of library management in United Kingdom schools of librarianship* Leeds Polytechnic, School of Librarianship, 1977, 138p.

Danton J P 'British and American library school teaching staffs: a comparative inquiry' *J Educ Libp* 1978 19(2) 97-129.

Jones N *Continuing education for librarians* Leeds Polytechnic, Department of Librarianship, 1977, 304p. Based on a thesis U of Bradford.

— 'Continuing education for librarians: results of a survey' *J Libp* 1978 10(1) 39-55.

O'Hanlon M J 'British Library Research and Development: current projects and future trends' *Info Scientist* 1975 9(3) 99-106.

Gilder L ed *Some recent developments in library research in Britain: a summary of the proceedings of a seminar held by the Library Management Research Unit, U of Cambridge August 1976* The Unit, 1977, 34p.

RADIALS bulletin — Research and development — Information and library science LA, 1975-. 3 a year. Part of Unesco ISORID System.

Moore N *Public library research: a study of the development and current state of public library research* British Library, 1978, 40p. (BLRD report 5419).

Taylor P J 'Research at Aslib 1958-1977' *Aslib Proc* 1978 30(3) 104-14.

Kanevskii B P 'Kritika anglo-amerikaniskikh sravnitel 'nykh issledovanii v oblasti bibliotekovedeniya' *Bibliot Bibliog za Rubezhom* 1974 (50) 8-37.

Peele D 'Evaluating library employees' *Lib J* 1972 97(16) 2803-7, refs.

Monick S 'British librarianship today: the death of a profession' *Rhod Libn* 1975 7(2) 21-9.

Report of the Commission on the Supply and Demand for Qualified librarians LA, 1977, 47p.

Anderson U *Career patterns in library/information research* British Library, 1978, 77p. (BLRD report 5459).

Department of Education and Science *Census of staff in librarianship and information work in the United Kingdom 1976* HMSO, 1978, 35p.

Harrison D J 'The staffing of public libraries: an appraisal of the 1976 LAMSAC report' *J Libp* 1979 11(3) 183-96.

School Library Association *The way ahead: the organization and staffing of libraries and learning resources in schools in the 1980s* SLA, 1980, 28p.

Marshall M and Nettlefold M eds *Report: survey on children's library staffing carried out in April 1975* LA, Youth Libraries Group, 1976, 13p.

Montgomery A C *Professionalism in British librarianship — its growth since 1945* LA, 1979, 303p.

Weibel K et al *The role of women in librarianship 1876-1976: the entry, advancement and struggle for equalization in one profession* Mansell, Oryx P, 1979, 510p, bibl.

Layzell Ward P 'Women and librarianship in 1975' *Lib Ass Rec* 1975, 77(4) 82-3. Changes since the author's survey in 1963.

Maidment W R 'Trade unionism in public libraries' *J Libp* 1976 8(3) 143-52.

Nayce J-L 'Librarians for social change — alternative library work in Great Britain: a new necessary movement and its periodical' *Buch Biblioth* 1977 29 880-3.

3a

Britain: an official handbook 1981 HMSO, 1981, 498p. Annual.

Henderson G P and Henderson S P A eds *Directory of British associations and associations in Ireland (1980-81)* 6th ed CBD Research, 1980, 486p.

Libraries, museums and art galleries yearbook J Clarke.

Taylor L J *A librarian's handbook: volume 2* LA, 1980, 1181p. Updates and supplements: *A librarian's handbook*, 1976 (ie: [Vol 1]).

Library Association handbook of organisation 1980-81 and membership directory.

Library Association yearbook.

Batten W E ed *Handbook of special librarianship and information work* 4th ed Aslib, 1975, 430p. (3rd edition edited by W Ashworth) Emphasis on new techniques.

Whatley A ed *International and Comparative Librarianship Group Handbook*, LA, 1977, 198p.

Library Association *Libraries in the United Kingdom and the Republic of Ireland* 8th ed LA, 1979, 173p.

'The 1975 NLW Directory of Library Authorities' *New Lib World* 1975 76(899) 8p insert.

Cudby L H ed *Dictionary of London public libraries* 7th ed Association of London Chief Librarians, 1982, 167p.

Eyre J J *Directory of UK library school teachers* 3rd rev ed Bingley/Linnet, 1972, 79p.

Codlin E M ed *Aslib directory* 4th ed Aslib, 1980, 2 vols. (3rd ed, 1970, published by B J Wilson).

Robert S A et al, eds *Research libraries and collections in the United Kingdom: a selective inventory and guide* Bingley/Linnet Books, 1979, 285p.

Houghton B ed *ARLIS directory of members — 1974-75* ARLIS, 1974, 31p.

Long M W ed *Music in British libraries* 3rd ed LA, 1981, 456p.

International Association of Music Libraries *Directory of UK Branch members* 1972, 12 leaves.

Library Association. Medical Section *Directory of medical libraries in the British Isles* 4th ed LA, 1976, 199p.

Edwards P I 'List of libraries in the field of pure and applied biology' *Biol J Linnean Soc* 1971 3(3) 173-88.

Burkett J ed *Special libraries and information services in the United Kingdom* 3rd rev ed Vol I: *Industrial and related library and information services* LA, 1972. Vol II: *Government and related library and information services* LA, 1974, 217p.

Guide to government department and other libraries 25 ed British Library, 1982, 95p.

British scientific documentation services British Council, 1974, 72p. Bodies supplying abstract and index services.

Finer R comp *Guide to selected computer-based information services* Aslib, 1972, 113p.

Finer R and Bowden P L *A guide to selected British non-computer-based*

commercially available information services Aslib, 1975, 106p.
Wilson C W J *Directory of operational computer applications in United Kingdom libraries and information units* 2nd ed Aslib, 1977, 169p.
Wall J comp *Directory of British photographic collections* Heinemann, 1977, 226p.

3b

Raynard W B 'Some developments in nineteenth century bibliography: Great Britain' *Libri* 1977 27(2) 97-107.
Linford J E et al *BNB/MARC Project: report on the period September 1970-March 1973* Council of the BNB Research and Development Section, 1974, 48p.
Clements F A ed *Proceedings of a conference held at Plymouth on 16 and 17 April 1975* MARC Users' Group, 1975, 35p. On the British Library MARC services.
British National Bibliography (BNB) 1950-. Weekly lists. Monthly, quarterly, annual cumulations.
Bookseller 1858-. Monthly and: *Cumulative Book List*. Annual.
British Books in Print Whitaker, 1874 -. Title varies.
Downs R B *British library resources: a bibliographic guide* ALA/Mansell, 1973, 332p.
Higgens G *Printed reference material* LA, 1980, 520p.
LA *Catalogue of the library* 1958, 519p.
LA and Aslib *Library and Information Science Abstracts* (LISA). 1969 -. Formerly *Library Science Abstracts*. 1950-68.
Sections in:
Aslib Proceedings; *Journal of Documentation*; *Library History:* 'Library history theses'.
Keeling D F comp *British library history: bibliography 1962-1968* LA, 1972, 164p.
— *Ibid: bibliography 1969-1972* LA, 1975, 150p. (First supplement).
Mann M *Library manpower planning: a bibliography* BLR&D report 5614.
Taylor P J ed *Library and information studies in the United Kingdom and Ireland 1950-1974: an index to theses* Aslib, 1976, 69p.
Five years' work in librarianship. 1951/55-1961/65 LA, 1958-65. Superseded by:
Whatley H A *British librarianship and information science 1966/1970* LA, 1972, 712p; *1971-1975* LA, 1977. 379p.
Hay W *Library services to disabled people in Britain: an annotated bibliography, 1970-1981* LA, 1982, 40p.
Atkin P 'Bibliography of use of surveys of public and academic libraries, 1950-November 1970' *Lib Info Bull* 1971 (14) 82p.
Wilson C W J 'A bibliography on UK computer based circulation systems' *Program* 1970 4(2) 55-60.
West M W et al 'Library automation: a bibliography, 1973-77' *J Lib Autom* 1978 11(4) 339-65. Mostly concerned with Great Britain.

3c

Current British journals: a subject guide to periodicals 3rd ed British Library, 1982.
Gresham J 'The abandoned switchboard: library/information journal' *Lib Rev* 1979 28 143-7, refs. Development of professional use of printed journals.
Roberts N 'Ten years of library journals in Great Britain, 1969-1979' *J Libp* 1979, 11(3) 163-82, refs.

Seaton J 'Readability tests for UK professional journals' *J Libp* 1975 7(2) 69, 83. Comparative study of British library journals.
Library Association Record. 1899-. Change of format in 1976. See comments in *Lib Ass Rec* 1975 77(11) 257-60 and 77(12) 279-80.
LA *Journal of Librarianship*. 1969-.
LA *Library History*. 1967-.
LA. International and Comparative Librarianship Group *Focus on International and Comparative Librarianship*. 1967-. In printed form since 1973/4.
LA. RSIS Group *REFER*. 1980-.
Circle of State Librarians *State Librarian*. 1952- . Previously: *Bulletin of the Circle of State Librarians* (1948-51).
ARLIS *Art Library Journal*. 1976- . Supersedes *ARLIS Newsletter*. 1969-76 (Nos 1-26).
ABTAPL *Bulletin*. 1956- . New format December 1974 (1)-.
Aslib Proceedings. 1949- .
Aslib *Journal of Documentation*. 1945- .
Institute of Information Scientists *Journal of Information Science* 1979 - . Replaces *Information Scientist*. 1967-78.
- *Inform*. Quarterly newsletter. 1975- .
Welsh Library Association/Cymdeithas Llyfrgelloedd Cymru *Y Ddolen* 1970- : Irregular.
Library Review. 1927- .
Kinninmont T 'Fifty years of *Library Review*' *Lib Rev* 1976/77 25(8) 299-301.
Library World. 1898-1971. Now *New Library World* 73 (854)-.
Murison J 'The old hundredth' *New Lib World* 1979 80(952) 189-90.
British Library Journal. 1975- . Replaces the section of the *British Museum Journal* concerned with the British Library.
Interlending Review: journal of the BLLD. 1971- . Formerly: *BLL Review*.
Information Storage and Retrieval. 1963- .
LA and Aslib Audio-Visual Groups *Audiovisual Librarian*. 1973- .
University College, London and Aslib *Journal of Informatics*. 1977- .
Program. 1966- . Current awareness on the use of computers in librarianship.
Loughborough U, Department of Library and Information Studies *Library Management News*. 1977- .
Librarians for Social Change. 1972- .
Socialist Librarians Journal. 1980- . From Community and Trade Union Centre.

3d

Walker M A *Reviews of United Kingdom statistical sources*Pergamon (for SSRC), 1981, 430p.
CSO *Facts in Focus* 5th ed Penguin/HMSO, 1980, 255p.
CSO *Annual abstract of statistics* HMSO.
Office of Population Censuses and Surveys *International migration: migrants entering or leaving the United Kingdom and England and Wales 1976* HMSO, 1979, 68p.
EUROMONITOR book readership survey, 1978 EUROMONITOR Publications Ltd, 1978, 74p. 3rd survey. Book readership and trade.
Moore N *Statistical series relevant to libraries* BLRDD, 1976, 36p.
Public library statistics Institute of Municipal Treasurers and Accountants then Chartered Institute of Public Finance and Accountancy, 1958/59- .
Public libraries statistics. Estimates 1980/81 CIPFA, 1980, 8p.
'Survey of college libraries in the United Kingdom, 1970: complete report' *Lib Info Bull* 1971 (15) 1-26, 48 tables.

[Statistics of university libraries] published by UGC 1919/20-.
LA Colleges of Technology and Further Education Section *College library statistics*.
Department of Education and Science *Statistics of libraries in major establishments of further education in England, Wales and Northern Ireland, 1977-78* DES, 1980, 16p.
Libraries and their finance: information prepared for a Working Party on Resources set up by the Library Advisory Council for England in February 1975, and the Working Party commentary on it DES, 1975, 27p.
'Library finance and figures: DES issues paper on library spending from 1967 to 1973(?)' *The Bookseller* 1975 (3638) 1640-2. See also:
'Books in a siege economy' (Series of statistics-based papers on the effect of cuts - Holborn conference 1975) *The Bookseller* 1975.
'Libraries and their finance' *J Libp* 1976 8(1) 1-20.

3e

Government publications HMSO, 1972-73- . Previously *Catalogue of Government publications*. Also *Consolidated list*, 5-yearly. Subject index.
Copyright and designs law: report of the Committee to consider the law on copyright and designs. (J Whitford, chairman) HMSO, 1977.
McFarlane G 'Towards a new British copyright law' *Solicitors J* 1977 121(35) 584-6.
Taylor L J *Copyright for librarians* Tamarisk, 1980, 164p.
DES *Public Lending right: report of the working party appointed by the Paymaster General* (H T Hookway, chairman) HMSO, 1972, 30- .
— *Public lending right: second report of the Technical Investigation Group* DES, 1974, 81p.
— *Public lending right: final report of an investigation of technical and cost aspects* HMSO, 1975, 28p.
— *Public lending right: an account of an investigation of technical and cost aspects* HMSO, 1975, 53p.
'Public lending right: a symposium' *The New Rev* 1975 2(21) 3-40.
Bell R 'Legal deposit in Britain' (Part I) *Law Libn* 1977 8(1) 5-8; (Part II) *Law Libn* 1977 8(2) 22-6.
O'Higgins P *Censorship in Britain* Nelson, 1972, 232p.
Dixon J 'Book selection, racism and the law of the land' *Assist Libn* 1979 72 (7/8) 94-9, refs.
Moys E M ed *Manual of law librarianship: the use and organisation of legal literature* A Deutsch, 1976, 733p.
Kaula P N 'Library legislation in Great Britain' *Herald Lib Sci* 1977 16(4) 353-64.
Morris R J B *Parliament and the public libraries: a survey of legislative activity promoting the municipal library services in England and Wales, 1850-1976*, Mansell, 1977, 477p.
Hewitt A R *Public library law in England and Wales, Scotland and Northern Ireland* Association of Assistant Librarians, 1975.
DES Library Advisory Council for England *Aspects of public library management: the application of new management processes to the public library service. Report of the working party* (J D Stewart, chairman) HMSO, 1973, 22p.
DES *The public library service: reorganisation and after* HMSO, 1973, 29p.
Phillips B J et al *Public libraries legislation, administration and finance* LA and CIPFA, 1977, 35p.

'The standards of public libraries' *New Society* 1979 48 (866) 332.

LA *Hospital libraries: recommended standards* Rev ed 1972.

Lewis J 'Legislation and official pronouncements relating to the English health and welfare library services' *New Zeal Lib* 1975 38(4) 179-88, refs.

UGC *Report of the Committee on libraries* (T Parry, chairman) HMSO, 1967, 292p. University libraries.

Capital provision for university libraries: a report of a working party [of the UGC] (R Atkinson, chairman) HMSO, 1976, 42p.

Colleges of Education libraries: recommended standards for their development LA, 1972.

LA *School library resources centres: recommended standards for policy and provision* LA, 1970, 15p.

Gopinath MA 'Standards for use in the planning of library and documentation systems: comparative data from India, UK, USA and Canada' *Lib Sci Slant Doc* 1974 11(3/4) 107-13.

3f

Bennett H S *English books and readers, 1475 to 1557* 2nd ed CUP, 1969, 337p.

Mann P H *Books: buyers and borrowers* A Deutsch, 1971, 208p.

Dobrynina N E 'Nekotorye aspekty sovremennykh issledovanii chteniya vo Frantsii i Velikobritanii' *Bibliot Bibliog za Rubezhom* 1974 (50) 38-62. Sociology of reading.

Breaking the reading barrier: papers of a conference held at the Library Association headquarters . . . on 23rd April 1974 LA, 1975, 41p.

Monk D *Social grading of the National Readership Survey* 4th ed rev Joint Industry Committee for National Readership Surveys, 1978, 18p.

Kedney R J ed *The adult illiterate in the community* Bolton College of Education, 1975.

A report on the National Deaf Literacy Scheme: a pilot project, September 1975-March 1976 National Deaf Literacy Scheme, 1976, 26p.

Hargreaves D *On the move: the BBC contribution to the Adult Literacy Campaign in the United Kingdom between 1972 and 1976* BBC, 1977, 43p.

Armour J *Take off* LA, 1980, 180p. Adult literacy education.

Irwin R *The English library: sources and history* Allen & Unwin, 1966, 312p.

Olle J G *Library history* Bingley/Saur, 1979, 114p. Largely based on British libraries.

Kaufman P *Libraries and their users: collected papers in library history* LA, 1969, 233p.

Savage E A *Old English libraries: the making, collection and use of books during the Middle Ages* Methuen, 1912, 298p. (Reprinted: Gale Research, 1968).

Wormald F and Wright C E *The English library before 1700* Athlone P, 1958, 273p.

Krivatsy N H *Libraries in 17th century England* Catholic U of America, 1965. (Thesis).

Whatley H A 'Non-librarianship: yesterday's closed libraries' *Lib Rev* 1979 28 78-87. 1930s.

Brown E 'War damage, 1939-1945 and postwar reconstruction in libraries in the Federal German Republic and England: a comparison' *J Libp* 1975 7 288-308.

Francis F C and Bloomfield V *Independent libraries in England: a survey of selected institutional proprietory and endowed libraries October 1973-December 1975. Report presented to the Council on Library Resources* Aylesbury, The Author, 1977, 143p.

Laroze M et al 'Voyage d'étude en Grande Bretagne' *Bull Biblioth Fr* 1978 23(2)

83-135. Three reports.
Tracy J I 'British librarianship: an American view' *PNLA Q* 1979 43 4-9.
Saunders W L ed *British librarianship today* LA, 1976, 378p.
Ashworth W 'Hard times are ripe times' *New Lib World* 1977 78 (919) 7-8.
Higham N 'Priority services in a stress situation' in *Proceedings, papers and summaries of discussions at the National Conference held at Scarborough, 6th September-9th September 1976* LA, 1976, 18-20.
Coping with cuts: proceedings of a conference held at Holborn Library, 13th July 1977 National Book League, 1977, 98p.
Harrison K C *Prospects for British librarianship* LA, 1976, 299p.
Library Advisory Council *Future development of libraries: the organizational and policy framework* 1978.
[Debate on the LAC report] *Lib Ass Rec* 1979 81(10) 481, 483.
Hookway H T *National library planning in Britain. A paper* (IFLA 40th Meeting, Washington, 1974), 14p.
Whibley V ed *Librarianship 1999. Papers at the conference of the LA Home Counties Branch, May 1977* The Branch, 1977.
Maidment W R *Librarianship* David & Charles, 1975, 151p.
Plumb P W 'Development of library cooperation in Great Britain' *Herald Lib Sci* 1977 16(4) 347-52, refs.
'Anglo-Soviet Conference on Library Co-operation' *Interlending Rev* 1979 7(2) 52-6, supplement: 6 microfiches.
Davey J 'Interlibrary lending in the United Kingdom and Ireland, 1978-79' *Interlending Rev* 1979 7(4) 119-25.
For conference activities involving cooperation with or interest in foreign libraries see the Anglo-Scandinavian Conferences, 1953- and the conferences of the LA International and Comparative Librarianship Group.
The British commitment overseas LA ICLG, 1979, 70p.
Dyson A J 'Organising undergraduate library instruction: the English and American experience' *J Acad Libp* 1975 1(1) 9-13.
Fjällbrant N *A comparison of user instruction in Scandinavian and British academic libraries* Chalmers U of Technology, 1975, 37p.
Mauperon A 'La formation des utilisateurs en Grande Bretagne et en République Fédérale d'Allemagne' *Documentaliste* 1976 13(1) 13-6.
Ford G ed *Users studies* Sheffield U, 1977, 92p, refs.
Stevenson M 'Education of users of libraries and information services' *J Doc* 1977 33(1) 53-78.
Progress in educating library users Bowker, 1978. Canada, Scandinavia, Great Britain.
Jones A *Educating and training for using secondary school libraries: teachers, librarians and pupils* LA, 1979, 313p.
Robson A 'The intellectual background of the public library movement in Britain' *J Lib Hist* 1976 11(3) 187-205.
Hassenforder J *Développement comparé des bibliothèques publiques en France, en Grande Bretagne et aux Etats Unis dans la seconde moitié due 19e siècle (1850-1914)* Cercle de la Librairie, 1967, 210p.
Kelly T *Early public libraries: a history of public libraries in Great Britain before 1850* LA, 1966, 281p.
— *Books for the people: an illustrated history of the British public library* A Deutsch, 1977, 271p.
— *History of public library in Great Britain, 1845-1975* 2nd rev ed LA, 1977, 582p.
Pemberton J E *Politics and public libraries in England and Wales, 1850-1970* LA, 1977, 149p.

Sykes P *The public library in perspective: an examination of its origins and modern role* Bingley, 1979, 184p.

Sturges R P 'Context for library history: libraries in 18th century Derby' *Lib Hist* 1976 4(2) 44-52.

Hunter J D 'The early years of the Birmingham Friends Reading Society' *J West Midlands Region Soc* 1968 2 44-76.

Noyce J 'Libraries and the working classes in the 19th century' *Libns for Soc Change* 1974/75 (7) 9p.

Tokiwa S [Mechanics' Institutes movement in 19th century England: influences to the Public Library Act (1850)] (In Japanese) *Lib Info Sci* 1976 (14) 311-23.

Gerard D E 'Subscription libraries (Great Britain)' in *Encyclopedia* 29 (1980) 205-21, bibl.

Williams D M 'English parochial libraries: a history of changing attitudes' *Antiquarian Book Monthly Rev* 1978 5(4) 138-47.

Knott J 'Newcastle-upon-Tyne newsrooms' *Lib Hist* 1977 4(4) 101-11.

Ball A W *The public libraries of Greater London: a pictorial history, 1856-1914* LA London and Home Counties Branch, 1977, 108p.

Stockham A *British county libraries, 1919-1969* A Deutsch, 1969, 126p.

Howley M and Orton I *Seventy five years, the first county library: a history of the Isle of Wight County Library, 1904-1979* The Library, 1980, 43p.

Ellis A *Public libraries and the First World War* Ffynnon P, 1975, 75p.

Kennington D and Pratt G *Public libraries and long range planning: an exercise in Delphi technique forecasting carried out on behalf of PLRG in 1973/74* PL Research Group, 1976, 81p.

Whibley V ed *Survival '76. One day conference of the London and Home Counties branch of the LA, 12th May 1976* LA, 1976, 46p.

Alfred J R 'Purpose of the public library: the historical view' *Lib Hist* 1972 2 185-204. Also in:

Public library purpose: a reader Bingley/Shoe String, 1978.

Barnard T D F *Libraries and the community: papers at the weekend conference of the London and Home Counties Branch of the LA, Eastbourne, May 1973* LA, The Branch, 1973, 86p.

Elliott J 'Where the pls went wrong' *New Lib World* 1976 77 (909) 47-8.

Morris R J B 'The adoption process for public libraries in the United Kingdom' *Local Gov't Rev* 1976 (140) 553-7.

— *Parliament and the public libraries* Mansell, 1977, 477p.

Thomas G 'Library services in rural areas' *Service Point* 1979 (17) 28-34.

Bowen J and Walley E *Report of a dissemination workshop to review progress and developments in community information services in the public libraries: project SI/G/257* Leeds Polytechnic, School of Librarianship, Public Management Research Unit, 1981, 53p. (BLRD report, 5597).

— *Design and implementation of a community information service in the library* Leeds Polytechnic, School of Librarianship, Public Library Management Research Unit, 1978, 137p.

Bunch A *Community Information Services* Bingley/Shoe String, 1982, 176p.

Library Advisory Councils *Public libraries and cultural activities* HMSO, 1975, 29p.

Foster A *Public libraries outreach to the disadvantaged* U of Sheffield, 1975.

Martin W ed *Library services to the disadvantaged* Bingley/Linnet Books, 1975.

Redfern M ed *New readers start here: a critical evaluation of reading schemes used by tutors of adult new readers . . .* LA, 1975, 59p.

Astbury R 'New adult readers and the public library in the United Kingdom' *Unesco Bull Lib* 1977 31(1) 26-34, refs.

Havard-Williams P 'Les loisirs et les biliothèques publiques en Grande Bretagne' *Ass Biblioth Fr Bull Info* 1976 (91) 87-91.

Corrigan P and Gillespie V *Class struggle, social literacy and idle time: the provision of public libraries in England as a case study in the organisation of leisure with indirect educational results* Brighton, J L Noyce, 1978, 37p.

Adult education and public libraries in the 1980s: a symposium LA, 1980, 94p, refs.

Croker S K *Immigrants: the problems they present public libraries in Sweden, the United Kingdom, the USA* College of Librarianship Wales, 1975, 54p.

Public library service for multi-cultural society: a report . . . of the Library Advisory Council and the Community Relations Commission Education Committee The Commission, 1976, 27p.

Winbank D A *Libraries' responses to a multi-cultural society: a traveller's notes* Western Australia Institute of Technology, Dept of Library Studies, 1978, 40p, refs.

Clough E and Quarmby J *A public library service for ethnic minorities in Great Britain* LA, 1978, 369p.

Cooke M *Public library provision for ethnic minorities in the United Kingdom: report of an investigation . . . 1979* Leicestershire Libraries and Information Service, 1979, 46p.

Simsova S 'The public library and the acculturation of migrants: a personal view of the British experience' *J Libp* 1979 11(4) 241-6, refs.

Going M E *Hospital library and work with the disabled* 2nd ed LA, 1973, 311p.

Hope R *In cabined ships at sea* Harrap, 1969. Seafarers Education Service.

Turner K *Hello sailors! Library services for British seamen yesterday and today* College of Librarianship Wales, 1977, 21p.

See also: *Lib Ass Rec* 1975 77(6) 134-5. *Assist Libn* 1976 69(7/8) 126-30.

Summer M A *Information services of trade unions* City U, Centre for Information Science, 1979, 71p. (MSc Thesis).

Home Office, Prison Department *Library facilities for people in custody* The Department, 1978, 19p.

Dyer C et al *School libraries: theory and practice* Bingley, 1970, 181p.

Ellis A *Library services for young people in England and Wales, 1830-1970* Pergamon, 1971, 198p.

Ellis A [Series of papers on the history of library services to children] *Lib Ass Rec* 1967 69(7); 1969 71(8); *J Libp* 1970 2(2); 1971 3(1).

Baudin G 'Origines et développement des bibliothèques publiques pour la jeunesse' *Médiathèques Publ* 1977 (42) 5-12. France, Great Britain, USA.

Shearing D K 'Aspects of 17th century grammar school librarianship' *School Libn* 1975 23(4) 305-9.

Hill J *Children are people — the librarian in the community* Hamish Hamilton, 1973.

Allan M *The school library resource centre* Crosby Lockwood Staples 1974, 165p.

Marshall M R *Libraries and literature for teenagers* A Deutsch, 1975, 300p.

'Children and crises' *Lib Ass Rec* 1976 78(4) 159-60. Effects of cuts.

[Library services and education] *Lib Ass Rec* 1978 80(4) 159-76.

Herring J E *Teaching library skills in schools* NFER, 1978, 96p.

Brake T 'The need to know: teaching the importance and use of information at school' *Educ Lib Bull* 1979 22(2) 38-51, refs. From the British Library project 'The need to know' — Community information at an inner London comprehensive school.

Hewitt V J *Toys and games in libraries* LA, 1981, 96p.

Marshall M R *Libraries and the handicapped child* A Deutsch, 1981, 205p.

Kearney H *Scholars, gentlemen: Universities and society in pre-industrial Britain, 1500-1700* Cornell U P, 1970, 214p.

Roberts N 'Aspects of British university librarianship, 1877-1977' *Coll Res Lib* 1977 38(10) 460-76.

Bryan H *A critical survey of university libraries and librarianship in Great Britain* Library Board of South Australia, 1966, 255p.

Research into library services in higher education Society for Research into Higher Education, 1968. Conference papers.

Neal K W *British university libraries* 2nd ed Wilmslow, The author, 1978, 138p.

Aspects of library services in a period of financial constraint: Papers delivered at a meeting of SCONUL . . .1975 SCONUL Secretariat, 1975, 49p.

Stearns J ed *New approaches to learning resources in higher education: selected papers delivered at a DES/ATCDE/LA Joint Conference . . . Bowness-on-Windermere, 1975* National Association of Teachers in Further Education, 1976, 87p.

Bryan H 'The perpetuation of inadequacy: a comment on the Atkinson Report' *Austr Acad Res Lib* 1976 7(4) 213-21.

Higham N 'The Atkinson Report and the self-renewing library' *Lib Ass CISE Newsletter* 1977 (13) 5-9.

'Librarianship for universities' *Lib Ass Rec* 1977 79(9) 471, 473, 475, 477, 479-81, 483.

Steele C ed *Steady-state, zero-growth and the academic library* Bingley/Linnet Books, 1978. Seven papers on the Atkinson Report.

Blackwood J W ed *The future of library collections: proceeding of a seminar held by the Library Management Research Unit, U of Technology, Loughborough, March 1977* LMRU, 1977, 83p.

Studies in the organisational structure and services in national and university libraries in the Federal Republic of Germany and in the United Kingdom: papers presented at a joint meeting . . . at the U of Bristol 1978 Saur/Bingley, 1979, 227p.

Gemeinsame Probleme von Staats- und Hochschulbibliotheken in Grossbritannien und der Bundesrepublik Deutschland . . ./ Common themes in academic librarianship in the Federal Republic of Germany and in the United Kingdom . . . Deutsches Bibliotheksinstitut/SCONUL, 1981, 285p. Meeting in Constance, May 1981.

McKinlay J 'British to the core: an Australian traveller's view of British university libraries' *Austr Acad Res Lib* 1979 10(4) 215-21.

Bendix D and Hall J B eds 'Library services and the Open University' *Drexel Lib Q* 1975 11(2) 1-92. Special issue.

Wilson T D 'Learning at a distance and library use: Open University students and libraries' *Libri* 1978 28(4) 270-82.

Wood J ed *College of education libraries and higher education: selected papers delivered at a DES/ATCDE/LA Joint Conference at Bowness-on-Windermere, 1973* Association of Teachers in Colleges and Departments of Education, Library Section, 1974, 72p.

Platt P 'The future of libraries of institutes and schools of education' *Brit J Teacher Educ* 1975 1(2) 221-6.

Ashworth W *Special librarianship* Bingley, 1979, 120p.

Burkett J *Industrial and related library and information services in the United Kingdom* 3rd rev ed LA, 1972, 263p?

Presanis A *The distribution of scientific and technical libraries and users in Great Britain* ASLIB, 1971, 32p.

Birks C I *Information services in the market place* BL, 1978, 70p.
Wilson T D et al 'Information needs in local authority social services departments: a second report on project INISS' *J Doc* 1979 35(2) 120-36, refs.
Davies R 'Dansk og engelske forskningsbiblioteker' *Bogens Verden* 1977, 59(3) 91-8.
Long M W *Musicians and libraries in the United Kingdom* LA, 1972.
Caloephead P *Libraries for professional practice* Architectural P, 1972, 127p.
Breem W W S 'Professional law libraries of Great Britain' *Law Lib J* 1971 64(3) 278-90.
'Art libraries and librarianship' *Lib Ass Rec* 1977 79(6) 309-18. Special feature, 6 papers.
Regional medical library systems: annual conference of the Medical Section of the LA, Liverpool U, 1976 LA, 1977, 78p.
Saunders G 'Medical school libraries in the United Kingdom: some statistics from 1977' *Aslib Proc* 1978 30(12) 404-15, refs.
Towards 2001 — 21st Annual Conference Institute of Information Scientists.
Barr K and Line M eds *Essays on information and libraries: Festschrift for Donald Urquhart* Bingley/Linnet Books, 1975, 211p.
Kenney B 'Die Plannung von nationalen Informationssystemen in der Bundesrepublik Deutschland, England und der USA' *Nachr Dok* 1975 26(4/5) 136-42.
Buchanan R 'Government attitudes to information.' (Paper at Aslib's 52nd annual conference). *Aslib Proc* 1979 31 53-63.
Stephen P 'Implications of the NATIS policy and of international cooperative schemes for the UK' *J Libp* 1977 9(3) 166-85.
Green S 'The organisation and planning of library activities in the United Kingdom in the context of NATIS' *Unesco Bull* 1977 31(2) 68-76. Bodies involved in establishing a comprehensive service.
Burkett J *Library and information networks in the United Kingdom* Aslib, 1979, 261p.
Andrew J ed *Developments in the organisation of non-book materials: papers and proceedings of a seminar on developments in the organisation and availability of non-book materials held at the Library Association on 18th November 1976* LA/Aslib Audiovisual Group/Council for Educational Technology, 1977, 64p.
Thomas P A *Towards a complete microform library* Hatfield, National Reprographic Centre for Documentation, 1976, 1 microfiche.
Cox N *Seminar on the utilisation of computers for the handling of information in libraries* Oriel P, 1967.
Loughborough U Library *Development and testing of automated library processes: report on OSTI-supported project* 1971, vp. (OSTI Report 5095).
Duchesne R M 'The use of computers in British libraries and information services: an analysis' *Program* 1974 8(4) 183-90.
Bidmead M ed *Use of computers in libraries and information centres: proceedings of a conference held by Aslib with the cooperation of the Aslib Computer Applications Group, London 19-20 May 1975* Aslib, 1976, 94p.

GREAT BRITAIN: SCOTLAND

1

National Library of Scotland, Edinburgh. 1680- .

- Lending Services. 1974- . Formerly: Scottish Central Library.

Brown W H 'The National Library of Scotland: a new role' *SLA News* 1974 (124) 168-81.

National Library of Scotland Staff 'Scotland, National Library of' in *Encyclopedia* 27 (1979) 98-109.

2b

Scottish Library Association (SLA)

McCorkindale N R 'Scottish Library Association: a brief history' *SLA News* 1970 (100) 169-70.

Aitken W R 'Scottish Library Association' in *Enclycopedia* 27 (1979) 131-6.

2c

Orr J M 'Aberdeen Library School' *SLA News* 1978 (143) 11-15.

Sked M J 'Further education and the continuing education of librarians' *SLA News* 1978 (145) 83-7.

3a

Library resources in Scotland 1980-1981 SLA, 1981, 149p. Recurrent publication of the SLA.

Macandrew H 'Art library resources in Scotland' *Art Lib J* 1979 4(3) 6-15.

Survey of Scottish art libraries' *Art Lib J* Part I: 1979 4(3) 6-15; Part II: 1979 4(4) 23-5.

Scottish libraries [1963-65, etc.]: a triennial review SLA, 1966- .

3b

Grant E G *Scotland* Clio P, 1982 (World Bibliographical Series, 34).

Walker R S 'Publications of the SLA, 1908-1971' *SLA News* 1970 (100) 164-6.

White B 'An index to SLA News, 1950-1967' *Indexer* 1969 6(4) 147-50. Followed by 2-yearly cumulations.

3c

SLA News 1950- .

Bibliotheck 1956- .

3d

Paton M W 'Public library statistics' *SLA News* 1971 (101) 191-3. New format following the new international standard.

3e

Scotland. Education Department *Standards for public library service in Scotland. Report. . .* HMSO, 1969.

Paton W B 'Local government reorganisation in Scotland: an assessment' *Assist Libn* 1976 69 22-5.

Hendry J D 'Towards the 1980s in Scotland' *New Lib World* 1977 78 187-8.

— 'The Scottish dimension' *Assist Libn* 1977 70(10) 154-5.

'Library legislation and policy planning: a Scottish Library Association policy statement based on the Report of the Working Party on Library Legislation/ Policy Planning' *SLA News* 1979 (150) 1-7 suppl.

Paton W B 'Scottish public library legislation' in *Encyclopedia* 27 (1979) 136-9.

3f

Alison W A G 'Scotland, libraries in' in *Encyclopedia* 27 (1979) 86-97. Followed by other papers on Scottish library activities.

McAdams F ed *Of one accord: essays in honour of W B Paton* SLA, 1977, 126p. (Scottish Library Studies, 4).

White A G D ed *Peebles '76: proceedings of the 62nd Annual Conference of the Scottish Library Association, 24-27 May 1976 — 'The role of the library in a changing society'* SLA, 1976, 104p.

'[SLA's summer school]' *SLA News* 1981 (158) 107-9. Two papers.

Aitken W R *A history of the public library movement in Scotland to 1955* SLA, 1971, 379p.

Ballantyne G H *Comparative studies in Scottish county library organisation and administration: a historical and critical survey* LA, 1965, 513p. (FLA thesis).

'Round the districts' Series of papers on city libraries in *SLA News* 1977- .

'[Library and reading services for children]' *SLA News* 1977 (140) Whole issue.

Bunch A J *Hospital and medical libraries in Scotland: an historical and sociological study* SLA, 1975, 186p.

Barr G R 'Music in Scottish libraries' *SLA News* 1977 (142) 381-3.

Royan B "SCOLCAP' — but I thought that was an on-line system' *MICRODOC* 1977 16(3) 82-4. Automation project; library cooperation.

GREAT BRITAIN: NORTHERN IRELAND

2b

Library Association. Northern Ireland Branch.

Carson W R H 'Some reflections on fifty years of the Northern Branch' *An Leabharlann* 1979 8(1) 4-6, 10, 12.

3b

Ulster yearbook: the official handbook of Northern Ireland [25th edition, 1981] Belfast, HMSO. First published: 1926.

Carson W R A and Morrow *A Directory of Northern Ireland libraries* 2nd ed LA, Northern Ireland Branch, 1977, 53p. First edition: 1967.

3c

Northern Ireland Libraries LA, Northern Ireland Branch 1962-71. Now merged with *An Leabharlann* 1972, New Series, No 1- .

3d

Summary of Education and Library Board's accounts for period. . . (Department of Education for Northern Ireland) Belfast, HMSO.

3f

Usherwood R C 'Libraries under stress: the effects of the Irish crisis' *Assist Libn* 1973 65 22-9. (Also in *Wilson Lib Bull* 1972).

Heaney H J 'Future library cooperation in Ireland' *An Leabharlann* 1972 1(4) 3-10. Joint weekend school: Association of Assistant Librarians (Northern Ireland Branch) and Irish Library Association, Assistant Librarians Section.

[Joint Conference of the Library Association of Ireland and the Library Association, Northern Ireland Branch, Dublin 1979] *An Leabharlann* 1979 8(3) 5-22.

Francis J 'Public libraries in Northern Ireland since 1973' *New Lib World* 1979 80(953) 213-4, 216.

Martin W J 'Closing the gaps: the problem of service to illiterates' *An Leabharlann/The Irish Library* 1974 3(4) 17-22. Analysis of a publication by the Northern Ireland Council for Educational Research *Reading standards in Northern Ireland.*

Latham S 'Northern Ireland: unusual system brings results' *Lib Ass Rec* 1978 80(4) 165. Special feature on school libraries 'AV provision in NI' *AV Libn* 1977 3 118.

Wintour B J C and McDowell B 'Automation at the new University of Ulster' *Program* 1976 10(2) 60-74.

Casey M ed *Applications of networking in Irish libraries — proceedings of a conference. . . March 1980, University College, Dublin* U College, Department of Library and Information Studies 1980, 61p.

GREECE

1

Ethniki Bibiotheke tes Ellados. Athens, 1828- .

Esdaille A 'Athens. The National Library of Greece' in *National libraries of the world* 2nd ed LA, 1957.

Library of Parliament, Athens, 1845- Second deposit library. Also acts as a public library.

Library of University College, Athens. Created with USAID funds. Promotes librarianship; holds training seminars.

Directorate of Documentation. Athens, 1972- Part of the Ministry for Culture and Science, Office of Scientific Research and Development.

Andrews K B *Greece: national documentation centre: [Mission] April 1972-April 1973* Unesco, 1973, 7p. (2972/RMO-RD/DBA).

Massil S W *Greece: establishment of a national documentation centre* Unesco, 1977, 31p.

2a

Ministry of Culture and Science — General Directorate of Cultural Affairs.

Ministry of Education — Directorate of Fine Arts, Belles-Lettres, Theatre and Libraries.

Greek Bibliographical Society, 1967- . Prepares the national bibliography.

2b

Enosis Ellenon Bibliothecarion, Athens, 1962- .

Cacouris G M 'The Greek Library Association' in *Encyclopedia* 10 (1974) 194-5.

2c

Carnovsky L *A library school for Greece: a prospectus* Unesco, 1961, 27p. Expert's report.

— 'Education for librarianship abroad: Greece' *Lib Trends* 1963 12(2) 158-65.

Cacouris G M 'Greece, library education in' in *Encyclopedia* 10 (1973) 190-5.

3b

Institut Français d'Athènes *Bulletin analytique de bibliographie hellénique* 1947- .

Phousaras G I *Bibliografia ton hellenikon bibliographion 1791-1947* Bibliopoleion tes Hestias, 1961, 284p.

General Council of Greek Libraries *National bibliography* 1930-39.

General Directorate of Press *Bulletin of Hellenic bibliography* 1960-67.

Greek Bibliographical Society *Ellenike bibliognosia* 1973- .

Ellenike bibliographia Libraririe Georgiades, 1946-50.

Bulletin bibliographique Kollaros & Co, 1952- . Trade list.

Clogg R and Clogg M J *Greece* Clio P, 1980, 224p. (World Bibliographical Series, 17).

3c

Enosis Ellenon Bibliothekarion *Deltion* (Bulletin) 1968- .

3d

Centre of Planning and Economic Research Library 1961- .

3e

Clément P *Études sur les droits des auteurs chez les Grecs et chez les Romains* Grenoble, 1867, 152p.

3f

Pfeiffer R *History of classical scholarship* OUP, 1968. Includes some information on libraries.

Doussis C *Notes on educational planning in Greece* Berlin, Tegal, 1963.

Fourre P *Problems of development: adult education techniques in developing countries: a Greek case study* OECD, 1963.

'Greek libraries' in Johnson E D and Harris M M *History of libraries in the western world* 3rd ed rev Scarecrow, 1976, 40-57.

Widmann H 'Buchformen, Buchherstellung und Buchvertrieb im alten Griechland und Rom' *Oberammergauer Vortrage* 1966 37-81.

Platthy J *Sources on the earliest Greek libraries with the testimonia* Amsterdam, Hakkert, 1968, 203p. (Thesis Catholic U of America, 1965).

Johnson E D 'Ancient libraries as seen in the Greek and Roman classics' *Radford Rev* 1969 23(2) 73-92.

Wright H C *Oral antecedents of Greek librarianship* Brigham Young U P 1977 237p.

White D A 'Origins of Greek librarianship: a philosophical exploration' *J Lib Hist* 1978 13 371-87. Review paper.

Sotiropaulos D *Organisation of libraries in modern Greece* U of Illinois, 1954.

Cacouris G M 'Greece, libraries in' in *Encyclopedia* 10(1973) 180-90.

Fessas R and Litsa C *The library: organisation and operation* Athens, Eugenides Foundation, 1970, 150p.

Sidorova A I 'Biblioteki Gretsii' *Bibliot i Bibliog za Rubezhom* 1971 (38) 46-71.

'First Panhellenic Congress of Librarians' *Herald Lib Sci* 1978 17 97.

Hopkins J and Vouteris K 'Public libraries in Greece: an experiment' *Lib Ass Rec* 1954 56(6) 215-6.

Frank J M *A public library service for Greece* Diploma in Librarianship, U of London (University College), 1957, 335p.

Kimsey M L 'Apollo outdone: the Greek library environment' *Lib Ass Rec* 1967 69(2) 40-2.

Carter M D 'The United States libraries in Athens and Cairo' *Lib Q* 1951 21(3) 206-13.

Ratcliff N 'Resources for music research in Greece — an overview' *Notes* 1979 36(1) 50-64.

Improving information transfer: Workshop in Rabat May 1976. Final report Unesco, 1976. Greece did participate.

IRELAND, Republic of

1

National Library of Ireland, Dublin. 1877- .

Henchy P 'The National Library of Ireland — plans and projects' *An Leabharlann* 1975 4(1) 5-15.

— 'Ireland, National Library of' in *Encyclopedia* 13 (1975) 82-8.

University College Dublin, Library. 1908- .

2a

Library Council/An Chomhairle Leabharlanna. 1947- .

2b

Bibliographical Society of Ireland, Dublin. 1918- .

Book Association of Ireland/An Leabhar-Cumann, Dublin.

Library Association of Ireland/Cumann Leabharlann nah Eireann, Dublin. 1928- .

Stockham K 'The role of the professional association in librarianship' *An Leabharlann* 1979 8(2) 22-3, 25. Golden Jubilee of the association.

Irish Association for Documentation and Information Services (IADIS), Dublin. 1967- . (1947-1967 as Irish Association for Documentation.)

Henchy P 'Irish Association for Documentation and Information Services (IADIS)' in *Encyclopedia* 13 (1975) 88-9.

Irish Association of School Librarians/Cumann Leabharlannaithe Scoile (CLS). 1962- .

British and Irish Association of Law Librarians.

2c

Power E 'Education for librarianship at University College Dublin [1928-]' *An Leabharlann* 1967 25(3) 109-15.

Taylor P J *Library and information studies in the United Kingdom and Ireland, 1950-1974: an index of theses* Aslib, 1976, 69p.

3a

Encyclopedia of Ireland Allen Figgis, 1968, 463p.

Henderson G P and Henderson S P A eds *Directory of British associations and associations in Ireland*, 1980-81 6th ed CBD Research, 1980, 486p.

Library Association *Libraries in the United Kingdom and the Republic of Ireland* 8th ed LA, 1979.

National Science Council *Scientific and technical information in Ireland: a review* NSC, 1972, 80p.

Sources of scientific and technical information in Ireland Institute for Industrial Research and Standards, 1972.

3b

University College Dublin School of Librarianship *Irish Publishing Record.* 1967- . Annual. National bibliography.

Hayes R J 'Irish national bibliography' *An Leabharlann* 1960 18 5-13.

An annual list of books deposited in the National Library is published in *An Leabharlann.*

The Irish Book Dublin, Dolmen Press, 1959-64 1-3 no. 1.

3c

Irish Library Association *An Leabharlann/The Library* 1930-71. From 1972 published jointly with the LA, Northern Ireland Branch as:

An Leabharlann/The Irish Library New Series Vol 1- .

Irish Association of School Librarians *CLS Bulletin.*

3d

Central Statistical Office *Statistical abstract of Ireland.*

3e

Government Gazette/Iris Oifigiuil.

Stationary Office *Consolidated list of government publications issued. . .* [1922/1925- .] Original lists published fortnightly.

Industrial and Commercial Property (Protection) Act 1927. Revised by the *Copyright Act* 1963. Legal deposit.

Jones G 'Irish local authorities and the public libraries acts, 1855-1914: a checklist of adoptions' *An Leabharlann* 1970 28(4) 118-9.

Casey R J 'Legislation on public libraries in the Republic of Ireland' *Int Lib Rev* 1969 1 341-50.

Havard-Williams P 'Library standards for Irish libraries in non-public libraries' *An Leabharlann* 1969 27(3) 92-102.

3f

Cole R C 'Smollett and the 18th Century Irish book trade' *Bibliog Soc Amer Papers* 1975 69 345-63.

Library World 1963 65(759). Issue devoted to Irish librarianship.

Havard-Williams P 'Libraries in Ireland: lessons from the past and lessons for the future' *Lib Info Sci* (India) 1971 (9) 133-42.

Power E 'Ireland, libraries in the Republic of' in *Encyclopedia* 13 (1975) 67-81, bibl.

Davey J 'Interlibrary lending in the United Kingdom and Ireland, 1978-79' *Interlending Rev* 1979 7(4) 119-25.

Joint conferences of the Library Association of Ireland and the LA Northern Ireland Branch are held regularly and reported in *An Leabharlann.*

Morton K G 'Mechanics' Institutes and the attempted diffusion of useful knowledge in Ireland, 1825-79' *Irish Booklore* 1972 2 59-74.

Powell J S 'Social and political influences on library provision in Ireland 1830-1925' *Lib Rev* 1980 29 20-6, refs.

Neylon M and Henchy M *Public libraries in Ireland* U College Dublin School of Librarianship, 1966, 34p.

Foley D 'The library and the reading public' *Books Ireland* 1976 (1) 13-6.

Marshall O and Power J 'Education libraries in the Irish Republic' *Educ Lib Bull* 1979 22(3) 9-20, refs.

Hurst F J E 'University libraries in Eire' *Lib World* 1963 65(766) 321-5.

Main L *The development of modern special libraries and their information services*

in the Republic of Ireland U of Wales, 1979, 493p.

O'Deirg I 'Libraries and information problems in the field of agricultural research: an Irish view' *An Leabharlann* 1970 28(4) 120-5.

Carroll B and Wood N *Scientific and technical information in Ireland: the findings of the National Documentation Use Study* National Science Council/An Chomhairle Eolaiodita, 1978, vol 1, 58p, Vol 2, 94p.

Sweeney G P 'On line networks in Ireland: present and future' *An Leabharlann* 1978 7(4) 116-7, 119, 121, 123, 125-7, 129-30, 132-3. Includes involvement with EURONET, etc.

ITALY

1

Biblioteca Nazionale Centrale Vittorio Emanuele II, Rome. 1876- .Its services include the Centro Nazionale di Informazioni Bibliografiche. 1931- .

Biblioteca Nazionale Centrale, Florence. 1747- .

Esposito E *Biblioteca Nazionale Centrale Vittorio Emanuele II* Ravenna, A Longo, 1974, 111p.

Barker N 'Biblioteca Nazionale at Florence' *Book Collector* 1969 18 11-22.

Crocetti L 'La Biblioteca Nazionale Centrale di Firenze dieci anni doppo' *AIB Boll* 1977 17(1) 3-6.

De Gregori G 'Ancora sui servizi bibliotecari nationali centrali' *AIB Boll* 1975 15(2) 126-33.

Consiglio Nazionale delle Ricerche (CNR), Rome, 1923- . Instituto per le Documentazione.

'Biblioteca centrale del CNR' *AIB Boll* 1976 16 427-8.

2a

Ministerio della Pubblica Istruzione. Direzione Generale delle Biblioteche, Rome, 1926- .

Carini-Dainotti V 'La politica della Direzione Generale delle Biblioteche dal 1926 al 1966' *Accad Bibliot Ital* 1967 25 396-418.

Istituto Centrale per il Catalogo Unico delle Biblioteche Italiane e per le Informazione Bibliografiche, Rome. 1951- . The union catalogue itself usually is referred to as CUBI.

Istituto di Patalogia del Libro, Rome, 1938- .

Di Franco Lilli M C 'Ruolo e funzioni dell'Istituto Centrale per la Patologia del Libro' *AIB Boll* 1976 16 342-5.

2b

Associazione Italiana Biblioteche (AIB), Rome. 1930- .

De Gregori G 'La base dell'Associazione' *AIB Boll* 1976 16(1) 33-9.

Alberani V 'L'AIB e i rapporti internazionali' *AIB Boll* 1978 18(3/4) 270-2.

Federazione Italiana delle Biblioteche Populari.

Ente Nazionale per le Biblioteche Populari e Scholastiche, Rome, 1917- .

Associazione Italiana per la Documentazione e l'Informazione (AIDI), Rome. 1966- .

Alberani V 'Library associations in Italy' *Herald Lib Sci* 1970 9 190-4.

2c

Roxas S A *Library education in Italy: an historical survey, 1870-1969.* Scarecrow, 1971, 248p.

Huckaby S 'Education for librarianship in Italy: an historical view' *J Lib Hist* 1971 6(1) 5-20, refs.

 Roxas S A 'Italy, library education in' in *Encyclopedia* 13 (1975) 139-53, bibl.

'La formazione professionale in Italia: un'analisi dell'estero' *AIB Boll* 1976 16(2) 143-5.

Botari A and Gragnani E 'Universitá formazione professionale dei bibliotecari' *Boll Bibliot* 1980 (23) 69-73.

3a

Stych F S *How to find out about Italy* Pergamon, 1970, 320p.

Ente Nazionale per le Biblioteche Populari *Guida delle biblioteche italiane* Rome, 1969, 622p.

AIB*Guide delle biblioteche scientifiche e techniche e dei centri di documentazione italiani* 1965.

'Biblioteche in possesso di fondi musicali' *Fontes Artis Mus* 1971 18(3) 107-57.

3b

Maltese D 'Appunti sul Centro Nazionale per il catalogo unico' *AIB Boll* 1971 11(4) 151-4.

Balsamo L 'Il primo catalogo collettivo delle biblioteche italiane' *Bibliofilia* 1963 65(2) 218-9.

Parsons A B *Italian National Bibliography, 1861-1960* U North Carolina, 1962, MA Thesis.

Pinto O *Le bibliografie nazionale* 2nd ed Olschki, 1969, 94p.

Revelli C 'Osservazioni sulla Bibliografia Nazionale Italiana' *AIB Boll* 1976 16 6-22.

Maltese D 'Sistema bibliografico nazionale e deposito legale' *AIB Boll* 1979 19(4) 264-70.

Biblioteca Nazionale Centrale di Firenze *Bibliografia nazionale italiana redatta a cura della Biblioteca.* . 1958- . Monthly. Published by Centro Nazionale per il CUBI. Cumulated: *Catalogo alfabetico annuale.*

CUBI-Catalogo cumulativo 1886-1957. Retrospective catalogue. Cumulation of:

Bolletino delle pubblicazioni italiane ricevute per diritto di stampa dalla Biblioteca Nazionale Centrale di Firenze.

Italia bibliografica (List of special Italian bibliographies) Sansoni, 1953-1961. Now included in the national bibliography.

Bologna. Concorzio Provinciale per la Pubblica Lettura *Dizionario bibliografico* 1967- . Il Mulino, 1972- .

Milano. Associazione Italiana Editori *Catalogo dei libri italiani in commercio* 1970- . Books in print.

Ottino G and Fumagalli G *Bibliotheca bibliographica italica* Rome and Turin, 1889-1896, 2 vols. *Supplements* I to IV, 1895/1900. Reproduzione Anastatica, Graz, 1957. List works on bibliography and libraries published in Italy or about Italy.

Vianello N 'Rassegna di recenti pubblicazioni italiane di bibliografia e biblioteconomia (1971-73)' *Accad Bibliot Ital* 1974 42 217-40.

Maraspin F *Bibliographie italienne sur les bibliothèques de province, 1945-1970* Matica Slovenská, 1970, 30p.

AIB Bollettino d'informazioni. From 1975 contains a section: 'Letteratura professionale italiana'. Index of current literature.

Centro Nazionale per gli Studi dell'Informazione *Bibliografia italiana nell'informazione (1962-1965)* 1969, 90p.

3c

Catalogo dei periodici 1958-1967. From new periodicals recorded in the national bibliography, 1972. Continues: *Catalogo dei periodici 1886-1957.*

Ministerio della Pubblica Istruzione *Accademie e Biblioteche d'Italia* 1927-43, 1950- . Supersedes: *Rivista delle Biblioteche e degli Archivi* Florence, 1883-1926.
AIB *Bolletino d'Informazioni* Rome. 1955- .
AIB *Quaderni.* Papers on special problems, bibliographies, etc.
AIB *Biblioteche Speciali e Servizi d'Informazione* 1962- .
AIDI *BID. Documentazione e Informazione* 1962- . With a supplement: *BID. Bollettino di Documentazione e Informazione Scientifico-Tecnica* 1962- .
Bibliofilia Florence, Olschki, 1899- .
Federazione Italiana delle Biblioteche Populari *La Cultura Populari*, Milan. 1911.
Ente Nazionale per le Biblioteche Populari e Scholastiche *La Parola e il Libro*, Rome. 1917- .
Istituto Nazionale dell'Informazione *Rivista d'Informazione* 1970- .
Istituto di Patalogia del Libro *Bollettino* 1939- .
Annali della Scuola Speciale per Archivisti e Bibliotecari dell'Università di Roma 1961- . Bimonthly.
Biblioteconomia e Bibliografia. Saggi e Studi Florence, Olschki. Publisher's series.

3d

Istituto Centrale di Statistica *Bollettino mensile di statistica* With supplements on library statistics.
- *Annuario delle statistiche culturali.*
Annuario delle biblioteche italiane Rome, Palombi, 1956/59- .
Annuario statistico delle biblioteche lombarde 1972/73, I: Biblioteche communali, 1974.

3e

Ministerio del Tesoro *Pubblicazioni edite dallo Stato e col su concorso.*
Gazzetta ufficiale della Repubblica Italiana.
Balboni F and Marinelli O 'Prospettive per un sistema bibliotecario italiano dopo l'emanzione della legge delegata' *AIB Boll* 1972 12(2/3) 63-74.
[Laws and Libraries] *AIB Boll* October 1977 issue.
Balzamo L 'I primi standars italiani della biblioteca pubblica' *Bibliofilia* 1964 76 209-11. Comments on the standards prepared by the Association:
La biblioteca pubblica in Italia: compiti instituzionale e principi generali di ordinamento e funzionamento AIB, 1964.
Baffi M A 'La reolamentazione dell'usupubblico nelle biblioteche pubbliche statali in Italia' *AIB Boll* 1979 19(1) 20-5, refs. Review of current legislation.
Celuzza A and Pensato G 'Linee per la formulazione di una legge quadro per le biblioteche' *AIB Boll* 1978 18(3/4) 183-8.
Adversi A *Note sulla legislazione e sul'organizzazione delle biblioteche delle università* Milan, Guiffrè, 1967, 35p.
Gravina F ed *La legge toscana per le biblioteche* Giunta Regionale Toscana, 1977, 248p.
Rossato A M 'La biblioteca di fronte al sequestro di stampati' *AIB Boll* 1971 11(2/3) 81-6.

3f

De Felice Olivieri S L *La cultura, il libro, la scuola, le biblioteche* 2nd ed Naples, 1961. (Guida alla studia della civilta Romana antica).
Vleeschauer H J de 'Jules César et l'origine de la bibliothèque dans la Rome antique' *Mousaion* 1958 (28) 70p.

Cagnot R L V *Bibliothèques municipales dans l'Empire Romain* Paris, 1906, 25p.

Davis D G 'Christianity and pagan libraries in the later Roman Empire' *Lib Hist* 1970 2(1) 1-10, refs.

Berthoud J 'The Italian Renaissance library' *Theoria* (U Natal) 1966 26 61-80.

La Biblioteca Medicea-Laurenziana nel secolo della sua apertura al pubblico, Il giugno 1571 Olschki, 1971, 76p.

See also in Johnson E D and Harris M H *History of libraries in the Western world* 3rd ed Scareccow, 1976, 58-73.

Barberi F 'Le biblioteche italiane dall'Unità a oggi' *AIB Boll* 1976 16(2) 109-33.

Petrucci A and Barone G *Primo: non leggere* Milan, 1976.

Barberi F *Biblioteca e bibliotecario* Cappelli, 1967, 365p.

Accardo S 'Accademie e biblioteche per la diffusione della cultura' *Accad Bibliot* 1969 37(2) 80-99.

Iseppi F and Schena A eds *La biblioteca come servizio culturale* Rome, Coines, 1976, 209p.

'Funzione e prospettive nella società contemporeana, Roma, Jan 1978' (Proceedings of the Conference of Academic Libraries) *Accad Bibliot Ital* 1978. Whole January issue.

[AIB 28th congress on the theme 'Libraries and culture'] in *AIB Boll* 1978 18(3/4). Whole issue.

Roxas S A 'Italy, libraries in' in *Encyclopedia* 13 (1975) 122-39.

Hamlin A T 'The library crisis in Italy' *Lib J* 1967 92(13) 2516-22.

Humphreys K W 'Le biblioteche in Italia: impresssioni personali' *AIB Boll* 1971 11(2/3) 87-95.

Carpenter R L 'Contrasting developments in Italian libraries' *Int Lib Rev* 1976 8(1) 33-49.

Pecenko M D G 'Libraries in Italy: situation and prospects' *Libri* 1980 30(2) 164-71, bibl.

Whatley A *Libraries in Northern Italy: notes and impressions by members of a visiting party of British librarians in September 1971* LA, International and Comparative Librarianship Group, 1973, 53p.

Hamlin A T 'Florence, libraries in' in *Encyclopedia* 8 (1972) 532-45.

Caude L N *Study of book damage and restoration in the libraries of Florence* Long Island U, 1970, 170p. (Research paper).

Carini Dainotti V *La biblioteca pubblica in Italia tra cronaca e storia, 1947-1967* Olschki, 1969, 2 vols (Biblioteconomia e Bibliografia. Saggi e studi 5).

Frajese A 'Il Piano "L"' *Accad Bibliot Ital* 1963 31 195-7.

Maioli M 'Politica di piano e biblioteche pubbliche' *Accad Bibliot Ital* 1972 40(1) 23-6.

Balsamo L 'Siatemi bibliotecari comprensoriali e programazione regionale' *Accad Bibliot Ital* 1972 40(1) 35-42.

Raiteri D 'La biblioteca pubblica nella crisi degli enti locali: un'ipotesi di lavoro' *AIB Boll* 1978 18(2) 115-20.

Guglielmi G 'A world within this world' *Lib Assoc Rec* 1980 82(5) 226-7.

INTAMEL working party Italy 1972 — Italian studies' *Int Lib Rev* 1973 5(1). Whole issue.

Revelli C 'I sistemi bibliotecari urbani' *AIB Boll* 1978 18(1) 1-9.

Barberi F 'La biblioteca pubblica a Roma' *AIB Boll* 1977 17(2) 97-110.

Bassi A 'La Biblioteca Nazionale di Torino: formazione delle raccolte e sistemazione nella nuova sede. Parte I: Origini — 1956' *AIB Boll* 1975 15(1) 3-24.

— 'Parte II: 1957-1975' *AIB Boll* 1975 15(2) 89-107.

Celuzza A 'La Biblioteca Provinciale di Foggia' *AIB Boll* 1975 15(3) 177-92. 1937- . New headquarters 1975.

Vianello N 'Situazione e prospettive delle biblioteche nel Veneto' *Accad Bibliot Ital* 1976 44(3) 228-39.

Colombo G 'Regioni e biblioteche: documentazione sullo sviluppo delle biblioteche pubbliche in Italia negli anni 1972-1975' *AIB Boll* 1976 16(4) 372-90.

Baracchetti G 'Mountain shepherds of Lombardy: socialization and the role of libraries' *Unesco J* 1979 1(1) 41-3.

Boarini V 'La Cineteca communale di Bologna' *AIB Boll* 1976 16(3) 318-23.

Bulgarelli S 'La biblioteca militare centrale dello Stato Maggiore dell'Esercito' *Accad Bibliot Ital* 1977 45(4/5) 314-24.

'Biblioteca per ragazzi a Torino' *Accad Bibliot Ital* 1968 36 405-8.

Stein A M 'Esperienza di biblioteca in un liceo sperimentale' *AIB Boll* 1976 16 138-43.

Gerevini S 'The organization and problems of university libraries in Italy' *Lib Trends* 1964 12(4) 550-7.

Hamlin A T 'Le biblioteche dell'università italiana: studia sui servizi e le raccolte librarie' *Accad Bibliot Ital* 1965 34(3) 121-38.

Coiro G 'Problemi delle biblioteche universitarie e prospettive' *Accad Bibliot Ital* 1969 37 275-84.

Firpo L 'Biblioteche e università' *Accad Bibliot Ital* 1979 47(1/2) 63-81.

Valenti M and Carosella M P 'Special libraries in Italy' *INSPEL* 1969 4(1) 28-34.

Sartori C 'Le biblioteche italiane: la situazione generale' *Fontes Artis Mus* 1971 18(3) 94-106. Music libraries.

Furlani S 'Die Geschichte der Bibliothek des italienischen Parlaments und die Entwicklung des italienischen Bibliothekswesens' *Zentralbl Biblioth* 1977 91 553-9.

Bisogno P *Programma di sviluppo dei servizi di documentazione ed informazione delle stazioni sperimentali per l'industria* Consiglio Nazionale delle Ricerche, 1969.

Ballarin M and Carosella M P 'Sistemi informativi in Italia: participazione a reti internazionali ed iniziative nazionali' *AIB Boll* 1975 15 269-82.

Maltese D *Razionalizzazione a automazione nella Biblioteca Nazionale Centrale di Firenze — incontro di studi . . . Ottobre 1968* Biblioteca Nazionale, 1970, 315p.

Bisogno P *Schema per una retedi informativa nel settore della documentazione cientifico-tecnica: elementi preliminare* CNR, 1972, 133p.

Carosella P M and Valentii M *Progetti di automazione nelle biblioteche italiane* AIB, Gruppo di Lavoro 7, 1973.

De Cosmo A *L'automazione in biblioteca* Foggia, Amministrazione Provinciale di Capitanata 1976, 32p.

Vinay A 'Problems of management and automation in the National Central Library of Rome' *Network* 1974 1(9) 15-7.

LUXEMBOURG

1

Bibliothèque Nationale, Luxembourg. 1798- . Legal deposit. Has a Service de Documentation et de Recherches Bibliographiques.

Centre d'Etudes et de Documentation Scientifiques.

2c

Bibliothèque Nationale. In-service training.

3a

Van der Vekene E *Répertoire des bibliothèques scientifiques ou populaires au Grand Duché du Luxembourg* Editions de l'Imprimerie St Paul, 1971, 56p.

3b

Hury C *Luxemburgensia. Eine Bibliographie der Bibliographen* Imprimerie St Paul, 1964, 186p. Covers 1846-1962.

Bibliothèque Nationale. Service des Luxemburgensia. *Bibliographie luxembourgeoise* 1944/45- , 1946- .

Van der Vekene E *Die Luxemburger Drucker und ihre Drucke bis zum Ende des 18. Jahrhunderts. Eine Bio-Bibliographie* Harrassowitz, 1968, 571p.

Blum M *Bibliographie luxembourgeoise. . . Première partie: Les auteurs connus* Vols 1-2 Luxembourg, 1902-1932. Left unfinished (A-Siegen). Covers the period to 1900.

Bibliothèque Nationale *Bibliographia Luxemburgensis* 1959- . Series of special bibliographies.

MALTA

1

Royal Malta Library, Valetta. 1776- . Founded by the Knights of St John. Legal deposit 1925.

Leopardi E R *Il-bibjoteka nazzjonali ta'Malta, 1555-1955.*

Caruana A *The Royal Public Library of Malta* Malta Government Printing Office, 1898.

The Library is part of the Public Library Deparment together with the other public libraries:

- Public (Lending) Library at Beltissebh and
- Public University in Gozo. Shares the legal deposit right.

Royal University of Malta Library, Msida.

Cassar Pullicino J 'The University Library, 1839-1842' *J Fac Arts* (R U Malta) 1(3) 213-43.

2a

Department of Public Libraries.

2b

Ghaqda Bibljotekarji (Malta Library Association — MLA), Msida. 1969- .

'Malta Library Association held its inaugural meeting in March 1969' *Unesco Bull Lib* 1969 23 275-6.

3a

Malta yearbook St Michael College of Education, 1953- . Includes: Lists of current publications and information on libraries. Now: *Malta Library Association yearbook.* 1971- . Second edition: 1973; Tenth anniversay issue: 1979, 53p.). Contains a directory of members and of libraries, a bibliography, etc.

3b

Guarnaschelli T and Valenziani E 'Saggio di una bibliografia di Malta e del Ordine di San Giovanni di Gerusalemme' *Arch Storia di Malta* 1938 9 436-93.

Royal Empire Society *Subject catalogue of the library 1930-1937* (Dawson reprints 1967).

Ministry of Defence Library *Malta* Booklist series No 620. Latest issue: June 1970.

Xuereb P *Melitensia — A catalogue of printed books and articles in the Royal Malta Library referring to Malta* Malta U P, 1974, 76p.

Malta Library Association Yearbook (See under 3a). Contains a bibliography on libraries and librarianship in Malta.

3c

Public Libraries Department *Annual report.*

MLA *Newsletter*, 1969- . Quarterly.

MLA *Occasional papers*, 1970- .

3d

Central Bank of Malta *The Maltese economy in figures.*

See also annual reports and yearbooks of the MLA, the Royal Library and the University library.

3e

Malta Government Gazette.

The laws of Malta Cap 142: Public Libraries; Cap 117: Registration of publications under the Press Ordinance.

Xuereb P 'Public libraries and legal deposit in Malta' *COMLA Newsletter* 1978 (21) 60-1.

3f

Bowen-Jones H et al *Malta: background for development* U of Durham, 1961.

Owen C *The Maltese Islands* David & Charles, 1969. Contains a bibliography.

Clair C *The spread of printing: Eastern hemisphere — Malta* Amsterdam, 1969.

[Il-Ktieb Malta] 'Symposium on book production and marketing in Malta' *Unesco Bull Lib* 1973 27(2) 122. Symposium organized by the MLA in June 1972. Papers available from the MLA; with English synopses.

Birkley A E 'Why does Malta want help?' *Focus Int Comp Libp* 1969 (8) 7.

Biggs P T 'Problems of librarianship in Malta' *Focus Int Comp Libp* 1973 4(3) 19-20.

— 'Malta: the library scene and its setting' *Int Lib Rev* 1973 5(2) 163-82, refs.

Sapienza A F 'Focus on young public library services: the need for cooperation in Malta' *Focus Int Comp Libp* 1974 5(4) 27-8.

Kazem M et al 'School library services: Egypt, Israel and Malta' *IFLA J* 1976 2(4) 266-70.

Gibbon F 'Studying the NATIS in Malta' *Focus Int Comp Libp* 1979 10(3) 28-30.

THE NETHERLANDS

1

Koninklijke Bibliotheek (Royal Library), The Hague, 1798- .

De Jonge A A 'Koninklijke Bibliotheek (Royal Library), The Netherlands' in *Encyclopedia* 13 (1975) 450-5.

Landelijke Bibliotheek Centrale (National Library Centre)

Stein F 'De Landelijke Bibliotheek Centrale' *Bibliot en Samenleving* 1979 7(7/8) 191-5.

2a

Bibliotheekraad (Library Council), 1975- . Advisory body insuring the liaison with the government. Has taken over the functions of the various Advisory Committees: for public libraries and for research libraries.

Commissie Algemene Vraagstukken Universitair Bibliotheekwesen (CAVUB), 1971- . For university libraries.

Nederlands Orgaan voor de Bevordering van de Informatieverzorging (NOBIN), 1971- . Coordinates information policies. Has taken over the functions of the Nederlands Instituut voor Informatie, Documentatie en Registratuur (NIDER) with an official status.

Wolfgram M J 'NOBIN in een nieuwe fase' *Open* 1977 9 74-7.

Stichting Gemeenschappelijke Opleiding (GO), 1950- Foundation for Joint Training Courses.

2b

Federatie van Organisaties op het Gebied van het Bibliotheek-Informatie en Documentatiebestel (FOBID), 1975- . Created by amalgamation of the Nederlands Vereniging van Bibliothekarissen (NVB) and the Nederlands Bibliotheek en Lektuur Centrum (NBLC). The NBLC itself had been created in 1972 by amalgamation of a number of existing associations. Among its services it runs a professional library:

Raadschelders J C 'Bibliotheekbeschrijving: de vakbibliotheek van het Nederlands Bibliotheek en Lektuur Centrum' *Open* 1976 8(12) 591-4.

The 1970s reorganization of the Netherlands library services and their effects on the associations' functions are detailed in:

— *Bibliotheek en Samenleving* 1977 5(3). Whole issue.

— *Encyclopedia* 19 (1976) in the Netherlands entry. (See under 3f).

2c

Brummel L 'Education for librarianship abroad. The Netherlands' *Lib Trends* 1963 12(2) 147-52.

Paul H 'Education for librarianship in the Netherlands' *J Educ Libp* 1974 15(2) 75-94.

Goossens J et al 'De DBA: Kontakten tussen opleiding en praktijk' *Bibliot en Samenleving* 1975 3(3) 97-103.

Van Leeuwen H 'De GO vijfentwintig jaar' *Open* 1975 7(10) 462-81. [Gemeenschappelijke Opleidingscommissie: part time courses organizing body].
Grader C 'Einde van de NBLC-Kursussen' *Bibliot en Samenleving* 1976 4(10) 587-8.
Spier J M 'Het beroepskeeld van de speciale bibliotecaris' *Open* 1971 3 (11) 669-722; 1971 3(12) 775-86. Image of the special librarian.
Ameringen S van 'Bedrijfsvergelijking van bibliotheken' (Professional comparison in libraries) *Bibliotheekleven* 1967 52 381-4.

3a

CVOB *Bibliotheekterminologie — Engels-Frans-Duits-Nederlands* 1967, 294p.
Pyttersen's Nederlandse Almanak Zaltbommel, Koninklijke Drukkerij van de Garde. Includes libraries and librarians; covers the Dutch West Indies and Suriname.
Afdeeling van Binnenlandse Zaken *Staatsalmanak voor het Koninklijk der Nederlanden* The Hague, Staatsdrukkerijen Uitgeverijbedrijf.
NVB *Libraries and documentation centres in the Netherlands* 1966, 61p.
Wegwijzer Bibliotheken en Documentaties Maatschappijwetenschappen Amsterdam, North Holland, 1971- .
Loosjes T P et al *Bibliotheek en documentatie: handboek ten dienste van de opleidingen* Rev ed Kluwer, 1977, 421p.
NBCL *Jaarboekje Openbare Bibliotheken*. Part I.

3b

Mackenzie Owen J S 'Het Nederlands Bibliografisch Centrum: een discussie-bijdrage' *Open* 1976 8(10) 470-4.
Brinkman's catalogus van boeken Leiden, A W Sijthoff, 1850- . Monthly.
Brinkman's cumulatieve catalogus van boeken A W Sijthoff, 1846- . Both include Belgian publications in Flemish. Indexes.
Nieuwe uitgaven in Nederland The Hague, 1909- . Selective bibliography of new publications.
Studia bibliographica in honorem Herman de la Fontaine Verwey Amsterdam, Menno Hertzberger, 1968, 480p.
Koninklijke Bibliotheek *Bibliografie van in Nederland verschenen officiële en semi-officiële uitgaven* Staatsuigeverij. Annual.
Dijk G van Jr 'Bibliografie van Lopende bibliografien op het gebied van het boeken-en bibliotheekwezen' *Bibliotheekleven* 1968 53 May 57-70F.

3c

CVOB and NVB *Bibliotheekleven* 1916-1969. Now superseded by:
Open 1969- . Now sponsored by FOBID and NVBA (Dutch Society for Industrial Archivists).
[10th anniversary of *Open*] *Open* 1979 11(1) Whole issue.
NVB and CVOB (then NBLC) *Openbare Bibliotheek* 1958-1972. In 1973 merged with *Mens en Boek* and in 1974 with *Boekenbeeld* and became:
NBLC *Bibliotheek en Samenleving* (Library and Society) 1973-.
NIDER *Tijdschrift voor efficiëntie en documentatie* 1928-1970.
Het Boek 1912- . M Nijhoff.

3d

Centraal Bureau voor de Statistiek (CBS), Woorburg [Created in 1899 — Has a library].

— *Maandschrift* (monthly bulletin).
— *Statistical Yearbook of the Netherlands.*
— *Statistisch zakboek* (pocket yearbook).
— *Statistiek van de Openbare bibliotheeken* Annual.
NBLC *Jaarboekje Openbare Bibliotheken.* Part II.

3e

Cohen Jehoram H 'Bibliotheekrecht voor auteurs' *Bibliot en Samenleving* 1977 5(6) 163-6.
Wijnstroom M 'De voorgeschiedenis van de Wet op het Openbare Bibliotheekwerk 1851-1971' *Bibliot en Samenleving* 1974 2(9) 346-51.
Ministerie van Cultuur, Recreatie en Maatschappelijk *Voorstel voor de normering van het openbare bibliotheekwerk in Netherland* 1970, 98p.
— *Voorontwerp wet op het openbare bibliotheekwerk* 1970, 43p.
The Public Libraries Act and The Library Council Act in the Netherlands The Hague, Ministry of Cultural Affairs, Recreation and Social Welfare and Dutch Centre for Public Libraries (NBLC) 1979, 30p.
Jongh-Helmig K de *The Public Library Act 1975 and its consequences for the public libraries in the Netherlands* Loughborough U of Technology, 1979, 51p, refs.
Richtlijnen voor de normering van het openbare bibliotheekwerk NBLC, 1980, 136p.

3f

Youngsman C L *Library development in the Netherlands* Thesis, U of Pittsburgh, 1964.
Maltha D J 'The Netherlands, libraries and information centers in' in *Encyclopedia* 19 (1976) 239-81.
International librarianship *Liber amicorum in honour of G A Riemsdijk* Amsterdam, Library Progress, ca 1969, 4 parts.
Court W de la 'De bibliotheek in de toekomstige maatschappij' (Library in the future society) *Open Bibliot* 1972 15(1) 7-10.
Schaafsma H 'De toekomstije bibliotheek als communicatiemiddel naast radio, televisie en pers' (Future of libraries as a communication medium compared to radio . . .) *Open Bibliot* 1972 15(1) 2-6.
'Interbibliothecair leenverkeer NVB-vergadering' [Conference papers] *Open* 1980 12(3) 117-47.
Riemsdijk G A van *Geschiedenis van de openbare bibliotheek in Nederland* NBLC, 1978- . 1. *Van de beginjaren tot mei 1940.* 1978, 168p. 2. *Mei 1940-mei 1945* 1979, 174p.
Court W de la *Openbare bibliotheek en permanente educatie* H D Tjeenk Willink, 1974, 175p.
Van Ommen L B 'Permanente educatie en de openbare bibliotheek' *Bibliot en Samenleving* 1975 3(10) 531-7.
Egas C 'De politieke impikaties van het openbare bibliotheekwerk' *Bibliot en Samenleving* 1973 1(1) 2-7.
Tilstra A 'Samenspel tussen openbare bibliotheken, regionale wetenschappelijke bibliotheek en provinciale bibliotheekcentrale' (Cooperation between the public library, the provincial library centre and the regional science library) *Open* 1969 1(2) 80-5.
Benders L and Duyf A 'De provinciale plannen 1980-1982 voor de openbare bibliotheekvoorziening' *Bibliot en Samenleving* 1980 8(5) 147-51.
Court W de la 'De Bijlmermeer: planning van het openbare bibliotheekwerk als

geintegreerd onderdeel van de culturele uitrusting van een nieuw stadsdeel' (Public library as part of a cultural centre in a new town) *Open Bibliot* 1971 14(10) 453-8.

Deetam H 'Les discothèques de prêt aux Pays-Bas' *Ass Bibliot Fr Bull Inf* 1975 89 231-4.

Van Zijderveld B 'Speel-o-theken: een snel opkomend verschijnsel in Nederland' *Bibliot en Samenleving* 1977 5(1) 3-5.

Woltjer L D 'Schoolbibliotheekwerk: moeilijkhedenen mog elijkheden' (School library work: difficulties and opportunities) *Open Bibliot* 1972 15(1) 11-25.

Bartling M 'De realisering van het schoolbibliotheekwerk in Nederland' *Bibliotheekgids* 1976 52(4) 237-41.

Waltz R 'De aktiviteiten van een schoolbibliotheekdienst' *Bibliot en Samenleving* 1976 4(10) 572-5.

Constan A 'De internationale kinderbibliotheek in Rotterdam' *Bibliot en Samenleving* 1979 7(9) 256-7.

[Mobile libraries] *Open Bibliot* 1972 15(4/5) Whole issue.

Sicking L M C J 'De bibliotheekvoorziening van bedrijven, (overheids?) en particuliere instellingen in Nederland' *Open* 1971 3(6) 378-82.

NBLC *Bibliotheekwerk voor bejaarden, zieken en gehandicapten: zeven inleidingen, gehouden op de bibliotheekdag voor het bejaardenwerk, het ziekenhuiswezen en de gehandicaptenzorg 16 Oct 1974* The Centre, 1975, 44p. Library work with handicapped, etc.

Brown R *Outreach in the Netherlands: an experiment in public library service to disadvantaged groups, with particular reference to the role of the NBLC: report to the BLRD* Brighton Central Library, Public Libraries Research Group, 1981, 23p (BLR&D report 5689).

Simonis-Rupert S 'Het bibliotheekwerk voor bejaarden, zieken en gehandicapten' *Bibliot en Samenleving* 1980 8(1) 3-6. Libraries for isolated, handicapped, etc.

Klages W 'Bibliotherapie bij psychiatrische patiënten: reikwijdte en grenzen' *Bibliot en Samenleving* 1976 4(3) 115-21.

Lems O 'Het is heir koud onbekend en vreemd': bibliotheekwerk voor immigranten' *Bibliot en Samenleving* 1979 7(11) 319-25, refs. Library services for immigrants.

'Lektuurvoorziening voor gedetineerden: een gespeek in de Bijlmerbages' *Bibliot en Samenleving* 1979 7(6) 159-63. Libraries for prisoners.

Rijkscommissie van Advies inzake het Bibliotheekwezen *De wetenschappelijke bibliotheken in Nederland; programma voor een belied op lange termijn* Staatsuitgeverij, 1969, 72p. Coordination programme for research and academic libraries.

'The structure and organization of the library of the Technological University at Eindhoven' *Bibliotheekleven* 1966 51(9) 548-80.

Elderink C M 'Open Universiteit en bestaande bibliotheekvoorzieningen' *Open* 1979 11(10) 484-98, refs. Plan for the Open University (1981-).

Burkett J *Special libraries and information centres in the Netherlands* Pergamon Press, 1968, 103p.

[Dutch music librarianship] *Fontes Artis Musicae* 1974 21(3) 87-138. Whole issue.

Normering muziekbibliotheken: eindrapport van de werkgraep normering muziekbibliotheken gevolgd door funkiie-omschrijvingen muziekbibliotheekpersoneel Nederlands Bibliotheek en Lektuur Centrum, 1975, 39p.

[Music librarianship] *Bibliot en Samenleving* 1976 4(9) 493-541. Whole issue.

Rusche C J 'De fonotheek van de NOS [Dutch Broadcasting Corporation]'

Open 1980 12(1) 22-5.
Hogeweg-de Haart H P 'Social science libraries in the Netherlands' *Inspel* 1978 13(3/4) 134-72.
Walker M 'Bibliotheekbeschrijving: de Amerikaanse bibliotheek' *Open* 1978 10(5) 255-6.
Mattha D J 'Documentation in a small, densely populated country' *Libri* 1965 15(1) 9-16.
Sicking L M C 'Verwachting voor morgen: automatisering, integratie, bibliotheken informatie' *Open* 1970 2 589-600.
[Papers of a conference on library automation and the project for integrated catalogue automation (1969-), The Hague, 1979.] *PICA Mededelingen* 1979 2(6/7).

PORTUGAL

1

Biblioteca Nacional, Lisbon. 1796- .
University of Coimbra. Library.
Instituto de Alta Cultura. Centro de Documentação Cièntífica, Lisbon. 1937- .

2a

Ministerio da Educação Nacional. Inspecção Superior das Bibliotecas. 1887- . Has a professional library.
Academia das Ciências. Comissão de Bibliografia Portuguesa, Lisbon. 1938- .
Fundação Calouste Gulbekian. Serviços de Bibliotecas.

2b

Associação Portuguesa de Bibliotecários, Arquivistas e Documentalistas, Lisbon.

2c

University of Coimbra.
Centro de Documentação Científica, 1956- . For documentalists.

3a

Centro de Documentação Científica *Guia das bibliotecas portuguesas* 1963, 365p.
'Repertorio das bibliotecas de Lisboa' in *Anais das bibliotecas e Arquivos.*

3b

Biblioteca Nacional *Boletim de bibliografia portuguesa* 1933- . Published 1937- . Monthly. Includes important periodicals.
Comissão de Bibliografia *Bibliografia geral portuguesa.*
Livros do Portugal 1941- . Trade list.
Serviços bibliográficos da livraria Portugal Trade List.
Centro de Documentação Científica Ultramarina *Boletim bibliográfico* 1957- . Classified index of articles.
Instituto Gulbekian de Ciência *Bibliografia e informação* Lisbon, 1973, 231p.
Dorn G M comp *Latin America, Spain and Portugal: an annotated bibliography of paperback books* 2nd ed rev Library of Congress 1976, 323p. (Hispanic Foundation bibliographical series, 14).
Gladden E M 'Books in Portuguese' *Booklist* 1978 74 804-5.

3c

Biblioteca Nacional *Repertorio das publicaçoes periodicas portuguesas.* Annual.
— *Boletim informativo.* Semi-annual.
Cuadernos de biblioteconomia, arquivistica e documentação, Coimbra. 1964- .
Fundação Gulbekian. Serviço de Bibliotecas *Boletim informativo* 1960- .
— *Boletim das bibliotecas itinerantes e fixas.* Seria III, No 1- 1975- .

3d

Instituto Nacional de Estatística *Anuario estatístico. Metropole.*
— *Anuario estatistico. Ultramar.*
— *Estatistica de educação.* Annual.

3e

Biblioteca Nacional *Bibliografia das publicaçoes ofiçiais portuguesas* 1967- . *Diario de Governo.*

3f

Bradford S *Portugal* Walker, 1973, 176p.

Lottman H R 'Publishing in Portugal: the '74 revolution was a watershed — dramatic effects — for publishers' *Publ Weekly* 8/5/1978 213 29-35.

Skorge S *Das portugiesische Bibliotheswesen der Gegenwart* Cologne, Greven Verlag, 1967, 143p. (Arbeiten aus dem Bibliothekar-Lehrinstitut Des Landes Nordrhein-Westphalen, 30).

Lasso de la Vega J 'University libraries in Spain and Portugal' *Lib Trends* 1964 12(4) 339-49.

Hjerppe R *Revised programme proposal for the Swedish-Portuguese cooperation in the field of scientific and technical information and documentation* Stokholm, Royal Institute of Technology, 1978, 42p (ERIC report ED-167 096).

Hjerppe R 'Introducing modern information services to research and development in Portugal' *Tisk Dok* 1977 33(2) 17-20. Role of the Centro de Documentação Científica e Tecnica (CDCT).

See also some references under Latin America; Spain.

SPAIN

1

Biblioteca Nacional, Madrid. 1712- . Created as Biblioteca Real.

Monroy Baigen G 'La Biblioteca del Escorial' *Bol Bibliog Nacion* (Mexico) 1955 6(3) 43-8.

Andres G de *La Real Biblioteca de El Escorial* Madrid, Impr Aldus, 1970; Incluces a complete bibliography on the National Library.

Garcia y Mas R *Die Biblioteca Nacional in Madrid* Berlin, Colloquium Verlag, 1975, 120p, refs.

Williams M 'El Escorial's Royal Library treasures' *Wilson Lib Bull* 1979 53(10) 690-3.

Biblioteca Central de la Diputación de Barcelona. 1923- .

2a

Ministry of Culture, Directorate of Books and Libraries, 1977- . Previously, to 1974, Ministerio de Educación. Dirección General de Archivos y Bibliotecas. Then the Directorate combined with the Directorate of Fine Arts to form the Directorate General of the Artistic and Cultural Patrimony.

Instituto Bibliográfico Hispanico. 1970- .

Instituto Nacional del Libro Español (INLE). 1931- .

Consejo Superior de Investigaciones Científicas (CSIS). Centro Nacional de Información y Documentación Científicas (CENIDOC).

2b

Asociación Nacional de Bibliotecarios, Archiveros y Arqueologos (ANABA), Madrid. 1949- .

— Delegación de Cataluna y Baleares, Barcelona.

Asociación Española de Amigos de las Bibliotecas. 1975- .

2c

Lasso de la Vega J 'Spain' in 'Education for librarianship' issue of *Library Trends* 1963 12(2) 153-7.

Ricart-Ribera R 'Barcelona library school: tradition and change' *Focus Int Comp Libp* 1972 3(2) 30-1.

'Activitas de la Escuela' *Biblioteconomía* 1975 32(79) 131-3. Barcelona school.

3a

Enciclopedia de la cultura española Editora Nacional, 1962-68, 5 vols.

Buonocore D *Diccionario de Bibliotecología* 2nd ed aumentada Buenos Aires, Ed Marymar, 1976, 452p.

Ministerio de Educación Nacional, Servicio de Publicaciones *Guia de las bibliotecas de Madrid* 1953, 556p.

3c

Instituto Bibliográfico Hispanico *Bibliografía española.* Previously *Boletin del desposito legal.* Monthly with annual cumulations which include periodicals.

Instituto Nacional del Libro Español *Libro Español* 1958- .

Perrino-Rodriguez F *Repertorio bibliográfico de 'El libro espanol'* INLE, 1969.

INLE *Libros españoles. Catalogo ISBN* 1973- . Continue the annual directory of books in print:

Libros españoles 1953- .

España e Hispanoamérica. Catalogo de libros españoles y publicaciones extranjeras sobre España y Hispanoamérica Bibliotheek der Rijksuniversiteit te Utrecht.

Libros en venta en Hispanoamérica y España Buenos Aires, Turner Ediciones. *Suplemento* 1974.

Wilgus A C *Latin America, Spain and Portugal: a selected and annotated bibliographical guide to books published in the United States, 1954-1974* Scarecrow, 1977. 910p.

Mateu y Llopis F 'Biblioteconomía retrospectiva en español' *Biblioteconomia* 1969 26 146-54.

Mateu Ibars M D 'Papeletas para el estudio de las bibliotecas españolas' *Biblioteconomia* 1965 22 59-84. Every year from then on.

— *Aportación bibliográfica para el estudio de las bibliotecas universitarias españolas* Madrid, 1958, 72p.

Garcia Ejarque L 'Bibliografía de las bibliotecas rurales españolas: aporte y llamada para su elaboración' *Bol ANABA* 1970 (56) 211-26.

Valle F comp *Bibliografía basica en español sobre teoria y técnicas de la información documentaria: guia para los estudios de documentación* U de Argentina, 1976, 154p.

IREBI. Indices de revistas de bibliotecología 1973- . Madrid, IABE (Ibero-American Bureau of Education). (See details under: Latin America, 3b).

3c

Instituto Bibliográfico Hispanico *Revistas españolas en curso de publicación.* Annual.

Dirección General *Boletin.* 1952-1974.

Boletin de bibliotecas y bibliografía. 1934/35- ?

Dirección General *Revista de archivos, bibliotecas y museos* 1871- .

ANABA Boletin. 1949- .

Escuela des Bibliotecarios, Barcelona *Biblioteconomía.* 1944- .

CENIDOC *Revista española de documentación científica* 1977- .

3d

Instituto Nacional de Estadística *Boletin de Estadística.*

— *España: annuario estadiístico.*

Servico Nacional de la Lectura *Memoria estadística.*

Instituto Nacional de Estadística *Estadística de bibliotecas: Año 1974.*

3e

Boletin oficial del Estado.

Gallent G G *El deposito legal de obras impresas en España. Su historia, su reorganización y resultados, 1958-1961* Madrid, Art Graf Clavileno, 1962, 264p.

3f

'Historia y situación de las bibliotecas' in *Primeras jornadas de bibliografía* Fundación Universitaria Española, 1977, 387-570.

Valentinelli G 'Della biblioteche della Spagna' *Sitz k. Akad Wiss* 1859 33 4-178.

Rubio y Borras M *Bibliotecas españolas* Barcelona, La Raza, 1926.

Sintes y Obrador F 'Libraries in Spain' *Unesco Bull Lib* 1956 10(4) 73-5.

Boletin de la Dirección General 1956 5(36) 256p. Special issue on Spanish librarianship.

Carrion M 'Spain, libraries in' in *Encyclopedia* 28 (1980) 328-60.

Hallewell L et al *Report to the Library Association on the visit to Spanish libraries by four British librarians, 4-10 October 1976* (np, np), 1976, 27p.

Thomson J 'A British view of Spanish libraries' *Focus Int Comp Libp* 1978 9(1) 3-5.

Schmolling R 'Mañana. . . das spanische Bibliothekswesen zwischen Gestern und Morgen' *Buch Biblioth* 1978 30(11) 817-8, 820-3, refs.

Diaz y Perez N *Las bibliotecas de España en sus relaciones con la educación popular y la instrucción publica* 2nd ed M G Hernandez, 1885.

Perez Rioja L *Las casas de la cultura* ANABA, 1971, 107p.

Ribé M del C 'Importancia social y cultural de prestamo de livros' *Biblioteconomía* 1968 25 49-60.

Spangen I C 'Et lite stykke Spania — fra innsiden' *Bok bibliot* 1974 41(6) 299-300.

Escolar-Sobrino H 'Audio visual materials and rural libraries' *Unesco Bull Lib* 1972 26(1) 8-12.

Lasso de la Vega J 'La biblioteca en el Plan de Reforma de la Enseñanza' *Bol ANABA* 1970 (56) 227-9.

Diaz Plaja A 'La biblioteca infantil en los espacios verdes' *Biblioteconomía* 1968 25 86-9.

Cot y Miralpeix N 'El prestamo en las bibliotecas infantiles y juveniles' *Biblioteconomía* 1968 25 44-8.

Lasso de la Vega J 'University libraries in Spain and Portugal' *Lib Trends* 1964 12(4) 339-49.

Spain: a review of national scientific and technical information policy Paris, OECD, 1974, 170p.

SWITZERLAND

1

Schweizerische Landesbibliothek/Bibliothèque Nationale Suisse/Biblioteca Nazionale Svizzera. Bern, 1895- .

Egger E 'Dokumentation am der Schweizerische Landesbibliothek' *Biblos* 1960 9(3) 125-38.

Helbing H et al '75 Jahre Schweizerische Landesbibliothek' *Nachrichten* 1970 3 97-112.

Stoddart Kropf L 'The Swiss National Library: its history, collections and prospects' *J Lib Hist* 1974 9(4) 352-60.

Stadt- und Universitätsbibliothek, Bern, 1528- .

Ecole Polytechnique Fédérale, Zurich, 1855- . Its library assumes the functions of a national technical library.

2a

Schweizerischer Bibliotheksdienst (Library Service), 1969- .

2b

Vereinigung Schweizerischer Bibliothekare (VSB)/Association des Bibiothécaires Suisses (ABS)/Associazione dei Bibliotecari Svizzeri (ABS), Bern, 1897- .

- Schweizerische Arbeitsgemeinschaft der Volksbibliotheken. A division of the VSB.

Borgeaud M-A 'L'ABS a 75 ans' *Nachrichten* 1972 48(5/6) 221-7.

Schweizerische Vereinigung der Dokumentation (SVD), Bern, 1939- .

'L'Association Suisse de Documentation' *FID Info* Apr/May 1952 4-5 16.

Schweizerische Gemeinschaft für Allgemeine, Öffentliche Bibliotheken, 1937- .

Schweizerische Volksbibliothek/Bibliothèque Pour Tous, 1920- . Organized on a regional basis.

2c

Cornaz M-L 'L'Ecole de Bibliothécaires de Genève [1918] et son developpement' *Nachrichten* 1962 38(1) 1-6.

Courten R de *Cours de bibliothéconomie pratique. . .* Rev ed Bibliothèque Nationale, 1972.

VSB/ABS *Aussbildung und Prüfungsordnung. . . vom 26 September 1970 — Statuts de la formation professionnelle et des examens* 1970, 10p.

— *Ausführungsbestimmungen zur Ausbildungs- und Prüfungsordnung. . . vom 26 September 1970 — Règlement d'application des statuts de la formation professionnelle et des examens* 1971, 22p.

Diederichs R et al, eds 'Bibliothekarische und dokumentalistische Ausbildung in der Schweiz' *VSB/SVD Nachr* 1976 52(6) Whole issue. Comparative study with West Germany, Austria, Great Britain and Scandinavia.

Stickler M 'Die Volksbüchereien der Schweig' *Erwachserenbildung in Österreich* 1977 28(1) 5-12.

3a

Flueler N et al, eds *La Suisse: de la formation des Alpes à la quête du futur* Ex Libris Verlag, 1975, 699p.

Luck J M ed *Modern Switzerland* Soc for the Promotion of Science & Scholarship (USA), 1978, 515p.

Archive, Bibliotheken und Dokumentationsstellen der Schwiez/Archives, bibliothèques et centres de documentation en Suisse/Archivi, biblioteche e centri di documentazione in Svizzera 4th ed Office de la Science et de la Recherche, 1976, 805p.

3b

Schazmann P-E 'Jean-Jacques Schenchzer 1672-1733 et les débuts de la bibliographie nationale' *Libri* 1972 22(2) 130-6, 15 refs.

Courten R de and Kamer J *Bibliographie analytique des bibliographies suisses courantes-Analytische Bibliographie der Laufenden schweizerischen Bibliographien* Bibliotheque Nationale Suisse, 1972, np. Classified.

Bibliothèque Nationale *Schweizer Buch — Le livre suisse — Il libro svizzero* Société Suisse des Libraires et Editeurs, 1901- . Monographs, periodicals, music, maps. Abt A: commercial publications; Abt B: academic and official publications. Cumulated as:

Katalog der Schweizerischen Landesbibliothek . . . 1901/1920-1941/1947. Then by:

Schweizer Bücherverzeichnis — Répertoire du livre suisse — Repertorio del libro svizzero 1948-1975.

Schweizer Buchhandel 1948- . Trade list.

VSB/ABS Schweizerische Volkbibliothek/Bibliothèque pour Tous Entscheidungen von Volks- und Bildungsbibliotheken über Neuerscheinungen — Bulletin critique des bibliothèques de lecture publique 1949- . Selection for public libraries.

Bibliothèque Nationale *Bibliographie der schweizerischen Amtsdruckschriften/Bibliographie des publications officielles suisses* 1946- .

- Sonderheft: *Periodische Amstdruckschriften von Bund, Kantonen und Gemeinden im Jahre. . .*1967- .

Giger U *Bibliographie für Jugend- und Volkbibliotheken in der Schweiz* VSB Diploma, 1967, 71p.

3c

Bibliothèque Nationale Suisse *Schweizer Zeitschriftenverzeichnis/Repértoire des périodiques suisses* 1951-55, 1956-60, 1961-66, 1966-70, 1971-75. Classified.

VSB/ABS and SVD *Nachrichten VSB-Nouvelles ABS-Notizie ABS* 1925- . Includes book reviews. In French or German.

VSD/ABS *Reports.*

VSB/ABS *Publications* 1907- .

SVD *Mitteilungen der SVD-Communications de l'ASD* 1953- . In French or German.

Outlook on Research Libraries 1978- .

3d

Eidgenössisches Statistisches Amt/Bureau Fédéral de la Statistique *Statistiques des bibliothèques suisses* ABS, annual.

3e

Communauté de Travail 'Bibliothèques d'Étude et de Formation' *Recomman-*

dations pour l'établissement de réglements d'utilisation à l'usage des bibliothèques publiques Nachr/Nouv/Notiz 1978 54(1) 22-32.

3f

Switzerland Bern Kümmerly & Frey 1970- .

Scherrer-Bylund P et al *Schweizerische Biblioteksprobleme heute* VSB/ABS 1967, 61p. (Publications, 22). Present conditions of librarianship.

Coen E et al *Bibliotheken in der Schweiz/Bibliothèques en Suisse/Biblioteche in Svizzere/Bibliotecas in Svizza* Bern, VSB, 1976, 192p. (Prepared for the IFLA meeting, Lausanne 1976).

Hoffmanova L 'Kuihovuictví ve Švýcarsku' *Čtenár* 1978 30(9) 331-6.

Tschudi H P 'Ausprache von Bundesrat Tschudi am 75 jährigen Jubiläum der VSB' *Nachr* 1972 48(5/6) 227-34. See the whole commemorative issue.

Courten R de 'Le prêt interurbain et le prêt international dans le cadre du Catalogue collectif suisse' (Congrès de Dijon, 14 mai 1966) *ABF Bull Info* 1967 56) 147-52. Cooperation.

Wirz H G 'Les bibliothèques publiques en Suisse' in *Bibliothèques populaires et loisirs ouvriers* Paris, 1933.

'Cinquantenaire de la Bibliothèque pour Tous' *Nachr* 1970 46(6). Whole issue.

Maier F G 'Bern und seine Bibliotheken' *Berner Jugend-Berner Schule* 1968 (3) 28p.

Lassere B and Tacchini C *La lecture publique en suisse romande: enquête du Groupe de travail des bibliothèques de lecture publique* (Thesis) Bern, Groupe de travail des bibliothèques de lecture publique, 1977, 198p.

Wendler F 'Die Situation der schweizerischen Schul- und Jugendbibliotheken, aufgezeit am Beispiel des Kantons Zürich' *Nachr* 1971 47(2) 71-80.

— 'Von der Bibliothek zum Informationszentrum — das neue Gesicht der Schulbibliotheksarbeit in der Schweiz' *Schulbiblioth Aktuell* 1976(4) 167-76, 193-4.

Chaiz P 'La bibliothèque publique et universitaire de Genève' *AID Boll* 1963 2(3) 27-8.

Strahm H 'Das Verhältnis der zentralen Universitätsbibliothek zu den Fach- und Institutsbibliotheken' *Nachr* 1971 47(3) 137-45.

Coen E 'La nouvelle bibliothèque des sciences humaines de Lausanne-Dorigny' *Nachr* 1978 54(1) 32-5.

Boesch M 'Sozialwissenschaftliche Bibliotheken und Dokumentationsstellen der Schweiz' *Inspel* 1976 11(4) 152-4.

Brüderlin P 'Grosse Dokumentationsprobleme in der Schweiz' *Nachr* 1972 48(1) 2-5.

Baer H 'Möglichkeiten und Bedingungen der Zusammenarbeit in der Dokumentation auf nationaler und internationaler Ebene' *Nachr* 1972 48(4) 162-6.

Sydler J-P 'La collaboration en documentation' *Nachr* 1972 48(4) 166-72.

Baer H 'Dokumentation: von der Bibliographie zu den Informationswissenschaften' *Nachr* 1973 49(1) 1-12, 12 refs.

SIBIL: système intégré pour les bibliothèques universitaires de Lausanne Bibliothèque Cantonale et Universitaire de Lausanne, 1976.

'SIBIL: an integrated system for university libraries in Lausanne' *Unesco Bull Lib* 1977 31(3) 180-1.

Gavin P 'Automation of cataloguing: some effects on library organization' *Unesco Bull Lib* 1977 31(5) 298-304.

 See also some references under Federal Republic of Germany.

SCANDINAVIA

Includes Iceland

2a

Scandinavian Library Centre 1968- . Based on the Bibliotekscentralen in Copenhagen. Cooperative centre.

Alster L 'Scandinavian Library Centre' *Scand Publ Lib* Q 1972 5(1) 13-5.

Cooperation in information transfer is organized through various bodies. See:

Hakli E 'Det Nordiska samarbetet på forskningsbiblioteks- och dokumentation sområdet: en översikt av utvecklingen sedan 1972' *Nord Tidsk* 1977 64(2) 33-40.

— 'The official framework of Scandinavian cooperation' *Int Forum Info Doc* 1979 4(4) 6-9, refs. (See more general references under 3f).

Nordiska Forskningsbibliotekens Samarbetskommitteé (NFBS) 1973-. Coordinating body of the national councils of research libraries.

Nordic Coordinating Body for Scientific and Technical Information (NORDDOK) 1970- .

In 1977 these two bodies came together to form:

NORDINFO, the Nordic Council for Scientific Information and Research Libraries.

'Nyt nordisk samarbejdsorgan: NORDINFO' *Bogens Verden* 1976 58(6) 299-300.

Ginman M 'NORDINFOn toiminta vuonna' *Signum* 1977 10(10) 175-8.

'NORDINFO — a new Nordic body for cooperation' *Unesco Bull Lib* 1977 31(2) 117.

Peace Research Institute, Oslo. Coordinates collection of material on developing countries for Scandinavian libraries.

Nordisk Dokumentationscentral for Massekommunikationsforskning (NORDICOM).

2b

Nordiska Vetenskapliga Bibliotekarieforbundet (NVBF) 1947- . Federation of the Scandinavian Research Libraries; administers the Scandia Plan (See under 3f).

2c

'[Some possibilities of education for librarians and information specialists in Scandinavia]' *Tidsk Doc* 1972 28(3) 54-73.

Lindsay M 'Library education in Scandinavia' *New Lib World* 1979 80 27-8.

Viirman E 'Library ressearch in Sweden and other Scandinavian countries: a report on research project and current debate' *Scand Publ Lib* Q 1970 3(3/4) 129-47.

3a

Nielsen T *Vocabularium bibliothecarii nordicum* NVBF, 1968, 278p.

Bibliotekstermer: svenska, engelska, fanska, tyska 2nd enlarged ed Bibliotekstjänst, 1965, 70p.

Birkelund P et al *Nordisk leksikon for bogvaesen* 1951-1962, 2 vols. Encyclopedia on books, bibliography and librarianship.

Directory of economic libraries in Scandinavia Helsingin Kauppakorkeakoulu Kirjasto, 1976, 105p. Part of a larger comprehensive guide project sponsored by IFLA.

Ruokonen K 'Survey of economic and business libraries in Scandinavia' *Unesco Bull Lib* 1977 31(5) 277-85.

3b

Nordisk bibliografi och bibliotekslitteratur 1913-33; 1950- . Bibliotekstjänst. Supplement to *Nordisk Tidskrift för Bok- och Biblioteksväsen.*

Kvamme J comp *Index Nordica: a cumulative index to English-language periodicals on Scandinavian studies* G K Hall, 1980 US, 601p.

Fraser S E and Fraser B J *Scandinavian education; a bibliography of English-language materials* Int Arts and Sciences P, 1973, 271p.

Soini A *Nordiskt bibliotekssamarbete 1873-1973: bibliografi/Library cooperation in Scandinavia 1873-1973: a bibliography* Helsingin Yliopiston Kirjasto, 1975, 102p.

3c

Kauppi H M 'A look at library periodicals, Scandinavian and others' *Scand Publ Lib Q* 1971 4(1) 37-46.

Nordisk Tidkrift för Bok- och Biblioteksväsen 1914- .

Scandinavian Public Library Quarterly 1968- . Scandinavian State directors of public libraries. In English, supersedes: *Reol: Nordisk bibliotekstidsskrift* 1962-68.

Scandiaplanen: informationsblad 1974- .

Scandiaplanen: Skriftserie 1976- .

3e

'Bibliotheksabgabe und Schriftstellerfonds in Skandinavien' *Buch Biblioth* 1971 23 405-8. Lending right.

Cook F E 'Legal responsibility for public library development in Scandinavia' *Lib Trends* 1960 9(1) 217-28.

3f

Connery D S *The Scandinavians* Eyre & Spottiswoode, 1966.

Lottman H R 'Scandinavia: book country' *Publ Weekly* 1980 217(15) 35-64.

Nordisk bibliotekers utvikling 1936-1947 Copenhagen, 1948. From the Scandinavian Library Conference, 1947.

Nordiska bibliotek 1947-1964: en översikt Gothenburg, 1964, 152p.

Harrison K C *Libraries in Scandinavia* 2nd rev ed A Deutsch, 1969.

Risager J Bibliotekspolitik i nordiskt perspektiv' *Biblioteksbladet* 1976 61(15/16) 225-6.

Kajberg L 'Die skandinavische Bibliotheks- und Informations-forschung' *DFW* 1980 28(2) 61-5, refs.

'Central book acquisition service in Scandinavia' *Scand Publ Lib Q* 1975 8(3) 90-8.

Hakli E *Tieteellisten kirjastojen pohjoismainen yhteistyö: katsans yhteisty-oorganisaatioihin* Yliopisto Kirjasto, 1975, 94p. (U Library Publication 39). With an English summary.

Ellsworth R C 'The Scandia Plan revisited' *Douglas Lib Notes* 1970 19(1) 18-25.

Both S 'Scandinavian library co-operation and the Scandia Plan' *ABQLA Bull* 1978 19(4) 33-7.

Sanners L-E 'Scandia Plan: collecting cooperation in the Nordic countries' *IFLA J* 1979 5(4) 282-7.

Törnudd E 'Scandinavian cooperation to further document delivery' *Int Forum Info Doc* 1979 4(4) 3-5.

Ottervik G 'The Scandia Plan' in *Encyclopedia* 29 (1980) 311-14.

Dahlø R 'Interlibrary in Scandinavia: a four library system in transition' *BLL Rev* 1975 3(4) 98-103.

Komarova E M 'Sovremennye formy mezhbibliotechnogo sotrudnichestva: opyt skandinavskikh bibliotek' *Bibliot Bibliog za Rubezhom* 1976 (56) 31-44.

Munthe G 'Samarbeidet mellom forskningsbiblioteker og folksbiblioteker' *Bok Bibliot* 1977 44(1B) 44-6.

Kajberg L 'Den 3 afro-nordiske biblioteksk onference i Helsingfors Sep 1979' *Borgens Verden* 1979 61(8) 398-402.

See also the annual Anglo-Scandinavian conferences.

Fjällbrant N ed *NVBF Anglo-Scandinavian Seminar on Library User Education* Gothenburg, Chalmers Tekniska Högskola Bibliotek, 1977, 141p.

Progress in educating library users Bowker, 1978. Covers Canada, Great Britain and Scandinavia.

Vaering K 'Nordisk konference om biblioteks-PR' *Bogens Verden* 1979 61(2) 71-4.

Kannila H 'A general view of Scandinavian public libraries' *Scand Publ Lib Q* 1968 1(1) 2-23.

Stickler M 'Besuch in skandinavischen Büchereien' *Erwachsenenbildung in Österreich* 1975 26(11) 541-6.

Oyler P 'Public libraries international: contemporary libraries in Scandinavia' in *Encyclopedia* 24 (1978) 339-58, refs.

Anglo-Scandinavian Public Library Conferences. 9th: *Public libraries and their users/non users* (1979) Copenhagen, State Inspection of Public Libraries, 1979, 100p.

Huotari H 'An international bookmobile' *Scand Publ Lib Q* 1979 12(4) 144-51.

Rose G 'The library service to seafarers' *Lib Ass Rec* 1975 77(6) 134-5.

Nilson M 'School libraries and international development: school libraries in Scandinavia' *Amer Lib* 1970 1(2) 183-5.

Jones H and Medlock L 'Children's libraries in Scandinavia: a first impression' *Lib Rev* 1970 22(5) 251-4.

[Children, environment and culture] *Bogens Verden* 1975 57(8/9) 248-98. Special issue.

Schulbibliothek Aktuell 1975 (3). Issue devoted to the 4th annual conference of the International Association of School Libraries, West Berlin, 1975. Papers mostly about West Germany and Scandinavia.

Stoklund Joahanson H V et al 'Barn och bibliotek: barnbibliotek, skolbibliotek, folkbibliotek' *Biblioteksbladet* 1976 61(18) 261-8.

Damgaard N 'Indvandrereleverne og skolebiblioteket' *Børn & Bøger* 1979 32(4) 194-5. Immigrant children.

Tveterås H L 'Scandinavian university and college libraries' *Lib Trends* 1964 12(4) 480-90.

Fjällbrant N *A comparison of user instruction in Scandinavia and British academic libraries* Chalmers U of Technology, 1975, 37p.

Tottie T 'Från forskningsbiblioteken' *Biblioteksbladet* 1976 61(5) 77-8.

Søholm E 'I al fald koordinering- den store nordiske styringsdebat' *Bibliotek 70* 1978 (14) 372-4. Report on a meeting of the NVBF.

Vig M-L 'Centralised control and coordination of research libraries — similarities and differences in the Nordic area' *Libri* 1979 29(2) 93-126.

Tell B 'Scandinavian collaboration in documentation: an organizational study' FID Regional Conference, Buenos Aires 1972 *Paper*, 14p.

— 'Scandinavian developments in documentation and information services' *Lib Trends* 1969 (3) 289-98.

Abrahamsson S 'SCANNET — Det nordiska datanädet för I&D-tjanster' *Nord Tidskr Bok Bibliot* 1977 64 97-101. Data base organised in 1976/77 by SINFDOK for Scandanavia.

DENMARK

1

Kongelige Bibliotek, Copenhagen. 1665- . Legal deposit; bibliographical activities through its National Bibliografisk Afdeling 1963- .

Birkelund P 'The Royal Library of Copenhagen: historical perspectives' *Lib Hist Rev* 1974 1(1) 83-96.

Dansk Teknisk Oplysningst Jeneste (DTO). 1955- . Technical Information Service.

Klintoe, K 'The story of DTO' *Ann Lib Sci* 1968 15(1) 1-6.

2a

Statens Bibliotekstisynet, Copenhagen. 1920- . Inspectorate of Public Libraries.

'Bibliotekstilsynet informerer: Bibliotekstilsynets virksomhed' *Bogens Verden* 1975 57 (2/3) 45-9.

Bibliotekscentralen. 1939-53 as Folkbibliotekernes Bibliografisk Kontor; 1954-62 as Dansk Bibliografisk Kontor.

Sørensen B 'Bibliotekscentralen — portraet af en virksomhed' *Bogens Verden* 1978 60(3) 99-102.

See also in Dewe M *Library agencies in Europe* Library Association, 1967. (Under Europe 3f).

On these central agencies see:

'Vore centrale instanser. En hjaelp? En byrde? En sutteklud? *Bogens Verden* 1975 57(5) 145-8. With special reference to their automated system FAUST.

National Advisory Council for Danish Research Libraries (Forskningsbibliotekernes Faellesråd). 1970- .

Danish Committee for Scientific and Technological Information and Documentation (DANDOK).

2b

Danmarks Biblioteksforening. 1905- . Danish Library Association.

Birkelund P 'Denmark, Library Association of' in *Enclyclopedia* 6 (197) 582-4.

Tennesen J 'Danmarks Biblioteksforenings hovedbestyrelse' *Bogens Verden* 1976 58(6) 301-2.

- Danmarks Videnskabelige og Faglige Bibliotekers. 1949- . Group for Scientific Librarians.

Bibliotekarforeningen for Folkbibliotekerne. 1939- .

Danmarks Skolbiblioteksforening.

Bibliotekfarforbundet. Union of Librarians.

'Bibliotekarforbundets beretning 1978/79' *Bibliotek* 1979 70(16) 462-81.

Bibliotekarforbundet for Forsknings- og Fagbiblioteker (Union of Librarians in Research and Special Libraries). In 1975 it merged with the Bibliotekarforening.

Nyeng A-G and Søholm E 'Focus på forskningsbibliotekerne (6): Fusioner vedtaget — hvad betyder det?' *Bibliotek 70* 1975 (8) 210-1.

2c

Riemsdijk G A van 'Danmarks Biblioteksskole' *Open Bibliot* 1969 12(1) 2-7.

Ørom A and Bach B 'Forsøgsuddannelsen i opløbssvinget' Bibliotek 70 1978 (3) 70-4.

Rasmussen R 'Internationalism in library education: a study tour of libraries in Denmark — Part I' *Focus Int Comp Libp* 1979 10(1) 3-7.

Kirkegaard P 'The Royal School of Librarianship Copenhagen' in *Encyclopedia* 26 (1979) 165-78, refs.

Krogh K 'Training for non-professional library assistants in Denmark' *Lib Ass Rec* 1967 69(8) 268-70.

Kajberg L 'Research in librarianship: a summarized report of the situation in Denmark' *Scand Publ Lib Q* 1977 10(4) 111-5.

Sørensen B 'Demand for librarians in Denmark, 1970-1985' *Scand Publ Lib Q* 1972 5(1) 16-21. Based on:

Betoenkning vedrørende behovet for bibliotekarer 1970-1985: en prognose Copenhagen, 1971, 206p.

Torfing G 'Dansk arbeidsundersøgelse (DAU): et hjaelpmiddel til bedre planiaegning' *Bogens Verden* 1976 58(6) 289-92.

— 'Work study in Danish public libraries (DAU)' *Scand Publ Lib Q* 1976 9(2) 59-66.

Hansen R 'Har Biblioteksfronten eksistensberettigelse?' *Bibliotek 70* 1975 (22) 558-61.

Kierkegaard E and Jørgensen H M 'Biblioteksfront, fagforening og socialistik biblioteksstrategi' *Bibliotek 70* 1976 (3) 70-2. Two papers criticizing the socialist 'Library Front'. Its history and aims are described in:

'Biblioteksfronten' *Bibliotek 70* 1975 (15) 360-2.

3a

Danish Ministry of Foreign Affairs *Denmark: an official handbook.*

— *Le Danemark: manuel officiel.* With bibliography.

Bibliotekscentralen Biblioteksvejviser. Annual. Guide to research libraries, public libraries, institutions, associations related to librarianship.

Danmarks Biblioteksforening *Biblioteksårbog* 1940- .

Pedersen E *Fører for firmabiblioteker. Dansk firma- og forskningsbiblioteker med tekniske og økonomiske specialer* 2nd rev ed 1974. Libraries in technology and economics.

3b

Munch-Petersen E *A guide to Danish bibliography* Royal School of Librarianship, 1965, 140p. With Supplements. Based on:

Larsen K *Fortgnelse over bibliografier* 2nd ed, 1961.

— 'National bibliographical services' *Unesco Bull Lib* 1961 15(6) 301-9.

Bibliotekscentralen *Dansk Bogfortegnelse* Annual with 5-year cumulations. Retrospective bibliography in progress.

— *Dania Polyglotta* 1901- . New series 1969- . Books on Denmark in foreign languages.

— *Dansk tidsskrift index* 1915- .

Bredsdorff A and Kajberg L 'Selected references on Danish libraries [1969-1979]' *Bogens Verden* 1979 61(10) 533-5. From English, French, German sources.

Kajberg L 'Danish documentation literature 1950-1975: some characteristics' *Tidskrift Dok* 1978 34(5) 77-9.

3c

Danish Library Association *Bogens Verden* 1918- .
Danish School Libraries Association *Børn og Bøger* 1948- .
Danmarks Biblioteksskole Birketinget *Bibliotek* 1970- .
Danmarks Biblioteksskole Skrifter. Monograph series.
Almindelige Danske Laegeforening *Bibliotek for Laeger*. Journal of the Medical Library Association.
Bibliotekarforbundet *Bibliotek 70* 1970- . Supersedes *Bibliotekar* 1959-70.
Scandinavian Public Library Quarterly 1968- . See details under Scandinavia.

3d

Danmarks Statistik *Statistik Årbog*.
For library statistics see in *Biblioteksårbog* and in journals of librarianship.

3e

Dansk Bibliografisk Kontor *Danish Public Libraries Act of May 27th 1950, with amendments of May 25th 1956 and March 21st 1959* 1961.
State Inspectorate of Public Libraries *Danish Public Libraries Act 1964* Bibliotekscentralen, 1965, 19p. Comments on this in:
Reol 1964 3(3) 131-40.
Wilson Library Bulletin 1965 39(7) 567-71.
Minister for Cultural Affairs *Public Libraries Act. Report No 607, 1971.*
'Lov om folke-og skolebiblioteker' *Bog Bibliot* 1971 38(1) 3-13.
Nilsen S 'Biblioteklovene — ofte gamle og svake' *Bok Bibliot* 1979 46(7) 374-5.
'Danish Libraries' Commission' *Scand Publ Lib Q* 1975 8 137- .
'Work of the Danish Library Commission' *Scand Publ Lib Q* 1978 11(1) 23-4.
Nielsen J and Sørensen B 'Bibliotekskommissionen — en statusrapport' *Bibliotek 70* 1979 (5) 145-9.
Nielsen O P 'En grundlov for danske biblioteker' *Bogens Verden* 1979 61(7) 280-7.
— English summary of the report: *Bogens Verden* 1979 61(7) 317-23.
Widding L and Jørgensen C 'The new 'Music Law' in Denmark' *Musikbibliothek Aktuell* 1977 (3) 59-61.
Plovgaard S *Folkebiblioteksbygningen: normer og typeplaner forbibliotekslokaler i omrader med 5.000 til 25.000 indbyggere* Bibliotekstilsynet, 1967, 135p.
— English translation: *Public library buildings: standards and type plans . . .* LA, 1971, 131p.
— German translation, 1971, 129p.

3f

Jones G W *Denmark* E Benn, 1970.
Kirkegaard P 'Denmark, libraries in' in *Encyclopedia* 6 (1971) 570-82, refs.
Westermann H 'The library system in Greenland: an account of current developments' *Scand Publ Lib Q* 1969 2(3) 137-48.
'Le biblioteche in Danimarca' *AIB Boll* 1974 14(4) 189-96.
Kajberg L 'Libraries and librarianship in Denmark' *IFLA J* 1979 5(2) 78-90.
Aquilina A 'Struttura del servizio bibliotecario in Danimarca' *AIB Boll* 1978 18(3/4) 24-65, refs.
'Temunummer: naerdemokrati og bibliotekar' *Bogens Verden* 1976 58(4) 157-86. Special section: libraries, information services, participation in democracy.
Van der Bosch L 'Verslag van een reis: Denemarken 31 Mei-9 Juni 1975' *Bibliotheekgids* 1975 51(3/4) 98-122. Visit to Denmark.

'Dansk biblioteksvaesen 1972-1976' *Bogens Verden* 1976 58(4) 191-7.
Tortzen V *Biblioteks-samarbejede i Danmark* 1964, 70p.
— 'The Danish interlibrary loan system' *Spec Lib* 1964 55(4).
Kirkegaard P *Public libraries in Denmark* Dansk Selskab, 1950.
Drehn-Knudsen E *Public libraries in Denmark* Bibliotekstilsynet, 1967, 118p.
Danmarks Biblioteksforening. Rationaliweringskomité *Rationalisering i danske folke biblioteker* Bibliotekscentralen, 1964, 310p.
— Abridged edition in German Harrassowitz, 1967, 129p.
— Abridged edition in English Library Association, 1969, 256p.
Bibliotekstilsynet. Arbejsfordelingsplanudvalget *Organisationsplalaegning i danske folkebiblioteker* Bibliotekscentralen, 1970, 288p.
Yayoschi M '[Public library services in Denmark]' *Tosh Zasshi* 1971 65(4) 192-4; 65(5) 244-7. In Japanese.
'[Danish public libraries]' *Scand Publ Lib Q* 1974 7(2) 34-80. Special issue commemorating the Danish libraries exhibition in Paris, May 1974.
Koefoed I 'Role of the public library in a grass-roots democracy: an attempt to provide the public with better information on local and central government activities' *Scand Publ Lib Q* 1977 10(4) 125-30.
Koefoed I '[Danish public libraries]' *Scand Publ Lib Q* 1979 12(1) 1-51. Whole issue.
Ballagi A G 'Közmüvelődési könyvtárügy Dániában' *Konyv Fygyelo* 1980 26(1) 59-64. Review of Danish libraries, based on the above publication.
Juul I 'Brems ikke for kraftigt op for kulturen' *Bogens Verden* 1980 62(6) 272-7. Effect of financial crisis.
Sørenson B 'Some problems of library service in sparsely populated areas in Denmark' *Scand Publ Lib Q* 1976 9(3/4) 73-6.
Petersen J 'Biblioteksbetjening i halvfjerdserne af firestore grupper: blinde og svagsteende, gaestearbejdere, militaert personel, søfolk' *Bogens Verden* 1979 61(1) 15-22. Services to special groups.
Invadrarna och biblioteket 1973. Survey by a committee set up by the Danish State Inspectorate on foreign workers.
Bibliotekstilsynet *De udenlandske arbejdere og folkebibliotekerne* Biblioteks-centralen, 1975, 80p.
'[Books for migrant workers]' *Bog Bibliot* 1976 43(5). Special section.
'The immigrant worker and the Danish public library system' *Unesco Bull Lib* 1978 32(1) 23-32.
Bibliotekscentralen *Biblioteksbetjening af aeldreinstitutioner. Biblioteket kommer* 1975, 41p.
Bibliotekstilsynet *Betaenkning om sygehusbiblioteker, afgivet af den af Bibliotektilsynet for sygehusbiblioteker* 1973, 51p. Report by the State Inspectorate on hospital library work.
Petersen J 'Library service for seamen in Denmark' *Scand Publ Lib Q* 1978 11(3) 69-72.
Enderson M *Visioner og virkelighed: traek af børnebibliotekernes historie i USA og Danmark 1870-1930* Danmarks Biblioteksskole, 1977, 84p.
Rostrup S 'Skolebibliotekernes — pä jajt efter ny identitet?' *Bibliotek 70* 1979 (5) 124-7.
Gammeltoft I 'Kultur — skole — skolebibliotek' *Børn og Boger* 1979 32(3) 103-7.
Damgaard N 'Indvandrereleverne og skolebiblioteket' *Børn og Boger* 1979 32(4) 194-5; 1980 33(1) 23-6; 33(4) 164-9.
Koch-Klose A 'Das wissenschaftliche Bibliothekswesen Dänmarks in der Gegenwart' *Z Bibl Bibliog* 1971 18(1) 1-18, refs.

Davies R 'Danish academic libraries' *J Libp* 1976 8(4) 229-43.

'Focus pä forskningsbibliotekerne' Series of papers in *Bibliotek 70* 1975, various issues.

Birkelund P 'Danmark: planlaegning af det samlade forskningsbiblioteksvaesen' *Nordisk Tid* 1975/76 62/63(4) 138-40.

Davies R 'Dankse og engelske forskningbilioteker' *Bogens Verden* 1977 59(3) 91-8.

Nyeng P 'Danske faglige og videnskabelige bilioteker (5): folkebibliotekernes platoniske forhold til U-landslitteratur og Mellemfolkeligt Samvirkes Bibliotek' *Bibliotek 70* 1977 (20) 562-4. Library of the Association for International Cooperation which collects material from the Third World.

DANDOK *Informationsformilding for forskning, udvikling og teknologi* [1976?]. Report on the reorganization of scientific and technological information.

Eisenberg A 'Processen mod FAUST' *Bogens Verden* 1975 57(6) 198-200. Critical assessment of FAUST (Folkebibliotekernes Automation System).

Werner B 'Toangsfaustisering af folkebibliotekerne' *Bogens Verden* 1975 57(7) 215-6. Compulsory introduction of FAUST into the public library system.

Barnholdt B 'ALIS — Danmarks Tekniske Biblioteks bogdatabank med tolhørende udlansstyringssystem' *Tidsk Dok* 1976 32(5) 87-92. Cooperative data base for a group of libraries.

FINLAND

1

Helsingin Yliopiston Kirjasto (Helsinki University Library). Created at Turku in 1640; legal deposit in 1707; transferred to Helsinki in 1828.

Helsingin Teknillisen Korkeakoulun Kirjasto (TKK). 1849- . In 1972 became the national central library for science and technology.

2a

Kirjastopalvelu (Library Bureau, part of the National School Board) 1962- .

Selén G 'Kirjastopalvelu' *Scand Publ Lib Q* 1968 1 163-9.

Tieteellisten Kirjastojen Lautakunta (Council of Research Libraries). Under the Ministry of Education. 1954-1972. Replaced by:

Tieteelisen Informoinnin Neuvosto (Council for Science Information and Research Libraries), Helsinki. 1972- . (TINFO).

Tammekann E M 'Tinfo-tausta, toiminta ja tulevaisuus' *Kirjastolehti* 1979 72(9) 408-11.

Suomen Nuorisokirjallisuuden Instituutti/Finlands Barnbokinstitut, Tampere, 1978- . Institut of Literature for young people.

'Suomen Nuorisokirjallisuuden' *Kirjastolehti* 1979 72(2) 64-6.

2b

Suomen Kirjastoseura (Finnish Library Association), Helsinki. 1910- .

'Kirjastoseuran tavoitteet' *Kirjastolehti* 1979 72(11) 510-5. Discussion of a report on future plans of the association.

'Suomen Kirjastoseuran tavoiteohjelma' *Kirjastolehti* 1979 72(4) 172-7. Long-term plans.

Kauppi H M 'Finnish Library Association' in *Encyclopedia* 8 (1972) 487-90.

Suomen Tieteellinen Kirjastoseura (Finnish Association of Research Libraries), Helsinki. 1929- .

Suomen Kirjallisuuspalvelun Seura (Association for Documentation). 1948- .

Kirjastonhoitajien Keskusliitto/Bibliotekariers Centralförbund (Central Association of Librarians). 1967- .

Tieteellisten Kirjastojen Toimihenkilöt (Association of non-professional staff of research libraries). 1970- .

2c

Tammekann E M 'Mitkä ovat koulutustarpeen perusteet' *Kirjastolehti* 1977 70(6) 265-7.

Meri S-L 'Current trends of library research in Finland' *Unesco Bull Lib* 1971 25(3) 158-60.

'Tieteeliset kirjastot' *Kirjastolehti* 1976 (10) 368-72.

Meri S-L 'Millainen on suomalainen kirjastonhoitaja?' *Kirjastolehti* 1970 63(9) 257-9.

— 'Kirjastonhoitajan ammattikuva' *Kirjastolehti* 1971 64(9) 316-21.

'Yleisten kirjastojen virat 1976' *Kirjastolehti* 1978 71(2) 65-6.

3a

Suomen Kirjastoseura *Kirjastokäsikirja Biblioteksliandbok för Finland* 1973.
— *Suomen kirjastonhoitajat/Finlands Bibliotekarier* 1968, 133p.
Liinama M and Heikkila M comps *Suomen tieteellisten kirjastojen opas/Vetenskapliga bibliotek i Finlands* 5th ed Finnish Research Libraries Association, 1976, 149p.

3b

Helsinki University Library *Suomen kirjallisuus/Finlands litteratur* 1878- . Monthly. Retrospective bibliography from 1544/1877- is available.
Association of Publishers and Booksellers *Suomessa ilmestyneen kirjallisuuden luettelo /. . ./ List of books published in Finland* 1968-71.
Screen J E O *Finland* Clio, 1981, 244p. (World Bibliographical Series, 31).
Turku University Library *Suomen aikakauslehti-indeksi/Index to Finnish periodicals 1803-1863* The Library, 1974. Then annual.
Soisalon-Soininen M *Suomen vapaan kansansivistystyön bibliografia 1820-1955* 1961, 292p. (Adult education including librarianship).
Finnish Library Association *Advances in library and information science in Finland* 1972, 28p.

3c

Suomen Kirjastolehti *Kirjastolehti* 1908- . 1921-1948 as *Kansanvalistus ja kirjastolehti.*
Suomen Tieteellinen Kirjastoseura *Signum* 1968- .

3d

Tilastollinen Keskustoimisto/Statistika Centralbyrán *Suomen tilastollinen vuosikirja/Statistik Årsbok för Finland.*
— *Tilstokatsauksia.* (Bulletin).
Statistics for libraries in *Kirjastolehti.* See:
'Tieteelliset kirjastot 1976' *Kirjastolehti* 1977 70(7/8) 304-7.
'Kuntien kirjastot' *Kirjastolehti* 1979 72(6) 272-4, 279-92.

3e

Library of Parliament *Valtion virallisjulkaisut/Statens officiella publikationer.* Annual.
— *Valtion painatuskeskuksen luettelo.* Catalogue of publications on sale at the Government Printing Office.

3f

Nickels S et al *Finland: an introduction* Praeger, 1973, 377p.
Perălă A 'Suomalaiset kirjanlukijat kirjastonkăyttăjină' *Kirjastolehti* 1980 73(2) 76-7, 89. Summary of a research project on 'Reading in Finland'.
Kauppi H M *Libraries in Finland* 3rd ed Finnish Library Association, 1971, 62p.
Sievanen-Allen R 'Finland, libraries in' in *Encyclopedia* 8 (1972) 477-87.
Rauta K 'Kirjasto muttuvassa yhteiskunnassa' *Kirjastolehti* 1971 64(9) 314-6.
Rautalin M-L ed 'The Finnish library scene' *New Lib World* 1975 76(903) 179-87, 189. Special section: 6 papers.
Rauta K and Häkli E 'Finsk bibliotekvaesen 1972-76' *Bogens Verden* 1976 58(6) 275-81.
[Librarianship in Finland] *Adult Educ Finland* 1978 15(3). Whole issue on the topic.
Hatch L 'Public libraries in Finland' *J Lib Hist* 1971 6(4) 337-59, refs.

Vakkari P 'Objectives and developing of the Finnish library system: report by the Library Committee of 1973, submitted in January 1976' *Scand Publ Lib Q* 1976 9(1) 12-7, 18-23.
Lehtinen M 'The economic resources in Finland of the public library system' *Scand Publ Lib Q* 1976 9(2) 40-7.
— 'The new government subsidy system for public libraries in Finland' *Scand Publ Lib Q* 1979 12(3) 97-101.
Numminen J 'Yleisten kirjastojen kehitysnäkymiä' *Kirjastolehti* 1979 72(7/8) 314-7. Organization and prospects.
Sakki P et al 'Jengit ja haïriöt' *Kirjastolehti* 1979 72(3) 100-5. Groups of youths causing disturbance and damage in public libraries.
Boldt B 'Swedish minority libraries in Finland, some aspects of biblingualism' *Scand Publ Lib Q* 1969 2(1) 33-41.
Lebväshaiho V 'Problems of the library service in Finnish Lapland' *Scand Publ Lib Q* 1971 4(2) 87-99.
Karvinen I 'The library in a sparsely inhabited area: general and special aspects of a municipal library' *Scand Publ Lib Q* 1978 11(4) 98-105.
Äyräs A 'Library problems in Finland's Northern and Northeastern developing regions' *Scand Publ Lib Q* 1977 10(3) 97-104.
Saarinen H 'The library in Lapland: an institution for spreading knowledge' *Adult Educ Finland* 1978 15(3) 15-21.
Nyberg M 'Favoured by law: an outline of hospital library activity in Finland' *Scand Publ Lib Q* 1969 2(4) 201-10.
Koster A and Voorpostel R 'Bibliotheekwerk voor bejaarden, zieken en gehandicapten in Zweden en Finland' *Bibliot en Samenleving,* 1980 8(1) 21-5.
Ryömä S 'He lukevat sormillaan' *Kirjastolehti* 1971 64(10) 370-1. Library for the blind, children's department.
Kautto V 'Korkeakoulukirjastojen kurssi' *Kirjastolehti* 1972 65(4) 140-3. Comments on the report of the adhoc committee on the reorganization of university libraries.
Saarinen H 'Lapin korkeakoulun kirjasto' *Kirjastolehti* 1979 72(5) 210-3. Laplan university library, 1979- .
Häkli E 'A unified approach to science information and research libraries in Finland' *Unesco Bull Lib* 1974 28(5) 245-8.
Chamerska H 'Biblioteki finskie: wrazenia ze slubowego wyjazdu do Finlandii' *Przeglad Bibliot* 1977 45(1) 61-8.
Ruokonen K 'Aktualne kierunki rozwoju bibliotek naukowych w Finlandii' *Bibliotekarz* 1977 44(6) 166-9.
Dube W 'Das finnische Projekt eines nationalen Bibliotheks- und Informations-systems' *Zentrbl Biblioth* 1977 91 517-21.

ICELAND

1

Landsbókasafn Íslands, Reykjavík. 1818- .

Hanson G *The National Library of Iceland during the 20th century* Chicago U, School of Librarianship, 1963. Thesis.

Gudmundsson F 'Landsbókasafn Islands 150 ára' *Lesbók Morgunbladsins* 1968 43 32-3. Reprinted in *Nordisk Tidkrift för Bok-och Biblioteksväsen* 1969 56(4) 155-69.

— 'Iceland National Library' in *Encyclopedia* 11 (1974) 144-51.

Háskólabókasafn (University Library), Reykjavik. 1940- .

Háskólabókasafn *Leidarvísir* 1971. Guide to the library.

Norroena Húsid (Nordic House) 1968- .

2a

Menntamálaráduneytid. Upplýsingablad Bókafulltrúa Rikisin (Ministry of Education. Directorate of Public Libraries). 1955- .

2b

Bókavardafélag Islands (Reading Society) Reyjkavik. 1960- .

Icelandic Library Association.

- Deild Bókavarda i Islenzkum Rannsóknarbókasöfnum (Division of Librarians in Research Libraries). 1966- .

Felag Bokasafnsfroedinga (Association of Professional Librarians). 1973- .

Einardottir E M *Association of Professional Librarians founded in Iceland* The Association, 1976, 4p.

2c

Sigurdsson E *Bokasafnspistill. Sérprentum úr bókinni mennt er máttur* 1968.

— 'Menntum bókavarda' *Landsbókasafn Årbók* 1970 27 121-31.

Bókasafnsfroedi: námstilliögun og lestrarefni 3rd ed University Library, 1971. Manual for the librarianship course, with reading material.

Bury S 'Library education in Iceland' *Int Lib Rev* 1977 9(3) 303-18.

3a

Iceland . . . Handbook Central Bank of Iceland. Chapter on: Libraries and museums.

Landsbókasafn Islands Arbók. 1944- . Covers the whole field of librarianship: laws, education, bibliography, etc.

3b

National Library *Ritaukaskrá Lansbókasafnsins* (Library catalogue) 1888-1944. Annual.

— *Lansbókasafns Årbok.* Section on bibliography 1944-73. Includes all materials received by the library.

— *Islenzk bókaskrá* (Iceland National Bibliography) 1974- .

3c

Frettabréf Bokavardafélag Islands (Library Association Bulletin) 1971- .
Bokasafnid (The Library) 1974- .
Annual reports worth looking at:
Háskólabókasafn *Årsskýrsla* (University Library report), 1969- . Previously included in the university report.
Borgarbókasafn Reykjavíkur *Årsskýrsla* (Central library of Reykjavik), 1966- .

3d

Hagstofa Islands (Statistical Bureau) *Hagtidindi* and *Hagskýrslur.*

3e

See in *Landsbokasafn Islands Arbok.*
Menntamalaraduneytid *Lōg og reglugerd um almenningsbákasafn* 1964. Laws and regulations for public libraries.

3f

Griffiths J C *Modern Iceland* Praeger, 1969, 226p.
Benedikz B S *Iceland* Vengendt/Routledge and Kegan Paul, 1969, 64p. (Spread of printing; Western Hemisphere series).
— *Libraries in Iceland: an historical survey* University College London, 1959. Thesis.
Sigurdsson E 'Iceland, libraries in' in *Encyclopedia* 11 (1974) 128-44, bibl.
Scott C F 'Libraries in Iceland' *Lib Ass Rec* 1965 67(12) 423-33.
— 'Recent developments in Iceland librarianship' *Focus* (London) 1971 2(2) 29-39, refs.
'Islands biblioteksvaesen 1972-76' *Bogens Verden* 1976 58(4) 197-201.
Lindall P 'Island behöver bättre samordning' *Biblioteksbladet* 1976 61(15/16) 229-30, 232-4. Need for better coordination.
Koefoed F 'Bogkultur og biblioteker: rejseindtryk fra Island' *Bogens Verden* 1972 54(10) 674-7.
Rautalin M-L 'Islannin yleiset kirjastot' *Kirjastolehti* 1975 68(10) 342-4. Public libraries.
Renborg G 'Utflykt i Isländsk biblioteksfilosofi' *Biblioteksbladet* 1976 61(13) 193-6.
Petursdottir K H 'Library resources to the sick and handicapped in Iceland' *Book Trolley* 1971 3(3) 9-12.
Häkli E 'Islannin tiekeelliset kirjastot' *Kirjastolehti* 1974 67(12) 458, 463. Research libraries.
Carter E and Tveteras H L *Iceland: proposal to amalgamate the National and University libraries in Reykjavik and to build a new National and University Library* Unesco, 1969.

NORWAY

1

Universitetsbiblioteket, Oslo. 1811- . University and National Library.

Norges Teknisk-Naturvitenskapelige Forskningsräd (Council for Scientific and Industrial Research). Norsk Senter for Informatik, Oslo. 1944- .

2a

Statens Bibliotektilsyn (Directorate of Public and School Libraries), Oslo. 1949- . Under the Ministry for Church and Education. 1902-35 as Library Office; 1935-49 as Office of Public Education.

Mathisen K 'Det statlige organ for folke- og skolsbibliotekar' *Bok Bibliot* 1977 44(4) 225-7.

Riksbibliotektjenesten (National Office for Research and Special Libraries). Set up in 1969 under the National Library Association to deal with planning and coordination.

Tveterås H L 'A national agency for library planning and coordination: Riksbibliotektjenesten in Oslo' *Unesco Bull Lib* 1970 24(3) 139-42.

'Riksbibliotektjeneste for de faglige og vitenskapelige biblioteker i Norge' *Bok Bibliot* 1969 36 145-53.

Riksbibliotektjenesten bygges opp: melding om virksomheten 1969-1973 Riksbibliotektjenesten, 1974, 56p. Report of activities. English summaries.

Biblioteksentralen, Oslo. Cooperative organization serving public libraries; includes bibliographical activities.

Hernes T 'Biblioteksentralen — the Norwegian Library Bureau' *Scand Publ Lib Q* 1968 1 81-91.

Norwegian Cultural Council (NCC). Amongst its activities administers the Norske Kulturfonds (Norwegian Cultural Fund). Cooperation with the Directorate of Libraries.

Granheim E 'The Norwegian Cultural Fund and its support to Norwegian literature' *Scand Publ Lib Q* 1971 4(2) 69-86.

Boksentralen. Booksellers' organization. Bibliographical activities.

2b

'Lønnsorganisasjoner sam organiser ausatte i bibliotekene' *Bok Bibliot* 1979 46(2) 76-83. Set of review papers on various organizations dealing with librarians.

Norsk Bibliotekforening (NBF) (Norwegian Library Association), Oslo. 1913- .

Rognmo P 'The Norwegian Library Association (NBF)' *Scand Publ Lib Q* 1975 8(1) 43-4. History, aims etc., reorganization.

NBF. Committee on Developing Countries. 1975- .

Norsk Bibliotekarlag (Norwegian Public Librarians Association), Oslo. 1946- .

Kommunale Bibliotekarers Forening (KBF) (Association of Municipal Librarians).

Norske Forskningsbibliotekarers Forening (Association of Norwegian Research Librarians), Oslo. 1946- .

Norsk Dokumentasjongruppe (Norwegian Documentation Group).

2c

Rugaas B 'Statensbibliotekskole 1975' *Bok Bibliot* 1975 42(4) 160-66.

— 'Statens bibliotekskole: virksomhetsoversikt for perioden 1975-77' *Bok Bibliot* 1977 44 394-7.

Proposals for a college of librarianship.

Andresen L 'Norges Bibliotekhøgskole: teori — men ikke praksis?' *Bok Bibliot* 1976 43(6) 328-9 (Part 1).

Hauge M 'Innstilling om Norges Bibliotekhøgskole, del II' *Bok Bibliot* 1978 45(3) 133-4.

Harbo O 'De enkelte elementer i de foreslåede norske bibliotekaruddanelser' *Bogens Verden* 1978 60(2) 56-9.

L'Abbate Widmann M 'Formazione dei bibliotecari a tempo limitato: l'esperienza norvegese' *AIB Boll* 1976 16(3) 245-51.

3a

NBF *Håndbok over norske biblioteker.*

Hernes T *Norsk bibliotekarmatrikkel* Biblioteksentralen, 1969, 167p.

Riksbibliotektjenesten *Norske vitenskapelige og faglige biblioteker og dokumentasjonssentraler* 1972. Previous edition: 1963.

Økonomiske Bibliotek i Norge Bergen, 1974, 38p.

3b

Universitetsbiblioteket *Norsk bokfortegnelse.* Weekly with cumulations. Does not include foreign books on Norway.

The bibliography includes the annual sections:

- *Liste over innenrikske blad og tidsskrifter.*

- *Bibliografi over Norges offentlige publikasioner.* 1956- .

Pettersen H *Biblioteca Norvegica* Chra, 1899-1924, 4 vols. Foreign works on Norway and translations from the Norwegian.

Raabe G *Norsk litteratur og bøker om Norge tryky i utlandet 1926-1930, 1931-1935* Oslo, 1935-41.

Bibliographies also exist for particular languages: English, French, German, Dutch, etc.

Norsk tidsskriftindex, 1964-1965 Oslo, 1970-71.

Norsk Senter for Informatik *Artikkelindex.* Annual.

3c

NBF and Norsk Bibliotekarlag *Bibliotek og Forskning Årbok.* 1952- .

Statens Bibliotektilsyn *Bok og Bibliotek* 1934- . 1916-33 as *For Folkeopplysning.*

— *Bokbladet* 1959- . For school and children's libraries.

Norsk Bibliotekarlag *Meldinger* Notodden, 1952- . Monthly.

KBF *Kontakten* Oslo, 1957- . Four to six per year.

Riksbibliotektjenesten *Synopsis: informasjon om informasjon.*

3d

Statistik Sentralbyrä Oslo, 1876- . *Norges offisielle statistik.*

— *Statistik årbok.*

3e

Granheim E 'The new Norwegian Public and School Libraries Act' *Scand Publ Lib Q* 1972 5(1) 9-12.

See also by the same author:

Bok Bibliot 1971 38(4) 282-90.

Bogens Verden 1971 58(8) 498-501.

Granheim E 'Has the new Norwegian Act concerning public and school libraries counteracted the economic crisis?' *Scand Publ Lib Q* 1976 9(2) 54-8.

Nordgarden A 'Norwegian standards for library book stocks' *Scand Publ Lib Q* 1978 11 12-7.

3f

Langslet L R 'Kulturolitikens nya norska dimensioner' *Biblioteksbladet* 1976 61(15/16) 226, 228-9. Paper at the 13th Scandinavian Library Congress.

Danton J P *United States influence on Norwegian librarianship* U of California P, 1957, 91p.

Yuoneva T S 'Biblioteki Norvegii' *Bibliot Bibliog za Rubezhom* 1961 8 66-83.

Kildal A *Haakon Nyhuus* Deichmanske Bibliotek, 1966, 62p. Includes information on the development of libraries.

Ellsworth R C 'Emerging patterns in Norwegian librarianship' *Lib Q* 1968 38(2) 168-83, bibl.

'Norsk bibliotekvesen 1972-76' *Bogens Verden* 1976 58(5) 233-9.

Munthe G 'Norway, libraries and information centers in' in *Encyclopedia* 20 (1977) 243-74.

Mellbye E and Hauge M '[Is there a lack of co-operation between special and public libraries]' (In Norwegian) *Bok Bibliot* 1968 35(3) 232-8.

Munthe G and Granheim E 'Arbeids-og oppgavefordelingen mellom fagbiblioteker og folkebiblioteker' *Bok Bibliog* 1972 39(3) 196-204.

Hasselberg I 'Interlibrary lending in Norway' *Scand Publ Lib Q* 1976 9 24-8.

Hauge M 'Investigation into rationalisation in Norwegian public libraries' *Scand Publ Lib Q* 1971 4(3/4) 151-70. Work of the NBF's Rationalization Committee.

— 'Norwegian public libraries today' *Scand Publ Lib Q* 1975 8(1) 5-12.

Kolodiziejska J 'Biblioteki publiczne w Norwegii' *Bibliotekarz* 1975 42(10) 225-9.

Hauge M 'Noe er forskjellig, men stort sett er vi like' *Bok Bibliot* 1979 46(3) 140-2. Comparison with Sweden.

— 'Regional central libraries in Norway' *Scand Publ Lib Q* 1968 1(4) 193-212.

Juvik L H 'Library activity in a minority area' *Scand Publ Lib Q* 1971 4(3/4) 176-87, refs. Services to Lapps.

Dette er også oppsokende bibliotekvirksombet Norway Library Association, Public Library Section Conference 1978. Outreach librarianship.

Heie B 'The outreach library service in Norway: where do we stand? What are our objectives? *Scand Publ Lib Q* 1980 13(2) 41-3.

'Bokbussen' *Bok Bibliot* 1980 47(1) 3-25. Section on bibliobus.

Barstad M 'The library boat in West Norway, a cultural centre afloat' *Scand Publ Lib Q* 1969 2(4) 217-28.

Vibstad B 'Library services for Norwegian seamen' *Scand Publ Lib Q* 1969 2(2) 102-16.

Jorstad A L 'The role of libraries in Norwegian distance learning' *Scand Publ Lib Q* 1978 11(4) 93-7. Concept of 'Norsk Fjernundervisning'.

Heie B 'Literature and library services for the handicapped in Norway' *Scand Publ Lib Q* 1976 9(3/4) 92-7.

Varsi T 'Funksjonshemmede i samfunnet' *Bok Bibliot* 1979 46(4) 174-6. Handicapped.

Frisvold O 'Boker i fengsel' *Bok Bibliot* 1977 44(3) 169-72. Services to prisons.

Ugland L and Gamst I 'The combination library — a Norwegian speciality?'

Scand Publ Lib Q 1975 8(1) 12-6. Public/school libraries using the same premises.
Lund B *Skolbibliotek i Norge* Biblioteksentralen, 1967 86p.
Granheim E 'Den nye bibliotekloven — forventninger og virkelighet' *Bok Bibliot* 1975 42(4) 144-50.
Byberg L 'Library service to children in Norway' *New Lib World* 1976 77(907) 16-7.
Tveteras H L *Universitets biblioteket i Oslo 1876 - 1911 - 1961* Grøndhal Søn, 1962.
Terland I and Terland H 'Friends, foes or partners: a city library watches an academic library grow' *Scand Publ Lib Q* 1979 12(2) 73-9.
Tveterås H L 'Forskningsbibliotekene i gar-idag-morgen' *Bok Bibliot* 1971 38(4) 290-0.
Munthe G 'Midveis i 70-rene: oppgaver og arbeidsmål for norsk fag- og forskningsbiblioteker' *Bok Bibliot* 1975 42(4) 152-9.
Hasselberg I 'Use of computers by Norwegian public libraries — proposed pilot project' *Scand Publ Lib Q* 1979 12(4) 118-21.

SWEDEN

1

Kungliga Biblioteket, Stockholm. Open to the public in 1632. Served the university until 1977. Legal deposit 1977. Bibliographical functions through its:

- Bibliografiska Institutet. 1953- . Responsible for LIBRIS.

Tottie T (Secretary to the Committee for University and College Reform) *Utredning och förslag rörande gräusdragnings problems i samband med kungl. bibliotekets nuvarande service till utbilding och forskning* Biblioteksgruppen, 1976 (From Stokholm U). Summary of these proposals in: *Unesco Bull Lib* 1976 30 300-1.

Svenska Institutet för Kulturellt Utbyte med Utlandet, Stokholm, 1945- . Cultural institute, represented in most European countries.

Kungliga Tekniska Högskolans Bibliotek (KTHB), Stokholm. 1827- .

2a

Government Committee for Cultural Affairs. Section for Literature and Libraries.

Kulturrådet (Cultural Council). 1974- . Now in charge of public libraries and their activities. See its report 1978 on the status and development of regional libraries.

Statens Råd för Vetenskaplig Information och Dokumentation (SINFDOK). 1968- . Coordination and support of research. Now partly superseded by a new body. See below.

Forskningsbibliotesrådet (Council of Research Libraries) (FBR). 1965- . Functions also altered in 1977 after the legislative reform of the library system following a joint report of two government commissions: SINFDOK and BIDOK (Biblioteks- och Dokumentationssamverkanskommittén). The new body responsible for planning, developing and coordinating the information service would be a:

Delegation for Scientific and Technical Information Transfer.

Ottervik G 'Coordinating agencies' in *Encyclopedia* 29 (1980) 317-22. Gives a summary of the reform, which also involves the Royal Library. For other references see under 3f: Documentation/Information.

2b

Sveriges Allmänna Biblioteksförening (SAB), Lund. 1915- .

'SAB:s organisation: organisationskommitterro förslag' *Biblioteksbladet* 1977 62 205-8.

Ottervik G 'Sveriges Allmänna Biblioteksförening 1915-1975: glimtar frän de förgangna första 60 ären' *Biblioteksbladet* 1975 60(11) 187-208. Jubilee issue.

The Association has established and run as a business company:

Bibliotekstjänst (BTJ). 1951- . Supply agency, cooperative services.

Ekberg N *Bibliotekstjänst: une courte introduction* Bibliotekstjänst, 1964, 23p.

Gumpert J 'Bibliotekstjänst: the Swedish library Bureau' *Scand Publ Lib Q* 1968 1(1) 24-34.

Svenska Bibliotekariesamfundet (SBS), Uppsala. 1921- . Research Librarians.

Tekniska Litteratursällskapet (TLS), Stokholm. 1939- . (Swedish Society for Technical Documentation). There have been plans to create a coordinating body for these three societies:

Janson B 'En ny nationell Samarbetsorganisation' *Biblioteksbladet* 1979 64(12/13) 215, 217.

Sveriges Vetenskapliga Specialbiblioteks Förening (SVSF), Stokholm. 1945- .

Some other associations are union oriented in their aims and activities:

Svenska Folkbibliotekarieförbundet, Varberg. 1939- .

Vetenskapliga Bibliotekens Tjänstemannaförening.

Both are affiliated to Sveriges Akademikers Centralorganisation (SACO: Swedish Confederation of Professional Associations).

Bibliotek i Samhälla (BIS). 1969- . (Library in Society). Association for library workers and library users.

Sandblad H and Ristarp J 'BIS: the library in society, a Swedish library association. An interview with H Sandblad' *Scand Publ Lib Q* 1971 4(3/4) 171-5.

2c

Akerstedt J 'Utbildningsreformen: bibliotekshögskola och utbildning i informatik nyheter i BU:s forslag' *Biblioteksbladet* 1969 54(9) 874-6. Reform in education for librarianship.

Persson E *Biblioteksforskning. Förutsättningar och former diskuterade mot bakgrunden av material från andra länder* Bibliotekstjänst, 1969, 91p. (Biblioteksstudier, 6).

Anastasiou J 'Training for librarianship in Sweden' *Spec Lib* 1978 69(2) 71-6.

3a

Swedish Institute *Facts about Sweden* 1969.

Bibliotekstjänst *Svensk biblioteksmatrikel* 1949- . Updated at irregular intervals.

Erikson E comp *Information and documentation services in Sweden* National Swedish Board for Technical Development, 1977, 87p. Includes a list of research libraries.

Berg B *Svenska specialbibliotek och dokumentationscentrale: Förteckning* 2nd rev ed TLS 1974, 123p. (Handbok, 8).

3b

Bibliografiska Institutet *Svensk bokföteckning*. Current national bibliography. Cumulated under the title:

— *Svensk bokkatalog*. Five yearly publication.

— *Suecana extranea* 1968- . Two a year. Books in foreign languages and foreign books on Sweden. Continues:

Holmbäck B 'About Sweden 1900-1963: a bibliographical outline' Special issue of *Sweden illustrated* 1968 (18) 1-94.

BTJ *Svenska tidskriftsartiklar*. Monthly with cumulations. Index to periodicals.

Furuland L and Brundin B *En bok om biblioteksforkning* Lundequistka Bokkandeln, 1969, 239p. Handbook on library research.

3c

Bibliografiska Institutet *Svensk tidskriftsföteckning* 1967/68- . Cumulated as *Svensk tidskriftskatalog* 1961-65- .

SAB *Biblioteksbladet* 1916- .
BTJ *Barn och Kultur/Children and Culture* 1955- . Began as *Skolbiblioteket.*
FBR *FBR Aktuellt* 1973- . FBR News.
BIS *Bibliotek i Samhälle* 1969- .
TLS *Tidskrift för Dokumentation* 1945- . (1945-48 as *Teknisk Dokumentation*).
Svenska Folkbibliotekarieförbundet *Bibliofack.*

3d

Statistika Centralbyrän *Statistik Årsbok för Sverige.*
Gouledo L 'Sweden new public library statistics' *Scand Publ Lib Q* 1977 10 88-95.

3e

Riksdagsbiblioteket *Arsbibliografi över Sveriges offentliga publikationar.* Government publications.
Boken: litteraturutredningens huvudbetånkande Statens Offentliga Utresningar, 1974.
Regeringens proposition 1977/78: 97, om åtgärder för att bevara skrifter och ljud- och bildupptajningar. Legal deposit bill.
Regeringens proposition 1977/78: 114, om ett centralt organ för informationsförsöjning, m.m. Bill on the reorganization of the library and information system.
'Litteraturpropositionen: stöd med näppe' *Biblioteksbladet* 1975 60(4) 65-7. Literature bill.
Östling E 'Folkbiblioteken och lagen' *Biblioteksbladet* 1977 62(2) 28-9.
Johnson K 'Länsbiblioteken: stor variationsbredd och betydande standardskillnader' *Biblioteksbladet* 1979 64(9) 172-3.

3f

Kulturrådet *A new cultural policy: report* 1972.
Ottervik G and Möhlenbrock S *Svenska bibliotek: historia — organisation — funktion*, 2a väsentligt omarb.uppl. Bibliotekstjänst, 1973, 135p. First edition: 1964. (SAB Handböcken, 15).
Ottervik G 'Sweden, libraries in' in *Encyclopedia* 29 (1980) 258-322, refs. Series of papers.
Heyworth B M *An outline of the Swedish library system* Leeds Polytechnic, Department of Librarianship, 1971, 49p.
Biblioteken. Archive und Informatik. Schwedische Dokumente zur Bibliothekarausbildung und zur Rolle der Bibliotheken in der modernen Gesellschaft DBV, Arbeitsstelle für das Büchereiwesen, 1971, 67p. Trends in Swedish librarianship.
'Svensk biblioteksvaesen 1972-1976' *Bogens Verden* 1976 58(5) 240-2; (6) 273-4.
Svensson G 'Svenska bibliotek i skuggan av reformer' *Biblioteksbladet* 1976 61(15/16) 234-6.
Schwarz S and Willers U *Knowledge and development: reshaping library and information services for the world of tomorrow. A Festschrift for Bjorn Tell* Royal Institute of Technology Library, 1978, 307p.
Östling E 'Bibliotek 90' *Biblioteksbladet* 1977 62(8) 127-8.
— 'Bibliotekspolitik i Sverige' *Bibliotek* 1980 70(5) 147-8.
Gumpert J 'Bibliotekstjänst informerar' *Biblioteksbladet* 1977 62(9) 154-8. On coordination.
Wiman K *Interurbanldn vid Svenska bibliotek-undersökning.*

Zethson S-E 'Interurban lending centres in Sweden' *Scand Publ Lib Q* 1976 9 18-23.

Hellmer S O 'Ländsbiblioteken efter kommunreformen' *Biblioteksbladet* 1969 54(7/8) 712-4.

Svensson S-O 'Economic regression and Swedish public libraries' *Scand Publ Lib Q* 1976 9(2) 48-53.

Carlen A 'Im gelobten land der Bibliotekare' *Nachrichten* 1979 55(2) 35-40.

Tripet J 'Modèle suédois pour le développement des bibliothèques de lecture publique' *Nachrichten* 1979 55(2) 40-4.

Hauge M 'Noe er forskjellig, men stort sett er vi like' *Bok Bibliot* 1979 46(3) 140-2. Comparison with Norwegian public libraries.

Hellgren B 'Mobile library in a Swedish forest region' *Scand Publ Lib Q* 1969 2 229-36.

Nydrén G 'Bokbus i glesbygd och stortstad' *Biblioteksbladet* 1978 63(2) 36-9. Bibliobus in sparsely populated areas.

Henriksson A 'A 'culture bus' in Swedish Lapland' *Scand Publ Lib Q* 1974 7(3) 96-8.

Josefsson W 'En båt lastad med böcker' *Biblioteksbladet* 1975 60(13) 237-8. Boat library along the coast.

Nyman G 'Talboken — viktig för nya grupper av läsare' *Biblioteksbladet* 1977 62(3) 40-2. Handicapped and hospital patients.

Koster A and Voorpostel R 'Bibliotheekwerk voor bejaarden, zieken en gehandicapten in Zweden en Finland' *Bibliot Samenleving* 1980 8(1) 21-5.

Gulyas M 'Invandrare till biblioteket I: dagens biblioteksfolk är oengagerade' *Biblioteksbladet* 1975 60(15) 269-70.

— II: 'En person med ett annat modersmål' *Biblioteksbladet* 1975 60 (16) 289-90, 292.

— III: 'Känner att man är isolarad' *Biblioteksbladet* 1975 60(17) 305-6.

Sandblad D H 'Swedish public library service for immigrants' *Scand Publ Lib Q* 1974 7(4) 131-6.

Croker S K *Immigrants: the problems they present public libraries in Sweden, the United Kingdom, the USA* College of Librarianship Wales, 1975, 54p.

Ochsner F *Gefängnisbüchereien in Schweden* DBV 1970, 48p. Prison libraries.

Östling E 'Books at the job, Swedish version: act II' *Scand Publ Lib Q* 1976 9(3/4) 70-2.

Elmqvist I 'The labour movement and the libraries' *Scand Publ Lib Q* 1980 13(2) 44-9. Libraries at the place of work.

Larsen H 'Samhällstrycket' *Bibliotelsbladet* 1979 64(2) 31-4. Community information role.

Karlsson K and Bergman A 'Library activities for children: a Swedish example' *Scand Publ Lib Q* 1976 9(3/4) 81-4.

Kylber A-M et al 'Biblioteken och barnåret' *Biblioteksbladet* 1979 64(7) 129-33.

Fjallbrant N *User education programmes in Swedish academic libraries: a study of developments in the years 1973-1977* Chalmers Tekniska Högskola Biblioteket, 1977, 53p.

'[Libraries and audio-visual media]' *Biblioteksbladet* 1978 63(1) 3-20. Whole issue.

Det Svenska informations- och biblioteksomradet en läesrapport FBR, 1975, 69p. Report on current situation; role of FBR and SINFDOK.

Vetnskaplig och teknisk informationsförsöjning: betänkande av BIDOK- och SINFDOK — utredningarna Liberförlag/Allmänna Forlaget, 1977 (Statens offentliga utredningar 1977, 71). Joint report of the two commissions. English summary:

Scientific and technical information provision in Sweden: proposal for a new organisation Stokholm, Ministry of Industry and Ministry of Education and Cultural Affairs, 1978, 36p.

Tynell L 'Informationsförjningens nya centralorgan' *Biblioteksbladet* 1979 64(5) 85-6, 88, 90. Also published as:

— 'Nya topporgan för den svenske informationsförjningen' *Bogens Verden* 1979 61(6) 230-2.

Szántó P 'Tudományos és müszaki tájékoztatás Svédorszagban' *Könyvtári Figyelö* 1979 25(6) 599-609.

Hjerppe R *Revised programme proposal for the Swedish-Portuguese cooperation in the field of scientific and technical information and documentation* Stokholm, Royal Institute of Technology, 1978, 42p. (ERIC Report ED-167 096).

'The Swedish LIBRIS network' *Network* 1974 1(8) 9-14. (LIBRIS: Datorbaserade informationssystemet för vetenskapliga bibliotek).

Sandels M *LIBRIS — The Swedish Library network system* FBR, 1975. (Reprinted from a paper in Schwarz S ed *The interactive library* pp 175-200). (See International, 3f: Networks).

Government Auditors *The data-based information system for scientific libraries — LIBRIS — a report* 1977. Comment on the report:

Hagström T 'Riksdagrevisorerna och LIBRIS' *Biblioteksbladet* 1977 62(13) 226, 228-30.

EASTERN EUROPE AND USSR

See also under: Europe.

1

Osipova I P 'The national library in a socialist society' *Libri* 1978 28(4) 255-69, refs. Comparative study of the Eastern European national libraries, their functions and role. From:

— 'Tipologicheskie osobennosti natsional'noii biblioteki v razvitom sotsialisticheskom obschestve' *Bibliot Bibliog za Rubezhom* 1978 (69) 3-24, refs.

Havasi Z 'Nemzetközi kutatás a nemzeti könyvtár tipológiai sajátosságai ról' *Konyv Figyelö* 1979 25(6) 533-8.

International Information Centre for Soviet and East European Studies, Glasgow.

International Scientific and Technical Information System (ISTIS).

Klimashevsky V A et al 'Specialized and sectoral subsystems of ISTIS' *Int Forum Info Doc* 1978 (April) 3 11-17.

Mezhdunarodnyi Tsentr Nauchnoi i Tekhnicheskoi Informatsii (MSNTI), Moscow. 1969- .

Sumarokov L N 'Zu den Aufgaben des Internationalen Zentrums für wissenschaftliche und technische Information' *Informatik* 1979 26(5) 6-10. Serves the socialist countries.

2a

Osteuropa-Institut München. Under the Bavarian Department of Education and Culture. 1952- .

Böss O '25 Jahre Bibliothek des Osteuropa-Instituts München' *DFW* 1978 26(1) 17-24.

2b

International Committee for Soviet and East European Studies. University of Birmingham.

SCONUL. Advisory Committe on Slavonic and East European Materials (SCONUL/ACOSEEM). Previously: Slavonic and East European Group.

Bibliotheken und Dokumentationsstellen der Osteuropa-, Südösteuropa- und DDR- Forschung. Arbeitsgemeinschaft, Cologne.

'Köln, ABDOSD Arbeitstagung' *Bibliotheksdienst* 1976 (7/8) 357-60. Activities of the Working Group. See also:

'VIe session du Groupe de Travail des bibliothèques et centres de documentation pour l'étude de l'Europe de l'Est, du Sud-est et de la RDA, en République Fédérale Allemande' *Bull Bibliot Fr* 1977 22 668-70.

2c

Drtina J *Knihovna: vedecko-teoretický sbornik, 1959* Prague, Statni Pedagogicke Nakladatelstvi, 1959, 336p. East European congress on development and unification of training. In German, Russian and French.

Bulletin d'Information des participants de la Conférence sur l'Enseignement Supérieur des Bibliothécaires Nos. 1-2 Prague, 1952-60; No. 3 Berlin, 1962. In German and Russian.
Malek K 'Organizace vzedelání knihovniku v evropských socialistických zemích' *Tech Knihovna* 1965 (9) 282-4; 1965 (10) 313-4; 1965 (11) 347-8.
[Third International Conference on University Training for Librarians in the Socialist States, 26-28 June 1969, Leningrad] *Papers*.
Unger R 'Die bibliothekarische Ausbildung in den europäischen socialistischen Ländern' *Zentrbl Biblioth* 1965 79(4) 193-224.
Magaloni de Bustamante A M 'Entrenamiento de especialistas de información en paises europeos de economia socialista' *Bol Inst Invest Bibliog* 1972 (8) 393-428.
Schwarz G 'Funktion und Tätigkeit methodischer Zentren in den sozialistischen Ländern' *Libri* 1968 18(2) 81-94.
Walker G M P 'The organisation of research in library science in Eastern Europe' in Saunders W L *University and research library studies* Pergamon, 1968, 159-212.
'VIII narada ośrodków bibliotekoznawczych i metodycznych krajów socjalistycznych' *Bibliotekarz* 1977 44(1) 2-25. Report on the 8th meeting of the library science research and method centres.

3a

The Soviet Union and Eastern Europe: a handbook London, A Blond, 1970- .
Lewanski R C *Bibliography of Slavic dictionaries.* Vol 1: Polish 1965 repr.; Vol 2 Bulgarian, Czech, Serbo-croation, Slovak 1963; Vol 3 Russian, 1963.
Slovnik knihovnických terminu v sesti jazycich Prague, Central Technical Library, 1958, 634p. Dictionary in 6 languages.
Simova V and Nalevkova M *Lexíkografická práca v informatike.* In 4 sections published in *Knižnice a Vedecké Informácie* 1979.
— *Slovak-Czech terminological dictionary of informatics* Bratislava, 1975.
Horecky P L and Kraus D H *East Central and Southeast Europe: a handbook of library and archival resources in North America* ABC/Clio, 1976, 467p.
Walker G *Directory of libraries and special collections on Eastern Europe and the USSR* Crosby Lockwood/Archon 1971, 159p.
— *Resources for Soviet, East European and Slavonic studies in British libraries* Mansell Info, 1980, 208p.
Lewanski R C *Eastern Europe and Russia: a handbook of Western European archival and library resources* K G Saur, 1980, 471p.
Kraus D H et al *National science information systems: a guide to science information systems in Bulgaria, Czechoslovakia, Hungary, Poland, Romania and Yugoslavia* MIT P, 1972, 325p.

3b

Nowak A ed *Typologia dokumentów: referaty z II Międzynarodowego spotkania ekspertów sjolistyczny d/s bieźącej bibliografii narodowej, Warszawa, 21-26 kwiecień 1975* Warsaw, Biblioteka Narodowa, 1976, 104p. (Prace Instytutu Bibliograficznego, 21). Second international meeting on UBC in socialist countries. For a short account see: *Przeglad Bibliot* 1975 43(4) 350-3.
Horecky P *East Central Europe: a guide to basic publications* ALA, 1969, 956p.
Ruggles M J and Mostecky V *Russian and East Europe publications in the libraries of the United States* Columbia U P, 1960 (Repr Greenwood, 1973, 396p).
Library of Congress *East European accessions list.* 1951- .

Hnik T ed *European bibliography of Soviet, East European and Slavonic studies* U of Birmingham, International Committee for Soviet and East European Studies, 1975?- .

Shaffer H G *Periodicals on the socialist countries and on Marxism: a new annotated index of English-language publications* Praeger, 1977, 135p.

Svodnyi sistematicheskii katalog inostrannych knig po biblioteko vedeniiu, 1957-1963 Leningrad, Biblioteka Akademii Nauk, 1966, 147p. Classified union catalogue of foreign books on librarianship, but the bulk of the entries is from Eastern European countries. (See also volumes for 1917-45, 1946-56 and more recent ones).

State Library for Foreign Literature *Informacija o bibliotechnom dele i bibliografii za rubezhom. Sbornik materialov.* 1962- .

3c

Horecky P L and Carlton R G *The USSR and Eastern Europe: periodicals in Western languages* 3rd rev ed 1967, 89p.

Riedel H 'Bibliothekarische Fachperiodica in der UdSSR und den anderen Ländern der sozialistischen Staatengemeinschaft' *Bibliothekar* 1978 32(5) 389-95; 32(6) 500-3, refs; 1979 33(2) 99-102; 33(6) 497-502.

Lenin Library *Bibliotekovedenie i Bibliografiia za Rubezhom.* 1958- . Cumulative index in No 30, 1969.

'50 vypuskov sbornika 'Bibliotekovedenie i Bibliografiya za Rubezhom' ' *Bibliot Bibliog za Rubezhom* 1974 (50) 3-7.

Opyt raboty bibliotek s inostrannoi literaturoi. Sbornik statei 1957- .

ZIB (Leipzig) *Bibliothekswesen der Sowjetunion und der Länder der Volkdemokratie.* 1955- .

SCONUL/ACOSEEM Newsletter, London. 1974 as *SCONUL/SEEG Newsletter.*

International Information Centre for Soviet and East European Studies *International Newsletter.*

3d

Shoup P *The East European and Soviet data handbook: political, social and developmental indicators, 1945-1978* Columbia U P, Hoover Institution, 1980.

3f

Fröschner G 'Die internationale Beratung der Spezialisten zur Problematik der soziologischen Erforschung der Lektüre vom 15 bis 18 Nov 1977 in Prag' *Zentbl Biblioth* 1978 92(2) 67-71. International conference of specialists in the sociology of reading.

Schuster H 'Die Verbreitung der Sowjetliteratur — ein bedeutender Beitrag zur Entwicklung sozialistischer Persönlichkeiten' *Bibliothekar* 1975 29(1) 1-7.

Molnar P 'The conception and interrelation of bibliology and library science formulated in recent debates in socialist countries' *Libri* 1968 18(1) 1-34.

Şkripkina T I *Istorija bibliotečnogo dela za rubežom. Europejskie socialističeskie strany. Učebnoe posobie* Leningrad Institut Kul'tury, 1974, 70p.

Vaneev A N 'Osnovnye zakonomernosti razvitiya bibliotechnoi nauki v zrelom sotsialisticheskom obshchestve' *Sovet Bibliot* 1978 (5) 35-50, refs. Features of development of library science in an advanced socialist country.

Kunze H 'Die Zusammenarbeit der Bibliotheken der sozialistischen Länder: Rückblick und Ausblik' *Zentbl Biblioth* 1970 84 156-62. Cooperation, retrospect and prospect.

[Fourth conference of European Socialist countries, Budapest 1970] *Bibliotekar* 1972 26(2) 79-84.

Rückl G and Riedel H 'Für eine höhere Stufe der Zusammenarbeit der sozialistischen Länder auf dem Gebiet des Bibliothekswesens' *Bibliotekar* 1971 25(2) 83-91. Fifth conference on cooperation.

'Medzinárodná porada vedúcich knižničných oddelení ministerštier Kultúry a riaditel'ov národných knižnic socialistických krajú' *Knizn Ved Info* 1975 7(4) 145-68. Conference of heads of ministries of culture library section, and directors of national libraries. Mongolia took part.

Kern W 'Kooperation des Bibliotheksverbandes der DDR mit Bibliotheksverbänden in sozialistischen Bruderländern' *Bibliothekar* 1977 31 707-10.

Schmidt K 'Sozialistische Öffentlichkeitsarbeit von Bibliotheken: Zielstellung — Inhalt — Methoden' *Zentbl Biblioth* 1976 90(8) 357-62.

Welsh D J 'Public libraries in Eastern Europe' *Lib Ass Rec* 1960 62(9) 280-3.

Irmler J 'Rural libraries — a comparative international study' *Int Lib Rev* 1970 2(1) 49-55. Largely on Eastern Europe. From the International Symposium on Librarianship, Prague, 1969.

Schietzel W 'Die Funktion der sozialistischen Arbeiterbibliotheken im Spiegel ihrer Fachzeitschrift' *Bibliothekar* 1968 22 1195-204 Functions of the socialist workers' library.

Sakálová E 'Študovňa pre deti a mládež' *Kniznicny Zbornik,* 1977 7-35, refs. Study libraries for young people.

Rojnic M 'University libraries in Yugoslavia, Czechoslovakia, Hungary, Rumania and Bulgaria' *Lib Trends* 1964 12(4) 583-605.

Reichardt G 'Trends of developments in the information systems of the Soviet Union and the COMECON countries' *Lib Trends* 1969 17(3) 318-25.

Zunde P 'Co-operation of the information agencies of the CMEA countries' *Int Lib Rev* 1969 1(4) 487-500.

Zircz P 'A KGST államok kulturalis-müveszeti információs tevékenysége és együttmüködése' *Konyv Figyelö* 1980 26(1) 14-9. Cultural and artistic information, activities and cooperation.

Gapotchka M P 'Cooperation of the Academy of Sciences of socialist countries on information and documentation in the social sciences' *Info Proc Manag* 1978 14(3/4) 145-8.

Bagdasaryan S M 'Informatsionnaya deyatel'nost' v oblasti meditsiny i zdravookhraneniya sotsialistichnikh' *Nauch Tech Info*, Ser 1 1974 (6) 19-27. English translation in *Sci Tech Info Process* 1974 (2) 58- . Medical information.

Kneitschei F 'Der Informationsbedarf aus gesellschaftlicher Sicht und einige Tendenzen seiner Entwicklung' *Informatik* 1972 19(3) 9-15. Information needs in science and technology.

Schwarz G 'VI Internationale Arbeitsberatung der nationalen wissenschaftlich-methodischen Zentren der europäischen sozialistischen Länder vom 1 bis 7 Okt 1972 in Sofia' *Zentbl Biblioth* 1973 87(2) 86-91.

ALBANIA

1a

Biblioteka Kombëtare, Tirana. 1922- . Also acts as a bibliographical and international exchange centre.
- Kabineti Metodik.

Universiteti Shtatëror i Tiranes, Biblioteka. 1957- . Shares some of the functions of the national library, in particular international exchanges.

2a

Ministria e Aresemit dhe Kultures se Republikes Popullore te Shqipërisë. Komiteti i Kultures dhe Arteve-Sektori i Librit.

Albanian Committee for Cultural Relations Abroad, Tirana.

Academy of Sciences, Tirana, 1972.
- Instituti i Kulturës Popullore, Tirana, 1947.

2c

Biblioteka Kombëtare. Kabineti Metodik. Coordinates research in librarianship and bibliography. Organizes courses for librarians and bibliographers.

3a

Keefe E K et al *Area handbook for Albania* American U P, 1971.

3b

Biblioteka Kombëtare *Bibliografia Kombëtare e R P Sh-Libri Shqip* 1958- . Quarterly.

— *Bibliografia Kombëtare e R P Sh-Artikujt e Periodikut Shqip* 1961- . Index of periodical articles. Quarterly 1961-64; bimonthly 1965; monthly 1966- . Supersedes:

— *Bibliografia e Republikes Popullore te Shqipërisë-Vepra origjinale dhe përkthime te vitit* 1958-65.

— *Bibliografia e librit Shqip per vitet 1945-1957* Ministria e Aresimit dhe Khultures, 1959, 185p.

— *Bibliografia retrospektive-Libri Shqip.*

— *Bibliografia retrospektive-Artikujt e Periodikut Shqip.*

— Catalogue of new acquisitions.

Stevanovic B Albanian books *Booklist* 1980 76 824-5.

Tirana University *Bulletin.*

3d

Statistical yearbook of the Popular Republic of Albania.

3f

Marmullakv R *Albania and the Albanians* Shoestring, 1975.

Pollo S and Puto A *The history of Albania: from its origins to the present day* Routledge and Kegan Paul, 1981, 322p. (Translation of: *L'Histoire de l'Albanie*).

152 Nasri W Z 'Albania, libraries in' in *Encyclopedia* 1 (1968) 146.

BULGARIA

1

Narodna Biblioteka 'Kiril i Metodii' (NBKM), Sofia. 1878- . Created as Darzavna Biblioteka 'Vasil Kolarov' it took its present name in 1954. It houses several 'commissions':

- Commission for Scientific Research and Library Work.
- Bibliographical Coordination Commission, 1959- . Attached since 1970 to the Council of Library Directors.
- Commission for Coordination of Recommended Bibliography, 1974- . Dealing mainly in material suitable for public libraries.

Kalajdžieva K and Mladenova Z *Cyril and Methodius National Library* The Library, 1969, 48p.

Kalajdžieva K 'Zadachi i funktsii Narodnoi Biblioteki imeni Kirilla i Metodiya' *Bibliotek Bibliog za Rubezhom* 1970 (33) 5-16.

Centr za Naučna Informacija i Centralna Biblioteka pri Blgarska Akademija na Naukite (Scientific Information Centre and Central Library of the Bulgarian Academy of Sciences), Sofia. The Centre was created in 1959 and was integrated with the Library in 1972.

Centralen Institut za Naučna i Techničeska Informacija (CINTI), (Central Institute for Scientific and Technical Information), Sofia. 1958- . Since 1973 the Centre includes the Central Scientific and Technical Library (created in 1962). Under the Committee of Science and Technical Progress.

2a

Komitet za Izkustvo i Kultura (Ministry of Arts and Culture).

Committee for Science, Technical Progress and Higher Education.

Council of Library Directors.

Since 1970 the main research libraries and information centres work as a 'corporation' under the supervision of the above bodies.

Kultura 1978- . New body responsible for arts, cultural activities and mass media. Coordinates cultural activities at regional level.

2b

Union of Public Libraries.

2c

Boncheva T 'Istoriya i razvitie na bibliotechnoto obrazovanie v Bulgariya' *Bibliotekar* 1976 23(12) 5-10.

Topalova T 'La formation des bibliothécaires en Bulgarie' *Knijižnica* 1967 11 114-22.

[25th anniversary of the State Library Institute (DBI)] *Bibliotekar* 1976 23(12) 1-48. Special Issue, 3 papers on professional education.

Ivkov S '[Improving the effectiveness of further training programmes]' *Bibliotekar* 1972 19(11) 30-2.

Chudziaková M 'Tridsat rokov socialistichej sútaže' *Čitatel* 1980 29(7/8) 246-7. Competition incentive scheme for public libraries.

Dimitrov D 'Tiya mladi mogat, a i znayat' *Bibliotekar* 1975 22(7/8) 61-2. Role of women in librarianship.

3a

Bulgaria annual. Includes information on libraries.

Subeva E *Nauchni ucherzhdeniia v Bulgaria* (Handbook of scientific institutions) BAN, Tsentralno Biblioteka, 1967, 188p.

Tosheva S et al *Spravochnik na bibliotekite v Balgariya* Sofia, Nauka i Izkustvo, 1963, 389p.

3b

Pundeff M V *Bulgaria. A bibliographic guide* Library of Congress, 1965, 98p.

BAN, Central Library 'Nauchna konferentsiia po problemite na spetsialnata bibliografiia i nauchnata informatsiia v NRB, 27 i 28 februari 1967, Sofia' *BAN Izvestiia* 1968 4 212p.

Zotova K 'Tekushtata natsionana bibliografiya pred novi zadachi' *Bibliotekar* 1971 18(12) 6-10.

— 'Súčasná národná bibliografia Bulharska: stav a problémy' *Knižnice Ved Info* 1976 8(1) 35-43.

The national bibliography is published in eight sections covering book and non-book materials. Of special interest here:

- Section 1: *Bălgarski knigopis,* 1897- . Annual cumulation 1969- . Books, prints, maps, musical scores.
- Section 2: *Bălgarski knigopis*, 962- . Monthly. Official publications and theses. This part is cumulated as: *Bălgarski disertacii,* 1973- .
- Section 4: *Bălgarski periodičen pečat*, 1965- . Newspapers and periodicals.
- Section 5: *Letopis na statiite ot bălgarskite spisanija i sbornici,* 1952- . Selected bibliography of articles in periodicals.
- Section 7: *Bulgaria v čuždata literatura*, 1966- . Annual bibliography of translations from Bulgarian works and foreign works on Bulgaria.
- Section 8: *Bibliografija na bălgarskata bibliografija*, 1963- . Annual bibliography of bibliographies.

NBKM *Bibliotekoznanie, bibliografija, knogoznanie naučna*, 1969- . Annual bibliography on library science, bibliography and information.

Committee for Science, Technical Progress and Higher Education, Technical Documentation Centre *Informacionen bjuletin*, 1968- .

3c

New periodicals are included in section 4 of the national bibliography.

NBKM *Izvestija.* 1963- . Annual.

— *Bibliotekar*. 1954- .

BAN Central Library *Izvestija*. 1965- .

3d

Tsentralno Statistichestvo Upravlenie pri Ministerskiia Suvet *Statisticheski godishinik na Narodna Republika Bulgariia.* 1910- .

NBKM *Knigozdavane i pecat N R Bulgaria statisticheski sbornik.* 1964- .

— [*Libraries in Bulgaria. Statistical data*]. 1965- . An analysis of Vols 1-11 was published as follows:

Laskeev N A 'Die Entwicklund des bulgarischen Bibliothekswesens von 1965 bis 1975' *Zentbl Biblioth* 1979 93(5) 216-9.

3e

Komitet za Izkustvo i Kultura *Bjuletin*. 1963- .

NBKM *Annals*.

3f

Mladzhov G *Bibliotechnoe delo v Bulgariia* NBKM, 1963, 52p.

Kraus D H 'Bulgaria, libraries in' in *Encyclopedia* 3 (1969) 471-84.

Savova E 'Biblioteche e bibliografia nella Repubblica Popolare Bulgara' *AIB Boll* 1977 17 216-9.

Krause F 'Zur deutsch-bulgarishen kulturellen Zusammenarbeit aus der Sicht der Deutschen Staatsbibliothek in Berlin' *Zentbl Biblioth* 1972 86(9) 513-21, refs. Mostly about the development of Bulgarian librarianship since 1944.

'Tridsset godini: po sotsialististicheski put' *Bibliotekar* 1974 21(9) 2-5.

Kalatdzhiena K '35 godini sotsialistichesko bibliotechno delo' *Bibliotekar* 1979 26(7/8) 1-11.

Heintze I 'Bulgarien: bibliotek i samhälle' *Biblioteksbladet* 1972 57(1) 5-10.

Kalaidzhieva K 'Po primeru strany sovetov' *Bibliotekar* (USSR) 1977 (11) 70-2.

Stanchev M 'Kum po-natatushno razvitie na sutrudnichestvoto mezhdy bibliotekite' *Bibliotekar* 1972 19(10) 19-24. Developments in cooperation.

— 'Primerni tipovi strukturi za otraslovoto sudurzhanie na fondovete v okruzhnite biblioteki' *Bibliotekar* 1979 26(7/8) 29-36.

Ivkov S 'Za tvorcheski podkhod v suvernovanieto' *Bibliotekar* 1974 21(9) 13-8. Relations with users in public libraries.

Khadzhikhristov K N 'Rol', zadachi i problemy okrizhnykh bibliotek Bolgarii' *Bibliotekovedenie* 1970 (33) 17-31. Regional libraries.

— 'Ravnosmetka — garantirashta novi uspekhi' *Bibliotekar* 1978 25(11/12) 4-13. Review of development of regional libraries.

Kralev S 'Sostoyanie obshcheobrazovatel' nykh bibliotek v narodnoi Respublike Bolgarii: problemy rukovodstva i organizatsiya' *Bibliotekovedenie* 1970 (33) 32-50. Organization and problems of public libraries.

Pavlova G 'Za efektivno bibliotechno obsluzhvane' *Bibliotekar* 1976 23(9) 6-12. Paper at a seminar on efficiency through centralization. See also the other papers.

Kalajdzieva K 'Rural libraries in Bulgaria' *Unesco Bull Lib* 1972 26(2) 80-3.

'Organizatsiya na bibliotechnoto obsluzhvane v selata' *Bibliotekar* 1973 20(4) 2-16.

Cholov P '[Educational reform and the tasks of libraries]' *Bibliotekar* 1972 19(6) 22-5.

— 'Sus zanakha na reformata v obrazovanieto' *Bibliotekar* 1974 21(9) 37-40.

Vasileva L 'Reformata v obrazovanieto i zadachite na uchilishtnite biblioteki' *Bibliotekar* 1975 22(9) 7-11.

Panajotova S 'Die bibliothekarische Betrenung der Kinde in Bulgarien' *Bibliothekar* 1979 33(6) 481-3.

Mitov Z 'Osnovni momenti v pravilnika za rabotata na profsnyuznite bibliotek' *Bibliotekar* 1972 19(7/8) 41-4. Trade union libraries.

— 'Vazhno zveno ot obshtiya bibliotechen kompleks' *Bibliotekar* 1974 21(11) 6-9. Trade union libraries.

Ivanova S 'The libraries of the Higher Technical Institutes and the movement to promote students' creativity in the field of science and technology' *Bibliotekar* 1973 20(1) 15-8.

Savova E 'Special libraries in the People's Republic of Bulgaria' *Inspel* 1975 10(1/2) 60-70.

— 'The libraries of the Bulgarian Academy of Sciences and their role in the

development of national science' *Bibliotekar* 1964 11(8) 20-6.

[*Problems of special libraries*] 1975. Progress of the libraries of the Academy of Sciences 1975-1990. Comments on this text in:

Savova E 'Tezisite za osnovnite nasoki na razvitieto na naukata i tekhnicheskiya progres i spesialnite biblioteki pri BAN' *Bibliotekar* 1976 23(3) 5-6.

Ivanova M 'Biblioteki, koito zasluzhavat poveche vnimanie' *Bibliotekar* 1976 23(4) 25-7. Special libraries.

Stanisheva L Kh and Mitusheva V D 'Rol' nauchnykh bibliotek v udovletvorenii professional'nykh potrebnostei spetsialistov' *Bibliot Bibliog za Rubezhom* 1978 (69) 33-46. Users' satisfaction and use of the major libraries: National Library, Academy of Sciences' library, Ivan Vazov National Library.

Khaladzhov R 'Sama biblioteko-sistema ot biblioteki' *Bibliotekar* 1977 24(3) 28-31. Suggest specialized centrales to serve smaller scientific libraries.

Kraus D H *Scientific and technical documentation and information in Bulgaria* Georgia Institute of Technology, School of Information Science, 1968.

Laskeev N A 'Das Netz landwirtschaftswissenschaftlicher Bibliotheken in Bulgarien' *Zentbl Biblioth* 1972 86 212-21.

Gabrovska S 'System of scientific information on social sciences in the People's Republic of Bulgaria' *Info Proc Manag* 1978 14(3/4) 161-73.

Kalaidzhieva K 'Der Aufbau eines einheitlichen Bibliothekssystems in Bulgarien' *Bibliothekar* 1976 30(7) 443-8.

— 'NATIS in Bulgaria' *Unesco Bull Lib* 1976 30(1) 9-10, 43.

Bulgaria Automated Centre for Scientific and Technical Information: project findings and recommendations Unesco, UN Development Programme, 1978, 35p.

Zelenkov G 'Automation prospects in university libraries' *Bibliotekar* 1979 26(1) 24-32. Experimental computer system at a specialized institute.

CZECHOSLOVAKIA

1

Státní Knihovna Československé Socialistické Republiky, Prague. 1959- . Complex of national services created by merger of existing libraries: Narodni Knihovna (National Library), Slovenska Knihovna (Slavonic Library), Universitní Knihovna (University Library), Ústředni Vědecko-metodický Kabinet Knihovníctví (Centre for Scientific Research and Methodology in Librarianship).

Státní Knihovny ČSR v Praze *Průvodce Státní Knihovnou ČSR v Praze* Státní Pedagogické Nakladetelstvi, 1970, 70p. Summaries in English, French, German, Russian.

Horák F '200 let veřejné Státni Knihovny ČSR' *Čtenář* 1977, 29(4) 106-10.

Matica Slovenska, Martin, 1863- . Since 1968 assumes the functions of a national library and bibliographical centre for Slovakia.

Matica Slovenska 1863-1963 Bratislava, Osveta, 1961.

Repčák J 'Od roku 1959 po dnešok' *Čitatel* 1979 28(4) 126-7. Role of the Matica Slovenska in networks.

Universita Karlova Knihovna (Library of the Charles University). Part of the above mentioned complex but worth singling out because of its important librarianship documentation contents.

ČSAV Základni Knihovna (ZK) Ústředi Vědeckých Informací (ÚVI) (Centre of Scientific Information of the Academy of Sciences, Main Library), Prague. 1963- .

Ústředi Vědeckých, Technických a Ekonomických Informaci (UVTEI) (Centre for Scientific, Technical and Economic Information), Prague. 1936- . Incorporates the: Státní Technická Knihovna (STK) (State Technical Library). 1707- .

2a

Slovak Ministry of Culture.

- Matica Slovenska Research Institute for Culture and Public Opinion. Created in the mid 1970s.

Central Office for Cultural Information. Coordinates the information system for Culture.

OBIS (Oborové Informační Stredisko pro Informatiku). 1969- . Part of the Central Office for the Scientific, Technical and Economic Information network.

Bibliographical Centre for Technical Literature (BCTL). 1962?- . Based in the State Technical Library.

2b

Ustřední Knihovnícka Řada (Central Library Council), Prague. 1955-1968. Replaced by unions.

'Union of Czech Librarians and Information Officers' *Unesco Bull Lib* 1970 24 227-8.

2c

Kase F J 'Education for librarianship abroad: Czechoslovakia' *Lib Trends* 1963 12(2) 166-87, refs.

Pasjar Š 'Visokoškolsko obrazovanje bibliotekara u Čehoslovačkoj' *Bibliotekar* (Belgrade) 1967 19 34-42.

Helbicová D 'Pomaturitni studium knihovníkú' *Čtenář* 1972 24(2) 55-7.

'Dobrovol'ní knihovnící' *Čitatel* 1975 24(12) 434-5. Volunteers as library workers.

Janátová A 'Professional aspects of information and library activities' *Int Forum Info Doc* 1978 3(3) 35-8.

Brosmannová Ž and Križanová H 'Knihovníci a knihovníčky' *Čitatel* 1975 24(2) 56-8. Male and female librarians.

3a

Strnadel J *Československé knihovny. Informativni přehled* Slovenská Knihovna, 1957, 193p.

Ardresář informačnich středisek v ČSSR UVTEI, 1970, 2 vols.

3b

Sturm R *Czechoslovakia: a bibliographical guide* Arno P, 1967, 157p.

Liba P 'Slovenska bibliografia na preloma' *Kniznice ved Info* 1971 3(4) 153-5.

Riško A 'Bibliographic practices in Czechoslovak libraries — progress and problems' *Int Cataloguing* 1978 7(3) 30-3, refs.

Hanušová K and Slapnička F 'Výsledky koordinační činnosti v oblasti technické bibliografie' *Tech knihovna* 1978 22(7/8) 205-11. Includes a list of the publications of the BCTL.

State Library *Soupis českych bibliografi*. 1956- . Annual list of bibliographies.

— *Bibliograficky Katalog CSSR — Česke knihy*. 1922- . Weekly.

— *Bibliografie české knižni tvorby 1945-1960*. Retrospective cumulation.

Supplements to the national bibliography:

— *Noviny a časopisy v českých-krakích*. 1951- . Newspapers and periodicals.

— *Clánky v ceských časopisech*. 1953- . Index of periodical articles.

Matica Slovenská *Slovenská narodná bibliografia - Knihy*.

— *Slovenská narodná bibliografia — Clánky*.

Previously (1960-1970): *Članky v Slovenských časopisech*. See:

Trancygier T 'Využivanie rozpisového radu Clánky slovenskej národnej bibliografie' *Knižnice Ved Info* 1978 10(6) 245-54.

State Library *Novinky literatury — Přehledy informativni literatury*. Abstracts of reference works: bibliographies, glossaries, textbooks, etc.

— *Československé disertace*. 1964- . Annual.

— *Soupis českých bibliografí. 1956-* . Annual list of bibliographies.

Cerná M L *Soupis české a slevenské knihovnické literatury z let 1945-1955* Prague U, 1956.

Kunc J et al *Patnáct let české knihovnické literatury 1945-1960* State Library, 1960, 47p. (Supplement to *Knihovnik*).

Jedlička J and Straka J *Bibliografie československého knihovnictvi* State Library, 1960/61-1967. Superseded by two separate publications:

State Library *Bibliographie českého knihovnictvi*. 1968/70- .

Matica Slovenska *Soupis slovenskej knihovnickej literatúry za rok. . .* 1967- .

Československá Informatika includes the annual feature 'Československá literatura z oblasti informatiky v roce. . .', 1970- . Annual review of literature on information science and special libraries.

UVTEI *Bibliografické prehledy*. Bimonthly. Index of library science.

— *Seznam vědecké a techniké literatury*. Index of scientific and technical information.

3c

Buocikova M 'České a slovenské knihovnické časopisy' *Čitatel* 1971 20(12) 429-30.

Matica Slovenská *Čitatel* (The Reader). 1952- .

Gabor F 'Casopis *Čitatel* a jeho zácnic' *Čitatel* 1975 24 (12) 436-8. Opinions on the journal.

Matica Slovenská *Knižnica.* 1952-68. Superseded by:

— *Knižničný a Vedecké informácie.* 1969- .

— *Knižničný Sbornik.* 1959- . Collected papers.

Ministerstvo Kultury a Informaci *Čtenar.* 1949- .

'A Czechoslovak library journal in 1968: selected extracts' *Int Lib Rev* 1969 1(2) 235-9.

Ministerstvo Kultury *Knihovnik.* 1956-68.

UBTEI *Metodika a Technika Informací.* 1959- .

— *Technika Knihovna.* 1957- .

Československá Informatika. 1959- . Contains bibliographies.

3d

Ustředni Úřaď Státni Kontroly a Statisky *Spravodag.*

— *Czechoslovakia — Statistical Abstracts.*

Statni Knihovna. Ustredni Vedecko-metodicky Kabinet Knihovnictvi *Lidové knihovni ČSSR. Statistický přehled o činnosti v roce. . .*

— *Knihovny vysokych škol v roce . . . Přehled výkazu o činnosti (College libraries).*

— *Statni vedecké knihovny v roce . . . Přehled výkazu o činnosti* (Scientific libraries).

3e

State Library *Novinky literatury — Stát a pravo.* Quarterly list of current laws and decrees.

Ústav Dějin KSČ 'Prohibitní literatura' *Knihovnik* 1968 13(8) 275-6.

'Purge of books in Czech libraries' *Times* 7 August 1973 5.

Mestitiz F 'Das neue tschechoslowakische Bibliotheksgesetz' *Zentbl Biblioth* 1960 74(1) 7-23.

Pasiar S 'Náš prvý knižničný zákon' *Čitatel* 1979 28(4) 123-5.

'K normàn pre ludové knižnice' *Čitatel* 1971 20(10) 362-3.

3f

Cejpek J *Stručni přehled dejin českého knihovnictví* Prague, 1967. History of librarianship until 1938.

Mostecky V *Library organization and policies in Czechoslovakia from 1945 to 1954, with a historical introduction* Catholic U of America, 1954, 90p. Thesis.

— 'Libraries under communism: Czechoslovak libraries from 1948 to 1954' *Lib Q* 1965 26(2) 105-17.

Černý V 'Uplynulých dvacet let a jak dál' *Čtenář* 1968 20(6) 203-5. Developments since 1948 and reorganization in 1968.

Vinář J 'Chvála šeskému myšleni' *Čtenář* 1968 20(11) 357-61. Errors of orientation before 1968.

Walker G 'Czechoslovak librarianship 1968-1969' *J Libj* 1970 2(2) 75-91, bibliography of recent writings in English. History of the 1968 changes.

Das Bibliothekswesen der Tschechoslowakei Oesterreichische Nationalbibliothek, 1966, 59p. (Biblos-Schriften, 43).

Horak F 'Libraries in Czechoslovakia' *Timeless Fellowship* 1966/67 (3/4) 39-52.

Library World 1967 69(807). Special issue on Czechoslovak libraries.

Cigánik M 'Czechoslovakia, libraries in' in *Encyclopedia* 6 (1971) 390-403, refs.
Kuzmik J *The past and the present of the libraries in Slovakia* Matica Slovenská, 1955, 8p.
Kútik V and Valinský M 'Libraries and librarianship in the Czechoslovak Socialist Republic' *IFLA J* 1978 4(2) 90-102.
Velinsky M 'Knihovnické služby v budoucnosti' *Čtenář* 1977 29(8/9) 270-6. Library service of the future.
Nilssen Koski L 'Studietur til Tsekkoslovakia' *Bog Bibliot* 1977 44(2) 105-9.
Maruniak P 'Slovensko-soveitske knihovnícke vztahy' *Čitatel* 1972 21(12) 429-31.
Malék R 'The educational functions of libraries in Czechoslovakia' *Unesco Bull Lib* 1970 24(4) 196-200.
Vojtášek J 'Úlohy osvetých knižnic pri práci s poliyickou literatúrou' *Čitatel* 1971 20(10) 345-7.
Velinsky M 'Úvahy o přítomnosti a gudoncnosti knihoven zejména lidových' *Čtenář* 1972 24(4)) 113-8; 24(5) 156-62; 24-6) 188-93.
Houšková J 'Okresmi knihovny mezi 20 let' *Čtenář* 1971 23(4) 123-4. District libraries and their development.
Maruniak P 'Metodika-súčast riadenia' *Čitatel* 1979 28(12) 425-6.
Klapitovs V 'Čo čaká na metodika okresnej knižnice' *Čitatel* 1979 28(12) 427-9. Two papers on Slovak departments of methodology.
Dvořáčková V 'Das Zentralbibliothekssystem im netz der öffentlichen Bibliotheken der ČSR' *Bibliothekar* 1977 31 389-92.
Čitatel 1977 26(12). Whole issue on public libraries. Several papers on services outside the library: to old people, the sick and handicapped, pre-school children.
Kleskeňová D 'Znovu k problematice školenich knihoven tentokrát však trochu jinak' *Čtenář* 1976 28(10) 326-9.
Trnka B 'Horizonti spolupráce: nové školské zákony a veřejné knihovny' *Čtenář* 1979 31(4) 100-5, refs. Effects of new education acts on school libraries.
Krizanova H 'Deti predškolského veku ako používatelia knižníc' *Čitátel* 1980 29(5) 171-3.
Sakalová E 'Nové úlohy pre školské knižnice' *Čitatel* 1980 29(7/8) 270-1. New tasks for school libraries.
Pelikan B 'Gottwaldovy knihovny' *Čtenář* 1971 23(11) 355-60. Party libraries integrated into public libraries and trade unions' libraries.
Novotný F *Československé knihovnické zákonodarstvi* State Library, 1962, 107p, bibl.
Karasová B and Germeran V 'Univerzitná knižnica v Bratislave' *Vlastivedný Časopis* 1969 18(1) 23-31.
Zahálková B 'Činnost vysokoskoloských knihoven v ČSR z hlediska rozvoje vysokých škol' *Knihovna Věd Sborník* 1979 (11) 153-86, refs. Role of university libraries in higher education.
Bisová-Cerná J 'Hudebni knihovnictví' *Knihovna Véd Sborník* 1979 (11) 305-39, 210 refs. Music libraries.
Wright G H 'The Czechoslovak scientific and technical library services' *Aslib Proc* 1969 21(9) 360-4.
— *Czechoslovakia: a study of scientific and technical library services* Hertis, 1968.
Risko A 'Teoretické otázky informačného systému kultúry' *Kniž Ved Info* 1974 6(3) 97-100. Proposal for the establishment of a cultural network. See also the following references.
— 'Kniznice a informačný systém kultúry' *Čitatel* 1974 23(11) 387-9. All-inclusive network: television and other mass media as well as libraries.

Zahradil J 'Information activities in the field of social sciences in Czechoslovakia'

Info Proc Manag 1978 14(3/4) 179-85.

Basl Z and Vítková A 'Usnesení vlády ČSSR č 237/77 k 'Zasadám rozvoje soustavy VTEI do roku 1980' *Českosl Info* 1977 19(9) 233-6. Resolution on the development of a scientific, technical and economic system of information.

Vondra J et al 'Deset let činnosti OBIS pro informatiku' *Českosl Info* 1979 21(9) 239-44. Information centre for information, part of VTEI.

Vitková H et al 'Činnost státních vědeckých knihoven v soustavé VTEI' *Tech Knihovna* 1979 23(1) 6-20. Comments on the official resolution cited above. See also in:

Tech Knihovna 1979 23(10) 265-76; *Ibid* 329-38.

Hylmar J 'Obzor sovremennogo sostaianiia mekhanizirovannykh informatsionno-polskovykh sistem na kartakh' *Nauk Tekh Info* Series I 1976 (11) 20-2.

Ràda V 'Komplexni automatizace provozu Státni Technek Knihovny v Praze' *Tech Knihovna* 1979 23(2) 41-6.

Gábor F 'Perspektívy uplatnovania novej techniky v knižniciach, *Čitatel* 1980 29(7/8) 264-7. Plan for the creation of a network with a national information centre.

GERMAN DEMOCRATIC REPUBLIC

For the pre-1945 period see: Germany — General

1

Deutsche Staatsbibliothek, Berlin. 1661- . Originally Preussische Staatbibliothek. Its collections were shared in 1945 and part of them went to West Berlin.

Deutsche Staatsbibliothek, 1661-1961 VEB, 1961, 3 vols.

Krause F 'Gedanken zur Entwicklung der Deutsche Staatsbibliothek im letzten Jahrzehnt' *Zentbl Biblioth* 1979 93(8) 359-67, refs.

Deutsche Bücherei (DB), Leipzig. 1912- .

Deutsche Bücherei 1912-1962: Festschrift zum fünfzigjährigen Bestehen der Deutschen Nationalbibliothek DB, 1962, 422p, bibl.

Bunke H 'Deutsche Bücherei (Leipzig)' *Börsenblatt Deutschen Büchhandel* 1980 36(51) 1574-5.

Rötzch H 'Zur Entwicklung der Deutschen Bücherei in den siebzigen Jahren' *Zentbl Biblioth* 1979 93(8) 367-73.

2a

Ministerium für Kultur. Sektor Bibliothekswesen der Abteilung Literaturverbreitung und Literaturpropaganda der Hauptverwaltung Verlag und Buchhandel. Public libraries.

Ministerium für Hoch- und Fachschulwesen, Wissenschaftliche Information und Museen, Sektor Wissenschaftlische Bibliotheken. Planning and development of university and research libraries.

Zentralinstitut für Bibliothekswesen (ZIB), Berlin. 1950- .

'Das Bibliothekswesen der DDR und sein Zentralinstitut' *Bibliothekar* 1975 29(3) 145-74. 25th anniversary.

Zentralinstitut für Information und Dokumentation (ZIID), Berlin. 1963- .

Humbolt Unversität. Institut für Bibliothekswissenschaft und wissenschaftliche Information, Berlin. 1955- . Training and research in librarianship and information work.

'20 Jahre Institut für Bibliothekswesen und wissenschaftliche Information der Humbolt-Universität zu Berlin' *Zentbl Biblioth* 1975 89(6) 241-301. Special issue.

Deutsche Bücherei. Bibliographisches Institut (BI). (See under 3b).

2b

Bibliotheksverband der Deutschen Demokratischen Republik Berlin, 1964- .

'Bibliotheksverband der Deutschen Demokratischen Republik' *Zentbl Biblioth* 1974 88(9) Two papers on the history, organization and role of the Association.

Kern W and Rannacher E 'Enwicklung und Arbeitsweise der Bezirksgruppen des Bibliotheksverbandes der Deutschen Demokratischen Republik' *Bibliothekar* 1976 30 601-9.

Schmidmaier D 'The work of the Technical Libraries Section of the Library Association (GDR) during the last ten years' *IATUL Proc* 1974 7(2) 83-6.
Göhler H 'Zu den objecktiven und subjektiven Bedürfnissen nach Literatur und Bibliotheksbenutzung [I]' *Bibliothekar* 1975 29(5) 303-8.
— [II] *Bibliothekar* 1976 30(1) 5-9.

2c

Kunze H 'The training of librarians and documentalists in the German Democratic Republic' *J Libp* 1970 2(1) 43-55.
'25 Jahre Fachschule für Bibliothekare "Erich Weinert"' *Bibliothekar* 1972 26(4) 219-29.
Burrington G A 'Outline of education and training in librarianship in the German Democratic Republic' *Res Libp* 1971 3(16) 113-9.
Werner R 'Stand und Entwicklungstendenzen der bibliothekarischen Fachschulausbildung in der DDR' *Zentbl Biblioth* 1974 88(9) 587-91.
Siek E 'Die neue Ausbildungsunterlage für den Bibliotheksfacharbeiter' *Bibliothekar* 1977 31(5) 297-304.
Ewert G 'Zehn Jahre Erwachsenenqualifizierung am Institut für Bibliothekswissenschaft und wissenschaftliche Information der Humboldt-Universität zu Berlin' *Zentbl Biblioth* 1979 93(2) 54-61, refs.
Zentralblatt für Bibliothekswesen 1979 93(6). Whole issue on library and information science education in East Germany.
Schwarz G 'Zur Hochschulausbildung von Bibliothekaren und Informatoren' *Zentbl Biblioth* 1975 89(10) 449-57.
Riedel H 'Postgraduale Studienmöglichkeiten an der Fachschule für Bibliothekare Erich Weinert, Leipzig' *Bibliothekar* 1976 30 831-4.
Kürschner G 'Zum Ausbildungsprofil von Informatoren an der Fachschule für wissenschaftliche Information und wissenschaftliches Bibliothekswesen, Berlin' *Zentbl Biblioth* 1977 91 564-7.
Kummer D 'Das neue einheitliche Berufsbild des Bibliothekars' *Bibliothekar* 1974 28(8/9) 590-600.
Rovelstad M 'Socialistic librarianship: cuius regio eius bibliotheca' *J Lib Hist* 1974 9(4) 318-33.

3a

Introducing the GDR Verlag Zeit im Bild, nd, 255p.
Taschenbuch für Bibliothekare BI, 1967, 298p. Includes information on West Germany.
Kunze H and Rückl G *Lexikon des Bibliothekswesens* 2. neubearbeiterte Auflage, VEB Bibliographisches Institut, 1974-75, 2 vols.
Liste der Bibliotheken der Deutschen Demokratischen Republik 5. erweiterte Auflage Deutsche Staatbibliothek, 1975.
BI *Jahrbuch der Bibliotheken, Archive und Informationsstellen der DDR* 1959- .
Deutsche Bücherei *Jahrbuch* 1965- .
Statsbibliothek *Jahrberichte* 1956- .

3b

Zur Arbeit des Beirats für Bibliographie bei der Deutschen Bücherei' *Zentbl Biblioth* 1972 86 410-5. Set up in 1971 for coordinating and developing bibliographical activities in DDR.
Deutsche Bücherei *Bibliographie des deutschen Bibliographien.*
— *Deutsche Nationalbibliographie und Bibliographie des im Ausland*

erscheinenen deutschsprachigen Schriftums 1931- . Weekly. Annual and multi-annual cumulations. Published in 3 sections; includes materials from other German-speaking countries.

— *Deutsches Bücherverzeichnis 1911/1915-* . 1916- . 5 yearly. Cumulative index of German books.

— *Jahresverzeichnis der Verlagschriften und einer Auswahl ausserhalb des Buchhandels erschienenen Veröffentlichungen der DDR, der BRD und Westberlins sowie der deutschsprachigen Werke anderer Länder* 1948- . Annual.

— *Bibliographie fremdsprachiger Germanica* Leipzig 1972- . Quarterly.

Bücher aus der DDR. Katalog 1972/73 and *Nachtrag* Deutscher Buch-Export und Import, 2 vols, and supplement.

Humbolt-Universität. Institut für Bibliothekswissenschaft und wissenschaftliche Information 'Neue Dissertationen aus dem Institut für Bibliothekswissenschaft und wissenschaftliche Information der Humboldt-Universität zu Berlin' *Zentbl Biblioth* 1976 90 111-18.

Kunz F and Wille M 'Auswahlbibliographie wichtiger Literatur zum Bibliothekswesen der DDR' *Bibliothekar* 1969 23(7/8) 848-55.

Auswahlbibliographie zum Entwicklung des ländlicher Bibliothekswesens in der DDR, 1945-1971 Matica Slovenska, 1971, 28p.

Das ländliche Bibliothekswesen der DDR 1945-1972: annotierte Auswahlbibliographie ZIB, 1973, 42p.

Tröger, E 'Literatur zum Bibliothekswesen im Verlag VEB Bibliographisches Institut Leipzig' *Zentbl Biblioth* 1976 90 553-6.

ZIB *Informationsdienst Bibliothekswesen* 1971- .

Literatur zum Bibliothekswesen. Schnellinformation und Bibliographie der deutschsprachigen Fachliteratur Methodisches Zentrum und ZIB, 1966- .

ZIID *Informationsdienst Information/Dokumentation. Annotierte Titelliste und Mitteilungen* 1968- . Supersedes:

ZIID-Mitteilungen 1964-68 and

ZIID-Schnellinformation 1966-68.

ZIID *Informationsmittel aus dem Informationssystem Wissenschaft und Technik der DDR*

See also section: 'Neue Bücher und Aufsätze zum Bibliothek und Büchwesen' in *Zentralblatt für Bibliothekswesen*.

3c

ZIB *Der Bibliothekar* 1946- .

BI *Zentralblatt für Bibliothekswesen* 1884- . Supplements: *Beihefte*.

'Verpflichtung und Auftrag: internationale Stimmen anlässlich des 90. Jahrganges des Zentralblattes fur Bibliothekswesen' *Zentbl Biblioth* 1976 90(8) 345-9.

'Zwei Zeitschriften — eine Redaktion: zur Arbeitswese der Redaktion der bibliothekarischen Fachzeitschriften der DDR' *Bibliothekar* 1976 30(8) 506-10.

Ministerium für Kultur. Beirat für das wissenschaftliche Bibliothekswesen *Mitteilungen aus dem wissenschaftlichen Bibliothekswesen der DDR* 1963- .

ZIB *Mitteilungen und Materialen* 1963- .

ZIID *Informatik* 1969- . Previously:

Dokumentation 1953-64. ZIID *Zeitschrift* 1965-68.

ZIID *Information/Dokumentation.* Monthly.

3d
Ministerrat der DDR. Staatliche Zentralverwaltung fur Statistik *Statistisches Jahrbuch der DDR* Staatverlag der DDR.
— *Stand und Entwicklung von Kunst und Kultur in der DDR* 1958- .
ZIB *Bibliotheksstatistik* 1961- .
Horscht W and Meister K-H 'Bibliotheksstatistik' *Bibliothekar* 1969 23 (7/8) 829-37. Covers the period 1958-67. See also *Ibid* pp 837-47 for a chronology showing the development of library activities.
Horscht W *Bibliotheksstatistiche Methoden als Hilfe für die Leitung und Plannung der Entwicklung staatlichen Allgemeinbibliotheken* Zentralinstitut für Bibliothekswesen, 1974, 44p. Theory and practice in DDR 1966-70.
Horscht W and Peter H 'Ergebnisse der statistischen Jahreserhebungen 1971-1974' *Bibliothekar* 1975 29(12) 796-802.
Annual report in *Bibliothekar*, such as:
Horscht W 'Bibliotheksarbeit der staatlichen Allgemeinbibliotheken in Spiegel statistischer Zahlen' *Bibliothekar* 1979 33(5) 393-8.

3e
Staat und Recht der Deutschen Demokratischen Republik. Bibliographie. Potsdam, Akademie fur Staats- und Rechswissenschaft der DDR, 1972- . Quarterly.
Gesetzblatt der DDR Teil I and Teil II.
The regulations following this new legislation may be found, as well as comments in:
Bibliothekar 1971 25(1) 10-3; 1st regulation concerning the ZIB.
Zentralblatt für Bibliothekswesen 1971 85(1) 18-25; 2nd and 3rd regulations concerning the Deutsche Bücherei and the Staatbibliothek.
Zentralblatt für Bibliothekswesen 1971 85(3) 148-51; 4th regulation concerning the various grades and categories of librarians and the list of regional libraries entitled to the copyright deposit.
See also:
Rückl G 'Ein neuer Abschnitt in der Entwicklung des ZIB' *Bibliothekar* 1971 25(1) 4-9.
VEB Bibliographisches Institut Rechts-ABC für Bibliothekare Das Institut, 1975, 498p.
Beiträge zum Bibliotheksrecht Berlin, Deutsche Bibliotheksverband, Arbeitsstelle für das Bibliothekswesen, 1978, 78p.
Bibliotheksverband der Deutschen Demokratischen Republik. Geschäftsstelle. *Die Bibliotheksverordnung der DDR und mit ihr in engem Zusammenhang stehende rechtliche Regelungen und Vereinbarungen* 2. erw. Auflage. Berlin, Geschäftsstelle des Bibliotheksverbandes des DDR. 1978.
Kabus E *Richtwerte für wissenschaftliche Bibliotheken* Methodisches Zentrum, 1969, 38p.

3f
Mellor R E H *The two Germanies* Harper & Row, 1978, 448p.
François E 'Le livre en République démocratique allemande' *Bull Biblioth Fr* 1976 21(4) 171-8.
Die Deutsche Demokratische Republik und ihre Bibliotheken: ein informativer Uberblick DVB, 1969, 32p. Development since 1945, associations, periodicals, problems.
Schumann I *Das Bibliothekssystem der DDR* 3rd ed Leipzig, Fachschule für Bibliothekare, 1961, 80p.

Thielo M *Das Bibliothekswesen in der Sowjetischen Besatzungszone Deutschlands* Bundesministerium für Gesamtdeutsche Fragen, 1965, 243p.
Schenbarth-Engelscholl K 'East Germany, libraries and information centers in' in *Encyclopedia* 9 (1972) 533-45.
Kaula P N 'Libraries and information activities in socialist countries (1): German Democratic Republic' *Her Lib Sci* 1975 14(1) 32-51.
Marks E '1945-Eine Werde in unserem Bibliothekswesen' *Bibliothekar* 1975 29(5) 289-96.
ZIB *Bibliotheksarbeit heute: Aufsätze und Diskussionsbeiträge* 1967, 137p.
'20 Jahre Bibliothekswesen der DDR' Special issue of *Bibliothekar* 1969 23(7/8) 190p. Mostly ideological; bibliography pp 176-83.
Bibliotheksarbeit in der Deutschen Demokratischen Republik: Sonderheft zum 25. Jahrstag der DDR' *Bibliothekar* 1974 28(8/9) 507-648.
Korluss W '30 let NDR: Německá demokratická republika a její knihovny' *Čtenář* 1979 3(8/9) 280-6.
Kerm V 'GDR — strana bibliotek' *Bibliotekar* 1979 (10) 58-60.
'Die Parteiorganisation in der Bibliothek: ein Bericht aus Aulass des 25 Jahrestages der Gründung der SED' *Bibliothekar* 1971 25(3) 166-72.
Fleck W and Langner H 'Bibliotheken im gesellschaftlichen Gesamtsystem' *Zentbl Bibl* 1968 82(10) 577-98.
Meyer G 'Die Entwicklung des sozialistischen Bibliothekswesens der DDR seit anfang der sechziger Jahre' *Zentbl Bibl* 1979 93(8) 341-58. refs.
Ziegler E M 'Weshalb wir uns von Bibliothekswesen der BDR abgrensen müssen' *Zentbl Bibl* 1973 87(1) 26-34, 15 refs. Divergence of aims in East and West Germany.
Krause F 'Zur deutsch-sowjetischen bibliothekarischen Zusammenarbeit seit dem siege der grossen sozialistischen Oktoberrevolution, gezeigt am Beispiel der Deutschen Staatsbibliothek zu Berlin' *Zentbl Bibl* 1977 91 449-55.
Plotz K *Cooperation of libraries to ensure the satisfaction of requirements in information and literature by the broad masses of people: development and experience in the German Democratic Republic* ERIC, 1977, 14p. (ERIC Report ED-176 755).
Mühle W 'Von der Volksbücherei zur staatlichen allgemeinbildenden Bibliothek' *Bibliothekar* 1969 23 694-709.
Horscht W 'Zur Entwicklung der staatlicher Allgemeinbibliotheken' *Bibliothekar* 1976 30(11) 726-36.
Göhler H 'Zur Problematik der bewusstseinsbildenden Funktion und Ideologiefunktion der staatlichen Allgemeinbibliotheken' *Bibliothekar* 1972 26(7) 435-70, 7 refs.
Vodisek P 'Bibliotheksarbeit in der DDR: die staatlichen Allgemeinbibliotheken' *Buch u Biblioth* 1978 30(1) 15-8, 20-4.
Riedl H and Rükl G 'Die staatlichen Allgemeinbibliotheken-Produkt und aktives Instrument des sozialistischen Aufbaus in der DDR' *Bibliothekar* 1979 33(4) 282-301, refs.
ZIB *Bereiche der ländlichen Zentralbibliotheken in der DDR. Ergebnisse einer Sondererfassung* 1971 231p. Survey of the central rural libraries, 1960-1971 with statistical tables and bibliography.
Rimkeit A 'German Democratic Republic 1970: the development of patients' libraries' *Int Lib Rev* 1972 C 361-4.
Plesske H M 'Zwanzig Jahre Kommission Gewerkschaftsarbeit in Bibliotheken, Archiven und Museen des Zentralvorstandes der Gewerkschaft Wissenschaft' *Zentbl Biblioth* 1976 90 537-42.

Peter H 'Gewerkschaftsarbeit und Gewerkschaftsbibliothek' *Bibliothekar* 1974 28(8/9) 526-36.

— 'Bibliotheksarbeit der Gewerkschaften' *Bibliothekar* 1979 33(4) 301-7, refs.

Gemmel A 'Die Literaturversorgung von ausländischen Werktätigen mit originalsprachiger Literatur in Betrieben der DDR' *Bibliothekar* 1977 31(4) 225-8.

Dressler I *Kinderbibliothekarbeit in der DDR* DBV, 1965, 63p.

'Bibliotheksarbeit mit Kindern: ein Schwerpunkt der Arbeit in staatlichen Allgemeinbibliotheken' *Bibliothekar* 1977 31 73-6.

Hüttner H and Harych I 'Lesen in der Mittelstufe' *Bibliothekar* 33(5) 399-401.

Paul P 'Die Bibliotheken einer Universitat als Einheit' *Zentbl Biblioth* 1972 86(7) 402-8.

Dube W 'Uber der Stand der bibliothekswissenschaftlichen Forschungstätigkeit in der Deutschen Demokratischen Republik' *Libri* 1971 21(4) 361-8, 8 refs.

'Pläne, Projekte, Vorhaben: massnahmen wissenschaftlichen Bibliotheken zur Erfüllung der Beschlüsse des IX Parteitages' *Zentbl Biblioth* 1976 90(11) 489-500.

Kroh A 'Zu einigen Problemen der Bildung von Netzen der Fachbibliotheken' *Zentbl Biblioth* 1972 86(5) 279-81.

Meyer G 'Zur Diskussion um die Bildung von Netzen der Fachbibliotheken' *Zentbl Biblioth* 1972 86(5) 257-63, 9 refs.

Schwarz G 'Die Fachnetzbildung im Bibliothekswesen der DDR' *Zentbl Biblioth* 1974 88(9) 565-75.

Zentrale für medizinisches Bibliothekswesen und Literaturinformation *Medizinische Bibliotheken und Informationsstelle in der DDR* 2nd ed 1969, 175p.

Mante E 'Netzarbeit der medizinischen Fachbibliotheken in Grosstädten' *Zentbl Biblioth* 1976 90 542-8.

Langhans S 'Wissenschaftlich-technische Information und Bibliothekswesen' *Bibliothekar* 1974 28(11) 725-30.

Stein H and Bauer R 'Die Anwedung des SOPS AIDOS im Kombinat Wälzlager und Normteile' *Informatik* 1979 (2) 26-8.

HUNGARY

1

Orzságos Szechényi Könyvtár (OSZK), Budapest. 1802- .

The National Széchényi Library: a guide OSZK, 1966, 55p.

Kiss J 'National Széchényi Library: history and scope' *Lib Hist Rev* 1974 1(2) 1-17.

Havasi Z 'Current and future goals of development in the Hungarian National Library' *J Lib Info Sci* 1978 3(1) 63-73. Indian viewpoint.

Állami Gorkij Könyvtár, Budapest. 1956- . Foreign Language Library.

Magyar Tudományos Akadémia Könyvtára (MTAK), Budapest. 1826- . Centre of the research institutes network.

Rózsa G ed *The library of the Hungarian Academy of Science, 1826-1976* MTA Könyvtár, 1976, 43p, 70pl. There is also a Russian edition.

Csapodi C '150 Jahre Akademiebibliothek in Budapest' *Biblos* 1977 26(2) 192-8.

Országos Müszaki Könyvtár és Dokumentaciós Központ (OMKDK), Budapest. The Library of the Technical Museum was created in 1883. The Technical Documentation Centre was created in 1949. The library under its more recent name of Central Technical Library was attached to the centre in 1951 and the complex took its present name in 1962, when it was brought under the State Committee for Technical Development. Coordination centre for the network of scientific and technical libraries and information system.

Benedek J 'Ninety years of the Hungarian Central Technical Library, 1883-1973' *Tudom Musz Tájék* 1973 20(4) 262-73.

25 ev a müszaki-tudományos tájékoztatás szolgálatában OMKDK, 1974, 146p. Report on 25 years of activities.

'[OMKDK. Two papers on its reorganization and new functions]' *Tudom Musz Tájék* 1980 27(2/3) 45-8; 50-3.

Országos Pedagógiai Könyvtár és Muzeum (OPKM), Budapest. 1906- . Centre of the network of school libraries.

Országos Orvostudományi Könyvtár és Dokumentációs Központ (OOKDK), Budapest. 1949- . Centre of the network of medical libraries.

2a

Kulturalis Miniszterium. Library Department with an advisory council: Országos Könyvtarügyi és Dokumentációs Tanács (OKDT) 1956- . Two departments to be noted:.

- National Commission for Bibliography.
- Centre for Library Science and Methodology: Konyvtártudományi és Módszertani Központ (KMK). 1959- . Based on the National Library.

The Centre for Library Science and Methodology, Budapest: a short guide 1972.

Papp I 'A KMK tevékenységének néhány vonásáról' *Könyv Figyelö* 1978 24(3) 262-73, refs. Some features of its activities.

Perälä A 'Unkarin kirjastotieteen ja metodologian keskus' *Kirjastolehti* 1979 72(5) 228-31.

Council of University Library Directors. Now includes the directors of college libraries.

Fenyes M 'Az Egyetemi Könyvtarigarizgatök Tanaczanok 1978-1979' *Könyv Figyelö* 1980 26(4) 388-90.

Bilincsi L '*Ibid*: Evi tevekenységéröl' *Könyv Figyelö* 1980 26(4) 391-4.

Magyar Tudományos Akademia. Könyvtártudományi Bizottság. (Academy of Sciences. Committee for Libraries).

2b

Magyar Könyvkiadók és Könyvteriasztók, Budapest. Union of Publishers and Booksellers.

Magyar Könyvtárosok Egyesülete, Budapest. 1935- . Association of Hungarian Librarians.

2c

Kovacs M 'The education of librarians in Hungary' *Libri* 1966 16(1) 18-48.

Katsanyi S '[Facilities, requirements and problems of the education of librarians]' *Könyv Figyelö* 1972 18(4) 402-11.

Kovacs M 'Planification des recherches bibliothéconomiques en Hongrie' *Unesco Bull Lib* 1967 21(5) 278-85.

'Könyvtartudomanyi kutatasok, 1970-1971' *Könyv Figyelö* 1971 17(4) 300-4.

Papp I 'Research in library science: the Hungarian scene' *Unesco Bull Lib* 1976 30(4) 199-205.

Pinter M 'Library science researches in Hungary' *Res Libp* 1975 5(30) 185-91. Includes a summary of library organization in Hungary.

— 'Library and information science researches, 1972-1973' *Res Libp* 1976 6(31) 20-32. Survey by questionnaires, with a list of newly reported projects.

Khavashi Z 'Organizatisiya bibliotekovedchekikh issledovanii v Vengerskoi Narodnoi Respublike' *Bibliot Bibliog za Rubezhom* 1978 (68) 3-12.

Kamarás I 'Reading research in Hungary, 1962-1972' *Res Libp* 1974 5(27) 87-103. Originally published in *Könyv Figyelö* 1973 19(5/6) 489-502, refs. See also in section 3b.

Jobórú M 'Women librarians and documentalists in Hungary' *Unesco Bull Lib* 1975 29(6) 315-8.

3a

Pipics Z *A Könyvtáros gyakorlati szótára/Dictionarium bibliothecarii practicum* National Library, 1963, 317p.

— *Vocabularium bibliothecarii: supplementum Hungaricum* Akadémiai Kiadó, 1971, 251p.

Erdei F *Information Hungary* Pergamon, 1968, 1160p.

OMKDK *Directory of Hungarian research institutions* 1975 OMKDK, 1976, 134p.

OSZK *Hungarian library directory* 1965, 2 vols.

Kiss J *Libraries in Hungary* National Library, 1972, 95p.

3b

Kabdebo T *Hungary* Clio P, 1980, 236p. (World Bibliographical Series, 15).

Szentmihalyi J 'Bibliographische Arbeit in Ungarn' *Biblos* 1971 20(1) 1-18.

OSZK *A Magyar bibliografiak bibliografidja/Bibliographia bibliographiarum Hungaricum* 1956/57- .

Moravek E 'Die ungarische Nationalbibliographie' *Museion* 1970 N.s. 4 706-14.

OSZK *Magyar nemzeti bibliográfia/Bibliographia Hungarica* 1945- . Two a

month, with annual cumulations as:

— *Magyar könyveszet: a magyarországon nyomtatot könyvészet térképek és szöveges hanglemesek sziakositott cimjegyzéke* 1961- .

A number of retrospective cumulations are published or in preparation:

Magyar könyvteszet 1920-1944; 1945-1960; 1961-1975. In classified order of subjects.

Some useful sections or supplements can be mentioned:

OSZK *Hungarika irodalmi szemle.* Quarterly. Books and articles on Hungary published abroad in foreign languages.

— *Magyar nemzeti bibliográfia: Magyar folyóiratok repertóriuma* Repertory of periodicals. 1946- . And as a supplement to this:

— *Kulföldi magyar nyelvü folyóiratok repertóriuma/Repertorium bibliographicum periodicorum extra Hungariam lingua Hungarica editorum.* 1972- . Quarterly list of articles published abroad in Hungarian.

— *Hungarica külföldi folyóiratszemk.* 1971- . Quarterly list of articles in foreign periodicals by Hungarian authors and/or about Hungary.

Hungarian book review. 1958- . Quarterly. Hungarian Publishers' and Booksellers' Association. English/French/German editions.

MTAK *Magyar könyvszemle.* 1876- . Book reviews with a section on librarianship: 'A magyar könyvtörténeti szakirodalom'.

Deszényi-Szemzö P 'Hundert Jahre ungarische Buchrundschau' *Biblos* 1977 26(3) 278-89. Comment on the above publication.

KMK *Gyorstatjékoztato a Magyar könyvtártudományi irodalmrol* (Express information on Hungarian library and information literature). 1965- . Cumulated with retrospective additions as:

— *Magyar könyvtártudományi bibliográfia* 1962/64- .

— *Könyvtári és dokumentációs szakirodalom. Referálo lap* Foreign library literature for Hungarian librarians.

— *Vengerskaia literatura po bibliotekovedenii i informatike/Hungarian library and information science abstracts.* 1972- . Half-yearly selection of Hungarian library literature for foreign use.

See also:

Barsa G and Szelestei L N 'Bibliografia: a magyar könyvtörténeti szakirodalom 1971-1975, II: nyomda -, könyv-, könyvtar- és sajtotörténet' *Magyar Könyvszemle* 1977 93(3) 289-303. History of publishing, press book and librarianship.

Tarr L *Problems of the village library: a selected bibliography* KMK, 1970, 27p.

KMK *Reading research in Hungary: 1960-1977 — a bibliography* OSZK, 1977, 70p.

3c

KMK *Könyvtári Figyelö* (Library observer). 1955- . 1955-57 as: *Könyvtári tájékoztató.* Bimonthly.

OPKM *Könyv és nevelés* (Book and Education). 1959- . 1959-66 as: *Iskolai könyvtárosok tájékoztatója.* Bimonthly.

Ministry of Culture *Könyvtaros* (The Librarian). 1951- .

OMKDK *Tudományos és Müszaki Tajékoztatás* (Scientific and technical information). 1954- . Monthly.

3d

Központi Statisztikai Hivatal (1867-). *Magyar Statisztikai Evkönyv* (Statistical yearbook).

 Statistical pocketbook of Hungary Statistics Publishing House.

Központi Statisztikai Hivatal — Kömyvtár és Dokumentációs Szolgálat (Library and Documentation Centre) *Statisztikai Irodalmi Figyelö*. Monthly.

Ministry of Culture. Department of Statistics *Közmüvelödesi Könyvtárak . . .évi adatai* (Data on public libraries for the year. . .). 1961- . Annual.

— *Tudományos és szakkönyvtśrak . . .évi adatai* (Data on academic and special libraries for the year. . .). 1961- . Every two years.

Szabó-Andras E *Könyvtári adatok, 1884-1962* Népmüvelési Propaganda Iroda, 1966, 230p.

OSZK — KMK *Településeink könyvtári ellátása 1970. A tanácsi és a szakszervezeti könyvtárak statisztikai adatai* Népmüvelési Propaganda Iroda, 1971, 35p. Statistics on council and trade union libraries. English translation of headings.

3e

Bereczky L 'Ungarn Büchereigesetz 1956' *Bibliotheksdienst, Beiheft* 22 35-50.

'The Library Act of Hungary' *Int Lib Rev* 1970 2 211-6.

Papp I '[Preparation of the new library law]' *Könyv Figyelö* 1972 18(1) 5-22.

— 'Néhány új vonás közmüvelödési könyvtaraink fejlödésében' *Könyv Figyelö* 1977 23(1/2) 7-15. Standards for library service.

Tabacs J *A könyvtari szolgalat jogi szabalyozasa* OKDT, 1966, 360p.

Kondor M and Futala T 'Bibliotechnoe zakonodatel' stvo sotsialisticheskoi Vengrii' *Bibliothekar* 1979 (7) 50-2. 1976 onward.

3f

Boldiszár I *Nouvelle relation entre culture et démocratie: les expériences de la politique culturelle en Hongrie* 1969, 45p.

Ministry of Culture *Education and cultural activities in Hungary, 1954-1970* 1970, 72p.

Weyr T 'Hungarians have an appetite for reading — and a rich larder to delve into' *Publ Weekly* Oct 1977 212 26-8.

Szente F 'Teoretyczne i praktyczne problemy centralisacji zaopatrywania bibliotek w miejscach zamieszkania i w miejscach pracy' *Bibliotekarz* 1977 44(1) 16-20. Problems of acquisition in densely populated areas.

Csapodi C 'Geschichte der ungarischen Bibliotheken' *Biblos* 1970 19(4) 276-85. History to 1944.

Kovaszanay A *The Hungarian library organisation 1945-1963, with a short historical introduction* Catholic U of America, 1965. Thesis.

Kovács M 'Die Entwicklung des Bibliothekswesens in Ungarn nach dem zweiten Weltkrieg' *Biblos* 1970 19(4) 285-99. Includes statistics.

Szabo C *Development of Hungarian librarianship* U of Chicago, School of Library Science, 1964. Thesis.

Réthi C 'Das ungarische Bibliothekswesen' *Bibloth u Wissenschaft* 1967 4 120-224. Comprehensive account of development.

'Bibliotechnoe delo Vengrii za 30 let (1945-1975gg)' *Bibliot Bibliog za Rubezom* 1977 (64) 16-29.

Sallai I 'A sjovjet könyvtárügy 60 éve és hatása a magyar közmüvelödesi könyvtarügure' *Könyv Figyelö* 1977 23(5/6) 459-68 Influence of Soviet librarianship.

Kraus D H 'Hungary, libraries in' in *Encyclopedia* 11 (1974) 84-123, bibl.

Nagy E 'Das ungarische Bibliothekswesen der Gegenwart' *Zentbl Biblioth* 1976 90(7) 297-305.

Whatley H A 'Hungary and Bulgaria: notes on two British Council study tours made in September-October 1968' *Lib World* 1969 80(828) 341-6, 348.

Klingner H 'Eindrücke aus dem ungarischen Bibliothekswesen' *Bibliothekar* 1977 31 454-8. Impressions of Hungarian libraries.

Sargeant P 'The Hungarian library system' *J Libp* 1979 11(4) 261-76, refs.

'A közmüvelödési könyvtárak helyzete és fejlödése' *Könyv Figyelö* 1969 (1) 5-24. Brief history of public libraries, problems.

Seydelmann G 'Offentliche Bibliotheken in Ungarn' *Büch u Bildung* 1970 22(11/12) 508-13.

Futala T 'New steps to an improved library service for different ethnic groups in Hungary' *Könyv Figyelö* 1972 18(5) 506-14.

Halász L and Nagy A 'Impact of the library' *Int Lib Rev* 1977 9 485-90.

Szente F 'A hátrányos helyzetü települesek könyvtarai' *Könyv Figyelö* 1974 20(6) 525-9. Libraries in disadvantaged areas.

Takács M 'Work and organisation of village libraries in Hungary' *Unesco Bull Lib* 1972 26(1) 30-2.

Gönczi I 'Aktuelle Probleme und Entwicklungstendenzen der Gewerkschefts-bibliotheken in der Ungarischen Volksrepublik' *Bibliothekar* 1974 28(12) 799-806. Trade union libraries.

'Könyv- és könyvtárhasználati ismeretek és as új általános iskolai tanterv' *Könyv Figyelö* 1979 25(4) 329-40. Revised curriculum and involvement of libraries.

Karolyi A 'Die Kinderbibliotheken in Ungarn' *Bibliothekar* 1979 33(6) 486-9.

Bánlaky P et al eds *Camp for young readers: a Hungarian educational experiment* Tankönyvkiadó, 1979.

Csapodi C et al *Biblioteca Corviniana* Magyar Helikon, 1967, 386p. English translation published by the Corviniana P, 1969, 398p.

— 'Bibliotheka Corviniana und die Ergebnisse der neueren Forschungen' *Zentbl Biblioth* 1971 85(10) 577-88.

Nagy E 'A förskolai könyvtárak helyzete és fejlesztési lehetöségei' *Könyv Figyelö* 1976 22(6) 504-11.

Zsidai J 'Die Probleme des fachbibliothekarischen Berufs in Ungarn' *Int J Spec Lib* 1971 6(3/4) 72-6.

Szepesi Z *A Magyar orvosi könyvtárügy és documentació 20 éve* OOKDK, 1969, 196p.

'Az orvosi könyvtárosok és orvostanacsadok — VIII Jubileumi ertkezlete (Budapest 1979) Programja' *Orvosi Könyv* 1980 20(1/2) 1-167. Special issue on the 8th Jubilee Conference of Medical Librarians and Medical Advisers.

Walleshausen G 'Az orvostudományi szakkönyvtári hálózat *Könyv Figyelö* 1974 20(5) 451-63. Network of medical libraries.

La politique scientifique et l'organisation de la recherche scientifique en Hongrie Unesco, 1971, 119p.

Rózsa G *Some considerations on the role of scientific libraries in the age of the scientific and technical revolution: an essay and approach to the problem* Hungarian Academy of Sciences, 1970, 25p.

Kraus D *Scientific, technical and economic documentation and information in Hungary* Atlanta, Georgia Institute of Technology.

Mohor J and Sardy P 'A kulturális és müvezete információ helyzete és perspektivái magyarországon' *Könyv Figyelö* 1979 25(6) 549-54.

Rózsa G 'Information and documentation on social sciences in Hungary' *Info Proc Manag* 1978 14(3/4) 235-41.

Kraus D H et al *National science information systems* MIT, 1972. (Hungary pp 153-178).

Orosz G *A szakirodalmi tájékoztatás gépeitese magyarországon* KMK, 1970, 88p. Mechanization of information in special libraries.

POLAND

1

Biblioteka Narodowa, Warsaw. 1928- .

The National library in Warsaw Biblioteka Narodowa, 1974.

See also in 3f *Encyclopedia.*

Wilska U 'Der Bau der neuen Nationalbibliothek in Warschau' *Börsenblatt Deutschen Buchhandel* 1980 36(38) 1128.

The National Library has several departments of interest:

- Instytut Bibliograficzny. 1928- .

- Instytut Książki i Czytelnictwa. 1955- . (Book and Reader's Institute).

Kadzielski J 'Badania Instytutu Książki i Czytelnictwa Biblioteki Narodowej nad ksiaźka, bibliotekami i czytelnictwen' *Rocz Bibliot Narod* 1969 (5) 363-7. Research at the Institute.

Kolodziejska J 'Instytut Książki i Czytelnictwa: 20-decie pracy' *Przegad Bibliot* 1977 45(1) 23-31.

Ankudowicz J and Kolodziejska J '25 lat Instytutu Książki i Czytelnictwa Biblioteki Narodowej' *Bibliotekarz* 1980 47(2) 27-33.

- Zaklad Informacji Naukowej. 1951- . (Department of Scientific Information).

Warsaw University — Library.

Bednarski H J 'Warsaw University Library' *Can Lib J* 1975 32(1) 34-9.

Warsaw University — Instytut Bibliotekoznawstwa i Informacji Naukowej.

Czekajewska-Jedrusik A 'Instytut Bibliotekoznawstwa i Informacji Naukowej 25 lat historii, kierunki rozwoju' *Przegl Bibliot* 1978 46(2) 115-28.

Ośrodek Dokumentacji i Informacji Naukowej Polskiej Akademii Nauk, Warsaw. Documentation and Information Centre of the Academy of Sciences.

Dembrovska M '[The library of the Polish academy of Sciences as an information centre for science and prognostics]' (In Russian) *Bibliot Bibliog za Rubezhom* 1972 (40) 25-33, refs.

Centrum Informacji Naukowej, Technicznej i Ekonomicznej (CINTE) and Instytut Informacji Naukowej, Technicznej i Ekonomicznej (IINTE). Created in 1972 as part of the reorganization of the information services (IINTE existed since 1950 as CIINTE). Central organisms of the information system (SINTO), for which see under 3f.

2a

Ministerstvo Kultury i Sztuki.

Ministerstvo Nauki, Szkolnictwa Wyzszego i Techniki.

Panstowa Rada Biblioteczna. 1969- . State Council for libraries.

Paliński E 'Dzialalność państwowej rady bibliotecznej w latach 1969-1977' *Przegl Bibliot* 1978 46(4) 407-11, refs.

2b

Stowarzyszenie Bibliotekarzy Polskich (SBP), Warsaw. 1917- .

Kolodziejska J 'The Polish Library Association 1917-1967' *Libri* 1967 17(4) 246-57.

Wróklewski A *Stowarzyszenie Bibliotekarzy Polskich 1917-1967* SBP, 1968, 47p.

2c

The training of documentalists in Poland CIINTE, 1960.

Czekayenska-Jedrusik A 'Dzialnošć Komisji Egzaminacyjnej dia Dyplomowanych Pracowników Dokumentacji Naukowej' *Przegl Bibliot* 1979 47(3) 317-27. Activities of the Board of Examination in Information Science.

Cwickowa J 'Dzialnošć Komisji Egzaminacyjnej dia Bibliotekarzy Diplomowanych (1962-1978)' *Przegl Bibliot* 1979 47(3) 299-316. Activities of the Examination Board for Library Science.

Dunin C et al '[Special issue for candidates to the library profession]' (In Polish) *Poradnik Bibliot* 1975 27(9/10) 206-53.

Kuzminska K 'Bemerkungen zum neuen Bildungssystem und zur Ausbildung der Bibliothekare in Polen' *Zentbl Biblioth* 1979 93(3) 97-103. School reform, 1978, and implications for the training of librarians.

Walczak M 'Państwowy Ośrodek kształcenia bibliotekarzy w Jarocine' *Bibliotekarz* 1980 47(1) 4-7.

Kolodziejska J 'Research on library science in Poland' *Libri* 1972 22(2) 97-106, refs.

— 'Metodologia badán w zakresie bibliotekoznawstwa' *Bibliotekarz* 1975 42(11/12) 263-70. Research methods in librarianship.

3a

Slownik pracowników książki Polskiej Pańtswowe Wydawnictwo Naukowe, 1972, 1042p. Dictionary.

Encyklopedia wiedzy o książce Zaklad Narodowy im Ossolińskich, 1971, 2874p.

Glombiowski K et al, eds *Encyklopedia wspólczesnego bibliotekarstwa polskiego* Zaklad Narodowy im Ossolińskich, 1976, 337p.

Pigoń E 'Encyklopedia wspólczesnego bibliotekarstwa polskiego' *Bibliotekarz* 1977 44(1) 28-31. Review of the encyclopedia.

Luczyńska A and Remerowa K *Libraries in Poland. Information guide* Polonia, 1961, 108p.

Klimowiczowa I and Suchodolska E *Informator o bibliotekach i ośrodkach informaji w Polsce* Biblioteka Narodowa, 1973, 541p. (1976- editions).

Lewański R *Guide to Polish libraries and archives* Boulder, East European Quarterly, 1974, 220p. (East European monographs, 6).

PAN Biblioteka *Biblioteki polskiej Akademii Nauk i towarzystw naukowych* 1969, 83p. Libraries of the Academy of Science and of scientific societies.

3b

Pekowa J and Lenartowicz M *Bibliographie sur la Pologne — Pays, histoire, civilisation* 2nd ed Panstwowe Wydawnictwo Naukowe, 1964, 300p.

Korpala J *Dzieje bibliografii w Polsce* PLA, 1969, 439p. History of bibliography in Poland.

Grefkowicz A 'Poczatki informacji bibliotecznej w Polsce' *Bibliotekarz* 1976 43(7/8) 197-200. Beginning of bibliographical services.

Biblioteka Narodowa *Przwodnik bibliograficzny*. 1945- . Weekly, with annual indexes. 1928-1939 as: *Urzedowy wykaz druków wydanych w Rzeczypospolitej Polskiej.*

Wilgat J 'Bibliografiya polska 1901-1939' *Przegl Bibliot* 1977 45(2) 117-34. On the retrospective bibliography project which should run to 30 vols.

Piusińska W *Problemy selekcji w polskiej bibliografii narodowej 1901-1939* Bibliographical Institute, 1969, 65p.

Biblioteka Narodowa *Bibliografia zawartości czasopism.* 1947/48, 1951- . Index of periodical articles.

— *Polonica zagraniczne. Bibliografia.* Bibliography of foreign materials on Poland.

Wojciechowski K *Bibliografia oswiaty doroslych w wyborze* 3rd ed Wydawnictwa Zwiazkowe CRZZ, 1971, 203p. Adult education.

Eychlerowa B comp. *Bibliografia bibliografii i Nauki o książce* 1937- . Annual, in two parts:

— Part 1: *Bibliografia bibliografii Polskich.* (Polish bibliographies).

— Part 2: *Polska bibliografia biblioloczna.* (Bibliology). Both are published by the Bibliographical Institute. There are cumulations.

'Bibliografia analityczna bibliotekoznawstwa i informacij naukowej'. 1969- . Supplement to *Przeglad Biblioteczny.* Supersedes: 'Przeglad piśmiennictva o książce' (1951-1968).

Prace Instytutu Bibliograficznego. 1964- . (1947-64 as *Biuletyn*) Monographs series including bibliographies and essays on bibliographical work.

Koperska T et al *Bibliography of problems facing public libraries in villages 1946-1969: Poland* Matica Slovenská, 1970, 30p.

Cwiekowa J 'Bibliografia dotyczaca problematyki polskich bibliotek naukowych' in Cwiekowa J and Przelaskowski R *Polskie biblioteki naukowa,* Warsaw, Państwowy Oświdek Ksytalcenia Korespondencyjnego Bibliotekarzy, 1971.

For review of bibliographical publications on books, librarianship, etc. see:

Trzcinska J 'Polnische Monographien über das Buch- und Bibliothekswesen' *Zentbl Biblioth* 1970 84 544-8. And:

Suchocka E 'Polnische büch- und bibliothekswissenschaftliche Literatur (1970-1973)' *Zentbl Biblioth* 1975 89(3) 110-6, refs.

On documentation and information see:

- 'Przeglad dokumentacyjny zagadnien informacji i dokumentacji' 1951- . Section in *Aktualne Problemy Informacji i Dokumentacji.* CINTE Bibliographical bulletin. Annual.

- *Przeglad Piśmiennictwa Zagadnień Informacji.* Contains a section of abstracts.

3c

Korpala J 'Przeglad polskich czasopism bibliotekarskich' *Przegl Bibliot* 1977 45(3) 251-79. Survey of Polish periodicals in librarianship, 1945-75.

SBP *Bibliotekarz.* 1946- . 1929-39 as: *Biuletyn biblioteki publicznej m.st. Warszawy.*

— *Poradnik Bibliotekarza.* 1949- .

— *Przeglad Biblioteczny.* 1927-39, 1946- . Published in cooperation with PAN Library. English summaries.

IINTE *Aktualne Problemy Informacji i Dokumentacji.* 1956- . 1956-61 as: *Aktualne Problemy Dokumentacji.*

3d

Glowny Urzad Statistyczny Polskiej Rzeczypo *Rocznik Statistyczny.*

— *Concise Statistical Yearbook of Poland.*

— *Rocznik Statistyczny Kultury.*

Bibliographical Institute *Ruch wydawniczy w liczbach/Polish publishing in figures.* 1955- . Annual.

Podzimek J 'Odborné knihovny a informačni střediska Polské lidové republiky' *Knihovna* 1973 16(4) 113-9. Special libraries.

3e

Monitor Polski.
Kolodziejska J 'Stan badan bibliotekoznawczych w Polsce' *Bibliotekarz* 1970 37(7) 193-9. On the 1969 library act.
Biblinski L et al *Zbiór przepisów prawnych dla bibliotek publicznych* SBP, 1974, 298p. Regulations for public libraries.
Zarzebski T *Przepisy prawne dla bibliotek naukownych i fachowych* SBP, 1968, 370p. Special and scientific libraries.
Harewicz M et al *Przepisy prawne dla służb informacji naukowej, technicznej i ekonomicznej* CIINTE, 1967, 506p. Scientific, technological and economic information.

3f

Arnold S and Zychowski M *Outline history of Poland — From the beginning of the state to the present time* 2nd ed Polonia, 1965, 284p.
Preibish A 'Polish libraries: their structure, organization and aims' *Int Lib Rev* 1977 9(2) 161-74.
Derentowicz M et al 'Poland, libraries and information centers in' in *Encyclopedia* 23 (1978) 1-93, refs.
Lamure C 'Bibliothèques de Pologne' *Ass Biblioth Fr Bull* 1971 (71) 73-82.
Kosmanowa B 'Uwagi o periodyzacji historii bibliotek poliskich' *Przegl Bibliot* 1976 44(1) 25-37.
Pazyra S *Z dziejów książki polskiej w czasie drugiej wojny światewej* PIW, 1970, 452p. Polish books during the Second World War.
Wormell I 'Det fanns inte mycket kvar: polskt bokväsen sedan kriget' *Biblioteksbladet* 1975 60(8) 131-5. Book world after the war.
Usherwood R C 'Rising from ruin: impressions of Polish libraries' *Wilson Lib Bull* 1976 50 792-6.
Baumgart J 'Bibliotekarstwo polskie: rozwój, stan aktualny i perspektywy rozwójowe' *Przegl Bibliot* 1973 (1) 27-55. Problems and perspectives.
Kocowski B ed *Twórcy nowoczesnego bibliotekarstwa polskiego* Zaklad Narodowy im. Ossolińskich, 1974, 342p. Pioneers of modern librarianship.
'O dalsza modernizacje bibliotek polskich: VII Zjazd Bibliotekarzy Polskich, Zielona Gora, 6-8 czerwca 1975r' *Przegl Bibliot* 1976 44(3) 219-321.; 44(4) 325-452. 7th conference of Polish librarians: Towards further modernization.
'Program rozwoju bibliotekarstwa polskiego' *Bibliotekarz* 1976 43(10). Whole issue on developments in librarianship.
Stankiewicz W 'Bibliotechnoe delo v Pol'skoí Narodnoí Respublike' *Bibliot Bibliog za Rubazhom* 1977 (64) 64-82. Bases of the plan described in the previous reference for the development of libraries to 1990.
Koziol M 'Program rozwoju bibliotekarstwa polskiego do 1990r' *Poradnik Bibliot* 1978 30(11/12) 239-42. More comments on same.
Maugham T J 'Biblioteki publiczne w Polsce' *Bibliotekarz* 1969 36(3) 65-71.
Gorechki D M 'The development of public libraries in Poland: some socio-historical considerations' *J Lib Hist* 1976 11(1) 6-25.
Jankowiak H 'Biblioteki publiczne po reformie struktury administracyjnej kraju' *Poradnik Bibliot* 1979 31(5) 109-10. Public libraries after the reform of the country's administrative structure.
'Rola biblioteki gromadzkiej w roswoju oswiaty na wsi' *Bibliotekarz* 1971 38(10/12) 290-376. Special issue on the role of rural libraries in educational development.

Burakowski J 'W 30-lecie powatania bibliotek gminnych' *Poradnik Bibliot* 1979 31(11/12) 273-8. Parish libraries since 1949.

Krazniewska K 'Czytelnictwo robotników' *Bibliotekarz* 1972 39(5) 129-33.

Nagórska I and Ksiazek I 'Praca kulturalno-oświatowa bibliotek zwiazkowych w Lodzi' *Bibliotekarz* 1972 39(5) 138-43. Educational work of the trade union library at Lodz.

Javurková M 'Čternářské zájmy dělníku' *Čtenâr* 1976 28(7) 220-4. Workers' reading habits.

Zieliński K 'Dwiescie lat polskich bibliotek wojskowych' *Bibliotekarz* 1967 34(11/12) 322-6. Army libraries.

Kamińska H 'Biblioteki szpitalne — nowa perspektywa organizacyjna' *Bibliotekarz* 1976 43(5) 115-9. Hospital libraries.

Niemczykowa A 'Najpilniesze spawy bibliotek szkolnych' *Bibliotekarz* 1974 41(4). Urgent problems of school libraries.

Gutri M 'Razvitie detskikh bibliotek Pol'shi na protyazhenii Poluweka' *Bibliot Bibliog za Rubezhom* 1975 (52) 14-23. Development of children's libraries in the last 50 years.

Andrzejewska J 'Rola bibliotek szkolnych w systemie oświaty i wychowania' *Poradnik Bibliot* 1979 31(1/2) 5-10, refs. Role of school libraries in the educational system.

Chorýnski P 'Biblioteki szkolne a reforma systemu nauczania poczatkowego' *Poradni Bibliot* 1979 31(3) 53-7, refs. School libraries in the educational reform.

Bialakowska B 'Biblioteki publiszne dia dzieci i ich uzytkownicy' *Przegl Bibliot* 1979 47(3) 289-97, refs. Children's libraries.

— 'Die offentlichen Kinderbibliotheken in Polen' *Bibliothekar* 1979 33(6) 483-6, refs.

Niewlaczyn K 'Biblioteki szkolne dla dzieci niewidomych' *Bibliotekarz* 1976 43(7/8) 181-8. Libraries for blind children.

Klossowski A *Dzialalnośé bibliotek szkól wyszych resortu Oświaty i Szkolnictva Wysźego w XXV-lec u Polski Ludowej* PWN, 1970, 51p. Libraries under the control of the Ministry of Education. English summary.

Blundell K 'Pioneering with the White Eagle — academic libraries in Poland today' *Assist Libn* 1975 68(10) 170-5.

Wieckowska H 'Akademicke ksztalcenie bibliotekarzy postulaty raportu o stanie bibliotek i próby ich realizacji' *Przegl Bibliot* 1975 43(3) 219-31.

Prokopowicz M 'Traditions and achievements of music libraries and library science in the Polish People's Republic' *Fontes Artis Mus* 1979 16(1) 36-43, refs.

Loś L *Biblioteki Naukowe* Książki o Książce, 1980, 178p.

Hancko R and Jopkiewicz Z 'Wybrane problemy szkolenia pracowników i uzytkowników informacji naukowej, technicznej i ekonomicznej' *Aktual Probl Info Dok* 1975 20(2) 3-9. Educating readers and information users.

Derentowicz M 'Puti i perspektivy razvitiia informatsionnoi sistemy v Pol'skoi Narodnoi Respublike v 1976-1980gg' *Nauk Tech Info* Serie 1 1977 (4) 22-6. Development of the information system.

Nitecki J Z 'National network of information in Poland' *J Amer Soc Info Sci* 1979 30(5) 274-9, refs.

Dembowska M 'Informacja naukowa w Polsce: rozwoju informacji naukowej, technicznej i ekonomicznej' *Przegl Bibliot* 1973 (3) 279-97. Present situation and future development of the information system.

Stankiewicz W 'Stan i perspektywy rozwoju informacji i dokumentacji naukowej' *Rocz Bibliot Narod* 1973 9 5-41.

Derentowicz M 'Założenia dolszego intensywnego rozwoju informacji naukowej, technicznej i ekonomicznej' *Aktual Probl Info Dok* 1974 (3) 10-5.

Kulikowski J 'System informacji naukowej, technicznej i organizacyjnej — SINTO: zarys koncepeji i perspektywa realizacji' *Przegl Bibliot* 1975 (1) 3-29. Scientific, technical information network.

Fialkowski 'A SINTO szükségleteit szolagáló tudományos kutások' *Tudom Musz Tajek* 1977 24(7/8) 303-6.

Derentowicz M 'Polský systém vědeckých a technických informací 'SINTO' ' *Českosl Info* 1978 20(3) 65-8.

Maciejwicz J 'Tla Prognozy rozwocju informacji naukowej, technicznej i ekonomicznej w Polsce do roku 2000' *Aktual Probl Info Dok* 1976 21(6) 3-7. Prognosis to the year 2000.

Korzon K 'Zastowanie metody delfickiej do prognozowania rozwoju dzialalności informacyjnej' *Aktual Probl Info Dok* 1976 21(6) 16-21. Use of the Delphi method to forecast the development of the information system.

Kunicki M 'Applications of the Delphi method in studies forecasting information activity in Poland up to the year 2000' *Int Forum Info Doc* 1978 3(4) 20-4, refs.

Korzon K 'A Delphi módszle felhasználása a tákekoztatási tevekenység fejlesztéséhek prognosztizalá saban' *Tudom Musz Tajek* 1978 25(5) 224-30, refs.

Chelifiski R 'Information and documentation on social sciences in the Polish People's Republic' *Info Proc Manag* 1978 14(3/4) 267-72.

ROMANIA

1

Biblioteca Centrală de Stat a Republicii Socialiste România, Bucharest. 1955- .

Biblioteca Akademiei Republicii Socialiste România, Bucharest. 1867- . Legal deposit since 1885.

Mironescu N 'La bibliothèque de l'Académie de la République Socialiste de Roumanie' *Rev Roum Hist* 1969 6(1) 77-89.

'Biblioteca Academiei Republicii Socialiste România' *Probl Info Doc* 1979 13(2) 87-92.

Centrul de Documentare Stiintifică al Akademiei.

Institutul National de Informare şi Documentare Stiintifică şi Tehnică (INID). 1949- . Under the National Council for Science and Technology. Previously Institutul Central de Documentare Tehnica (IDT).

Centrul de Informare şi Documentare in Ştiinţele Sociale şi Politice, Bucharest.

2a

Consiliul Culturi şi Educatiei Socialiste.

2b

Asociaţia Bibliotecarilor din RSR, Bucharest. 1956- .

2c

Lázárescu G '[Documentary information science — a subject matter for learning]' *Studii Cerc Doc* 1970 12(4) 32(638), refs.

Taraboi V and Loucki C '[Achievement of the IDT in the training and improvement of documentary information specialists in the field of scientific and technical information]' *Probl Info Doc* 1972 6(1) 2-8.

Loucki C 'Stepping up efficiency of documentary information training' *Probl Info Doc* 1972 7(1) 5-27, refs.

See also Dima-Dragan C in *Biblos* below in 3f.

3a

Biblioteca Academiei RSR *Vocabular de Bibliologie* 1965, 179p. Useful appendices.

Moldoveanu V et al *Ghidul bibliotecilor din România* Editura Enciclopedică Română, 1970, 476p.

Biblioteca Centrală Universitară *Ghid de documentare al bibliotecilor universitare din România* 1970, 111p.

3b

Biblioteca Centrală *Bibliografia Republicii Socialiste România.* 1952- . Now in 10 series, the following three most relevant:

- *Bibliografia bibliografilor* (Series 5). Every two years.
- *Teze de doctorat* 1972- . Annual. Cumulations.

- *Articole din publicatii periodice şi în serie* 1953- .
- *Repertoriul bibliografilor nepublicate*. 1960- . Lists of unpublished bibliographies.
- *Buletin de informare in bibliologie*. 1965- .
- *Revista de referate i bibliogie*. 1965- . Quarterly.

Aleman V 'Considerati privind publicatiile de informare documentara din RSR' *Probl Info Doc* 1972 (11) 29-49.

INID *Bulletin analytique de la littérature scientifique et technique roumaine*. In English, French, Russian.

3c

Comitetual de Stat pentru Cultură şi Artă *Revista bibliotecilor* (Library review). 1948-1965 as *Călăuza bibliotecarului*. In 1974 it merged with:

Consiliul Culturi şi Educatiei Socialiste *Indrumattorul cultureal: revista lunara a Consiliului/Culturii şi Educatiei Socialiste*. 1948- .

Comitetul de Stat pentru Cultură şi Artă *Probleme de bibliologie*.

INID *Probleme de informare şi documentare*. 1967- . Contains a section of abstracts with English, French and Russian summaries.

University of Bucharest School of Librarianship *Studia bibliologica*. 1965- .

Centrul de Documentare al Akademiei *Studii şi cercetari de documentare şi bibliologie*. 1955- . 1955-63 as *Studii şi cercetări de bibliologie*.

Centrul de Informare şi Documentare in Ştiinţele Sociale şi Politice *M & SI: metodologia şi sociologia informaţiei*. 1974- .

New periodicals are listed in the national bibliography (series 4): *Publicatii periodice şi in series*.

3d

Directia Centrală de Statistica *Anuarul statistic al RSR*.

— *Breviarul statistic al RSR*.

3e

Biblioteca Centrala *Bibliografia RSR. Publicatii officiale*. 1970- .

3f

Tomescu M '[The book and the library in the Roumanian People's Republic]' *Probl Bibliol* 1963 5-25.

Harrison K C 'The library situation in Rumania' *Lib Ass Rec* 1972 74(10) 183-6.

Stoica I 'Citeva probleme actuale ale bibliotecomiei romanesti' *Probl Info Doc* 1972 (12) 39-49.

Dima-Drăgan C *Ex libris — bibliologie şi bibliofilie* Cometitul de Cultură şi Educatie Socialistă, 1973, 398p. Collected papers.

— 'Das rumänische Buch- und Bibliothekswesen' *Biblos* 1978 27(4) 350-73; 1979 28(1) 33-48; 1979 28(2) 119-32.

Moldeoveanu V 'Romania, libraries and documentation centres in' in *Encyclopedia* 26 (1979) 41-154.

Sonevend P 'Romániai konyvtárakról: adolékok egy tanulmányut nyomán' *Könyv Figyelö* 1975 21(3) 309-17. Study tour.

'[National conference of the directors of municipal and city libraries, December 1970]' *Rev Bibliot* 1971 24(3) 142-60.

Lebel G 'Trois bibliothèques bucarestoises: trois types de réalisations' *Bull Biblioth Fr* 1971 6 187-205.

Mihit A M 'Bibliotecile sindicatelor — biblioteci publice?' *Rev Bibliot* 1971 24(4) 216-8.

Valasoglu I 'Les bibliothèques de l'Université de Bucarest 1864-1964' *Rev Roum Hist* 1964 3(4) 747-54.
Stoica I 'The central university library, Bucharest: over 75 years in the history of a collection' *Unesco Bull Lib* 1972 26(2) 94-6.
— 'Relaţiişi limite in dezvoltarea complexelor biblioteconomice universitare' *Probl Info Doc* 1974 8(11/12) 578-88. Development of university centres.
— 'Principles governing the information activities of Romanian university libraries' *Unesco Bull Lib* 1975 29 271-5.
Mârza I 'Unfamiliar libraries: the Batthyaneum, Alba Julia' *Book Collector* 1975 24 558-64.
Oldson W O 'The research libraries of Romania' *Int Lib Rev* 1979 11(3) 373-85.
Studi şi cercetari de documentare şi bibliologie 1967 9(2/3) 414p. Special commemmorative issue on the library of the Academy of Sciences.
Avramesar A et al '[Documentary information research within the Scientific Documentation Centre of the Academy of the SRR]' *Studi Cerc Doc* 1971 13(3) 203-11, refs.
Dragulanescu D and Moldoveanu V *The history of documentation in Romania* [In Romanian] Bucharest, 1976.
Manea A 'Consideratii cu privire la organizarea informării documentare in instituele de cercetare' *Probl Info Doc* 1970 4(10) 555-72. Documentation in research institutes.
Crăcea P 'Methodological guiding in documentary information network' *Probl Info Doc* 1971 5(11) 67-80.
Adler E 'O anchetă a beneficiarilor privind necesitătile de informare' *Probl Info Doc* 1975 9(6) 328-47. Users' needs in the field of science and technology; role of INID.
Taraboi V 'Principles of the setting-up of a national scientific, technical and economic documentary information system' *Probl Info Doc* 1971 5(5) 5-46.
— *Organisation, functioning and activities of national documentary information systems in the scientific, technical and economic fields* INID, 1973, 90p. Editions in Romanian, English, French and Russian.
Ioanid M 'Information and documentation in the social sciences in the Socialist Republic of Romania' *Info Proc Manag* 1978 14(3/4) 267-73.

YUGOSLAVIA

1

Narodna Biblioteka Socijalističke Republike Srbije, Belgrade. 1832- .

Zivanov M 'Istorijski razvoj Narodne Biblioteke Srbije' *Narodna Biblioteka Srbije Godišujak* 1978 43-60.

Narodna Biblioteka. Jugoslovenski Bibliografski. Institut. 1949- .

Bacé M 'The Yugoslav Bibliographical Institute' *Unesco Bull Lib* 1959 13(10) 228-30.

Nacionalna i Sveučilišna Biblioteka, Zagreb. 1776- . Deposit for Croation material.

Rojnič M *Nacionalnai Sveučilišna Biblioteka* Zagreb, Hrvatsko Bibliotekarsko Društvo, 1974.

—'Die national- und Universitätsbibliothek in Zagreb', *Biblos* 1977 26(4) 401-19.

Narodna in Univerzitetna Knjižnica, Ljubljana. 1774- . Slovene material.

Cveljo K 'Special librarianship in Yugoslavia: the central Technical Library at the University of Ljubljana' *Spec Lib* 1979 70 239-48.

Every republic and autonomous province of the federation has its deposit library.

Slovenska Akademija Znanosti in Umetnosti (Slovene Academy of Arts and Sciences), Ljubljana.

Klanencic M *Biblioteka in publikavije Slovenske Akademije Znanosti in Umetnosti v latin 1952-1971* The Academy, 1973, 298p.

Academy of Sciences and Arts in Zagreb.

Jakič T 'Die Bibliothek der Jugoslawischen Akademie der Wissenschaften und Künste in Zagreb' *Biblos* 1977 26(4) 420-31.

Centre for the Study of Librarianship, Documentation and Information Science (Zagreb University). 1964- .

Jugoslovenski Centar za Tehničku i Naučnu Dokumentaciju (JCTND), Belgrade. 1952- . Has a science policy research unit.

2a

Sekretariat za Kulturu. In every state.

2b

Savez Drustava Bibliotekara Jugoslavije (Federation of Library Associations in Yugoslavia), Belgrade. 1949- .

2c

Bromberg E 'Education for experts in information in Yugoslavia' *Spec Lib* 1965 56(6) 375-8.

Hanž B 'Yugoslavia: library education in Yugoslavia' *Int Lib Rev* 1971 3(1) 113-20.

Cveljo K 'A recent development in library education in Yugoslavia' *J Educ Libp* 1977 18(1) 53-62. First graduate course in Sarajevo University, 1972- .

Mikačič M 'Die Fachausbildung der Bibliothekare in Kroatien' *Biblios* 1977 26(4) 393-400.

Vidovič D 'Sadrzaj i glavni pravci istrazivackog radu u podrucju bibliotekarstva/informacije' *Bibliotekar* (Belgrade) 1976 28(5) 557-61. Main trends in research, seen through the literature.

Jankovic M 'Sistematsko merenje delatnosti i razvoja javnih biblioteka' *Bibliotekar* 1971 23(2) 179-88. Method for staff evaluation.

3a

Enciklopedija Jugoslavije 1955- .

Central Office of Information Belgrade *Informativni priručnick o Jugoslaviji.* 1948- . Quarterly.

Rječnik *Bibliotekarskih stručnih izraza/Vocabularium Bibliothecarii* Zagreb, Izdavačko Produzece Skolska Knijiga 1965, 184p. English/Croatian-Serbian edition.

Janovič S and Rojnič M comps *A guide to Yugoslav libraries and archives* American Association for the Advancement of Slavic Studies, 1975, 113p.

Stipcevic A *Libraries in Croatia* Zagreb, Croation Library Association, 1975.

Vodnič po dokumentacijskih in informativnih službah SRS Ljubljana, Svera Inzenirjev in Tehnikov SRS, Sekcija Dokumentacija, 1964, 61p.

Vodič kroz naučne i stručne biblioteke u Bosni i Hercegovini Sarajevo, Narodna Biblioteka SRBIH, 1970, 86p.

3b

Bibliographical Institute *Bibliografija Jugoslavije, knige, brošure i muzikalije.* 1950- .

— *Jugoslavenska retrospektivna bibliografska gradja-knige, brošure i musikalije, 1945-1967.* 21 volumes.

— *Bibliografija Jugoslavenske periodike.* 1956- . Quarterly.

— *Bibliografija Jugoslavije, članci i prilozi.* In three subject sections. Periodical articles.

University Library, Belgrade *Popis rukopisnih doktorskih disertacija.* 1970- . Bibliography of unpublished theses.

Zagreb, Council of the Academies of Sciences and Arts *Scientific bulletin/Bulletin Scientifique.* Section B: *The Humanities/Les Sciences humaines* includes library science. Selection of abstracts published in English and French since 1965.

Lazic K 'Les données bibliographiques sur la bibliothéconomie en Serbie de 1848 à 1944' *Bibliotekar* 1963 15 285-312.

Jovanovic B *A classified index of Yugoslav library periodicals published in Serbo-Croatian, 1959-1965* Catholic U of America, 1965, Thesis.

'Jugoslovenska bibliotekarska bibliografija' Section in *Bibliotekar* 1961- .

Cveljo K 'Libraries and education for librarianship in Yugoslavia: a bibliographical overview' *Int Lib Rev* 1977 9(3) 319-50.

JCTND *Bilten dokumentacije* (Bulletin of Documentation). In 23 series.

3c

Mesiček M 'Une contribution à l'étude des périodiques de bibliothéconomie en Yougoslavie' *Vjesnik Bibliot Hrvatske* 1962 8 145-53.

Crvcanin M 'Bibliotekarski časopisi Jugoslavije (1948-1971)' *Bibliotekarstvo* 1973 19(3) 17-39.

Društvo Bibliotekara Srbije *Bibliotekar* Belgrade. 1948- .

Društvo Bibliotekara Bosne i Hercegovine *Bibliotekarstvo.* 1955- .

Društvo Bibliotekajev Slovenije *Knjižnica.* 1957- .
Društvo Bibliotekara Hrvatske *Vjesnik Bibliotekara Hrvatske.* 1968- .
JCTND *Informatika.* 1955- .
Zagreb Referalni Centar *Informatologia Jugoslavica.* 1969- .

3d

Savezni Zavod za Statistiku *Statistički godisnjak.*

3e

Bibliographical Institute *Bibliografija zvanicnih publikacija* 1971- . Annual list of official publications.

Mudri-Skunca V 'No zakon o bibliotecnoj djelatnosti i bibliotekama' *Vjesnik Bibliot Hrvatske* 1973 19 1-6.

3f

Galič P *Povijest Zadarskih knižnica* Društvo Bibliotekara Hrvatske, 1969, 143p. With an Italian summary. History of libraries in Zadar (Dalmatia).

Basovic L 'A brief survey of libraries and librarianship in postwar Bosnia and Hercegovina' *J Lib Hist* 1978 13(1) 1-10.

Bachaldin B 'Sem'dnei v Yugoslavii' *Bibliotekar* (Moscow) 1970 (8) 54-8. Study tour.

Brochard C 'Bibliothèques de Belgrade. Rapport d'un voyage d'étude, 15-23 décembre 1969' *Ass Biblioth Fr Bull Info* 1970 (67) 101-10.

Papič M 'Das Bibliotheksnetz und die organization des Bibliotheken in der SFR Jugoslaven' *Zentbl Biblioth* 1966 80(2) 66-71.

'Sonderheft Kroatien' — 1 Teil: *Biblos* 1977 26(4) 343-431, refs; 2 Teil: *Biblos* 1978 27(1) 1-48.

'Sonderheft Slowerien' 1Teil: *Biblos* 1975 24(3) 173-224; 2 Teil: *Biblos* 1975 24(4) 275-310.

Tafuri di Melignano M T 'Biblioteche in Montenegro: a Cettigne' *Accad Bibliot Ital* 1977 45 333-43.

Mudri-Skunca V 'Zagrebake javne kniznice u procesu integracije' *Vjesnnik Bibliot Hrvatske* 1970 16(3/4) 131-48.

— 'La bibliothèque ouvrière de Zagreb: matériaux pour son historique' *Bull Sci Sect B* 1967 13 83.

[Conference: The worker as reader] *Bibliotekar* 1973 25(3/4) 237-318.

Alkorva-Balagovic S 'Zagrebin kirjastoauto' *Kirjastolehti* 1977 70(3) 126-7. Bookmobile.

Jugovic M *Children and school libraries in the Federal People's Republic of Yugoslavia* U of Chicago, 1967, Thesis.

Kasapinovič S 'Saradnja dečje biblioteke i škole' *Bibliotekar* 1971 23(3) 371-6. Cooperation between children's and school libraries.

Zagrbu S V 'School libraries in Yugoslavia' *Int Lib Rev* 1978 10(4) 368-9.

Vasijevič M 'Stanje i perspektive hasih vojvih biblioteka' *Bibliotekar* 1970 22(4) 327-32. Military libraries.

Pruett L 'Music research in Yugoslavia' *Notes* 1979 36(1) 23-49. Visit to music libraries.

Grothusen K D *Die Entwicklung der wissenschaftlichen Bibliotheken Jugoslawiens seit 1945* Cologne, Greven Verlag, 1958, 176p.

Gašpersič Z and Dernuluc V 'De l'état de certaines bibliothèques techniques spécialisées de Lubliana dans les années 1965 et 1966' *Knjižnica* 1966 10 42-6.

Slajpah M 'Education of students as users of scientific and technical information in Yugoslavia' Paper in *Developing library effectiveness for the next decade* —

IATUL Conference, Louvain, 1977 IATUL, 1978, 181-5.

Živkovic B 'Uniform library information system in Yugoslavia' *Int Lib Rev* 1979 11(3) 367-71.

Pantič V 'System of social science information in Yugoslavia' *Info Proc Manag* 1978 14(3/4) 311-3.

Tell S V *Plan for a Yugoslav scientific-technical information network: Yugoslavia (Mission) December 1972* Unesco, 1973, 42p.

Wesley-Tanaskovič I 'An information system for science and technology in Yugoslavia' *Unesco Bull Lib* 1975 29(6) 327-30.

UNION OF SOVIET SOCIALIST REPUBLICS

(Soiuz Sovetskikh Sotsialisticheskikh Respublik). The former Russia now is Rossiiskaia Sovetskaia Federativnaia Sotsialisticheskaia Respublika (RSFSR). Most of the All-Union institutions have their headquarters in this 'Federal' state.

1

A number of libraries have all or some of the functions of a national library within their area of interest.

- Gosudarstvannaia ordena Biblioteka SSSR im V I Lenina (Lenin Library). Created in 1862 it received its present name in 1925. It has received the order of Lenin.

Istorija Gosudarstvenoj ordena Lenina Biblioteki SSSR imeni V I Lenina za 100 let, 1862-1962 Lenin Library, 1972.

Nabatova M B 'Inostrannaya pechat' o biblioteke imeni Lenina i ee izdaniyakh' *Bibliot Bibliog za Rubezhom* 1975 (53) 64-90. Foreign press reports on the Lenin Library.

Khrenkova A 'Glavnaya v strane: 50 let s imeni Lenina' *Bibliotekar* 1975 (1) 48-55.

Kartashov N 'Rol' natsional'noi biblioteki v merzhvedomstvennoi koordinatsii' *Bibliotekar* 1980 (1) 39-41. Coordination of readers' services in all types of libraries, etc.

Based on the Lenin Library is the:

- Nauchno-metodicheskij Otdel Bibliotekovedniia i Bibliografij 1950- . Reorganized in 1959 as a separate institute. Research in methods and techniques applicable to Soviet librarianship. Publishes reading lists, conference papers, etc.

Osipowa L P 'Dzialalnose Nauchowo-badawcza paustwowej biblioteki ZSRR im V I Lenina' *Bibliotekarz* 1970 37(9) 267-77. Research activities.

Ratnikova E J 'Experiment po prognozirovenyn v gosudarstvennoy biblioteke SSSR im V I Lenina' *Bibliot SSSR* 1972 (53) 46-52.

Nazmutoinov I 'Biblioteka imeni V I Lenina obshchesoyuzny Nauchno-metodicheskii tsentr' *Bibliotekar* 1974 (11) 28-33.

- Vsesoiuznaia Gosudarstvennaia Biblioteka Inostrannoi Literatury Moscow. 1921- . All-Union State Library of Foreign Literature. Acquires and exchanges foreign materials, publishes indexes, etc.

Peleh E B 'Az Össz-szövetségi állami idegen njelvii könyvtár (Moszkva) olvasószolgálati tapasztalataibó' *Konyv Figyelö* 1980 26(1) 77-83.

Kuhtarina I P 'Reference services in the All-Union State Library of Foreign Literature USSR (VGBIL)' *Unesco J* 1980 2(1) 42-9.

- Gosudarstvennaia Publičnaia Naučno-Tehničeskaia Biblioteka SSSR, Moscow. 1958- . State Public Scientific and Technical Library. (GNPTB). Deals with science and technology. Research in librarianship, automation and mechanization of processes; methodological centre for science libraries.

Lebel G 'La bibliothèque publique Scientifique et Technique d'Etat de l'USSR à Moscou' *Bull Biblioth Fr* 1972 17(5) 227-40.

- Gosudarstvennaia ordena Trudovogo Znameni Publičnaia Biblioteka im M E Saltykova-Shchedrina, Leningrad. 1932- . Leningrad public library.
- Akademiia Nauk SSSR. Has a chain of branches and libraries.

Varfolomeeva M V 'The libraries of the USSR Academy of Sciences over the past sixty years' *Unesco Bull Lib* 31(6) 360-71.

—'Tsentralizatsiia v sisteme akademicheskikh bibliotek' *Sov Bibliog* 1977 (1) 94-102.

The academy also fulfills some information functions through some of its departments:

- Nauchnoj Informacii i Fundamental'naja Biblioteka po Obshshestvennym Naukam, Moscow. 1918- . Institute of information and central library for the social sciences.
- Vsesojuznij Institut Naučno-Tehničeskoj Informacij (VINITI), Moscow, 1952- . All-Union Institute of Scientific and Technological Information. Set up by the Council of Ministers on Science and Technology. Research and publication of abstracts (See under 3b).

Fomin A A *Vsesojuznij Institut Naučnoj i Tehniceskoj Informacii i ego dejatel'nost* VINITI, 1968, 61p. Activities of the institute.

Chernyi A I 'VINITI: science information activities over twenty-five years' *Int Forum Info Doc* 1977 2(4) 3-9.

Finally an important library for Soviet studies outside the USSR:

- Helsinki University Library.

'Largest Russian collection outside USSR: the Helsinki University Library' *Herald Lib Sci* 1977 16 445-6.

NB: For broader references about some of the above institutions see under 3f.

2a

Ministry of Culture. USSR Library Council, Moscow.

Efimova A N 'Library Council of the USSR. Ministry of Culture' *Unesco Bull Lib* 1976 30 240-1.

Ministry of Higher Education.

Gosudarstvennogo Komiteta pri Sovete Ministrov SSSR po Nauke i Tehnike. State Committee of the Council of Ministers on Science and Technology.

Vsesoiuznaia Knizhnaia Palata. Created in 1920 and renamed in 1931. Coordinates bibliographical activities and acts as publisher.

Fartunin I I '60 let Vsesoiuznoi Knizhnoi Palate — tsentru gosudarstvennoi bibliografii' *Sov Bibliog* 1977 (5) 6-13.

2b

Trade Union of Cultural Enlightenment Workers. Since 1957 a library section groups librarians. Membership mandatory.

2c

Gastfer M P 'The training of Soviet librarians' *Unesco Bull Lib* 1967 21(6) 327-33.

Serov V V 'Library science and some problems of library education in the USSR' *Libri* 1969 19 175-90.

Lebedeva N F and Bykova N P 'Advanced training of librarians in the USSR' *Unesco Bull Lib* 1971 25(6) 338-43.

Zazersky E J 'System of librarians training in the USSR' *Int Lib Rev* 1974 6 219-29.

Davinson D 'Library education in USSR' *New Lib World* 1975 76(906) 255-7.

Publichnaia Biblioteka (Moscow) *Problemy sovershenstvovaniia vyshego bibliotechnogo obrazovaniia no sobremennom etape obzornaia informatsiia* The

Library, 1975, 43p. Problems of improving higher education for librarianship: review of the literature.
Mankevich A I A and Shekhurin D E 'Problemy podrotovki kadrov dlya spetsial 'nykh bibliotek informatsionnykh sluzhb' *Nauch-Tekh Info*, Ser 1 1974 (10) 3-9. Translated in *Sci Tech Info Process* 1974 (4) 1-9. Problems of training for special librarians in the information services.
Burova N 'Universitet dlya spetsialistov' *Bibliotekar* 1979 (2) 49-50. Course for special librarians at the: Universitet Bibliotechno-bibliograficheskikh Znanii (ULBK), Novosibirsk.
Arutjunov N B 'Training and refresher courses for information specialists in the USSR' *Unesco Bull Lib* 1974 28 29-33.
Belyakov L 'Problemy zaochnogo obrazovaniya' *Bibliotekar* 1976 (8) 45-8.
Chernyshev L 'Issledovaniyam-novoe kachestvo' *Bibliotekar* 1972 (1) 49-52. New approach to library research.
Dressler I *N K Krupskaja und die bibliothekarische Beruf* Berlin, Zentralinstitut für Bibliothekswesen, 1975, 62p. Krupskaia and the library profession.
Fioux L 'L'image de la bibliothèque et du bibliothécaire en URSS dans la revue professionnelle *Bibliotekar*' *Médiathèques Publ* 1977 (44) 5-30, refs; 1978 (45) 7-36, refs.

3a

Yelizarenkova T P ed *Russkoangliskii slovar knigoredcheskikh terminov/Russian-English bookman's dictionary* Moscow, 1969.
Zhdanova G S et al *Russko-anglo-frantzuskii terminologicheskii slovar po informatsionnoi theorii i praktike* Nauka, 1968, 240p.
Walker G P M *Russian for librarians* 2nd ed Bingley, 1983, c128p.
Arsenov S T et al *Terminologicheskii slovar po informatika* Mezhdurarodnyi Tsentr Nauchnoi i Tekhnicheskoi Informatsii, 1975, 752p.
Bol'shaia Sovetskaia Entsiklopediia 3rd ed Izd'vo 'Sovetskaia Entsiklopediia', 1970- . 30 volumes.
Great Soviet Encyclopedia (Translation of the above) Macmillan/Collier Macmillan, 1973- . 30 vols. General but useful for USSR.
Evaluation of the encyclopedia in:
Wilson Lib Bull 1975 49(10) 728-40. Reply from Macmillan in *Ibid* 1976 50(1) 20-1.
The Far East and Australasia Europa Yearbooks. Includes: The USSR in Asia.
Annuaire de l'USSR. Droit, économie, sociologie, politique, culture Paris, CNRS.
Biblioteki SSR obshchestvenno-politicheskogo filoliskusstvoved cheskogo profil-ja. Spravodnik Kniga, 1979, 343p. By subjects, with socio-political profiles.
See also guides to individual libraries.

3b

Tysakevich N F 'Problems of Universal Bibliographic Control and present trends in research in the USSR State Public Library for Science and Technology' *Inspel* 1974 9(1/2) 45-52.
Kartashov N S 'Aktualne voprosy bibliograficheskoi deyatel' nosti Gosudarstvennoi Biblioteki SSSR im. V I Lenina' *Sovet Bibliog* 1979 (5) 3-10.
Golovanova L G 'Tsentr Rekomendatel'noi Bibliografii' *Sovet Bibliog* 1975 (149) 11-23. Prepares recommended bibliographies for public and related libraries. Based on the Lenin Library.
Thompson A *Russia/USSR: a selected, annotated bibliography of books in English* Clio P, 1979, 289p.

Library of Congress *Monthly list of Russian accessions*. 1948-1969. In Dewey order.

Mashkova M V *Istoriia russkoi bibliografii nachala XX veka (do oktobria 1917 gada)* Kniga, 1969. Beginning of the 20th century — to 1917.

Fonotov G B '60 let sovetskoi Bibliografii: osnovnye itogi i zadachi' *Sovet Bibliog* 1977 (4) 3-11.

Maichel K *Guide to Russian reference books* Hoover Institution 1962- .

Nagel-Arbatskii K S 'Vypusk bibliograficheskikh posobii v SSSR 1967-1975' *Sovet Bibliog* 1977 (4) 27-9. Survey of bibliographical tools published in USSR.

All-Union Book Chamber *Bibliografija sovetskoj bibliografii.* Annual.

Vladimirov L 'Soviet centralized bibliography: its strength and weakness' *Coll Res Lib* 1966 27 185-90.

Gosudarstvennaia bibliografiia SSSR. Spravodnik 2nd ed Kniga, 1967, 112p. Guide to USSR bibliographies.

Whitby T J and Lorkovic T *Introduction to Soviet national bibliography* Libraries Unlimited, 1979, 229p. Includes a translation of the above work.

All-Union Book Chamber *Knizhnaia letopis*. 1907- . Weekly with a monthly section for official publications. Annual index as:

Ezhegodnik knigi SSSR (USSR Book Annual).

Letopis zhurnalnych statei. 1927- . Index of periodical articles.

Beletskaia Z G 'Letopis zhurnal'nykh statei 'na sovremennom etape: k 50-letilu so dnia osnovanila' *Sovet Bibliog* 1976 (5) 3-8. On the periodical index and its 50th anniversary.

VINITI *Referativnye Zhurnaly*. 1960- . Abstracts on all subjects, currently in 184 sections.

Periodicheskaia pechat SSSR 1917-1949: bibliograficheskii ukazatej 1955-58, 10 vols. (Vol. 9 is about librarianship and related subjects).

Bibliograficheskaia rabota oblastnoi biblioteki, prakticheskoe posobie Kniga, 1967, 244p. Bibliographical work in regional libraries. They publish in particular bibliographies related to their own states.

Yoo Y comp *Soviet education: an annotated bibliography and readers' guide to work in English, 1893-1978* Greenwood P, 1980, 408p.

For sources on the history of librarianship see under 3f:

Abramov K I *Istoriia biblioteknogo delo v SSSR*.

Nabotova M B 'Sovremennoye sostoyanie i perspektivi razvitya informatsii v Oblasti bibliotekovedenniia i bibliografovedenniia' *Sovet Bibliog* 1972 (133) 3-19. Analysis of sources for research on librarianship and bibliography.

Aav Y *Russian bibliographies* Helsinki U Library, 1970. (Biblioteca Slavica, 7). Bibliographies and books on librarianship in cyrillic characters.

Simmons J S G *Russian bibliography, libraries and archives: a selective list of bibliographical references* Anthony C Hall, 1973, 76p.

Deutsche Staatbibliothek *Sowetisches Bibliotheks- und Buchwesen. Bibliographie 1945-1972* The Library, 1975, 293p. Russian sources.

Lenin Library *Bibliotekovedenie i bibliografiia. Ukazatel sovetskoj literaturi* 1955- . Since 1967 deals only with USSR material. Another series deals with foreign libraries and material.

All-Union Book Chamber *Sovetskaia bibliografiia. Sbornik statei i materialov* 1933- . History, practice and development of librarianship and bibliography.

Rubrikator osnovnyh informacionyh izdanij SSSR VINITI, 1974.

VINITI *Nauchno-tekhnicheskaia informaciia.* 1963- . One of the series of the *Referativnye Zhurnaly*. Since 1967 in two sections: 'Organisation and method' (Organizatsiia i metodika) and 'Processing and information'. For comment on the service see:

Fokin S J 'Nauczno-techniczeskaia Informacja — rola i zadania pisma w rozwoju informacji' *Aktual Probl Info Dok* 1978 23(5) 23-6.

Scientific and technical information processing, New York. 1974- . English translation of material from Russian sources in the NTI Section 1.

VINITI *Ekspress-Informacija — Teoriia i praktika nauchnoi- informacii* 1965- .

3c

All-Union Book Chamber *Letopis periodicheskikh izdanij SSSR*. Every five years. Series 1 deals with periodicals. Annual amendments and additions in the main national bibliography.

RSFSR Ministry of Culture *Bibliotekar.* 1923- . Not published during 1942-45. 1923-41 as *Krasnyi Bibliotekar.*

Lenin Library *Sovetskoje Bibliotekovedenije.* 1973- . Supersedes: *Biblioteki SSSR* 1949-72.

State Public Library for Science and Technology *Technicheskie Biblioteki SSSR.* 1961-68. The, 1969- : *Nauchnye i technicheskie Biblioteki SSSR.*

Akademiia Nauk. Biblioteka *Bibliotechno-bibliograficheskaia Informaciia.* 1951- .

For journals of a broader scope, see in: Eastern Europe, 3c.

3d

Centralnoe Statisticheskoe Upravlenie *Kulturnoe stroitelstvo SSSR: Statisticheskii sbornik.*

— : *Statisticheskii ezhegodnik.*

— : *Dostzheniia sovetskoi vlasti za 40 let v tsifrakh.* 1957.

Poluboyarinov M M 'Statistika kulturi i sovershenstovanie bibliotechnogo dyela' *Biblioteki SSSR* 1972 (53) 34-45. Study of developments based on statistical returns.

In'kova L M 'Smotr nauchnykh sil Rossii' *Sovet Bibliot* 1977 (6) 45-54. Library resources.

3e

Rogers A R 'Censorship and libraries in the Soviet Union' *J Lib Hist* 1973 8(1) 22-9, refs.

Moody C 'Book censorship in the Soviet Union' *South Afr Lib* 1974 41(4) 163-71.

'Nash osnovnoi zakon' *Bibliotekar* 1977 (10) 4-5. Fundamental law.

'Model statutes for information services in the USSR' *Unesco Bull Lib* 1971 25(2) 94-101.

Serov V V ed *Rukovodiashshie materialy po bibliotechnomu delu: pravodnik* Kniga, 1975, 224p. Directives on library affairs.

Novoselov V I 'Voprosy bibliotechnogo zakonodatel'stva' *Sovet Bibliot* 1979(6) 34-45, refs. Need for revision of regulations in libraries.

Haritonov R P 'Standardization of the principal processes in scientific and technical information and librarianship in the USSR' *Unesco Bull Lib* 1971 25(5) 260-2, 266.

3f

Cohen S F et al *The Soviet Union since Stalin* Macmillan/Indiana U P, 1980, 342p.

Zvorykin A A *Cultural policy in USSR* Unesco, 1970, 68p.

Hotimsky C M *The acquisition of Russian books* Bingley, 1974, 37p. Publishing, exchanges, sources for selection.

 Puzikov A L et al *Kniga v SSSR* Tskusstvo, 1975.

Walker G *Soviet book publishing policy* CUP, 1978, 164p.
'Russia — USSR,' book printing and libraries' in *Encyclopedia* 26 (1979) 180-245, bibliography of Russian sources.
Horecky P L *Libraries and bibliographic centres in the Soviet Union* Indiana U P, 1959, 287p.
Ruggles M J and Swank R C *Soviet libraries and librarianship. Report of the visit* . . . ALA, 1962, 147p. With a bibliography by P L Horecky.
Francis S *Libraries in the USSR* Bingley/Linnet Books, 1971, 182p. Translation from *Biblioteki SSSR*, 1967.
Bibliotekovedenie, bibliografiia i informatika: tematicheskii sbornik trudov, vyp 1 Moskovskii Gosudarstvennyi Institut Kultury 1974 194p. Collected works.
Greguletz A 'Bibliotheksgeschichte in der UdSSR' *Zentrbl Biblioth* 1977 91 353-62, 397-405, 471-80.
Slukhovskii M I *Bibliotechnoe delo v Rossii do XVIII veka* Kniga, 1968, 231p.
'50 let SSSR: sovetskaya mnogonatsionalnaya' *Bibliotekar* 1972 (12) 2-58. Fifty years development of a multinational country.
Chandler G *Libraries, documentation and bibliography in the USSR 1917-1971: survey and critical analysis of Soviet studies 1967-1971* Souvenir P, 1972, 183p.
'[Libraries and library science since 1917]' *Bibliothekar* 1977 31(10). Whole issue.
Dergacheva L D 'God za godom; kratkaia khronika sobytii bibliotechnogo dela v SSSR [1917-1941]' *Sovet Bibliot* 1977 (4) 43-52.
Vaks I A — [1941-1973] *Sovet Bibliot* 1977 (5) 68-85.
— [1974-1977] *Sovet Bibliot* 1977 (6) 104-9. Brief chronology.
Abramov K I *Bibliotechnoe stroitel'stvo v pervye gody sovetskoi viasti: 1917-1920gg* Kniga, 1974, 264p.
Davidova L I and Krasovitskaya T Yu 'Arkhivnye documenty po istorii bibliothechnogo dela (1917-1920)' *Sovet Bibliot* 1976 (5) 69-81.
Istoriia bibliotechnogo dela v SSSR: dokumenty i materialy 1918-1920gg Kniga, 1975, 297p.
- : *Sbornik nauchykh trudov, vyp 1* Kniga, 1975, 69p. *Vyp 2* Kniga, 1976, 96p.
Poluboyarinov M M 'Bibliotechnoe delo v 1960-1972gg: nekotorye tsifry, itogi' *Sovet Bibliot* 1974 (5) 34-41.
Annual feature prepared by the Lenin Library and published by Kniga. Keeps up this survey of developments, under the title: 'Bibliotechovedenie v . . . (year): obzor literatury'.
Serov V V Novyi etap bibliotechnogo stroitel'stva v SSSR Kniga, 1975, 48p. New stage of development.
— 'A new stage in library development in the USSR' *Unesco Bull Lib* 1976 30(1) 37-45.
Simsova S *Lenin, Krupskaia and libraries* Bingley/Linnet Books, 1968, 73p.
Fonotov G P 'Lenin and libraries' *Unesco Bull Lib* 1970 24(3) 118-25.
Lenin i sovremmenye problemy bibliotekovedenija Kniga, 1971.
Abramov K I 'Der leninsche Plan der Bibliotheksentwicklung und seine Verwiklichung in der UdSSR' *Zentrbl Biblioth* 1977 91 461-7.
Raymond B *Krupskaia and Soviet Russian librarianship, 1917-1939* Scarecrow, 1979 223p.
Suput R *The contribution of E I Shamurin to Soviet librarianship* Case Western Reserve U, School of Librarianship. Thesis.
Pahin A I 'Rukovodiashchaia rol' Kommunisticheskoi Partii v razvitii bibliotechnogo dela' *Sov Bibliot* 1977 (6) 14-27. Role of the communist party in the development of libraries.
Zaicev V 'Bibliotheken in der entwickelten sozialistischen Gesellschaft'

Bibliothekar 1977 31 651-9. Libraries in a developed socialist country.

'O významu úlohy knihoven w komunistické výchově pracujíeich a vědeckotechnickém pokroku' *Čtenář* 1974 26(10) 294-6.

Kanevskii B 'Na sluzhbe mira i sotsialnogo progressa' *Bibliotekar* 1977 (1) 4-8.

Nazmutdinov I K 'Libraries of the USSR's one hundred nationalities' *Unesco Bull Lib* 1972 26(6) 307-14.

Chubaryan O S 'La science des bibliothèques en URSS' *Bull Bibl Fr* 1972 17(11) 469-81, refs.

— 'Development of the Soviet library system' *Indian Libn* 1972 27(3) 133-45.

Miller L H 'Aspects of libraries in the Soviet Union' *Lib Trends* 1973 22(3). Whole issue.

'U istokov tsentralizatsii i obrazovenie i deiatel 'nost' Tsentral'noi Bibliotechnoi Komissii 1920-1922gg' *Sov Bibliot* 1977 (4) 3-12. Centralization organized by the Central Library Committee.

Sikorskii N M 'Sovetskoe bibliotekovedenie: osnovnÿe napravleniya razvitiya, neotlozhnÿe zadachi' *Sov Bibliot* 1978 (2) 3-23, refs.

Frumin I 'Bibliotechovedenie: ob'ekt, predmet, funksii' *Bibliotekar* 1977 (2) 64-8.

Harris G ed *Four studies in Soviet librarianship* [Papers presented at the Library Association International and Comparative Librarianship Group Conference: 'Books and Libraries in the USSR', Bodleian Library, 24 September 1976]. The Group, 1977, 67p. (Occasional papers, 3).

Delougaz N P et al 'Libraries and information services in the USSR' *Spec Lib* 1977 68(7/8) 252-65. Study tour.

[Franco-Soviet Seminar, 1976] (In Russian) *Bibliot Bibliog za Rubezhom* 1977 65 5-42.

The First Soviet-American Seminar: a summary ERIC, 1979, 57p. (ERIC Report ED-176 723).

'Anglo-Soviet Conference on Library Co-operation' *Interlend Rev* 1979 7(2) 52-6, Suppl: 6 microfiches.

Grichanov Y A 'Zu Problemen der Schaffung eines Systems von Depositbibliotheken in der UdSSR' *Zentrbl Biblioth* 1974 88(10) 619-31.

Samokhina N 'Mezhbibliotechnyi abonment v SSSR na sovremennom etape' *Sov Bibliot* 1977 (5) 38-50. Interlibrary loans.

Biblioteki SSSR 1972 (54) 22-34, 35-53, refs. Experiments with recommended bibliographies at the Lenin Library.

Dobrynina N E and Stelmah V D 'Reseach on reading and readers' interests in the USSR' *Unesco Bull Lib* 1973 27(3) 160-6, 183.

Zhabistskaia L K 'Psikhologicheskie mekhanismy vospriyatia khudozhestvennoi literatury' *Sovet Bibliot* 1973 (1) 53-61. Research on readers' comprehension.

Cook G 'Civic criticism and public libraries in early nineteenth century Russia: interplay or isolation?' *J Lib Hist* 1977 12(1) 27-41.

Vasilenko V I 'Distributing centres for libraries in the USSR' *Unesco Bull Lib* 1966 20(3) 136-9.

Isayev Y V and Sirotkina E I 'Einige Probleme der Organisation eines Büchereinetzes inder Sowjetunion' *Bibliotheksdienst. Beiheft* 1971 (66) 21-8.

Obrosov J P and Pachshenko F N *Massokye biblioteki v gorodakh: struktura seti, pomeshchenija i izdanija* Izd. Literatury po Stroitel'stvy, 1973, 174p.

Varfolomeeva M V *Rol' massovyh bibliotek v kulturnoj revoljucii v SSSR (1928-1942gg)* Nauka, 1974, 231p.

Spiegel H *Die Entwicklung der Sowjetischen Massenbibliotheken unter besonderer Berücksichtigung der Neuordnung und Zentralisierung ihres Netzes* Berlin, Zentralinstitut für Bibliothekswesen, 1974, 135p. Development of

public libraries and reorganization of their network.

Belen'kii I 'Literatura o problemakh mezhvedomstvennoi tsentralizatsii massovykh bibliotek' *Bibliotekar* 1980 (4) 43-5.

Spiegel A 'Zentralisierung im ländlichen Bibliothekswesen der Sowjetunion' *Bibliothekar* 1980 34(4) 159-61, refs.

Lenin Library *V Pomoshch massovym bibliotekam* Kniga, 1976, 87p. In support of public libraries collections.

Fenelonov E A 'Libraries in rural areas in the USSR' *Unesco Bull Lib* 1972 26(1) 13-7.

'[Rural libraries]' *Bibliotekar* 1973 (3) 2-38. Series of papers on the subject.

Ponomareva E S 'Library services for the peoples of the Far North of the USSR' *Unesco J* 1979 15 252-5.

Misserey J 'Bibliothèques d'Asie centrale soviétique' *Lecture Biblioth* 1976 (39/40) 5-11.

Shapishnikov A 'I govoryashchie knigi i 'brail', i diapozitivy' *Bibliotekar* 1976 (8) 65-9. Provision of books in Braille and of 'talking' books.

Nefedchenko M 'Hospital libraries in the USSR' *Unesco Bull Lib* 1970 24(5) 248-50, 283.

Efebovskii I V 'V pomoshch' obucheniyu i vospitoniyu sovetskikh voinov' *Sovet Bibliog* 1976 (160) 14-21. Use of recommended bibliographies for the education of the armed forces.

Medvedeva N 'Scientific research on children's reading and library work with children' *Unesco Bull Lib* 1972 26(4) 203-9.

Miller E C *Reading guidance in Soviet children's libraries* Birmingham Polytechnic, n.d., 30p.

'Bibliotheksarbeit mit Kindern in der UdSSR' *Bibliotheksdienst. Beiheft* 1971 (65) 36p.

Ganickaia I 'Das System der Bibliothekarischen Betruung der Kinder bis zu 14 Jahren in der UdSSR' *Bibliothekar* 1977 31 660-6.

Gitter N M and Isaev Yu V 'Organizatsiya bibliotechnogo obsluzhivaniya yunoshestvannoi sistemy' *Sovet Bibliot* 1979 (6) 71-9. Special services for teenagers.

Pozdnjakova G I 'Ideologische und pädagogische Probleme der bibliothekarischen Betreuung der Kinder in der sowjetischen Bibliothekswissenschaft' *Bibliothekar* 1980 34(3) 102-8.

Seuberlich W 'Die Universitätsbibliotheken der Sowjetunion, insbesondere die Universitätsbibliotheken Moskau und Leningrad' *Z Biblioth Bibliog* 1962 9(2) 155-71.

Vladimirov L 'The accomplishment of university libraries in the Soviet Union' *Lib Trends* 1964 9(2) 155-71.

Thirion G 'Aperçu sur l'enseignement supérieur et ses bibliothèques en URSS' *Ass Biblioth Fr Bull Info* 1976 (93) 213-23.

Libe V and Lisauskene M 'Kompleksnoe planirovanie idelnoevospitatel'noi raboty' *Bibliotekar* 1976 (8) 22-6. Complex planning for ideological education.

Karatygina T F 'Coordination and cooperation of special libraries in the USSR' *Inspel* 1977 12(1) 39-48.

Balatova E 'Dlya masterov stsený' *Bibliotekar* 1979 (8) 42-4. On the All-Union Theatre Society's central library.

Sudwell W E *Policy of Soviet scientific and technical libraries, history and development, 1917-1965* Catholic U of America, 1967. Thesis.

Karatygina T F *Technicheskie biblioteki SSSR za 50 let Sovetskoj vlasti* GPNTB SSSR, 1967, 66p. Technical libraries during 50 years of Soviet rule.

— 'Central scientific and technical libraries serving different branches of the Soviet economy' *Unesco Bull Lib* 1973 27(2) 92-7.

Aktualnije voprosy raboty naucnyl bibliotek Saltykova-Shchedrin Library, 1974.

Karatygina T F 'Development of scientific and technical libraries in the USSR' *Inspel* 1975 10(1/2) 38-48.

Tyshkevich N I 'O razvitii nauchno-tekhnicheskikh bibliotek' *Nauch-Tekh Info* -Ser 1 1976 (10) 3-7. Translation in *Sci Tech Info Process* 1976 (4) 1-7.

Osipova I P 'Gosudarstvennaya Biblioteka SSSR im. V I Lenin — golovnoe nauchno-issledovatel'skoe uchrezhdenie' *Sovet Bibliot* 1974 (6) 26-42. Lenin Library as a main research organization.

Solov'eva N N 'Gosudarstvennaya Biblioteka SSSR im V I Lenin v sisteme bibliotek strany' *Sovet Bibliog* 1976 (5) 9-25. Lenin Library in the library system.

Varfolomeeva M V 'Osnovnye napravleniya rukovodstva set'yu akademicheskikh bibliotek' *Nauch Tech Bibliot SSSR* 1978 (12) 32-5. Network of the Soviet Academy of Sciences libraries.

Kartashov N 'Glavnaya biblioteka Sibiri' *Bibliotekar* 1978 (9) 75-8. Academy of Sciences, Siberian Department library.

The USSR scientific and technical information system: a US view: report of the US participants (to a US/USSR Symposium on Scientific and Technical Information, Moscow June 1973) National Science Foundation, Office of Scientific Information Service, 1973, 69p.

Nakashima M 'Information dissemination in the multi-lingual nations' (In Japanese) *Annals J S L S* 1974 20(1) 1-13.

Belkin J 'Some Soviet concepts of information for information science' *Amer Soc Info Sci J* 1975 26(1) 56-64.

Kamala Rao B 'On Soviet national information system' *Annals Lib Sci Doc* 1975 22(1) 5-11.

Kedrovskij O 'The State Science and Technology Information System in the USSR' *Unesco Bull Lib* 1977 31(2) 86-97.

Arutiunov N B 'Razvitie gosudarstvennoi sistemy nauchnotekhnicheskoi informatsii v SSSR' *Nauch Tech Info*, Ser 1 1977 (11/12).

— 'The system of international exchange of scientific and technological information: the USSR's participation' *Unesco J* 1979 1(3) 210-4.

Vinogradov V A 'Information service for the social sciences in the USSR' *Info Proc Manag* 1978 14(3/4) 301-10.

Basova I M and Matvejeva J M 'Verkesserter Informationsversorgung sdienst Informatik des VINITI' *Informatik* 1980 27(1) 21-4.

LARC *A survey of automated activities in the libraries of the Soviet Union* LARC, 1973.

Ryabov A B 'Automatizatsiya bibliotechno-bibliograficheskikh protsessov — odna iz vazheishikh form povysheniya effektivnosti raboty bibliotek' *Sovet Bibliok* 1975 (5) 107-16.

Baranov V M 'Automatizatsiia biblioteknovye podkhody i rezul'taty issledovanii' *Sovet Bibliog* 1977 (5) 90-4.

Sokolov A V (Problemy i perspektivy avtomatizatsii bibliograficheskikh protsessov v SSSR' *Sovet Bibliog* 1978 (6) 27-36. Plan for automated bibliographical services and catalogues.

SECTION 3

THE AMERICAS

THE AMERICAS

NORTH AMERICA

This area will only include information common to Canada and the United States. But see also under United States as a number of organizations publish material relevant to Canada as well.

1

Institute for Scientific Information (ISI).

Lazarow S 'Institute for Scientific Information (ISI)' in *Encyclopedia* 12 (1974) 89-97.

2a

American Library Association and Canadian Library Association Joint Committee.

2b

American Libary Association (ALA), Chicago. 1876- . See references under United States, 2b.

Association of Research Libraries (ARD), Washington. 1932- . See references under United States, 2b.

Association of American Library Schools (AALS). 1915- .

Council of National Library and Information Associations, Haverford 1942- . Created as Council of National Library Associations.

Wiener T 'Council of National Library Association' *L of C Info Bull* 1977 36 20-1.

National Librarians Association, Alma, Mich. 1975- . Affiliated to the ALA.

Dollard P 'My child, the *librarian*librarian — a report on the National Librarians Association' *Wilson Lib Bull* 1979 53(9) 636-8.

— 'The National Librarians Association' *Argus* 1979 8(3/4) 28-32.

American Society of Information Science (ASIS). 1968- . 1937-67 as: American Documentation Institute.

2c

International Library Information Center (ILIC) University of Pittsburgh. 1964- . Based on the Graduate School of Library and Information Sciences.

North American library education directory of statistics ALA. Published every few years.

Bidlack R E ed *The ALA accreditation process, 1973-1976: survey of library schools whose programs were evaluated under the 1972 standards* ALA, 1977.

Graduate schools accredited by the ALA ALA Office for Library Education.

Directory of Institutions in the United States and Canada offering or developing courses in library technology Council of Library Technology.

Directory of educational programs in information science ASIS. Annual.

Information on courses and statistics can also be found in: *Journal for Education in Libararianship.*

Carroll C E *Professionalization of education for librarianship with special reference to the years 1940-1960* Scarecrow, 1970, 355p. (PhD Thesis, U of California, Berkeley, 1969, 453p).

Houser L J and Schrader A M *Search for a scientific profession: library science education in the United States and Canada* Scarecrow, 1978, 180p, bibl.

Shera J H and Anderson M *Education for librarianship in the United States and Canada* Liverpool Polytechnic, Department of Library and Information Studies, 1975. (Occasional papers, 3).

Ripin A L and Kasman D 'Education for special librarianship: a survey of courses offered in accredited programs' *Spec Lib* 1976 67(11) 504-9.

Laliberté M 'Sujets des thèses de doctorat nord-américaines récentes en bibliothéconomie et science de l'information' *Argus* 1979 8(2) 15-7, refs. Topics chosen for librarianship theses in recent years.

3a

See also under United States, 3a.

Klein B ed *Guide to American directories* 10th ed Klein Pub, 1977. By subjects: section on librarianship.

Palmer A M ed *Research centers directory* 5th ed Gale Research, 1975. Updated by a supplement: *New research centers.*

Ash L *Subject collections: a guide to special book collections and subject emphases as reported by university, college, public and special libraries and museums in the United States and Canada* 4th ed Bowker, 1974, 108p.

Simora F comp *Bowker annual of library and book trade information* 26th ed Bowker 1980, 700p. Extremely important for basic facts and figures about all aspects of librarianship in the USA and Canada. Statistics, laws, salaries, directories, organizations, bibliography, and recently: completed surveys of individual health sciences and academic libraries.

LRMP: Library Resources Market Place Bowker. Current volume: 1980.

American library directory: a classified list of libraries in the United States and Canada. Plus a selected list of libraries around the world Bowker, 1964- . Current editor: J. Cattell Press. (32nd ed: 1979, 1666p).

Ash L ed *Bibliographical directory of librarians in the United States and Canada* ALA. Between editions updated by *ALA membership directory*. Annual.

Lenroot-Ernt L ed *Directory of special libraries and information centers in the United States and Canada* 7th ed Gale Research, 1982. (*Directory of special libraries and information centers*, Vol 1).

— *Subject directory of special libraries and information centers: a subject classified edition of material taken from 'Directory of special libraries and information centers* 5th ed Gale Research, 1979, 5 vols:

— *Business and law libraries.*

— *Education and information science libraries.*

— *Health sciences libraries.*

— *Social sciences and humanities.*

— *Science and technology libraries.*

Special Libraries Association *Special libraries directory: institutions where SLA members are employed* SLA, 1977, 163p.

'Directory of state library agencies and related organizations [including US territories, Canadian provinces and USOE regional offices]' *ASLA Press News*, 1978 8(1) 3-4.

Parch G D *Directory of newspaper libraries in the United States and Canada* SLA, 1976.

Weber O S *North American film and video directory: a guide to media collections and services* Bowker, 1976, 284p.

School library supervisors directory Bowker, 1966- .

Directory of library consultants Bowker.

Foreign service directory of American librarians University of Pittsburgh Book Center.

ALA Association of College and Research Libraries — Asian and African section *Directory of Asian and African librarians in North America* The section, 1978, 33p. Librarians specialized in Asian and African affairs.

NB. For directories of individual associations see in *Bowker annual* and *ALA handbook.*

3b

Dissertation abstracts. Humanities and social sciences University Microfilms. See section: 'Library science' and the *Cumulated indexes.*

Lee J M ed *ALA publications checklist* ALA, 1979, 112p. (Latest edition noted).

Tryon J S 'Theses and dissertations accepted by graduate library schools: 1976 through August 1978' *Lib Q* 1979 49 182-96. Recurrent feature in this journal.

Copenhaver C and Boelke J comps *Library service to the disadvantaged* ERIC/CLIS, 1968, 19p. Selected bibliography 1960-68.

3c

Advances in librarianship Academic P, 1970- . Annual. General papers and papers on North America.

NLA newsletter: the National librarian 1976- .

Council of National Library and Information Associations *Update.* 1977- . Irregular.

3d

Annual statistics of medical school libraries in the United States and Canada 1978-1979 Houston Academy of Medicine, 1980, v. paging.

3e

Gopinath M A 'Standards for use in the planning of library and documentation systems: comparative data from India, UK, USA and Canada' *Lib Sci Slant Doc* 1974 11(3/4) 107-13.

3f

Jackson S L et al, eds *A century of service: librarianship in the United States and Canada* ALA, 1976, 354p.

Munthe W *American librarianship from a European angle* ALA, 1939, Reprinted: Shoe String, 1964, 191p.

Morel E *Bibliothèques: essai sur le développement des bibliothèques publiques et de la librairie dans les deux mondes* Mercure de France, 1908, 2 vols. Public libraries in Europe and America.

'A la découverte des bibliothèques publiques canadiennes et américaines' *Lecture et Bibliothèques* 1968 (5) 5-42.

'Regional public library systems' *Lib Trends* 1964 13(3) 107p. Series of papers on the problems caused by the variety of systems in Canada and the USA.

Libraries and popular education Dalhousie U, 1978, 67p.

New horizons for academic libraries. Papers of the ACRL conference 1978 Saur, 1979.

Beatty W K and Beatty V L 'Medical school libraries in the United States and Canada built between 1961 and 1971' *Med Lib Ass Bull* 1975 63(3) 324-36.

'Information in America' *Library J* 15 September 1979. Whole issue.

Patrinostro F S comp *A survey of automated activities in the libraries of the United States and Canada* 2nd ed LARC Association, 1971.

CANADA

1

National Library of Canada (NLC), Ottawa. 1953- .

Lamb W K 'Canada National Library' in *Encyclopedia* 4 (19) 165-9.

Donnelly F D *The National Library of Canada: forces in its emergence and in the identification of its role and responsibilities* CLA, 1973, 281p.

Wees I 'The National Library of Canada: the first quarter-century' *Can Lib J* 1978 35(3) 153-63.

— *The National Library of Canada: twenty five years after* NLC, 1978, 59p. (ERIC Report ED-168 591).

The future of the National Library of Canada NLC, 1979, 88p.

Amongst the various services of the library the following are of interest here:

Multilingual Biblioservice.

Library Documentation Service. Professional information service.

Bibliographical Services. Prepares the national bibliography.

Canadian Book Exchange Centre. 1974- . Clearinghouse for the exchange of unwanted library material.

Preibish A 'Canadian Book Exchange Centre: a contribution to library resources development' *Austral Acad Res Lib* 1979 10(1) 51-4.

National Research Council (NRC). National Science Library (NSL), Ottawa. Official functions assumed 1953- . In 1970 becomes responsible for developing a national scientific and technical information network (STI) of which it is the centre.

Brown J E 'National Science Library of Canada' in *Encyclopedia* 19 (1976) 177-81.

2a

National Library Advisory Board.

Ministries of Education of the provinces and states.

Canadian Institute for Scientific and Technical Information/Institut Canadien de l'Information Scientifique et Technique.

International Center for Research on Bilingualism, Quebec. 1967- .

2b

NLC. Library Documentation Centre *Directory of Library Associations in Canada* Annual since 1974. English and French versions.

Garry L S 'Canadian library associations' in Garry L S and Garry C eds *Canadian libraries in their changing environment* 315-342, refs. (See under 3f).

American Library Association/Canadian Library Association Joint Committee. Coordinates the activities of the two associations.

Canadian Library Association (CLA)/Association Canadienne des Bibliothèques, Ottawa. 1947- .

Kitchen P 'Canadian Library Association' in *ALA yearbook.*

Morton E H 'Canadian Library Association' in *Encyclopedia* 4 (1970) 170-92, refs.

The main subdivisions of the CLA are:
- Canadian Association of Children's Librarians.
- Canadian School Library Association.
- Canadian Association of Public Libraries (CAPL).
- Canadian Library Trustees Association.
- Canadian Association of College and University Libraries (CACUL). In 1976 the sub-division: Division of Academic Research Libraries separated from the Association to become the: Canadian Association of Research Libraries/ Association des Bibliothèques de Recherche du Canada.

Canadian Health Libraries Association. 1976- .

Canadian Association for Information Science (CAIS). 1969- .

Institute of Professional Librarians of Ontario (IPLO).

Houser L 'The Institute of Professional Librarians of Ontario: an analysis, 1954-1975' *IPLO Q* 1975 17(1/2) 3-119. Collection of documents.

Association pour l'Avancement des Sciences et des Techniques de la Documentation (ASTED), Montreal. 1974- . Supersedes: Association Canadienne des Bibliothécaires de Langue Française (ACBLF). 1943- .

Desrochers E 'Association Canadienne des Bibliothécaires de Langue Française' in *Encyclopedia* 2 (1970) 38-42.

Corporation des Bibliothécaires Professionnels du Québec. 1969?- .

[Tenth Anniversary Conference] *Argus* 1979 8(3/4) 4-35.

Bibliographical Society of Canada, Toronto. 1944- .

2c

White J H and Prodrick R G 'Education for librarianship in Canada — 1960-1973: a selected bibliography' *IPLO Q* 1975 16(3) 121-44.

Foster M 'Philosophy of librarianship' *Can Lib J* 1979 36(3) 131-7, refs. Survey of library schools and students' idea of librarianship.

Schrader A M 'Library science education in Canada' *IPLO Q* 1976 17(4) 199-264, refs.

Denis L G and Houser L J 'Study of the need for PhDs in library science in large Canadian universities' *Can Lib J* 1972 29 19-27.

Bassam B *The Faculty of Library Science, University of Toronto and its predecessors, 1911-1972* The Faculty, 1978, 141p.

Tague J M 'Information science in graduate library programs' *Can Lib J* 1979 36 89-99.

Lajeunesse M 'Education and training of information specialists in French-speaking countries: a comparative study' *Unesco J* 1979 1(2) 124-37, refs.

CLA Education for Library Manpower Committee 'Summary of a survey of library technician training courses in Alberta, British Columbia, Manitoba and Ontario, 1968-1969' *Feliciter* 1969 14(10), (11), (12). Revision of *CLA Occasional Paper* 71 (1968) and *Feliciter* 1968 13(2).

Campbell A and Dawson I eds *The library technician at work: theory and practice — proceedings of a workshop . . . May 1970* CLA, 1970, 232p.

Bassnett P J 'Library research in Canada' *Can Lib J* 1972 29 307-9.

Pannu G S 'Research in librarianship and the Canadian Library Association' *Can Lib J* 1972 29 300-6.

Packer K H 'A study of job opportunities in Canada for professional librarians' *Ontario Lib Rev* 1979 63(1) 4-11.

Klement S ed 'Alternatives in librarianship' *Can Lib J* 1977 34(2) 77-140, bibl. Special issue on the use of library education for pursuing non-library careers.

Smart A 'Women — the 4/5 minority' *Can Lib J* 1975 32(1) 14-7. Background to the 1975 conference on women in librarianship.

3a

Encyclopedia Canadiana Toronto, Grolier Society, 1958, 10 vols.

Canada yearbook, 1905- .

Quebec yearbook/Annuaire du Québec, 1950- .

Canada annual review U of Toronto P.

Fyfe J and Deutsch R H *Directory of special collections in Canadian libraries* CLA, 1968, 2 vols.

CLA organization handbook and membership list.

Canadian library directory/Répertoire des bibliothèques canadiennes CLA, 1963, 2 vols.

Quebec Bibliothèque Nationale *Répertoire des bibliothèques du Québec* Ministère des Affaires Culturelles du Québec, 1970, 101p.

Anderson B L comp *Special libraries and information centres in Canada: a directory* (1970 revision) CLA, 1970, 168p.

NLC. Library Documentation Centre *Federal government libraries in Canada: a list/Les bibliothèques du gouvernement fédéral canadien: une liste* NLC, 1977.

— *Ibid. Departmental and keyword indexes* NLC, 1977.

Preibish A ed *Co-operation among libraries in Canada 1972 (a preliminary checklist)* NLC, 1972, 82p.

3b

Lockhead D *Bibliography of Canadian bibliographies/Bibliographie des bibliographies canadiennes* 2nd ed rev and enlarged U of Toronto P, 1972, 312p.

Rider L H 'The state of Canadian bibliography: a CACUL report' *Can Lib J* 1975 32(4) 309-11.

Ryder D E *Canadian reference sources: a selective guide* CLA, 1973, 185p. Supplement in *Can Lib J* July/August 1973.

— 'Canada reference sources' *Can Lib J* 1978 35(4) 289-93.

— 'Canadian reference sources 1978 — a selection' *Can Lib J* 1979 36(4) 197-9.

Forget L J S 'L' automatisation de la bibliographie nationale du Canada: Canadiana' *Doc et Biblioth* 1974 20(4) 184-9; 1975 21(1) 23-35.

Wilson M C 'Canadiana: changes in the national bibliography' *Can Lib J* 1977 34 417-9.

Canadiana: Canada's national bibliography — description and guide NLC, 1978, 53p (ERIC report ED-169 891).

NLC *Canadiana.* 1951- . Monthly, with annual cumulations. Previously: *Canadian catalogue*, 1921-1949.

Canadian books in print/Catalogue des livres canadiens en librairie, 1967- . U of Toronto P, 1968- .

— *Author and title index.*

— *Subject guide to Canadian books in print*. 1973- .

Québec. Bibliothèque Nationale *Bibliographie du Québec.* 1968- . Quarterly, in two sections: government publications and others. Cumulations.

Répertoire de l'édition au Québec, 1972- . Edi-Québec for various bodies: Association des Editeurs Canadiens, Société des Editeurs de Manuels Scolaires du Québec, Conseil Superieur du Livre and Bibliothèque Nationale.

Canadian periodical index, 1948- . Monthly with annual cumulations. Now published by CLA. Cumulated author and subject indexes: 1938-1947; 1948-1959.

Periodex: index analytique des périodiques de langue française Montreal, Centrale des Bibliothèques, 1972- . Monthly with annual cumulations. Supersedes:*Index analytique, 1966-1972.*

Library science update 1976- . U of Toronto, Faculty of Library Science. Monthly.

Revue de la Sociéte de Bibliothéconomie canadienne 1 (1977)- . Vancouver, Parabola Systems. Annual review and selection from Canadian library journals.

Amey L J 'The combination school and public library: a bibliography with special emphasis on the Canadian experience' *Can Lib J* 1976 33(3) 263-5, 267. (See paper on the same subject in 3f).

Bonneau L-P 'Scientific and technological information in Canada — 1969-1978' *Can J Info Sci* 1979 4 7-12.

Swanick E L *Canadian library architecture: an introductory bibliography* Vance Bibliographies, 1980, 10p. (Architecture series, bibliography A-189).

3c

Pluscauskas M ed *Canadian serials directory/Répertoire des publications sériées canadiennes* U of Toronto P, 1976, 534p.

Henry G *Répertoire des périodiques québecois* Bibliothèque Nationale du Québec, 1974- .

Canadian Library Association *Canadian Library Journal*. 1944- . Bimonthly. 1944-68 as *Canadian library*.

— *Feliciter*. 1954- . 8 issues a year. In 1975 the divisional newsletters were amalgamated with this magazine:

CAPL Newsletter ceased with December 1974 issue.

CACUL Newsletter ceased with 1975 6(1).

Agora (Canadian Association of Special Libraries) ceased with 1975 9(2).

CLA Occasional papers. 1953- .

ASTED *Documentation et Bibliothèques*. Previously *ACBLF Bulletin*. 1955- .

Corporation des Bibliothécaires Professionnels du Québec *Argus* 1971- .

IPLO Quarterly. 1959- .

CAIS/ACSI *Information science in Canada*. Toronto, 1970- . Quarterly.

— *Canadian Journal of Information Science/Revue Canadienne des Sciences de l'Information*. 1976- . Annual.

NLC *National Librarv News/Nouvelles de la Bibliothèque Nationale,* Ottawa, 1969- .

3d

Canada Yearbook includes statistics.

Dominion Bureau of Statistics *Survey of libraries*. 1931- . Annual since 1958-59. In two sections: 'Public libraries' and 'Academic libraries'.

Public libraries in Canada/Bibliothèques publiques au Canada . . . Statistics Canada, Education, Science and Culture Division. Annual.

Gagnon G *Découpage du territoire québecois en régions de bibliothèques* Québec, Ministère des Affaires ulturelles, 1967, 145p.

'Statistiques des bibliothèques publiques du Québec' *Biblio-Contact* 1979 5(1) 3-15.

Anderson B L *Special libraries in Canada: a statistical analysis and commentary* CLA, 1969, 13, 20 leaves, tables. (CLA Occasional paper 76).

3e

Canadian government publications: consolidated annual catalogue Ottawa, Queen's Printer, 1953- . 1895-1952 as: *Annual catalogue of government publications*. Cumulation of:

Daily checklist of government publications/Liste quotidienne des publications fédérales Information Canada, 1952- .

Ellsworth R C 'Library royalties in Canada: a status report' *Libri* 1977 27(3) 195-203.

National Library Act 1953. Copyright.

Canada public library laws 1966 4th ed CLA, 1967, 183p. *Supplement* 1968, 8p.

Public library standards CLA, 1967, 23p. *Appendix*, 1969, 23p

Normes pour les bibliothèques municipales Québec, Ministère des Affaires culturelles, Service des Bibliothèques Publiques, 1974, 62p.

3f

Morton E 'Library history of Canada — a panoramic review. Part I' *Lib Hist Rev* 1974 1(4) 65-98; Part II: *Lib Hist Rev* 1975 2(1) 82-102.

Drolet A *Les bibliothèques canadiennes 1604-1960* Ottawa, Cercle du Livre de France, 1965, 234p, bibliography 215-31.

Peel B ed *Librarianship in Canada, 1946 to 1967: essays in honour of Elizabeth Homer Morton* CLA, 1968, 205p.

Into the seventies, challenge of change CLA, 1971, 88p. Proceedings of the CLA 25th annual conference.

Garry L S and Garry C eds *Canadian libraries in their changing environment* York U (Ontario), Centre for Continuing Education, 1977, 593p.

Campbell H C *Canadian libraries* 2nd ed Pendragon, etc., 1971, 114p.

Morton E H 'Canada, libraries in' in *Encyclopedia* 4 (1970) 71-157. (See also with this paper other more specialized ones on various aspects of Canadian librarianship).

Reicher D 'Le gouvernement et les bibliothèques' *ACBLF Bull* 1971 17 3-6.

Beard J R *Canadian provincial libraries* CLA, 1967, 300p. Originally PhD Thesis, Columbia U, 1965.

Gifford H 'Canadian participation in IFLA: its growth and problems' *Can Lib J* 1975 32(2) 127-31.

Murray-Lachapelle R 'La coopération du Canada avec l'Afrique francophone dans le domaine des bibliothèques et de la documentation' *Doc et Biblioth* 1979 25(2) 81-6, refs.

'Swedish-Canadian problems of mutual interests' *CLA Occasional paper* 57. Report of a conference and discussion, September 1967.

Progress in educating library users Bowker, 1978. Canada, Great Britain, Scandinavia.

Chartrand G A ed *Livre, bibliothèque et culture québecoise* ASTED, 1977.

Gale P *Development of public libraries in Canada* Catholic U of America, 1965. Thesis.

Morton E H *Developing public libraries in Canada 1535-1983* Dalhousie U Libraries and School of Library Service, 1975, 16p. (Occasional paper 9).

Manley-Casimir M E et al *The right to know: policies, structures and plans for the development of library services in Alberta: a report to the Department of Culture, Youth and Recreation* L W Downey Associates, 1974, 113p.

Hamilton M F 'Resources for community information centres' *Ont Lib Rev* 1974 58(4) 223-38.

Dewdney P 'The Crouch experience: an inter-agency approach to neighbourhood services [1970-]' *Can Lib J* 1979 36(1/2) 5-14.

Wertheimer L 'The Metro bilingual project' *Can Lib J* 1974 31(6) 497-501.

— 'New Canadians and the public library a decade later' *Unesco Bull Lib* 1974 28(3) 139-45.

Zielinska M F 'Multiculturalism and library services to ethnic communities' *Unesco Bull Lib* 1978 32(1) 15-22.

Mott H 'Some practical implications of multilingual library service' *Ont Lib Rev* 1979 63(1) 41-4.

Amey L J and Smith R J 'Combination school and public libraries: an attitudinal study' *Can Lib J* 1976 33(3) 251-9. See also a bibliography in 3b.

Amey L J *The Canadian school-housed public library* Dalhousie U Libraries and School of Library Service, 1979, 481p.

Scott M B 'School libraries in Canada 1971' *Can Lib J* 1972 29 118-38.

Szpakowska J K *Profils culturels des jeunes montréalais: livres, lecture et loisirs: une enquête . . . 1969-1970* U de Montréal, 1970, 314p.

— *Profil d'un centre documentaire multimédia: bilan d'une enquête réalisée en 1974 dans 279 écoles secondaires au Québec* U de Montréal, Ecole de Bibliothéconomie, 1975, 450p.

Wertheimer L 'Serving children in multilingual communities' *Can Lib J* 1978 36(1/2) 37-41.

Marshall J G 'Clinical librarians join health care team to provide information directly' *Can Lib J* 1979 36 23-8.

Cartwright M J 'Survey of the history of academic libraries in Canada' *Can Lib J* 1968 25(2) 98-102, bibl.

University research libraries: report of the Consultative Group on University Research Libraries Canada Council, 1977, 44p.

Darvall B 'Law libraries in Australia and Canada: a note on two recent surveys' *Austr Acad Res Lib* 1976 7(4) 245-8.

Sharing resources — sharing costs. Seventh annual conference on Information Science, Banff 1979 CAIS, 1979, 426p. See also other conferences on Information Science sponsored by CAIS.

Canadian library systems and networks, their planning and development. Papers presented at a symposium at the CLA conference, Winnipeg, June 1974 CLA, 1974, 50p.

NLC — Canadian Union Catalogue Task Group *Final report to the National Librarian of Canada [on the establishment of a library network]* NLC, 1976, 86p.

Wu J M 'The Agriculture Canada Libraries Information Network' *Can J Info Sci* 1979 4 68-73.

Automation in libraries [1967-]. Proceedings of CACUL annual conferences.

Canadian MARC. A report of the activities of the MARC Task Group NLC, 1972, 242p.

UNITED STATES OF AMERICA

1

Library of Congress, Washington DC, 1800- . Created to serve the Congress, it assumes the functions of a national library and bibliographical centre. It plays a central part in coordinated library and information systems (for this see below under 3f).

Cole J Y *For Congress and the nation: a chronological history of the Library of Congress* The Library, 1979, 196p.

Goodrum C A *The Library of Congress* Praeger, 1974, 292p.

Cole J Y *The Library of Congress in perspective: a volume based on the reports of the 1976 Librarian's Task Force and Advisory Groups* Bowker, 1978, 281p.

Metz P 'The use of the general collection in the Library of Congress' *Lib Q* 1979 49(4) 415-34.

National Archives of the United States, Washington DC.

National Library of Medicine, Bethesda Md, 1836- . Formerly the Surgeon General's Library, then the Armed Forces Medical Library. It is the centre of a national network and an international information data base.

National Agricultural Library, Washington.

Institute for Scientific Information (ISI).

Lazerow S 'Institute for Scientific Information (ISI)' in *Encyclopedia* 12 (1974) 89-97.

Educational Resources Information Center (ERIC), Bethesda MD.

Slansky D A and Brandhorst T *A bibliography of publications about the Educational Resources Information Center* ERIC, Processing and Reference Facility, 1978, 18p. (ERIC Report ED-169 955).

Booth B 'A look at ERIC after ten years' *Educ Lib Bull* 1975 18(3) 1-11.

Chesley R E *Dissemination of educational information through the Educational Resources Information Center (ERIC)* ERIC, 1979, 16p. (ERIC Report ED-171 285).

Survey of ERIC data base research services ERIC, 1974 (EDO-94 750).

Knapp S D and Zych M L 'The ERIC data base and the literature of library and information science' *RQ* 1977 16(3) 209-12.

Drazan J G *The unknown ERIC: a selection of documents for the general library* Scarecrow, 1981.

International Library Information Center. University of Pittsburgh.

Center for Documentation and Communication Research, Cleveland, Case Western University.

Kent A and Perry J W 'The Center for Documentation and Communication Research at the Western Reserve University' *Unesco Bull Lib* 1959 13(11/12) 256-61, 265.

Department of Commerce. National Technical Information Service (NTIS). 1970. Created as Clearinghouse for Federal Scientific and Technical Information (1964-) by expansion of the Office of Technical Services (1946-).

Hoshovsky A G and Album H H 'Toward a national technical information system' *Amer Doc* 1965 16(4) 313-22.

Chitty M G *NTIS: concept of the clearinghouse, 1945-1979* North Carolina U, 1979, 74p. (NTIS Report BP-300 947).

A new centre is under discussion:

National Periodicals Center. Project of the National Commission on Libraries and Information Science (See under 2a), to make literature more easily available.

Effective access to the periodical literature: a national program NCLIS/US GPO, 1977, 92p.

Gull C D *National periodicals center concept reconsidered: alternatives and costs* Gull and Associates, 1979, 31p. (NTIS Report PB-296 351).

Savage N 'A National Periodicals Center: the debate in Arlington' *Lib J* 1979 104(10) 1108-15. Report on a forum discussing the need for such a centre.

A specialized centre exists in the Library of Congress for the purpose of directing inquirers to the relevant institutions and publishing specialized directories (See under 3a): National Referral Center (Part of the Science and Technology Division) (NRC). 1962- .

McFarland M W 'The National Referral Center (NRC)' *Spec Lib* 1975 66(3) 126-32.

For other federal or federally supported libraries and information centres see under 3a.

2a

US Department of Health, Education and Welfare. Office of Education. Library Services and Educational Facilities. 1938- .

Main agencies created by the government or by professional organizations with the aim of coordinating services and maintaining standards of services and performance:

National Commission on Libraries and Information Science (NCLIS). Created by an act of Congress in 1970, under the Office of the Secretary for Health, Education and Welfare. Its creation was the result of recommendations made by the National Advisory Commission on Libraries set up in 1966 to investigate library performance in the USA.

'National Commission on Libraries and Information Science signed into law' *Lib Congress Info Bull* 30/7/1970 29 374-7.

Stevens C H 'National Commission on Libraries and Information Science' in *Encyclopedia* 19 (1976) 64-84.

Council on Library Resources (CLR), 1956- . Supported by the Ford Foundation.

Clapp V W 'Council on Library Resources' in *Encyclopedia* 6 (1971) 219-27, refs. Includes a list of publications.

Council of Library Resources. The year 1977-78 The Council, 1978, 61p. (ERIC Report ED-168 495).

Gwinn N E 'The Council of Library Resources: a 20 year report' *Lib J* 1977 102(3) 330-4.

Council of Library Technology (COLT). 1967- .

Council of Planning Librarians (CPL). 1960- .

Federal Library Committee. 1965- . Under the Librarian of Congress, funded by the Council on Library Resources. Coordinates the activities of the federal libraries.

Howard P and Morissey M eds 'The Federal Library Committee' *Drexel Lib Q J* 1970 6(3/4) 205-341. Series of papers.

Robisheaux J *The Federal Library Committee* Texas Women's University, 1971, 59p.

 United States Information Agency (USIA). Maintains libraries abroad as US

Information Services (USIS) and book procurement centres.

Henderson J W *The United States Information Agency* Praeger, 1969.

A list of the USIS is included in Kruzas A T *Directory of special libraries and information centers* (See in: North America, 3a).

US Book Exchange (USBE), Washington. 1948- . Operates in the US and abroad.

Rovelstad H 'The economics of the Universal Serials and Book Exchange (USBE)' *Interlending Rev* 1979 7(3) 98-101.

Farmington Plan. Sponsored by the Association of Special Libraries, for cooperative acquisition of foreign material.

Williams E E 'Farmington Plan' in *Encyclopedia* 8 (1972) 361-8.

URBANDOC. Mainly for public libraries.

Sessions V S and Sloan L W *Urbandoc: a bibliographic information system. Demonstration report* New York City U, 1971.

National Book Committee. 1954- . Created by the ALA and The American Book Publishers Council. Research in the field of reading. See for details in *Bowker Annual* (In North America, 3a).

Federal Council for Science and Technology. Committee on Scientific and Technical Information (COSATI). Specialized panels on types of activities, eg: Information analysis and data centres.

Other bodies also have activities in the field of librarianship or information science. See in particular:

National Science Foundation (NSF) in scientific information.

Adkinson B W 'National Science Foundation — Science information' in *Encyclopedia* 19 (1976) 154-77.

Carnegie Corporation, New York. 1911- .

Anderson F 'Carnegie Corporation of New York' in *Encyclopedia* 4 (1970) 200-7.

Ford Foundation, New York. 1935- .

Mayer R A 'Ford Foundation' in *Encyclopedia* 8 (1972) 592-600.

Rockefeller Foundation, New York. 1913- .

2b

Sullivan P 'Library associations' *Lib Trends* 1976 25(1) 135-52.

Riss Fang J and Songe A H *International guide to library, archival and information science associations* 2nd ed Bowker, 1980, 302-65.

Bowker Annual (See in North America, 3a).

American Library Association (ALA), Chicago. 1876- .

ALA *A handbook of organization. . .* (Annual). Structure, divisions and subdivisions, chapters, etc.

ALA yearbook: a review of library events. . . Covers all activities, problems, current developments of the ALA.

ALA, policies, procedures and position statements 2nd ed ALA, 1970, 176p.

Thomison D *A history of the American Library Association, 1876-1972* ALA, 1978, 301p.

Downs R B 'Assessing the American Library Association: a review essay' *J Lib Hist* 1979 14 191-9.

Young A P 'Aftermath of a crusade: World War I and the enlarged program of the American Library Association' *Lib Q* 1980 50(2) 191-207, refs.

Holley E G '1969-1979: a troublesome, tumultuous decade revisited' *Amer Lib* 1979 10(6) 302-4, 305-8, 310, refs.

Amongst the ALA Divisions a few can be mentioned:

- American Association of School Librarians (AASL).

Pond P 'Development of a professional school library association: American

Association of School Librarians' *School Media Q* 1976 5(1) 12-8.
- Association of College and Research Libraries (ACRL).
- Information Science and Automation Division.
- Library Education Division.
- International Relations Division.
- Public Library Association (PLA).
- Resources and Technical Services Division.

Other librarianship (and related fields) associations include:

Association of Research Libraries (ARD), Washington. 1932- .

Kaplan L 'The Association of Research Libraries: a study of organizational effectiveness' *J Acad Libp* 1975 1(4) 8-11.

Special Libraries Association (SLA), New York. 1909- .

McKenna F E 'Special libraries and Special Libraries Association (SLA)' in *Encyclopedia* 28 (1980) 386-443.

Association of American Law Libraries, Chicago. 1906- .

Medical Library Association, Chicago. 1898- .

Music Library Association, Washington. 1931- .

Association of American Library Schools (AALS). 1915- .

National Librarians Association.

American Society for Information Science (ASIS). 1968- . Created in 1937 as American Documentation Institute.

'Organization profile: American Society for Information Science' *Information* May 1971 3 177-80. Also in *Info Hotline* 1976 8(2) 29-31.

Schultz C 'ASIS: notes on its founding and development' *ASIS Bull* 1976 2(8) 49-51.

National Federation of Science Abstracting and Indexing Services (NFAIS), Philadelphia. 1957- .

National Federation of Voluntary Literacy Schemes (NFVLS).

National Federation of Voluntary Literacy Schemes: a valuable contribution NFVLS, 1980, 40p.

Bibliographical Society of America, New York. 1904- .

American Book Publishers Council.

2c Education and training — General-history-trends.

Journal of Education for Librarianship Surveys of courses, projects, statistics and prospects of new professional placements, etc.

Nasri W Z 'Education in library and information science' in *Encyclopedia* 7 (1971) 414-65, 73 refs. Includes history of library education, as well as present situation.

Debons A 'Education in information science' in *Encyclopedia* 7 (1971) 465-74.

Davis D G 'Education for librarianship' *Lib Trends* 1976 25(1) 113-34.

Bramley G *History of library education* 2nd ed Bingley/Saur, 1980. Development in USA and UK and influence on other countries.

Williamson C C *Williamson reports of 1921 and 1923, including 'Training for library work' (1921) and 'Training for library service' (1923)* Reprinted by Scarecrow, 1971, 276 and 165p.

Vann S K *Williamson reports: a study* Scarecrow, 1971, 212p.

Slanker B O *Reminiscences: seventy five years of a library school* U of Illinois P, 1969, 133p.

White C M *A historical introduction to library education: problems and progress to 1951* Scarecrow, 1976, 296p. (Less descriptive) Rev. enl. ed. of his *The origins of the American library school,* 1961.

 Churwell C D *The shaping of American library education* ALA, 1975, 130p.

Asheim L 'Trends in library education — United States' *Adv Libp* 1975 5 147-201.

Vance K E et al 'Future of library education: 1975 Delphi study' *J Educ Libp* 1977 18(1) 3-17. A Delphi study.

Galvin T J 'Change in education for librarianship' *Lib J* 1976 101(1) 273-7.

Wilson P 'Impending change in library education: implications for planning' *J Educ Libp* 1978 18(3) 159-74.

Reed S R 'Library education 1977-1987' *J Educ Libp* 1978 19(2) 87-96.

Conant R W *The Conant report: a study of the education of librarians* MIT, 1980, 210p.

Trejo A D 'Modifying library education for ethnic imperatives' *Amer Lib* 1977 8(3) 150-1.

Marco G 'Library schools in North America and elsewhere: co-operative agreements' *Unesco* 1980 2(3) 189-94, 208.

Peace N E and Chudacoff N F 'Archivists and librarians: a common mission, a common education' *Amer Archivist* 1979 42(4) 456-62.

Saracevic T 'Essay on the past and future of information science education: historical overview' *Info Proc Man* 1979 15 1-15.

Fosdick H 'Library education in information science: present trends' *Spec Lib* 1978 69(3) 100-8, bibl.

2c Education and training — Schools, programmes, curricula, continuing education.

Library education directory Office of Education, 1962-63. Annual.

Graduate schools accredited by the ALA ALA, Office for Library Education.

Association of American Library Schools *Directory*, 1943- in *J Educ Libp*.

Wilkie L C ed *Directory of educational programs in information science 1971-72* American Society for Information Science, 1971, 111p.

— *1972-1973*, suppl. ASIS, 1972.

Reed S R 'Federally funded training for librarianship' *Lib Trends* 1975 24(1) 85-100.

Cassata M B and Totten H L eds *The administrative aspects of education for librarianship: a symposium* Scarecrow, 1975, 407p.

Boll J J 'A basis for library education' *Lib Q* 1972 42(2) 195-211, 30 refs.

Goldhor H ed *Education for librarianship: design of the curriculum of library schools* (Proceedings of a Conference, University of Illinois, Graduate School of Library Science, 6-9 Sep 1970) U of Illinois, 1970, 195p.

Fryden F N 'Post-master's degree programs in the accredited US library schools' *Lib Q* 1969 39(3) 233-44.

Slavens T P 'Opinions of library science PhD's about requirements for the PhD degree in Library Science' *Coll Res Lib* 1969 30 525-32.

Danton J Periam *Between MLS and PhD* ALA, 1970.

Belzer J et al 'Curricula in information science analysis and development. Bibliography' *ASIS J* 1971 22 193-223.

— 'Curricula in information science: four year progress report' *ASIS J* 1975 26(1) 17-32.

Schlachter G and Thomison D 'The library science doctorate: a quantitative analysis of dissertations and recipients' *J Educ Libp* 1974 15(2) 95-111, refs.

Totten H L 'A survey and evaluation of minority programs in selected graduate library schools' *J Educ Libp* 1977 18(1) 18-34.

Danton J P 'British and American Library School teaching staff: a comparative inquiry' *J Educ Libp* 1978 19(2) 97-129.

Library Education Experimental Project (LEEP). Reports of progress published in a special periodical *LEEP* 1969 1(1/3) Syracuse University, 1969.

Sable M H and Deya L 'Outline of an introductory course in international and comparative librarianship' *Int Lib Rev* 1970 2 187-92.

Kanevskii B P 'Kritika anglo-amerikanskikh sravnitel' nykh issledovanii v oblasti bibliotekovedeniya' *Bibliotekoved Bibliog za Rubezhom* 1974 50 8-37. Critical study of Anglo-American studies in comparative librarianship, methodological problems, etc.

Roper F W *Special programs in medical library education, 1957-1971.*

— 'Part I: Definition of the problem and research design' *Med Lib Ass Bull* 1973 61(2) 225-7.

— 'Part II: Analysis of the programs' *Med Lib Ass Bull* 1973 61(4) 387-95.

— 'Part III: The trainees' *Med Lib Ass Bull* 1974 62(4) 397-404.

— 'Part IV: Career characteristics of two groups of medical librarians' *Med Lib Ass Bull* 1974 62(4) 405-12.

Solow L I 'Education for music librarianship in the United States' *Fontes Artis Musicae* 1979 16(1) 44-7.

Casey G M 'Education for institutional library service' *Lib Trends* 1978 26(3) 431-45.

Sollenberger J K *In service training: a bibliographical survey* revised edition 1964 ALA, 1965.

Penland P R 'Inservice training' in *Encyclopedia* 12 (1974) 46-79.

Case R et al *Evaluation of alternative curricula* ALA, 1975, 183p.

Continuing education for librarians ALA Recurrent lists of workshops, seminars and short courses.

Stone E W ed 'Personnel development and continuing education in libraries' *Lib Trends* 1971 20(1) 3-183.

Stone E W et al *Continuing library and information science education: final report to the National Commission on Libraries and Information Science (NCLIS)* ASIS, 1974, 189p. Recommends CLENE: Continuing Library Education Network and Exchange.

Stone E W 'Continuing education for librarians in the United States' *Adv Libp* 1978 8 241-331.

Education of state library personnel: a report with recommendations relating to the continuing education of state library agency professional personnel ALA, 1971, 62p.

Kenney L A 'Continuing education for academic librarians' *Calif Libn* 1969 30(3) 199-202.

Allen L A *Continuing education needs of special librarians* New York, SLA.

2c Research.

Dalton J 'Library education and research in librarianship: some current problems and trends in the United States' *Libri* 1969 19(3) 157-74.

Eaton A J 'Research in librarianship in the USA' *Libri* 1971 21(4) 350-60.

[Section on library research] *J Educ Libp* 1979 20(2).

Ferguson D 'Disseminating library and information science research in the United States' *Unesco Bull Lib* 1975 29(6) 319-28, refs.

Fry B M and Libbey M A 'Status of library research in the Federal Government' *Drexel Lib Q* 1970 6 290-305.

Janaske P C 'Federally funded research in librarianship' *Lib Trends* 1975 24(1) 101-14.

2c Professional issues.

212 *Program of Research into the Identification of Manpower Requirements, the*

Educational Preparation and the Utilization of Manpower in the Library and Information Profession Office of Education.
Kortendick J J and Stone E W *Job dimensions and educational needs in librarianship* ALA, 1971, 503p.
Ricking M and Booth R E *Personnel utilization in libraries: a system approach* ALA, 1974, 158p.
Wasserman P 'Elements in a manpower blueprint: library personnel for the 1970's' *ALA Bull* 1969 63 581-99.
Reed S R 'Library manpower planning in the USA' *Libri* 1975 25(4) 332-47.
Cooper M D 'An analysis of the demand for librarians' *Lib Q* 1975 45(4) 373-404.
Bureau of Labor *Library manpower: a study of demand and supply* USGPO, 1975, 94p.
Nyren K *Personnel in libraries* New York, Library Journal, 1979, 63p, refs. (LJ special report, 10).
Wasserman P *The new librarianship: a challenge for change* Bowker, 1972, 287p.
Presthus R *Technological change and occupational response: a study of librarians. Part of a Program. . .* Office of Education, Bureau of Research, June, 1970, 141p.
Stone E W *Factors related to the professional development of librarians* Scarecrow, 1969, 281p.
D'Elia G P 'Determinants of job satisfaction among beginning librarians' *Lib Q* 1979 49 283-302.
Patterson Wahba S 'Job satisfaction of librarians: a comparison between men and women' *Coll Res Lib* 1975 36(1) 45-51.
Mugnier C *The paraprofessional and the professional job structure* ALA, 1980, 157p.
Josey E J et al *Opportunities for minorities in librarianship* Scarecrow, 1977, 201p.
Busha C H 'Intellectual freedom and censorship: the climate of opinion in midwestern public libraries' *Lib Q* 1972 42(3) 283-301.
Lewis Guyton T *Unionization: the viewpoint of librarians* Chicago Amer Lib Ass, 1975, 204p.
Schlipf F A ed *Collective bargaining in libraries* U of Illinois Grad Sch of Lib Sci, 1975, 179p.
Walters J H *Image and status of the library and information services field. Part of a Program. . .* Office of Education, Bureau of Research, July 1970, 89p.
'Who we are: a national profile of the American librarian on the 100th anniversary of ALA's founding' *Amer Lib* 1976 7(6) 333-87.
Holley E G 'Librarians, 1876-1976' *Lib Trends* 1976 25(1) 177-207.
Newmyer J 'The image problem of the librarian: femininity and social control' *J Lib Hist* 1976 11(1) 44-67.
Weibel K et al *The role of women in librarianship 1876-1976: the entry, advancement and struggle for equalization in one profession* Mansell, Oryx P, 1979, 510p.
'Women in librarianship' *Lib J* 1971 96(15). 3 articles.
Schiller A R 'Women in librarianship' *Adv Libp* 1974 4 103-47.
'Beyond awareness: women in libraries organize for change' *Sch Lib J* 1977 23(5) 31-6.
Garrison D 'The tender technicians: the feminization of public librarianship 1876-1905' *J Soc Hist* 1972/73 6(2). Repr. in *J Acad Libp* 1977 3(1) 10-9, refs.
Milden J W 'Women, public libraries, and library unions: the formative years' *J Lib Hist* 1977 12(2) 150-8.

Tze-Chung, Li 'A profile of Chinese-American librarians' *J Lib Info Sci (USA/Taiwan)* 1979 5(1) 43-50.

Josey E J ed *The black librarian in America* Scarecrow, 1970, 336p.

— *What black librarians are saying* Scarecrow, 1972, 317p.

— 'Can library affirmative action succeed?' *Lib J* 1975 100(1) 28-31.

Downs R B 'The role of the academic librarian 1876-1976' *Coll Res Lib* 1976 37(6) 491-502.

Hartz F R 'Health sciences librarians and mental health laws' *Med Lib Ass Bull* 1978 66 441-6.

Lawrence G G 'C.M.L.: Clinical Medical Librarian' *Online* 1979 3(3) 60-3.

3a

See also: North America 3a.

Directory Info Service no. 1 April 1977- Detroit, Information Enterprises, 1977- .

Library of Congress. National Referral Center *Directory of information resources in the United States* Serial directory.

Chronologies and documentary handbooks of the States Oceana Publications, 1978(?)- .

Bernardo S *The ethnic almanac* Doubleday, 1981.

Wynar L R and Buttlar L *Guide to ethnic museums, libraries and archives in the United States* Kent State U, School of Library Science, 1978, 378p.

Encyclopedia of associations 16th ed Gale Research, 1981:

- 1 National organizations in the US (Subject order) 1631p.
- 2 Geographic and executive indexes.
- 3 New associations and projects. Quarterly supplement to Vol. 1.

Our nation's libraries: an inventory of resources National Commission on Libraries and Information Science, nd, 16p.

'Acronyms and initialisms of library networks' *Information Reports and Bibliographies* 1976 5(6) 16-9.

Index of opportunity in library science and index of opportunity in computer sciences Princeton, Resource Publications, 1969, 2 vols. 32 and 52p.

Foreign service directory of American librarians U of Pittsburgh Book Center.

Garnett A B *School library supervisors directory* 1966- . Bowker.

Josey E J and Shockley A A eds and comps *Handbook of black librarianship* Libraries Unlimited, 1977, 392p.

Leonard L E and Erteschick A M *Federal programs for libraries: a directory* Washington, Bureau of School Systems, Office of Libraries and Learning Resources, 1978, 67p. (ERIC report ED-165 812).

Benton M and Ottersen S *Roster of Federal libraries* George Washington U, 1970, 282p.

Schick F L *Survey of special libraries serving the Federal government* US Office of Education, 1968, 108p.

ALA. Government Documents Round Table *Directory of Government document collections and librarians* 2nd ed Washington, Congressional Information Service, 1978, 528p.

Library of Congress. National Referral Center *A directory of information resources in the United States: Federal Government* The Center, 1974.

Survey of public library facilities, 1963-64 US Office of Education, 1968.

Nelson Associates Inc *Public library systems in the United States: a survey of multijurisdictional systems* ALA, 1969, 368p.

Delanoy D D and Cuadra C A *Directory of academic library consortia* System Development Corp, 1972, 304p.

Schick F L and Crawford S *Directory of health science libraries in the US, 1969* American Medical Association, 1970, 197p.

United States. Directory Service *Directory of major medical libraries in the United States* The Service, 1978, 64p.

Irvine B J *Slide libraries: a guide for academic institutions, museums and special collections* 2nd ed Libraries Unlimited, 1979.

Kruzas A T *Encyclopedia of information systems and services* 4th ed, 1981, 933p. With interedition supplements. Ann Arbor, Edwards Bros.

Library of Congress. National Referral Center *A directory of information resources in the United States, Vol. 8: social sciences* Rev ed The Center, 1973.

Sessions V S *Directory of data bases in the social and behavioral sciences* New York, City U and Science Associates International, 1974, 300p.

Directory of federally supported information analysis centers 4th ed National Referral Center, 1979, 95p. (NTIS report AD-AO82 470) Weinberg report.

Westby B M 'Commercial processing firms: a directory' *Lib Resour Tech Serv* 1969 13(2) 209-86.

National Technical Information Service *Directory of computerized data files and related software* 1974- . Annual.

3b

Avram H D and Maruyama L S eds *The library bibliographic component of the national library and information service network* USGPO (for Library of Congress), 1977, 87p.

Bookstein A et al, eds *Prospects for change in bibliographic control* U of Chicago P, 1977, 138p. (Proceedings of 38th Conference of the Graduate Library School, 1976).

Watson P G ed *On-line bibliographic services: where we are, where we're going* ALA, Reference and Adult Services Division, 1977, 91p. Part of the ALA Centennial Conference.

Library of Congress catalog of printed cards to 1942; supplement 1942-47, then:

Library of Congress author catalog 1948-52, now:

Library of Congress — The National union catalog.

Library of Congress and National Catalogue. Author lists 1942-1962: a master cumulation Detroit, Gale Research, 1969, 152 vols.

National Union catalogue, pre-1956 imprints Mansell, 1969- . Cumulations of early volumes of the Library of Congress catalogues.

Library of Congress catalog — books: subjects Quarterly, with cumulations.

Library of Congress *Catalog of copyright entries* Copyright Office. In 13 sections. Includes periodicals and non-book materials.

Zink S D *United States government publications catalogs* SLA 1981 (SLA bibliographies, 8).

Library of Congress *Monthly catalog of United States Government Publications.*

— *Cumulative index. . . 1900-1971* Carollton P, 1973, 14 vols.

— *Non-GPO imprints received in the Library of Congress* Annual *Publishers' weekly* New York, Bowker, 1872- .

American book publishing record (BPR) Bowker, Monthly.

American book publishing record cumulative 1950-1977 Bowker, 1979, 14 vols.

Books in print and *Subject guide to Books in print* Bowker. Both annual.

American reference books annual Libraries Unlimited Inc. In classified order of subject.

Guide to the National Archives of the United States National Archives and Records Services, 1975, 884p.

Nakata Y *From press to people: collecting and using US Government publications* ALA, 1979, 212p.

Mitterling P I *U.S. cultural history: a guide to information sources* Gale Research, 1979. (American Government and history information guide series, 5).

Robinson B J *The Mexican American: a critical guide to research aids* JAI Press, 1979, 300p.

National Federation of Science Abstracting and Indexing Services *NFSAIS member service descriptions 1969-1970* NFSAIS, 1969, 57p.

Systems Development Corporation *A system study of abstracting and indexing in the US* The Corporation, 1966, 228p.

3b Library and information science.

Library literature H W Wilson Co, 1921- . International coverage but all aspects of US librarianship are extensively covered. In classified order of subjects, multiple entries.

Library and information science today (LIST) 1971- . Annual. Science Associates Publ. On research.

Current awareness — library literature 1972- .

Information science abstracts. Previously *Documentation abstracts*, 1966- . American Society for Information Science.

Annual review of information science and technology 1966- . American Society for Information Science. ERIC/Center for Library and Information Science Series of bibliographies and review papers.

Lee J M ed (for 1979) *ALA publications checklist [1979]: a list of materials currently available from the American Library Association* ALA, 1979, 112p. Annual.

University of Illinois, School of Library Science *Occasional papers* Mostly bibliographies on various aspects of library problems.

Schlachter G A and Thomison D *Library science dissertations 1925-1972: an annotated bibliography* Libraries Unlimited, 1974, 293p.

Tryon J S 'Theses and dissertations accepted by graduate library schools: 1976 through August 1978' *Lib Q* 1979 49 182-96. Annual.

Downs R B *American library resources: a bibliographical guide* ALA, 1951, 428p.

— *Supplement 1950-1961* 1962, 226p.

— *Supplement 1961-1970* 1972, 244p.

Jackson W V *Resources of research libraries: a selected bibliography* U of Pittsburgh Book Center, 1969, 65p.

A selected bibliography of library and information service Case Western University, Center for Documentation and Communication Research, 1970, 16p.

Schon A E *Government documents in the library literature 1909-1974* Ann Arbor, Pierian P, 1976, 110p.

Hsu K and Diodato V P 'Library and information sciences textbooks-in-use: a master checklist' *Information Reports and Bibliographies* 1976 5(2) 2-37.

Ellsworth D J and Stevens N D eds *Landmarks of library literature 1876-1976* Scarecrow, 1976, 520p.

ERIC/CLIS *Library surveys and development plans: an annotated bibliography* 1969, 45p. Complements:

Rike G E *Statewide library surveys and development plans: an annotated bibliography*, 1956-67 (ERIC document ED-023 439).

Harris M H *A guide to research in American library history* Scarecrow, 1968, 186p. Lists 496 titles, 1908-1965.

Jackson S L 'Material for teaching library history in the USA' *J Educ Lib* 1972 12 178-92.

Harris M H and Davis D G *American library history: a biliography* U of Texas P, 1978, 260p.

Davis D G and Harris M H 'Three years' work in American library history, 1971-1973' *J Lib Hist* 1974 9(4) 296-317.

— 'Two years' work in American library history, 1974-1975' *J Lib Hist* 1976 11(4) 276-96.

Bach H 'Bibliographical essay on the history of scholarly libraries in the USA, 1800 to the present' U of Illinois, Library School, *Occasional paper* 1959 (54), 24p, mimeo.

Stenstrom R H *Cooperation between types of libraries, 1940-1968: an annotated bibliography* ALA, 1970, 159p.

Chang D M 'Academic library cooperation: a selective annotated bibliography' *Lib Resour Tech Serv* 1976 20(3) 270-86.

Murfin M E and Wynar L *Reference service: an annotated bibliography* Libraries Unlimited, 1977, 294p.

Farina V 'Library and information services for older adults: an annotated bibliography' *Drexel Lib Q* 1979 15(2) 83-91. Part of a special issue on the subject.

Stoffle C 'Public library service to the disadvantaged: a comprehensive annotated bibliography, 1964-1968' *Lib J* 1969 94(2) 141-52; 1969 94(3) 507-15. See also under North America, 3b.

Poole J *Library services for the blind and physically handicapped: a bibliography, 1968-1978* Library of Congress, National Library Service for the Blind and Physically Handicapped, 1979, 73p.

Development of an integrated Bibliographic Information System for the Blind and Physically Handicapped (BIS/BAH) Library of Congress, Division for the Blind and Physically Handicapped (DBPH) 1975-77. 1st phase: Design and testing.

Pratt A D 'Libraries, economics and information: recent trends in information science literature' *Coll Res Lib* 1975 35 33-8.

Martin S K 'A selective annotated bibliography on library networking' *Information Reports and Bibliographies* 1976 5(6) 20-8.

Leonard L L 'Cooperative and centralized cataloging and processing: a bibliography, 1850-1967' U of Illinois Library School, *Occasional paper* 1968 (93).

Stockard J 'Selective survey of MARC literature' *Lib Resour Tech Serv* 1971 15(3) 279-89.

3c

Springman M A and Brown B M *The directory of library periodicals* 2nd ed Drexel P, 1967, 192p.

Moon E 'The library press' *Lib J* 1969 94(20) 4104-11. Critical review of the main professional journals in the USA.

Shields G R 'The library press: national and state magazines' *Drexel Lib Q* 1979 15(1) 3-24, refs. Whole issue on library literature.

Edgar N L 'Library periodical literature: a centennial assessment' *Serials Libn* 1978 2(4) 341-50, refs.

Katz W A ed *Library literature: the best of [1971]* Scarecrow. Annual.

There are over 800 library periodicals in the USA. Only the most general in scope can be mentioned:

ALA *American libraries*, 1970- . Previously *ALA Bulletin*, 1907-69.

Library Journal, New York, Bowker, 1876- .

Library trends, Urbana, 1952- .

Library quarterly, Chicago, 1930- .

Top of the news, ALA, 1944- .

Wilson library bulletin, New York, 1914- .

Journal of education for librarianship, Urbana, 1960- .

Library resources and technical services, ALA, 1957- .

Library of Congress quarterly journal

ERIC/CLIS *Newsletter*, 1968- .

Library research, 1979- . Quarterly.

Public library quarterly, New York, 1979- .

Center for the Study of Rural Librarianship, School of Library Science, Clarion State College *Rural Libraries*. 1980- .

College and research libraries, Chicago, 1939- .

Journal of academic librarianship, Boulder, Col., 1975- . 6 pa.

Special libraries, SLA, 1910- .

ALA, Health and Rehabilitative Library Services Division *Health and rehabilitation library services*, 1975- . Formerly *AHIL quarterly*.

US Scientific and Educational Administration, Technical Information Systems *Agricultural libraries information notes*, 1975- . Monthly.

Film Libraries Information Council, New York *Film library quarterly*, 1967- .

Serials librarian, New York, 1976- . Quarterly.

National Taiwan Normal University, Department of Social Education and Mid-West Chinese American Librarians Association *Journal of library and information science*, 1975- . 2pa.

ASIS journal October 1969- . Previously *American documentation,* 1950- .

ASIS *Collective index to the Journal of the American Society for Information Science, vols 1-25, 1950-1974* The Society, 1976, 282p.

ASIS bulletin, 1974- . 10 pa.

Information-news/sources/profiles, Science Associations/International Inc. 1959- . Supersedes: *Scientific information notes*.

Information-part 2, 1972- . Full texts of studies, bibliographies, state of the art, etc. Special bibliographical supplements.

Information and referral: the journal of the Alliance of Information and Referral Systems Phoenix, The Alliance of Information and Referral Systems, 1979- . 3 pa.

Information manager Information and Records Management Inc., 1978- . 6 pa.

Advanced technology/Libraries, 1972- . Los Angeles, Becker & Hayes. Microforms, video-recording, etc.

Microform review, 1972- . Weston, Microform Review Inc.

Journal of library automation (JOLA). ALA, Information Science and Automation Division.

Resource sharing and library network, 1980- .

Online: the magazine of online information systems, 1977- . Weston, Conn., Online Inc.

3d

Wasserman P and Paskar J *Statistics sources: a subject guide* 4th ed Gale Research, 1974, 892p.

 Rather J C and Cohen N M *Statistics of libraries: an annotated bibliography of*

recurring surveys US Office of Education, 1961, 50p.

Schick F L 'Century of library statistics of national scope' *Bowker annual* 1970 5-11.

— 'Library statistics: a century plus' *Amer Lib* 1971 2(7) 727-31.

Palmer D C ed *Planning for a nationwide system of library statistics. Final report . . . submitted in May 1970* (by the ALA) USGPO, 1970, 117p.

Ladd B *National inventory of library needs, 1975: resources needed for public libraries and academic libraries and public school library/media centers: a study submitted to the National Commission on Library and Information Science, March, 1977.*

[Library finances] *Amer Lib* 1977 8(10) 549-80. Special issue.

Rockwood C E and Rockwood R H *Quantitative guides to public library operation* U of Illinois, 1967, 26p. (Occasional paper no 89).

Library statistics. Part I: Selected statistics of public libraries serving populations of 35,000 and above. Institutional data. US Office of Education. Recurrent record.

— *Part II: Selected statistics of public libraries serving populations of less than 35,000. Institutional data.*

Lyle Eberhart W 'A closer look: Gallup survey of American adults assesses the role of libraries in America' *Amer Lib* 1976 7(4) 206-9.

Library statistics of colleges and universities. Institutional data.

— *Analytical report.* USGPO.

Dunn O C and Seibert W F *The past and likely future of 58 research libraries, 1951-1980: a statistical study of growth and change* 4th ed Purdue U, 1968, 70p.

US Office of Management and Budget *National plan for federal library statistics* Approved 26 June 1970; tested 1971-72; implemented 1972-73.

Kruzas A T *Special libraries and information centers: a statistical report on special library resources in the US* Gale Research, 1945, 42p.

Lewis A J '1978 statistical survey of law school libraries and librarians' *Law Lib J* 1979 72 302-39.

3e

Chee L 'How to research copyright law' *Law Lib J* 1977 70(2) 171-83, bibl.

Roberts M T comp *Copyright: a selected bibliography of periodical literature relating to literary property in the United States* Scarecrow, 1971, 416p.

Copyright, the librarian and the law Proceedings of the 8th annual symposium. . . Rutgers U, 1972, 83, 13p.

Cambridge Research Institute *Omnibus copyright revision: comparative analysis of the issues* ASIS, 1973, 280p.

Goldberg M D *Chairman Current development in Copyright Law 1977: volumes 1 & 2* New York City, Practising Law Institute, 1977, 2 vols.

For comments on the revision of the copyright law and its implications for libraries see:

Amer Lib 1976 7(10) 609-11.

Info Hotline 1976 8(8) 2-3; 1976 8(10) 1-31.

Int J Law Lib 1977 5(1) 121-30; 1978 6(2) 151-8.

Law Lib j 1977 70(2) 121-52.

De Grazia E *Censorship landmarks* Bowker, 1969, 657p.

ALA, Office for Intellectual Freedom *Intellectual freedom manual* ALA, 1974, 148p.

Flanagan L N 'Defending the indefendable: the limits of intellectual freedom' *Lib J* 1975 100(18) 1887-91.

Krug J F and Harvey J A 'Intellectual freedom and librarianship' in *Encyclopedia* 12(1974) 169-85.

Vagianos L 'Libraries and censorship' *APLA Bull* 1979 43(1) 4-6.

Oboler E M *Defending intellectual freedom: the library and the censor* Greenwood P, 1980, 246p. (Contributions to Librarianship and Information Science, 32).

Kerbec M J ed *Legally available US Government information as a result of the Public Information Act* Arlington, Output Systems Corp, 1970, 2 vols.

— 'Public Information Act: a potent tool for librarians and citizens seeking information from the Government' *Lib J* 1970 95 4229-31.

Ladenson A ed *American library laws* 4th ed, ALA.

— *1st suppl. 1973-74* ALA, 1975, 244p.

Angelo D et al *State library policy: its legislative and environmental contexts* ALA, 1971, 128p.

Fry J W 'LSA and LSCA, 1956-1973: a legislative history' *Lib Trends* 1975 24 7-15.

The Federal Government and public libraries: a ten year partnership, 1957-1966 US Office of Education, 1966, 20p.

Mersel J et al *An overview of the Libraries Services and Construction Act — Title I. Final report* Office of Education, Bureau Research, 1969, 374p. (Bowker, 1969, 373p.)

- *Text and amendments* in Bowker annual.

Hall F H 'Public laws/public libraries: the Federal Information Centers Act' *Pub Lib* 1979 18 21-2.

Schubert J F 'The impact of the Federal Library Services and Construction Act' *Lib Trends* 1975 24 27-44.

Ottersen S comp 'A bibliography on standards for evaluating libraries' *Coll Res Lib* 1971 32 127-44. Part 2 of a 'Critique on standards for evaluating library collections'.

Hirsch F E ed 'Standards for libraries' *Lib Trends* 1972 21(2) 159-355.

Minimum standards for public library systems, 1966 ALA, 1967, 69p.

Bloss M 'Standards for public library service — quo vadis?' *Lib J* 1976 101(11) 1259-62.

Standards for library services for the blind and visually handicapped: adopted July 14, 1966 by the Library Administration Division ALA, 1967, 54p.

Standards for school media programs ALA/AASL, 1969, 66p.

ACA/ALA Health and Rehabilitative Library Services Division *Library standards for juvenile correctional institutions* American Correctional Association, 1975, 7p.

3f General.

Lafeber W and Polenberg R *The American century: a history of the United States since the 1890's* Wiley, 1975, 536p.

Ehrlich P R et al *The golden door: international migration* Ballantine Books, 1979.

Tebbel J *A history of book publishing in the United States* Bowker, 1972-81, 4 vols.

The 1978 Consumer Research Study on Reading and Book Purchasing: a study inquiring into the nature of reading and book buying habits of the American public Book Industry Study Group, 1978, 333p.

Wynar L R 'The study of the ethnic press in the United States' *Unesco J* 1979 1(1) 56-62.

Thomassen C E ed *CATV and its implications for libraries* U of Illinois Graduate

School of Library Science, 1974, 91p. (Conference).

Ben-David J *Centers of learning: Britain, France, Germany, US: an essay* McGraw Hill, 1977, 208p.

[Library and information science in America] *ASIS Bull* 1976 2(8) Whole issue. History, survey.

Rebenak J H 'Contemporary libraries in the United States' in *Encyclopedia* 24(1978) 291-338.

Harris M H ed *Reader in American library history* NCR Microcard Editions, 1971, 242p.

Anderson M T *History of colonial American libraries, 1607-1776* Thesis, U of Mississippi, 1966.

O'Loughlin Sister M A *Emergence of American librarianship: a study of influence evident in 1876* Thesis, Columbia U, 1971, 264p.

Stone E W *American library development 1860-1899* Wilson Co, 1977, 367p.

Harris M H ed *The age of Jewett: Charles Coffin Jewett and American librarianship, 1841-1868* Libraries Unlimited, 1975, 166p. (Heritage of Librarianship Series, 1.)

Shera J H 'Failure and success: assessing a century' *Lib J* 1976 101(1) 281-7.

Harris M H 'Portrait in paradox: commitment and ambivalence in American librarianship, 1876-1976' *Libri* 1976 26(4) 281-301.

Winger H W (issue ed) 'American library history: 1876-1976' *Lib Trends* 1976 25(1) 1-416.

Boyd Rayward W 'Librarianship in the New World and the Old: some points of contact' *Lib Trends* 1976 25(1) 209-26.

Miksa F L ed *Charles Ammi Cutter, library systematizer* Libraries Unlimited, 1977 (Heritage of Librarianship, 3.)

Vann S K ed *Melvil Dewey, his enduring presence in librarianship* Libraries Unlimited, 1977.

Birdsall W F 'Archivists, librarians and issues during the pioneering era of the American archival movement' *J Lib Hist* 1979 14(4) 457-79, refs.

Metcalf K De Witt *Random recollections of an anachronism: or 75 years of library work* Readex Books, 1980, 401p.

Elliot K M *Chronology of librarianship, 1960-69* Kent State U, Research paper, 1971, 24p.

Maryland U, School of Librarianship and Information Science *Frontiers in librarianship: proceedings of the Change Institute 1969* Greenwood, 1972, 440p.

'Change 1969-79' *Amer Lib* 1979 10(6) 30-373. Series of papers.

McCrimmon B comp *American library philosophy: an anthology* Shoe String, 1975, 248p.

Knight D M and Nourse S E eds *Libraries at large: tradition, innovation and the national interest. The source book based on the National Advisory Commission on Libraries* Bowker, 1969, 664p.

Curley A 'Social responsibility and libraries' *Advances in Librarianship* 1974 4 77-101.

Monat W R 'The role of the social and behavioral sciences in determining library operation and impact' *Lib Trends* 1976 24(3) 583-96.

Dain P and Steig M F eds 'Libraries and society: research and thought' *Lib Trends* 1979 27(3) 221-417. Whole issue.

Libraries and the life of the mind in America ALA, 1977. Includes influence on Europe and of Europe on America.

See also:

American Library Association Conferences. On a topical theme. Annual.

Lettman M 'Our librarians abroad: a Jamaican looks at libraries in the US' *Jamaica Lib Ass Bull* 1975 23-6.

Sanner L-E *Studieresa i USA, hösten 1974* Stockholm, Karolinska Institutets Bibliotek, 1975, 45p.

Kemp D A 'American librarianship: a British view' *PNLA Q* 1979 (Winter) 43 10-8.

New Library World 1979 80- . Quarterly series on library activities in the USA.

'American librarians abroad' *Lib Trends* 1972 20(3) 475-591.

Vosper R 'A century abroad' *Coll Res Lib* 1976 37(6) 514-30.

Brewster B J *American overseas library technical assistance, 1940-1970* Scarecrow 1976 434p.

Plotnik A et al 'Washington library power: who has it, and how it works for you' *Amer Lib* 1975 6(11) 647-74.

Casey G M (issue ed) 'Federal aid to libraries: its history, impact, future' *Lib Trends* 1975 24(1) 153p. Whole issue.

Gwyn A et al 'Friends of the library' *Coll Res Lib* 1975 36(4) 272-82, refs.

Wright C 'Current developments in Federal support for libraries in the United States' *Libri* 1976 26(2) 96-107.

Molz R K *Federal policy and library support* MIT, 1977, 118p.

The White House Conference on Library and Information Services, 1979: summary USGPO, 1980, 101p.

- [Extensive summaries in] *Spec Lib* 1980 71(2).
- *Info Hotline* 1980 12(5).
- *Lib J* 1980 105(2) 149-66.

Towards a national program for library and information services: goals for action NCLIS, 1975, 106p.

- *Final report* ASIS, 1975, 115p. (ERIC report ED-107 312).

For summaries see:

- *Information Reports and Bibliographies* 1975 4(3) 1-30.
- ERIC report ED-167 128, 15p.

Nyren K ed *Making cooperation work* New York, Library Journal, 1979, 56p. (Library Journal special report, 9.)

Patrick R J et al *A study of library cooperatives, networks and demonstration projects: final report* (For the Office of Planning, Budgeting and Evaluation, US Office of Education) K G Saur, 1980. Vol. 1: Findings and recommendations. Vol. 2: Case Study reports.

Kanevskiĭ B P 'Problemy koordinatsii komplektovaniya i otbora literaturȳ v deyatel' nosti krupnȳkh nauchnȳkh bibliotek SShA' *Bibliot Bibliog za Rubezhom* 1976 (60) 6-24

'The need to know' *Lib J* 1976 101(1) 292p. Special issue.

Lubans J ed *Educating the library user* Bowker, 1974, 435p.

— *Progress in educating the library user* Bowker, 1978, 230p.

3f Public libraries and children's libraries.

US Dept of the Interior, Bureau of Education *Public libraries in the United States of America: their history, condition and management — special report* The Bureau, 1876.

Sessa F B 'Public libraries, International history of the public library [in USA]' in *Encyclopedia* 24(1978) 267-91.

Garrison D *Apostles of culture: the public librarian and American society, 1876-1920* Free Press, 1979, 319p, refs.

Mickelson P 'American society and the public library in the thought of Andrew Carnegie' *J Lib Hist* 1975 10(2) 117-38.

Blayney M S ' "Libraries for the millions": adult public library services and the New Deal' *J Lib Hist* 1977 12(3) 235-49.

Public Library Association *The public library mission statement and its imperatives for service* PLA, 1979, 16p.

Schuman P G *Social responsibilities and libraries: a Library Journal/School Library Journal selection* Bowker, 1976, 402p.

Seymour W N comp *The changing role of public libraries: background papers from the White House Conference* Scarecrow, 1980, 270p.

Kirchfeld F 'Radikale Bibliothekare im öffentlichen Dienst' *Buch u Bibl* 1976 28 353-66.

Erteschik A M *Public library construction 1965-1978. The Federal contribution through the Library Services and Construction Act* Washington, Bureau of School Systems, Office of Libraries and Learning Resources, 1978, 31p. (ERIC report ED-165 813).

McCrossan J A ed 'State library development agencies' *Lib Trends* 1978 27(2) 109-217. Whole issue.

Brown J W 'A nationwide survey reveals . . . new media in public libraries' *Wilson Lib Bull* 1976 51(3) 232-9.

'Films in public libraries' *Lib Trends* 1978 27(1) 3-105. Whole issue.

Jennison P S and Sheridan R N eds *The future of general adult reading in America* ALA, 1971, 160p.

'The librarian and the teaching of reading' *Wilson Lib Bull* 1970 45(3) 239-307. Series of papers.

The Right to Read Committee of the AASL and ALA *The right to read and the nation's libraries* ALA, 1974, 109p.

Penland P R and Mathai A *Library as a learning service center* Dekker, 1978, 237p.

Forinash M R ed 'Public library and adult basic education' *Drexel Lib Q* 1978 (Oct). Whole issue.

Kozol J 'How we can win: a plan to reach and teach twenty-five million illiterate adults' *Wilson Lib Bull* 1980 54(10) 640-4.

Stevenson G 'The wayward scholar: resources and research in popular culture' *Lib Trends* 1977 25(4) 779-818.

Bouvy M 'Démocratie et choix des livres' *Médiathèques publiques* 1979 (51); (52) 5-21. Includes texts of ALA Declaration of library rights, etc.

Penland P R 'Floating librarians' in *Encyclopedia* 8 (1972) 501-30, 125 refs.

Penland P R et al, eds *Institute on the floating librarian in the emerging community, Pittsburgh, 1970* U of Pittsburgh, 1970, 261p.

— *Advisory counseling for librarians* Proceedings of an Institute on readers advisory services, Pittsburgh, 1969 U of Pittsburgh, 1969, 179p.

Earl Bone L ed 'Community analysis and libraries' *Lib Trends* 1976 24(3) 429-643.

Samore T *Progress in urban librarianship: a seminar on community needs and the designing of library education programs to meet these needs* U of Wisconsin Milwaukee, School of Library Science, 1974?, 128p. (Library science studies, 4).

Childers T *The information-poor in America* Scarecrow, 1975, 182p. Final report of a study 'Knowledge/information needs of the disadvantaged 1972' — Grant Bureau of Libraries and Learning Resources.

Turick D *Community information services in libraries* Bowker, 1978, 80p. (Library Journal special report, 5).

Jones C S ed *Public library information and referral service* Gaylord Professional Pub, 1978, 265p.

Bunch A *Community Information Services* Bingley/Shoe String, 1982, 176p.
Budington W S ed 'Library services in metropolitan areas' *Lib Trends* 1974 23(2) 179-317. Whole Issue.
Ruhig de Mont R *Reform and reaction: the big city public library in American life* Greenwood P, 1977, 153p.
Croker S K *Immigrants: the problems they present public libraries in Sweden, the United Kingdom, the United States* College of Librarianship, Wales, 1975, 54p.
Winbank D A *Library responses to a multi-cultural society: a traveller's notes* Western Australia Institute of Technology, Dept of Library Studies, 1978, 40p, refs.
Wynar L R 'Library services to ethnic communities' *Cath Lib World* 1977 49 156-61.
Townley C T 'American Indian library service' *Adv Libp* 1978 8 135-80.
Dudley M S *Chicano library program* U of California Library, 1970 (UCLA Lib Occasional papers, 17).
Haro R P and Smith E M eds 'Service to the Spanish speaking, 1978' *Wilson Lib Bull* 1978 53(3) 228-67, refs.
Casey G M 'Services to the disadvantaged' *Lib Trends* 1974 23(2) 271-85.
Eisman H L 'Public library programs [for elderly readers]' *Wilson Lib Bull* 1979 53(8) 564-9, refs.
'Library programs and services to the disadvantaged' *Lib Trends* 1971 20(2) 187-471.
Brown E F *Library services to the disadvantaged* Scarecrow, 1971, 560p.
Lipsman C K *The disadvantaged and library effectiveness* ALA, 1972, 197p.
'Library services to the aging' *Lib Trends* 1973 21(3) 359-458.
Appel J and Casini B P eds '[Library and information services for older adults]' *Drexel Lib Q* 1979 15(2) 1-93. Whole issue.
Posell E Z 'Libraries and the deaf patron' *Wilson Lib Bull* 1977 51(5) 402-4, refs.
Stetten K J *Telebook center for the blind: phase 1, final report* Washington D.C., The Mitre Corporation, 1976, 116p.
Lovejoy E ed 'Library service for the blind and physically Handicapped' *Health and Rehabilitative Library Services Division Journal* 1976 2(2) 2-19, refs.
Strom M G ed *Library services to the blind and physically handicapped* Metuchen, N.J., Scarecrow Press, 1977, 285p.
National Library Service for the Blind and Physically handicapped *Library services to the blind and physically handicapped: a state of the art review* The Service, 1979.
Rosen G K 'Hospital libraries and collections' in *Encyclopedia* 11 (1974) 22-61, bibl.
'Bibliotherapy' *Libri* 1975 25(2) 133-62. Special section.
Phinney G ed *The librarian and the patient: an introduction to library services for patients in health care institutions* ALA, 1977, 352p.
Farmer J 'Full members of the team: medical librarians in the patient care setting' *Lib Ass Rec* 1977 79(2) 81, 83, 85.
Harris C L 'Hospital-based patient education programs and the role of the hospital librarian' *Med Lib Ass Bull* 1978 66(2) 210-7.
Developing a public library type service adapted for mentally retarded citizens California U Library, 1977, 13p. (ERIC report ED-167 142).
Forrer, A-M and Zajac M *Library service to the mentally retarded* Pennsylvania State Library, 1978, 16p. (ERIC report ED-165 728).
Kupstas K *Library programs for long-term chronic psychiatric patients*

Pennsylvania State Library, 1978, 73p. (ERIC report ED-167 079).
McClasky H C ed [Institution libraries] *Lib Trends* 1978 26(3) 301-446. Whole issue.
Association of Hospital and Institution Libraries *Jails need libraries too: guidelines for library service programs to jail* ALA, 1974, 15p.
Rubin R J ed 'Breaking in: library service to prisoners' *Wilson Lib Bull* 1977 51(6) 496-533. Set of papers.
Cheeseman M 'Prison (correctional) libraries' in *Encyclopedia* 24 (1978) 117-24, refs.
Madden S B 'The right of young adults in correctional institutions' *Top of the News* 1979 35(3) 247-55.
Lopez M D 'Children's libraries: nineteenth century American origins' *J Lib Hist* 1976 11(4) 316-42.
Enderson M *Visioner og virkelighed: traek af bornebibliotekernes historie i USA og Danmark 1870-1930* Danmarks Bibliotekskole, 1977, 84p. Comparative study Denmark, USA.
Baudin G 'Origines et développement des bibliothèques publiques pour la jeunesse' *Médiathèques Publ* 1977 (42) 5-12. Comparative study, and US aid to Europe.
Shapiro L L 'Libraries for tomorrow children: grim fairy tale' *Lib J* 1976 101(1) 101-6.
Richardson S K ed *Allerton Park Institute 1977: Children's services of public libraries* U of Illinois, Graduate School of Library Science, 1978, 178p.
Krueger K ed 'Public library facilities for children' *Illinois Lib* December 1978. Whole issue.
Rogers J-A V *Libraries and young adults: media, services and librarianship* Libraries Unlimited, 1979, 238p.
Braverman M *Youth, society, and the public library* ALA, 1979, 289p.
Rudser R *A study of combination school/public libraries in North Dakota* Bismark, State Library Commission, 1977, 88p.
Woolard W L B *Combined school/public libraries: a survey with conclusions and recommendations* Scarecrow, 1980, 184p. Revision of a thesis, 1977.
Davies R A 'School libraries' in *Encyclopedia* 26 (1979) 361-71. Developments, standards, etc.
Fain E 'The library and American education: education through secondary school' *Lib Trends* 1979 27(3) 327-52, refs. Part of an issue 'Libraries and society'.
Penland P R 'Instructional media centers' in *Encyclopedia* 12 (1974) 99-149, refs.
Bock D J and Lajeunesse L R *Learning resources center: a planning primer for libraries in transition* Library Journal, 1977, 64p.
Prostano E T and Prostano J S *The school library media center* 3rd ed Libraries Unlimited, 1982.
Barber R W and Waldro P R eds 'Supervision of instructional media service' Part I *Drexel Lib J* 1977 13(2); Part II *Ibid* 1978 14(3) 1-133.
Babin L J *The library media center in the public school* Wethersfield, Pyquag Books, 1979, 52p.

3f Academic and special libraries.

Hamlin A T *The university library in the United States: its origins and development* U of Pennsylvania P, 1981.
Byrd P et al *Guide to academic libraries in the United States* Prentice Hall, 1981, 184p.

Holley E G 'Academic libraries in 1876' *Coll Res Lib* 1976 37(1) 15-47.
Kaser D 'A century of academic librarianship as reflected in its literature' *Coll Res Lib* 1976 37(2) 110-27.
Farber E I and Walling R eds *The academic library: essays in honor of Guy R Lyle* Scarecrow, 1974, 171p.
Weber D C 'A century of cooperative programs among academic libraries' *Coll Res Lib* 1976 37(3) 205-21.
Rosenthal J A *The research Libraries Group: proposals for cooperation among the libraries of Columbia, Harvard and Yale universities and the New York Public Library* 1974, 161p.
Poole H ed *Academic libraries by the year 2000: essays honoring Jerold Orne* Bowker, 1977, 205p.
Edelman H and Tatum G M 'The development of collections in American university libraries' *Coll Res Lib* 1976 37(3) 222-45.
Tuttle H W 'From Cutter to computer: technical services in academic and research libraries, 1876-1976' *Coll Res Lib* 1976 37(5) 421-51.
Moore E L ed *Junior college libraries: development needs and perspectives* ALA, 1969, 104p. (ACRL monographs, 30).
Dyson A J 'Organising undergraduate library instruction: the English and American experience' *J Acad Libp* 1975 1(1) 9-13.
Gwinn N E 'Academic libraries and undergraduate education: the CLR [Council on Library Resources] experience' *Coll Res Lib* 1980 41(1) 5-16, refs.
Smith J C 'The impact of Black study programs on the academic libraries' *Coll Res Lib* 1972 33(2) 85-92.
Haro R P 'Academic library services for Mexican Americans' *Coll Res Lib* 1972 33(6) 454-62.
Bendix D and Hall J B eds 'Library services and the Open University' *Drexel Lib Q* 1975 11(2) 1-92. Special issue.
Orne J 'Academic library buildings: a century in review' *Coll Res Lib* 1976 37 316-31.
Vosper R G 'The private collector and the research library; a goodly company' *Imprint of the Stanford Libraries Associates* 1978 4(1) 5-12.
Jackson E B ed *Special librarianship: a new reader* Scarecrow, 1980, 759p.
— 'Special libraries in 1980 as seen in 1968 and 1978' *Sci Tech News* 1979 33(2) 32-4.
Smith J I *Library and information servies for special groups* Science Associates, 1974.
Harvey J F ed *Church and synagogue libraries* Scarecrow, 1980.
Crawford S and Dandurand G L 'Health science libraries in the United States: a five year perspective' *Bull Med Lib Ass* 1975 63(1) 7-13, refs.
Buxton C A *Health sciences libraries in the United States* 1976, 65p.
Roussel A 'Les bibliothèques médicales américaines, organisation en réseau, octobre-novembre 1977' *Bull Biblioth Fr* 1979 24(5) 223-30.
Lindberg D A B *The growth of medical information systems in the United States* Lexington Books, 1979.

3f Information, automation, networks.

ASIS *Key papers in information science* ASIS, 1971.
Husbands C W and Tighe R L eds *Information revolution: proceedings of the 38th ASIS annual meeting, Vol 12, Boston, October 1975* ASIS, 1975, 170p (Part I) and 2 microfiches (Part II: Abstracts of selected papers).

Hammer D P ed *The information age: its development, its impact* Scarecrow, 1976, 290p. Developments 1965-75.

Brenner E H ed *The information age in perspective* (ASIS annual meeting 1978) Knowledge Industry Pub, 1978, 381p. All aspects, including transfer to the Third World.

Becker J *The information decade* ERIC, 1978, 18p. (ERIC report ED-158 753).

Meredith J C 'NTIS update: a critcal review of services' *Govern't Public Rev* 1974 (4) 343-61. NTIS: National Technical Information Service, clearinghouse for scientific, technical and industrial information.

Martin S K ed *Information politics: proceedings of the 39th ASIS annual meeting, Vol 13, San Francisco, October 4-9, 1976* ASIS, 1976, 176p (Part I) and microfiches (Part II).

See also other meetings of ASIS.

Haas W J et al 'Managing the information revolution: CLR's bibliographic service development program' *Lib J* 1979 104 1867-70. Center for Library Resources.

Cacaly S 'L'information scientifique et technique aux Etats Unis' *Documentaliste* 1977 14(1) 27-33; 14(2) 17-24.

Bush in A A and Yurow J H *The foundations of United States information policy* National Telecommunications and Information Administration, 1980, 20p. (NTIS report PB80-204019).

Kenney B 'Die Planung von nationalen Informationssystemen in der Bundesrepublik Deutschland, England und der USA' *Nachr Dok* 1975 26(4/5) 136-42.

Kent A and Galvin T J eds *The structure and governance of library networks. Proceedings of the 1978 conference in Pittsburgh co-sponsored by the National Commission on Libraries and Information Science and the University of Pittsburgh* Dekker, 1979, 352p.

Library of Congress. Network Development Office *The role of the Library of Congress in the evolving national network: a study commissioned by the Library of Congress. . . and funded by the National Commission on Libraries and Information Science* The Library, 1978, 141p.

Avram H D 'US Library of Congress networking activities' *Unesco Bull Lib* 1978 33(2) 71-80.

Donohue J C 'The Library of Congress: a proposed role in a national information and referral network' *ASIS J* 1979 30(4) 202-4.

Ackoff R L et al *Designing a national scientific and technological communication system: the SCATT report* U of Pennsylvania, 1976, 174p.

Goldstein S and Miller M R eds *Library networks 1974-1975* Knowledge Industry Pub, 1974, 110p.

Martin S K *Library networks 1976-1977* Knowledge Industry Pub 1976, 131p.

Guilloux R comp *Réseaux et systèmes de documentation* Gauthier-Villars, 1975, 340p. Europe, USSR, USA.

Bullard S R et al, eds 'Multitype library networking: a symposium' in *Library acquisitions* 1978 2(3/4) 159-91, refs.

Nöthiger R 'Bibliotheksautomatisierung und Bibliotheknetzwerke in den USA' *Nachrichten* 1979 55(4) 149-60, refs.

Kaplan L *Reader in library services and the computer* NCR Microcard Editions, 1971, 239p.

Fasana P J 'Impact of national developments on library technical services and public services' *J Lib Autom* 1974 7(4) 249-62.

Moldoveanu V 'Automatizarea bibliotecilor in SUA' *Stud Cerc Dok* 1975 17(1/2) 211-32.

Martin S K *Technology in libraries: 1960-2000* ERIC, 1978, 15p. (ERIC report ED-158 764).

Divilbiss J L *Proceedings of the 1976 Clinic on Library Applications of Data Processing: the economics of library automation* U of Illinois, Graduate School of Library Science, 1977, 164p.

Spigai F G et al, eds *Information roundup: a continuing education session on microform and data processing in the library and information center: costs/benefits/history/trends. Proceedings of the 4th ASIS mid-year meeting. Portland May 1975* ASIS, 1975, 179p. 16 papers.

Lancaster F W ed *Problems and failures in library automation. Proceedings of the 1978 Clinic on Library Applications of Data Processing* U of Illinois, Graduate School of Library Science, 1978, 109p.

Meyer R W and Panetta R 'Two shared cataloguing data bases: a comparison' *Coll Res Lib* 1977 38(1) 19-24. Comparison of OCLC and B/NA Blackwell North America.

Allison A M and Allan A eds *OCLC: a national library network* Enslow Pub, 1979, 248p. Ohio Computer Library Center. On-line resources sharing. See also other similar schemes such as: SOLINET, SLICE, etc.

Gore D et al, eds *Requiem for the card catalog: management issues in automated cataloguing* Aldwych P, 1979, 200p.

Mason M 'United States special libraries and Universal Bibliographical Control' *Inspel* 1974 9(1/2) 53-63.

LATIN AMERICA

The term is taken here to cover the American countries with a Spanish or Portuguese background. But as the Caribbean countries with British, French or Dutch associations are involved in many regional activities, they are treated under this heading. See the relevant subsections under: Caribbean Region.

1

'The role of national libraries in national and international information systems. Latin American supplement' *Working paper* for the Meeting of Directors of National Libraries, Oslo, 1975. Rio de Janeiro, Biblioteca Nacional, 1975, 7p.

Gropp A E *Bibliografía sobre las bibliotecas nacionales de los paises Latinoamericanos y sus publicaciones* PAU, 1960, 58p. (PAU Bibliographic series, 50).

Pan American Union (PAU) Columbus Memorial Library/Biblioteca Commemorativa de Colón.

Wilson J and Shepard M D 'Organization of American States (OAS). General Secretariat, Columbus Memorial Library' in *Encyclopedia* 21 (1977) 16-35.

Casa de las Américas, Havana. Specializes in Latin American culture.

Hansen D et al 'Casa de las Américas og Cubas kulturoffensiv in Latinamerika' *Bibliotek 70* 1978 (10) 247-9.

For specialized libraries in North America see under North America and USA, 3a, subject collections and similar publications. See also:

Miller K E and Fort G V *Major Latin American collections in libraries of the United States* OAS, 1970, 38p. (Cuadernos Bibliotecologicos, 1 revised).

Jackson W V 'Binational center libraries' in *Encyclopedia* 2 (1969) 470-81. Mainly on the US Centers in Latin America.

Jackson W V ed *Latin American collections* Nashville, The Author, 1974, 142p. (Vanderbilt U Bookstore).

Crow M *Scholar's guide to Washington, DC: Latin American and Caribbean studies* Smithsonian Instn P, 1979, 346p. Mainly on collections.

Naylor B et al *Directory of libraries and special collections on Latin America and the West Indies* [in the UK] Athlone P, 1975, 161p.

See also under 2a: American Studies; and 3b for catalogues, etc.

2a

Organization of American States (OAS)/Organisación de Estados Americanos (OEA), Washington, 1890- . Created as: International Union of American Republics. Its General Secretariat, the Pan American Union (PAU) administers the Columbus Memorial Library. It also has a Department of Cultural Affairs with an Interamerican Committee of Bibliography.

Shepard M Daniels *Organization of American States and its potential for collaboration in the improvement of scientific documentation in Latin America* OAS, 1970, 27p. (Limited distribution).

Economic Commission for Latin America (ECLA).

Center for Interamerican Relations, New York.

Organisación Internacional de Cultura y Educación Latinoamericana. Based on Peru.

Unesco. Centro Regional en el Hemisferio Occidental, Havana.

- Centro Regional de Educación de Adultos y Alfabetisación Funcional para América Latina. 1951- .

Centro Regional para el Fomento del Libro en la América Latina (CERLAL), Bogota. Bibliographic activities.

Plazas A 'Los objectivos y realizaciones del CERLAL' *Working paper* B-8 at SALALM, 1975 U of Texas 1978, 158-67.

Fundación Interaméricana de Bibliotecología Franklin, Buenos Aires.

2a Latin American Studies: Centres, their activities and publications.

A short list of institutions or of references to institutions for research on Latin America. See also under 3b for catalogues, etc.

Zarubezhnye tsentry po izuchentiiu latinskoi Ameriki Moscow, Institut Latinskoi Amerika, 1970, 2 vols. Vol 1: Centres in Latin America; Vol 2: Centres in Western Europe.

Mesa-Lago C *Latin American studies in Europe* Pittsburgh, Center for Latin American Studies, 1979, 190p.

- Oficina de Educación Iberoamericana (OEI), Madrid.
- Lateinamerkia-Institut, Freien U, Berlin.
- Österreichisches Lateinamerika-Institut, Vienna.
- Institut des Hautes Etudes de l'Amérique Latine, Paris.
- Nordiska Samfundet för Latinamerika-forskning, Stockholm. Institute of Latin American Studies.

Hilton R *Handbook of Hispanic sources: material and research organizations in the United States* 2nd ed Stanford U P, 1956, 448p.

Haro R P *Latin American research in the United States and Canada: a guide and directory* ALA, 1971, 111p.

Gormly M *Resources for Latin American studies* Rev ed UCLA, Latin American Center, 1977, 284 leaves.

Léon P R 'Los estudios sobre Iberoamérica en el Canada' Sevilla, Escuela de Estudios Hispano-Americanos, *Historiografía y Bibliografía Americanista* 1972 16(1) 71-98.

Andrade G 'Latin American studies in Japan' *Lat Amer Res Rev* (U of Texas) 1973 8(1) 147-56. Institutions, activities, review of publications.

Most Latin American countries have a research centre on Latin America, usually attached to a university.

2b

Seminars on the Acquisition of Latin American Library Materials (SALALM), 1956- . Since 1975 its secretariat is at the University of Massachusetts Amherst. Formerly at the University of Texas, Austin. The reports and papers of the annual meetings are a most valuable source of information on bibliographical and library development, activities and plans. Since 1969 the meetings are organized around a theme: type of material, acquisitions in a region or other topic relevant to library material. Each seminar generates the publication of:

Final report and working papers now available from the SALALM Secretariat. These or individual papers will be cited where relevant, but for general information and guidance see:

- *Facts about the SALALM* Annual brochure.

- Abella R et al *Index to the SALALM progress reports, 1956-1970* SALALM Secretariat, 1975, 163p. These reports are included every year in the conference papers.

- *SALALM Newsletter* 1973- . Three a year.

Read G F 'SALALM: thoughts on the birth and development of an organisation' Paper in *Acquisitions from the Third World LIBER Seminar September 1973* Mansell, 1975, 177-91. (Edited by D A Clarke).

FID. Comisión Latinoaméricana (FID/CLA). 1960- . Meetings are held in different Latin American Countries every other year: Mexico, 1967; Rio de Janeiro, 1969; Lima, 1971; Bogota, 1973, etc. Since 1969 the reports of the meetings have been published by the FID as *Annals*. For information on the activities of FID/CLA see:

FID/CLA Newsletter. 1964- .

IFLA. Grupo Regional de América Latina (FIAB/GRAL).

Convenio Andrés Bello (for educational, scientific and cultural integration). Grupo de Trabajo para el Desarrollo de los Servicios de Bibliotecas y de Información Científica y Técnica en los paises signatorios del Convenio Andrés Bello (DEBICYT). The countries involved are Bolivia, Chile, Colombia, Ecuador, Peru and Venezuela. The work group organized itself during the first meeting, in Caracas, November 1971.

Primera reunión, Caracas, 15-18 noviembre 1971. Informe final. Known as DEBICYT-1. A plan of development was formulated; then a second meeting was convened to study the proposed plan:

Seconda reunión, Bogota, 19-25 noviembre 1972 (DEBICYT-2). Both reports published by the Madrid Officina de Educación Iberoamericana. (Report on the second meeting in *Fenix* 1973 23 225-39).

Long E 'The role of library associations in Latin America' *Focus Int Comp Libp* 1976 7(3) 28-9.

Inter-American Bibliographical and Library Association (IABLA). Now based on North Miami Beach. 1930- .

Asociación Latinoaméricana de Bibliotecarios (ALBOR), Medellin 1968- .

Asociación Latinoaméricana de Escuelas de Bibliotecología y Ciencias de la Información (ALEBCI). 1970- . Based on the School of Librarianship, U of Minas Gerais, Brazil; but its seat changes. ALEBCI *Estatutos* Belo Horizonte, 1972.

Asociación Interamericana de Bibliotecarios y Documentalistas Agricolas (AIDBA), Turrialba (Costa Rica). 1958- . Revived in 1965.

Paz de Erickson A M 'Asociación Interamericana de Bibliotecarios y Documentalistas Agricolas (AIDBA), Turrialba' *ACB Bol* 1975 3(22/23) 37-44.

— 'Inter-American Association of Agricultural Librarians and Documentalists (AIDBA)' in *Enclyclopedia* 12 (1974) 185-7).

2c

Mesas de Estudio de la Preparación de los Bibliotecarios en la América Latina, 1963-65. Publications generated by these meetings, published by Editorial Universidad de Antioquia:

- *Normas para escuelas de bibliotecología* [Vol 1], 1968, 55p.
- *Trabajos de base presentados a las 3 mesas de estudio* Vol 3, 1969, 363p.
- *Conclusiones y recomendaciones, programa y bibliografías* Vol 2, 1970, 160p.

Sabor J E *Las normas y conclusiones de Medellin en la formación de bibliotecarios en América Latina* (Reunion de Consulta sobre los Programas de la OEA para la Formación de Bibliotecarios, Medellin, 1974) Medellin, 1974.

— *Trabajo No 2* Medellin, 1974.

Jackson W V 'Education for librarianship in Latin America' *Lib Trends* 1963 12(2) 322-55.

Sanz M T 'Training of librarians and documentalists in Latin America' *Unesco Bull Lib* 1967 21(6) 318-26.

Shepard M Daniels 'Education for librarianship in Latin America' *J Educ Libp* 1967 7(3) 119-34.

Jackson W V 'Library education in Latin America: a look backward and forward' in Goldstein H and Goudeau J eds *Library history, Seminar No 4. Proceedings* Florida State U, 1972, 316-31.

Carvalho M M de and Vieira A da Soledad 'A ALEBCI e a formação do bibliotecario' *Rev Escu Bibliot UFMG* 1974 3 131-5.

Tanodi A 'Archival training in Latin America' *Unesco J* 1979 1(2) 112-23.

[Education and training of librarians for area collections] *Working paper* in SALALM XVII, 1972. Published 1975.

Levi N de 'El entrenamiento de especialistas de la información' *Bol Inst Invest Bibliog* 1972 (8) 355-71, tables.

Tomé M Y 'Avance en la preparación de bibliotecarios especializados y de especialistas en información an América Latina: analisis de la problematica en este proceso educativo' *IAALD Q Bull* 1978 23 39-45.

Saračevic T 'Training and education of information scientists in Latin America' *Unesco J* 1980 2(3) 170-9, bibl.

'Escuelas de bibliotecarios en América Latina (lista provisional)' *Fenix* 1967 5 364-6.

Penna C V and Daniels M *Guia de escuelas y cursos de bibliotecología en América Latina* 3rd ed PAU, 1964, 66p. (Revised by: C Rovira).

Curras E comp *Catalogo de cursos sobre ciencias documentarias, biblioteconomía y archivología impartidos en los paises iberoaméricanos* U Complutense de Madrid, 1979, 92p.

Arenas J L de 'Información estadística de las escuelas de bibliotecología en América Latina' *ALEBCI Bol Info* 1974 3 Suppl.

Alguero M S 'The Inter-American Library School as a major training facility for Latin America' *J Educ Libp* 1966 6(4) 243-51.

'Escuela Interaméricana de Bibliotecología' in *Encyclopedia* 8 (1972) 184-204.

Freiband Sé ' "Library planning" in the Interamerican Library School curriculum' *J Educ Libp* 1976 17(1) 47-54.

Juarroz R *América Latina: curso audio-visual de bibliotecología 15 de junio- 15 de agosto de 1969* Unesco, 1970, 57p.

Penna C V *Resultados de la primera mesa de estudios sobre la formación de bibliotecarios y mejoramiento de bibliotecarios en servicio en la América Latina* Escuela Interamericana de Bibliotecología, 1965, 36p. Vol 1. See also, published as an annex:

Sanz M T *Analisis de los informes nacionales sobre el estado actual de la profesión bibliotecaria en América Latina* 1965, 284p.

Penna C V *Comments on the suggestions approved by the round table on training and in-service training of librarians in Latin America, Quito, 1966* Unesco, Document LBA/Conf 29/4.

'Research in librarianship and professional training' *Unesco Bull Lib* 1968 22(1) 29-32.

3a

Delpar H ed *Enclyclopedia of Latin America* McGraw Hill, 1974, 651p.

232 Massa G B et al *Diccionario técnico de Biblioteconomía Espanol-Inglés/*

Technical dictionary of librarianship Spanish-English Mexico, Editorial F Trellos, 1964.

Buonocore D *Diccionario de bibliotecología* 2nd ed aumentada Buenos Aires, Ediciones Marymar, 1976, 452p.

Barbosa D *Lista de siglas latino-americanas* Economic Commission for Latin America, 1978, 379p.

Latin America and the Caribbean: a handbook London, A Blond, 1967- .

South American handbook London, Davies, 1968.

Brooks J ed The 1976 *South American handbook* 52nd ed Bath, Trade and Travel Pub, 1976, 984p.

Wilgus A C ed *Latin American historical dictionaries* Scarecrow, 1967- . Series on individual countries.

Unesco. Centro Regional *Directorio de organismos rectores de la politica científica nacional en América latina* Montevideo, 1968, 355p. (World directory of national science policy-making bodies, Vol 3, Spanish edition).

Sable M H *Master directory for Latin America containing ten directories covering organizations, associations and institutions in the fields of. . .* UCLA, Latin American Center, 1965, 438p.

Instituto de Cultura Hispanica. Centro Iberoamericano de Cooperación Universitaria y Científica *Guia de estudios superiores de Iberoamerica* Madrid, Edicione Cultura Hispanica, 1973, 508p.

La empresa del libro en América Latina: una guia seleccionada de las editoriales, distribuidores y librerias en América latina 3rd ed Bowker Editores Argentina, 1973, 300p.

Lofquist W S *The market for books in Latin America* US Department of Commerce, 1960- .

Guia de bibliotecas de la América latina.

Bibliotecas públicas y escolares en América latina PAU, 1963, 136p.

Hilton R *Scientific institutions of Latin America with special reference to their organization and information facilities* Stanford, Institute of International Studies, 1970, 748p.

IBBD *Guia de bibliotecas especialidades e centros de documentação da America Latina* 1970, 1 vol. (FID/CLA Publição especial, 3; FID Publ 470).

Library of Congress, Hispanic Foundation *National directory of Latin Americanists* 2nd ed 1971, 684p.

3b

Shepard M Daniels *An Inter-American bibliographic institute: a proposal for comprehensive international bibliographic and cataloguing control* PAU, 1963, 12p. (Cuadernos bibliotecológicos, 16).

Cohen I V 'Ein bibliographisches Zentrum' *Übersee Rundschau* 1978 30(4) 35-6. On the Centro Bibliografico Iberoamericano, Mexico City, 1976- .

Unesco 'Latin American seminar on the control and acquisition of bibliographic material, Bogota 13-17 October 1975 (SAMBLA)' *Int Catalog* 1976 5(2) 3-4.

Pariseau E J ed *Latin America: an acquisition guide for college and public libraries* Consortium of Latin American Studies Programs (CLASP) Gainesville, and Latin American Studies Association (LASA) Secretariat, 1975, 754p. (CLASP Publ, 7).

Riasco Sanchez B 'Bibliografía latinoamericana: programa del CERLAL' *Working paper* in SALALM, Bogota 1975 U of Texas, 1978, 163-6.

Monte-Mór J 'ISBD application to Latin American national bibliographies' *Unesco Bull Lib* 1977 31(4) 233-9, 254, bibl.

3b Bibliographies of bibliographies and reference works.

Conover H F *Records of current publishing in Latin America.* List updating the list of national bibliographies published in her *Current national bibliographies* Library of Congress, 1955.

Zimmerman F *Current national bibliographies of Latin America: a state of the art study* U of Florida, Center for Latin American studies, 1971, 139p.

Geoghegan A R *Obras de referencia de América latina — repertorio selectivo y anotado* Buenos Aires, The Author, 1965, 280p. In UDC order, indexes.

Sabor J E *Manual de fuentes de información. Obras de referencia, enciclopedias, diccionarios, bibliografías* 2nd ed Kapelusz, 1967, 342p.

Stein B H *Latin America: a guide to selected reference sources, bibliographies and introductory texts in the Princeton University Library* The Library, 1977, 190p.

Peraza Sarausa F *Bibliografías corrientes de la América latina* 6th ed U of Florida, 1969. (Biblioteca del Bibliotecario, 65).

Bayitch S A *Latin America and the Caribbean: a bibliographical guide to works in English* U of Miami P, 1967, 943p.

Woods R D *Reference materials on Latin America in English — the humanities* Scarecrow, 1980, 639p.

Foster D W and Foster V Ramos *Manual of Hispanic bibliography* U of Washington P, 1970, 206p.

Vivo P *Latin America: a selected list of sources* Washington, Latin American Service, 1972. (Revision of *Sources of current information on Latin America,* 1971).

Gropp A E *A bibliography of Latin American bibliographies* Scarecrow, 1976, 2 vols. (First published, 1968, 515p.).

Cordeiro D R et al *A bibliography of Latin American bibliographies: social sciences and humanities* Scarecrow, 1979, 272p. Supplement to Gropp.

— 'A bibliography of Latin American bibliographies' *Working paper* A-2 in 21st SALALM U of Massachusetts, SALALM Secretariat 1976, 21 leaves.

Delorme R L *Latin America; social sciences information sources.* 1967-1979 ABC-Clio P, 1981, 262p.

3b Bibliographies — General.

Turner M C ed *Libros en venta en Hispanoamérica y España* 2nd ed Bowker (Buenos Airies), 1974, 2 vols. Supplements between editions.

Fichero bibliográfico Hispanoamericano 1961-. Monthly listing; basis of the above publication.

New Latin American books: an advance checklist of newly published titles just acquired under the Latin American Cooperative Acquisitions Program (LACAP) Stechert Hafner, 1960- . (On LACAP see Savary M *The Latin American Cooperative Acquisitions Program: an imaginative venture* Hafner, 1968, 144p.).

Comentarios bibliográficos américanos Montevideo, CBA Editores, 1969- . Bimonthly.

Bibliografía de Centroamérica y del Caribe, Argentina y Venezuela Imprento Nacional de Cuba, 1956.

Millares Carlo A *Prontario de bibliografía general* U Católica Andrés Bello, 1973, 144p.

Woodbrisge H C and Newberry D eds *Basic list of Latin American materials in Spanish, Portuguese and French* U of Massachusetts Library, 1975, 205p (SALALM Bibliography, 2).

North American Congress on Latin America *NACLA's bibliography on Latin America* 1975, 48p.

Dorn G M *Latin America, Spain and Portugal: an annotated bibliography of paperback books* 2nd rev ed Library of Congress, 1976, 323p (Hispanic Foundation Bibliographic Series, 14).

Jamison E A *Introduction to Latin America; manual for an interdisciplinary course: an annotated bibliography* U of Wisconsin, 1976, 206p.

Rocio Guadarrama M del and López A *Bibliografía de América Latina (Economia, política, sociología)* Mexico, UNAM, Centro de Estudios Latinoamericanos, 1976, 335p. By countries.

Wilgus A C *Latin America, Spain and Portugal: a selected and annotated bibliographical guide to books published in the United States, 1954-1974* Scarecrow, 1977, 910p.

Hallewell L ed *Latin American bibliography* U of London, Institute of Latin American Studies, 1978, 227p.

3b Latin American Studies — Aids to research.

Sable M H 'Methods of bibliographical compilation in Latin American studies' *Herald Lib Sci* 1979 18(1/2) 117-20.

— *A guide to Latin American Studies* UCLA, 1967, 2 vols. (UCLA Reference series, 4).

— *Latin American studies in the non-Western world and Eastern Europe: a bibliography on Latin America in the languages of Africa, Asia, the Middle East and Eastern Europe (excluding USSR)* Scarecrow, 1970, 701p.

Latin America in Soviet writings: a bibliography Vol 1: *1917-1958*; Vol 2: *1959-1964* Johns Hopkins (for Library of Congress), 1966, 2 vols. (Hispanic Foundation publications, 1/2).

Historiografía y bibliografía Americanistas Seville, Escuela de Estudios Hispano-Americanos. Biblioteca.

Ban I *Bibliografía de publicaciones Japonesas sobre América latina* Tokyo, Sofia U, Instituto Iberoamericano, 1978, 38p.

Handbook of Latin American studies (HLAS) 1936- . U of Florida P Annual. Covers books and periodicals. Classified: librarianship in general references section.

Carvalho T et al *Catálogo da Biblioteca Frederico Edelweiss.* Vol 1: *Salvador, Brazil* U Federal da Bahia, Centro de Estudios Baianos, 1975, 184p. First volume of a comprehensive set.

PAU Columbus Memorial Library *List of books accessioned and periodical articles indexed* 1950- .

Latin American collections in the UCLA Library — Guides. See for instance:

Lauerhass L *Library resources on Latin America: research guide and bibliographic introduction* UCLA Latin American Center and U Library, 1978, 95p (Guides, Series A, No 2).

University of Florida Libraries *Catalog of the Latin American collection* G K Hall, 1973, 13 vols. Updated by supplements.

Hilton R *A bibliography of Latin America and the Caribbean* Scarecrow, 1980, 675p. (Catalogue of a private collection: the Hilton Library).

University of Texas Library *Catalog of the Latin American collection* 1969, 31 vols. Supplements 1-4 to date. Latest published: 1977.

Bibliographic guide to Latin American studies 1978 (Based on the collection of the University of Texas, with addition from the Library of Congress). G K Hall, 1979, 3 vols.

Hispanic and Luso-Brazilian Councils Canning House (London) *Catalogue* G K Hall, 1967.

— *British bulletin of publications on Latin America, the West Indies, Portugal and Spain.*

University of London. Institute of Latin American Studies *British union catalogue of Latin Americana.* Also published various series.

— *Latin American studies in the universities of the UK; Staff research in progress; Theses.*

Bibliotheek der Rijksuniversiteit te Utrecht *España e Hispanoamérica: catálogo de libros españoles y publicaciones extranjeras sobre España e Hispanoamérica.*

— *Supplementos.*

Amsterdam. Centro de Estudios y Documentación Latinoamericanos *Boletin informativo sobre estudios Latinoamericanos en Europa* No 10- as: *Boletin de estudios Lantinoamericanos.*

PAU *Inter-American bibliography review/Revista Interamericana de bibliografía* 1951- . Quarterly. Index to Vols 1-15.

Latin America: a catalog of dissertations Xerox University Microfilms, 1974, 70p.

Sable M H *Guide to nonprint materials for Latin American studies* Ethridge, 1979, 141p.

OAS Columbus Memorial Library *Index to Latin American periodical literature 1929-1960* G K Hall, 1962, 8 vols.

— *First supplement 1961-65* G K Hall, 1968; *Second supplement: 1966-70*, G K Hall, 1980.

Grossman J ed *Index to Latin American periodicals: humanities and social sciences/Indice general de publicaciones periodicas latinoaméricanos: humanidades y ciencias sociales* G K Hall, 1961-1971. No more published. Eventually replaced by:

Valk B G ed *Hispanic American periodical index (HAPI)* UCLA, Latin American Center, 1975- .

Information to be found too in the following:

Latin American research review Library of Congress 1965- .

Latin American bibliography series UCLA 1971?- .

PAU Columbus Memorial Library *Bibliographic series* 1933- . Lists, bibliographies, directories, etc.

Amérique latine: bulletin analytique de documentation Toulouse, Groupe de Recherche sur l'Amérique Latine (GRAL) Dec 1978- .

3b Special bibliographies — Librarianship.

OAS Secretaria General *Documentos oficiales. . . ; indice analitico* 1960- . Annual.

PAU. Columbus Memorial Library *Bibliography of books and articles in periodicals on the Organization of American States* Washington, 1977, 22p.

Weaver J L *Latin American development: a selected bibliography* ABC-Clio, 1969, 87p. Period: 1950-1961.

Gardner M A *The press of Latin America: a tentative and selected bibliography in Spanish and Portuguese* U of Texas, Institute of Latin American Studies, 1973, 34p. (Guides and bibliographies, 4).

Centro de Educación para el Desarrollo de la Communidad en América Latina (Patzcuaro) *Bibliografía sobre alfabetización* Vol 1, 1969, 157p; Vol 2, 1969, 134p.

Lauerhass L and Oliveira de Araúja Haugse V L *Education in Latin America: a bibliography* G K Hall for UCLA Latin American Center, 1980, 431p. (UCLA, LA Center Publication and Reference series, 9).

OAS. Centro Interamericano de Promoción de Exportaciones (CIPE) *Red interaméricana de información comercial: guia bibliografica para el establicimiento de centros de información comercial en función de las exportaciones* Bogota, CIPE, 1975, 99p.

Kinard S R *Working papers of the SALALM: list and index*. Kept up to date. *Basic documents of the SALALM* 2nd ed Amherst, 1975, 55p.

Linares E *Bibliografía bibliotecológica* PAU 1960, 233p. Mimeo. (Bibliographic series, 49).

Rovira C *Bibliografía bibliotecológica. Suplemento 1960-1962* PAU, 1964, 92p. (Bibliographic series, 49, Suppl 1).

Cantañeda J del G *Bibliografía bibliotecológica Latino-americana Parte 2: analiticas de publicaciones periodicas* U de Antioquia 1967, 275p. Part 1 not traced.

Jackson W V *Bibliografía del planeamiento de los servicios bibliotecarios* U de Antioquia, 1968, 15p. Mimeo.

Universidad de Antioquia. Escuela Interamericana de Bibliotecológía *Boletin de adquisiciones*. Section: 'Indice bibliotecológico latinoamericano'. From Latin American periodicals.

Gropp A E 'Bibliographical activities of special libraries in Latin America: a bibliography of publications: 1950-1964' *Inspel* 1968 3 111-46.

Valle F *Bibliografía basica en español sobre teoria y tecnicas de la información documentaria: guia para los estudios de documentación* U de Argentina, 1976, 154p. Period 1953-1975.

Indices de revistas de bibliotecología (IREBI), Madrid. 1973- . Current contents type of index published by the Ibero-American Bureau of Education, Madrid, with the Centro de Documentación Bibliotecológica (CDB), Universidad Nacional del Sur, Argentina and the Instituto Bibliográfico Hispánico (IBH), Madrid.

IABLA *Inter-American bibliography review* 1941-1944.

PAU *Inter-American review of bibliography/Revista interaméricana de bibliografía*. 1951- . Quarterly. Cumulative index Vols 1-15. Bibliographies, articles, etc. on librarianship.

3c

Zubatsky D S *Research sources for Ibero-American studies: a union list of serials in the fields of the humanities and social sciences held by Washington University libraries* Washington U, 1969, 20p. *Supplement: September 1969/June 1971*, 32p.

Zimmerman I *Guide to Latin American periodicals: Humanities and social sciences* Gainesville, Kallman Pub Co, 1961, 357p. Extensive annotations. Includes the West Indies.

Widener Library Shelflist Vols 5-6: 'Latin America and Latin American periodicals' Harvard University P.

Mesa R Q comp *Latin American serial documents: a holding list* [in the library of Congress, New York Public Library and 16 University libraries in the USA] Xerox University Microfilms 1968- . One volume per country. Vol 1: Colombia, etc. Latest noted: Vol 11: Uruguay.

Foster D W 'An annotated registry of scholarly journals in Hispanic studies' *Rev Interamer Bibliog* 1978 28(2) 131-47.

Research institutes and departments of Latin American studies usually publish periodicals, see for instance:

Österreichisches Latinamerika-Institut *Zeitschrift für Latinamerika*, Vienna.

Cahiers des Amériques Latines Paris. Miscellaneous documents.

Scandinavian Association for Research on Latin America (NOSALF) Institute of Latin American Studies *Ibero-Americana* 1970?- .

Latinamerika-Institutet, Stockholm *Latino-americana*. 1978- . Irreg.

See also periodicals published by university libraries specializing in Latin America.

Boletin interamericano de archivos Córdoba, Argentina School of Archivists. 1974- .

PAU Columbus Memorial Library *Inter-American library relations*. 1955- ?. No more published. Spanish edition as: *Noticiero bibliotecario interaméricano* 1963- .

PAU *Bulletin* 1893-1948. Superseded by *Américas*. 1949- .

OAS Library Development Program (1956-). Publication Program (Subsection: Planeamiento nacional). Publication series:

Estudios bibliotecarios 1958- . Surveys, studies, etc.

Cuadernos bibliotecologicos 1960- . Occasional papers on various topics.

University of Florida *Biblioteca del bibliotecario*. Series.

SALALM *Newsletter* 1973- .

Unesco Boletin de la Unesco para las bibliotecas, Havana. Spanish edition of the *Unesco Bulletin for Libraries*. Now: *Revista de la Unesco de la información, bibliotecología y archivología* (1979-).

FID/CLA *Newsletter* 1964- .

Asociación Latinoamericana de Escuelas de Bibliotecología y Ciencias de la Información (ALEBCI) *ALEBCI Boletin informativo* 1972- . Quarterly.

Escuela Interamericana de Bibliotecología *Revista Interamericana de bibliotecología* Medellin, 1978- .

Fundación Interamericana de Bibliotecología Franklin *Noticiero Franklin* Buenos Aires 1964- .

AIBDA *Boletin informativo,* Turrialba 1966-79. Now:

— *Revista AIBDA,* Turrialba 1980- .

Reforma newsletter Association of Spanish Librarians in USA 1973- .

3d

UN/ECLA *Economic Bulletin for Latin America* 1948- . With a: *Statistical supplement* which, after 1964, was published separately as:

Statistical bulletin for Latin America 1965- .

UCLA Latin American Center. Statistical and Computer Support Committee *Statistical abstract of Latin America* 1956- . General statistics; since the 1976 edition includes also a 'Special issue' section, dealing with problems of current interest. (Present editor: J W Wilkie).

OAS Instituto Interaméricano de Estadística *Estadística* 1943- . Includes bibliographies of statistical sources of Latin American countries.

— *La structura demográfica de las naciones americanas* 1960 Section 'Analfebetismo y nivel de educación' (Vol 1(4)).

— *América en cifras*. See issues on topics: culture, etc.

Latin America 1978- . New York, Facts on file, 1979- .

3e

Library of Congress *A guide to the official publications of the other American republics* 1945-49, 19 vols. By countries.

Finó J F 'Bases para una legislación bibliotecaria integral' *As Costaric Bibliot Bol* 1959 1(10/11) 6-17.

Comité Redactor de Normas Bibliotecológicas Latino-Américanas (CORBLA) 1970- . No publications traced so far.

3f General background.

Wilgus A C *Latin America 1492-1942: a guide to historical and cultural development before World War II* Scarecrow Reprint, 1973 [1941], 941p.

Bailey H M and Nasatri A P *Latin America: the development of its civilization* 3rd ed Prentice Hall, 1973, 822p.

Blakemore H and Smith C T *Latin America: geographical perspectives* Methuen, 1974, 60p. Society, economic conditions, etc.

Lewald H E *Latinoamérica: sus culturas y sociedades* McGraw Hill, 1973, 436p.

Cozean J D *Latin America* Washington, Stryker-Post, 1979, 107p.

Phillips R N and Marquez O *Visiones de Latinoamérica: a cultural reader* 2nd ed Harper and Row, 1980.

Alisky M *Latin American media: guidance and censorship* Iowa State U P, 1981.

Guttentag Tichauer W 'Glances on book distribution in Latin America' *Working paper* B-18 at SALALM 1975 U of Texas, 1978, 173-9.

Klasse I 'Problemas de la distribución del libro en America Latina' *Working paper* B-15 at SALALM 1975 U of Texas, 1978, 167-72.

Schiro H 'Producción y distribución en América Latina: algunos problemas' *Working paper* B-7 at SALALM 1975 U of Texas, 1978, 147-57.

Grenz W *Das Bildungswesen in der gesamtentwicklung Latein-Amerikas* Hamburg, Institut für Iberoamerika-Kunde, 1966, 271p. (Bibliographie und Dokumentation, Heft 9).

Valderrama F 'El analfabetismo en America Latina' *Rev Ecuador Educ* 1966 19 152-7.

Seminario del CREFAL sobre alfabetisación funcional en América latina, First, Quito 21-30 mayo 1969 *Informe final* CREFAL, 1969, 64p.

Seminario operacional de alfabetisación, Pátzcûaro, 21 de septiembre-8 de octubre de 1970 Un método de formación para el desarrollo: alfabetisación funcional. *Informe* CREFAL, 1970, 4 vols. Mimeo.

Aguirre R G *Evaluación de la literature existente en español para la educación permanente de adultos. Algunos problemas y orientaciones* Buenos Aires, Ministerio de Educación, 1970, 153p. Mimeo.

Abad Grijalva G 'El planeamiento educativo y la explosión demográfica en América latina' *Bol Inst Int Niño* 1969 43(169) 241-57.

Harrell W A ed *Education and population in Latin America: a conference* U of Texas (Houston), Latin American Studies Program, 1975, 199p.

Freire P *La educación como práctica de la libertad* Siglo Veiutiuno Ed, 1976.

Whitmore M 'The role of education in Latin American librarianship' *Int Lib Rev* 1978 10(2) 137-50.

3f Librarianship — History, development and trends.

Thompson L S 'Las bibliotecas en la Hispanoamérica colonial' *Bol Bibliot General* (Maracaibo) 1963 3(5) 33-46.

Millares C A 'Bibliotecas y difusión del libro en Hispanoamérica colonial' *Bol Hist* (Caracas) 22 Jan 1970 25-72.

Penna C V *Bibliotecología Latinoaméricana* Havana, Ed Anuario Bibliográfico Cubano, 1959, 46p. Also published: Bogota, ACB, 1959, 46p and Tucuman, Biblioteca Nacional, 1960, 66p.

Jackson W V *Aspects of librarianship in Latin America* Illini Union Bookstore, 1962.
— *Report to the Department of State on 1967 visit to Latin America* Pittsburgh, 1967, 19p. Mimeo. Visit to Argentina, Brazil, Chile, Colombia, Jamaica.
Green G H 'Latin American libraries and the revolution of rising expectations' *Progress Lib Sci* 1966 129-39.
Johnson E R 'Library development in Latin America: a scalogram' in Williamson W L *Assistance to libraries in developing nations: papers on comparative studies* U of Wisconsin, Library School, 1971, 68p. See in General: Developing countries 3f.
Krzys R and Litton G 'Latin American librarianship' in *Encyclopedia* 14 (1975) 51-74.
Freudenthal J 'Librarianship in South America: a kaleidoscopic view' *Wilson Lib Bull* 1976 50(10) 784-91. Report on a tour.
Rieser H 'Bibliotheken und Bibliotekare in Südamerika' *Biblos* (Austria) 1976 25(4) 388-99.

3f Planning library services.

OAS *Analysis of the library situation in Latin America* OAS, 1970, 7p. (Cuadernos bibliotecologicos, 52).
Shepard M Daniels 'State of library planning in Latin America' *Missouri Lib Ass Q* 1969 30(4) 307-25.
OAS Library Development Program 'To gain access to knowledge.' Report OAS, Secretariat General, 1971; (Cuadernos bibliotecologicos, 55). Also in Spanish.
Shepard M D *Planeamiento nacional de servicios bibliotecarios*. Vol 1: *La infrastructura bibliotecológica de los sistemas nacional de información* OAS, Secretaria General, 1972, 136p. (Estudios bibliotecarios, 8). Document prepared for the conference on the Application of Science and Technology to the Development of Latin America (CACTAL), Brazil, 1972.
— Vol 2 was a review of the situation in Latin American countries. (Estudios bibliotecarios, 8).
Penna C V et al Seminario Interamericano sobre la Integración de los Servicios de Información, de Archivos, Bibliotecas y Centros de Documentación en America Latina y el Caribe, Washington, 1972 *Informe final* OAS, 1973, 143p.
Penna C V *Servicios de bibliotecas y de información: nueva concepción latinoamericana* Madrid, Asociación Nacional de Bibliotecarios y Archíveros y Arqueólogos, 1973, 141p.
Sabor J E *El planeamiento bibliotecario a traves de los congresos y reuniones celebrados en América latina* Washington, OAS?, 1974, 39p.
— 'Planning library services: conferences in Latin America' in *Encyclopedia* 22 (1977), 314-37, bibl.
[National, regional and international planning for library services in Latin America], 18th SALALM, Port of Spain, Trinidad 1973 *Final report and working papers* SALALM Secretariat, U of Massachusetts Library, 1975, 456p.
Shepard M D 'Informe del programa de desarrollo de bibliotecas y archivos de la Organización de los Estados Americanos' *Working paper* A-4 at SALALM 1975, Bogota U of Texas, 1978, 114-36.
Hazen D C ed *Library resources for Latin America: new perspectives for the 1980s* [25th SALALM final report and working papers] SALALM Secretariat, 1980, 318p.

3f Aid and cooperation in library development.

'ALA Committee on Library Cooperation with Hispanic Peoples. Report' *Hispanic Amer Hist Rev* Nov 1929 516-20.

Milani C H 'Some possibilities of library cooperation with Latin America' *ALA Bull* April 1939.

Sandvig M M and Dudgeon L 'The library program of the USIA in Latin America' *Inter-Amer Bibliog Rev* 1955 5 291-8.

Murrow E R 'USIA's library program in Latin America' *Lib J* 1961 86(20) 3887-9.

Penna C V 'Unesco aids Latin American libraries' *Lib J* 1956 81(20) 2633-5.

Piñeiro M A 'Unesco and library services in Latin America' *Unesco Bull Lib* 1966 20(5) 245-51.

On some meetings planned by Unesco see also *Unesco Bull Lib* 1966 20(6) 278-98; 1968 22(4) 166-72; 1975 29 108-9.

Rivera R O 'Cooperation among the libraries of the Western Hemisphere' *Inter-Amer Bibliog Rev* 1941 1(2) 112-6.

Jackson W V 'Cooperation in Latin America' *Lib Trends* 1975 24(2) 379-97, refs. Development programme of the OAS.

For the meetings organized by the OAS see in the series:

Reuniones bibliotecológicas which contains working papers, final reports of meetings.

Shepard M D 'A solicitud de los paises: asistencia que la OEA brinda a Latinoamérica en el campo de la información' *Working paper* D-9 at 19th SALALM, 1974, 27p. (Cuadernos bibliocológicos, 62).

See also 'Congresso Latinoamericano de Biblioteconomia e Documentação' First congress at Salvador, Brazil, 1980.

3f Public libraries — Children and school libraries.

Development of public libraries in Latin America — The São Paulo Conference Unesco, 1952, 189p. (Public library manuals, 5). Also published in French and in Spanish.

Shepard M D 'El programa de fomento de bibliotecas de la OEA y la Alianza para el Progresso' *Fenix* 1964 14 96-109.

Acosta Hoyos L E *Bibliotecas populares parroquiales para América latina* Washington, Catholic Library Association, 1967, 100p. Thesis, Catholic U of America.

Freudenthal J R 'Public libraries International: Contemporary libraries in Latin America' in *Encyclopedia* 24 (1978) 422-55, bibl.

Seminario sobre planeamiento de un servicio de bibliotecas escolares, Bogota, 1961 *Informe final* Havana, Unesco, 1962.

Daniels M *Bibliotecas públicas y escolares en América latina* PAU, 1963, 136p. Mimeo.

— 'Children's library services in Latin America' *Lib Trends* 1963 12(1) 106-18.

Van Dyke F Z 'Library services to children in Latin America' *Int Lib Rev* 1969 1 439-44.

'Venezuela fue la sede de la 9a Conferencia Internacional de Bibliotecarios Escolares (June 1980)' *Ekaré* 1980 (25) 16-8 Theme of the conference 'Library services in Latin America and other countries: the present and the future'.

3f University and Research libraries — Special libraries.

Seminario regional sobre el desarrollo de las bibliotecas universitarias en América latina, Mendoza, 1962 *Informe* (prepared by J Lasso de la Vega).

'Regional seminar on the development of university libraries in Latin America' *Unesco Bull Lib* 1963 17(2) Suppl 123-36.

Barboza de la Torre P 'Sintesis del seminario regional sobre el desarrollo de las bibliotecas universitarias en America latina' *Educación* (Cararcas) 1962 23(99/100) 95-118. Papers of the meeting published as Unesco documents.

Milczewski M A *Estructura de la biblioteca universitaria en la América latina* PAU, 1967, 48p.

Instituto Interaméricano de Ciencias Agricolas 3a Mesa redonda del programa interamericano de desarrollo de bibliotecas agricolas, Rio de Janeiro, Nov 19-21, 1969 *Documentos y recomendaciones* Turrialba, The Institute, 1970, 300p. (IICA Bibliotecología y documentación, 18).

Paz de Erickson A M 'The role of professional organizations in the development of agricultural librarianship and documentation in Latin America' in Chaplin A H ed *The organization of the profession* Munich, Verlag Dokumentation, 1976, 94-103.

— 'Agricultural libraries and the spirit of cooperation: a continuing process' in Fusionie y Moran A and L eds *International agricultural librarianship: continuity and change* Greenwood, 1979, 29-51.

3f Information — Automated systems.

Unesco *La politica científica en América latina* 1969, 178p.

Dextre S G 'Industrial information in Latin America' *Info Scientist* 1976 10(4) 149-56.

Penna C V 'Seminar on planning of national scientific and technical information structure, Madrid, 23-28 November 1970' *Unesco Bull Lib* 1971 25(4) 186-90.

Seminario sobre planeamiento de estructura nacionales de información científica y técnica *Informe final* Madrid, Oficina de Educación Iberoamericana, 1971, 107p.

Conferencía Iberoamericana sobre información y documentación científica y tecnologica, Madrid, 1978 *Actas* 1979, 339p. Conference sponsored by Unesco, OAS and the Spanish National Scientific and Documentation Centre (CENIDOC).

CLADES and a future information and documentation network for Latin America New York, Unesco, Latin American Center for Economic and Social Documentation (CLADES), 1971, 21p.

Da documentação à informática. Seminario sobre Documentação e Informática, 1971, Rio de Janeiro (INDOC Seminar) Fundação Gerúlio Vargas, Instituto de Documentação, Servicio de Publicações, 1974, 240p.

Information for Development in Latin America and the Caribbean: summary of a meeting held in Cali, California, October 1977 Ottawa, International Development Research Centre, 1979, 28p

Saracevic T et al 'Information systems in Latin America' *Ann Rev Info Sci Tech* 1979, 14 249-82.

Patrinostro F S *Survey of automated activities in the libraries of Mexico, Central America and South America* LARC Association 1972, 85p. (World survey series, 4).

Shepard M D *An inter-American network for the transmission of bibliographic information: plans and progress* ERIC, 1977, 10p. (ERIC Report ED-176 759). OAS plans based on the use of USA databanks to coordinate its activities in the field of library and information science.

Towards improved information transfer in Latin America and the Caribbean: the role of Unesco Paper at regional seminar for Latin America and the Caribbean, Mexico, 1979 Unesco, 1979 (PGI-79/WS 9).

'Latin American developments in library automation' *Int Catal'g* 1980 9 15-8.

MEXICO

1

Biblioteca Nacional de Mexico, Mexico City, 1833- . Now one of the institutes of the Universidad Nacional Autonoma de Mexico (UNAM). Legal deposit and Library Directorate.

Barbarena B E 'One hundred years of the National Library of Mexico' *Mex Q Rev* 1968 3(1) 56-63.

Torre Villar E de la 'Palabras en la ceremonia commemorativa del primer centenario de la Biblioteca Nacional, 1967' *Bol Inst Invest Bibliog* 1969 1(2) 11-25.

— 'La Biblioteca Nacional: su trayectoria y finalidades' *Bibliot Arch* 1967 1(1) 5-21.

'Documentos para la historia de la Biblioteca Nacional' *Bibliot Nacion Bol* (New series) 1955 6(1) 3-28.

Archivo General de la Nación.

Civeira Taboada M and Bribiesca M E *Guia descriptiva de los ramos que constituyen el Archivo General de la Nación* The Archives, 1977, 124 leaves.

Centro de Servicios de Información y Documentación del Consejo Nacional de Ciencia y Tecnología (CONACYT/CSID), Mexico City. 1971- . Scientific information.

2a

Secretaría de Educación Pública. Dirección General de Publicaciones y Bibliotecas. Also has a library.

Instituto de Investigaciones Bibliográficas, Mexico City. 1967- . Under the administration of UNAM. It incorporates the Biblioteca Nacional, which it has reorganized, and a centre for bibliography and library science.

2b

Asociación Mexicana de Bibliotecarios A C (AMBAC). 1954- . Created in 1924 as Asociación de Bibliotecarios Mexicanos.

Asociación de Bibliotecarios de Instituciones de Enseñanza Superior y de Investigaciones (ABIESI). 1957- . College and Research Libraries Division of AMBAC.

Ruz Menéndez R 'La Asociación de Bibliotecarios de Enseñanza Superior y de Investigaciones (ABIESI)' *U Yucatan Rev* 1977 19(111) 127-30.

2c

UNAM Colegio de Bibliotecología y Archivología. 1956- .

Escuela de Capacitación Bibliotecaria. 1962- .

AMBAC *Mesa Redonda sobre formación de recursos humanos para las bibliotecas* 1980. Second Round Table: 1981.

3a

Enciclopedia de Mexico, en diez tomos Instituto de la Enciclopedia de Mexico, 1966- .

Weil T E et al *Area handbook for Mexico* American U P, 1975, 450p.

Briggs D C and Alisky M *Historical dictionary of Mexico* Scarecrow, 1981, 259p. (Latin American Historical Dictionaries, 21).

Secretaría de Educación Pública. Dirección General de Publicaciones y Bibliotecas *Directorio de bibliotecas de la República Mexicana* 6a ed La Dirección, 1979, 2 vols. (Comp.: C Culebra y Vives).

Anzoleaga de Lopez F et al, comps *Directorio de bibliotecarios y documentalistas* AMBAC, 1977, 500p.

Barbarena B E *Directorio de bibliotecas de la ciudad de Mexico/Directory of Mexico City libraries* 2nd ed U de las Americas, 1967, 259p.

Lindvall K *Research in Mexico City: a guide to selected libraries and research centers* U California, San Diego, Instructional Services Dept, 1977, 45p.

3b

Saenz Cirlos V J *Guia de obras de consulta sobre Mexico en el campo de las ciencias sociales* U Texas P, 1968, 146p. Section on libraries and librarianship.

Instituto de Investigaciones Bibliográficas *Bibliografía Mexicana* 1967- . Bimonthly.

— *Anuario bibliográficio* 1958-66. Retrospective bibliography published 1967- : *Bibliografía del siglo XVII* also in progress.

— *Boletin* contains lists of bibliographies issued in Mexico.

Centro Mexicano de Escritores *Recent books in Mexico* 1954- . Book reviews.

— *Catalogo de publicaciones mexicanas* 1959, 262p.

Texas University Library, Latin American Collection *Recent Mexican acquisitions* 1962/64 (1) - . Irregular.

Mercader Martinez Y N *Bibliografía selectiva: la educacion en Mexico 1910-1970* Escuela Nacional de Biblioteconomía y Archivonomía, 1974, 290 leaves.

3c

UNAM Dirección de Bibliotecas *Anuario de bibliotecología y Archivología* 1970 2a epoca, vol. 1- . Previously *Anuario de Biblioteconomía y Archivonomía.*

AMBAC *Noticiero de la AMBAC* 1966- . Irregular.

ABIESI *Archivos Cuadernos* 1976- . Series.

Escuela Nacional de Bibliotecarios y Archivistas (Then Escuela de Capacitación Bibliotecaria) *Bibliotecas y Archivos* 1967- .

3d

Secretaria de Economía *Revista de Estadística.*

3e

Ker A M *Mexican Government publications: a guide to the more important publications of the national government of Mexico, 1821-1936* USGPO, 1965, 333p.

Fernandez Esquivel R M *Las publicaciones oficiales de Mexico: guia de publicaciones periodicas y seriades, 1937-1970.* UNAM, 1970.

Instituto de Investigaciones Bibliográficas *Bibliografía de las publicaciones del Gobierno de Mexico* (1935-) 2 vols.

De la Torre Villar E *Mexico: ley de depósito legal. Informe . . .* Bogotá, 1975.

3f

Humbert M *Le Mexique* Paris, PUF, 1976, 126p.

Bixler P *The Mexican library* Scarecrow, 1969, 129p. Two studies by experts who made a survey of Mexican libraries in 1966.

Rice K E *Library services and development in Mexico* Pittsburgh U, 1964. Thesis.

Avando-Sanz G 'Dos bibliotecas coloniales de Potosi' *J Inter Amer Studies* 1961 3(1) 133-42.

'Las primeras jornadas mexicanas de biblioteconomía, bibliografía y canje' (Mexico, 1956) *AMBAC Bol* 1957 1(1) 6-15.

'Las secondas jornadas mexicanas de biblioteconomía, bibliografía y canje' (San Luis, Potosi, 1959) *U Yucatan Rev* 1959 1(2) 107-11.

White C M *Mexico's library and information services — a study of present conditions and needs* Totowa, Badminster P, 1969, 106p.

Martinez J L 'Bibliotecas en Mexico: analisis y programa' *Cuad Amer* 1975 200(3) 35-54.

La problematica de las bibliotecas en Mexico y sus soluciones. Memorias (8 Jornades Mexicanas de Biblioteconomía, Mayo 1977) AMBAC, 1977, 386p.

Morales Campos E and Perez Paz N *La planeación del servicio nacional bibliotecario: proyectos presentados de 1956-1976* AMBAC, 1977, 250p. (Monografias, 1).

Chavez Campomanes M T 'La biblioteca pública en Mexico: su historia, su funcionamiento y organisación y perspectivas para el futuro' *Bol Inst Invest Bibliog* 1969 1(2). Whole issue.

Segura Garcia B 'Bibliotecas, escuelas y bibliotecarios de Mexico' *Educación* (San José) 1963 9(37/38) 110-3.

Pérez Poire M *Las bibliotecas escolares circulantes: plan una biblioteca escolar universitaria circulante* 1970, 97p.

Casa Tiroa B *Bibliotecas y educación* Compañia Editorial Impresora y Distribuidores (CEID), 1974, 125p.

Garza Mercado A *Programa de necesidades del edificio de la biblioteca del Colegio de Mexico* ABIESI, 1976, 35p.

Sandoval A M 'A university information centre in the Third World' *Unesco Bull Lib* 1978 32(1) 42-8, 68. On the Centro de Informacion Cientifica y Humanistica, Mexico.

Goldman M K 'Technical information services in Mexico' *Spec Lib* 1978 69(9) 355-60.

Consejo Nacional de Ciencia y Tecnología 'La información y documentación de ciencia y tecnologia en Mexico' *Comercio Exterior* 1976 26(10) 1219-35.

CARIBBEAN REGION

For the purpose of this work the term covers Central America and Mexico, all the Caribbean islands, Guyana and the Guinas. Some items are not comprehensive in scope.

1

University of Florida Libraries. Belong to the Farmington Plan with the special responsibility of collecting material from, but not exclusively, the West Indies.

University of Puerto Rico Library.

Caribbean Regional Library (CRL), Hato Rey, Puerto Rico. Originally the library of the Caribbean Commission (1947-60), based on Trinidad; then of the Caribbean Organization (1960-65), when it moved to Puerto Rico. When the Organization was dissolved the library passed on to the Government of Puerto Rico on Trust, then to the Caribbean Economic Development Corporation (CODECA). Its aims are to increase the collection of materials on the region and to update the *Current Caribbean Bibliography*.

Easton J D 'The Caribbean Commission Library' *Caribbean* 1955 8(8) 166-8.

2b

Caribbean Archives Association. Regional Branch of CARBICA.

Association of Caribbean University and Research [Institute] Libraries (ACURIL). 1969- . About its formation see:

Zimmerman I in *South Eastern Latin Americanist* 1969 13(1) 14.

Outgrowth of the cooperative movement in the Caribbean universities: Association of Caribbean Universities and Research Institutes (UNICA). Holds annual meetings: see under 3f.

3a

Freudenthal J R *Caribbean acronym list* Austin, SALALM Secretariat/U of Texas, Latin American Collection, 1979, 6p. (Working paper C-4 at 24th SALALM).

Caribbean Yearbook — 1979/80 is the 50th Anniversary edition Caribook Ltd, 1980, 922p.

Gropp A E *Guide to libraries and archives in Central America and the West Indies, Panama, Bermuda and British Guiana* Tulane U, Middle American Research Institute, 1941, 741p.

Vaughn R V comp *West Indian library and archival personnel: a directory* The Author, Christiansted, V. Is, 1972, 89p.

Dower C A 'Libraries with music collections in the Caribbean islands' *Notes* (Music Lib Ass), 1977, 34(1) 27-38.

3b

Daniels M 'Proposal for an Inter American bibliographic institute to be initiated by a pilot center for bibliographic information for the Caribbean' *Working paper* at the 6th SALALM, 1961.

Breen J J *The establishment of a bibliographic center for the Caribbean* Fall Church, System Development Corp, 1967, 37 leaves.

Seminario bibliográfico de Centro-América y del Caribe, Panama, 1958 *Informe final*, 2 vols.

Chang H C *A selected, annotated bibliography of Caribbean bibliographies in English* St Thomas, Caribbean Research Institute, 1975, 54p.

Comitas L comp *Caribbeana 1900-1965: a topical bibliography*U of Washington P (for the Research Institute for the Study of Man), 1968, 909p.

— *The complete Caribbeana 1900-1975: a bibliographic guide to the scholarly literature.* Vol 1: *People*; Vol 2: *Institutions*; Vol 3: *Resources*; Vol 4: *Index* Millwood, NY, KTO Press/Kraus-Thomson, 1977, 4 vols. Updates the above bibliography.

Bibliografía actual del Caribe/Current Caribbean Bibliography/Bibliographie courante de la Caraībe CODECA, Biblioteca Regional del Caribe 1951- . Classified.

'Current bibliography' section in *Caribbean studies*, U of Puerto Rico, Institute of Caribbean Studies, 1961- .

Caribbean bibliographic series U of Puerto Rico, Institute of Caribbean Studies, 1970- .

University of Florida *Caribbean acquisitions* 1957/58 (1959) - . In subject order.

University of Texas Library *Recent acquisitions for the Caribbean Islands (excluding Cuba) and Guyana, French Guiana and Surinam* 1962/March 1967- . Irregular.

Baa E M *Doctoral dissertations and selected theses on Caribbean topics accepted by universities of Canada, United States and Europe from 1778-1968* St Thomas, USVI, Bureau of Public Libraries and Museums, 1969, 91p.

— *Theses on Caribbean topics 1778-1968* U of Puerto Rico P, 1970, 146p. (Caribbean Bibliographic Series, 1).

Dossick J J 'Doctoral research on the Caribbean and Circum-Caribbean accepted by American, British and Canadian universities, 1966-67' *Canad Stud* 1968 8(2) 89-96; . . . 1968-1970' *Canad Stud* 1971 11(2) 127-55.

Mevis R comp *Inventory of Caribbean studies: an overview of social research on the Caribbean conducted by Antillean, Dutch and Surinamese scholars in the period 1945-1973* Leiden, Royal Institute of Linguistics and Anthropology, 1974, 181p.

3c

List of West Indian periodicals in the library U of West Indies, Mona, 1969, 24p.

Caribbean studies Puerto Rico U, Institute of Caribbean Studies. 1961- . Quarterly.

Caribbean review Hato Rey. 1969.

Caribbean quarterly U of the West Indies.

Caribbean Archives Caribbean Archives Association, 1975- . 2 a year.

ACURIL *Carta informativa/Newsletter* 1973- .

3e

Avafia K 'Legal deposit problems in the West Indies' *Unesco Bull Lib* 1976 30(3) 147-57, 161. English speaking countries.

3f

Easton D K 'Patterns and problems of publishing in the Caribbean area' *Working paper* 5 at 5th SALALM, 13p.

Cox M and King O The problem of the acquisition of Caribbean materials in the English speaking Caribbean' *Guyana Lib Ass Bull* 1977 6(3) 1-16.

Jordan A T 'Caribbean library activities' *Working paper* A-4, Part E at 20th SALALM, Bogota, 1975, 141-2.

Pagán Jiménez N 'Los recursos bibliotecarios sobre el Caribe en Puerto Rico' *Working paper* B-3 at 24th SALALM, UCLA, 1979, 14p.

Jordan A 'Library planning in the Caribbean area' *Working paper* at the 18th SALALM, Port of Spain, 1973, 407-21.

— 'Sharing library resources in the English speaking Caribbean' *Interlending Rev* 1978 6(1) 10-7.

Conference on interlibrary cooperation and exchange, San Juan, April 30-May 2, 1969 St Thomas, USVI, Department of Conservation and Cultural Affairs, 1969, 251p.

ACURIL Conferences:

- Jordan A *Research library cooperation in the Caribbean* ALA, 1973, 145p. First and second meetings of ACURIL.
- First Caribbean Conference on University and Research Institute Library Cooperation, 14-17 June, 1969 *Agenda and working papers* U of Puerto Rico, 1969, 1 vol.
- *Los recursos bibliotecarios para la investigación en el Caribe: documentos oficiales* ACURIL, 1978, 459p. Third annual conference, Caracas, 1971.
- *The management of library personnel in the Caribbean: official documents* ACURIL IV, San Juan (Puerto Rico), 1972 ACURIL, 1975, 92p.
- [Education for librarianship in the Caribbean ACURIL VII, Willemstad (Curaçāo), 1975]. See 'ACURIL VII' *Open* 1976 8 43-4.
- [8th annual conference of ACURIL] Kingston (Jamaica), 1976 *Unesco Bull Lib* 1977 31(3) 252-3.
- 'Association of Caribbean University and Research Libraries 8th annual meeting' *Herald Lib Sci* 1977 16 97-8.
- Benjamin J and Stephenson Y 'Report on ACURIL IX' *Guyana Lib Ass Bull* 1977 6(4) 15-6. The theme was 'Caribbean resources: sharing, conservation and photoduplication'.
- Kahler M E 'Report of the 9th annual meeting of ACURIL, Willemstad, Curaçāo, Netherlands Antilles, November 6-12 1977' *Lib of Cong Info Bull* 1977 36 82-3.
- 'ACURIL IX' *IFLA J* 1978 4 205-6, 309.

Unesco/ACLA meeting of Caribbean librarians and documentalists, Port of Spain, November-December 1977. Announcement, but publication not traced.

Benjamin J P and Cox M A 'The development of science communication in the Caribbean: a brief survey' *Guyana Lib Ass Bull* 1977 6(1/2) 10-9.

'Workshop on the planning of NATIS, library and documentation networks for the Caribbean area, Kingston, Jamaica, November 1975' *Guyana Lib Ass Bull* 1976 5(2) 1-4.

CENTRAL AMERICA

2a

Organisación de Estados Centro-Americanos (ODECA), San Salvador, 1965- . Departmento de Asuntos Culturales.

US Agency for International Development. Regional Office for Central America and Panama.

2b

Consejo Superior Universitario Centro-Americano (CSUCA), San José. Unión Bibliotecológica Centroamericana.

'Unión Bibliotecológica Centroamericana' *Honduras Bibliot Arch* 1959/60 1(2) 5-6.

Federación de Universidades Privades de América Central y Panamá (FUPAC).

2c

Sabor J A 'Posibilidades de crear una escuela centroaméricana para el adiestramiento y formación de personal bibliotercario' Primera Reunión de Bibliotecarios de las Universidades Centroamericanas *Memoria* U de Costa Rica, 1962 (Publicaciones, Serie bibliotecología, 15).

3b

Rodriquez M and Peloso V C *A guide for the study of culture in Central America* PAU, 1969, 88p. Basic bibliographies, 5).

'Bibliografía seleccionada de ciencias sociales sobre los paises centroamericanos' *Ciencias Polit Soc* (Mexico) 1965 11(40/41) 273-376.

Texas University, Latin American Collection *Recent acquisition of books . . . from Central America* 1962/65 (1967)- ?.

3c

ODECA. Departamento de Asuntos Culturales *Boletin informativo* 1956- .

CSUCA *Repertorio.*

3f

Rojas Rojas E *Centroamérica: bibliotecas escolares y centro de formación de bibliotecarios, septiembre-diciembre 1966. Estudio preliminar* Unesco, 1967, 45p. Also: Tucuman, Arg., Biblioteca Central U National, 1968.

Reunión de expertos sobre el desarrollo de las bibliotecas en América Central, Antigua (Guatemala) 29 de julio-2 de agosto de 1968 *Informa final* Unesco, 1968, 41p, annex. (BIBCENTRAM/4).

— *Ibid* English edition Unesco, 1968, 29p.

'School libraries in Central America: a shortened version of the final report' *Int Lib Rev* 1970 2 287-305.

Penna C V 'School libraries in Panama and Central America: a Unesco meeting 249

of experts' *Amer Lib 1970 1(2) 182-3, See also in Unesco Bull Lib* 1969 23(1) 46-7.

CSUCA Primera Reunión de Bibliotecarios de las Universidades Centroamericanas, San Pedro, 1962, *Memoria* U de Costa Rica, 1962, 165p. See in particular.

Rojas Rojas E 'Situación actual de los servicios bibliotecarios en las universidades centroaméricanas'. Also published in *As Costarric Bibliot Bol* 1962 2(14/15) 16-43.

Deal C W et al *The libraries of Central American universities: a report to CSUCA* US Agency for International Development, Regional Office, 1965. Spanish edition as: *Las bibliotecas de las universidades centroamericanas.*

COSTA RICA

1

Biblioteca Nacional, San José. 1888- . Legal deposit library. Previously San Tomas University Library.

Universidad de Costa Rica, Biblioteca, San José, 1946- . Shares the legal deposit privelege. Has a librarianship department.

2a

Ministerio de Educación Pública. Departmento de Bibliotecas. 1958- .

Consejo Nacional de Investigaciones Científicas y Technológicas. (CONICIT). Some bibliographical functions: union catalogue of periodicals, etc.

2b

Colegio de Bibliotecarios de Costa Rica, San José. 1974- .

Asociación Costarricense de Bibliotecarios (ACB), San José. 1949- .

Kopper N 'La Asociación Costarricense de Bibliotecarios' *As Cost Bibliot Bol* 1975 3(22/23) 9-20.

2c

Alvares Brenes M 'La formación del bibliotecario' *As Cost Bibliot Bol* 1958 1(9) 6-8.

Masis Rojas T *Programa del curso de bibliotecología* Dirección General de Servicio Civil, 1968, 12p.

3a

Blutstein H I *Area handbook for Costa Rica* American University, 1970, 323p.

Creedman T S *Historical dictionary of Costa Rica* Scarecrow, 1977, 251p. (Latin American Historical Dictionaries, 16).

CONICIT *Guia de bibliotecas, archivos, servicios y centros de información y documentación en Costa Rica* CONICIT, 1975, 81p.

3b

Kopper N 'The book trade in Costa Rica: the present state of Costa Rica bibliography; the state of exchange in Costa Rica' *Working paper* 14 at 10th SALALM, 1965, 13p.

Dobles Segrada L *Bibliografía de Costa Rica*, 1933, 10 vols.

— *Indice bibliográfico de Costa Rica* Imprenta Lehmann 1927-1967, 11 vols By subjects.

Biblioteca Nacional *Boletin bibliográfico* 1935/38-1955, published 1939-56. Superseded by:

Comité Nacional de Bibliografía, the ACB *Anuario bibliográfico costarricense,* 1956- . Imprenta Nacional, 1958- .

3c

CONICIT *Catalogo colectivo de publicaciones periódicas existentes en Costa Rica* CONICIT, 1976, 479p.
ACB *Boletin,* San José. 1955- . Irregular.
Publicaciones de la Universidad de Costa Rica — Serie Bibliotecología.

3d

From: Dirección General de Estadística y Censos, San José. Has a library.

3e

Legal deposit Law No 40 of 27th June 1896. Amended by Decree No 2834 of 18th October 1961.
Rojas Rojas E 'Estudio sobre el estado actual de la profesión bibliotecaria en Costa Rica — y leyes y decretos relativos' *As Cost Bibliot Bol* 1964 2(16) 13-99.

3f

Rovinski S *Cultural policy in Costa Rica* Unesco, 1977, 61p.
Rojas Rojas E 'Costa Rica, libraries in' in *Encyclopedia* 7 (1972) 207-14.
Obregón L R 'Nuestras bibliotecas antes de 1890' *As Cost Bibliot Bol* 1955 1(2/3) 4-18.
Rojas Rojas E 'Miguel Obregón Lizano, iniciador del movimiento bibliotecario nacional' *As Cost Bibliot Bol* 1961 2(13) 7-21.
Meléndez Chaverri C 'Don Miguel Obregón Lizano, primer crusado de las bibliotecas en Costa Rica' *As Cost Bibliot Bol* 1955 1(6) 12-8.
Hartog J 'Boeken te kust en te keur: in Costa Rica' *Open* 1970 2 826-7.
Cruz Brenes B 'La promoción de la biblioteca popular' *Educación* 1955 9(37/38) 20-3.

EL SALVADOR

1

Biblioteca Nacional, San Salvador. 1870- . Previously: Library of the University of El Salvador.

Velasquez de Doumakis R 'El Salvador, National Library in' in *Encyclopedia* 8 (1972) 1614.

Escamilla Salavedra J 'Breve historia de la Biblioteca Nacional de El Salvador' *Anaqueles* 1971/72 1 9-21.

Romero M 'La Biblioteca Nacional y la reforma educativa' *Anaqueles* 1971/72 1 67-71.

Castro E 'La Biblioteca Nacional y la Subsecretaría de Cultura en el Ministerio de Educación' *Anaqueles* 1971/72 1 77-82.

Universidad de El Salvador, San Salvador.

Centro Nacional de Documentación.

2a

Ministerio de Educación. Subsecretaria de Cultura.

Ministerio de Relaciones Exteriores. Departamento de Archivos y Bibliotecas, San Salvador.

2b

Asociación de Bibliotecarios de El Salvador (ABES) 1958- .

Asociación General de Archivistas de El Salvador, San Salvador.

3a

Flemion P F *Historical dictionary of El Salvador* Scarecrow, 1972. (Latin American Historical Dictionaries, 5).

Blutstein H et al *El Salvador: a country study* American University P, 1979, 260p. (Reprint of the 1970 handbook).

3b

Dirección General de Bibliotecas 'Book publishing in El Salvador' *Working paper* 17 at 10th SALALM, 1965, 21p.

Alvarenga A C *Algunas consideraciones sobre los metodos de control bibliográfico y el funcionamiento del depósito legal en la Republica del Salvador* Bogotá, 1975. Mimeo.

Biblioteca Nacional *Anuario bibliográfico salvadoreño* 1952 (Published 1954, 39p)- ?. Supplement to *Anaqueles*.

Garcia Villas M comp *Listo preliminar de la bibliografía salvadoreña de las obras existentes en la Biblioteca Nacional* Biblioteca Nacional, 1952, 430p.

Biblioteca Nacional *Boletin bibliográfico, lista de obras incorporadas, autores y materiales* 1968 1- . The national library has published from time to time (1896, 1897, 1920-23, 1932) catalogues of publcations received, general or sectional, some of them in its *Boletin* and other publications.

Catálogo impreso de libros de la Biblioteca Central de la Universidad de El Salvador. With regular supplements.

3c

Biblioteca Nacional *Anaqueles*. Irregular.

Universidad de El Salvador. Biblioteca Central *Boletin*. 1975- .

ABES *Boletin Bibliotecario* Superseded by:

— *ABES Informa: boletin mensuel.*

3d

Dirección General de Estadística y Censo *Primer inventorio nacional de los servicios y recursos estadísticos, deciembre 1965* The Dirección, 1966, 76p.

— *Anuario estadístico.*

— *Boletin estadístico.*

— *El Salvador en cifras.*

3e

Diario oficial.

3f

Universidad 1969 94(3/4). Whole issue on the educational system in El Salvador.

Gunnar Mendoza L *El Salvador — Situación y planificación del servicio de documentos publicos, enero-febrero de 1973* Unesco , 1974, 113p.

'Bibliotecas del Caribe: bibliotecas de El Salvador' *Anuario Bibliog Cubano Bol* 1942 (Oct/Dec) 58-9.

'Cien bibliotecas ambulantes en 1953' *Info de El Salvador* Mayo 14 1953 20-1.

'Situación de las bibliotecas en la Universidad de El Salvador' Reunión de Bibliotecarios de las Universidades Centro-americanas, 1962 *Memoria* U de Costa Rica, 1962.

GUATEMALA

1

Biblioteca Nacional de Guatemala, Guatemala. 1879- .

Vola D 'Historia de la fundación de la Biblioteca Nacional' *Bibliot Nacion Bol* August 1934 347-53.

'Bibliotecas del Caribe: bibliotecas de Guatemala' *Anuario Bibliog Cubano Bol* Oct/Nov 1942 56-8.

Universidad de San Carlos. Biblioteca Central, Guatemala. 1965- . Legal deposit library, and bibliographical functions, 1975- , taken over from the National Committee for Bibliography.

2a

Ministerio de Educación Pública.

Consejo Nacional de Investigaciones Científicas y Tecnológicas.

2b

Asociación Bibliotecológica Guatemalteca, Guatemala. 1969- .

2c

Universidad de San Carlos. Facultad de Humanidades. Escuela de Bibliotecología (1948-) *Estatuto de Estudios* The Faculty, 1962, 16p.

3a

Area handbook for Guatemala American University, Foreign Area Division, 1970, 361p.

Moore R E *Historical dictionary of Guatemala* Scarecrow, 1973, 285p. (Latin American Historical Dictionaries, 1). Originally published 1967, 187p.

Peraza Sarausa F *Directorio de bibliotecas de Guatemala* Anuario Bibliográfico Cubano, 1946, 24p. (Biblioteca del Bibliotecario, 17).

3b

Dardón Córdova G 'Four topics concerning books in Guatemala' *Working paper* 11 at 7th SALALM, 1962, 21p.

— *La bibliografía en Guatemala, su desarrollo durante los siglos XIX y XX* U de San Carlos, Escuela de Bibliotecología, 1969, 118p. Mimeo.

— *Anuario bibliográfico guatemalteco* Biblioteca Nacional, 1960- .

Bibliografía guatemalteca y catálogo general de libros, folletos, periodicos, revistas (1660-1960) Tipografía Nacional, 1960-64, 10 vols. Compilers vary.

San Carlos University Library *Indice bibliográfico guatemalteco* 1974- . The library has the legal deposit privilege since 1975, and replaces the National Committee for Bibliography.

Franklin W B *Guatemala* Oxford, Clio P, 1981, 109p. (World Bibliographical Series, 9).

Revista universitaria includes special bibliographies and indexes of periodicals.

Biblioteca Nacional *Boletin* contains lists of printed works received in the national library on legal deposit.

3d

Ministerio de Economia. Dirección General de Estadística *Primer inventorio de los servicios y recursos estadísticos nacionales* 1965, 36p.

— *Anuario estadístico de la Dirección General de Estadística.*

3e

El Guatemalteco.

Seminario sobre situación de la aplicación del ancerdo ministerial No 502 Universidad de San Carlos, 1971.

3f

Samayoa Guevara H H 'Documentos para la historia de la educación en Guatemala' *Antropol y Hist Guatem* 1968 20(1) 95-104.

Raul Osegueda P 'Factores de desarrollo: la investigación científica y la educación en Guatemala' *Humanidades* (U San Carlos) 1970/79 6(11) 18p.

Flores R et al 'Guatemala, libraries in' in *Encyclopedia* 10 (1973) 237-46.

'Guatemalan librarian visits LC on fact-finding tour' *Lib Congr Info Bull* 1978 37 450-1.

Harto J 'Boeken te kust en te Keur: in Guatemala' *Open* 2/12/70 827-8.

'Crease le biblioteca de cultura popular guatemalteca "15 de Septiembre" ' *El Guatemalteco* Aug 31, 1956 313.

'Guatemala public libraries' *Unesco Bull Lib* 1966 20(1) 49.

Juarroz R *Guatemala: plan de operaciones para el desarrollo de las bibliotecas públicas y escolares, 20 de enero-6 abril de 1968* Unesco, 1968, 51p. (Also published by Universidad Nacional de Tucuman, Biblioteca Central, 1969, 64p.) Contains statistical data.

HONDURAS

1

Biblioteca Nacional de Honduras, Tegucigalpa. 1880- . Has a Centro Nacional de Información Bibliográfica.

2a

Ministerio de Educación Pública.

2b

Asociación de Bibliotecarios y Archiveros de Honduras (ABAH).

3a

Meyer H K *Historical dictionary of Honduras* Scarecrow, 1976, 399p. (Latin American Historical Dictionaries, 13).

3b

Durón J F *Repertorio bibliográfico hondureño* Imprenta Calderon, 1943, 68p.

— *Indice de la bibliografía hondureña* Imprenta Calderon, 1946, 211p.

Garcia M A *Anuario bibliográfico hondureño: 1961-1971* Banco Central de Honduras, 1973, 512p. In progress.

— *Bibliografía hondureña Vol 1: 1620-1930* Banco Central de Honduras, 1971, 486p. In progress.

— 'Las publicaciones hondureñas de 1971' *Acad Hondur Lengua Bol* 1972 15(15) 7-38.

3c

Honduras rotaria 1943- . Rotary Club. Contains bibliographies.

ABAH *Honduras bibliotecológica y archivistica* 1959- ?.

Revista del Archivo y de la Biblioteca Nacionales 1940- ?.

3d

Dirección General de Censos y Estadísticas *Anuario estadístico.*

Estadísticas educaciones. Annual.

3e

Presupuesto General de la República *La Gaceta: periodico oficial.*

Prontuario de leyes de Honduras.

3f

Ayes J A *Directory and inventory* of libraries ABAH, 1972. Review of the situation with a list of libraries.

Durón J F 'Republic of Honduras, libraries in' in *Encyclopedia* 25 (1978) 239-41.

Carias F G 'Consideraciones sobre el estado actual de la Biblioteca y Archivos Nacionales' *Arch Bibliot Nacion Rev* 1954 33(3/4) 88-94. Now separated.

'Primeras jornadas bibliotecológicas hondureñas' *Honduras Bibliot Arch* 1959 1(1) 7-11.

Ballon A 'Primary school library system in Honduras' *Unesco Bull Lib* 1969 23(6) 293-9.

'Apuntes generales sobre los servicios bibliotecarios de la Universidad Nacional Autonoma de Honduras' Reunión de Bibliotecarios de las Universidades Centroamericanas, San Pedro de Montes, 1962 *Memoria* Universidad de Costa Rica, 1962.

Hallam D M 'Starting a library from scratch' *Lib Ass Rec* 1969 71 328-9. On the university library.

NICARAGUA

1

Biblioteca Nacional, Managua. 1882- . Under the Academia Nicaragüense.

Zepeda Henriquez E 'Escorzo historico de nuestra Biblioteca Nacional' *Rev Cons Pensiamento Centro-Amer* 1969 20(100) 5-6.

Biblioteca Centroamericana. Collection on the region.

Vega Bolaños A 'La Biblioteca Centroamericana' *Elite* Sep 1940 5-6.

2a

Ministerio de Educación Pública.

2b

Asociación de Bibliotecas Universitarias y Especializadas de Nicaragua (ABUEN), Léon. 1969- .

Asociación Nicaragüense de Bibliotecarios (ASNIBI). 1965- .

3a

Ryan J M et al *Area handbook for Nicaragua* American U, Foreign Area Studies, 1970, 391p.

Meyer H K *Historical dictionary of Nicaragua* Scarecrow, 1972, 503p. (Latin American Historical Dictionaries, 6).

3b

Bibliotecá Américana de Nicaragua *Bibliografía de trabajos públicados en Nicaragua* 1943-1945/7 published 1944-48, 3 vols.

Banco Central de Nicaragua *Boletin Nicaragüense de bibliografía y documentación* 1974 (1)- . Quart. To establish a national bibliography.

Ministerio de Educación *Educación.* Includes a section 'Raseña de libros y revistas'.

3c

Aviles J 'Publicaciones periodicas de Granada' *Bol Nicarag Bibliog Doc* 1975 (8) 14-8.

ASNIBI *Novedades.* 1973- . Irreg.

3d

Dirección General de Estadística *Boletin de estadística.*

3e

La Gaceta.

3f

Mayorga-Rivas R 'La biblioteca americana de Nicaragua y el concepto democrático de la biblioteca pública' Ministerio del Instrucción Pública *Publicaciones* Feb/June 1944 29-31.

Hartog J 'Boeken te kust en te keur: in Nicaragua' *Open* 1970 2 762-3.

PANAMA

1

Biblioteca Nacional, Panamá. 1892- .

Universidad de Panamá. Biblioteca. The University has a School of Librarianship. 1941- .

2a

Ministerio de Educación Pública.

Comisión Nacional de la Unesco. Comité de Bibliotecas.

Consejo Superior de Bibliotecas.

2b

Asociación de Bibliotecarios Graduados del Istmo de Panamá, Panamá, 1955- .

2c

Informe sobre el proyecto para la formación de bibliotecarios escolares Panama U, Departmento de Bibliotecología, 1975, 68p.

Riba A G de 'La Biblioteca Nacional y la formacion del personal en servicio en las bibliotecas bajo su direccion' *Unesco Com Nacion Panama Bol* 1960 2(1) 7-10.

Herrera C de 'Los estudios de bibliotecologia en la temporada de verano de la Universidad de Panama' *Unesco Com Nacion Panama Bol* 1960 2(3) 7-9.

3a

Hedrick B C and Hedrick A K *Historical dictionary of Panama* Scarecrow, 1970, 105p. (Latin American Historical Dictionaries, 2).

Peraza Sarausa F *Directorio de bibliotecas de Panamá* Havana, Anuario Bibliográfico, 1948, 34p. (Biblioteca del Bibliotecario, 21).

Alvarado A A 'Guia de bibliotecas de Panamá' in *Seminario bibliográfico de Centro-América y del Caribe, Panama 1958. Informe final,* Vol. 2, 40p.

3b

Susto Lara J A *Panorama de la bibliografía en Panamá (1616-1967)* Editorial Universitaria, 1971, 102p.

Biblioteca Nacional *Bibliografía panameña 1953* 66p.

Universidad de Panamá. Grupo Bibliográfico *Bibliografía de libros y folletos, 1958-1960* 1960, 44 leaves.

Herrera F A 'Bibliografía de Panamá de 1960 a 1963' *Loteria* 1965 2 epoca 10(118) 67-96.

Loteria Nacional de Beneficiencia *Loteria* 1941- . Contains lists of publications.

The Reference Department of the University Library compiles lists of theses from the University Departments including the Department of Librarianship.

Heraldo 1959- . Trade list.

Grupo Bibliográfico *Bibliografía retrospectiva de las publicaciones periodicas aparecidas en la República de Panamá* Working paper at the Segundo Seminario Bibliográfico de Centro Americana y del Caribe, Panamá Feb 1958. Covers 1954-57.

Biblioteca Nacional *Bibliografía bibliotecología Panameña desde el 10 de enero de 1948 hasta la fecha septiembre 25 de 1951* 1952, 6p. Mimeo.

Theses in librarianship will include bibliographies relevant to this subject.

3c

Asociación de Bibliotecarios . . . *Boletin.*

Comisión Nacional de la Unesco *Boletin.* 1959- .

Boletin de la Escuela de Bibliotecología. 1967- .

Universidad de Panamá *La Voz de la biblioteca universitaria.* 1966.

Loteria. See under 3b.

3d

Dirección de Estadística y Censo *Panamá en cifras.*

3e

Gaceta oficial.

'Organizase el servicio nacional de bibliotecas. Ley No 5 de enero de 1956' *Gaceta oficial* 1956 53 (12936) 1-3.

3f

Herrera C D de et al 'The booktrade, bibliography and exchange of publications in Panama' *Working paper* 14 at 7th SALALM 1962, 14p.

Mendieto O V U 'La industria y el comercio del libro en Panamá' *Working paper* B-9 at SALALM, Austin 1974 Vol 2, 123-46.

Susto J A 'Desarrollo de las bibliotecas en Panamá en el siglo XIX' *Loteria* 1957 2 epoca 2(20) 41-7.

Castillero Reyes E de Jesus 'Historia de las bibliotecas en Panamá en el siglo XX' *Loteria* 1957 2 epoca 2(20) 56-63; 2(22) 59-63.

'Bibliotecas del Caribe: bibliotecas en Panamá' *Anuario Bibliog Cubano Bol* Oct/Dec 1942 53-5.

Hartog J 'Boeken te kust en te keur: in Panama' *Open* 1970 (Nov).

Patiño G *Base financiera para el desarrollo de un servicio regional de bibliotecas* Biblioteca Nacional, 1952, 21p.

Alvarado A A 'La Asociación y las bibliotecas públicas' *As Panam Bibliot Bol* 1959 2 epoca 2(4/5).

Penna C V 'School libraries and international development: school libraries in Panama' *Amer Lib* 1970 1(2) 182-3.

WEST INDIES

CUBA

1

Biblioteca Nacional José Marti, Havana. 1901- . Legal deposit and bibliographical functions. Centre of the library network.

Ramos S 'Twelve years' work at the National Library of Cuba' *Unesco Bull Lib* 1972 26(4) 210-3.

Pérez de la Riva J 'Los 75 anos de nuestra casa' *Rev Bibliot Nacion* 1976 18(3) 5-11.

Garcia-Carranza A et al 'Las caracteristicas tipológicas de la Biblioteca Nacional de Cuba en el periodi 1959-1976' *Rev Bibliot Nacion* 1978 20(1) 5-52.

Academia de Ciencias de Cuba. Biblioteca Central. 1962- . Prepares union catalogue, distributes scientific material; library school.

Instituto de Documentación e Información Científica y Técnica (IDICT).

Casa de las Américas, Havana. 1960- . Cultural centre; link with other Latin American countries.

Hansen D et al 'Casa de las Américas og Cubas kulturoffensiv i Latinamerika' *Bibliotek 70* 1978 (10) 247-9.

Instituto Cubano del Libro. 1967-77. Production and distribution of teaching material. Its functions have been taken over by other institutions.

2a

Ministerio de Educación.

Consejo Nacional de Cultura. Dirección Nacional de Bibliotecas.

2b

There are no library associations in modern Cuba. In the pre-revolution period there were:

Asociación Cubana de Bibliotecarios.

Colegio Nacional de Bibliotecarios Universitarios.

Organisación Nacional de Bibliotecas Ambulantes (ONBAP), now integrated in the national network.

2c

Aguayo J 'Informa sobre la creación de una escuela de bibliotecarios en la Universidad' *Univ Habana* 1947 (70/72) 292-306.

Massip S 'The School of Librarianship of Havana University, Cuba' *Unesco Bull Lib* 1958 12(2/3) 37-9.

'Curso para directores de Bibliotecas de la Red Nacional de Consejo Nacional de Cultura en la Biblioteca Nacional durante los dias 25 de enero al 25 de febrero de 1967' *Bibliotecas* 1967 5(2).

 'Formación y superación del personal de la Red Nacional de bibliotecas del

Consejo Nacional de Cultura. Encuentro del 1° al 12 septiembre 1969. Programa' *Bibliotecas* 1969 7(4/5) 5-7.
See also other papers in that issue.
Bueno S 'El quince aniversario de la Escuela de Técnicos de Biblioteca' *Rev Bibliot Nacion* 1977 19(3) 170-7.
Hansen D et al 'Den cubanske bibliotekaruddannelse' *Bibliotek 70* 1978 (14) 370-1.

3a

Baez V ed *La Enciclopedia de Cuba* 2nd ed San Juan, Puerto Rico, 1975-77, 14 vols.
Marinello J et al *Cuba* Paris, Editions du Burin, 1968, 247p.
Mesa R Quintero *Cuba* U Microfilms, 1969, 207p.
Block J K *Area handbook for Cuba* 2nd ed American U, Foreign Area Studies, 1976, 550p.
Unesco Centro Regional en el Hemisferio Occidental *Breve repertorio cultural de la Habana* 2nd ed 1974, 35p. Includes libraries.
Peraza Sarausa F *Directorio de bibliotecas de Cuba* U of Miami P, 1968.
Dirección Nacional de Bibliotecas *Guia de bibliotecas y centros de documentación de la República de Cuba* 3rd ed Biblioteca Nacional, 1970, 101p.

3b

Fernandez Robaina T comp *Bibliografía de bibliografías cubanas: 1859-1972* Biblioteca Nacional, Departamento de Hemeroteca e Información de Humanidades, 1973, 340p.
Pariseau E J *Cuban acquisitions and bibliography: proceedings and working papers of an international conference, Library of Congress, April 13-15, 1970* Library of Congress, 1970, 164p. Holdings in American and some European libraries.
Texas University Library *Recent acquisitions for Cuba of the Latin American collection* 1962/March 1967 (1)- .
Zimmerman I 'National bibliographer in exile: Fermin Peraza Sarausa of Cuba, 1907-1969' *Wilson Lib Bull* 1970 44 1060-3.
Peraza Sarausa F *Bibliografía cubana* 1937-1965 (1937-52 as *Anuario bibliográfico)* 1938-66, later volumes published by U of Miami.
— *Revolutionary Cuba*, 1966-68 U of Miami P, 1967-69. Mostly foreign sources.
Dulatova A N 'Izdaniia Kubinskoi natsional 'noi bibliografii' *Sovet Bibliog* 1976 (5) 94-7.
Biblioteca Nacional *Bibliografía cubana* 1963-64 (1967)- . Continues the publication compiled by F Peraza Sarausa.
The Biblioteca Nacional is also publishing a retrospective national bibliography *Bibliografía cubana* (1917-1936).
Catalogo general de libros Editorial Orbe, 1976, 90p. Trade list published since 1968.
Fernandez Robaina T 'Los indices de publicaciones periodicas en Cuba' *Bibliotecas* 1970 8(5).
Biblioteca Nacional El Equipo Bibliográfico Carlos M Trelles *Indice general de publicaciones periódicas cubanas: Humanidades y ciencias sociales* 1972?-. Annual.
Pereza Sarausa F *Bibliografía bibliotecológica cubana* 1948 (1967), 1949-55.
Biblioteca Nacional *Bibliografía sobre bibliotecología* 1971, 94p.
— *Bibliografía sobre documentación e información* (Suplemento) 1970, 47p.
— *Bibliografía sobre documentación e información* 1972, 35p. No more recent volumes traced.

Ministerio de Educación, Centro de Documentación e Información Pedagogica *Referativa* 1974- . Abstracts of selected articles on education; socialist countries mainly.

3c

Instituto Cubano del Libro *Revistas y periódicos cubanos* 1977, 79p.
Biblioteca Nacional *Boletin de Anuario bibliográfico cubano* 1938-52.
— *Revista* 1909- . 3 series: 1909-12, 1949-58, 1959- .
— *Informacion y documentación bibliotecológica* 1965- .
— *Folletos de divulgación técnica y científica.*
— Youth Department *Polillita.*
Consejo Nacional de Cultura *Bibliotecas* 1963- .
IDICT *Actualidades de la documentación* 1968- .
ONBAP *Islas* 1959- . *Indice 1-10, 1959-68* Published 1974, 189p.
Asociación Cubana de Bibliotecarios *Boletin* 1949-59.
Colegio Nacional de Bibliotecarios Universitarios *Cuba bibliotecológica* 1953-60.

3e

Gaceta oficial.
Bibliotecas. Includes information on laws related to libraries.

3f

Rossa G 'La organisación de la ciencia y la cultura en Cuba' *Rev Mexic Sociol* 1969 31(3) 633-41.
Cornejo Acosta M *Cuba: el sistema nacional de documentación e información pedagogica, diciembre de 1971- enero de 1972* Unesco, 1972, 35p.
Rovira C 'Cuba: libraries in' in *Encyclopedia* 6 (1971) 312-32, refs.
Dorf Rudich S M 'Library and documentation activities in Cuba' *Herald Lib Sci* 1974 13(1) 1-22.
'Presupuesto bibliotecológico cubano, 1949-50' *Bibliot del Bibliotecario* 1949 (27).
'Jornadas bibliotecológicas cubanas. Nuestras jornadas' *Cuba Bibliot* 1953 1(2) 15-23.
'Primer fórum de bibliotecarios' *Bibliotecacs* 1964 2(3) 4-10.
'Seminario sobre la modernisación progresiva de las bibliotecas. Ciclo de conferencias a cargo del Profesor Aubert Dulang de la Unesco' *Bibliotecas* 1971 9(1) 11-32.
Dulong A *Cuba: étapes à franchir en vue de la modernisation des bibliothèques, octobre-novembre 1970* Unesco, 1971, 41p. Also in Spanish.
Ramos S 'Das Bibliothekswesen in Kuba' *Zentbl Biblioth* 1971 85(8) 470-7. Development since 1959.
Hansen D et al 'Revolutionens biblioteker' *Bibliotek 70* 1978 (12) 312-5.
Jepsen I U et al 'Bibliotekerne arbejder med revolutionen — revolutionen arbejder med bibliotekerne' *Bibliotek 70* 1978 (13) 327-31. Visit to Cuba, miscellaneous libraries, in particular the National Library and its role.
'2° encuentro nacional de bibliotecas públicas' *Bibliotecas* 1970 8(6) 15-9.
'3° encuentro nacional de bibliotecas públicas, del 12 al 20 de octubre de 1971' *Bibliotecas* 1971 9(5/6) 3-6.
Siekierski S 'Biblioteki publiczne na Kubie' *Bibliotekarz* 1974 41(11-12) 337-41.
'O rabote bibliobusa odnoi iz publichnykh bibliotek tsentral'nogo paiona Kuby' *Bibliot Bibliog za Rubezhom* 1979 (74) 12-4.
Bacon B 'Cuba: books to the children' *Wilson Lib Bull* 1978 52(10) 783-8.

Giblin J C 'Conversations in Cuba' *School Lib J* 1978 25(1) 23-8. Report on a visit to Cuba.

'Seminario a trabajadores de la documentación e información técnica. Programa' *Bibliotecas* 1968 6(1) 5-6.

Bagdasaryan S M 'Informatsionnaya deyatel'nost' v oblasti meditsiny y zdravookhraneniya sotsialistichnikh' *Nauk-Tekh Info* Ser.1 1974 (6) 19-27. Translated in *Sci Tech Info Process* 1974 (2) 58- . Includes Cuba.

Valls J *Cuba: un sistema de recuperación de datos en el Instituto de Documentación e Información Científica y Técnica (IDICT) 22 de abril-16 de junio de 1974* Unesco, 1974, 19p (3061/RMO.RD/DBA).

Prochazka B 'Kuba: 20 let rozvoje ekonomiky, knihovnictví a informací' *Čtenář* 1980 32(4) 119-22.

DOMINICAN REPUBLIC

1

Biblioteca Nacional, San Domingo. 1971- . Legal deposit.

Perez C F 'Inauguración del edificio de la Biblioteca Nacional' *Rev Interamer Bibliog* 1971 21 357-8.

Universidad Autónoma de Santo Domingo. Biblioteca. 1458- . Legal deposit, bibliographical activities.

2a

Secretario de Estado de Educación, Bellas Artes y Cultura. Sección de Bibliotecas.

Servicio de Documentación y Bibliotecas, San Domingo. 1958- . Under Unesco.

2a

Asociación Dominicana de Bibliotecarios (ASODOBI). 1974- .

Association of University Libraries. 1978- . By resolution of the National Council of Institutions of Higher Learning.

3a

Secretaria de Educación [List of libraries and holdings] Mimeo list prepared in 1969.

3b

Floren Lozano L *Bibliografía de la bibliografía dominicana* Ciudad Trujillo (San Domingo), 1948, 68p.

Hitt D S et al *A selected bibliography of the Dominican Republic: a century after the restoration of independence* American U, 1968, 142p.

Universidad Autónoma *Bibliografía dominicana.* 1971- .

Boletin Bibliográfico dominicano 1945.

Anuario bibliográfico dominicano 1946-1947.

Columbus Memorial Library holds the typescript of the Dominican bibliography for 1950-1951.

Universidad Pontificia Boliviana *Revista* 20(73) contains the Dominican bibliography for 1955.

Universidad Autónoma *Anales* Supplement contains the bibliography for 1956-1960.

Biblioteca de la Universidad Autónoma *Boletin de adquisiciones* 1969- . Contains a section 'Libros dominicanos'. In Dewey Order.

Universidad Nacional Pedro Henriquez Ureña. Biblioteca *Boletin de adquisición.*

Postigo J D ed *Libros dominicanos* Libreria Hispaniola, 1971.

Cuadernos dominicanos de cultura. Contain information on bibliographical works.

Pensiamento dominicano Libreria Dominicana. Series of bibliographical works.

3c

ASODOBI *El Papiro* 1976- . 3 a year.

3d

Oficina Nacional de Estadística *Anuario estadístico de la República Dominicana.*
— *República Dominicana en cifras* 1968.
— *Bibliotecas municipales.* 1968.

3e

Gaceta oficial.
Castro Cotes M M *Situación actual de la Biblioteca Nacional: legislación sobre el deposito legal y mecanismos para su funcionamiento* Bogotá, 1975.

3f

Bell I *The Dominican Republic* Westview/Benn, 1981, 392p. Historical review, 1844-1979.
Moushey E W 'Dominican Republic, libraries in' in *Encyclopedia* 7 (1972) 293-6.
Baa E M and Espinal de Hoetink L 'Library and bibliographic activities in the Dominican Republic' *Working paper* No 4 at the 9th SALALM, 1964, 32p.
'Las bibliotecas populares' *Inst Investig Psicopedagog Bol* 1951 2(5) 5.
Patin E *Apuntes de bibliotecología* Oficina Nacional de Administración y Personal, 1969, 269 leaves. (Publicaciones, 3).

HAITI

1

Bibliothèque Nationale, Port-au-Prince. 1940- .

'On September 10, 1939, at Port-au-Prince, the corner stone of the new national library laid' *PAU Bull* 1940 (Jan) 74 56.

Centre de Documentation, Port-au-Prince. 1960- .

Centre de Documentation Pédagogique, Port-au-Prince. 1958- .

Institut Français d'Haïti.

2a

Département de l'Education Nationale.

Conseil National des Recherches Scientifiques.

3a

Lacombe R 'La République d'Haïti' Paris, Direction de la Documentation *Notes et études documentaires* 1977 (4436/37) 1-96.

Perusse R I *Historical dictionary of Haiti* Scarecrow, 1977. (Latin American Historical Dictionaries, 15).

3b

Ballantyne I and Lygia M F C *Haitian publications: an acquisition guide and bibliography*. Madison, SALALM Secretariat, 1980, 52p.

Bissainthe M *Dictionnaire de bibliographie haïtienne* Scarecrow, 1951, 1052p. Covers 1804-1949.

— *Ibid — Premier supplément* Scarecrow, 1973, 269p. Covers 1950-1970.

Bertrand W *Publications haïtiennes des années 1973-1975* 1975.

Peraza Sarausa F *Haitian bibliography, 1950-1967* U of Miami, Center for Advanced International Studies, [1970?].

Institut Français d'Haïti *Conjonction* includes a section 'Bibliographie haïtienne'. 1949- .

3c

Institut Français d'Haïti *Conjonction: revue franco-haïtienne* 1942- .

Louis D and Montas M 'Bibliographie: 1957-1977 index des textes et articles parus dans *Conjonction*' *Conjonction* 1978 (138) 97-135.

3d

Institut Haïtien de Statistique *Bulletin trimestriel de statistique*. 1951- .

— *Guide économique de la République d'Haïti* 1977, 667p.

3e

Le Moniteur.

'Réglement des bibliothèques nationales de la République' *Le Moniteur* 1940 95(29) 225-7.

'Ley organica de las bibliotecas públicas de Haiti' *Anuario Bibliog Cubano Bol* 1950/51 14 (52/55) 89-91.

'Décret formant un cadre technique de bibliothécaires, d'archivistes et de muséologues pour les services d'administration' *Le Moniteur* 1958 Special issue 114(23) 128.

3f

Centre de Documentation Pédagogique *Tableau de l'école haïtienne* [1968?].

Bertrand J W 'Bibliothèques haïtiennes aujourd'hui' *Conjonction* 1975 (127/128) 9-53. Review of present conditions, need for a library school.

Delmas B *Haïti: état des systèmes d'information des pouvoirs publics et proposition de réorganisation et développement* Unesco, 1979.

PUERTO RICO

1

University of Puerto Rico (UPR). General Library, Rio Piedras. 1903- .
- Graduate School of Librarianship. Library.
- Institute of Caribbean Studies.

Institute of Puerto Rican Culture. Biblioteca General de Puerto Rico.

CODECA Biblioteca Regional del Caribe/Caribbean Regional Library (CRL), Hato Rey. Originally the library of the Caribbean Organization, 1961-64. Caribbean collections. See under Caribbean Region.

Puerto Rican Research and Resources Center.

2a

Departamento de Instrucción Pública. School Libraries Division.
- Public Libraries Division 1956- . In 1975 recommendation to make it autonomous.

State Advisory Council on Libraries 1974- .

2b

Sociedad de Bibliotecarios de Puerto Rico, Rio Piedras 1961- .

2c

Pérez de Rosa A 'Training and manpower needs of Puerto Rican libraries' *Libri* 1969 19(2) 107-20, refs.

3a

Báez V *La Gran enciclopedia de Puerto Rico* Madrid, C Corredera, 1976, 14 vols.

Farr K R *Historical dictionary of Puerto Rico and the US Virgin Islands* Scarecrow, 1973. (Latin American Historical Dictionaries, 9).

Toro J del comp *Guia de bibliotecas de Puerto Rico* Rev ed UPR for Sociedad de Bibliotecarios de Puerto Rico, 1971, 63p.

3b

Vivo P *The Puerto Ricans: an annotated bibliography* Bowker, 1973, 299p. Sponsored by the Puerto Rican Research and Resources Center.

Velasquez G ed *Anuario bibliográfico puertorriqueño* UPR Biblioteca, 1948-1952. Later published by the Department of Education. Irregular.

Parker F and Parker B J eds *Education in Puerto Rico and of Puerto Ricans in the USA: abstracts of American doctoral dissertations* Puerto Rico, Inter-American U P, 1978, 601p.

See also in *Caribbean Studies*. Contains bibliographies.

3c

Sociedad de Bibliotecarios *Boletin* 1961- . 3 a year.

— *Cuadernos bibliotecológicos* 1970- . Monographs.

3d

See United States sources.

3e

Las publicaciones oficiales del Gobierno del Estado Libre Asociado de Puerto Rico: bibliografía UPR, Colegio Regional de Cayey Biblioteca, 1968, 76p.

Jimenez de Leon C H *Legislación bibliotecaria en Puerto Rico* Sociedad Bibliotecarios, 1970, 13p. Mimeo. (Cuadernos bibliotecológicos, 4).

Thomas de Dominguez E et al *La base de los servicios bibliotecarios escolares en Puerto Rico* Sociedad de Bibliotecarios, 1971, 17p. Mimeo (Cuadernos bibliotecológicos, 4) Covers 1903-1969.

3f

Wagenheim K *Puerto Rico: a profile* 2nd ed Praeger, 1975, 294p.

Woll A L *Puerto Rican historiography* Gordon P, 1978, 134p.

Maldonado-Denis M *Puerto Rico: a socio-historic interpretation* Vintage Books, 1972, 336p.

Mapp E ed *Puerto Rican perspectives* Scarecrow, 1974. Includes Betancourt J A 'Library service to Puerto Ricans: an overview', pp 97-103, and Lopéz L and Belpré P 'Reminiscences of two turned-on librarians' pp. 83-96.

Reimer E et at *Comprehensive educational planning in Puerto Rico; final report* Department of Education, 1968, 111, 4 leaves.

Cruz Monclova L *El Libro y nuestra cultura literaria* Sociedad de Bibliotecarios, 1974, 11 leaves (Cuadernos bibliotecológicos, 9)

Vasquez M W *Puerto Rico and its libraries* Pittsburgh U Thesis, 1964.

Delgado R R and Hyning J van 'Puerto Rico, libraries in' in *Encyclopedia* 25 (1978) 16-27.

Velasquez G *Puerto Rico State plan for further extension of public library service to rural areas* 1962, 1 vol.

Lewis C 'Bootstrap library drive succeeds in Puerto Rico' *Lib J* 1970 95 1813-5.

Departamento de Instrucción Pública *Public library needs: survey and analysis. Final report* The Department, 1975, 1 vol. Recommends the University Library to become the national library and the centre of the country's library network.

Gaver M G and Velasquez G *School Libraries of Puerto Rico* 1963, 116p.

Velasquez G 'El programa de servicios bibliotecarios del Departamento de Instrucción Pública de Puerto Rico' *Soc Bibliot Puerto Rico Bol* 1962 1(2) 5-12.

Santoni Ortiz M *Como estimular en los educandos un interés permanente por la lectura a través de las diferentes etapes de su enseñanza: aprestamiento, enriquecimiento y refinamiento* UPR, 1970, 105p. MA Thesis.

Toro J del *Estudios sobre las bibliotecas de los colegios regionales de Puerto Rico* San Juan, 1969, 23 leaves.

AMERICAN VIRGIN ISLANDS

Three main islands: St Croix, St John, St Thomas. US Governor with an administrator for each island.

1

Public Library, St Thomas. With branches. It is also the seat of the Bureau of Public Libraries and Museums.

2a

Department of Conservation and Cultural Affairs. The Bureau is administered by this department.

Caribbean Research Institute, St Croix.

2b

St Croix Library Association.

2c

Chang H C *Narrative evaluation report on the Institute for Training in Librarianship* St Croix, 1976?, 121p.

3b

Caron A *Inventory of French documents pertaining to the US Virgin Islands* St Thomas Bureau of Libraries, 1978, 62p. (Occasional paper, 3).

3c

Bureau of Libraries. *Information* St Thomas.

3f

Creque D D *The US Virgins and the Eastern Caribbean* Whitmore, 1968, 266p.

Department of Education *Annual reports* includes figures on public libraries.

Conference on sharing Caribbean resources for instruction and research, St Thomas, March 17-19, 1969 *Proceedings* St Thomas, 1970, 182p.

Franklin R D *Report on the library situation in the Virgin Islands* Toledo, Ohio, Public Library, 1967, 25p.

'Virgin Islands survey urges library growth' *Lib J* 1968 93(4) 698.

Library resources in the Virgin Islands of the United States St Thomas, Bureau of Libraries, 1977, 32p (ERIC Report ED-156 116).

Espinosa-Almestica J *Bookmobiles in the Virgin Islands: a study of mobile services in St Croix* USVI St Croix Library Association, 1972, 8p.

BRITISH ASSOCIATED WEST INDIES

With Belize and Guyana.

1

Lashley C 'West Indian national libraries and the challenge of change' *Jamaica J* 1972 6(2) 31-3.

University of the West Indies (UWI) Libraries in every campus: Mona (Jamaica), St Augustine (Trinidad and Tobago), Cave Hill (Barbados). They act as bibliographical centres for the rest of the West Indies.

Institute of Jamaica. West India Reference Library, Kingston. See details under: Jamaica, 1.

Caribbean Community (CARICOM) (and Common Market). Based on Georgetown, Guyana. 1973. Has its own library.

Collins C 'The Caribbean Community (CARICOM) Secretariat Library' *Guyana Lib Ass Bull* 1974 4(3) 5-7.

Eastern Caribbean Regional Library (ECRL). Created in the 1930s lasted until 1962. See references below under 3f.

2c

Benge R 'Library education in the West Indies' *LATT Bull* 1961 1 2-9.

Collings D 'Library education in the English speaking Caribbean' *Unesco Bull Lib* 1973 27(1) 12-7.

— 'Library education in the English speaking Caribbean' *Working Paper* in 18th SALALM, 1973 373-85.

3a

Yearbook of the West Indies and countries of the Caribbean London, 1926/27-1952. Title varies.

Lux W *Historical dictionary of British Caribbean* Scarecrow, 1975 (Latin American Historical Dictionaries, 12).

3b

Gocking W E 'Exchange of publications in the West Indies' *Working paper* No 11 at 5th SALALM, 1960, 12p.

Richards J E 'Bibliographical aids for building reference collections on the British Caribbean' *Working paper* at 12th SALALM, 1967, 33p.

Gocking W E 'The University of the West Indies and its regional collections' *Working paper* No 25 at 12th SALALM, 1967.

Gill M E 'Planning meeting on national bibliographies of the English speaking Caribbean' *Unesco Bull Lib* 1974 28(6) 308-10.

McMurdoch A 'Regional workshop on national bibliographies of the English speaking Caribbean, Georgetown, Guyana, 25-29 November 1974' *Unesco Bull Lib* 1975, 29(3) 148-50. Report on the meeting which aimed at establishing a collective regional bibliography based on the improved bibliographies from

Jamaica, Trinidad and Tobago, Barbados and Guyana, but expanded to the other CARICOM members. It should be the *CARICOM bibliography*. (1976?-).

Institute of Jamaica *The catalogue of the West India Reference Library* Kraus International, 6 vols. From the *Accessions lists*.

Trinidad and Tobago Central Library *Accession list of West Indian material.*

Cundall F *Bibliography of the West Indies* (*Excuding Jamaica*) Johnson Reprint, 1971 (1909).

University of the West Indies, Cave Hill. Institute of Social and Economic Research *A bibliography of the Caribbean* Cave Hill, 1974, 167 leaves. (Occasional bibliography series, 1)

Benewick A *A list of books on West Indian Federation* 2nd ed West India Reference Library, 1962.

Stephenson Y *Bibliography on the West Indian Federation* U of Guyana Library, 1972, 34p. Mimeo. (U of Guyana Library series, 6).

3d

Quarterly economic report Port of Spain 1951- . Statistics by areas.

3f

Guerin D *The West Indies and their future* D Dobson, 1961.

Guy H A ed *Women in the Caribbean: a record of career women in the Caribbean, their background, services and achievements* Port of Spain, Quick Service Printing Co, 1968, 173p.

Cave R *Notes towards the history of printing and related trades in the West Indies* U of the West Indies, Mona, Department of Library Studies, 1975, 17p.

Bennett E 'British West Indies libraries' in *Encyclopedia* 3 (1969) 345-59.

Thompson L S 'Library development in the English speaking West Indies' *Libri* 1955 5(3) 256-66.

Jackson M M 'Libraries abroad: review of significant developments in 1967: the Caribbean area' *J Lib Hist* 1968 3(4) 357-60.

Jordan A *The development of library service in the West Indies through interlibrary cooperation* Columbia U, School of Library Service 1966/67. University Microfilms, 1967; Scarecrow, 1970, 433p. Thesis.

— 'Library cooperation in the West Indies: the state of the art' *Libri* 1973 23 18-51. Supplement to the above.

Easton D K 'Public library service in the British territories of the Eastern Caribbean' *Unesco Bull Lib* 1951 5(12) 421-6.

Hockey S W 'Library services in the Eastern Caribbean' *Unesco Bull Lib* 1957 11(8) 185-7.

Jordan A 'Public libraries in the British Caribbean' *Lib Q* 1964 34(2) 143-62; 34(3) 258-63.

Collins C 'The public library services in the less developed countries of the Caribbean Community member states' *Guyana Lib Ass Bull* 1976 5(4) 1-5.

Eastern Caribbean Regional Library *ECRL, a regional experiment: a report of the progress of the ECRL 1941-1950* Port of Spain, 1951.

ECRL progress report, 1952-1958 Port of Spain, GPO, 1959. The West Indies Federation was dissolved in 1962 and the library transferred to the University of West Indies, Port of Spain.

Jordan A 'Cooperative technical services in the West Indies' *Jamaica Lib Ass Bull* 1968 2(4).

BAHAMAS

1

Nassau Public Library.

3f

Reid D G *Bahamas: public library service, February 1970* Unesco, 1970, 45p. Mimeo.

Boultbee P G 'Library service in the Bahamas' *Int Lib Rev* 1978 10(2) 151-4.

BARBADOS

1

Public Library, Bridgetown. 1947- . Legal deposit, bibliographical activities.
University of the West Indies (UWI). Cave Hill Campus. 1963- .

2a

Ministry of Education and Youth Affairs.

2b

Library Association of Barbados (LAB), Bridgetown. 1968- .

2c

Bennett H and Shinebourne J 'Report on the Library Association of Barbados' library assistants' training course, July-September 1978' *COMLA Newsletter* 1979 (23/24) 15-7.

3b

Cruikshank J G 'A bibliography of Barbados' *J Barbados Hist Soc* 1935 2(3) 155-65; 2(4) 220-5.

Public Library *Barbadiana: a list of works pertaining to the history of the island of Barbados* 1966, 44p.

— *The National Bibliography of Barbados* 1975- . Quarterly.

Barbados takes part in a combined bibliography for the English-speaking Caribbean (CARICOM). See under British Associated West Indies, 2a.

3c

Library Association of Barbados *Journal*. Irregular. Originally: *Bulletin*.

3f

Ministry of Education and Youth Affairs *The educational system in Barbados* Bridgetown, 1975.

St Hill C 'Barbados, libraries in' in *Encyclopedia* 2 (1969) 251-7.

See also in Chandler G *International librarianship* (Section on Barbados) under General: Developing countries, 3f.

Newton V 'The role of libraries in developing countries: focus on libraries in Barbados and Jamaica' *Bull East Caribbean Affairs* 1977 2(12) 1-7.

Ifill E L V *The public library movement in Barbados and Jamaica* London, Library Association, 1968, FLA Thesis.

Foster B 'Black reading power' *Int Lib Rev* 1976 8(3) 265-70.

St Hill C 'School libraries in Barbados' *Int Lib Rev* 1978 10(4) 385-8.

BELIZE

1

National Library Service. Central Library, Belize City. 1935- .

2a

Ministry of Education, Housing and Labour.
Library Service Statutory Board.

2b

Belize Library Association (BLA), Belize City. 1976- .

2c

National Library courses and in-service training.

3a

Gregg A R *British Honduras* HMSO, 1968.

3b

National Library Service *British Honduras collection* 1967?.

Bradley L H ed *A bibliography of published material on the country as found in the national collection: supplement to the second edition* Belize, British Honduras Library Service, 1966, 10p.

Minkel C and Alderman R H *A bibliography of British Honduras, 1900-1970* Michigan State U, Latin American Studies Center, 1970, 93p. (Research Report, 7).

Woodward R L comp (Herstein S R ed) *Belize* Clio, 1980, 229p. (World bibliographical series, 21).

3c

Belize Library Association *Bulletin* 1976- . Quarterly.
National Library Service *The Lighthouse*.

3f

Belize: new nation in Central America Independence Secretariat, 1972, 72p.

Cave R 'Printing in 19th century Belize' *Lib Q* 1976 46(1) 20-37.

Hutchison L *Development and present status of the Public Library Service in Belize* U of Chicago, 1975, 82p. MA Thesis.

BERMUDA

1

Bermuda Library. Reference Department, Hamilton. 1839- .

Thomson G 'The Bermuda Library — of books and blooms, and little white devils' *Wilson Lib Bull* 1979 53(10) 700-3.

2a

Department of Education. Advisory role.

3a

Great Britain. Foreign and Commonwealth Office *Bermuda report*.

3f

Gray M E and Skiffington M 'Bermuda, libraries in' in *Encyclopedia* 2 (1969) 343-7.

GUYANA

1

National Library, Georgetown. Originally the Public Free Library 1909- .

Deposit library; bibliographical activities through its Editorial Board 1974- . University and Government take part. University of Guyana Library. Legal deposit.

Kabdebo T and Stephenson Y 'University of Guyana Library: past, present and future' *Lib Ass Rec* 1970 72 258-60.

Benjamin J 'University of Guyana Library — the role of its Caribbean Research Library' *Guyana Lib Ass Bull* 1977 6(4) 1-4.

2a

Ministry of Education.

National Science Research Council.

Knee C 'The role of the National Science Research Council of Guyana in the dissemination of scientific information' *Guyana Lib Ass Bull* 1976 5(4) 13-9.

2b

Guyana Library Association (GLA). 1968- .

Cornelius J 'Impressions of the revised Constitution and Rules of the Guyana Library Association' *Guyana Lib Ass Bull* 1976 5(2) 11-12.

2c

Jackson J 'Labour relations and the library' *Guyana Lib Ass Bull* 1976 5(3) 7-11.

3a

Guyana handbook Manufacturers' Association and U of Guyana, Faculty of Education, 1976, 255p.

Mitchell W B ed *Area handbook for Guyana* American U, 1969, 378p.

Guyana Library Association *Guide to library services in Guyana*.

3b

Cummings L P and Stephenson Y *A selection of documents on Guyana* 1969, 24p. Mimeo.

Cummings L P *Bibliography — section 2* (of a bibliography on the Guianas) 1968, 45p.

A select bibliography of the works of Guyanese and on Guyana Georgetown Public Library, 1967, 51p.

National Library *Guyanese National Bibliography: a subject list of new books printed in the Republic of Guyana . . .* 1973- . Quarterly with annual cumulations.

University of Guyana Library Series 1970 (1)- . Mainly bibliographies.

3c

Guyana Library Association *Bulletin*. 1969- .

3e

Laws of Guyana. Legal deposit: Publications and Newspapers Act 23 September 1972 (Cap 21:01 of 1973, para. 1).

3f

Memorandum on education policy by the Minister of Education, January 4, 1968 Government Printery, 1968, 15p.

Seymour A J *Cultural policy in Guyana* Unesco, 1977, 68p.

Merriman S E *A national library system for a developing country, with special reference to Guyana, South America* London, FLA Thesis, 1970. Published by University Microfilms, 1971.

GLA [Report to the Government of Guyana on the state of libraries in Guyana]. Details not traced. Resulted in the establishment of a national policy for information.

Kabdebo T 'Guyana, libraries in' in *Encyclopedia* 10 (1973) 246-9.

[Papers presented at the Annual General Meeting of the Guyana Library Association on 8th March 1974] *Guyana Lib Ass Bull* 1974 4(2) 1-11.

Georgetown Public Library *Diamond Jubilee, Public Free Library, 1909-1969.* (Now the National Library).

McGuire W 'The need for school library service' *Guyana Lib Ass Bull* 1971 1(3) 5-10.

Craigwell J 'Libraries, archives and public relations' *Guyana Lib Ass Bull* 1976 5(2) 5-7.

Dos Ramos P 'Coordination of Guyana government libraries — a step in the right direction' *Guyana Lib Ass Bull* 1974 4(3) 1-4.

Benjamin J P 'Bringing back the rare materials' *Guyana Lib Ass Bull* 1976 5(3) 1-6.

Stephenson Y V 'Problems of information systems: a brief review of the Guyana position' *Guyana Lib Ass Bull* 1977 6(1/2) 1-9.

JAMAICA

1

Institute of Jamaica (1879-). West India Reference Library (WIRL) Kingston. 1894- .

Breckner M A 'The libraries of the Institute of Jamaica' *Lib Ass Rec* 1958 60(10).

Robertson G 'The West India Reference Library of the Institute of Jamaica' *Jam J* 1972 6(1) 15-20.

University of the West Indies (1948-) Mona Campus. Library.

- Department of Library Studies. Library, Kingston 1973- .

Jamaica Library Service (JLS). Central library, Kingston. 1948- .

2a

Office of Prime Minister. National Council on Libraries, Archives and Documentation Services. 1974- .

Ferguson S 'The National Council on Libraries, Archives and Documentation Services' *Jam Lib Ass Bull* 1975 16-7.

2b

Jamaica Library Association, Kingston. 1949- .

2c

Collings D 'University of West Indies Library School: progress report, 1971/72' *Jam Lib Ass Bull* Jan 1973 30-7.

University of the West Indies Department of Library Studies Kingston, 1972, 21p.

'Guidelines on condition of service for library staff in Jamaica' *COMLA Newsletter* 1979 (25) 37.

3a

The Handbook of Jamaica Kingston, GPO, 1881- . Regularly updated.

Weil T E et al *Area handbook for Jamaica* American U P, 1976, 332p.

Richards J E *Directory of Jamaican libraries. Part I: Jamaica Library Service, University of West Indies, libraries of the government departments and statutory boards* Jamaica Library Association, 1967, 99p.

3b

Delattre R *A guide to Jamaican reference material in the West India Reference Library* Institute of Jamaica, 1965, 76p.

Jamaica Library Service *Jamaica: a select bibliography 1900-1963* Jamaica Independence Festival Committee, 1963, 115p.

— *Jamaica: a select reading list* 1975, 11p.

Institute of Jamaica *Jamaica National Bibliography* 1964- . Annual. 1964-67 as *Jamaican Accessions.*

Williams R I comp *Jamaican national bibliography: 1964-1970* WIRL, 1973, 322p. Cumulation of the annual lists.

Institute of Jamaica *The Jamaican national bibliography, 1964-1974* Kraus International Publications, 1980.

3c

Jamaica Library Association *Bulletin* 1950- . Annual.
— *Newsletter* 1969- . Irregular.
Institute of Jamaica *Jamaica Journal* 1967- . Quarterly. General.

3d

Department of Statistics *Annual abstracts of statistics.*

3e

Hinds S *Jamaica government publications: a bibliography* Institute of Jamaica, 1971, 14p. Mimeo.
Government publications on sale at the Government Printing Office GPO, 1969, 18p.
The acts of Jamaica passed in the year . . . GPO, Kingston.
Standards for school libraries, with plans for the establishment of a department of library studies, University of West Indies (1971).

3f

Institute of Jamaica *Cultural policy in Jamaica* Unesco, 1977, 53p.
Cave R 'Printing comes to Jamaica' *Jam J* 1975 9(2/3) 11-7.
Newton V 'The role of libraries in developing countries: focus on libraries in Barbados and Jamaica' *Bull East Carib Affairs* 1977 2(12) 1-7.
Bateson N *Library planning for Jamaica* GPO , 1945.
Robinson J L 'National planning for libraries in developing countries: with special reference to the Jamaican situation' *Jam Lib Ass Bull* 1976 (8/9) 11-21.
— 'Jamaica, libraries in' in *Encyclopedia* 13 (1975) 169-205, bibl.
Donovan D G *Report of a visit to Jamaica, November 14-18, 1967* ALA, 1968, 16 leaves.
Danton J Periam *Report of a library mission to Jamaica 20-28 September 1968 undertaken on behalf of Unesco* Kingston, 1968, 58 leaves. Also published as *Jamaica: library development* Unesco, 1968, 56p.
Bennett H 'Private and subscription libraries in Jamaica before 1879' *J Lib Hist* 1968 3(3) 242-9.
Cave R 'Early circulating libraries in Jamaica' *Libri* 1980 30(1) 53-65, refs. Period 1779-1844.
Bennett H E *The Jamaica Library Service: its foundation and development* Southern Connecticut State College, 1966, 127p. MA Thesis.
Warmington C et al *Jamaica Library Service: 21 years of progress in pictures, 1948-1969* The Service, 1972, 367p.
Harrison K C 'How Jamaica is tackling illiteracy' *Lib Ass Rec* 1976 71(11) 529.
Robinson J L 'Rural library development in Jamaica' *Unesco Bull Lib* 1973 27(4) 213-8.
Allen G 'The Public libraries' Bookmobile Service in Jamaica' *Jam Lib Ass Bull* 1975 28-30.
Eng A K *Role of the school library service in the development and promotion of school libraries in Jamaica* Long Island U, 1970, 81p. Research paper.
National Council on Libraries *Plan for a national documentation, information and library system for Jamaica* Kingston, Documentation Services, 1978, 96p. (ERIC Report, ED-168 594).
 See also under Latin America, 3f Jackson W V; Barbados, 3f Ifill E.

TRINIDAD AND TOBAGO

1

University of the West Indies, St Augustine Campus. Library. Legal deposit library.

University of the West Indies, St Augustine *Development of the University Library, St Augustine: ten year plan, 1965-1975* The Library, 1965, 20p, tables.

Central Library of Trinidad and Tobago, Port of Spain. Centre of the Library Services. Legal deposit library.

Carnegie Free Library, San Fernando. 1919- .

Introducing your Central and Carnegie library services Government Printery, 1965, 19p.

2a

Ministry of Education and Culture.
Trinidad Public Library Committee.
Carnegie Free Library Committee.

2b

Library Association of Trinidad and Tobago (LATT), Port of Spain, 1960- .

2c

Goring A E 'Professional education' *LATT Bull* 1963 2(1).

'Library assistant today' *COMLA Newsletter* 1979 (25) 41. Originally published in *LATT Bull* 1977 4(2).

3a

Trinidad and Tobago Yearbook Port of Spain, Guille Printery, 1866- .

Black J K et al *Area handbook for Trinidad and Tobago* American U, 1976, 304p.

3b

Central Library *Accession list of West Indian material*, and:

— *Trinidad and Tobago imprint list*. Published since 1965 under various titles: *Classified list of accessions; Trinidad and Tobago and West Indian bibliography: monthly accessions*.

— *Professional paraphernalia: a selective bibliography of books on librarianship and related topics* Government Printing Office, 1963, 17 leaves. Prepared for the first library seminar held at Port of Spain, June 1963.

3c

Library Association of Trinidad and Tobago *Bulletin* 1961- . Also known as: *BLATT*.

— *Biblio*. Newsletter.

3d

Institute of Social and Economic Research.

Central Statistical Office *Annual statistical digest* 1967- . Includes libraries.

— *A digest of statistics on education* 1950/56, 1966/67- .

3e

Government Printer *Trinidad and Tobago gazette.* Contains lists of official publications.

Laws of Trinidad and Tobago.

'Trinidad and Tobago Government serials in the University of the West Indies Library' Working paper, 12th SALALM, Mona, 1967. *Final report and working papers*, Vol 2, 218-30.

3f

Trinidad and Tobago: the making of a nation London, COI, 1962. (Reference pamphlets, 53).

Adams E B 'An English library at Trinidad, 1633' *Américas* 1955 12(1) 25-41.

Solomon P 'The role of libraries in our changing community' *LATT Bull* 1965 2(4) 9-19. Special issue.

Morton E H *Trinidad and Tobago: development of library services, October-December* 1972 Unesco, 1974, 202p. (3044/RMO.RD/DBA).

Raymond U 'Planning for library services in Trinidad and Tobago' *Working paper* at 18th SALALM 1973 University of Massachusetts, 1975 pp 327-40.

LEEWARD and BRITISH VIRGIN ISLANDS

1

Public Library, Tortola. 1943- .
Antigua Central Library. 1907- .
Montserrat Public Library. 1899- .
St Kitts, Nevis, Anguilla Public Library, Basseterre, 1890- .

2a

Montserrat Ministry of Education, Health and Welfare.

2b

Tortola. Friends of the Library Association. To promote public library services.

3a

British Virgin Islands — report of the Constitutional Commission 1965.
Great Britain. Foreign and Commonwealth Office *British Virgin Islands, report* London, HMSO, Latest noted: for 1972 published 1973, 61p.
Great Britain. Colonial Office *Leeward Islands, report* HMSO Latest, 1960.
Penn V *Report of the Public Library for the year . . .* Tortola Public Library. Noted: 1970.

3b

Penn V *Tortolana: a bibliography* Tortola Public Library 1968 1(1)- .

3c

Leewards Islands: an economic survey Barclays Bank, 1960.

3f

Johnson P 'Caribbean librarian' *Lib J* 1978, 103(4) 432-4. About Verna Penn, her work in the Virgin Islands and development of libraries under her charge.
Smeaton J 'New children's library in Antigua' *Lib Ass Rec* 1954 56(6) 216-7.

WINDWARD ISLANDS

1

Dominica. Public Library, Roseau. 1902- .
Grenada. Public Library, St George. 1845- .
St Lucia. Central Library, Castries. 1924- .
St Vincent. Public Library, Kingstown. Before 1900- .

2a

Dominica. Ministry of Information, Roseau.
Grenada. Ministry of Information and Social Affairs.
St Lucia. Ministry of Education and Culture.
St Vincent. Ministry of Education and Youth Affairs.

3a

Great Britain Foreign and Commonwealth Office (Formerly: Colonial Office) *Dominica — report*. Latest 1964/65.
— *Grenada — report*. Latest 1965/66.
— *St Lucia — report*. Latest 1963/64. Published 1967.
— *St Vincent — report*. Latest 1964/65.
St Lucia yearbook Castries, Voice Pub Co, 1967, 126p; 1968, 112p. Contains the national bibliography.

3b

See *CARICOM bibliography* under British Associated West Indies, 3b.

3d

Government of St Lucia Statistical Unit.
Windward Islands: an economic survey Barclays Bank, 1960.

3e

St Lucia ordinances, acts, statutory rules and orders for the year, 1967- . GPO, 1968- .

3f

Boromé J A 'Origin and growth of the public libraries of Dominica' *J Lib Hist* 1970 5(3) 200-36.

DUTCH ASSOCIATED WEST INDIES

Curaçāo, Bonaire and Aruba, Leeward Islands (Saba, St Eustatius and part of St Martin) and Surinam (or Dutch Guiana) constitute the Dutch associated West Indies. See also sources on Netherlands.

1

Nederlandse Stichting voor Culturele Samenwerking met Suriname en de Nederlandse Antillen (STICUSA) (Dutch Foundation for Cultural Cooperation with Suriname and the Dutch Antilles), Amsterdam.

Carrilho-Fazal Ali Khan C 'Het bibliotheekwerk van het Cultureel Centrum Suriname' in *STICUSA Jaarverslag* 1971 59-63.

Curaçāo. Stichting Weterschappelijke Bibliotheek, Willemstad. 1950- . The library assumes the functions of a national library for the group.

Curaçāo Public Library, Willemstad. 1922- .

Aruba Public Library. 1949- .

Surinam. STICUSA Library, Paramaribo.

2a

Surinam. Ministry of Education and Community Development, Department of Librarianship, Paramaribo.

2b

Asociation di Biblioteka i Archivo di Korsow (ABAK). 1972- .

3a

Wijers de Bruijin A T M ed *Bibliotheek- en documentatiegids voor Nederland, Suriname en de Nederlandse Antillen* 3rd ed NIDER, 1971, 491p.

Felhoen Kraal J L G 'Libraries and archives for research in West Indian history' *West Indische Gids* 1956/57 37 71-92.

3b

Felhoen Kraal J 'Netherlands Antilles and Surinam: developments 1946-1956 as reflected in publications on these countries' *Current Carib Bibliog* 1956.

West-Indisches Gids 1919-59 then *Nieuwe West-Indische Gids* 1960- . Section on bibliography. See:

Wagenaar-Hummelinck P comp 'Bibliografie' *Nieuwe West Indische Gids* 1975 50(2/3) 148-80; 50(4) 217-36.

STICUSA *Opgave van litteratuur betreffende Suriname* Amsterdam, 1967, 76p.

Ensberg L *Boeken over Suriname: bibliografie van boeken bestaande uit op bevattende een beschrijving van Suriname als geheel* Amsterdam, Bibliotheek- en Documentatieschool, 1969, 40p. Thesis.

Nagelkerke G A comp *Literatuur — oversicht van Suriname tot 1940* Koninklijk Instituut voor Taal- Land- en Volkkunde Bibliotheek, 1972, 199p.

— *1940 tot 1970* The Institute Library, 1971, 96p.

— *Literatuur — oversicht van de Nederlandse Antillen vanaf de 17e eeuw tot 1970* The Institute Library, 1973, 147p.
Gordijn W ed *Bibliografie van Suriname* STICUSA, 1972, 256p.
STICUSA *Nederlandse Antillen* 1975, 271p.

3c

Stichting Wetenschappelijke Bibliotheek *Jaarverslag/Annual report* Willemstad.

3d

Bureau voor de Statistiek *Statistisch jaarboek.*

3f

Goslinga C C *A short history of the Netherlands Antilles and Surinam* Nijhoff, 1979, 198p.
Hartog J 'De openbare boekerijen op de Nederlandse Antillen' *Bibliotheekleven* 1951 36 44-8.
— 'De grote groei van Aruba's Leeszaal' *Bibliotheekleven* 1956 41(1) 11-4.
Foster B 'Curaçāo and Aruba — libraries in the sun' *Wilson Lib Bull* 1979 53(10) 704-7.
*De openbare bibliotheken op de Antillen-verslag van een werkbezoek*NBLC, 1980, 47p.
ACURIL VII (1975) took place in the Dutch Antilles and stimulated library development. Report:
'ACURIL VII' *Open* 1976 8 43-4.

FRENCH ASSOCIATED WEST INDIES

Three French 'départements' with the same status as metropolitan ones: Guadeloupe, Martinique and French Guiana. See also under France.

1

Guiana. Bibliothèque Franconie, Cayenne. Centre ORSTOM de Cayenne 1952- . Scientific information.

Guadeloupe. Bibliothèque Centrale de Prêt de la Guadeloupe, Basse Terre. 1966- . Has a bookmobile service.

Martinique. Bibliothèque Victor Schoelcher, Fort de France.

Bibliothèque Universitaire Antilles-Guyane. Branches in the three countries.

Centre d'Etudes Régionales Antilles-Guyane.

2a

General Council of Guadeloupe.

Guiana. Ministère de l'Education.

3a

Almanach de la Martinique Imprimerie Martiniquaise.

Lasserre G et al 'Les départements d'Outre-mer: la Guadeloupe' *Notes et Etudes Documentaires* 1974 (4135/7) 1-84.

Brasseur G *La Guyane française: a bilan de 30 années* Paris, Direction de la Documentation Française, 1978, 184p. (Notes et Etudes Documentaires, 4497).

[Martinique] *Notes et Etudes Documentaires* 1974 (4060).

3b

Canton B E 'The French Caribbean Departments: sources of information 1946-1955' *Current Caribbean Bibliography* 1954 4 1-36.

Abonnenc E et al *Bibliographie de la Guyane française* Vol 1: *Ouvrages et articles de langue française concernant la Guyane et les territoires avoisinants* Paris, Larose, 1957.

Debien G 'Antilles de langue française — bibliographie' *Caribbean Studies* 1967 7(2) 53-70.

— 'Informaciones bibliográficas americanas: Antillas de lengua francesa' *Anuario Estud Amer* 1965 22 1017-39. Also as: 'Antillas de lengua francesa' *Hist Bibliog Amer* 1965 11 129-51.

Jardel J-P et al 'Bibliographie de la Martinique' *Cahiers du CERAG* 1973, Special issue, 231p.

3d

Institut National de la Statistique et des Etudes Economiques (Paris) *Annuaire statistique de la Guadeloupe* 1963/67 Imprimerie Nationale, 1969, 111p.

3e

St Pierre et Miquelon *Journal officiel des Iles St Pierre et Miquelon* St Pierre, Imprimerie du Gouvernement. Bimonthly.

3f

Hervieu J-P 'Les archives de la Guadeloupe' *Bull Soc Hist Guadeloupe* 1968 (9/10) 153-7.

Morel J 'Libraries in the French Antilles and cooperation' in Jordan *A Research library cooperation in the Caribbean* ALA, 1973, 28-35.

ARGENTINA

1

Biblioteca Nacional, Buenos Aires. 1810- as Public Library of Buenos Aires. National Library 1884- .

Torre Revello J 'La Biblioteca Nacional de la Republica Argentina' *Rev Hist Amer* (Mexico) June 1938 68-72.

Universidad de Buenos Aires. Instituto Bibliotecológico (CID).

Gravenhorst H 'Instituto Bibliotecológico (Institute for Librarianship) of the University of Buenos Aires' in *Encyclopedia* 12 (1974) 97-9.

Universidad de Buenos Aires. Centro de Investigaciones Bibliotecológicas (CID) 1967- . See in *Encyclopedia* 4 (1970) 405-6.

Centro de Documentación Bibliotecológica de la Universidad Nacional del Sur (CDB), Bahia Blanca. 1962- .

Matijevic N 'Centro de Documentación Bibliotecológica (CDB)' in *Encyclopedia* 4 (1970) 404-5.

Centro de Investigación Documentaria (CID), Buenos Aires. 1960- .

Centro de Documentación Científica (CEDOC). 1963- . Under the Consejo Nacional de Investigaciones Científicas y Tecnicas.

2a

Ministerio de Educación de la Nación. Subsecretaria de Cultura, Buenos Aires.

- Dirección Nacional de Bibliotecas Populares. 1870- . Has a professional library: Biblioteca del Bibliotecario, 1944- .

Consejo Nacional de Investigaciones Científicas y Tecnicas (CNICT).

The provinces have their ministries and other official bodies.

2b

Fundación Interaméricana de Bibliotecología Franklin, Buenos Aires.

Asociación Archivistica Argentina, Buenos Aires.

Asociación Argentina de Bibliotecas y Centros de Información Científica y Técnica, Buenos Aires. 1937- . Created as Comité Permanente de Bibliotecarios.

Asociación de Bibliotecarios Gradados de la Republica Argentina (ABGRA), Buenos Aires. 1953- as Asociación de Bibliotecarios Gradados de la Capital Federal. Continues the work of the Centro de Estudios Bibliotecológicos del Museo Social Argentino. 1943-?

Asociación Bibliotecarios Economicos y Administrativos (ABEA), Ciudad de Cordoba.

Asociación de Bibliotecarios Profesionales, Santa Fé.

Asociación Argentina de Bibliotecarios Biomedicos, Buenos Aires.

There are also regional associations.

2c

CNICT *Guia de Escolas y cursos de bibliotecología en la República Argentina* 1965, 31p.

Andreozzi M R *La experiencia de Tucuman: curso audio-visual de bibliotecología* U de Buenos Aires, 1969, 15 1. Mimeo.

Universidad de Buenos Aires *Guia de escuelas y cursos de bibliotecología: Argentina, Chile, Uruguay* Ed preliminar, 1973.

Garza Mercado A *Enseñanza bibliotecológica: dos ensayos y un proyecto* Asociación Nacional de Universidades y Institutos de Enseñanza Superior, 1974, 81p.

The *Boletin informativo ABGRA* contains information on development in professional education.

3a

American University. Foreign Area Studies Division *Area Handbook for Argentina* US-GPO, 1969, 446p.

Wright I S and Nekhom L M *Historical dictionary of Argentina* Scarecrow, 1978, 1113p.

OCDE *Education, resources humaines et développement en Argentine* Paris, 1967, 495p.

Giuffra C A *Guia de bibliotecas argentinas* Fundación Interamericana de Bibliotecologia Franklin, 1967, 334p.

CDB *Guia de las bibliotecas universitarias argentinas* 1965, 1970. Latest edition: 1976, 207p.

Matijevic N *Guia de las bibliotecas patagonicas* 1970, 43p.

'Lista general de bibliotecas populares' *Libros y Bibliot* Oct 1926 161-253.

Universidad de Buenos Aires *Guia de las bibliotecas de la Universidad de Buenos Aires*.

Matijevic N *Quién es quién en la bibliotecología argentina* CBD, 1965, etc.

3b

'Argentina — Foundation of a bibliographic research center in Santa Fé' *Bookbird* 1977 15(4) 29.

Geoghegan A R *Bibliografía de bibliografías argentinas, 1808-1970* Buenos Aires, Casa Prado, 1970, 130p.

Fundación Franklin *Estado actual de la bibliografía corrente nacional argentina* 1966.

Boletin bibliográfico nacional (1937-49 as *Boletin bibliográfico argentino*). Now published by the Biblioteca Nacional. Irregular.

Boletin bibliográfico Lajouane Libreria y Editorial. Quarterly trade list.

Provincia de Buenos Aires. Biblioteca Pública Central *Catálogo temático de publicaciones periódicas. Boletin bibliográfico.*

Matijevic N *Bibliografía bibliotecológica argentina (hasta 1967)* CDB, 1969, 314p.

Peralta A 'Bibliografía bibliotecológica argentina' (1968-1969) *Documentación Bibliotecológica* 1971(2), 48p.

— 1970 *Documentación Bibliotecológica* 1972 (3) 1-19. See in general:

Documentación Bibliotecológica 1970 (1)- . Published by CDB, which also publishes:

Indices de revistas de Bibliotecología (*IREBI*) 1973- , jointly with the Oficina de Educación Iberoamericana (Madrid) and the Instituto Bibliográfico Hispanico (Madrid).

3c

Mesa R Q comp *Argentina. Latin American serial documents: a holding list* Bowker, 1971, 693p.

Fundación Franklin *Noticiero Franklin* 1964-?

Camera Argentina del Libro *Biblos* 1941-66.

ABGRA *Bibliotecologia y Documentación Argentina* 1979- . Previously *Boletin informativo ABGRA*.

Instituto Bibliotecológico *Boletin informativo* and *Publicaciones*.
CID *INTI*. Irregular; contains abstracts and articles.

3d

Instituto Nacional de Estadística y Censos *Boletin mensual de estadísticas* 1956- .
— *Anuario estadistico de la República Argentina*.

3e

Boletin oficial. Contains lists of material deposited with the Registro Nacional de la Propriedad Intelectual. 1971- .
Marco del Pont de Pacheco V L *Legislación bibliotecaria argentina*. La Plata, Colegio de Bibliotecarios, 1968, 70p.
Legal deposit: Law 11723 Article 57 and Decree 3.079/57.

3f

Agency for International Development *Brazil and Argentina: a survey report on publishing, books and library resources* National Book Committee Inc, 1967, 155p.
Buonocore D *Libreros, editores e impresores de Buenos Aires: esbozo para una historia del libro argentino* Buenos Aires, Bowker, 1974, 360p.
Graham-Yooll A *The Press in Argentina, 1973-1978* Writers and Scholars Educational Trust, 1979, 171p.
Sabor Riera M A *Contribución al estudio histórico del desarrollo de los servicios bibliotecarios de la Argentina en el bibliotecarios de la Argentina en el siglo XIX: Parte 1: 1810-1852; Parte 2: 1852-1910* U Nacional del Nordeste, Dirección de Bibliotecas, 1974-75, 2 vols.
Fino J F and Hourcade L A 'Evolución de la bibliotecologia en la Argentina, 1757-1952' *Universidad* (Santa Fé) 1952 25 265-301.
Sabor J E 'Argentine, libraries in' in *Encyclopedia* 1 (1968) 520-9.
Giuffra C A 'Bibliothèques de la République argentine' *Museo Soc Arg Bol* 1965 43(323) 68-72.
Deransart P *Bibliothèques et systèmes documentaires en Argentine et au Brésil* Le Chasnay, 1977, 145p.
Comisión Nacional de Alfabetización *Programa nacional de alfabetización y educación de adultos. Nivelos objectivos y contenidos minimos del programa* 1965, 13p.
— *Reunión sobre funcción y desarrollo de las bibliotecas escolares y populares y su relación con el programa nacional intensivo de alfabetización y educación de adultos, Santiago del Estero, 1965*. Report and recommendations from the Ministry of Education.
Velasquez L H 'Popular libraries in Argentina' *Unesco Bull Lib* 1956 10(5/6) 105-6.
Sabor J E 'El libro, los lectores, las bibliotecas' *Limen* 1972 10(36/37) 97-9.
Heguy de Ballastero N J et al 'Bibliotecas escolares: resultados de una investigación' *Rev Educ* (La Plata) 1969 (21) 65-9.
Zago N 'La biblioteca escolar y su importancia' *Rev Educ* 1969 (22) 65-6.
Sánchez B 'La biblioteca escolar' *Limen* 1972 10(36/37) 105-6.
Mirabelli J J 'Situación de la universidad argentina' *Rev Ci Econ* 1969 57(3) 223-47.
Giuffra C A 'Bibliotecas universitarias argentinas' *Universidad* (Santa Fé) 1963 (58) 295-307.
Van Dijk M and Van Slype G *El servicio de documentación fronte a la explosión de la información* CEDOC, 1972.

BOLIVIA

1

Biblioteca y Archivo Nacionales, Sucre. 1836- .
Universidad Mayor de San Andrés. Biblioteca, La Paz.
Banco del Libro, La Paz. Has branches in the provinces.
Centro Nacional de Documentación Cientifica y Tecnológica, La Paz 1968- .

2a

Consejo Nacional de Educación, La Paz.
Dirección de Cultura, La Paz. 1832- .

2b

Asociación Boliviana de Bibliotecarios (ABB), Cochabamba. 1974- .

2c

Professional education at:
Universidad Mayor de San Andrés, La Paz.
Fundación Patiño. Centro Pedagogico y Cultural de Portales, Cochabamba.
Centro Pedagogico y Cultural de Portales *Formación profesional del bibliotecario en Bolivia* The Centre, 1973, 11p.

3a

Heath D *Historical dictionary of Bolivia* Scarecrow, 1972, 324p. (Latin American Historical Dictionaries, 4).
Universidad Mayor de San Andrés. Centro Nacional de Documentación Científica y Tecnológica *Guia de bibliotecas, centros y servicios documentarios de Bolivia* La Paz, 1973, 113p.

3b

Siles Guevara J *Bibliografía de bibliografías bolivianas* Imprenta del Estado, 1969, 38p.
— 'Bibliografía de bibliografías bolivianas' 2nd ed *Estudios Andinos* 1970 1(1) 148-70.
Boletin bibliográfico boliviano La Paz 1965- .
Guttentag Tichauer W *Bibliografía boliviana* Amigos Del Libro, 1963- . Annual. Not based on legal deposit.
Costa de la Torre A *Catálogo de la bibliografía boliviana* U Mayor de San Andrés, 1968/73, 2 vols (1255, 1069p). Twentieth century imprints; contains a 'Historia de la bibliografia boliviana' Vol 1 pp 23-236.

3c

Revista de la Biblioteca Nacional Sucre. 1920-41. Not published in 1921-35, 1938.

3d

 Banco Central de Bolivia *Boletin estadístico*.

3e

Anuario de leyes, decretos y resoluciones supremas.

3f

Jackson W V 'Bolivia, libraries in' in *Encyclopedia* 2 (1969) 655-9.

Guttentag Tichauer W 'Survey of the library situation in Bolivia' in *Papers—18th SALALM, Port of Spain, 1973* SALALM Secretariat, 1975, Working Paper B-5, 365-71.

Benktson L G 'Bolivias väg till bibliotek' *Biblioteksbladet* 1976 61(14) 216-8. Developments.

Plotnik A 'Born again in the Andes' *Amer Lib* 1977 8(8) 409-12. General progress.

Calderon M 'Notas bibliotecarias' *Bibliot Municip Rev* 1949 1(3) 97-102.

Burtillos J A 'Fin y objeto de las bibliotecas para la infancia, adolescencia y juventud' *Bibliot Municip Rev* 1949 1(1) 88-9.

Mettini I J L *Plan para el desarrollo de las bibliotecas públicas y escolares* U Nacional de Tucumán, Biblioteca Central, 1975, 85p. Survey of resources and strategies 1971-1991 in the context of economic and social development.

Benktson L G 'Bolivia: a plan for the development of public and school libraries' *Int Lib Rev* 1978 10(1) 71-5. Based on the above paper.

BRAZIL

1

Biblioteca Nacional, Rio de Janeiro. 1808- .

Universidad de São Paulo. Divisão de Biblioteca e Documentação (DBD-USP). 1970- . Merger of the Central library and documentation service.

Conselho Nacional de Pesquisas. Instituto Brasileiro de Bibliografia e Documentação (IBBD), Rio de Janeiro. 1954- .

Universidade Federal do Paraná. Centro de Bibliografia e Documentação (CBD). 1956- . By agreement with IBBD and on the same pattern.

Instituto Brasileiro de Informação em Ciência e Tecnologia. (IBICT).

2a

Ministerio da Educação e Cultura. Departamento de Asuntos Culturais. Serviço Nacional de Bibliotecas, Brasilia. 1961- . (Title varied).

Conselho Federal de Biblioteconomia (CFB), São Paulo, now Brasilia 1962- . With regional councils in provinces (Conselhos Regionais).

Conselho Nacional de Pesquisas. Scientific documentation.

Fundação do Livro Infantil e Juvenil. São Paulo State, Secretariat of Education.

2b

Federação Brasileira de Associações de Bibliotecários (FEBAB) São Paulo. 1959- .

'Federação Brasileira de Associações de Bibliotecários' *FEBAB Bol* 1964 9(5/6) 88-102.

Moreno Musso L G 'Federação Brasileira de Associações de Bibliotecários' in *Encyclopedia* 8 (1972) 368-70.

Both references contain a list of member associations. See for instance:

Comisão Brasileira de Bibliotecas Centrais Universitárias (FEBAB/CBBCU).

Comisão Brasileira de Bibliotecas Publicas e Escolares (FEBAB/CBBPE). The latest member is the:

Comisão Brasileira de Documentação em Ciências Sociales e Humanidades. 1978- .

Associação Paulista de Bibliotecários (APB). 1938- .

Associação Profissional de Bibliotecários do Estado do Rio de Janeiro (APIBERJ). 1949- .

Associação Brasileira de Escolas de Biblioteconomia e Documentação (ABEBD) based on São Paulo School of Librarianship. 1967- .

Rede de Bibliotecas de Amazónia (REBAM), Belém.

Pereira M and Coelho Lopes M *A Rede de Bibliotecas da Amazónia (REBAM): instrumento para o desenvolvimento da Amazónia* Ministério do Interior, 1973, 1 vol.

2c

Jackson W V 'Brazil, library education in' in *Encyclopedia* 3 (1970) 237-59, bibl.

Ferreira L M A G et al 'Currículo mínimo de biblioteconomia' *Rev Escol Bibliot* (U Minas Gerais) 1977 6(1) 92-9.

Da Soledade Vieira A 'A formação de administradores de bibliotecas: na berlinda o programa da UFMG [U Federal de Minas Gerais] *Rev Escol Bibliot* (U Minas Gerais) 1977 6(2) 136-60.

— and Lima E 'A pós-gradação em biblioteconomia e a formação de uma líderança nacional' *Rev Escol Bibliot* (U Minas Gerais) 1977 6(2) 125-35.

Oliveira Carvalho A de 'Pos-graduação em biblioteconomia e ciencia da informação: reflexoes, sugestoes, experienceias' *Rev Escol Bibliot* (U Minas Gerais) 1978 7(2) 289-309, refs.

IBBD *Cursos especializados e de pós-graduação* 1970, 12p.

Alonso F R 'Educational program at the PAHO's Regional Library of Medicine in São Paulo, Brazil' *Med Lib Ass Bull* 1974 62 63.

Overmeyer L *Training in the automation of library processing: Brazil (Mission) 6 September-26 October 1973* Unesco, 1974, 11p.

Bastos da Cunha M 'O bibliotecario brasileiro na atualidade' *Rev Escol Bibliot* (U Minas Gerais) 1976 5(2) 178-94.

Athayde Polke A M et al 'Análise do mercado do trabalho do bibliotecário em Belo Horizonte' *Rev Escol Bibliot* (U Minas Gerais) 1976 5(2) 165-77.

Bastos da Cunha M 'O papel do bibliotecário na sociedade brasileira' *Rev Escol Bibliot* (U Minas Gerais) 1978 7(1) 7-26, refs.

See also 3b: Garcia Moreno Russo L.

3a

Grande enciclopedia Portuguesa e Brasileira Part II: *Brasil* Lisbon and Rio, 1967- . 4 vols.

Brazil at a glance Editoria Barnes, 1967, 255p.

Instituto Nacional do Livro *Guia das bibliotecas brasileiras* 4th ed 1969.

IBBD *Bibliotecas especializadas brasileiras*. List of members of the documentation network.

— *Quem é quem na biblioteconomia e documentação no Brasil* 1971, 544p. Directory of librarians and documentalists.

Da Terra Caldeira P *Guia das bibliotecas do Estado de Minas Gerais* Belo Horizonte, Conselho de Extensão da UFMG 1977, 113p.

Secretaria de Cultura *Guia de Bibliotecas do Estado de São Paulo* 1978, 399p.

APB Grupo de Trabalho em Tecnologia. Comissão de Levantamento de Bibliotecas . . . *Levantamento de bibliotecas da area tecnológica* IBBD, 1974, 418p.

APB *Relação dos bibliotecários no interior do estado: até setembro 1973* APB, 1973, 1 vol.

Conselho Nacional de Desenvolvimento Ciêntifico e Tecnológico *Siglas de entidades brasileiras: versão preliminar* The Council, 1979, 950p.

3b

Bastos da Cunha M 'O controle bibliográfico da literatura científica e tecnológica no Brasil' *Rev Escol Bibliot* (U Minas Gerais) 1977 6(1) 26-44.

Basseches B *A bibliography of Brazilian bibliographies/Uma bibliografía das bibliografias brasileiras* Detroit, Blaine Etheridge Books, 1978, 185p.

Harmon R M and Chamberlain B J *Brazil: a working bibliography in literature, linguistics, humanities and the social sciences* Arizona State U, Center for Latin American Studies, 1975, 101p (Special study, 14).

Instituto Nacional do Libro *Bibliografia brasileira* 1938-1955. 11 vols.

— *Revista do libro*. Section 'Bibliografia brasileira corrente' 1956-1963.

— *Bibliografia brasileira* 1964-66, 3 vols.

— *Bibliografia brasileira mensal* 1967-73.

In 1973 merged with the:

Biblioteca National *Boletim bibliográfico* 1951- . Under this title.

Jackson W V *Catalog of Brazilian acquisitions of the Library of Congress, 1964-1974* G K Hall, 1976.

Meurer C T 'A Library of Congress e a aquisição de publicações oficiais brasileiras' *Rev Bibliot Brasilia* 1976 4(2) 201-12.

Sindicato Nacional dos Editores de Livros *Ediçoes brasileiras* 1964- . Quarterly.

McNeil M R *Guidelines to problems of education in Brazil: a review and selected bibliography* Teachers College P, 1970, 66p.

Leipziger F T 'Brazilian library literature' *Int Lib Rev* 1976 8(4) 379-95. As it reflects developments in librarianship.

Garcia Moreno Russo L *A biblioteconomia brasileira, 1915-1965* Instituto Nacional do Libro, 1966, 356p. On library school organization with a 659 items bibliography on librarianship.

DBP-USP *Bibliografia bibliotecologica brasileira* 1952, 41p.

— *Bibliografia brasileira de biblioteconomia* (De Carvalho O) 1959, 97p.

— *Indice de periodicos correntes Serie: Biblioteconomia e documentação* 1968- .

IBBD *Noticias* Contains a current list of accessions. Classified.

— *Bibliografia brasileira de documentação* Vol 1, 1960: 1811-1960 Vol 2, 1972: 1960-1970; etc.

Instituto de Planejamento Economico e Social. Setor de Documentação *Bibliografia seletiva e analitica sobre transferência de tecnologia para o Brasil e para paises em desenvolvimento e/ou subdesenvolvidos* (CN Ferreira comp) 1972, 1 vol.

3c

Biblioteca Nacional *Anais* 1876- . Irregular.

— *Biblioteca e bibliotecários* 1954- . Monthly.

INL *Revista do Libro* 1956-70.

FEBAB *Revista Brasileira de Biblioteconomia e Documentação* 1973- . Replaces *FEBAB Boletim informativo* 1960-72.

Associação de Bibliotecários do Distrito Federal *Revista de Biblioteconomia de Brasilia*, 1973- .

UFMG *Revista da Escola de Biblioteconomia* 1972- .

APIBERJ *Noticias*.

IBBD *Ciência da informação* 1972- .

3d

Instituto Brasileiro de Geografia e Estatistica. Conselho Nacional de Estatistica *Anuario estatistico do Brasil*, Rio. 1916- .

Oliveira R R de 'A documentação estatistica básica no Brasil' *Amér Latina* 1966 9(1) 148-81.

Ministerio de Educação e Cultura. Serviço de Estatistica *Bibliotecas 1960* The Service, 1962, 105p.

3e

Diario oficial Brasilia.

Chaia J *Algumas notas para a historia das bibliotecas do Brasil: basedas na legislação de 1808-1889* Marilia, Biblioteca Publica João Mesquita Valença, 1967, 80 leaves, tables.

Gelfand M A 'Brazil's library law' *Lib J* 1966 91 1362-4.

Legislação da profissão de bibliotecario Conselho Federal de Biblioteconomia, 1971, 38p. Previous ed 1966.

3f

Bello J M *A history of modern Brazil, 1889-1964* Stanford U P, 1966.

Monbeig P *Le Brésil* 4th ed Paris, PUF, 1967, 127p.

Villegas J E *Brazil as a model for developing countries* Vantage P, 1979, 77p.

Havighurst R J and Moreira J R *Society and education in Brazil* Pittsburgh U, 1965, 263p.

Agency for International Development *Brazil and Argentina: a survey report on publishing, books and library resources* National Book Committee Inc, 1967, 155p.

Andrade O de Souza *O livro brasileiro: progressos e problemas: 1920-1971* Rio, Editora Paralelo (and INL) 1974, 127p.

Jackson W V *The national textbook program and libraries in Brazil* U of Pittsburgh Book Center, 1967. (Portuguese edition by Agencia Norte-Americana para o Desenvolvimento Internacional).

INL *Programa nacional do livro didactico* INL, 1973, 72p.

Fonseca E N da 'Libraries in Brazil' *Lib J* 1961 86(20) 3891-5.

Ferraz T A 'Library conditions in Brazil' in *Unesco course for Teachers of Librarianship* Copenhagen, 1970.

Deransart P *Bibliothèques et systèmes documentaires en Argentine et au Brésil* Le Chasnay, 1977, 145p.

Fonseca E N da *A biblioteconomia brasileira no contexto mundial* Rio de Janeiro, 1979.

McCarthy C *Developing libraries in Brazil, with a chapter on Paraguay* Scarecrow, 1975, 207p.

Jackson W V 'Brazil, libraries in' in *Encyclopedia* 3 (1970) 166-237, bibl.

Encontro de Responsaveis pela Execução do Programa de Bibliotecas no Brasil I° Brasilia, 1973, Anais Brasilia, 1973, 32p. To implement the programme: Programa Nacional do Libro do Plano Setorial de Educação e Cultura.

Congresso Brasileiro de Biblioteconomia e Documentação, 7°, Belem, 1973. Anais IBICT, 1977, 474p.

'Integration of information systems in national development' Theme of the 9th congress (*Unesco Bull Lib* 1977 31 121).

Escolar H *Brasil: desarollo de las bibliotecas públicas en el Brasil. Creación de la biblioteca pública de Brasilia, octubre — diciembre de 1968* Unesco, 1969, 63p.

Jackson W V 'Fifty million books for Brazil' *Wilson Lib Bull* 1969 44 197-202.

A biblioteca nos programas de alfabetização de adultos Fundação Movimento Brasileiro de Alfabetização (MOBRAL), 1975, 21p.

Souza F de B 'O desenvolvimento das bibliotecas públicas e sua influência sobre a indústria editorial brasileira' *Rev Bibliot Brasilia* 1977 5(1) 91-8.

Suaiden E J 'Perspectivas das bibliotecas públicas no Brasil' *Rev Bibliot Brasilia* 1978 6(1) 77, 82.

Negrao M R 'A evolução do departamento de bibliotecas públicas, 1907-1978' *Rev Bibliot Brasilia* 1979 7(2) 186-209. City library system.

'Bibliotecas públicas' *Rev Brasil Bibliot Doc* 1973 2 119-25. Small public libraries.

Garcia Moreno Russo M *Estado de São Paulo: bibliotecas públicas municipais, situação e sugesões* FEBAB, 1973, 90p.

Pessoa E L C 'Sistema estadual de bibliotecas públicas de Rio Grande do Norte' *Rev Bibliot Brasilia* 1979 7(2) 158-61.

Oliveira M de F P de 'Sistemas de bibliotecas públicas do Estado do Ceará' *Rev Bibliot Brasilia* 1979 7(2) 162-73.

Silva K M de C 'Sistema de bibliotecas públicas do Estado da Bahia: situação actual' *Rev Bibliot Brasilia* 1979 7(2) 174-85.

Sperandio L 'Historico da biblioteca pública do Paraná' *Rev Bibliot Brasilia* 1974

2(2) 199-202.
Tavares D F *As bibliotecas infanto-juvenis de hoje* Salvador (Bahia) Biblioteca Infantil Monteiro Lobato, 1970, 52p.
A responsibilidade social da biblioteca no plano setorial da educação, I U Brasilia, 1977, 575p. Conference, Brasilia, 1975.
'Basic proposal for a network of school libraries in Rio de Janeiro, Brazil' *Bookbird* 1978 16(2) 26-35. First part of a survey.
Góes L P S 'Bibliotecas infantis de São Paulo' *Rev Brasil Est Pedagogicas* 1977 62(141) 97-102.
Lemos A A Briquet de and Macedo V A A 'A posição da biblioteca na organização operacional da universidade' *Rev Bibliot Brasilia* 1974 2(2) 167-74.
Gelfand M A 'Política de aquisição em bibliotecas universitárias: planos e programas, individuais e cooperativos, de formação de acervos' *Rev Bibliot Brasilia* 1974 2(2) 155-65.
Miranda A *Bibliotecas dos cursos de pós-graduação em educação no Brasil: estudo comparado* (Paper at the 9th Congress of librarians). Brasilia, Ministerio da Educação e Cultura, MEC/DAU/CAPES, 1977, 94p.
— 'Postgraduate education libraries in Brazil: a comparative study' *Focus Int Comp Libp* 1978 9(2) 15-7.
Figueirido N 'Bibliotecas universitarias e especializadas: paralelos e contrastes' *Rev Bibliot Brasilia* 1979 7(1) 9-25, refs.
Da Silva A F S 'Levantamento do 'status quo' da biblioteca do INPA' *Rev Bibliot Brasilia* 1979 7(1) 91-117. Library services to a research institute.
Nobrega Cesarino M A de 'Bibliotecas especializadas, centros de documentação, centros de analise da informação: apenas uma questao de terminologia?' *Rev Escol Bibliot* (U Minas Gerais) 1978 7(2) 218-41, refs. Differences between special libraries, documentation centres, information centres: is it only a question of vocabulary.
Vincenti A L 'The organization of national documentation and information services in Brazil' *Lib Trends* 1969 17 245-57.
Conselho Nacional de Pesquisas 'Directrises básicas para a implantação do Sistema Nacional de Informação Científica e Tecnológica (SNICT)' *Ciência Info* 1973 2(1) 69-73.
Daniels Shepard M 'Library automation in Brazil as an element in an inter-American network for transmitting bibliographic information' *Int Catalog* 1977 6(4) 45-7. US/Latin America cooperation. In Brazil the Fundação G Vargas's library might be linked with the Library of Congress for a multilingual network.

CHILE

1

Biblioteca Nacional, Santiago. 1813- .

Silva Castro R 'Los primeros años de la Biblioteca Nacional de Chile (1813-1824)' *Rev Hist Amer* (Mexico) 1956 (42) 355-407.

'La extension cultural de la Biblioteca Nacional' *Mapocho* 1963 1(3) 276-84.

Universidad de Chile. Biblioteca Central, Santiago.

- Departamento de Bibliotecológia.

Centro Nacional de Información y Documentación (CENID), Santiago 1962- . Coordinates activities of libraries and documentation centres. Manages the documentation network SIDOC/CHILE.

Johnson de Vodanovic B 'Centro Nacional de Información y documentación (CENID)' in *Encyclopedia* 4 (1970) 406-8.

2a

Dirección de Bibliotecas, Archivos y Museos, Santiago. 1930- .

Comisión Nacional de Investigación Cinetífica y Tecnológica (CONICYT).

2b

Colegio de Bibliotecarios de Chile, Santiago. 1969- . Supersedes the Asociación de Bibliotecarios de Chile 1955-66.

'The Society of Librarians of Chile' *Unesco Bull Lib* 1970 25(4) 285.

2c

Villalón-Galdames A and Pimstein-Lamas A 'Chile, University of Chile, School of Library Science' in *Encyclopedia* 4 (1970) 623-7.

3a

Salvatore B *Historical dictionary of Chile* Scarecrow, 1972 (Latin American Historical Dictionaries, 7).

CENID *Guia de bibliotecas y centros de documentación de Chile* CENID, 1971, 119p. Mimeo. (Serie directorios, 1).

3b

Freudenthal J R *Development and current status of bibliographic organization in Chile* U of Michigan, PhD Thesis, 1972, 367p. See also in *Libri* 1972 22(4) 273-80.

Laval R A 'Bibliografía de bibliografías chilenas' *Rev Bibliog Chile y Extranjera* 1915 3(1/2).

Biblioteca Nacional *Anuario de la prensa chilena* 1886- .

Servicio bibliográfico chileno Zamoran y Caperan, 1940- . Quarterly trade list.

Dirección de Bibliotecas *Las publicaciones de la Biblioteca Nacional, 1854-1963; informe elevado al Ministerio de Educación* 1964.

Anrique Reyes N 'Bibliografía de las principales revistas y periodicos de Chile' *U Chile Anales* 1957 114-115 212-6.

Anuario de publicaciones periódicas chilenas Biblioteca Nacional, 1923- . Suspended 1938-51.

Anuario bibliográfico de la Facultad de Filosofia y Educación Universidad de Chile 1962 (for 1960)- . The school of librarianship belongs to this Faculty.

3c

Asociación de Bibliotecarios de Chile *Boletin* 1956-66.

Colegio de Bibliotecarios de Chile *Boletin* 1969- .

— *Noticia bibliotecaria.*

Biblioteca Nacional *Mapocho* 1963- . Quarterly.

Universidad de Chile. Departamento de Bibliotecología *Revista Chilena de Bibliotecología y Documentación* 1975- . Includes a section of bibliography.

CENID *Notas informativas* 1963- .

3d

Dirección de Estadística y Censo *Anuario.*

3e

Diario oficial.

Freudenthal J R 'National report: Chile — library legislation' *Int J Law Libns* 1974 2(2) 71-4).

Scarpa R E *Chile: Ley n° 17.336 sobre propriedad intelectual. Presentación y analisis* Bogotá, 1975. Mimeo.

3f

Sanz M T 'Chile, libraries in' in *Encyclopedia* 4 (1970) 615-22.

Feliu Cruz G *El problema bibliotecario nacional* Biblioteca Nacional, 1963, 61p.

Problemas de los servicios bibliotecarios en Chile Terceras jornadas bibliotecarias chilenas. Inform final Asociacion de Bibliotecarios, 1964, 43p.

Freudenthal J R *Current status of libraries and librarians in Chile.* Paper at 18th SALALM, Port of Spain, Trinidad, April 29-May 3, 1975 OAS, 1975, 19p. (Working Paper B-4).

Harrington C W 'Library consulting, Chile style' *Louisiana Lib Ass Bull* 1969 32 104-13.

Rooney E M 'Jesuit libraries go public' *Cathol Lib World* 1971 42 487-91.

Arce Rovedy L and Watt Torres E 'Proyecto de creación de un sistema nacional de bibliotecas escolares para Chile' *Rev Chil Bibliot Doc* 1975 1(1/2) 9-13.

Keren C and Robredo J *Chile: estudio de factibilidad sobre la créación de uno red nacional de información cientifica y técnica* Unesco, 1972, 78p.

Improving information transfer: workshop in Rabat, May 1976. Final report Unesco, 1976. Chile was one of the participants.

Freudenthal J R 'Information and documentation in Chile: progress report and bibliography, 1970-1975' *ASIS J* 1977 28(1) 58-60, refs.

COLOMBIA

1

Biblioteca Nacional de Colombia, Bogotá. 1939- . Created in 1868.

Forero L E 'La Biblioteca Nacional de Bogotá' *Bibliot Nacion Rev* Jan 1930 299-330.

Hernández de Alba G and Carrasquilla Botero J *Historia de la Biblioteca Nacional de Colombia* Instituto Caro y Cuervo, 1977, 447p. (Publicación 38). Traces its history over 200 years.

Posada E 'Biblioteca Nacional' *Bol Hist Antigüedades* 1977 64(717) 254-70.

Instituto Caro y Cuervo, Bogotá. 1942- . Legal deposit library.

'Investigar, enseñar y difundir' *Espiral* 1973 (127) 5-18. Report on the objectives of the Institute.

Universidad Social Católica de la Salle. Faculdad de Ciencias de la Información, Bogotá. 1971- . Library school, bibliographical activities.

2a

Ministerio de Educación Nacional. Sección de Servicios Bibliotecariós, Bogotá.

Instituto Colombiano para el Fomento de la Educación Superior. División de Documentación y Fomento Bibliotecario, Bogotá.

Instituto Colombiano de Cultura. División de Bibliotecas y Centros Culturales (COLCULTURA).

Fondo Colombiano de Investigaciones Científicas y Proyectos Especiales 'Francisco José de Caldas' (COLCIENCIAS). To establish and develop the information system (Sistema Nacional de Información (SNI)).

2b

Asociación Colombiana de Arquivistas, Medellin.

Asociación Colombiana de Bibliotecarios (ASCOLBI), Bogotá. 1956-.

Bibliotecarios Agrícolas Colombianos, Bogotá.

Colegio Colombiano de Bibliotecarios (CCB), Medellin. 1968-. Merger of: Colegio de Bibliotecarios Colombianos (1963-) and Asociación de Egresados de la Escuela Interamericana de Bibliotecología (ASEIB).

2c

The main feature of librarianship education in Colombia is the creation in Medellin of the Interamerican Library School serving other Latin American countries, beside the purely Colombian institutions.

Krzys R A 'Library training in Colombia before the Inter-American Library School' *J Educ Libp* 1966 6(4) 234-43.

Flóren Lozaino L 'The Inter-American School of Library Science, University of Antioquia: origins and future plans' *Unesco Bull Lib* 1966 20(4) 177-83. See other references in Latin America, 2c.

Krzys R A *Education for librarianship in Colombia* Western Case Reserve University, Thesis, 1965.

Krzys R A and Litton G L *History of education for librarianship in Colombia* Scarecrow, 1969, 203p.

3a

Blustein H I et al *Area handbook for Colombia* 3rd ed American U, Foreign Area Studies, 1976, 508p.

Davis R H *Historical dictionary of Colombia* Scarecrow, 1977. (Latin American Historical Dictionaries, 14).

Gorman de Alzate M and Espinosa Bermeo X comps *Guia de editoriales, distribuidoras y librarias de Bogotá* Centro Regional para el Fomento del Libro en la América Latina, 1977, 214p. Directory of publishers, booksellers, etc.

Directorio de la Educación superior en Colombia Instituto Colombiano para el Fomento de la Educación Superior, 1977, 254p. Includes departments of librarianship and libraries of the institutions.

Directorio Colombiano de bibliotecas públicas Instituto Colombiano de Cultura, 1977, 81p.

Flóren Lozano L *Guia de las bibliotecas de Medellin* Escuela Interaméricana de Bibliotecología.

Directorio Colombiano de unidades de información Fondo Colombiano de Investigaciones Científicas, 1976, 182p.

Sanchez Toro S and Aceved de Espinal N *Quien es quien en la bibliotecología Colombiana* Pereira, U Tecnológica, Departamento de Bibliotecas, 1974, 199p.

3b

Moreno de Angel P and Toro Duque, C *El deposito legal y el control bibliográfico en la Biblioteca Nacional de Colombia* Bogotá, 1975.

Romero-Rojas F S 'La bibliografía en Colombia' Working paper B33, SALALM 1975 *Final report and papers* U of Texas Austin, 1978, 331-6.

Giraldo Jaramillo G *Bibliografía de bibliografías Colombianas* 2nd rev ed Instituto Caro y Cuervo, 1960, 204p.

Watson G H *Colombia, Ecuador and Venezuela: an annotated guide to reference materials in the humanities and social sciences* Scarecrow, 1971, 279p.

Flóren Lozano L *Obras de referencia y generales de la bibliografía Colombiana* U de Antioquia, 1968, 204p. Mimeo. 1900 onwards, on Winchell's guide pattern.

Anuario bibliográfico colombiano 1951/56- . Instituto Caro y Cuervo. Retrospective bibliography on the way.

Londono Benveniste F and Ochoa Núnez H comps *Bibliografía de la educación en Colombia* Instituto Caro y Cuervo, 1976, 678p.

Bibliografía bibliotecológica colombiana U de Antioquia, 1961- .

Escuela Intéramericana de Bibliotecología. Biblioteca *Boletin de adquisiciones* 1955- . Books, periodicals on librarianship.

Ballesteros Lopez D *Bibliografía sobre la Biblioteca Nacional* U de la Salle, 1975, 38p.

Bohorquez J I *Indice del Boletin de la Asociación Colombiana de Bibliotecarios, 1957-67.*

Boletin cultural y bibliográfico. Indice general 1958-1966; 1966-1973 Biblioteca Luis-Angel Arango, 1973, 2 vols.

3c

Moreno Mattos A *Publicaciones periodicas en Colombia 1964* Departemento Administrativo Nacional de Estadística, 1965, 52p.

Boletin de la Asociación Colombiana de Bibliotecarios, Bogota. 1957-79. Now superseded by:

Carta al Bibliotecario 1979- .

Escuela Interaméricana de Bibliotecología *Revista interaméricana de bibliotecología* 1978- .
Carta trimestrial de Bibliotecarios Agricolas Colombianos, 1965- .

3d

Departamento Administrativo Nacional del Estadística *Boletin mensual de estadística.*
— *La biblioteca en Colombia* (1964) 5th ed 1966.
Escuela Interaméricana de Bibliotecología *Estadísticas de la EIB 1956-1972* U de Antioquia, 1973; *Suplemento* 1973-1976 Published 1977, 73p.
See also annual feature in the *ASCOLBI Boletin* and *Carta al Bibliotecario.*

3e

Diario oficial.
Bohorquez J I *La legislación bibliotecológica colombiana.*
'Colombian legislation on information systems and books' *Unesco Bull Lib* 1975 29(1) 50-1.

3f

Aprile-Gniset J *Colombie* Paris, Seuil, 1977, 190p.
Ruiz J E *Cultural policy in Colombia* Unesco, 1977, 93p.
Amaya de Heridia M 'Distribución, producción, comercio del libro y bibliotecas en Colombia, 1955-1971'. Paper B-1, SALALM 1975 *Final report and papers* U of Texas Austin, 1978, 204-60.
Santa E ed *El libro de Colombia: antologia* Instituto Colombiano de Cultura, 1973, 241p. Collected papers on books, publishing, etc. Includes Posado E 'La Biblioteca Nacional' pp 183-199.
Tarr T S 'Organization of the royal public library of Santa Fé de Bogota' *J Lib Hist* 1970 5(1) 20-34.
Jackson W V 'Colombia, libraries in' in *Encyclopedia* 5 (1970) 282-315, refs.
Florén Lozano L 'El pais necesita bibliotecarios si queremos acelerar nuestro desarrollo científico y cultural' *U de Antioquia* 1965 42(161) 131-8.
Jackson W V *Steps towards the future development of a national plan for library services in Colombia* Vanderbilt U Bookstore, 1971, 66p.
Bohorquez C J I *Estado actual de las bibliotecas en Colombia* Fondo Colombiano de Investigaciones Científicas, 1971, 82p. (Bibliotecología y documentación 2).
Yeamans S *The Medellin pilot public library: development and influence* Kent State U, Thesis 1965.
Riascos Sánchez B *Proyecto de programa para el fomento de bibliotecas públicas* Instituto Colombiano de Cultura, 1970.
Ministerio de Educación *Seminario sobre bibliotecas escolares para inspectores nacionales de educación, 11-22 de enero de 1968, Informe* 1968, vp. Mimeo.
Asociación Colombiana de Universidades *Plan general de desarrollo para bibliotecas universitarias colombianas* 1967, 17p.
Freiband S J 'Reference service in Colombian university libraries' *Unesco Bull Lib* 1978 33(2) 92-4.
Sanchez Juliao D 'La universidad y el pueblo: bibliotecas para el pueblo' *Desarrollo Indoamericano* 1977 12(36) 13-4.
Carabelli A et al *Creación de un sistema nacional de bibliotecas y documentación agraria para Colombia: informe final* Instituto Colombiano Agropecuario (ICA), 1970.
Agudelo C 'Red de documentación y información de Colombia: REDIC' *Rev Fuerzas Armadas* 1971 21(63) 521-52.

Becker J et al *Sistema colombiano de información científica y técnica* Quirima, 1970, 59p. Mimeo.

'Establishment of a national information system (SNI) in Colombia' *UNISIST Newsletter* 1974 2(4).

Schur H *Colombia — Information specialists for development* Unesco, 1977, 64p. Also in Spanish.

Monge F and Urbine M J 'Un sistema para la automatizacion de bibliotecas en Latinoamérica: experiencia del INCORA en Colombia' *U Antioquia* 1969 45(172) 411-26.

ECUADOR

1

Biblioteca Nacional, Quito. 1792- .

Universidad Central del Acuador. Biblioteca General, Quito.

Biblioteca Municipal, Quito.

2a

Ministerio de Educación Pública.

Casa de la Cultura Ecuatoriana, Quito. 1944- . Bibliographical activities.

2b

Asociación Ecuatoriana de Bibliotecarios (AEB), Quito. 1945- .

Asociación Ecuatoriana de Administradores de Documentos y Archivos, Quito.

2c

Universidad de Guayaquil. Escuela de Bibliotecología.

3a

Bork A W and Maier G *Historical dictionary of Ecuador* Scarecrow, 1973 (Latin American Historical Dictionaries, 10).

3b

Chaves A *Fuentes principales de la bibliografía ecuatoriana* Casa de la Cultura, 1958, 24p.

Espinosa Cordero N *Bibliografía ecuatoriana* Cuenca, Colegio Nacional Benigno Malo, 1934.

Watson G H *Colombia, Ecuador and Venezuela: an annotated guide to reference materials in the humanities and social sciences* Scarecrow, 1971, 279p.

Bibliografía ecuatoriana/Ecuadorian bibliography/Bibliographie de l'Equateur/Ecuadorianische Bibliographie Quito, Universidad Central del Ecuador, Biblioteca General 1975- . Six a year. Cumulations as:

Anuario bibliográfico ecuatoriano.

Casa de la Cultura *Catálogo general de publicaciones, 1944-65* 1965, 218p.

— *Catálogo* 1965- . Classified by subjects.

U of Texas Library. Latin American Collection *Recent Ecuadorian acquisitions* 1962 No 1, etc.

3c

Museo Historico, Quito.

AEB *Unidad Bibliotecaria*. 1973- .

3d

Instituto Nacional de Estadística *Ecuador en cifras*.

3e

Registro oficial Quito.

3f

Burbano Martinez H *La educación y el desarrollo economico y social del Ecuador* Casa de la Cultura, 1966, 191p.

El sistema de educación nacional del Ecuador (Paper presented at the meeting of experts on the national planning of library services, Quito, 1966) Unesco, 1966, 8p.

Moreira D *Cultural policy in Ecuador* Unesco, 1979, 94p.

Bravo J G 'Ecuador, libraries in' in *Encyclopedia* 7 (1972) 387-96. Includes the text of the following report on Ecuador:

Goicoechea C *Examen actual de los servicios de bibliotecas en el Ecuador* (Paper presented at the meeting of experts on the national planning of library services, Quito, 1966).

'Meeting of experts on the national planning of library services in Latin America, Quito 1966' *Unesco Bull Lib* 1966 20(6) 278-85. Special reference to Ecuadorian problems.

Mitchell E 'Ecuador: pilot project in the Andes' *Lib J* 1968 93(20) 4264-7.

Albertus U 'Role of libraries in the functional literacy programme: library services for new literates' *Unesco Bull Lib* 1970 24(4) 201-4.

Uzcategui E 'El problema de la alfabetización y la producción de libro' *Rev Ecuat Educ* 1969 21(60) 187-201.

PARAGUAY

1

Biblioteca, Museo y Archivo Nacionales, Asunción. 1869- .

Universidad Nacional de Asunción. Biblioteca.

Centro Cultural Paraguaya-Américano, Asunción. 1942- .

2b

Asociación de Bibliotecarios del Paraguay.

2c

Universidad Nacional de Asunción. Escuela de Bibliotecología. 1971-.

3a

Kolinski C J *Historical dictionary of Paraguay*Scarecrow, 1973. (Latin American Historical Dictionaries, 8).

3b

Bibliografía paraguaya Asuncion, 1959- . Occasional trade list.

Fernández-Caballero C F S comp *The Paraguayan bibliography: a retrospective and enumerative bibliography of printed works of Paraguayan authors* Washington, Paraguay Arandú Books, 1970, 143p.

— *Paraguái tai hũme, tove Paraguái arandu taisarambi ko yvy apére — The Paraguayan bibliography* Vol 2 U of Massachusetts, Library, 1975, 221p. (SALALM, Bibliographies, 2). Foreign works on Paraguay, 18th century to 1974.

Jones D L *Paraguay, a bibliography* Garland P, 1979, 499p.

U of Texas Library. Latin American Collection *Recent Paraguayan acquisitions* 1962/Febr 1967, No 1, etc.

3c

Universita Católica, Asunción *Estudios Paraguayos.*

Asociación de Bibliotecarios del Paraguay *Revista de Bibliotecología y Documentación Paraguaya.* 1972- . Irregular.

3d

Banco Central del Paraguay *Boletin estadístico mensual.*

3f

Heisecke G 'Aspectos estructurales de la educación en el Paraguay' *Aportes* 1969 12 85-110.

MacCarthy C *Developing libraries in Brazil; with a chapter on Paraguay* Scarecrow, 1975, 207p.

Paraguay: plan para el establicimiento de un centro nacional de documentación, agosto de 1974 Unesco, 1975, 44p. (3147/RMO.RD/DBA).

PERU

1

Biblioteca Nacional del Perú, Lima. 1821- . Burned down in 1943, reopened in 1947. Part of the National Institute of Culture, with the functions of a coordinating body. Bibliographical activities through its Oficina de Bibliografía Nacional y registro de Derechos de Autor (1944-).

'La destrucción de la Biblioteca Nacional' *Mercurio peruano* 1945 25(194) 198-207.

'Seis audaciones de la Biblioteca Nacional' *Bibliot Nacion Bol* 1946 3(9) 21-44.

Campbell M V 'The third National Library of Lima' *Libro* 1959 9(3) 194-200.

Valderrama L 'Cronología esquemática de la Biblioteca Nacional' *Fénix* 1971 (21) 5-16.

Universidad Nacional Mayor de San Marcos. Biblioteca Central.

Arbulu Vargas R 'La Biblioteca Nacional y la Universidad Peruana: algunos datos retrospectivos' *Apuntes* 1977 3(6) 83-7.

Universidad Nacional Mayor de San Marcos. Centro de Información Bibliográfica (CIB). 1969- . Part of the university's Dirección de Biblioteca y Publicaciones.

2a

Ministerio de Educación.

Ministerio de Cultura.

Cámera Peruana de Libro. Involved in organizing libraries for young people and prisoners; works with the Library Association.

Consejo Nacional de Bibliotecas (Pan-American Union).

2b

Asociación Peruana de Archiveros, Lima.

Asociación Peruana de Bibliotecarios, Lima. 1945- .

Asociación de Bibliotecas Agrícolas, Lima.

Agrupación de Bibliotecas para la Integración de la Información Socioeconomica (ABIISE), Lima. 1969- .

2c

National Institute of Culture. Escuela Nacional de Bibliotecarios. See also in the *Boletin de la Biblioteca Nacional.*

Ojedo O 'Escuela de Bibliotecarios. Cursillo de entronamiento para el personal en funcciones de la Biblioteca Popular de la Camera de Diputados' *Bol Bibliot Nacion* Sep 1946 7-14, 15-9.

3a

Guia de bibliotecas del sistema nacional de la universidad peruana CONUP, Dirección de Evaluación de Universidades, Oficina de Evaluación, 1975, 97p.

3b

Vargas Ugarte R *Manual de estudios peruanistas* 4th ed Gil, 1959. (With a chapter on libraries and collections).

Biblioteca Nacional. Oficina de Bibliografía *Anuario bibliográfico peruano* 1943- . Includes periodicals, official publications, theses, etc. and books published abroad on Peru.

Universidad Nacional Mayor de San Marcos, Biblioteca Central *Boletin bibliográfico*. 1923- . Has a section of abstracts of periodicals received in the library.

Biblioteca Nacional *Fénix*. Section 'Noticias bibliográficas'.

Benavides Balbin A 'Bibliografía de bibliografías y biblioteconomía 1936-1948' *Bol Bibliog* (U San Marcos) 1949 22(1/2) 3-28.

3c

Biblioteca Nacional *Boletin*. 1943- . Quarterly.

— *Fénix*. 1944- . Cumulative index in No 19 (1969).

— *Gaceta bibliotecaria del Perú*. 1963- . Quarterly; on public libraries.

Asociación Peruana de Bibliotecarios *Boletin*. 1956- .

Universidad Nacional de Trujillo . . . División de Bibliotecas *Libri-UNT*. 1973- . Quarterly. On libraries, documentation and related fields.

3d

Oficina Nacional de Estadísticas y Censos *Anuario estadístico del Perú*. 1919- .

— *Cuentas nacionales del Perú 1950-1978* The Oficina, 1979, 158p.

— *Ibid, 1970-1978: cuadros suplementarios* The Oficina, 1979, 283p.

ABIISE *Informe de la Comisión de normalización de estadísticas para bibliotecas especializadas* La Agrupación, 1975, 24p. Norms of statistics for special libraries.

3e

El Peruano.

Gaceta bibliotecaria del Perú. See 1964(8) for public library laws.

Chávez de Ontaneda E et al 'Legislación bibliotecaria' *Fénix* 1968 (18) 146-52.

Valderrama L *El deposito legal y su incidencia en el control bibliográfico* Bogotá, 1975. Mimeo.

3f

Werlich D P *Peru: a short history* Southern Illinois U P/Feffer 1978, 434p.

Valcárcel C D *Breve historia de la educación peruana* Editorial Educación, 1975.

National Institute of Culture *Cultural policy in Peru* Unesco, 1977, 70p.

Bonilla de Gaviria M C 'Peru, libraries in' in *Encyclopedia* 22 (1977) 86-118.

Olivera R I 'Mesas redondas bibliotecológicas (Nov 1967)' *Fénix* 1968 (18) 54-152. Whole issue on all aspects of librarianship.

Congreso Nacional de Bibliotecología y Información, Lima 1977. Papers not traced.

Cordova de Castillo N 'La biblioteca de Ocopa: su historia y organización' *Fénix* 1973 23 71-127. History of the oldest library in Latin America.

Pouncey L 'The library convent of Ocopa' *Lat Amer Res Rev* 1978 8(3) 147-54.

Brownridge H 'To Peru on exchange' *Assist Libn* 1977 (4) 58-61.

Ballón D M 'Public library development in Peru' *Unesco Bull Lib* 1959 13(8/9) 184-6, 208.

Summers B 'Una experiencia de biblioteca pública' *Gaceta Bibliot Perú* 1964 (7) 6-7.

Arbulu Vargas R 'El problema máximo de las bibliotecas minimas' *As Peru Bibliot Bol* 1964 (8) 35-8.

Ballón D M 'Actividades culturales de la biblioteca pública' *Gaceta Bibliot Perú* 1964 (6) 2, 7.

Checa de Silva C 'Servicio de extensión en Lima' *Fénix* 1966 (16) 5-40.

Ministerio de Educación. Oficina de Investigación y Desarrollo *Diagnóstico y programación de las bibliotecas escolares del Perú. Documento de trabajo* La Oficina, 1969, 65p, annexes.

Cueto Fernandini C and Cueto Fernandini L *Pongamos en marcha las bibliotecas* escolares Tipografia-Offset Sesator, 1969, 174p, bibl. Manual, with a description of school library development.

Olivera R I 'Bibliotecas al servicio de la communidad de negocios en el Perú' *Fénix* 1968 (18) 153-66.

URUGUAY

1

Biblioteca Nacional, Montevideo. 1793- . Legal deposit and bibliographical activities. Runs the:

- Instituto Nacional del Libro 1964- . Promotion of library services, and a:
- Centro de Documentación Científica, Técnica y Economica.

Biblioteca del Poder Legislativo, Montevideo. 1929- . Legal deposit and bibliographical activities.

Universidad de la República. Biblioteca.

Consejo Nacional de Educación Secundaria Básica y Superior. Biblioteca Central. 1833- .

2a

Ministerio de Educación y Cultura.

Instituto de Investigaciones Bibliotecológicas del Uruguay (IIBU).

2b

Asociación de Bibliotecarios del Uruguay (ABU), Montevideo. 1945- .

Agrupación Bibliotecológica del Uruguay (ABU), Montevideo. 1957- .

Asociación de Bibliotecólogos y Afines del Uruguay. 1978- .

2c

Ziegler de Cabrera N 'Evolución y estado actual de la enseñanza bibliotecológica en el Uruguay' *Bibliot Artigas-Washington Bol* 1969 2a epoca Vol 1.

See also under Argentina, 2c.

3a

Willis J L *Historical dictionary of Uruguay* Scarecrow, 1974. (Latin American Historical Dictionaries, 11). *Guia de bibliotecas de Montevideo* Universidad, 1948, 30p.

Musso L A *Archivos del Uruguay* Estado Mayor de Ejército. Departamento de Estudios Historicos, 1974, 49p. Directory of archives, with an appendix, a list of important libraries.

3b

Musso Ambrosi L A *Bibliografía de bibliografías uruguayas* Castro, 1964, 102p. In Dewey order.

Vener J S 'La bibliografía en el Uruguay' *Rev Inter-Amer Bibliog* 1954 4(1) 35-42.

Bibliografía y documentación en el Uruguay Bahia Blanca, U Nacional del Sur/Montevideo, 1972. (By L A Musso).

Vener J S 'Pedro Mascaro y la bibliografía uruguaya' *Rev Inter-Amer Bibliog* 1961 10 343-55.

Mascaro P comp *Anales de la bibliografía uruguaya* 1895. First attempt at producing a current national bibliography.

Biblioteca Nacional *Anuario bibliográfico uruguayo* 1946/49 (1/4) 1968- .
Biblioteca del Poder Legislativo *Bibliografía uruguaya* 1962- .
— Cumulation for *1962-68* published in 1971.
— Cumulation for *1969-72* published in 1977, 2 vols.
U of Texas Library. Latin American Collection *Recent uruguayan acquisitions* 1962/March 1967 (1)- .
Biblioteca Pedagogica Central *Bibliografía uruguaya sobre educación.*
Musso Ambrosi L A *Bibliografía bibliotecológica del Uruguay* Modellin, Escuela Interaméricana de Bibliotecológia, 1964, 199p.
— *Bibliografía bibliotecológica y bibliográfica del Uruguay, 1964-1969* Centro de Estudios del Pasado Uruguayo, 1970, 52p.

3c

Biblioteca Nacional *Revista.* 1966- .
Biblioteca Artigas-Washington *Boletin*, Montevideo. 1945-59 1-5 Primera epoca; 1969 1- Seconda epoca.
Centro de Documentación Científica, Técnica y Economica *Boletin informativo.*

3d

Dirección General de Estadística y Censos *Anuario estadístico.*
Blanco de Paolillo J *La estadística en las bibliotecas* Montevideo, 1977, 20p.

3e

Diario oficial.
Musso Ambrosi L A *Indice de la legislación bibliotecaria del Uruguay 1830-1969: principales leyes . . . con una bibliografía auxiliar* Montevideo, The Author, 1969, 24p. Mimeo.
— *Legislación uruguaya de archivistica* Estado Mayor del Ejército, 1970. (Offprint from *Boletin* (125) and (126)).
Massa H *Normas que regular el depósito legal de impresos* Bogotá, 1975.

3f

Alisky M *Uruguay: a contemporary survey* Praeger, 1969, 174p.
Musso Ambrosi L A 'Aportes para la historia de la bibliotecológía en el Uruguay' *Bibliot Artigas-Washington Bol* 1969 2a epoca 1 19-34.
Gropp A E 'A portrait of libraries in Uruguay' *Louisiana Lib Ass Bull* 1949 12(5) 153-9.
Musso Ambrosi L A *Mesa redonda sobre servicios bibliotecarios realizada en la Asociación de Bibliotecarios del Uruguay* Montevideo, The Author, 1968, 8p.
Espinosa Borges, I A *Problemas bibliotecarios del Uruguay; el libro en nuestra sociologia cultural* Fuentes de Informacion Uruguaya, 1968, 268p.
Helguera N and Rodriguez de Ferro M *Centralización de las bibliotecas de enseñanza secundaria básica y superior: una utopía o una realidad?* Montevideo, EUBCA, 1977.
Bachetta C *Cooperación y coordinación en las bibliotecas universitarias* EUBCA, 1969.

VENEZUELA

1

Biblioteca Nacional, Caracas. 1833- . Now part of the Instituto Autónomo Biblioteca Nacional y Servicios de Bibliotecas, following the NATIS system. Its services includes the Centro Bibliográfico Venezolano.

'Creación de la Biblioteca Nacional de Venezuela' *Arch Gen de la Nación Bol* 1965 55 295-9. Includes laws, statutes, etc.

'La Biblioteca Nacional depositaria de la cultura venezolana' *Rev Nacion Cultura* 1977 39(233) 266-76.

Muñoz E 'La nueva sede de la Biblioteca Nacional' *Rev SINASBI* 1978 (1) 57-60.

Universidad Central de Venezuela (UCV). Biblioteca Central, Caracas. 1850- .

Archivo General de la Nación. 1910- .

Biblioteca del Instituto Venezolano de Investigaciones Científicas (IVIC), Caracas. 1959- .

Centro Nacional de Información Científica y Técnica (CENICIT), Caracas.

2a

Consejo Nacional de la Cultura (CONAC). The National Library reports to this council.

Ministry for Intellectual Development.

Banco del Libro. 1960- . To establish networks of public libraries.

Consejo Nacional de Investigaciones Científicas y Técnicas (CONICIT), Caracas.

2b

Asociación Venezolana de Archiveros, Caracas.

Colegio de Bibliotecólogos y Archivólogos de Venezuela (COLBAV), Caracas. 1962- .

Asociación Interaméricana de Bibliotecarios y Documentalistas Agrícolas (AIBDA). Filial Venezuela. 1971- .

2c

Courses at UCV, Facultad de Humanidades y Educación. Escuela de Bibliotecononomía y Archivos.

Cortés A V *Venezuela: reorganización de la formación de archiveros y de las estructuras archivísticas, octubre-noviembre de 1974* Unesco, 1975, 19p. (3129/RMO.RD/DBA).

3a

Rudolph D K and Rudolph G A *Historical dictionary of Venezuela* Scarecrow, 1971, 142p. (Latin American Historical Dictionaries, 3).

Marin O comp *Directorio de bibliotecas venezolanas* UCV, 1973, 99p.

Directorio de recursos de información especializada en Venezuela CONICIT, 1976.

3b

Biblioteca Nacional. Centro Bibliográfico *Anuario bibliográfico venezolano* 1916-1954, 1975- . 1955-1974 being published.

— *Bibliografía venezolana* 1(1) 1970-74. Quarterly.

Villasana A R *Ensayo de un repertorio bibliográfico venezolano: años 1808-1950* Banco Central de Venezuela, 1969- .

Watson G H *Colombia, Ecuador and Venezuela: an annotated guide to reference materials in the humanities and social sciences* Scarecrow, 1971, 279p.

3c

Biblioteca Nacional *Boletin*. 1959- .

— *Informe annual*. Review of aims and achievements.

Colegio de Bibliotecólogos . . . *COLBAV*. 1964- .

Codex: boletin de la Escuela de Biblioteconomía. 1966- .

Escuela de Biblioteconomía *Temas biblioteconómicos* 1956- .

Universidad del Zulia *Boletin de la Biblioteca Central*, Maracaibo. 1960/61- . Section on bibliography and library science.

Revista del SINASBI 1978- . Two a year. Sistema Nacional de Servicios de Bibliotecas e Información Humanística (with Información Científica y Tecnológica, de Archivos y de Estadísticas e Informática). The review published by the Comisión Coordinadora SINASBI.

Banco del Libro *Ekare:boletin informativo*. 1976-.

3d

Oficina Central de Estadística e Informática (Previously: Dirección General de Estadística y Censos) *Catálogo de series estadísticas* 1965, 492p.

— *Anuario estadístico de Venezuela.*

— *Boletin trimestrial de estadística*. Includes statistics of libraries in the section: [Statísticas] 'Culturales y Sociales'.

Venezuela up to date, Washington. 1949- .

3e

Gaceta oficial.

Duran A *El deposito legal en Venezuela. Informe* Bogota, 1975.

3f

Perez Villa M Bibliotecas coloniales de Venezuela U de Zulia, 1962, 14p. Also published in *Revista Bolivar* (Bogota) 1957/58 11 (49) 77-86.

Ospina C 'Libraries in Venezuela' *Louisiana Lib Ass Bull* 1949 12(5) 159-63.

Moncada Moreno J 'El problema bibliotecológico en Venezuela' *Temas Bibliot* 1957 2(3) 8-11.

Diaz L E and Padrón L E 'Developing a public library system for the metropolitan area of Caracas: outline of a plan' *Unesco Bull Lib* 1976 30(4) 191-8, refs.

'Red experimental de bibliotecas públicas del Banco del Libro' *Ekare* 1977 2(7) 3-8.

'El Banco del Libro comparte su esperiencia' *Ekare* 1977 2(8) 12-4.

Piñiero M A 'Bibliotecas de la escuela de enseñanza secundaria' *Educacion* (Caracas) 1962 29(96/97) 41-54.

Horowitz R G de 'School library services of the Banco del Libro: a taxonomy' *Illinois Lib* 1972 54 512-22.

Betancourt de Perez V 'Modernizing education in Latin America through school libraries' *School Lib* 1971 20(2) 36-40. Guyana Plan.

Beroin L J 'Guyana plan for school libraries in Venezuela' *Unesco Bull Lib* 1971 25(4) 205-11.

Alvarez G M 'La biblioteca de la Universidad del Zulia' *U del Zulia, Bibliot Central Bol* 1973/74 14/15 (23/24) 113-25.

Diakonova O [Report of the National Commission set up for the establishment of a national information system (based on infrastructure of documentation, libraries and archives)] Unesco, 1974?.

Tell B V *Venezuela: a national scientific and technological information system* Unesco, 1974, 28p (3058/RMO.RD/DBA).

SECTION 4

AFRICA SOUTH OF THE SAHARA

AFRICA SOUTH OF THE SAHARA

1

Panovsky H 'National libraries and bibliographies in Africa' in Jackson M M ed *Comparative and international librarianship* Bingley/Greenwood, 1970, 225-55.

Aje S B *The role of the national libraries in national and international information systems — the African region;* supplement to the working paper for the meeting of Directors of National Libraries, Oslo 1975 [See main documents of the conference in General, 1] National Library of Nigeria, 20p.

For information on collections of Africana see:

'Collections of Africana' *Unesco Bull Lib* 1961 15(5) 277-87. Europe and USA.

Scolma directory of libraries and special collections on Africa 3rd ed (J Roe comp) Crosby Lockwood, 1973, 118p. In Great Britain.

Benewick A J *Asian and African collections in British libraries — problems and prospects* Peregrinus, 1974, 139p.

Witherell J W 'Africana in the Library of Congress: the role of the African section' *Lib Congress QJ* 1970 27(3) 184-96.

Duignan P *Handbook of American resources for African studies* Stanford, 1967, 218p.

2a

Rupp B 'Inventaire des principaux répertoires d'institutions de sciences sociales et humaines en Afrique au Sud du Sahara' *Social Sciences information* 1966 5(2), 16p.

'Directory of research organisations and institutes devoted to Africa' in *Africa* 1968- . African P Associates (Paris)/Africana Pub Co (New York).

'Research institutes, associations and institutions studying Africa' in *Africa South of the Sahara* Europa Pub, 1971- . By countries with their main publications. See also 'Regional organizations' section II of the yearbook.

International guide to African studies research/Etudes africaines, guide international de recherches Enlarged rev ed of *International register of organisations undertaking africanist research in social sciences and humanities* London, IAI, 1975.

Only a few of the organizations concerned with Africa are listed below as possible sources of information.

- Organisation of African Unity (OAU), Addis Ababa. 1963- .
- UN Economic Commission for Africa, Addis Ababa. 1958- .
- Centre Africain de Formation et de Recherche Administratives pour le Développement (CAFRAD)/ African Training and Research Centre in Administration for Development.
- Unesco Regional Office for Science and Technology for Africa, Nairobi. 1965- .
- Unesco Bureau Régional pour l'Education en Afrique, Dakar. 1970- . (BREDA).

Bibliographical and cultural centres:

- Africa Bibliographic Centre (ABC), Dar es Salaam.

Jordan R T and Wadood T A *Africa Bibliographic Center (ABC) — a proposal to the OAU* Addis Ababa, 1974. Mimeo.

Darch C 'The Africa Bibliographic Centre (ABC) in Dar es Salaam: its origins and immediate future' *Afr Res Doc* 1977 (14) 11-4.

Mascarenhas O C *Africa Bibliographic Centre (ABC): an experiment in African documentation and library resource sharing* ERIC, 1977, 12p (ERIC Report ED-176 753).

- University of Ibadan. Institute of African Studies 1962- .
- Université de Dakar. Institut Fondamental d'Afrique Noire (IFAN). 1936- . (See under Senegal).
- Africa Institute of South Africa, Pretoria. 1960- .
- Centre d'Etudes et de Documentation Africaines (CEDAF), Brussels 1970- .
- Centre d'Analyse et de Recherche Documentaire sur l'Afrique Noire (CARDAN), Paris. 1965- . See:

Lib Mater Afr 1967 5(1) 14-31, 37-8.

African Studies Bulletin (Boston) 1967 10(3) 66-87.

- Institut fur Afrika-Kunde, Hamburg. 1963- .
- International African Institute (IAI), London. 1926- .
- Istituto Italiano per l'Africa, Rome.

Bossi G R 'La biblioteca dell 'istituto Italiano per l'Africa' *Ass Afr Ital Boll* 1970 3(1/2) 8-18.

- Afrika Instituut, The Hague. 1946- .
- Instituto de Estudios Africanos, Madrid. 1945- .
- Nordiska Afrika Institutet, Uppsala.
- USSR Academy of Sciences. Africa Institute.

The Africa Institute, USSR Academy of Sciences: a decade of activities, 1959-1969 Moscow, Social Sciences Today Editorial Office, 1970, 48p.

- Boston University. African Studies Center. 1953- .
- African Bibliographic Center, Washington. 1963- .
- Committee on African Studies in Canada, Montreal.

For other centres in North America, see Duignan P above: Africa, 1.

2b

Associations for cultural research.

- Société des Africanistes, Paris.
- Deutsche Afrika Gesellschaft, Bonn. 1960- .
- African Studies Association of the United Kingdom, Birmingham University. 1963- .
- Standing Conference on Library Material on Africa (SCOLMA). 1962- . See:

Afrika-Spektrum (Hamburg) 1970 2 163-9.

Ass Afr Ital Bol 1970 3(3/4) 28-36.

Lib Mater Afr 1971 8(3) 196-206.

Simpson D H 'Fifteen years of SCOLMA' *Afr Res Doc* 1977 (13) 1-6.

- African Studies Association — Archives-Libraries Committee of USA. 1958- .

Organizations concerned with librarianship and related problems.

- Unesco. See its annual programme in *Unesco Bulletin for Libraries* and (1979-) *Unesco Journal of Information Science, Librarianship and Archives Administration*. See in particular:

Gardner F M 'Unesco and library and related services in Africa' *Unesco Bull Lib* 1966 20(5) 212-8.

- IFLA. See:

'Cooperation IFLA/ICAE in Africa' *IFLA J* 1979 5(1) 50-1. Cooperation for literacy with the International Council for Adult Education.

- African Adult Education Association (AAEA), Nairobi. 1968- .
- Association of African Universities (AAU), Accra. Documentation Centre, 1972- .
- Standing Conference of African University Libraries (SCAUL). Lagos. 1964- . Has regional divisions:
- SCAUL Eastern Area (SCAULEA), Nairobi. 1971- .
- SCAUL Western Area (SCAULWA), Nsukka- . 1972- .
- SCAUL Central Area.
- SCAUL Northern Area. These last two not active.

Anafulu J C 'The Standing Conference of African University Libraries, 1964-1974' *Int Lib Rev* 1976 8 397-415, refs.

- Standing Conference of African Library Schools (SCALS), Dakar. 1973- . Created after the Dakar Seminar, part of the conference on 'Harmonization of librarianship Training Programmes in Africa', February 1974.
- International Association for the Development of Documentation, Libraries and Archives in Africa (IADLA)/Association Internationale pour le Développement de la Documentation, des Bibliothèques et des Archives en Afrique (AIDBA), St Louis then Dakar. 1957- as Association pour le Développement des Bibliothèques en Afrique. 1960-Association Internationale pour le Développement des Bibliothèques en Afrique. Present name 1968- .

Dadzie E K W 'The International Association for the Development of Documentation, Libraries and Archives in Africa (AIDBA)' *ECARBICA J* 1973 (Sep).

2c

Willemin S 'The training of librarians in Africa' *Unesco Bull Lib* 1967 21(6) 291-300.

Ogunsheye F A 'The future of library education in Africa' *Libri* 1976 26(4) 268-80.

'The Dakar Seminar and its recommendations (1974)' *SCALS Newsletter* 1975 1(1) 1-5.

'Standing Conference of African Library, Archives and Information Studies Schools Second meeting, Ibadan, 1978' *Doc Term Bibliog* 1978 (6) 289. Subsequent conference in Ghana, 1980.

Dale D C 'Library schools in Africa: a preliminary survey' *Illinois Lib* 1972 54 481-6.

Oby D S *The curriculum needs of the Sub-Saharan African Library school: a study in comparative education for librarianship* U of Pittsburg, 1974. PhD thesis in library science.

Johnson A F 'African studies in comparative librarianship' *Afr Res Doc* 1975 (8/9) 15-21.

Evans D W 'African studies and British library schools' *Afr Res Doc* 1978 (16/17) 12-7.

Nzotta B C 'Education for library management in African schools' *J Libp* 1977 9(2) 130-43.

Dean J 'The training of African documentalists for the social sciences' *Nig Lib* 1967 3 101-9.

'Inter-university Council for Higher Education Overseas, Manpower and Training Committee: Report of the working party on the training of library staff of overseas universities' *SCAUL Newsletter* 1971 (6) 52-61. Mainly on African librarians.

[Training and status of African librarians, archivists and documentalists] Conference, Dakar, 1977. *Papers and documents* from the Director of the School of

Librarianship, University of Dakar. (EBAD, 1977, 18p).

Darch C 'The status of professional librarians in African universities' *Int Lib Rev* 1975 7(4) 497-502. A survey.

Sène H 'Les statuts du personnel des bibliothèques, dépôts d'archives et centres de documentation en Afrique Noire et au Maghreb: étude comparative' *BLIBLAD* 1977 (3) 9-19.

3a

Africa South of the Sahara Europa Pub, 1971- . Annual. History, economic and social conditions, government, resources etc.

Africa contemporary record. Annual survey of documents 1970/71- . London, Rex Collins, 1971- . Political, social, economic, military.

Africa guide 1980 Saffron Walden, World of Information, 1979, 430p. Annual.

Africa 1968- . Paris, African P Associates; New York, Africana Pub Co.

Fordham P *The geography of African affairs* Penguin (3rd ed, 1972).

Hornburger J M and Whithey A *African countries and cultures: a concise illustrated dictionary* McKay, 1980.

Taubert S ed *African book trade directory 1971* Verlag Dokumentation/Bowker, 1971, 319p.

Zell H M ed *The African book world and press: a directory/Répertoire du livre et de la presse en Afrique* 2nd rev ed Oxford, H Zell (USA and Canada: Gale Research), 1980, 372p. Compiled by African Book Publishing Record. Previous ed: 1977.

Unesco Field Science Office for Africa (Nairobi) *Survey of the scientific and technical potential of the countries of Africa/Enquête sur le potentiel scientifique et technique des pays d'Afrique* (1969/70).

Unesco Regional Office for Education (Dakar) *Repertory of documentation and education research centres in Africa* The Office, 1976, 86p.

Zidouemba D *Directory of documentation, libraries and archives services in Africa/Répertoire des services de documentation, de bibliothèque et d'archives en Afrique* 2nd ed (Rev and enlarged by E de Grolier) Unesco, 1977, 311p. Supersedes:

Dadzie E W and Strickland J T *Directory of archives, libraries and schools of librarianship in Africa* Unesco, 1965. Includes North Africa.

Association of College and Research Libraries (USA) Asian and African Section *Directory of Asian and African librarians in North America* The Section, 1978, 33p.

3b Bibliographic services — Developments, problems.

Book development in Africa: problems and perspectives Unesco, 1969, 37p. Also in French: *La promotion du livre en Afrique: problèmes et perspectives*, 41p.

Darch C 'Bibliographic control in a multi-lingual situation: Africa, The Soviet Union and India' *Ethiopian Lib Ass Bull* 1975 3(2) 10-3.

Aje S B 'ISBD application to African national bibliographies' *Unesco Bull Lib* 1977 31(4) 216-22. Survey of African national bibliographies and prospects of introducing the International Standard Bibliographical Description.

Conferences:

Pearson J D and Jones R *The bibliography of Africa. Proceedings and papers of the International Conference on African bibliography, Nairobi, 4-8 December 1967* Frank Cass, 1970, 362p. Papers on general issues and on individual countries. Lists bibliographical services on Africa and Africana periodicals.

See also:

Pearson J D and Jones R *African bibliography* OUP, 1968, 38p. Summary of the proceedings. And in:

Africa 1968 38(3) 293-331.

Molnos A 'Whither African bibliographies? an observer's afterthoughts to a recent conference' *East Afr J* 1968 5(2) 17-9, 22-5.

Bloomfield V *Conference on the acquisition of material from Africa, Birmingham University, 25 April 1969. Report and Papers* Zug, Inter-Documentation, 1970, 154p.

SCOLMA 'Conference on developments in African bibliography since the Nairobi conference, Rhodes House, Oxford, April 1970. Papers and proceedings' *Lib Mater Afr* 1970 8(1) 9-71.

Voss H 'Colloquium on Africa documentation, Hamburg, July 1970' *Afrika-Spektrum* 1970 2 159-62.

SCOLMA *Progress in African bibliography: SCOLMA conference, Commonwealth Institute, 17-18 March 1977. Proceedings* SCOLMA, 1977, 318p.

Evans D W 'The SCOLMA conference: Progress in African bibliography' *Afr Res Doc* 1977 (13) 7-21. Three papers.

'Developments in the bibliographic control of African materials: report on the SCOLMA conference, March 1977' *Int Cataloguing* 1977 6 19-21.

Bourna R 'The Unesco Regional Seminar on Bibliographical Control in Africa, Lagos, 1978' *Int Cataloguing* 1978 7(2) 17-9. Eleven countries represented from all parts of Africa.

'Second Unesco Seminar on Bibliographic Control in African countries, Dakar 1979' *Int Cataloguing* 1979 8(2) 15-6.

Anderson D P 'Second Unesco Seminar on Bibliographic Control in African countries' *IFLA J* 1979 5 255-6.

3b Bibliographies of bibliographies and reference sources.

South African Library *A bibliography of African bibliographies covering territories South of the Sahara* 5th ed The Library, 1971.

Garling A *Bibliography of African bibliographies* Cambridge, African Studies Centre, 1968, 138p. Mimeo.

Besterman T *A world bibliography of African bibliographies* Rev and updated by J D Pearson Blackwell, 1975.

Davis L G *An introductory bibliography of bibliographies on Africa* Council of Planning Librarians (USA), 1977.

Duignan P ed (Conover H F and Duignan P comps) *Guide to research and reference works on Sub-Saharan Africa* Standford, Hoover Institution P, 1971, 1102p. Retrospective and current bibliographies, reference periodicals, official publications, theses. General, regions, subject indexes. (Hoover Instn Bibliog Series, 46).

Conover H F *Research and information on Africa: continuing sources*. Library of Congress, 1954, 70p. Enlarged and updated in two volumes: *Africa South of the Sahara*, 1957; *North and North East Africa* 1957.

Skurnik W A E ed *Sub-Saharan Africa: a guide to information sources* Gale Research, 1977, 140p.

Panofsky H E *A bibliography of Africana* Greenwood, 1975, 350p. (Contributions to Librarianship and information Science, 11)

Kohl E 'Laufende afrikanische Nationalbibliographien' *Z Biblioth Bibliog* 1970 17(6) 355-67.

Liniger-Goumaz M *Bibliographies africaines: Energie-Politique-Population-Transports* Genève, Editions du Temps, 1971, 144p.

Nsubuga N 'African scientific papers: a bibliometric examination' *Ugandan Lib* 1980 3(1) 15-21.

3b Acquisition: methods, catalogues, trade lists.

Knoke S 'Report on a library acquisition trip to Africa, December 1969-March 1970' *Africana Lib J* 1970 1(4) 14-23.

James J R 'The establishment of an overseas acquisition center: a personal reminiscence' *Lib Congr Q J* 1970 27(3) 206-12.

African Books in Print: an index by author, title and subject U of Ife P/R Abel, Vol 1, 1973: English and vernacular; Vol 2: French, Portuguese, Spanish. Includes a directory of publishers.

African Book Publishing Record 1975- . Oxford, Hans Zell. Quarterly updating service to *African Books in Print.*

Africana Catalogue International U Booksellers, Africana Center, 1967-69. Superseded by *Africana Journal: a bibliographical review quarterly* 1970- . Africana Pub Co (New York).

African Books Newsletter, 1965-71. Superseded by *Bibliographia Africana*. Calcutta, K K Ray Ltd. Monthly.

3b Published library catalogues and lists.

(Sample listing. See also 'Collections' in section 1, and general sources).

Catalogue of Africana in Ibadan University Library [1948-72] G K Hall, 1973, 2 vols.

Paris. Musée de l'Homme *Catalogue systématique de la section Afrique* 2 vols.

London University. SOAS *Catalogue* G K Hall, 28 vols.

Africana in the library of the Scandinavian Institute of African Studies Uppsala, The Institute, 1963- . Two a year.

Widener Library Shelflist, 2: *Africa* Harvard U P, 1965, 2 vols.

Duignan P et al *African and Middle East collections: a survey of holdings at the Hoover Institution* Stanford U P, 1971, 37p.

3b Bibliographies, abstracts, indexes.

Afribiblios Lagos, Nigeria National Library, 1978- . Two a year.

Africa Bibliographic Centre *Africa index to continental periodical literature* Oxford, Hans Zell Pub, 1977 (for 1976)- . Annual.

Comité Interbibliothèques de Documentation Africaine 'Bibliographie française sur l'Afrique au Sud du Sahara, 1968 publications' [and subsequent years] in CARDAN *Recherche et Enseignement* 1970- .

Afrika-Schriftum: Bibliographie deutschesprachiger . . . Steiner, 1966-71, 2 vols. Continued in:

Deutsche Afrika Gesellschaft *Afrika Bibliographie* 1960/61- .

International African Institute *African abstracts* 1950- . French edition: *Analyses africanistes* 1967- .

— *International African bibliography* (Formerly published in *Africa*) 1971/72, 1/2, 1973 vol 3 etc. Prepared by SOAS, published by Mansell.

Wallenius A-B *Africana Scandinavica, 1960-1968* Scandinavian Institute of African Studies, 1971, 104p.

Glazier K M *Africa South of the Sahara: select and annotated bibliography, 1958-63* Hoover Institution, 1964.

— *1964-68* The Institution, 1969, 139p.

Miller E W *Tropical Eastern and Southern Africa: a bibliography on the Third World* Vance Bibliographies, 1981, 82p.

Library of Congress. African Section *Africa South of the Sahara: index to periodical literature, 1900-1970* G K Hall, 1971, 4 vols.
Asamani J O comp *Index Africanus* Hoover Institution P, 1975, 659p. (Hoover Institution Bibliographical Series, 53). Covers 1885-1965, periodicals, Feschriften, proceedings etc.

3b African research and studies. General.

Walreaert M *Les études africaines dans le monde* CEDESA, 1971, 104p.
CARDAN issues series in its Bulletin d'information et de liaison:
- *Etudes africaines* 1971-72, 274p.
- *Registre des recherches africanistes de langue française en cours* 1970- .
- *Inventaire des thèses et mémoires africanistes de langue française soutenus* 1969- .
- *Inventaire des thèses africanistes de langue française en cours* 1969- .

African Studies Association of the United Kingdom *Bulletin*. In 1973 this and SCOLMA *Library materials on Africa* were amalgamated under the title: *African Research and Documentation* 1973 (1)-.
IAI *Current Africanist Research* Nov 1971 (1)-.
- *Publications and theses on Africa* Frank Cass, 1963- .

Markov W *Afrika-Studien* Karl Marx U, 1967, 237p.
Pasqualini G A 'Studi africanisti en Spagna nell'ultimo decennio (1959-69)' *Ass Afr Ital Boll* 1970 3(1/2) 19-29.
Abramov V 'The current state of African studies in the Soviet Union' *Res Rev Inst Afr Studies* (Legon) 1970 6(2) 15-26.
African Studies Association (USA) *Directory of African studies in the USA* 1971- .
- *Research in progress . . .: selected listing of current research on Africa* 1970/71- .
- *African Studies Bulletin.*

Hofman L *US and Canadian publications and theses on Africa in . . .* 1969- . Hoover Institution P.
Canadian Association of African Studies *Resources for African studies in Canada.*

3b African studies. Sources on special subjects (Including libraries).

Washington, African Bibliographic Center *Special bibliographic series* Negro U P, 1968- . Volumes on regions, countries or topics.
- *Current bibliography on African affairs* 1962- .

Boston University. African Studies Center *Publications of the Development Program* series under the title: *Study guide for . . .* On countries or topics.
Library of Congress *Maktaba Afrikana*. Bibliographical series 1976?- . On topics, mainly political organization and international relations.
Sohn L B *Basic documents of African regional organizations* Vol 1- . Oceana Pub, 1971- .
Martello W E and Butler J E *The history of Sub-Saharan Africa: a select bibliography of books and reviews, 1945-1975* G K Hall, 1978, 158p. (Bibliographies and Guides in African Studies).
Hanson J W and Gibson G W *African education and development since 1960: a select and annotated bibliography* Michigan State U, 1966, 327p.
Conover H F *African libraries, book production and archives: a list of references* Library of Congress, 1962, 64p.
Murtagh D D *Education for librarianship in Africa: a bibliography* U of Witwatersrand, 1968, 32p.

3c

Library of Congress *Sub-Saharan Africa: a guide to serials* US-GPO, 1970, 409p. 4670 entries in Western and African transliterated languages. Monograph

series, yearbooks, directories, annual reports are included.

Paris. Maison des Sciences de l'Homme *World list of African periodicals.*

Africa South of the Sahara Europa Pub. Contains a list 'Select bibliography (Periodicals)' at the end of every edition. Research periodicals from countries in Africa and outside Africa, dealing with Africa or part of Africa.

Feuereisen F and Schmacke E *Africa: a guide to newspapers and magazines* Africana Pub Co, 1969, 251p.

Deutsches Institut für Afrika-Forschung *Periodika-Verzeichnis, Stand 1 mai 1970* The Institute, 1970, 57p.

Alman M *Periodicals published in Africa: a list and a union list* SCOLMA, 1972.

Travis C *Periodicals from Africa: a bibliography and union list of periodicals published in Africa* G K Hall, 1977.

Unesco *List of scientific and technical periodicals published in 32 countries of Africa from 1950 to 1970* Unesco, 1972, 69p.

Unesco. Bureau Régional pour l'Education en Afrique (BREDA) *Educafrica.* Two a year.

African Adult Education Association *Newsletter.*

— *Journal.*

SCOLMA *Library materials on Africa* 1962-72. Superseded by:

SCOLMA and African Studies Association *African research and documentation* 1973- . Contains papers on bibliography, collections, lists of periodicals, etc.

SCAUL *Newsletter* Dar es Salaam 1965- . Publication resumed 1977 at Lagos University.

SCALS *Newsletter* Dakar 1973- .

3d

ECA *Bibliography of African statistical publications, 1950-1965* Addis Ababa, UN-ECA, 1966.

Kpedekpo G M K *Social and economic statistics for Africa* Allen & Unwin, 1981, 224p.

3e

IFLA *Catalogue of African official publications available in European libraries as of 1 May 1971* Berlin, Staatbibliothek, 1971, 251p.

Evans E J A 'Library legislation in developing countries of Africa' *Libri* 1968 18(1) 51-68. French-speaking Africa, Gambia, Ghana, Nigeria, Zambia.

3f

Wiley M and Wiley D *Africa* West Haven, Pendulum P, 1973, 191p, bibl.

Fage J D *A history of Africa* Hutchinson, 1978.

Oliver R and Fage J D *A short history of Africa* Penguin (5th ed, 1975).

Unesco *General history of Africa* 1980- . 8 vols.

Oliver R and Atmore A *The African Middle-Ages, 1400-1800* CUP, 1981, 216p. By regions, comparative study.

— *Africa since 1800* 3rd ed CUP, 1981, 372p.

Gailey H *A History of Africa from 1800 to present* Holt, R & W, 1972.

Gann L H and Duignan P *Colonialism in Africa, 1870-1960* CUP, 5 vols. Vol 5 (1973): *Bibliography.*

Metrowich F R *Africa in the sixties* Africa Institute of South Africa, 1970, 329p.

Van Chi-Bonnardel R *The atlas of Africa* Free Press, 1973.

Robson P and Lury D A eds *The economics of Africa* Allen & Unwin, 1969.

Stamp L Dudley *Africa: a study in tropical development* 3rd rev ed (by W T W Morgan) Wiley, 1972, 520p.

Daley D *Language map of Africa and the adjacent islands* London, International African Institute, 1977.

Sow A I et al *Introduction to African culture: general aspects* Unesco, 1979, 184p. (Introduction to African Culture, 1).

Miller J C ed *The African past speaks: essays on oral tradition and history* Archon, 1980.

Conferences on education sponsored by Unesco:

Addis Ababa 1961. *Final report* 1961.

Tananarive 1963. On higher education *Report* 1963, 339p.

Abidjan 1964. On literacy programmes.

Court D and Ghai D *Education, society and development* Nairobi, OUP, 1974.

Blakemore K and Cooksey B *A sociology of education for Africa* Allen & Unwin, 1981, 274p.

Université et politique scientifique en Afrique Montreal, AUPELF, 1975.

Unesco *National science policies in Africa* Unesco, 1974. (Science Policy Studies and Documents, 31).

Bousso A A 'Programme pour l'Afrique: état présent et perspectives d'avenir' *IFLA J* 1977 3(3) 270-1.

Unesco *Books for the developing countries — Asia, Africa* Unesco, 1962, 31p.

Ayandele E A 'The textbook problem in African history for the secondary grammar school' *West Afr J Educ* 1967 11(3) 143-8.

Wegman E 'La promotion du livre en Afrique' *Unesco Chronicle* 1969 14(4) 153-7.

'Unesco meeting on book development in Africa, Accra, February 1968' *Unesco Bull Lib* 1968 22(4) 206-7.

Book development in Africa — problems and perspectives Unesco, 1969.

Zoue E E *Le rôle de la mission dans la pénétration du livre en Afrique* ENSB, Thesis, 1975, 37p.

Chantal J de 'Bibliothèques et archives du Tiers-Monde, problèmes et perspectives' *Doc Biblioth* 1975 21(2) 85-95.

Vanwijngaerden F 'Improving exchanges of publications with developing contries in Africa: a few suggestions' *Unesco Bull Lib* 1976 30(2) 90-2.

Fontaines R 'Le problème du livre face au lecteur en Afrique: quelques lignes d'action proposées' *Bull Biblioth Fr* 1976 21(1) 11-18.

Uya O E 'African cultural revival studies: implications for library development programmes' *Nigerbiblios* 1976 1(3) 18-9, 21.

Plumbe W J 'Africa, libraries in' *Encyclopedia* 1 (1968) 119-25.

Sitzman G L 'African librarianship, an overview' *Africa Report* Sep/Oct 1975.

Ojoade J O 'Private and public libraries in Roman Africa' *Niger Lib* 1975 11(1/2) 111-22.

Martin W 'African libraries: an indigenous concept' *Focus Int Comp Libp* 1972 3(3) 55-60.

Kwakwa M A 'African libraries in search of an image' *Lib Ass Rec* 1972 74(4) 72-3. Reprinted in Foskett D J ed *Reader in comparative librarianship* 1976 159-62.

IFIDON S E 'Special problems facing African librarians: the West African experience' *Libri* 1974 24(4) 310-8.

John M 'Libraries in oral-traditional societies' *Int Lib Rev* 1979 11 321-39. Based on African societies.

Amadi A O *African libraries: Western tradition and colonial brainwashing* Scarecrow, 1981, 265p.

'Library development in Africa' *Unesco Bull Lib* 1961 15(5). Whole issue.

Bell S *Comparative study of African library development* London U College,

Diploma in Library Science, 1967.
'Unesco sponsored meeting of African libraries and documentation centres, Nairobi, 1966' Documents?
Meeting of experts on the national planning of documentation and library services in Africa, Kampala December 1970 *Final report* Unesco, 1971, 28p. (COM/MD/18).
— *Main working document* Unesco, 1970, 81p. (COM/CONF 9/3).
Broome M 'The organisation and planning of library development in Africa: an account of a meeting of experts . . .' *Unesco Bull Lib* 1971 25(5) 246-50.
'Afro-Scandinavian library conferences' in *Encyclopedia* 1 (1968) 125-6.
Kajberg L 'Den 3 afro-nordiske bibliotekskonference i Helsingfors Sep 1979' *Bogens Verden* 1979 61(8) 398-402.
Jorstad A L 'Nordisk støtte til bibliotekutbygging i Afrika' [Report of 3rd Afro-Scandinavian Library Conference, Helsinki, 1979] *Bog og Bibliot* 1979 46(7) 388-9.
Uba D E 'The third Afro-Nordic Library Conference, 1979' *Bogens Verden* 1979 61(10). In English.
Gardner F M 'Unesco and library and related services in Africa' *Unesco Bull Lib* 1966 20(5) 212-8.
USIA operations in Africa . . . *Report* US-GPO, 1962, 22p.
Milburn S 'Achievement of Literature Bureaus in African territories' *Wilson Lib Bull* 1956 30(5) 698, 706.
Development of public libraries in Africa Unesco, 1954, 155p. (Unesco Public Library Manual, 6). Ibadan Seminar 1953. See also in *Lib Ass Rec* 1954 56(3) 80-4.
'Regional seminar on the development of public libraries in Africa' *Unesco Bull Lib* 1963 17(2), Suppl 106-22. Enugu Seminar, 1962. See also in *East Afr Lib Ass Bull* 1963 (3) 3-8.
Lalande-Isnard F 'The development of libraries in Africa: six years after the Enugu Seminar' *Unesco Bull Lib* 1968 22(5) 241-6.
Brothers S C '[Public libraries]: contemporary libraries in Africa' in *Encyclopedia* 24 (1978) 457-62.
Nyarko K 'Educationists and library awareness in Africa' *Lib Ass Rec* 1973 75(6) 107-9.
Beverley P R 'School libraries in the Division of African Education' *Rhod Libn* 1976 8(4) 64, 66, 68, 70.
Ogunsheye F A 'Abadina Media Resources Centre (AMRC): a case study in library service to primary schools (Papers at the International Association of School Librarianship meeting, Ibadan, 1977)' *Unesco J* 197? 1(1) 29-36.
Holdsworth H 'University and special libraries, and higher education in Africa' *Unesco Bull Lib* 1961 15(5) 254-8.
Ifidon S E 'The objectives of African university libraries: the Nigerian experience' *Int Lib Rev* 1978 10(1) 43-50. Need for an indigenous concept.
Williams G J 'African university libraries: a consumer viewpoint' *Lib Rev* 1979 28 239-46.
Mamoun Izz Eldin 'Agricultural libraries and documentation centres in Africa with particular reference to the D R of the Sudan' in *Proceedings of the 4th World Congress, Institut National de Recherche Agronomique, Paris 1971,* 299-303.
Phillips S 'Law libraries: a community service for modern Africa' *Int J Law Libr* 1976 4(2) 109-14.
Official reports of the African seminar for librarians and documentalists of administrative information services, 31st March-7th April 1975 Achimota,

Ghana Institute of Management and Public Administration, 1975, 243p, refs.

'First African Conference on Informatics in Administration, Algiers, 6-9 December 1976' *Unesco Bull Lib* 1977 31 253. Organized by CAFRAD.

El Hadi M M 'The African Integrated Network of Administrative Information (AINAI): a conceptual project proposal' *Afr Res Doc* 1976 (11) 13-20.

Hounsell J W *A plan for a system to provide developmental information in Africa* National Technical Information Service, Office of International Affairs, 1980, 44p. (NTIS Report PB80 — 189806).

Survey of the scientific and technical potential of the countries of Africa Unesco, 1970, 296p.

Unesco/UNISIST 'Assistance to countries of the African continent in the development of scientific and technical information infrastructures' *UNISIST Newsletter* 1974 2(4) 2-3.

Polinière J P *Situation and needs of national information systems in science and technology* Unesco, 1975. (Technical Report RP/1973-74/2.13.6, Serial No FMR/SC/STI/75/13 2(E)). East Africa, Burundi, Rwanda, Kenya, Tanzania, Uganda, Zambia.

Adimorah E N O 'Scientific information transfer and national development in Africa' *Unesco Bull Lib* 1978 32(5) 333-7.

Unesco Réunion d'experts sur la plannification des réseaux de services de documentation et des bibliothèques (NATIS), Brazzaville 5-10 juillet 1976 Unesco (CC.76/610/3). *Final report*; also published in English.

3b

International African Institute *Selected annotated bibliography of Tropical Africa* New York, Twentieth Century Fund Survey of Tropical Africa, 1956, 481p.

O'Connor A M *Urbanization in tropical Africa, 1960-1979, an annotated bibliography* G K Hall, 1981.

3f

Brass W et al *The demography of tropical Africa* Princeton U P, 1968, 539p.

Uchendu V C *Education and politics in tropical Africa* Oweri/New York, Conch Magazine, 1979, 301p.

Accra Meeting on Book Development in tropical Africa. Conclusions and suggestions Unesco, 1968.

'Unesco meeting on book development in Africa, Accra 13-19 February 1968' *Unesco Bull Lib* 1968 22(4) 206-7. See also *Publishers Weekly* 15/4/68. Statistics.

Curtain P 'The archives of Tropical Africa: a reconnaissance' *J Afr Hist* 1960 1(1) 129-47.

Varley D H 'Conference of university libraries in tropical Africa' *Unesco Bull Lib* 1965 19(2) 73-6.

— 'University library cooperation in tropical Africa: the Leverhulme library conference, Salisbury, 1964' *Libri* 1965 15(1) 64-71. Also reported in *East Africa Library Association Bulletin* 1965 (6) 19-22. SCAUL was created at the issue of this conference.

Plumbe W J *Preservation of books in tropical and subtropical countries* OUP, 1964, 72p.

— *Storage and preservation of books, periodicals, and newspapers in tropical climates: a select bibliography* Unesco, 1958, 9p.

— 'Furniture and equipment in tropical libraries' *Unesco Bull Lib* 1961 15(6) 271-6.

Rousset de Pina J 'Construction of libraries in tropical countries: general data' *Unesco Bull Lib* 1961 15(6) 263-70.

ENGLISH-SPEAKING AFRICA

1

Flood R 'British Council in Africa: its role and its libraries' *Lib Mater Afr* 1972 10(1) 14-6. Brief history 1947- .

2a

Commonwealth Development Corporation, London. 1948- as Colonial Development Corporation. With regional offices.

2c

Regional Training Centre for Archivists from English-speaking Africa. From October 1975- . Sponsored by Unesco.

3a

Great Britain. Colonial Office *Reports* on each territory until independence.

3b

Conover H F *The British Empire in Africa: selected references, I: General* Library of Congress, 1942, 37p.

Commonwealth Institute *Selected reading lists for advanced study*. Issues by regions or countries.

Kotei S I A 'Some notes on the present state of national bibliography in English-speaking Africa' *Africana Lib J* 1971 2 13-8.

3f

Bell S *Library development in Africa: a study of its foundations and administrative policy in Ghana, Nigeria, Sierra Leone, Uganda, Kenya, Tanzania and Zambia* London, University College, Diploma in Librarianship, 1967.

Commonwealth Foundation *Conference of librarians from Commonwealth universities in Africa, Lusaka, August 1969. Reports and proceedings* The Foundation, 1970, 70p. (Occasional papers, 8).

FRENCH-SPEAKING AFRICA

1

Instituts Fondamentaux d'Afrique Noire (IFAN). Main centre in Dakar. Most of them have now been integrated into national library and documentation systems.

Centre d'Analyse et de Recherche Documentaires sur l'Afrique Noire (CARDAN), Paris. See more details under: Africa.

2a

Organisation Commune Africaine et Mauricienne (OCAM). Library in Bangui, 1974- . Formerly in Yaoundé, 1966-74. Cooperation.

Conseil Africain et Malgache pour l'Enseignement Supérieur (CAMES). Headquarters in Ouagadougou (Upper Volta). 1968- .

2b

Association Internationale pour le Développement des Bibliothèques en Afrique (AIDBA). Most of the local sections now have evolved into national library associations. Dakar, 1957- .

2c

Main training facilities are:

Dakar. Ecole de Bibliothécaires, Archivistes et Documentalistes (EBAD) 1974. Previously (1967-74): Centre Régional de Formation de Bibliothécaires des Pays d'Afrique d'Expression Française.

Lyons (France). Ecole Nationale Supérieure de Bibliothécaires (ENSB).

Seguin L 'The regional centre for the training of librarians in Dakar' *Unesco Bull Lib* 1964 18(3) 101-4.

Bousso M A 'Centre Régional de Formation des Bibliothécaires' *SCAUL Newsletter* 1967 (4) 171-7.

— 'La formation des bibliothécaires à Dakar' *Bull ACBLF* 1967 13(4) 167-73.

— 'La formation des bibliothécaires des pays en voie de développement: politique à suivre' *Bull Unesco Biblioth* 1968 22(4) 194-7.

'La formation et le recyclage des bibliothécaires et documentalistes' in *Université et politique scientifique en Afrique* Montreal, AUPELF, 1975, 81-6.

Fontvielle J R and Merland M 'Library science in the context of French-speaking Africa: a new course at the National Institute of Librarianship (ENSB)' *Unesco Bull Lib* 1978 32(4) 266-78.

Orleans J d' *Centre régional de formation d'archivistes* Unesco, 1973.

Centre régional de formation d'archivistes, Dakar — résultats et recommendations du projet Unesco, 1976 (FMR/CC/DBA/76/271 (UDDP)).

Sane O 'Archives administration in the French-speaking countries of black Africa: EBAD's curriculum' *Unesco J* 1979 1(4) 260-6.

Brugghen W van der *Cours d'introduction à la documentation: aide mémoire synoptique* FID, 1972, 93p. Prepared for the African course.

Menou M J *Sénégal — Section des documentalistes, Ecole des Bibliothécaires, Archivistes et Documentalistes de l'Université de Dakar* Unesco, 1975, 155p (FMR/COM/DND/75/118).

Lajeunesse M 'Education and training of information specialists in French-speaking countries: a comparative study' *Unesco J* 1979 1(2) 124-37, refs.

Sène H *A comparative survey of the career structure of staff in libraries, archives and documentation centres in French-speaking Black Africa and the Maghreb — Working report* Dakar, EBAD, 1977, 18p.

3a

Encyclopédie africaine et malgache Paris, Larousse, 1964-68, 19 issues.

3b

Conover H F *French colonies in Africa. A list of references* Library of Congress, 1942, 89p.

France. Ministère de la Coopération *Indications bibliographiques à l'usage des bibliothèques africaines et malgaches* 1966, 262p.

Afrique noire d'expression française, sciences sociales et humaines — Guide de lecture CARDAN, 1968, 301p.

Rupp B 'Quelques notes sur la situation de la bibliographie africaniste en France' *Lib Mater Afr* 1970 8(1) 37-71.

Dadzié K E W 'Les services bibliographiques en Afrique tropicale de langue française et principalement au Sénégal' in Pearson J D and Jones R *The bibliography of Africa* 1970, 88-99. See under Africa, 3b.

Brasseur P 'The bibliography of the countries of French-speaking black Africa' *Africana Lib J* 1971 2(1) 13-6.

EBAD *Bibliographie nationale courante de l'année 1967 des pays d'Afrique d'expression française* 1969, 78p. Mimeo.

Africana I-IV. Catalogue of Tunisia National Library's holdings on African French-speaking countries.

Journal de la Société des Africanistes, Paris, 1931- . The second issue in every volume contains 'Bibliographie africaniste'.

Centre d'Etudes et de Documentation sur l'Afrique et l'Outre-Mer (CEDAOM), Paris *Afrique contemporaine* includes a section 'Revue des livres et des revues'.

CAMES *Répertoire des recherches en cours en Afrique francophone.*

3c

Thomassey M *Catalogue des périodiques d'Afrique noire francophone (1858-1962) conservés à l'IFAN* IFAN, 1965, 117p. (Initiations et Etudes Africaines, 19).

Notes Africaines 1949- . Dakar.

Bulletin des Bibliothèques de France contains articles and information on African libraries.

BLIBAD: bulletin de liaison à l'intention des bibliothécaires, archivistes et documentalistes africains Dakar, EBAD, 1976- .

3d

Institut National de Statistique et d'Etudes Economiques *Données statistiques africaines et malgaches* 1971- .

3f

Lewis W H *French-speaking Africa: the search for identity* New York, Walker, 1965, 256p.

Lusignan G de *French-speaking Africa since independence* Pall Mall P, 1969.

La croissance urbaine en Afrique noire et Madagascar (Colloque du CNRS) CNRS, 1972, 2 vols, 1109p.

Rupp B et al 'Inventaire des enseignements dispensés dans les pays francophones (1971-72); enquête avec l'appui de l' AUPELF' *Etudes Afr Bull Info Liaison* 1972 4(1/2) 273p.

Dadzié K E W 'Libraries, bibliography and archives in French-speaking countries of Africa' *Unesco Bull Lib* 1961 15(5) 242-53.

N'Diaye A G *Organisation commune africaine, malgache et mauricienne. Réorganisation du service de documentation, archives et bibliothèques, mai-août 1972* Unesco, 1972, 18p.

— *Ibid, avril-mai 1974* (Second report) Unesco, 1974, 28p.

Heissler N et al *Diffusion du livre et développement de la lecture en Afrique* Paris, Cujas, 1966, 300p.

Fontaine R 'Le problème du livre face au lecteur en Afrique: quelques lignes d'action proposées' *Bull Biblioth Fr* 1976 21(1) 11-8.

Murray-Lachapelle R 'La coopération du Canada avec l'Afrique francophone dans le domaine des bibliothèques et de la documentation' *Doc Biblioth* 1979 25(2) 81-6, refs.

'Archive policy for French-speaking African countries: regional seminar on archives, Dakar 15/3 — 9/4/71' *Unesco Bull Lib* 1972 26(2) 84-7, 96.

Arom S 'Rapport sur une mission d'information effectuée dans quelques pays d'Afrique Centrale et Occidentale' Conseil International de la Philosophie et des Sciences Humaines (CIPSH) *Bulletin* 1974/75 75-86. Central Africa, Cameroon, Ghana, Ivory Coast, Upper Volta, Sénégal. 'Phonothèques' (Recorded sound libraries).

See also sub-sections: French Associated Eastern Africa, French-speaking West Africa, French-speaking Central Africa.

EASTERN AFRICA

This is not a definite region and the references vary in scope.

2a

Commonwealth Development Corporation. Eastern African Office, Nairobi. Economic cooperation for development.

Regional Committee for the Development of Information Services in Eastern Africa. Under the East African Academy with sponsorship of the German Foundation for International Development.

Library of Congress Office in Nairobi. Procurement centre for Eastern Africa.

James J R 'The Library of Congress program in Eastern Africa' in Pearson J D and Jones R *The Bibliography of Africa* 1970, 75-82. See under Africa, 3b.

2b

Pankhurst Rita 'National and regional organizations in Eastern Africa' in Chaplin A H *The organization of the library profession* Verlag Dokumentation, 1973, 61-76.

Standing Conference of African University Librarians — Eastern Area (SCAULEA).

Standing Conference of Eastern, Central and Southern African Librarians (SCECSAL), Dar es Salaam. 1947- . Supersedes the Standing Conference of East African Librarians.

Harrison K C 'SCECSAL' *COMLA Newsletter* 1977 (15) 11.

2c

Co-ordinating Centre for Regional Information Training (CRIT), Nairobi. 1975- . Created and maintained by the German Foundation for International Development (DSE), Bonn and the East African Academy. Based on Kenya's National Academy for the Advancement of Arts and Sciences, Nairobi. Organizes training courses for the region.

Dean J *A regional library science program for Eastern Africa* Ford Foundation, 1974, 68p. (ERIC Report ED-156 113). Commissioned by SCAULEA.

Abidi S A H 'Library training facilities in Eastern Africa' *Indian Lib Ass Bull* 1976 12(3/4) 169-75. East Africa, Ethiopia, Mauritius.

— 'Library training programmes in East Africa: an evaluation *Unesco J* 1980 2(3) 159-69.

Abidi S A H and Moeller T eds [*Report of the meeting on introduction of information science into library training in Eastern Africa, Dar es Salaam, 26-29 February 1980*.] CRIT, 1980, 37p. (CRIT Series, 20/80).

3a

Davis S W *A preliminary directory of documentation centres in Kenya, Malawi, Tanzania, Uganda and Zambia* Makarere U, East Africa School of Librarianship, 1969.

3b

Library of Congress *Accessions list for Eastern Africa* Nairobi, 1968- .

Webster J B 'The research and activities of the bibliographic section of the program of Eastern African studies, Syracuse University' in Pearson J D and Jones R *The bibliography of Africa* 1970, 135-7. See under: Africa, 3b.

3f

Irwin J M 'A tour of East and Central Africa: some impressions and trends, November 1973' *Maktaba* 1974 1(1) 50-4. Kenya, Malawi, Tanzania, Uganda, Zambia.

Harrison K C *The importance and relevance of librarianship for developing countries* Commonwealth Foundation, 1975, 29p. Kenya, Malawi, Tanzania, Uganda, Zambia.

Johansen T 'Øst-og sørlige Afrika: biblioteksutbygging i Kenya, Tanzania, Zambia og Botswana' *Bok Bibliot* 1976 43(6) 310-7. Library development in the 70s.

Flood R A and Bentley A D 'Bibliotekutbyggingen i det østlige og sørlige Afrika' *Bok Bibliot* 1977 44(3) 174-6. Two papers on the part played by the British Council in library development; a critical reply to the above paper.

Kaumgamno E E and Llomo C S *Library services in West and East Africa* Tanzania Library Service/Transafrica Book Distributors, 1979, Vol 1, 273p.

Musis J S 'The Standing Conference of Eastern, Central and Southern Librarians, October 1976, Lusaka' *Maktaba* 1977 4(1) 39-42.

Sweeney W D et al, eds *Libraries and information services as instruments of transition to the 21st century in Africa* Zambia Library Association, 1976, 87p. Proceedings of SCECSAL II, Lusaka, 1976.

Thairu R W ed *The development of information: an African approach* Kenya Library Association, 1979, 143p. Proceedings of the 3rd SCECSAL, Nairobi, 1978.

Namushi N 'Third International Standing Conference of Eastern, Central and Southern African Librarians, Nairobi, 1978' *Zambian Lib Ass J* 1979 11(1) 50-3. With a pre-conference workshop including training of certified library assistants.

Xuereb P 'Africa: report on the 3rd SCECSAL' *COMLA Newsletter* 1979 (23/24) 22-4.

Larby P M 'The meeting of SCAUL (Eastern Africa) Addis Ababa, February 1971' *Lib Mater Afr* 1972 9(3) 166-72.

'SCAUL Eastern Area Conference, Addis Ababa, February 1971' *SCAUL Newsletter* 1971 (6) 1-9.

SCAULEA Conference, Addis Ababa Final report Haile Selassie U, 1971.

'Joint Conference of SCAULEA II and CRIT, Nairobi, 13-17 December 1977' *IFLA J* 1978 4 203-5.

'Role of university libraries in the development of the area' is the theme of the SCAULEA III and CRIT joint conference.

Ballard R M 'Special libraries and information centres in South Eastern Africa' *Spec Lib* 1979 70(7) 287-92. Central Africa and Tanzania.

'International Conference on the development of documentation and information networks in East Africa, held in Nairobi 24 July to 1st August 1973' *Unesco Bull Lib* 1974 28 52-3.

— *Report* German Foundation for International Development (Document DSE-DOK 701 A/a). Sponsored by Unesco.

Jumba-Masagazi A H K 'Documentation activities in Eastern Africa: the Nairobi conference' *Maktaba* 1974 1(1) 12-20.

'Information Services in East Africa International Conference on the Development of . . .' Arusha (Tanzania) April 1976. Announced in *Unesco Bull Lib* 1976 30 399. Follow up on the Nairobi conference.

Polinière J P *Situation and needs of national information systems in science and technology* Unesco, 1975 (Technical report: RP/1973-74/2.13.6; Serial No: FMR/SC/STI/75/13 2(E)).

Unesco *The use of documentation and information for planning and decision making;* seminars Khartoum November 1974, Kampala November 1974, Dar es Salaam December 1974, German Foundation for International Development (Document: DSE-DOK 790 A/a).

See also under Tropical Africa, English-speaking Africa.

ETHIOPIA

1

National Library and Archives, Addis Ababa. 1944- .

Wright S G 'National libraries in Ethiopia' *U Coll Rev* (Addis Ababa) 1961 1 41-6.

University of Addis Ababa Library. 1950- . In particular:

- Institute of Ethiopian Studies, Library and Documentation Centre, 1963- . Bibliographical activities. Legal Deposit.
- Documents Department, 1967- . Deposit for UN and agencies' publications.

2a

Ministry of Education.

2b

Library Association of Ethiopia, Addis Ababa. 1961- .

2c

Haile Selassie I University. Faculty of Education *Programme in library science* Addis Ababa, 1970.

Giorgis K W 'Library education in Ethiopia' *Int Lib Rev* 1973 5(4) 453-61.

Aldiga T 'Library training in Ethiopia, past and present' Paper in Abidi S A H and Moeller T eds Meeting on *Introduction of information science into library training in East Africa* See under: Eastern Africa, 2c.

Darch C 'The status of professional librarians at Haile Selassie University' *Ethiopian Lib Ass Bull* 1975 3(2) 33-41.

3a

Prouty C and Rosenfeld E *Historical dictionary of Ethiopia* Scarecrow, 1981, 436. (African Historical Dictionaries, 32.)

Amos G O *Directory of Ethiopian libraries* Addis Ababa, 1968.

Solomon G C *Survey of the major libraries of Ethiopia* U of Southern California, 1977, 202p. DLS thesis.

3b

Ethiopian publications: books, pamphlets, annuals and periodical articles Institute of Ethiopian Studies, 1965- . Annual bibliography.

Books of this month American Library.

Addis Ababa University *Current research on Ethiopia and the Horn of Africa.*

— *Ethiopian publications.*

Hidarv A and Rahmato D *A short guide to the study of Ethiopia: a general bibliography* Greenwood P (for the African Bibliographic Center, Washington), 1976, 176p.

Brown C F *Ethiopian perspectives: a bibliographic guide to the history of Ethiopia* Greenwood P., 1978, 264p. (Special Bibliographic Series — African Bibliographic Center; New Series no. 5).

Darch C *A Soviet view of Africa: an annotated bibliography on Ethiopia, Somalia and Djibouti* G K Hall, 1980, 200p.

3c

List of current periodical publications in Ethiopia Addis Ababa U, Institute of Ethiopian Studies, 1964- . 2 a year.

Library Club *Library news bulletin*, 1965- . Irregular.

3d

Central Statistical Office *Statistical abstract of Ethiopia* 1963- .

3f

Nicol C *From the roof of Africa* Hodder, 1972, 362p.

Kaula E Mason *The land and people of Ethiopia* Lippincott, 1972 [1965] 159p.

Jordan R T 'Running fast in Ethiopia: a report of first impressions' *Learning today* 1972 5 55-7.

Pankhurst Richard 'The foundations of education, printing, newspapers, book production, libraries and literacy in Ethiopia' *Ethiopia Observer* 1962 6(3) 241-92.

Teshome G W *Education in Ethiopia: prospect and retrospect* U of Michigan P, 1979, 256p.

Danton J Periam 'Libraries in the Land of the Lion of Judah' *Lib J* 1962 87(9) 1732-6.

Pankhurst Rita 'Libraries abroad: Ethiopia' *J Lib Hist* 1966 1(3) 187-92.

— 'Ethiopia, libraries in' in *Encyclopedia* (1972) 8 215-27.

Belcher S 'Libraries in Ethiopia' *PNLA Q* 1971 35(3) 8-15.

Darch C 'Towards the librarianship of scarcity: some recent trends in Ethiopia' *Focus Int Comp Libp* 1975 6(2) 15-6.

Mengteab A 'Library, documentation, archives and information network for Ethiopia's development' *Ethiop Lib Ass Bull* 1975 3(2) 43-6.

Giorgis K W 'Planning and organizing public libraries in Ethiopia for the period 1975-2000' *Unesco Bull Lib* 1976 30(2) 78-82, 100.

Paton W B *Ethiopia: development of public and school libraries, October 1968-January 1969* Unesco, 1969, 21p, appendix. (Report 1110/BMS-RD/DBA).

- Summary of the report in *Unesco Bull Lib* 1970 24(1) 27-32.

Pankhurst Rita *Haile Selassie I University: the library ten year development 1967/68-1976/77* Addis Ababa, 1967.

Peck T P 'Ethiopia's developing medical/health science information services' *Spec Lib* 1975 66(5/6) 273-80.

Demissie E 'Present situation of documentation centres in Ethiopia' *Int Forum Inf Doc* 1979 4(4) 23-5.

SOMALIA

1

State Council Archive. Legal deposit for official publications. Being organized as National Archives.

Lenz W *Mission to Somalia, 30 March-1 April 1976* International Council of Archives, 1976.

National University, Main Library, Mogadishu. 1949- .

National Library Service, Mogadishu.

2a

Ministry of Higher Education and Culture.

2c

Short courses organized by the Ministry and the University at the Somali Institute of Development, Administration and Management (SIDAM), and at the University College of Education.

See also under Ethiopia, 3b.

3b

Bibliografia Somala Mogadishu. Chamber of Commerce, 1958. Italian section.

Salad M K *Somalia: a bibliographical survey* Greenwood, 1977, 468p (African Bibliographic Center; Special bibliographic series; new series, 4).

3e

Library of Congress *Official publications of Somaliland, 1941-1949: a guide* The Library, 1960, 41p. British section.

3f

Lewis I M *Somali culture, history and social institutions: an introductory guide to the Somali Democratic Republic* London School of Economics, 1981, 54p.

Röhr H *Somalia: library development* Unesco, 1965, 5p. Mission, 1963.

EAST AFRICA

2a

East African High Commission (EAHC). 1948-61.

East African Common Services Organization (EACSO). 1961-1967.

East African Community (EAC). 1967- .

- East African Literature Service (EALS). 1967- .

Munn R F 'The East African Literature Service' *Unesco Bull Lib* 1973 27(1) 29-32.

East African Academy. Research Information and Publication Services, Nairobi. 1968- . Ford Foundation Grant. Collects research information. Originally: East African Research Information Centre (EARIC).

2b

East African Library Association (EALA), Nairobi. 1956-72. Superseded by national associations.

Fang J R and Songe A H 'East African library association *Lib J* 1973 98 2041-5.

Musisi J S and Abukutsa J L 'Evolution of library associations in Kenya' *Int Lib Rev* 1978 10(4) 345-53, refs. Traces the history of the EALA.

2c

EALA 'Conference on library training for East Africa' *EALA Bull* 1963 (4) 17-9.

Larsen K *East African School of Librarianship, March 1963-December 1964* Unesco, 1964, 13p. See also in *Unesco Bull Lib* 1964 18(3) 105-9. School created in 1964.

Gomm G 'Library education and training in East Africa' *EALA Bull* 1966 (7) 44-9.

'East African School of Librarianship' *SCAUL Newsletter* 1967 (4) 164-9.

Mukwato L E 'Training of librarians in East Africa: a talk to the Zambian Library Association' *ZLA J* 1(1) 11-8. Also in: *INSPEL* 1969 4 91-6.

Plant R 'The East African School of Librarianship' *Lib Rev* 1971 23(1/2) 39-42.

Saith S S 'East African School of Librarianship' in *Encyclopedia* 7 (1972) 327-37.

— *East African School of Librarianship: Uganda (Mission) July 1968-November 1972* Unesco, 1973, 79p. (2924/RMO.RD/DBA).

Kibirige H M 'Current trends in the training of library and information specialists in East Africa' *Libri* 1975 25(1) 34-9. Also in *Ugandan Lib* 1975 32-40. Special issue.

Kiyimba J N 'The East African School of Librarianship (EASL): its contribution to library development in Africa' *Unesco Bull Lib* 1978 32(4) 260-5.

Pala F O 'The library profession in East Africa: past and present' *EALA Bull* 1974 (14) 126-30. Paper at a conference, Nairobi, 1972.

3a

Marco Surveys Ltd *Research services in East Africa*East African Academy, 1966.

Makarere U College Library *Directory of East African Libraries* 2nd rev ed 1969. (Library Publ, 4). Regularly updated.

3b

Kibirige H M 'Bibliographical control in East Africa: state of the art' *Int Lib Rev* 1978 10(3) 313-26, refs.

Brothers S C 'Bibliographic organisation and control in Kenya' *Libri* 1974 24(3) 164-70. Largely about East Africa in general.

Pfukani B M 'East Africana collection of the University of Nairobi libraries — the first decade 1968-1978' *Unesco J* 1979 1 163-7.

East Africana publications — catalogues of publications held by the Makarere, Nairobi and Dar-es-Salaam university libraries. Union card catalogue.

Library of Congress Office (Nairobi) *Accessions lists: East Africa* 1967- .

London. Commonwealth Office *Kenya, Tanzania, Uganda.* Selected lists for advanced studies.

Molnos A *Sources for the study of East African cultures and development* EARIC, 1968. (Information circulars, 1). Also includes organizations, libraries, etc.

Howell J B comp *East African community: subject guide to official publications* USGPO, 1977, 272p.

Shields J J *A selected bibliography on education in East Africa, 1941-1961* 1962.

Makarere U Library *Education in East Africa* 1970- .

— National Institute of Education *Monthly accessions list* 1969- .

3c

SCOLMA 'Periodicals published in Africa. Part 8: East African Community, Kenya, Tanzania, Uganda' *Lib Mater Afr* 1969 6(3). Supplement.

Makarere U Library *Periodicals in East African libraries* 1966- . 8th ed 1974. Assist. R Munn. Originally at West Virginia U, now prepared from Makarere University. Title varies.

EARIC *Information circulars.*

EALA Bulletin 1962-1972.

3d

East African Statistical Office *Statistical abstract.* Now superseded by national services.

3e

Conover H *Official publications of British East Africa* Library of Congress, 1960-63, 4 parts. Updated by:

East Africa: subject guide to official publications of Kenya, Tanzania and Uganda 1975.

3f

Ingham K *A history of East Africa* 3rd ed Longmans, 1965.

Proctor J H 'The effort to federate East Africa: a post mortem' *Polit Q* 1966 37(1) 46-69.

Hughes A J *East Africa: Kenya, Uganda, Tanzania* Penguin, 1969.

East African Institute of Social and Cultural Affairs *East African cultural heritage* 1966.

Abukutsa J L ed 'The role of books in development: proceedings of the 5th Biennial Conference of the East African Library Association, Nairobi, September 25-29, 1972' *EALA Bull* 1974 (14) 1-142.

Kaungamno E E and Llomo C S *Books build nations. Vol 1: Library services in West and East Africa* Tanzania Library Services, 1979, 169p.

Hockey S W 'Development of library services in East Africa: a report to the governments of East Africa' 1960. And 'Six years after' in *EALA Bull* 1967 (8) 7-9.

— 'Library resources in English-speaking East Africa' *Unesco Bull Lib* 1961 15(5) 232-6.

Kawesa B M *Resource sharing in relation to library acquisition: a case for East Africa* ERIC, 1977, 25p (ERIC Report ED-176 762).

Kaungamno E E 'The East African library movement and its problems' *East Afr J* 1969 6(6) 36-9.

Matogo B W K 'Library trends in East Africa, 1945-65' *Int Lib Rev* 1977 9(1) 67-82.

Wallenius A B *Library work in Africa* Scandinavian Institute of African Studies, 1966, 72p.

— *Libraries in East Africa* Scandinavian Institute of African Studies, 1971, 219p.

Belton E J 'East Africa, Libraries in' in *Encyclopedia* 7 (1972) 324-7.

Kibirige H M 'Public libraries in East Africa in the mid-1970s: a comparative critique' *Unesco Bull Lib* 1977 31(6) 331-9, refs.

Komora Y 'The role of books and libraries in curriculum development' *EALA Bull 1974* (14) 115-9. Paper at the Nairobi conference 1972.

Luckman M E 'Development of special libraries in East Africa' *EALA Bull* 1966 (7) 29-37.

See also under: Eastern Africa.

KENYA

1

University of Nairobi Libraries. Main Library in particular: deposit library for local publications and for material from international bodies: UN, FAO, WHO etc., research reports. See under East Africa 3f Wallenius A B.

Nairobi City Library Services, Central Library. Created in 1931 as the Macmillan Library, taken over by Nairobi City Council in 1962.

2a

Ministry of Housing and Social Services. National Library Service Board (NLSB), Nairobi. 1967- . Operates the Kenya National Library Service (KNLS). See under East Africa, 3f Wallenius A B.

Ministry of Education.

2b

Kenya Library Association (KLA), Nairobi. 1973- . 1953-73 as: Kenyan Branch of the East African Library Association.

Musisi J S and Abukutsa J L 'Evolution of library associations in Kenya' *Int Lib Rev* 1978 10(4) 345-53, refs.

2c

Sinnette E Des Verney *Kenya: national training project in library, archival and information studies* Unesco, 1979, 24p.

3a

Horrobin D F *Guide to Kenya and Northern Tanzania* East Africa Publishing House, 1971.

London, Central Office of Information *Kenya* 1970. (Fact Sheets on the Commonwealth).

KLA Education Subcommittee *Survey of Kenyan libraries* KLA, 1975.

Njuguna J R *Directory of libraries in Kenya* Nairobi, Gazelle Books, 1977, 102p.

Nairobi City Library Services *Libraries for the young survey* 1970.

3b

Thairu R W 'Acquisitions in Kenya libraries' *Maktaba* 1977 4(1) 4-20.

Brothers S C 'Bibliographical organization and control in Kenya' *Libri* 1974 24(3) 164-70.

Pfukani B 'Towards the establishment of a national bibliographic agency in Kenya' *Maktaba* 1978 5(1) 3-6.

Wanjohi G 'The foundation of the national bibliography and the national bibliographic agency' *Maktaba* 1978 5(1) 7-14.

Library of Congress Field Office *Accession lists* 1967- . Office based on Nairobi. With an *Annual serial supplement.*

346 University of Nairobi Library *Accessions lists.*

Kenya National Library Services *Accessions lists.*
Nairobi City Library Services *Accessions lists.*
Webster J B *A bibliography of Kenya* Syracuse U, 1967, 461p. (East African bibliographical series, 2).
Martin L *Education in Kenya before independence: an annotated bibliography* Syracuse U.

3c
Maktaba Kenya Library Association, 1974- .
University of Nairobi *Library magazine* 1979- .

3d
Ministry of Finance and Planning *Kenya statistical digest.*

3e
Publications on sale at Government Printing and Stationery Department, Nairobi 12/8/1966 Kenya Government Printer.
Kenya Gazette 1957- . 1920-1956 as *Kenya official gazette.* Contains lists of government publications.
Books and Newspapers Act 1962 (Laws of Kenya, Cap 111).
Public Libraries Act 1965.

3f
Mwaura P *Communication policies in Kenya* Unesco, 1980, 94p.
Franklin Book Programs *A book development program for Kenya* 1966.
Dames T J 'The literacy centres in Kenya' *Afr Adult Educ* June 1967 25-7.
Kemp D A R 'A view of Kenya libraries' *Libn Book World* 1959 48 157-62.
Ndegwa J 'Documentation centres and libraries in Kenya' Paper at the International Conference on: *Development of Documentation and Information in East Africa*, Nairobi 1973. See under East Africa.
Munn R F 'Kenya, libraries in' in *Encyclopedia* 13 (1975) 432-5.
Carlqvist G 'Glimtar frán bibliotek i Kenya' *Biblioteksbladet* 1979 64(11) 206-9.
KNLS *Development Plan 1968/69 — 1972/73.*
— *The Kenya network of library services (Nairobi).*
Lmangu J 'Library services to children with special reference to Nairobi City Libraries (Eastlands Branch)' *Maktaba* 1977 4(2) 92-7.
Mumford B C L 'Royal College, Nairobi' *Canadian Lib* 1963 19 213-5.
Abukutsa J L 'The library in higher education: with special reference to the University of Nairobi' *Maktaba* 1974 1(1) 21-33.
University of Nairobi *Library Magazine* 1979 (2) 1-61. Issue on a workshop: Kabete Library and Agri-Vet information, September 1979.
Dosat N P 'The Mines and Geological library, Nairobi' *EALA Bull* 1967 (8) 18-20.
Kemp M E *A national documentation system in Kenya*. Conference on Dissemination of Scientific and Technological Information, Langata 1973. No document traced.
Gehrke U *Kenya. Planning for a national information system* Unesco 1975. (RP/1973-74/4.221.1; Serial No FMR/DBA/75/117).

TANZANIA

1

National Central Library, Dar es Salaam. 1967- . Deposit library, headquarters of the Tanzania Library Services.

'The National Central Library in Tanzania' *Unesco Bull Lib* 1968 22(4) 210-1.

University of Dar es Salaam, Main Library. 1969- . Deposit library.

Arunsi N O 'Ten years of growth of the University of Dar es Salaam Library, 1961-1970' *Unesco Bull Lib* 1971 25(5) 263-6.

2a

Ministry of Education. Tanzania Library Services Board (TLSB). 1963- . 1963-75 as Tanganyika Library Services Board. (See references in 3f).

2b

Chama Cha Ukutubi (CUTA)/Tanzania Library Association (TLA), Dar es Salaam. 1971- . 1964-71 as Branch of the East African Library Association.

2c

Tawete F K 'Library education in a developing Tanzania' *Someni* 1968 (3) 21-8.

3a

Hatch J *Tanzania: a profile* Pall Mall, 1972, 214p.

Tanzania directory Government Printer. 1966- . (Previously: *Tanganyika directory*).

3b

Langlands B W 'The amateur status of national bibliographies: some problems facing bibliographical work, based on Uganda and Tanzania experience' Working paper in Pearson J D and Jones R *The bibliography of Africa*, 66-74. (See under Africa South of the Sahara 3b).

Darch C 'The Africa Bibliographic Centre (ABC) in Dar es Salaam: its origins and immediate plans' *Afr Res and Docum* 1977 (14) 11-4.

Tanzania Library Service *Printed in Tanzania* 1969- The Service, 1971- . Retrospective volumes for 1964-68.

Tanzania Society *Tanzania notes and Records* contains 'Tanzania bibliography'. 1966- .

3c

TLA *Someni*. 1968- .

— *Matukio* (Events). Monthly newsletter.

Tanzania Library Service *Tanzania Library News*. Quarterly.

3d

Central Statistical Office *Statistical abstracts*.

3e

Laws and Statutes of Tanzania.

Libraries (Deposit of Books) Act 1962, amended by the Library (Deposit of Books) Order 1963. Since then superseded by the Tanzania Library Service Board Act 1975. (See references in 3f).

3f

Kimambo I N and Temu A J *A history of Tanzania* East African Publishing House, 1969.

Kaula E Mason *The land and people of Tanzania* Lippincott, 1972, 139p.

Kim K S et al *Papers on the political economy of Tanzania* Heinemann Educ, 1979, 294p.

Coulson A *Tanzania, 1800-1980* OUP, 1982, c320p.

Kaungamno E E *Mass media in Tanzania* Tanzania Library Service, nd, 21p. (TLS Occasional paper, 2).

Broome E M 'First steps in Tanganyika' *EALA Bull* 1966 (7) 18-25.

Tanzania Library Association *Planning for the future: the role of libraries and librarians* (3rd week-end conference 29-30 November 1969) TLS, 1970, 58p.

Rudberg C 'Bybliotek i Tanzania: underhäller läsförmågan' *Biblioteksbladet* 1978 63(12) 238, 240-1.

Kaungamno E E 'Tanzania, libraries in' in *Encyclopedia* 30 (1980) 101-20, refs.

Tawete F K *The need for resource sharing among libraries in Tanzania* ERIC, 1977, 17p. (ERIC report ED-176 760).

Tanganyika Library Service *What we do: books for all* 1971, 20p.

— *Introduction to librarianship, with special reference to the Tanganyika Library Service* 1971, 72p.

Kaungamno E E 'The Tanganyika Library Service and its role in adult education' *Libri* 1972 22(3) 190-9.

— 'A national plan for the development of library services' *EALA Bull* 1974 (14) 7-24.

— 'The functions and activities of Tanzania Library Service within the NATIS concept' *Unesco Bull Lib* 1975 29(5) 242-8.

Ilomo C S 'Books and Ujamaa: the Tanzania Library Service; its problems and prospects' *Afr Res and Docum* 1976 (10) 1-10.

— *Library development in mainland Tanzania* TLS, 1977. (TLS Occasional paper, 3).

Chelelo G M *Tanzania Library Service: the role of a national library service in the development and promotion of adult education in Tanzania* Loughborough U of Technology, 1978, 114p.

Kaungamno E E and Ilomo C S *Books build nations, Vol 2: Library services in Tanzania* Dar es Salaam, Transafrica Book Distributors/Tanzania Library Services, 1979, 273p.

Baregu M L M 'Library service for new literates and others in rural areas in Tanzania' *Focus Comp Int Libp* 1971 2(2) 21-8.

— 'Rural libraries in functional literacy campaigns' *Unesco Bull Lib* 1972 26(1) 18-24.

Frost E 'School libraries in Tanzania' *Unesco Bull Lib* 1969 23(6) 300-9, 325.

Brekke K 'Norsk bibliotekar i Tanzania' *Bok Bibliot* 1975 42(6) 296-8. School library in Mzumbe.

Bourne C P *United Republic of Tanzania. Planning for a National Research Information Centre, September 1974* Unesco, 1975, 23p. (3127/RMO.RD/DBA).

Ilomo C S *Tanzania: problems involved in developing a national information system for development* National Central Library, 1978, 109p.

See also: Ballard R M in Central Africa, 3f.

UGANDA

1

Makarere University Library, Kampala. 1959- . Deposit library. The National Institute of Education and the East African School of Librarianship are based on the university and have their own libraries.

Lwanga T K 'The library of Makarere University' in Wallenius A B *Libraries in East Africa* Uppsala, 1971, 131-43.

Barlow M M 'A special collection in a university setting: the Makarere University Library, Africana/Special collections' *Ugandan Lib* 1975, Special issue, 61-5.

Institute of Public Administration, Deposit Library and Documentation Centre, Kampala. 1969- .

Uganda Library Service, Kampala. 1948- as East African Literature Bureau to 1964. Central Library in Kampala.

2a

Ministry of Culture and Community Development. Public Library Board 1964- .

National Co-ordinating Committee for Documentation, Kampala.

2b

Uganda Library Association (ULA), Kampala. 1964- . Previously 1957-64, Uganda Branch of the East African Library Association.

Uganda School Library Association (USLA), Kampala. 1966- .

Uganda Special Libraries Association, Entebbe. 1970- .

2c

East African School of Librarianship, Kampala. See under: East Africa, for references.

Abidi S A H 'School librarians in Uganda' *Ugandan Lib* 1980 3(1) 23-36.

3a

Trowell K M *A handbook of the museums and libraries of Uganda* Uganda Museum, 1957, 16p.

3b

Makarere University *Library Bulletin and accessions list* 1954- . Includes a section: *Uganda bibliography*.

Uganda Society *Uganda Journal*. Includes lists of books and articles on Uganda.

The Institute of Public Administration publishes bibliographies.

Collison R L *Uganda* Clio P, 1981, 192p. (World Bibliographical Series, 11).

3c

Uganda Library Service *Newsletter*.

— *Annual report*. 1964/65- .

Uganda Library Association *Ugandan Libraries* 1972- . 1966-72 as: Uganda Library Association *Bulletin*.

350 USLA *Newsletter*. 1966- .

3d

Ministry of Planning and Economic Development, Statistics Division *Statistical abstracts* Entebbe, 1961- .

3e

Catalogue of Government publications prior to 1965 Uganda Printing Department.

List of Government publications, Bills, Ordinances, etc. Government Printer. Monthly.

Gray B A comp *Uganda: subject guide to official publications* Library of Congress, 1977, 271p.

Uganda Gazette, Entebbe. 1908-1939 as *Official Gazette of the Uganda Protectorate.*

Uganda. Laws, Statutes, etc *The Public Libraries Act,* 1964.

Karaza-Karumaya 'Burning books with Idi Amin: a personal reminiscence of censorship in Uganda' *Zambia Lib Ass J* 1978 10(2) 45-7, refs.

3f

Jørgensen J J *Uganda: a modern history* Croom Helm, 1981, 381p.

Thompson G A 'Uganda life and libraries' *Assist Libn* 1964 57(10) 171.

Serwada S 'The development of library services in Uganda' *East Afr Lib Ass Bull* 1966 (7) 26-8.

'[National needs and problems of library development in Uganda]' *Ugandan Lib* 1975, Special issue, 79p. Libraries and social development, legislation, etc.

Matogo B W K 'Leading issues in development of public libraries in emergent Uganda, 1960-1970' *Libri* 1975 25(4) 298-317.

Sitzman G L 'Uganda university library' *Coll Res Lib* 1968 29(3) 200-9, 212

See also East Africa, 3f: Wallenius A B.

CENTRAL AFRICA

1

National Archives of Rhodesia and Nyasaland, Salisbury. 1935- . Now serve Zimbabwe only.

University of Zambia. Institute for African Studies. Originally Rhodes-Livingstone Institute, 1937-65, and Centre for African Studies, 1967-71.

2a

Commonwealth Development Corporation. Central African Office, Lusaka.

Central Africa Library Services. Now replaced by countries' services.

See also under: Eastern Africa.

2b

Library Association of Rhodesia and Nyasaland, Bulawayo. 1960-63. Then Library Association of Central Africa. Now replaced by national associations.

At one time the region was organized as a branch of the South Africa Library Association. See:

Burke EE 'CABSALA?' *Rhod Libn* 1974 6(4) 61-5.

2c

James A 'Training for librarianship' *Lib Ass Centr Afr Newsletter* 1964 4(2) 31-5.

3a

Directory of libraries in the Federation of Rhodesia and Nyasaland Salisbury, U College, 1960, 42p. (Library occasional papers, 1).

3b

Bibliography of African education in the Federation of Rhodesia and Nyasaland (1890-1958) 2nd impr U of Cape Town Libraries, 1969, 29p.

London. Commonwealth Institute *Malawi, Rhodesia, Zambia*. Selected reading lists for advanced studies. Regularly updated.

3c

Central Africa Library Service *Bulletin*.

Library Association of Rhodesia and Nyasaland *Newsletter*. Superseded by Library Association of Central Africa *Newsletter*.

3e

Walker A A *The Rhodesias and Nyasaland: a guide to official publications* Library of Congress, 1965, 285p.

3f

Edwards J 'The National Archives of Rhodesia and Nyasaland' *Lib World* 1960 (723) 53-8.

Baxter T W 'National Archives of Rhodesia and Nyasaland' *Lib World* 1962 (748) 101-5.

Johnson N 'Library cooperation' *Centr Afr Lib Serv Bull* 1965 5(3) 36-43.

Stiles D E 'Libraries here and overseas' *Centr Afr Lib Serv Bull* 1965 5(3) 44-8.

Varley D H *Library services in the Rhodesias and Nyasaland. Report on existing facilities and recommendations on future developments* SALA, 1951, 115p. Mimeo. Available in the library of Zimbabwe University.

— 'Library services in the Rhodesias; twelve years after' *Lib World* 1962 (748) 92-5.

Johnson N 'An outline of public library development in the Federation of Rhodesia and Nyasaland' *Lib Ass Rec* 1961 63(11) 368-71.

Varley D H 'Library services for Africans in the Rhodesias and Nyasaland' *South Afr Lib* 1953 20(4) 108-16.

— 'Libraries, an integral part of education: a three point advance' *Centr Afr Lib Ass Newsletter* Dec 1964.

— 'School library work in the Rhodesias and Nyasaland' *South Afr Lib* 1952 20(2) 59-64.

Made S M 'University libraries in English-speaking Central Africa' *J Libp* 1969 1(4) 236-52.

Ballard R M 'Special libraries and information centers in South Eastern Africa' *Spec Lib* 1979 70 287-92. Malawi, Tanzania, Zambia, Zimbabwe. Preliminary work on a directory.

MALAWI

1

National Archives of Malawi, Zomba. 1947- . Created as a branch of Central African Archives.

Drew J D C 'The library of the National Archives of Malawi' *Rhod Libn* 1970 2(3) 74-8.

Malawi National Library Service, Lilongwe (Formerly at Blantyre). 1968- .

Johnson A F 'The Malawi National Library Service: the first two years' *Rhod Libn* 1970 2(3) 64-6.

University of Malawi Library, Zomba. 1965- .

Plumbe W J 'The University of Malawi Library' *Rhod Libn* 1970 2(3) 55-63.

Kanthambi P *The role of the University of Malawi — the Polytechnic Library in Malawi* Loughborough U of Technology, 1980, 195p. (MLS dissertation).

2b

Malawi Library Association, Zomba, 1976- .

3a

Malawi: an official handbook Dept of Information. Annual.

The year in review Dept of Information.

3b

National Archives *Malawi National Bibliography: list of publications deposited in the library of the National Archives* 1965- . Annual.

Malawi National Library Service *Books about Malawi: a select reading list* Blantyre, The Service, 1969, 23p.

Malawi University *An interim bibliography of development in Malawi* Limbe, Chancellor College Library, 1972, 26p.

— *Library accessions List* 1967- .

Syracuse University *A bibliography of Malawi* 1965, 161p.

3c

Malawi National Library Service *Bulletin*, 1968- .

MALA Bulletin (Journal of the Malawi Library Association) 1979- .

3e

Malawi Government Gazette 1964- . Lists Government publications.

Printed Publications Act Cap 19:01 of the Laws of Malawi 1948. Amended 1956, 1964, 1968.

National Library Service Act, 1967.

3f

'Malawi' *Times* 1973 30 June, Supplement, 4p.

Namponya C R 'History and development of printing and publishing in Malawi' *Libri* 1978 28 167-81.

Mwiyeriwa S S 'Libraries in Malawi' *Unesco Bull Lib* 1975 29(6) 361, 364.
Mabomba R S 'Malawi, libraries in' in *Encyclopedia* 17(1976) 1-56, refs.
Msiska A W C 'The Malawi collection in the University of Malawi Library at Chancellor College, Zomba, Malawi' *Rhod Libn* 1976 8(1) 1-6.
— 'An attempt to build up a local collection in the University of Malawi Library, Chancellor College: the formation years 1965-1975' *Zambia Lib Ass J* 1980 12(1) 12-7. (Part of the Africana Collection).

ZAMBIA

1

National Archives of Zambia Library, Lusaka. 1964- . Previously, 1947-64, part of the Central African Archives. Legal deposit library. Acts as a national documentation centre for the humanities and social sciences.

University of Zambia Library, Lusaka. 1966- .

Zambia Library Service, Central Library, Lusaka. 1962- .

National Council for Scientific Research. (1967-), National Documentation and Scientific Information Centre (NDSIC), Lusaka. 1969- .

2a

University of Zambia. Institute for African Studies (Formerly: Rhodes Livingstone Institute), Lusaka. 1937- . Created by merger of the Institute for Social Research and the Centre for African Studies, 1971- .

2b

Zambia Library Association, Lusaka. 1967- . Formerly: Library Association of Central Africa, (Zambia Branch).

Cheelo L Z 'Zambia Library Association: past history, present and future developments' *J Lib Hist* 1972 7 316-28.

2c

University of Zambia and Zambian Library Service. Conference on library training in Zambia, held at the University of Zambia, 3rd January 1967; *Report and resolutions*.

Spillers R E 'The importance of practical work in the ibrary studies curriculum: the Zambia experience' *Zambia Lib Ass J* 1978 10 85-7, refs.

Ballard R M 'Library studies and the library profession in Zambia: observations by an outsider' *Zambia Lib Ass J* 1978 10(3) 80-4.

Librarianship in Zambia: a careers guide Advisory Council of the Zambia Library Service, 1969, 27p.

3a

Zambia Lib Ass *School libraries handbook* 1978.

— *Who's Who in Zambian librarianship* 1978.

— *Directory of libraries in Zambia* 2nd ed, Lusaka, 1978.

Zambia Library Service *Directory of library centres* Annual.

3b

Sweeney W D 'Subject headings for Zambia, 1: languages and peoples' *Zambia Lib Ass J* 1978 10(4) (unnumbered).

Williams G J 'Bibliographic developments in Zambia since 1973' *Zambia Lib Ass J* 1977 9(4) 75-81.

Bibliography of publications deposited in the National Archives 1961-62 (1963-64).

Rehman K A comp *The National bibliography of Zambia, 1970-71* Lusaka, National Archives of Zambia, 1977, 115p. First vol of the national bibliography. Retrospective volumes in preparation.

Williams G J *Independent Zambia: an annotated bibliography* ca 1978. See also in *Zambia Library Association Journal.*

University of Zambia Library *Zambiana acquisitions.*

Parker F 'African education in Zambia: a partial bibliography of magazine articles, 1925-1963' *Afr Studies Bull* (Boston) 1967 10(3) 6-15.

3c

Institute for African Studies *Journal.*

Zambian Library Association *Journal* 1969- . Since 1978 includes: Zambia: bibliography.

3d

Central Statistical Office *Statistical yearbook* 1967- .

Rigg J A 'Secondary school libraries in Zambia: some statistics and comments' *Zambia Lib Ass J* 1979 11(2) 75-85.

3e

Printed Publications Ordinance. Cap 154 1964. Legal deposit law.

3f

Librarianship in Zambia UNZA, 1972.

Parr M W 'Libraries and humanism' *Zambia* 1968 Sep 27-31.

Asplund M 'Libraries and library problems in Zambia' in Wallenius A B *Library work in Africa*, Chap.3. (See Africa, 3f.)

Thompson A and Kelly N 'Two outlooks on libraries in Zambia — from visitor and participant' *Lib Ass Rec* 1977 79(7) 368-9.

Parr M W *Development Plan for Northern Rhodesia Library Service for the period 1965-1970.*

To introduce the Zambia Library Service Lusaka, The Service, pamphlet 31.

Parr M W 'Zambia Library Service and adult education' *Commonwealth Educ Liaison Cttee Newsletter* 1968 Nov 2(3) 7-8.

Kulleen P C 'Public libraries and continuing education' *Zambia Lib Ass J* 1977 9(1/2) 7-9.

Walubita M 'Functions and role of the Zambia Library Services' *Zambia Lib Ass J* 1978 10(3) 88-9.

Sherwood C 'How to soothe a lecturer: an experience in Zambia' *Can Lib J* 1972 29(6) 482-5. Brief overview of various features of the Zambian library system.

Brown E M 'Travels with a Kombi: among library centres in Zambia' *New Lib World* 1971 73 161-4.

Pollard L 'Focus on young public library services: starting a public library service in Northern Zambia' *Focus Int Comp Libp* 1974 5(4) 28-30. See also other papers on public libraries.

Bentley A D 'Zambia: Lusaka Branch Libraries project' *Unesco J* 1979 1(4) 264-6.

Parr M W *School mobile library pilot project.*

Mukwato L E 'School library service in Zambia: present position and future plans and work of the Zambia Library Service' *Focus* (London) 1971 2(3) 43-51.

Loveday A J 'The university library: an essential "laboratory"' *University* 1968 Sep 13, 18-9.

Loveday A J 'Zambia, an experiment in open plan librarianship' *Focus* 1974 5(3) 19-20. University of Zambia.

Agar J 'The Department of Agriculture Library, Zambia' *IAALD Q Bull* 1976 21(3/4) 122-5.

Lundu M C 'Development of information systems: the African humanistic approach' *Libri* 1978 28 283-92. (Originally prepared for the Standing Conference of Eastern, Central and Southern African Libraries, Nairobi 1978).

Library technology in Zambia.

Lungu C 'I: Considering a cooperative automated information system for research in academic libraries in Zambia' *Zambia Lib Ass J* 1979 11(2) 63-9, refs.

Rooke A 'II: Micrographics in Zambia' *Ibid* 70-4.

Dall F 'III: Some hints on the storage and use of audio-visual equipment in Zambia' *Zambia Lib Ass J* 1980 12(1) 8-11.

ZIMBABWE

1

National Archives. Library, Harare (Salisbury). 1935- . Previously Government Archives for Rhodesia and Nyasaland. Deposit privilege. Bibliographical activities.

Coggin C 'Rhodesia's National Reference Library' *South Afr Lib* 1973 40 258-63.

University of Zimbabwe Library, Harare. 1956- .

National Free Library of Zimbabwe, Bulawayo. 1896 as Bulawayo Public Library. Since 1943 functions as the National Lending Library and interlibrary loan service centre. Deposit privilege.

Worsley E 'The oldest public library in Rhodesia (Bulawayo)' *Lib World* 1962 (748) 106-11.

'Twenty five years: the National Free Library, 1944-1969' *Shelfmark* 1969 (17) June 1-8, and in *Rhod Libn* 1970 2 2-8.

2a

Ministry of Education and Culture.

Literature Bureau Zimbabwe, Harare. 1954- . To encourage literature production and publication.

Scientific Council of Zimbabwe, Harare. 1964- .

2b

Library Association of Rhodesia and Nyasaland 1961-64.

Library Association of Central Africa (Rhodesia Branch) 1964-67.

Rhodesia Library Association. Bulawayo and Salisbury Branches. 1967- .

- School Libraries Section, 1976- .

No evidence of activity has been found since 1979.

2c

Harrison A 'Academic and professional education in librarianship: a consideration of Rhodesia requirements' *Rhod Libn* part 1: 1970 2(4) 99-103; part 2 1971 3(1) 1-21, 26 refs.

[Papers of the Rhodesian Library Association's 14th Annual Meeting] *Rhod Libn* 1974 6(4) Whole issue. Reviewes current needs in all fields of librarianship.

3a

Hartridge D and Robarts T *Directory of Rhodesian libraries* National Archives, 1975. (New edition).

3b

Dellar G 'The pattern of Rhodesian publishing, 1961-1967' *Rhod Libn* 1969 1(3) 71-2, 74-6, tables.

Coggin C 'Rhodesian bibliography: a survey' *Rhod Libn* 1970 2(4) 81-98, 69 refs.

— 'Rhodesian bibliography: recent contributions' *Rhod Libn* 1971 3 70-2.

— 'The future of Rhodesian bibliography' *Rhod Libn* 1972 4 52-6.
— 'Rhodesian bibliography: part 3' *Rhod Libn* 1972 4 74-5.
National Archives of Rhodesia *Rhodesia National bibliography* 1967- . Supersedes:
— *List of publications deposited in the library of the National Archives* 1961-66. Until 1963 included Nyasaland publications.
Pollak O B and K *Rhodesia/Zimbabwe* Clio P, 1979, 195p. (World Bibliographical Series, 4).

3c

Rhodesia Library Association *Rhodesian librarian* 1969- . Quarterly. Supersedes:
— *Newsletter* 1961-68.
National Free Library *Shelfmark*.
National Archives *Current periodicals*.
Literature Bureau *Bulletin*. Quarterly.

3d

Central Statistical Office (1927-) *Monthly digest of statistics*.

3e

Government Gazette 1923- .
Rhodesia Statute law. Cap 75.
'Legislative provisions affecting libraries' *Rhod Libn* 1970 Suppl 43-9.

3f

Kumbula T J *Education and social control in Southern Rhodesia* R & E Res Associates, 1979, 168p.
Harrison A 'Rhodesia, libraries in' in *Encyclopedia* 25(1978) 402-38, refs.
Dellar G 'Libraries in a siege economy' *African Research and Documentation* 1979 (20) 1-5. (Lecture to SCOLMA, 1978).
Burke E E *Proposal for a Government library service* National Archives, 1967.
Rhodesia Library Association 'Evidence submitted to the commission of inquiry into library services in Rhodesia' *Rhod Libn* 1970 2(3). Supplement.
Rhodesia Library Commission, (Greenfield Commission) 1970 *Report* Government Printer, 1971, 70p.
'A National Public Library Service for Rhodesia? The Library Commission's findings' *Rhod Libn* 1971 3(2) 29-35.
Lashbrook J *A new library service* U Rhodesia Library, 1976 (Typescript).
— 'A new library service' *Rhod Libn* 1977 9(1) 1-2,4.
Russell J 'Aspects of library provision in African townships: the Bulawayo township libraries' *Rhod Libn* 1973 5 33-41.
Burke E E 'The Salisbury Public Library: a sideline in Rhodesian library history' *Rhod Libn* 1969 1 99-103.
Information Service *Libraries for Africans* Government Printer, 1961, 3p.
Rhodesia Library Association, Mashonaland Branch *Report on a survey of libraries for Africans in Mashonaland, 1967-8* Salisbury, The Branch, 1969.
'School libraries' *Rhod Libn* 1976 8(4) 61-80. Special features, 2 talks.
Dearling G M C 'School libraries: in the division of European, Asian and coloured education' *Rhod Libn* 1976 8(4) 70-2, 74-6.
Harrison A 'The academic library as a measure of civilization' *Rhod Libn* 1976 8 41-54.

SOUTHERN AFRICA

Some references include countries in Central Africa.

2a

Commonwealth Development Corporation, Southern African Office, Johannesburg.

3a

Overseas reference book of the Union of South Africa, including South West Africa, Lesotho, Botswana and Swaziland First published: London, Todd, 1945. Includes a bibliography.

Africa Institute of South Africa *Southern Africa data/Suider-Afrika data.* In separate issues by topics: *Population* 1969, 15p; *Health*, 1969, 12p; etc.

Rosenthal E ed *Encyclopedia of Southern Africa* Warne, 1979.

Pretoria, State Library *Handbook of Southern African libraries* The Institute, 1969.

3b

Willet S M A *A checklist of recent reference books on Lesotho, Botswana and Swaziland* Grahamtown, Rhodes U, Department of Librarianship, 1971, 6p.

3e

Basutoland, Bechuanaland Protectorate and Swaziland High Commissioner *Official Gazette* Pretoria, 1963. Now replaced by official gazettes for individual countries.

Balima M G *Botswana, Lesotho and Swaziland: a guide to official publications 1868-1968* Libbrary of Congress, 1971, 84p.

3f

Made S M 'Aspects of library provision in newly independent neighbouring countries' *Rhod Libn* 1977 9(4) 66-7, 69, 71-3. Botswana, Lesotho, Malawi, Swaziland.

SOUTH AFRICA, Republic of

1

State Library, Pretoria. 1887- .

South African Library, Cape Town. 1818- .

Pama C *The South African Library: its history, collections and librarians, 1818-1968* Balkema, 1968, 216p.

Robinson A M L 'The national library as a research institution' *South Afr Lib* 1965 33(2) 121-4.

— 'National libraries — their history and development — with special reference to South Africa' *Paper at SALA Conference 1978* SALA, 1978, 416-30.

University of Witwatersrand Library.

Johannesburg Public Library.

Kennedy R F *The heart of a city: a history of the Johannesburg Public Library* Cape Town, Juta, 1970, 636p.

2a

Department of National Education. Division of Library Services. 1955- .

Vink C M 'Die afdeling Biblioteekdienste (DLS), Departement van Nasionale Opvoeding' *South Afr Lib* 1975 42(4) 135-8.

Department of National Education. National Library Advisory Council (NLAC). 1967- .

Council for Scientific and Industrial Research (CSIR). Centre for Scientific and Technical Information (CSTI), Johannesburg. 1945- . Since the early 1960s the centre has a Library Service Division.

Kingwill D G 'The CSIR: its role in scientific and technical information' *South Afr Lib* 1977 45(2) 51-8.

2b

South African Institute for Librarianship and Information Science/Suid-Afrikaanse Instituut vir Biblioteek- en Inligtingwese (SAILIS). 1980- . Replaces the South African Library Association/Suid Afrikaanse Biblioteekvereniging (SALA), Potchefstroom, 1930-1979, and is open to all South African librarians.

'South african librarians renounce apartheid' *Am Lib* 1980 11(4) 183.

African Library Association of South Africa (ALASA). 1964-? .

Library League of South Africa. 1959-70 as Cape Library Association.

South African Indian Library Association. 1967- .

It is likely that these associations will disappear under the terms of the SAILIS.

2c

Vleeschauwer H J de 'The University of South Africa and its department of library science' *Mousaion* 1956 (12) 82p.

Wertheimer R M 'Education for librarianship abroad: South Africa' *Lib Trends* 1963 12(2) 260-72.

Malan S J 'Some issues in the training of librarians and information workers' *Mousaion* 1972 (99) 38p.

Dickson L E 'American library education for South African librarians' *South Afr Lib* 1973 41(2) 77-82.

Renewal in the education of librarians and information workers. Symposium, Pretoria, August 1973 *Mousaion* 1974 2(2) 237p.

Fouche B et al *Survey of institutions providing professional training in librarianship and information science and of full time tutors and researchers in library and information science in the Republic of South Africa in 1979* South African Institute for Librarianship and Information Science, 1980, 104p.

SALA *Librarianship as a career* 2nd ed, 1970, 10, 11p.

Zaaiman R B 'Die implikasies van professionalisering vir bibliotekarisse in Suid-Afrika en moontlike ontwikkelingstendense' *South Afr Lib* 1976 43(4) 121-30.

Viljoen A J 'Taakdifferensiasie en die professionalisering van die biblioteek — en inligtingsberoep' *South Afr Lib* 1977 45(1) 5-15.

3a

Vaktaalburo and SALA *Dictionary of library terms* Johannesburg, Voorhekkerpers, 1971, 149p.

South Africa. Africa Institute *Southern Africa data* Pretoria, The Institute, 1969.

Pretoria. State Library *Handbook of Southern African libraries* 1970, cxi, 939p. (Contributions to Library Science, 10). Also covers the 'Central African' region.

Boshoff MM comp, ed *Directory of Southern African libraries, 1975* 3rd rev ed State Library Pretoria, 1976, 301p. (Contributions to Library Science, 20.)

Musiker R *Special libraries: a general survey with particular reference to South Africa* Scarecrow, 1970, 215p, bibl.

SALA, Southern Transvaal Branch, Section for Special Libraries *List of special libraries and information sources in the Southern Transvaal* Johannesburg, The Section, 1974, 109p.

There exist directories for other provinces and states.

3b

Kingwill D G and Van Houten R 'Bibliographic and information services: progress in the 1960's and the 1970's' *South Afr Lib* 1976 44(2) 53-7.

Musiker R *South African bibliography: a survey of bibliographies and bibliographical work* Crosby Lockwood/Archon Books, 1970, 104p, index.

Reitz C *South African bibliography* Illinois U, Graduate School of Library Science, 1967, 18p, mimeo. (Occasional papers, 90).

Musiker R 'Bibliographical scene in South Africa' *South Afr Lib* 1971 38 278-83. Reprinted in *Lib Mater Afr* 1971 9(1) 24-33.

— 'Bibliographical progress in South Africa' *Africana Lib J* 1971 2 10-1; 1972 3 Summer 21-3.

— 'South African bibliography' *Lib Mater Afr* 1972 10(1) 17-9.

SALA newsletter. Regular review of progress.

State Library (Pretoria) *South African National Bibliography* (SANB), 1959- . Supersedes:

— *Publications received in terms of Copyright Act no 9 of 1916* 1933-58.

Mendelssohn S *South Africa, bibliography* Kegan Paul, 1910, 2 vols. It is now being revised and enlarged. See:

Smit D E 'The Mendelssohn revision project' *South Afr Lib* 1970 37 256-9.

State Library (Pretoria) *S.A. Unicat* Cumulative issues on fiche. Bimonthly

supplement to: *South African joint catalogue of monographs on microfiche, 1941-1975.*

South African Library *Africa nova* 1958-69. Included material about South Africa published abroad.

'Kongresreferate 1966-1975' *South Afr Lib* 1976 43(4) 131-7.

Coetzee J C *Annotated bibliography of research in education* Pretoria, Human Sciences Research Council, 1970, 181p.

Taylor C J *Coloured education: a bibliography* U of Cape Town Libraries, 1970, 21p.

Bibliographical series: consolidated list of bibliographies submitted for the Diploma in Librarianship of the University of Cape Town, 1964-66 The School, 1966. Updated in *SALA Newsletter*.

Public Library of Johannesburg *Index to South African periodicals* (M Richards ed), 1940-49, 1950-59, then annual. Also retrospective coverage.

Musiker R *Library science literature, 1965-69: a selective review* Rhodes U, 1970, 27 1.

- *1970-71*, 1972, 25 1, etc.

3c

State Library *Current South African periodicals: a classified list, July 1965* The Library, 1966, 167p.

- *Supplements:* 1967, 35 1, etc.

SALA *SALA Newsletter/SABV Nuusbrief* 1947-1980. Now:

SAILIS *SAILIS Newsletter/SAIBI Nuusbrief* 1980- .

SALA then SAILIS *South African Libraries/Suid-Afrikaanse Biblioteke* 1933- . Quarterly.

ALASA *ALASA Newsletter* 1970-?

Transvaal School Media Centre *School media centre* 1980- . Previously:

Transvaal School Library Association *Skoolbiblioteek/School Library* 1969-1980.

South African Library *Quarterly Bulletin/Kwartaal Blad* 1946- . Includes notes on Africana.

University of South Africa *Mousaion* 1955- . Irregular monographs.

State Library contributions to library science 1961- .

Cape Provincial Library Service *Cape Librarian/Kaapse Bibliotekaris* 1957- . 10 a year.

Orange Free State Provincial Library *Free State Libraries/Vrijstaatse Biblioteke* 1958- . 6 a year.

University of Cape Town *The Jaggerite* 1947- . Irregular.

3d

Department of Cultural Affairs. Division of Library Services *South African Government publications: Department of Statistics, 1910-1968* English 123p; Afrik. 123p.

Department of Statistics *Statistical yearbook.*

— *Education: principal statistics, 1970* (1971), 21p.

Official *South African municipal yearbook* Pretoria, 1909- . Statistics on public libraries included.

3e

South Africa 'Laws, Statutes' . . . in *SANB*.

State Library *Government Gazette.*

Willemse J 'The legal depost privilege with special reference to South Africa' *Mousaion* (68 and 69). No 69 deals with South Africa.

Aschenborn H J 'Copyright acts and legal deposit' *South Afr Lib* 1964 31(3) 93-102.

Westra P E 'Leenvergoeding' *South Afr Lib* 1978 45(4) 141-5.

'Censorship in South Africa' *South Afr Lib* 1971 38(4) 216-59. Whole issue.

Dutoit A B 'Sensuur in Suid-Afrika: politieke en akademiese aspekte' *South Afr Lib* 1975 43(1) 11-20.

De Klerk W A 'Sensuur in Suid-Afrika: die skrywer se standpunt' *South Afr Lib* 1975 43(1) 21-4.

Taylor E 'A survey of South African public library legislation, 1956' *South Afr Lib* 1957 24(3) 94-8.

Wertheimer R J 'Legal responsibility for public library development: South Africa' *Lib Trends* 1960 9(1) 30-4.

SALA Sub-Committee on Public Library Standards *Standards for South African public libraries* 2nd ed, rev. Potchefstroom, 1968, 47p.

3f

Cope J *South Africa* 2nd ed E Benn, 1967.

Taylor L E *South African libraries* Bingley/Shoestring, 1967, 101p. Includes bibliographies.

Kritzinger S J 'Historical survey of the more important libraries in the Union of South Africa' *South Afr Lib* 1945-54 13 to 21. Series of articles.

Interdepartmental Committee on the Libraries of the Union of South Africa *Report* Cape Town Printer, 1937, 66p. Main document in the history of South African libraries.

Dreyer B J 'Die 1978 SABV-konferensie' *South Afr Lib* 1979 46(3) 96-9. Theme: Librarianship in South Africa — development since the first conference 1928.

Van Houten R *Proposed framework for a national programme in the field of librarianship, information and documentation* National Library Advisory Council (NLAC), 1975, 27p.

Line M B 'National library planning in South Africa — some notes' *South Afr Lib* 1975 43(2) 43-5.

Malan S I 'n Nasionale biblioteek — en inligtingoovertreid vir die Republiek van Suid-Afrika- 'n terreinverkenning' *South Afr Lib* 1976 44(2) 59-73. A proposal.

— *'Library science and information service: a general orientation'* Durban, Butterworth, 1978, 185p, bibl. Survey of all aspects of library and information science in South Africa, needs and problems.

Overduin P G J ed *Biblioteekbeplanning vir die jaar 2000* (A symposium 1977) U of the O F S, 1977.

Potchefstroom University and SALA *Aspects of South African libraries* 1962, 52p.

Library World Special issue on South Africa 1963 64(755).

South African Libraries 1969 37(3) 120-7, 144-9. On structure, staffing, etc.

— 1970 38(3) also contains some 1970 Conference papers. Useful for a review of progress.

Egidy B von 'Das Südafrikanische Bibliothekswesen' *Biblioth Wissensch* 1975 9 1-36.

Kesting J G 'South Africa, libraries in the Republic of' in *Encyclopedia* 27(1979) 129-259 (Bibl. 237-259).

Switzer D and L 'South African libraries and the Black press' *South Afr Lib* 1978 46(2) 55-60.

Schauder D E 'Libraries and apartheid' *Int Lib Rev* 1978 10(4) 335-43, refs.

— 'Bibliotheekwerk en apartheid' *Biblioth Samenleving* 1979 7(2) 47-51, refs.

Hadley A T *Trends in inter-library lending in South Africa: report of a survey*

undertaken at the State Library during the period April to September 1969 State Library, 1971, 56p. (Contributions to Library Science, 12).
State Library seminar on library cooperation 2nd, August 1967. Pretoria, 1967, 92p. (Contributions to Library Science, 08).
Duvenage A P 'Library cooperation in the Vaal Triangle' *South Afr Lib* 1977 44(4) 153-6.
Wilson C J 'Resources centres in Natal' *South Afr Lib* 1977 45(2) 45-50.
Fouché B *Aspekte van die leserkunde* U of South Africa, 1977, 39p.
Kesting J G 'Formal education, literacy and the need for adult library service in South Africa' *Skoolbiblioteek/School Lib* 1978 10(2) 3-5.
Laurence P M 'Public library in South Africa' *The Library* 1897 January. Reprinted in *South Afr Lib* 1970 37 236-43.
Friis T *The public library in South Africa: an evaluative study* Deutsch, 1962.
Kesting J G et al, eds *Libraries and people: essays R F M Immelman* Cape Town, Struik, 1970, 163p.
Non-European library service, Transvaal: a brief history, 1931-1969 State Library, 1969, 14p.
Manaka S P 'Non-white library services in the Transvaal' *Mousaion* 1973 (100) 234p. (M. Bibl. dissertation).
Peters M A *The contribution of the (Carnegie) Non European Library Service, Transvaal, to the development of library services for Africans in South Africa* State Library, Pretoria, 1975, 227p.
Harris N 'City library service to the coloured community' *Cape Libn* 1971 Aug 13-7.
Jankowski I 'Südafrika: Bibliotheken in Kapstadt' *Buch und Biblioth* 1977 29(9) 683-9.
Vink C M and Frylinck J H 'Library services in the Black states of Republic of South Africa' *South Afr Lib* 1978 46(2) 47-53, refs.
Bekker J 'Raakpunte tussen biblioteekdienste vir bluides en siendes' *South Afr Lib* 1974 42(2) 59-63.
De Villiers P J A 'The South African Library for the Bluid: a diamond jubilee' *Cape Libn* 1979 Oct 10-2.
Mulder J 'Leesmotivering en die rol van belangstelling' *Mousaion* 1976 2(3) 47p.
Kruger J A *Die historiese ontwikkeling van skololbiblioteke in Suid-Afrika* in SALA Conference 1978, Paper SALA 1978 pp 43-82.
'Library services to children in South Africa' *Skoolbiblioteek/School Lib* 1978 10(2) 12-7.
Klette R R 'School libraries: as they might be' *Rhod Libn* 1976 8(4) 61-2, 64.
Villier I F A de 'Staatsdiensbiblioteke in Europe en Suid-Afrika — 'n vergelyking' *South Afr Lib* 1975 42(4) 139-42.
Kingwill D G 'The organisation of national documentation and information services in South Africa' *Lib Trends* 1969 17(3) 267-79.
Hooper A S C 'A library advisory service to South African industry' *South Afr Lib* 1974 42(2) 65-8.
Gorman G E 'The co-ordination and harmonisation of library-related information project' *South Afr Lib* 1979 46(4) 145-9.
De Bruin H 'Library computerisation in South Africa: the current scene' *South Afr Lib* 1980 47 125-30.
[Information systems] See Thairu R W ed *International Standing Conference (3rd) of Eastern Central and Southern African Libraries*, in: Eastern Africa, 3f.

BOTSWANA

1

National Library, Gaberone. 1968- .

Dale D C 'National libraries in developing countries: the case of Botswana' *J Lib Hist* 1971 6(3) 195-211, refs.

University of Botswana, Lesotho and Swaziland. Botswana Campus. Library.

Botswana Government Information Services, Gaberone.

2a

Ministry of Home Affairs. National Library Service (BNLS), Gaberone. 1967- . Includes the National Library.

Parker J S *Botswana National Library Services: the first three years: a report on the establishment and development of the Botswana National Library Service, from November 1966 to October 1969* Gaberone, 1969, 18p, mimeo.

Stiles D E 'The Botswana National Library Service (BNLS)' *New Lib World* 1976 77(914) 156-7.

2b

Botswana Library Association. 1978- .

Botswana Library Association Journal 1979 1(1) contains the proceedings of the inaugural meeting, August 1978, and the history of the association.

3a

Great Britain. Commonwealth Relations Office *Report on Bechuanaland* HMSO. To 1965. Annual.

The guide to Botswana Gaberone & Johannesburg, Winchester P, 1968- .

Mushonga B L B *Directory of libraries in Botswana* Gaberone, National Institute for Research in Development and African Studies. Documentation Unit, 1977, 55p.

3b

'Botswana. Notes on the national bibliography of Botswana' *Botswana notes and records* 1970 2 121.

Botswana National Library Service *Annual report: the National Bibliography of Botswana (NABoB)*. 1969- . 2 per year.

Middleton C *Bechuanaland: a bibliography* U of Cape Town, School of Librarianship, 1969, 27p.

Mohome P and Webster J B *A bibliography of Bechuanaland* U of Syracuse, 1966, 59p. (Occasional bibliography, 5).

— *Supplement 1968* (Occasional Bibliography, 12).

Stevens P E *Bechuanaland: a bibliography* U of Cape Town, School of Librarianship, 1969, 27p.

3c

National Library Service. Staff Guild *Bonesa*. 1969- .

National Library *Botswana notes and records* 1969- . Includes lists of theses on Botswana.

Botswana Library Association Journal, Gaberone. 1979- . 3 per year.

3d and 3e

Government Gazette. 1963- .

3f

Parker J S 'Libraries in Botswana' *Kutlwano* 1967 6(3) 4-5.

Matthews F 'Libraries in Botswana' in Kesting J C ed *Libraries and people* Cape Town, Struik, 1970, 191-7.

Phephana T 'The genesis of library development in Botswana' *Lib World* 1968 70 70-4.

Grove-Smith T 'Botswana blues' *Assist Libn* 1978 71(4) 46-8.

Cambell A 'The library of the National Museum and Art Gallery' *Botswana Lib Ass J* 1979 1(1) 15-6.

LESOTHO

1

Government Library and Archives, Maseru. 1958- .

Gregory R G *Archival records in Lesotho — a proposal for a cooperative project* 1975. Mimeo.

National University of Lesotho Library, Roma. The university was created in 1945 as Pius College; in 1964 became the Roma Campus of the University of Basutoland, Bechuanaland and Swaziland; national university since 1975.

2a

Ministry of Culture.

2b

Lesotho Library Association, Maseru. 1979- .

3a

Lesotho yearbook. Maseru, 1958- .

3b

Te Groen J C *Basutoland: a bibliography* U of Cape Town, School of Librarianship, 1946, 30p. (3rd impr 1972).

Webster J B *A bibliography of Lesotho* Syracuse U, 1968. (Occasional bibliography, 9).

Gordon L *Lesotho: a bibliography* U of Witwatersrand, Department of Bibliography, Librarianship and Typography, 1970, 47p.

Willet S M and Ambrose D P *Lesotho: a comprehensive bibliography* Clio P, 1980, 496p. (World Bibliographical Series, 3).

3e

Government Gazette. Maseru, 1963- .

3f

Commonwealth Institute *Lesotho* The Institute, 1980, 12p.

Hutton J 'Lesotho, libraries in' in *Encyclopedia* 14 (1975) 251-2.

NAMIBIA

1

Government Archives Library, Windhoek. 1939- .
Windhoek Public Library. 1966- .

2a

United Nations Institute for Namibia, Lusaka. 1976- . Training for development.

3a

Winter C *Namibia* Butterworths, 1977.

3b

Strohmeyer E 'Bibliographical services in Namibia in 1975' *Bibliog Doc Terminol* 1977 17 264-5.
Welch F J *South West Africa: a bibliograhy* U of Cape Town, 1967, 41p.

3f

Serfontein J H P *Namibia* Rex Collings, 1977.
Winter C *Namibia* Butterworth P, 1977.
Green R H et al *Namibia: the last colony* Longman, 1981, 310p.

SWAZILAND

1

National Archives.

University of Botswana, Lesotho and Swaziland. University College of Swaziland Kwaluseni, 1966- . Library, 1971- .

Swaziland National Library Service (SNLS), Manzini. 1971- .

3a

South Africa Institute of Race Relations *Swaziland: facts and figures* Johannesburg, 1968, 4p.

Kuzwayo A W Z and Ward M eds *Directory of Swaziland libraries* 1975?

3b

National Archives *National bibliography* 1973- .

SNLS *Monthly list of acquisitions.*

Arnheim J *Swaziland: a bibliography* U of Cape Town, 1950, 23p. (3rd impr 1969).

Wallace C S *Swaziland: a bibliography* U of Witwatersrand, 1967, 87p.

Webster J B *A bibliography on Swaziland* Syracuse U, 1968, 32p. (Occasional Bibliography, 10).

Nyeko B *Swaziland* Clio P, 1982. (World Bibliographical Series 44.)

3e

Government Gazette Mbabane, 1963- .

3f

Van Jackson W 'Library development in Swaziland' *Int Lib Rev* 1976 8(4) 367-77, refs.

Kuzwayo A W Z *Information systems and national information services in Swaziland* Kwaluseni, U College of Swaziland Library, 1978.

MAURITIUS

1

Mauritius Archives Department, Port Louis. 1815- . Deposit library, bibliographical work.

University of Mauritius Library. 1965- . Deposit library.

Chantal J de 'The University of Mauritius Library' *SCAUL Newsletter* 1971 (6) 43-5.

Bibliothèque de la Cité, Port Louis. 1851- . Open to the public in 1890.

Benoit G *The City Library of Port Louis: a brief history (1851-1968)* The Library, 1977, 19p.

Mauritius Institute Public Library, Port Louis. 1902- . Under the Ministry of Education and Cultural Affairs.

2a

Ministry of Education and Cultural Affairs.

2b

Mauritius Library Association, Port Louis.

Commission Technique des Bibliothécaires Municipaux, Curepipe.

3a

Great Britain. Colonial Office *Report on Mauritius*. HMSO. To 1967.

Riviere L *Historical dictionary of Mauritius* Scarecrow, 1982 (African Historical Dictionaries, 34.)

3b

Toussaint A and Adolphe H *Bibliography of Mauritius, 1502-1954* Mauritius Archives, 1956, 884p. Continued by:

Mauritius Archives Department *Annual report*. Bibliography in appendix. 1955- .

— *Government Gazette* 'Memoranda of books'. 1893- . Quarterly supplement.

3c

Mauritius Archives Department *Annual report*.

Mauritius Institute *Annual report*.

Bulletin des Bibliothèques Municipales de l'Ile Maurice March 1969 (1). Only issue published by the Commission Technique des Bibliothécaires Municipaux.

3d

Central Statistical Office *Yearbook of statistics* 1946-59.

— *Quarterly digest of statistics* 1961- .

3e

Government Gazette of the Island of Mauritius 1809- .

Legal deposit since 1893. *Archives Ordinance* No 71,1952; modified by *Archives (Amendment) Act* 1973.

3f

N'Diaye A G *Organisation commune africaine, malgache et mauricienne — Réorganisation du service de documentation, archives et bibliothèques, mai-août 1972* Unesco, 1972, 18p.

'Gaëtan Benoît, bibliothécaire d'aujourd'hui' *L'Express* 10/10/74 p.3.

Goordyal B R 'Mauritius, libraries in' in *Encyclopedia* 17 (1976) 287-304.

Benoît G 'Libraries in Mauritius' *COMLA Newsletter* 1978 61

Roda J-C 'La lecture publique à l'Ile Maurice: problèmes et perspectives' *Bull Biblioth Fr* 1976 21(9/10) 443-8.

Harrison K C 'Ideal size for national library service' *Lib Ass Rec* 1978 80 443, 445.

SEYCHELLES

2a
Ministry of Eduction and Culture, Victoria.

2c
Library assistant's course in technical services in Victoria, August 1978. Run by Unesco.

3a
Great Britain. Foreign and Commonwealth Office *Report on the Seychelles* HMSO. Biennial.

3b
Journal of the Seychelles Society. Contains the bibliography on the country.

3e
Government Gazette, Victoria. The *Supplements* contains the laws.

3f
Pala F O *The Seychelles: reoganisation and development of libraries, museums and archives* Unesco, 1977, 14p (Restr. Technical Report RP/1975-76/4.221.2).

ST HELENA and TRISTAN DA CUNHA

3a
Great Britain. Colonial Office *Report on St Helena* HMSO. Annual.

3b
Kitching G C *St Helena bibliography* Government Printer, 1947, 6p.
Brander J *Tristan da Cunha 1506-1950* Hoorn, 1952. History and bibliography.

3e
St Helena Government Gazette Government Printing Office.
— *Supplements* contains the laws. Include Tristan da Cunha.

3f
Cross T *St Helena: including Ascencion Island and Tristan da Cunha* David & Charles, 1981, 192p. History.

FRENCH ASSOCIATED EASTERN AFRICA

3b
Robequain C *Madagascar et les bases dispersées de l'Union française* PUF, 1958.

3e
See under: Madagascar, 3e.

COMORO ISLANDS

3e
Journal officiel, Tananarive, 1960- .

DJIBOUTI

2a
Ministry of National Education, Djibouti City.

3a
Guide annuaire de la Côte des Somalis Djibouti Publicité, 1954- .

3b
See under Ethiopia, 3b.

3e
Journal officiel de la Côte Française des Somalis 1900- ?

MADAGASCAR

1

Biblothèque Nationale, Tananarive (Antanarivo). 1920- . Originally 1920-24 as Bureau de Documentation du Gouvernement Général; 1925-61 as Bibliothèque du Gouvernement Général. Deposit library.

'Bibliothéque Nationale de Madagascar' *Bull Bibliot Fr* 1967 12(1) 17-8.

Razafindrakotohasina Rakato R R *La bibliothèque Nationale de Tananarive* Lyons, ENSB, 1977, 37p. Thesis.

Université de Madagascar. Bibliothèque Universitaire. 1960- .

Lamothe M S de Nucé de *Pour une meilleure connaissance de la Bibliothèque Universitaire de Antanarivo* Soc des Amis de la Bibliothèque, 1966, 54p. Mimeo.

— 'Les nouvelles installations de la Bibliothèque Universitaire de Madagascar' *Bull Biblioth Fr* 1969 14 503-12.

Archives Nationales de Madagascar. 1958- .

2a

Ministère des Affaires Culturelles et de l'Education Nationale. Service des Bibliothèques.

Ministère de l'Information, de l'Orientation Idéologique et des Relations avec les Institutions. Deposit rights.

Ministère de la Recherche Scientifique. Institut de Recherche Scientifique de la République Malgache (IRSM). 1946- . Previously Centre ORSTOM de Tananarive.

Office du Livre Malagasy. 1971- . Based on the National Library.

2b

Association pour le Développement des Bibliothèques de Madagascar (ADBM). 1966- .

'Association pour le Développement des Bibliothèques de Madagascar' *Lumière* (Madagascar) 23/10/66 (1592) 4.

Firaisan'ny Mpikaji ny Haren-Tsaim-Pirenena (Fimpihafi). 1976- . Association for archivists, librarians, documentalists and museologists. May be a new format of the above association.

2c

See under French Speaking Africa, 2c.

3a

Annuaire national de Madagascar. 1892- .

Rajemisa-Roalison R *Dictionnaire historique et géographique de Madagascar* Librairie Ambazontany, 1966, 384p.

Secrétariat d'Etat à la Jeunesse et aux Sports *Répertoire des bibliothèques spécialisées et services de documentation de Tananarive* 1968. Mimeo.

3b

Lamothe M S de Nucé de 'La bibliographie nationale à Madagascar' Paper in Pearson J D and Jones R *The bibliography of Africa* . . . 1970, 120-5. (See Africa, 3b).

Lyutova K V 'Stanovlenie natsional'noi bibliografii v Demokraticheskoi Respublike Madagaskar' *Sovet Bibliog* 1976 (156) 109-14.

Grandidier G *Bibliographie de Madagascar 1500-1955* Paris/Tananarive, Inst de Recherche Scientifique de Madagascar, 1905-57, 3 vols.

Fontvieille J *Bibliographie nationale de Madagascar 1956-1963* Montpellier, Inst de Psychologie; Tananarive, Trano Printy Loterana, 1971, 512p.

National Library *Bibliographie annuelle de Madagascar* 1964- . Includes all materials published in Madagascar and material published abroad on Madagascar.

— *Vao Niseho* (Current bibliography).

Valette J *Catalogue du fonds malgache du British Museum* Tananarive, Imprimerie Nationale, 1967, 56p.

Ministère de l'Information *Bulletin de Madagascar*. Includes lists of deposited material. See 1967 (253) 299-454 for a reprint of the above list.

Molet L 'Bibliographie critique récente sur Madagascar' *J Canad Etudes Afr* Nov 1967 (1) 52-63.

3c

Razafintsalama G *Périodiques malgaches 1866-1960* Paris, Bibliothèque Nationale, 1964, 107p. Mimeo.

Périodiques malgaches de la Bibliothèque Nationale The Library, 1970, 199p.

ADBM *Ny boky no loharonom-pandrosoana* (Le livre source de progrès). 1967- .

Archives Nationales *Tantara*.

Ministère de l'Information *Bulletin de Madagascar*. 1950- .

3d

Ministère des Finances et du Plan. Institut National de Statistiques et de Recherches Economiques (INSRA) *Annuaire statistique de Madagascar*.

3e

Witherell J W *Madagascar and adjacent islands: a guide to official publications* Library of Congress, 1963, 58p.

Gazetim-panjakanan'ny Repoblika Malagasy/Journal officiel de la République Malgache Tananarive, 1896- .

3f

Hesetine M *Madagascar* Pall Mall, 1971, 334p.

Hugon P *Economies et enseignement à Madagascar* Paris, Institut International de Planification de l'Education, 1976.

Ranivo M 'Madagascar (Malagasy Republic), libraries in' in *Encyclopedia* 16 (1975) 444-52.

'Library development' *Unesco Bull Lib* 1961 15(5) 226,247.

Saron G 'Les halls d'information à Madagascar: foyers culturels franco-malgaches' *Rev Madag* 1956 (29) 51-8.

'Bibliothèque Municipale de Tananarive' *Courrier Madag* 9/1/64 (470) 8.

'La bibliothèque territoriale (Tananarive) *Bull Madag* 1958 (147) 711-2.

Hardyman J T 'The documentation of Madagascar' *J Doc* 1947 3(1) 9-16.

Aries P *Madagascar, documentation scientifique* Unesco 1969 (1560/BMS. RD/SCP).

REUNION

1

Archives Départementales, St Denis.
Bibliothèque Universitaire, St Denis. 1972- .
Bibliothèque Départementale, St Denis. 1856- .
Bibliothèque Centrale de Prêt, St Denis. 1956- .

2a

Paris. Ministère de l'Education Nationale. Direction des Bibliothèques to 1975. See under France, 2a for changes.

3e

Journal et bulletin officiel de la Réunion, St Denis. 1910- . Previously *Bulletin officiel de l'Ile Bourbon* and *Bulletin officiel de l'Ile de la Réunion.*

3f

Drouhet Y 'Bibliothèques centrales de prêt. La Réunion' *Bull Biblioth Fr* 1959 4(9) 411-4.
— 'Vingt ans de lecture publique à la Réunion *Bull Biblioth Fr* 1975 20(11) 513-8.
Roda J-C 'Le nouveau bâtiment de la Bibliothèque du Centre Universitaire de la Réunion' *Bull Biblioth Fr* 1976 21(7) 329-35.

WESTERN AFRICA

2a

West African Office. Economic cooperation.

2b

West African Regional Branch of the International Council on Archives (WARBICA). Had its inaugural conference in Dakar in December 1977. English-speaking, French-speaking countries and Guinea-Bissau were represented.

RESADOC, Bamako (Mali). 1979- . African system of regional documentary information for the Sahel. To help development of resources.

N'Diaye G O 'RESADOC — vers la réalisation du premier système international africain d'information documentaire régional' *Documentaliste* 1980 17(2) 54-8.

Aguolu C C 'Library associations in West Africa and the concept of a profession' *Niger Lib* 1975 11(3) 153-61, refs.

— in *Int Lib Rev* 1976 8(1) 23-31. Discusses the possibility of reviving the West African Library Association (WALA) and extending it to include French-speaking West African countries.

2c

Akinyotu A 'A comparative study of education for librarianship in West Africa' *Int Lib Rev* 1976 8(4) 493-513. Includes the Dakar school.

3a

Harrison Church R J *West Africa* 8th ed Longman, 1979.

3e

Evans E J A 'Library legislation in the developing territories of Africa' *Libri* 1968 18(1) 51-78. Includes texts of laws for Ghana and Nigeria and comparison with French-speaking countries, in particular Ivory Coast.

3f

Dunn J ed *West African states: failures and promise* CUP, 1978.

Akinyotu A 'The state of education and library services in West Africa — a brief review' *Int Lib Rev* 1976 8(2) 217-29.

John M 'Libraries in traditional societies' *Sierra Leone Lib J* 1978 4(1) 2-23.

Stutzman M *The role and problems of libraries in developing countries — The West African experience* UCLA, 1978, 117p. (ERIC Report ED-176 744).

Akinyotu A 'Regional cooperation in library services: its potentialities for developing countries with special reference to West Africa' *Nig Lib* 1974 10(2/3) 91-107.

Tarzamon P *The role of international organizations in the development of libraries in West Africa: an assessment of their library technical assistance* Loughborough U, 1979, 119p, refs.

Lalande-Isnard F 'Typology of readers of public libraries in West Africa' *Unesco Bull Lib* 1977, 31(5) 292-7.

Fadiran D 'The role of libraries in the teaching and studying of French in secondary schools in West Africa' *West Afr J Educ* 1975 14(3) 415-22.

— also in *Int Lib Rev* 1976 8(4) 483-91.

Frewar L B 'SCAUL Western Area conference, 4-7 April 1972 at the University of Lagos — Report' *Lib Mater Afr* 1972 10(1) 20-5.

'Standing Conference of African University Libraries, Western area — Third meeting at the University of Ghana, April 1976' *Unesco Bull Lib* 1976 30(5) 296-7. Aims at fostering cooperation between English- and French-speaking West African countries.

Fourth meeting 1978 at Kinshasa Campus of the University of Zaire.

'Conference on documentation in West Africa, Abidjan, 11-17 September 1972' *Unesco Bull Lib* 1973 27(2) 121. Zaire also took part.

Armstrong C Wesley *Role of information resources in national development: a descriptive study and analysis of library resources in West Africa* Pittsburgh U, Graduate School of Library and Information Science, PhD, 1971.

Sheriff G M *Resource sharing in West Africa: some implications for the development of national information policies* ERIC, 1977, 14p. (ERIC Report ED-176 764).

UNISIST Meeting on Regional Information Policy and Planning in West Africa, Accra December 1978.

ENGLISH-SPEAKING WEST AFRICA

1

Evans E J A 'Presidential address (National libraries)' *WALA News* 1960 3(5) 211-8.

University of Ghana. Balme Library.

University of Ibadan. Institute of African Studies. Library.

2b

West African Library Association (WALA). 1954-62. Replaced by national associations. Reactivated with invitation to French-speaking West African countries to take part. See under: Western Africa.

2c

Ibadan University. Department of Library Studies. 1960- .

Peeler E 'Education for librarianship in West Africa' *Nig Lib* 1964 1(2) 61-7.

Dean J 'Ibadan Institute of Librarianship' *SCAUL Newsletter* 1967 (4) 177-8.

Ofori A G T 'The organisation of the library profession in West Africa' in Chaplin A H *The organisation of the library profession* Verlag Dokumentation, 1973, 77-84.

3a

West African directory London, J Skinner, 1965- .

Jacande L K *West Africa annual* Publishing and Distributing Co.

3b

Rydings H A *The bibliographies of West Africa* Ibadan U P, 1961, 36p.

Aguolu C C 'Bibliographic problems in Ghana, Nigeria and Sierra Leone' *Int Lib Rev* 1973 5(2) 199-207.

Keane C *Ghana, Sierra Leone and the Gambia: a basic annotated bibliography for students, librarians and general readers* Commonwealth Institute, 1977, 40p. (Commonwealth bibliographies, 10).

Davies H *Libraries in West Africa 1960-1971: a bibliography* Aberystwyth College of Librarianship, 1972, 14p. (Occasional papers, 1).

3c

WALA *West African Libraries*. 2 issues, 1954. Then:

— *WALA News* 1955 Vol 2- . Superseded by:

Nigerian Libraries 1964- .

3e

Knox-Hooke S A *The law relating to public libraries in West Africa: a comparative study with the UK library laws* London, FLA Thesis, 1966.

Dean J ed Seminar on standards of practice for West African libraries, 15-16 April 1967, University of Ibadan *Proceedings* U of Ibadan, Inst of Librarianship, 1969, 116p. (Occasional papers, 1).

3f

Gilfond H *Gambia, Ghana, Liberia and Sierra Leone* F Watts, 1981.

Thatcher P *West African history* New ed Longman, 1980, 119p. (Revision of Boahen A A *Topics in West African history*, 1974).

Hargreaves J D *The end of colonial rule in West Africa* Barnes and Noble, 1979, 141p.

Harrison K C 'Progress in West Africa' *Lib Ass Rec* 1980 82(1) 19. Ghana, Gambia, Sierra Leone.

Lancour H *Libraries in British West Africa: a report of a survey for the Carnegie Corporation in New York* U of Illinois Lib School, Occasional Papers, 53 1958.

Harris J 'Librarianship in West Africa' *New Zeal Lib* 1960 23(2) 43-51.

Evans E J A 'Library resources in English-speaking West Africa' *Unesco Bull Lib* 1961 15(5) 227-31.

Harris J *Pattern of library growth in English-speaking West Africa* U of Ghana, Dept of Library Studies, 1970, 28p. Mimeo.

Ifidon S E 'Special problems facing African librarians: the West African experience' *Libri* 1974 24(4) 310-8. Problems of book selection tools and of staff.

Kaungamno E E and Llomo C S *Books build nations.* Vol 1: *Library service in West and East Africa* Tanzania Library Service/Trans-Africa Book Distributors, 1979, 169p. Papers of a conference. (Vol 2 see under: Tanzania).

Dean J 'Organisation and services of university libraries in West Africa' in Jackson M M *Comparative and international librarianship* Bingley/Greenwood, 1970, 113-37.

Pretty M M 'The training college library in West Africa' *West Afr J Educ* 1964 3(1) 29-30.

GAMBIA

1

National Library, Banjul (Formerly Bathurst). 1976- . Centre of the National Library Service.

Granheim E 'Nytt sentralbibliotek i Gambia' *Bok Bibliot* 1977 44(3) 173.

2a

Department of Education.

2b

Gambia Library Association, Banjul. 1977- .

3a

Great Britain. Colonial Office *Report on the Gambia* HMSO, to 1964.

The Gambia London, COI, 1965. (Reference pamphlet, 70).

3b

Gamble D P *Bibliography of the Gambia* London, Colonial Office, 1958, 36p.

— *A general bibliography of the Gambia up to 31 December 1977* G K Hall, 1979.

3e

Government Gazette. 1883- .

Walker A *Official publications of Sierra Leone and Gambia* Library of Congress, 1963.

Gambia Library Board Act 1976.

3f

Rice B *Enter Gambia: the birth of an improbable nation* Houghton Mifflin, 1967, 389p.

Gray J *History of Gambia* Frank Cass, 1966.

Five-year Plan for Economic and Social Development, July 1975-June 1980. Libraries are included for the first time.

Flood R A *Library development in the Gambia — report to the British Council* 1970.

N'Jie S P C 'The Gambian library development' *Unesco J* 1980 2(1) 50-4.

GHANA

1

Research Library on African Affairs, Accra. 1961-66 as the Padmore Research Library. Funded by the Ghana Library Board.

University of Ghana. Balme Library. 1948- . Originally at Achimota, as University College of Ghana Library.

Dean J 'The Balme Library, University of Ghana: history, structure and development, 1948-1965' *Nig Lib* 1967 3(2) 79-82.

Kotei S I A 'Development of the Balme Library, University of Ghana' *Lib Mater Afr* 1971 8(3) 177-90.

University of Ghana. Department of Library Studies. 1965- . Previously Ghana Library School.

- Institute of African Studies Library. 1961- .

Council for Scientific and Industrial Research (CSIR). 1958- . Central Reference and Research Library (CRRL), Accra. 1964- .

Ghana Library Board. Accra Central Library, 1956- .

2a

Ghana Library Board, Accra. 1950- . Public libraries.

The Ghana Library Board Silver Jubilee 1950-1975: brochure The Board, 1975, 115p.

2b

Ghana Library Association, Accra. 1962- .

'Ghana Library Association' *Unesco Bull Lib* 1966 23(9) 326.

2c

Benge R C 'The Ghana Library School' *Lib World* 1963 64(752) 221-3.

— 'Library education in Ghana, 1961-1967' *Lib Ass Rec* 1967 69(7) 225-9.

Kotei S I A 'A proposed course for sub-professional personnel in libraries' *Ghana Lib J* 1969 3(1) 24-9.

Nitecki A *Department of Library and Archival Studies: background, courses, examinations, annual reports* U of Ghana Dept of Lib & Archival Studies, 1974, 95p.

3a

Ghana yearbook Accra, Daily Graphic, 1957- .

Ghana: an official handbook Ghana Ministry of Information, 1961- .

Nitecki A comp *Directory of libraries in Ghana* U of Ghana Dept of Lib & Archival Studies, 1974, 62p.

Agyei-Gyane L comp *Directory of special libraries in Ghana* CRSL, 1974, 71p.

3b

Kisiedu C O 'Ghana and the knowledge explosion — the problem of bibliography' *Afr Res & Doc* 1975 (8 & 9) 34-41.

De Heer A N 'A national bibliography for Ghana' *Ghana Lib J* 1969 3(2) 17-25.
Research Library of African Affairs *Ghana: current bibliography* 1967- . Bimonthly.
— *Ghana National Bibliography* 1965- . 1968- .
Cardinall A W *A bibliography of the Gold Coast* Accra, Government Printer, 1932- .
Johnson A F *A bibliography of Ghana, 1930-1961* Longmans, 1964, 210p. (Also published by Ghana Library Board).
— *Books about Ghana: a select reading list* Ghana Library Board, 1961.
Brockensha D and Kotei S I A 'A bibliography of Ghana 1958-1964' *Afr Studies Bull* (Boston) 1967 10(2) 35-79.
Kotei S I A *Select annotated bibliography of Ghana* Ghana Library Board, 1965, mimeo.
Aguolu C C *Bibliography of Ghana in the humanities and social sciences, 1970-71* Scarecrow, 1973.
Pitcher G *Bibliography of Ghana, 1957-59* Kumasi, Nkrumah U, 1960. Periodical articles. These now are included in the national bibliography.
Ghana University Library *List of theses* 1969-?

3c

Ghanaian periodicals and newspapers Research Library on African Affairs, 1969 (Bibliographical series, 6).
Ghana library journal Ghana Library Association, 1963- . Irregular.

3d

Ministry of Information. Central Office of Statistics *Statistical handbook* 1961- .

3e

Witherell J W and Lockwood S B *Ghana: a guide to official publications, 1872-1968* Library of Congress, 1969, 110p.
Ghana Book and Newspapers Registration Act, 1961 (Act 73).

3f

Buah F K *A history of Ghana* Macmillan, 1980, 229p.
Jones T *Ghana's first republic* Methuen, 1976.
Ministry of Economic Planning *Five year development plan 1975/76-1979/80* 3 parts, Accra, 1977.
Johnson A F 'The place of libraries in national economic development, Ghana' *Unesco Lib Bull* 1962 16(5) 247-8.
Evans E J A *A tropical library service: the story of Ghana's libraries* Deutsch, 1964, 174p.
Library World 1963 64(752). Issue devoted to all aspects of librarianship in Ghana.
Amedikey E Y 'Ghana, libraries in' in *Encyclopedia* 10(1973) 1-9.
Nilsson M 'Bibliotek i Ghana' *Biblioteksbladet* 1980 65(4) 65-7.
Ofori-Attah G T 'Library co-operation in Ghana: the public libraries' *Ghana Lib J* 1964 1(3) 60.
De Heer A N 'Rural library service project: draft proposal' *Zambia Lib Ass J* 1977 9(1/2) 1-6.
Otinkorang R A *The problem of mobile library planning, design, construction and development in Anglophone countries with particular reference to Ghana* Loughborough U of Technology, 1980, 95p. (MLS dissertation).
Sackey J U *Children's reading in Ghana* London, FLA Thesis, 1970.

Ofori-Attah G T 'School libraries and children's libraries in Ghana' *WALA News* 1958 3(1) 34-41.

Mensah-Kane J J 'Secondary school and training college libraries in Ghana' *Ghana Lib J* 1964 1(3) 1-5.

Ofosu-Appiah L H 'Libraries in Ghana's schools and training colleges' *Legon Observer* 1970 Feb.

Young R D E 'University library co-operation' *Ghana Lib J* 1964 1(3) 56.

Amadekay E Y 'Current problems of university libraries in Ghana' *Ghana Lib J* 1964 1(2) 36-41.

Azare-Bediako A *Reading habits of students: a survey of students at University College of Cape Coast* London, FLA Thesis, 1967.

Pitcher G 'The University of Science and Technology Library, Kumasi' *Nig Lib* 1967 3(2) 93-6.

Nii-Moi J B *The need for a national library and information service in Ghana* Loughborough U of Technology, 1980, 149p. (MLS dissertation).

Scientific and technical information in Ghana — report of a 'Legon Workshop on the pooling of resources' December 1972 Published 1973.

LIBERIA

1

National Library (Government Public Library), Monrovia. 1959- . Created in 1929 as the Department of Education, Central Library.

University of Liberia Library, Monrovia. 1862- . Deposit library.

Lancour H *The University of Liberia Library: report of a survey* 1960.

Department of Information, Cultural Affairs and Tourism. Liberian Information Service Library, Monrovia. 1947- . Is the reference service for the country. Holds a collection of Africana.

2a

Department of Education.

2b

Liberia Library Association (LLA), Monrovia. 1977- .

3a

Liberian Yearbook. Monrovia, 1956- .

Liberia: basic data and information Monrovia, Liberian Trading and Development Bank, 1968.

3b

Conover H F *Liberia: a selected list of references* Library of Congress, 1942, 13p.

Solomon M D and d'Azevedo W L eds *General bibliography of the Republic of Liberia* Evanston, I11., North-Western U P, 1967.

Holsoe S E *Bibliography of Liberia* U of Delaware, Liberian Studies Association of America, 1971, 2 vols.

3c

University of Liberia Library *Library Newsletter*.

Department of Education *Annual report*, 1959/60- .

3e

Liberian official gazette. Monrovia, 1922- . See Educational laws.

3f

Clapham C S *Liberia and Sierra Leone: an essay in comparative politics* CUP, 1976.

Evans E J A *Liberia: libraries* Unesco 1967, 25p.

Armstrong C W 'Liberia, Libraries in' in *Encyclopedia* 14 (1975) 257-91.

CARE-LIBERIA, National Library extension program: the library as a complement to the Community School Monrovia, 1972, mimeo. Proposal via the Department of Education for school libraries in rural areas.

Angel H E *Liberia: Government archives and records service: the William V S Tubman Library Museum, July-September 1974* Unesco, 1975 38p (3119/RMO-RD/DBA).

Cornell University at the University of Liberia—final report May 28, 1962-July 31, 1968 Cornell U.

NIGERIA

1

National Library of Nigeria, Lagos. 1962- .

Adeyemi N M 'National Library of Nigeria and Library development in Nigeria' *Libri* 1972 22(1) 77-84.

University of Ibadan Library. 1948- . (Institute of Library Studies, 1960-). Deposit for UN and OAU publications; collection of Africana.

Harris J *Ibadan University Library: some notes on its birth and growth* Ibadan U P, 1968, 60p.

University of Nigeria Libraries, Nsukka. 1960- . The University has an Institute of African Studies.

Afigbo A E 'The Institute of African Studies, University of Nigeria, Nsukka 1963-1971: a brief survey' *Ikorok* 1971 1(1) 3-9.

State Central Library, Enugu. 1956- . Deposit library; Nigerian collection.

National Scientific and Technological Development Agency. Library and Documentation Centre, Ibadan. 1973- .

2a

National Library Board. 1964- . With Library Boards in the various states of the Federation.

Nigeria Educational Research Council, Lagos. 1965- .

2b

Nigerian Library Association, Ilorin. 1962- . 1954-62 as West African Library Association (WALA), Nigerian Branch.

Oderinde N O 'Our professional association, 1948-1968' *Nig Lib* 1970 6(1/2) 65-100.

OBIDS 'Nigerian Library Assoociation' in *Encyclopedia* 20 (1977) 50-68.

Nigerian Association of Agricultural Librarians (NAALD). 1976- .

2c

Akinyotu A 'Training and education of library personnel in Nigeria: a historical survey' *West Afr J Educ* 1971 15(3) 195-200.

— 'Training and education of library personnel in Nigeria: comments and proposals on its objectives and content' *Nig Lib* 1972 8(2) 103-16.

'Report on the colloquium on education and training for librarianship in Nigeria held at the Conference Centre, University of Ibadan, 15-19 March 1974' *Nig Lib* 1975 11(1/2) 139-49.

Obi D S 'Education for librarianship in Nigeria' *Nig Lib* 1975 11(3) 221-51.

Ajia S A *Library education in Nigeria: a study of factors that influenced its development* Loughborough U of Technology, 1977, 154p.

Ogunsheye F A 'Formal program development in library education in Nigeria' *J Educ Libp* 1978 19(2) 140-50. Ibadan U Library School and Amhadu Bello U, Dept of Library Science.

Nzotta B C 'Postgraduate librarianship class of 1977 at Ibadan' *Int Lib Rev* 1979 11 113-24.
'Proceedings of the 1979 Teacher/Librarian's Refresher Course, April 1979 at State Central Library, Enugu' *Anambra/Imo State School Bull* 1979 8(2/3) 1-96, refs. Whole issue.
Onadiran G T 'Research in education for librarians in a developing nation, the Nigeria experience' *Pakistan Lib Bull* 1978 9(3/4) 1-8.
Oyemakinde A 'Nigerian librarians and the search for professional recognition' *Bendel Lib J* 1979 2(1) 26-7, refs.
Fadiran D 'Changing career patterns of professional librarians in Nigeria, 1950-80' *Int Lib Rev* 1979 11 105-12.

3a

Nigeria Yearbook Lagos, Daily Times, 1960- .
Nigeria Handbook Federal Ministry of Information Nigeria, 1953- .
Decalo S *Historical dictionary of Nigeria* Scarecrow P, 1979 (African Hist Dict 20).
NLN *Libraries in Nigeria: a directory* 1st edition for 1967-68 published in 1970. Regular revisions.

3b

Ogunsheye F A 'Problem of bibliographical services in Nigeria' *Nig Lib* 1969 5 62-8.
Shoyinka P H 'Bibliographic control in Nigeria' *Libri* 1978 28(4) 294-308, refs.
— 'Bibliographic control in Nigeria. Paper presented at the ALA Annual Conference 1978' *College and Res Lib* 1979 40 7-25.
NLN *A bibliography of biographies and memoirs on Nigeria* 1968.
National bibliography of Nigeria NLN, 1973- . Monthly. Includes all forms of publications. Supersedes:
Ibadan University Library *Nigerian publications: current national bibliography* 1950 352-1972.
National Library of Nigeria: a guide to the collection NLN, 1970.
NLN *Nigerian books in print* 1967- .
Harris J *Books about Nigeria: a select reading list* U of Ibadan P, 1959; 5th ed 1969, 83p.
Ibadan University Library *Bibliographical series*.
NLN *Theses and dissertations accepted for higher degrees in Nigerian Universities* 1966/67 (1969)- .
— *Index to selected Nigerian periodicals* 1965.
Belleh G S 'Medical librarianship in Nigeria: a review of the literature and some comments on some problems and prospects' *Med Lib Ass Bull* 1975 62 199-207.

3c

University of Ibadan Library *Nigerian periodicals and newspapers* 1950-1970, (latest edition), 1971. Includes supplements to the national bibliography since 1956.
National Library *Serials in print in Nigeria* 1967- .
— *Publications*. Monographs: bibliographies, directories, etc.
Newsletter, Nigeria London, International Communications, 1978 no 1- .
Nigerian Library Association *Nigerian libraries* 1964- . 3 a year. Supersedes *WALA News* for Nigeria.
NLN *Nigerbiblios* 1976- . Quarterly.

Bendel State Library Board *Bendel library journal* 1978- . Biannual.
— *Newsletter* 1977- .
NLA Lagos Division *Lagos librarian* 2 (1967)- . Vol. 1 1965/66 as *Information bulletin*.
University of Ibadan *Library record* 1949- .
- Institute of Librarianship *Occasional papers* 1969- .

3d

Nwoye S C 'Essence of library statistics' *Nigerbiblios* 1976 1(2) 17-8.

3e

Conover H F *Nigerian official publications: a guide* Library of Congress, 1959. Revised by:
Lockwood S B *Nigeria, a guide to official publications [1861-1965]* Library of Congress, 1966, 166p.
Federal Republic of Nigeria *Official Gazette*.
Olukemi Toye B 'Legal deposit in a Nigerian university library: its role in the field of Nigerian studies [1973-1978]' *Bendel Lib J* 1979 2(1) 12-8, refs.
Olaitan M O 'Publication laws in Nigeria, 1950-1971' *Nig Lib* 8(1) 35-44.
Agidee D 'Legal provisions for library development in Nigeria, 1948-1968' *Nig Lib* 1970 6(1/2) 53-63.
Nigeria 'National library decree' (No 29 of 1970) *Official Gazette, Suppl* May 14 1970 57(27) Part A.

3f

Ayandele E A *Nigerian historical studies* F. Cass, 1979, 305p.
Arikpo O *The development of modern Nigeria* Penguin, 1967.
Kirk-Greene A and Rimmer D *Nigeria since 1970* Hodder & Stoughton, 1981, 160p.
Fasurgi T A *Cultural policy in Nigeria* Unesco, 1973, 63p.
Anamaleze J *The Nigerian press: the people's conscience?* NY, Vantage P, 1979, 142p.
Oyeoku K K 'Publishing in developing countries: a programme for research based on the Nigerian situation' *Unesco Bull Lib* 1972 26(3) 150-4.
Dodson D and Dodson B 'Publishing progress in Nigeria' *Scholarly Publ* 4 Oct 1972 51-60.
Oduyoye M 'Nigerian books in Nigerian libraries: the responsibilities of librarians and publishers in developing authorship and promoting readership' *Nig Lib* 1974 10(2 & 3) 155-7.
Ali Z S 'Acquisition through legal deposit — National Library experience' *Nigerbiblios* 1976 1(2) 11-12, 16.
USAID A book development project in Nigeria 1964-68. *Final report* to the Ford Foundation Franklin Book Programs.
Nwafor B U 'The bookshops of Enugu — a Third World town' *Biblos* (Austria) 1975 24(2) 142-7.
Unoh S O 'The relationship between reading ability and experimental background in reading' *Nig Lib* 1975 11(1 & 2) 101-10.
Fafunwa A B *History of education in Nigeria* Allen & Unwin, 1974.
Ekpe F C 'Colonial situation and library development in Nigeria' *Int Lib Rev* 1979 11 5-18.
Omolewa M 'Adult readers in Nigerian libraries, 1932-1960: a study of library use in colonial Nigeria' *Nig Lib* 1974 10(1) 29-40.

Adegoke A 'The evolution of libraries in Nigeria' *Int Lib Rev* 1973 5(4) 407-52. Bibl, 447-52.

'Twenty years of library development' Nigerian Library Association Conference 1970 in *Nig Lib* 1970 6(1/2).

Oderinde N O 'Nigerian libraries in post-war reconstruction' *Lagos Libn* 1968 3(4) 9-20.

Enu C E 'The Nigerian civil war and its effects on the library services in the war-ravaged former Eastern Region of Nigeria' *Libri* 1970 20(3) 206-17.

Bowden R 'The recovery: Nigerian library developments 1970-1973' *J Libp* 1974 6(3) 179-202.

Oderinde N O 'A decade of progress' *Nigerbiblios* 1976 1(1) 5-7.

Ifidon S E 'New developments in the Nigerian library scene' *J Libp* 1978 10 201-11.

Aguolu C C 'Foundation of modern libraries in Nigeria' *Int Lib Rev* 1977 9 461-83.

Aina L O 'Factors affecting development of librarianship in Nigeria' *Int Lib Rev* 1979 11 57-67.

Mould R A 'The development of libraries in Northern Nigeria' *Lib Mater Africa* 1972 10(3) 179-83.

Uba D E 'Library co-ooperation in Nigeria' *Nig Lib* 1975 11 213-20.

Abimbola S O 'Management by objectives (MBO): its application to libraries' *Nigerbiblios* 1979 4(1) 8-9, 11-3.

Nwoye S C 'Nigeria, libraries in' in *Encyclopedia* 20(1977) 1-49, bibl.

'Nigerian studies' *Int Lib Rev* 1975 7(1) 39-113. Whole section.

Chandler R G ed [Nigerian librarianship] *Int Lib Rev* 1979 11(1) Whole issue.

Ogundipe O O *Aspects of Nigerian librarianship: talks and essays by the President of Nigerian Library Association for the period January 1978 to December 1979* U of Benin Library, 1979, 48p.

See also the Conferences of the Nigeria Library Association on specific themes:
- Libraries in the new national structure (Jos 1971).
- Service concept of libraries (Enugu, 1972).
- Toward scientific management in Nigerian libraries (Benin, 1974).
- Libraries in the cultural development of a nation (Kano, 1975) etc.

Oyedeji L 'Public library service and adult learning in metropolitan Lagos' *Nig Lib* 1975 11 159-68.

Tugbiyele E A 'Libraries and adult education' *COMLA Newsletter* 1979 (23/24) 19, 21.

Bonny H V 'Nigeria: pilot project on school libraries in Africa' *Unesco Bull Lib* 1966 20(2) 71-7.

Green L E *Report on visit to Nigeria school libraries 1968* Unesco, 1969.

Ita N O 'Educational planning and school library development in Nigeria' *Libri* 1969 19(4) 237-45, bibl.

Oni-Orisan B A 'Education, school libraries and Nigeria's Development Plan 1970-74' *Nig Lib* 1972 8(1) 21-7.

Olanlokun S O 'Education and libraries in Nigerian schools: a review' *Int Lib Rev* 1976 8(4) 477-82.

Izevbekhai Y A 'The Midwest Book Depot: a new dimension in library service in Nigeria [Benin region]' *Unesco Bull Lib* 1975 29(4) 188-91.

Agunwa C O 'The organisation of library services for primary schools in Anambra State' *Anambra/Imo States School Lib Ass Bull* 1979 8(2/3) 58-64.

Akomas C 'Children's library services in Nigeria' *NLA Newsletter* 1977 (61 & 62) 4-8.

Ogunsheye F A 'Abadina media resource centre (AMRC): a case study in library service to primary schools' *Unesco J* 1979 1(1) 29-36.

Kanu E N 'Role of the library in developing creativity' *Anambra/Imo States School Lib Ass Bull* 1979 8(4) 24-7.

Dike V W 'The school library and modern education' *Anambra/Imo States School Lib Ass Bull* 1979 8(2/3) 76-83, refs.

Atinmo M 'Public and school library services to the physically handicapped in Nigeria: an evaluation' *Int Lib Rev* 1979 11(4) 441-9.

'Papers at a workshop on Teacher Training College Libraries, March 1968, Ibadan' *Nig Lib* 1969 5(3) (Whole issue).

Nigerian Libraries 1967 3(2). Whole issue on university libraries.

Enu C E 'Problems of Nigerian university libraries' *Unesco Bull Lib* 1973 27(2) 84-91, 125.

Ratcliffe F W 'Western ways and Nigerian means: university librarianship in Nigeria' *Afr Res & Doc* 1975 (8 & 9) 29-34.

Ifidon S E 'Objectives of African university libraries: the Nigerian experience' *Int Lib Rev* 1978 10(1) 43-50.

Edoka B E *Circulation functions and staffing patterns in Nigerian university libraries* Loughborough U of Technology, 1979, 95p, refs.

Petrie C M 'Special libraries' *Nig Lib* 1966 2(2) 61-6.

Osundina O 'Elements of special librarianship' *Bendel Lib J* 1979 2(1) 20, 21-4.

Winjobi S A *Management problems of government special libraries in developing countries with particular reference to agricultural libraries in Nigeria* Loughborough U of Technology, 1979, 187p. refs.

Oguara E T A 'Special libraries in Nigeria: situation and outlook in development' *Nig Lib* 1975 11(3) 185-212.

Okwuowulu A O 'Role of libraries in the health service in Nigeria' *Int Lib Rev* 1979 11 163-74.

Belleh G S 'Hospital libraries in Nigeria' *Spec Lib* 1977 68(3) 122-6.

Hague H 'Further news from a Nigerian medical library' *Lib Ass Med Section Bull* 1976: Part I: (105) 5-7; Part II: (106) 4-5.

Adimora E N O 'Agricultural librarianship, documentation and information science in Nigeria' *Int Lib Rev* 1977 9 413-28.

Ogbeide N A 'Law librarianship in Nigeria: history development and problems' *Int J Law Lib* 1976 4(1) 19-26.

Olaitan M O 'Law librarianship in Nigeria, history and problems: a rejoinder' *Int J Law Lib* 1976 4(3) 202-5.

Onyechi N I C *Use of library and information resources by social science researchers in Nigeria: a pilot survey* Loughborough U of Technology, 1979, 127p.

Belleh G S 'Towards a national biomedical information network for Nigeria' *Int Lib Rev* 1978 10 179-85.

Ogunsheye F A *Nigerian library resources in science and technology* U of Ibadan, Institute of Librarianship, 1970, 44p. (Occasional papers, 2).

Odeinde T O 'Documentation and information services for science and technology in Nigeria' *Nig Lib* 1972 8(1) 1-13.

— 'Scientific and technological information needs and services' *Nig Lib* Apr/Aug 1975 11 1-10.

Oyemakinde A 'Automation at Ibadan University Library' *Program* 1979 13(3) 143-6.

SIERRA LEONE

1

Sierra Leone Library Board, Freetown. 1959- . Deposit library, exchange centre.
Fourah Bay College Library, Freetown.
- United Nations Library. 1973- .
- Documentation Centre. 1977- . Sierra Leone collection, U N collection.

2a

Ministry of Education. Library Board.

2b

Sierra Leone Library Association (SLLA), Freetown. 1969- .
Sierra Leone School Library Association. 1975- .

2c

Ogundipe O O 'Education for librarianship in Sierra Leone. I: The need' *Sierra Leone Lib J* 1974 1(1) 18-27. Also in: *Unesco Bull Lib* 1975 29(3) 151-7.

3a

Sierra Leone Yearbook Freetown.
SLLA *Directory of libraries and information services* 2nd ed SLLA, 1976. (First edition: 1971).

3b

Luke H C *Bibliography of Sierra Leone* OUP, 1925.
Zell H M *A bibliography of non-periodical literature on Sierra Leone, 1925-1966* Fourah Bay College Bookshop, 1966, 44p.
Williams G J *A bibliography of Sierra Leone, 1925-1967* Africana Pub Co/Meier & Holmes, 1971, 209p.
Fourah Bay College Library *Current bibliography of Sierra Leone* 1967/68- .
Sierra Leone Library Board *Sierra Leone publications: a list of books and pamphlets in English received by the Sierra Leone Library Board under the Publications Amendment Act, 1962* 1962/3. Government Printer, 1964- .
Catalog of the Sierra Leone collection, Fourah Bay College Library, University of Sierra Leone G K Hall, 1979, 411p.
Thompson J S T *Library development, bibliographical control, archives and book development in Sierra Leone: a list of references* U of Sierra Leone, 1978, 55p. First part: Synopsis; second part: Bibliography.

3c

SLLA *The Sierra Leone Library Journal*. 1974- .
Library Board. Children's Library *Read*.

3e

Walker A *Official publications of Sierra Leone and Gambia* Library of Congress, 1963.

Sierra Leone Library Board Ordinance: 1959- . Board took over the British Council libraries; the Central Library of the Board became one of the deposit libraries.

'Legal deposit of books' *Herald Lib Sci* 1971 10 411.

3f

Fyfe C M *The history of Sierra Leone: a concise introduction* Evans, 1981, 150p.

— *A short history of Sierra Leone* New ed Longman, 1979, 179p.

Clapham C S *Liberia and Sierra Leone: an essay in comparative politics* CUP, 1976.

One hundred years of university education in Sierra Leone Freetown Celebration Committee, 1976.

Strickland J T 'Library development in Sierra Leone' *Lib World* 1962 64(745) 3-9.

Thompson J S T 'Library development in Sierra Leone — report on the SCOLMA Seminar, 18 February 1969' *Lib Materials Afr* 1969 6(3) 91-4.

Lalande-Isnard F 'Les bibliothèques de Sierra Leone' *Afr Contemp* 1969 8(9/12).

Jusu-Sheriff G M 'Sierra Leone, libraries in' in *Encyclopedia* 27 (1979) 336-402. Includes statistics on individual libraries.

Sierra Leone Library Board 'The mobile library service in Sierra Leone' *Sierra Leone Lib J* 1977 3(1) 11-4.

FRENCH-SPEAKING WEST AFRICA

See also: French-speaking Africa, Western Africa.

1

Institut Fondamental d'Afrique Noire (IFAN). Main library in Dakar. Now part of the library of Dakar University. Deposit library for West Africa.

2c

Dakar University. Ecole de Bibliothécaires, Archivistes et Documentalistes. See details under French-speaking Africa.

3a

Annuaires des Républiques de l'Ouest Africain Dakar, Agence Havas Afrique, 1960- .

Dakar University. Centre d'Etudes des Sciences et Technique de l'Information *Les moyens d'information en Afrique de l'Ouest.*

3b

Joucla E *Bibliographie de l'AOF* Paris, Editions Géographiques . . ., 1937, 705p.

Brasseur P *Bibliographie générale du Mali* IFAN, 1964, 462p. (The Mali Federation in existence at the time included the French Soudan, the Niger and Haut Sénégal).

Dadzié E W 'Les services bibliographiques en Afrique tropicale de langue française et particulièrement au Sénégal' in Pearson J and Jones R *The bibliography of Africa*, 1970. See under Africa, 3b.

Witherell J W *French-speaking West Africa: a guide to official publications* Library of Congress, 1967, 201p.

3d

Service de la Statistique Générale de l'AOF *Bulletin statistique et économique mensuel* Dakar, 1949-59.

3e

Journal officiel de l'AOF Rufisque, 1905-59.

3f

Foltz W J 'From West Africa to the Mali Federation' *Yale Studies Polit Sci* 1966 12 214p.

Poncelet M '60 ans d'expériences fédérales en Afrique de l'Ouest francophone' *Canad J Afr Studies* 1967 (2) 85-109.

Lavergne de Tessan M de 'Inventaire linguistique de l'Afrique Occidentale Française et du Togo' *IFAN Memoires* 1963 (30) 241p.

Charpi G 'Les archives de l'AOF' *ABCD* Nov/Dec 1953 (12) 317-22.

Johnson G W 'The archival system of former French West Africa' *Afr Studies Bull* 1965 8(1) 48-58.

Monod T 'Bibliothèques africaines' *Notes Afr* 1948 (39) 18-9.

Hahn A 'L'oeuvre éducative, les bibliothèques et la lecture publique en AOF' *Bull Biblioth Fr* 1956 1(4) 499-514.

Froment-Guieysse G 'L'essor des centres culturels en AOF' in *Encyclopédie mensuelle d'Outre-mer* 1956 (71/72) 329-52.

Chauveinc M 'Situation et rôle d'une bibliothèque médicale en Afrique d'expression française' *Bull Biblioth Fr* 1967 12(11) 371-410.

BENIN

1

Bibliothèque Nationale, Porto Novo. 1975- . Previously library of the Institut de Recherches Appliquées, 1961- . See below.

Roberts K H *Bibliothèque Nationale, Bénin: rapport d'une mission . . . juillet 1976* Unesco, 1976 (CC/DBA.14).

Centre National de la Recherche Scientifique et Technique, Porto Novo. 1961- . Created in 1943 as an IFAN centre; 1961- as Institut de Recherches Appliquées (IRAD). Houses the national library but has its own library as well, and a documentation centre which keeps an index of documents concerning the Benin.

Université Nationale du Bénin. Bibliothèque Universitaire, Cotonou. 1970- . The university was the Institut d'Enseignement Supérieur, 1962-70.

2a

Ministère de la Jeunesse, de la Culture Populaire et des Sports. Service Central des Bibliothèques.

2b

National Association of Archivists, Librarians, Documentalists, Booksellers, Museologists and Museographers of Benin, Porto Novo.

3b

Da Silva G *Contributions à la bibliographie du Dahomey* Retrospective bibliography to 1959 which appeared in the *Etudes Dahoméennes* 1963.

3c

CNRST *Etudes Dahoméennes* 1948- . New series 1963-69.

3d

Institut National de la Statistique et de l'Analyse Economique.

3e

Journal officiel.

3f

Herskovits M J *Dahomey: an ancient West African kingdom* New York, J J Augustin, 1938.

Nzongola G *Essai sur le Dahomey* Brussels, CEDAF, 1971, 41p. (Cahiers du CEDAF, 5).

Marshall M R 'Dahomey, libraries in' in *Encyclopedia* 6 (1971) 404-6.

— 'Libraries in Dahomey' *Lib World* 1971 72(847) 208-12.

GUINEA

1

Bibliothèque Nationale, Conakry. 1960- . Deposit library.
Archives Nationales, Conakry. 1960- .
Institut National de Recherche et de Documentation de Guinée, (INRDG), Conakry. 1958- . Previously IFAN Centre.

2a

Secrétariat d'Etat à la Recherche Scientifique. Supervises all three bodies in one.

3b

Recherches africaines published by INRDG since 1959 has a bibliographic supplement. 1958-63 bibliography was published in 1964 (1).

3c

INRDG *Recherches Africaines* 1959- . Previously *Etudes guinéennes.*

3e

Journal officiel de la République de Guinée, Conakri. 1958- . Previously (1901-1958) *Bulletin officiel de la Guinée française* and *Journal officiel de la Guinée française.*

3f

Suret-Canale J *La République de Guinée* Paris, Editions Sociales, 1970, 423p.
Soriba Camara S *La Guinée sans la France* Presses de la Fondation Nationale des Sciences Politiques, 1977.
La Guinée d'aujourd'hui Europe d'Outremer, 1979.

IVORY COAST

1

Bibliothèque Nationale, Abidjan. 1968- . Deposit library; originally IFAN documentation centre. Has a documentation centre, deposit for classified official documents, and a bibliographical department. Its Office National d'Echange de Publications deals with domestic and international exchanges (See *Unesco Bull Lib* 1975 29(1) 105). Both set up in 1974.

Archives Nationales, Abidjan. 1913- . Deposit library. Complements the national library.

Delmas B *Côte d'Ivoire, Archives Nationales: réorganisation et développement* Unesco, 1973 (2285/RMO.RD/DBA). Second report: Unesco, 1974 (3070/RMO.RD/DBA). 22 and 21 pages.

Orleans J d' *Côte d'Ivoire, réorganisation et développement des archives* Unesco 1973 (2608/RMO.RD/DBA).

Université d'Abidjan. Bibliothèque Centrale. 1963- .

Bibliothèque Centrale de Lecture Publique de la Côte d'Ivoire, Abidjan. 1963- .

Office de la Recherche Scientifique et Technique Outre Mer (ORSTOM). Two centres 1946- and 1969- . Special bibliographies.

2a

Ministère de l'Education Nationale. Direction des Affaires Culturelles. Service des Bibliothèques et Publications. 1967- . Responsible for the national and the central public libraries and for school libraries.

2b

Association pour le Développement de la Documentation, des Bibliothèques et Archives de la Côte d'Ivoire (ABACI), Abidjan. 1972- .

3b

Bibliothèque Nationale *Bibliographie nationale courante pour les livres, brochures, périodiques et publications officielles parus en Côte d'Ivoire* 1969- .

Centre d'Etude d'Afrique Noire (Bordeaux) *Documentation Africaine I: République de la Côte d'Ivoire. Liste arrêtée au 1er novembre 1968: livres, journaux et autres documents disponibles au CEAN*, 9p.

Janvier G *Bibliographie rétrospective de la Côte d'Ivoire*, I: *Sciences de la vie*; II: *Sciences de l'homme*, 1972-74 in Annales de l'Université d'Abidjan, Special publication. (Vol III: *Sciences physiques et de la Terre*) (Published?).

3c

'Periodicals published in Africa. Ivory Coast' *Lib Mater Afr* 1965 3(1) Suppl, 4p.

National Archives *Warbica*.

3d

Direction de la Statistique *Bulletin mensuel de statistiques* 1950- .

3e

Journal officiel de la Côte d'Ivoire, 1895-1958.

Journal officiel de la République de Côte d'Ivoire. 1958- .

Legal deposit laws (1962 and 1969). See in *Le contrôle bibliographique* IFLA (IFLA Publ, 3) 133-7.

'Law on documentation in Ivory Coast' *Unesco Bull Lib* 1975 29 105.

3f

Glardon M *Structure d'animation culturelle en Côte d'Ivoire*. I *Inventaire critique des organisations et agents culturels en milieu rural et semi-urbain*. II *La vie socio-culturelle dans les centres semi-urbains* Paris, Culture et Développement, 1969, 168p.

Liguer-Laubhouet K-L 'Ivory Coast, libraries in' in *Encyclopedia* 13 (1975) 160-5.

Delrieu S *Côte d'Ivoire: bibliothèque pilote en Côte d'Ivoire* Unesco, 1966, 19p.

— 'La bibliothèque de l'Université d'Abidjan' *SCAUL Newsletter* 1971 (6) 9-12.

See also in Western Africa, 3e; in General, 3f: Penna C V *The planning of library and documentation services*.

MALI

1

Bibliothèque Nationale, Bamako. 1913- .

Archives Nationales du Mali, Bamako. 1913- . Both under the responsibility of the Institut des Sciences Humaines. See below.

Bekeny I *Mali, réorganisation des Archives, novembre-décembre 1969* Unesco, 1970, 17p (2231/BMS.RD/DBA).

2a

Ministère de l'Enseignement Supérieur et Secondaire et de la Recherche Scientifique. Inspection des Archives, des Musées et des Bibliothèques, Bamako.

— Institut des Sciences Humaines, Bamako. Created in 1944 as an IFAN centre.

Ministère des Arts et Culture.

2b

Association du Mali des Bibliothécaires, Archivistes et Documentalistes (AMBAD). 1978- .

3b

Brasseur P 'Les difficultés recontrées dans l'établissement d'une bibliographie de type national: l'exemple du Mali' in Pearson J D and Jones R *The bibliography of Africa* 103-12. See under Africa, 3b.

— *Bibliographie générale du Mali (anciens Soudan français et Haut-Sénégal-Niger)* Dakar, IFAN, 1964, 462p. To 1960. 1960-65 to follow (not traced).

'Mali: a bibliographical introduction' *Afr Studies Bull* 1966 9(3) 74-87.

Imperato P J and E M *Mali: a handbook of historical statistics* G K Hall, 1981.

3e

Journal officiel de la République du Mali 1959- . Previously: *Journal officiel du Soudan français.*

3f

'Mali: literacy and economic development' *Unesco Chronicle* 1966 12(3) 104-5.

MAURITANIA

1

Bibliothèque Nationale, Nouakchott. 1965- . Originally created in 1939 as the library of the Centre d'Etudes Mauritaniennes, became in 1943 the Section Mauritanienne of the IFAN Centre in St Louis (Senegal). Transferred to Nouakchott. (See 3f.) Deposit.

Archives Nationales, Nouakchott. Main centre, with other more specialized centres. Legal deposit.

2a

Présidence de la République. Secrétariat Général.

2b

Association Mauritanienne des Bibliothécaires, des Archivistes et des Documentalistes (AMBAD), Nouakchott. 1979- . Up to 1979: Section Mauritanienne de l'AIDDBA.

3a

Gerteiney A G *Historical dictionary of Mauritania* Scarecrow, 1981, 98p. (African Historical Dictionaries, 31).

3b

Toupet C 'Orientation bibliographique sur la Mauritanie' *IFAN Bull* 1959 (1/2) 201-39; 1962 (3/4) 594-613.

Bibliothèque Nationale *Liste mensuelle des nouvelles acquisitions* 1973- . From 1974 printed publication in three quarterly sections: National and official printed works; Foreign books; National and foreign periodicals.

3d

Direction de la Statistique *Bulletin statistique et economique* 1964- .

— *Annuaire statistique* 1969- .

3e

Journal officiel de la République Islamique de Mauritanie, St Louis then Nouakchott. 1959- .

Legal deposit: Loi 63.109 amended by Loi 65.047.

3f

Chartrand P *La Mauritanie en mutation, par les élèves du cycle A sous la direction de P Chartrand* Nouakchott, ENA (College of Administrative Studies), 1976, 187p.

Ould Hamidoun M and Leriche A 'Curiosités et bibliothèques de Chinguetti' *Notes Afr* 1950 109-12.

Gut C *Projet de réorganisation des Archives Nationales, février/mars 1976.*

Heymowski A *Mauritanie: organisation de la Bibliothèque Nationale de Mauritanie, Nouakchott, septembre 1964-février 1965* Unesco, 1965 (WS/0765.94-CUA).

— *Mauritanie: organisation de la Bibliothèque Nationale* [Second Mission.] Unesco, 1972 (2644/RMO.RD/DBA).

'Organising the National Library of Mauritania in Nouakchott' *Unesco Bull Lib* 1966 20(2) 98-9. These publications review the general library situation in the country.

See also some references under Middle East.

NIGER

1

Archives Nationales, Niamey. 1913- .

Université de Niamey. Bibliothèque universitaire. 1973- .

- Institut de Recherches en Sciences Humaines (IRSH). Attached to the university in 1973. Previously: Centre IFAN, 1944, then Centre Nigérien de Recherches en Sciences Humaines (CNRSH), 1964.

ORSTOM. Mission à Niamey. 1961- .

2a

Ministère de l'Education Nationale, de la Jeunesse et des Sports.

3c

IRSH *Etudes nigériennes*.

3d

Service de la Statistique *Bulletin trimestriel de la statistique* 1959- .

3e

Ministère des Finances *Journal officiel de la République du Niger* 1958/59- . 1938-58 as *Journal officiel du Niger*.

3f

Donaint P and Lancrenon F *Le Niger* Paris, PUF, 1972, 128p.

SENEGAL

1

Archives Nationales, Dakar. Legal deposit.

Université de Dakar. Bibliothèque Universitaire. 1952- .

- Centre d'Etudes des Sciences et Techniques de l'Information (CESTI). Library created in 1967.

- Institut Fondamental d'Afrique Noire (IFAN). 1936-59 as Institut Français d'Afrique Noire.

Centre de Recherche et de Documentation du Sénégal (CRDS), St Louis. 1962- . Previously Centre IFAN.

2a

Ministère de l'Education Nationale.

Ministère de l'Enseignment Supérieur.

2b

Association Nationale des Bibliothécaires, Archivistes et Documentalistes Sénégalais, Dakar. 1973- . Previously: Section Sénégalaise of AIDBA.

Association Sénégalaise pour le Développement de la Documentation, des Bibliothèques, des Archives et des Musées, Dakar. Has its Commission des Bibliothèques.

2c

Université de Dakar. Ecole des Bibliothécaires, Archivistes et Documentalistes (EBAD), Dakar. 1967- . Previously, 1962-67 as: Centre Régional de Formation des Bibliothécaires des Pays d'Afrique d'Expression Française (CRBF). Serves the other French-speaking African countries.

Bousso A 'University of Dakar School for Librarians, Archivists and Documentalists' *Unesco Bull Lib* 1973 27(2) 77-83, 107. As they are broader in their scope the other references to this school will be entered under French-speaking Africa, 2c.

3a

Colvin L G *Historical dictionary of Senegal* Scarecrow, 1981, 339p. (African Historical Dictionaries, 23).

CESTI *Les moyens d'information au Sénégal.*

3b

Archives Nationales *Bibliographie du Sénégal* 1972 (No 40) - . Supersedes:

— *Liste des ouvrages reçus et revues dépouillées au cours du mois de . . .* 1962-72. And:

— *Bulletin bibliographique des Archives du Sénégal* 1964- (1-39).

Porges L *Bibliographie des régions du Sénégal* (Origins to 1973) 2 vols Archives Nationales du Sénégal, Vol. 1; Mouton, Vol 2. Supersedes an earlier and shorter bibliography:

— *Elements de bibliographie sénégalaise, 1959-63* Archives Nationales, 1964, 141p. Mimeo.

See also the lists of acquisitions and the catalogues of the main libraries cited under 1.

3c

CRDS *Cahiers d'études sénégalaises*. These contains occasional bibliographies.

IFAN *Notes africaines*. 1949- .

— *Mémoires*, and *Bulletin*.

3d

Service de la Statistique *Bulletin statistique*.

3e

Journal officiel de la République du Sénégal.

Legal deposit: see texts in *IFLA Publications*, 3 156-62.

3f

O'Brien R C *White society in black Africa: the French of Senegal* Faber, 1972, 320p.

Monteil V 'Esquisses sénégalaises' *Initiations et Etudes Africaines* (IFAN) 1966 (21).

Gassama A and Kane F B *L'imprimé dans la société sénégalaise de tradition orale* ENSB Thesis, 1976, 30p.

Willemin S *Sénégal: développement des bibliothèques, octobre 1964-juin 1966* Unesco, 1966, 11p.

Bousso A 'Les bibliothèques du Sénégal' *Le Soleil* nd, (566), Suppl.

N'Diaye K *Les bibliothèques au Sénégal* ENSB Thesis, 1976, 37+10p.

Maack M N *Libraries in Senegal: continuity and change in an emerging nation* ALA, 1981, 280p. Originally: Thesis, Columbia U.

Hirsch-Pécaut C 'Une bibliothèque d'Afrique Noire: St Louis du Sénégal' *Ass Biblioth Fr Bull* June 1958 75-8.

N'Diaye K 'Misère des bibliothèques sénégalaises ou le paradoxe de l'école sénégalaise' *BLIBLAD* 1976 (1) 4- .

Melching M 'Meeting children on their own terms in Senegal' *Wilson Lib Bull* 1979 54(2) 109-11. Criticizes the large share of French material.

Ndoye A *Rôle des centres culturels étrangers au Sénégal* ENSB, 1977, 60p. Librarianship thesis.

Chauveinc M 'Situation et rôle d'une bibliothèque médicale en Afrique d'expression française' *Bull Biblioth Fr* 1967 12(11) 371-410.

Sénégal — Centre national de documentation scientifique et technique. Résultats et recommendations du projet Unesco, 1979, 48p.

TOGO

1

Bibliothèque Nationale, Lomé. 1937- as Service de la Documentation Générale; 1945 attached to IFAN centre; 1960: Institut Togolais des Sciences Humaines (INTSHU-BN).

Kiakoutassim E T *La direction de la Bibliothèque Nationale du Togo* Lyons, ENSB, 1977, 63p. Thesis.

University du Bénin. Bibliothèque Universitaire, Lomé. 1965-70 as Centre d'Enseignement Supérieur, Bibliothèque. (Not to be confused with the Université Nationale du Bénin, Abomey, Bénin). Institut National de la Recherche Scientifique, Lomé. 1965- .

2a

Ministère de l'Education Nationale. National and University libraries.

Ministère de la Jeunesse, des Sports, de la Culture et de la Recherche Scientifique. Direction des Affaires Culturelles. Service des Bibliothèques. For public libraries.

2b

Association Togolaise pour le Développement de la Documentation, des Bibliothèques, Archives et Musées, Lomé. 1959- . Originally Section Togolaise de l'Association Internationale pour le Développement des Bibliothèques en Afrique.

3b

Othily A *Eléments de bibliographie du Togo* Office de la Recherche Scientifique et Technique Outre-Mer (ORSTOM), 1968.

Santraille M and Noël O *Contribution à la bibliographie du Togo* ORSTOM, 1972.

Bibliothèque Nationale *Journal officiel* includes the national bibliography.

3c

Institut Togolais des Sciences Humaines *Etudes Togolaises* 1965- .

3f

Cornevin R *Histoire du Togo* 3rd rev ed Paris, Berger-Levrault, 1969; bibl:pp 475-528.

Pireaux M *Le Togo aujourd'hui* Paris, Editions Jeune Afrique, 1977.

Fontvieille J *Togo — les bibliothèques: enquête et propositions de développement* Unesco, 1977, 88p.

UPPER VOLTA

1

Bibliothèque Nationale, Ouagadougou. 1970- .

Centre National des Archives, Ouagadougou. 1970- .

Weilbrenner B *Haute-Volta, réorganisation et développement des archives* Unesco, 1973, 35p. (2849/RMO.RD/DBA).

Université d'Ouagadougou. Bibliothèque Universitaire.

Centre Voltaïque de la Recherche Scientifique (CVRS). Created in 1950 as IFAN Centre.

Centre Culturel Franco-Voltaïque, Ouagadougou.

2a

Ministère de l'Education Nationale et de la Culture. Commission Nationale pour les Bibliothèques, les Archives et la Documentation. 1969- . To organize and coordinate a national system of libraries and documentation centres.

2b

Association Voltaïque pour le Développement des Bibliothèques, des Archives et de la Documentation (AVDBAD). 1971- .

3a

McFarland D M *Historical dictionary of Upper Volta* Scarecrow, 1978.

3b

Izard F and Bonnefond P *Bibliographie de la Haute Volta*, Vol I: 1956-1965 CVRS, 1967, 188p. Vols II and III not traced.

3c

CVRS *Notes et Documents Voltaïques.*

3d

Institut National de la Statistique et de la Démographie. Section Documentation et Archives. *Bulletin mensuel de statistique.*

3e

Journal officiel de la République de Haute Volta. 1959- . Previously: *Journal officiel de la Haute Volta.*

3f

Table ronde sur l'organisation et le développement de la recherche scientifiqe en Haute Volta CVRS, 1970, 50p.

Zongo L and Auedrago Noraogo A *Essai d'analyse critique sur les centres culturels étrangers en Haute Volta* Lyons, ENSB, 1977, 31p. Thesis.

Roberts K *Propositions pour le développement des services de bibliothèque et de documentation en Haute Volta* Unesco, 1976 (COM/DND 14).

Cartry M and Izard F 'Note sur la situation de la documentation en Haute Volta' *Notes Docum Voltaïques* Jan/March 1968.

FRENCH-SPEAKING CENTRAL AFRICA

Former French and Belgian equatorial Africa.

1

Bibliothèque Publique de Brazzaville. Contains documents related to former French Equatorial Africa.

Université de Brazzaville. Bibliothèque Universitaire. Formerly part of the Fondation de l'Enseignement Supérieur en Afrique Centrale (FESAC).

2a

Centre d'Etudes et de Documentation Africaines (CEDAF), Brussels. 1970- . Mainly concerned with former Belgian territories.

Institut pour la Recherche Scientifique en Afrique Centrale (IRSAC), Bukavu. 1947- . Belgian territories.

2c

Museus- Mukis D M D 'La formation professionnelle en Afrique Centrale' in *Le contrôle bibliographique universel (UBC) dans les pays en voie de développement* Munich, 1975 (IFLA Publications, 3) pp 112, 115.

3a

Mbot F 'Inventaire des bibliothèques et centres de documentation en Afrique centrale' *Bull Info Liaison CARDAN* 1974 6(4). Cameroon, Congo, Gabon, République Centrafricaine, Chad, Zaire.

3b

Bruel G *Bibliographie de l'Afrique Equatoriale Française* Paris Larose, 1914, 326p.

Lambert J comp *Catalogue de la bibliothèque de l'Institut d'Etudes Centrafricaines* Montpellier, Imprimerie Charité, 1951, 153p (Mémoires de l'IEC, Vol. 4).

Kellerman L comp *Catalogue de la bibliothèque de l'IEC. Supplément No 1* Brazzaville, 1953, 232p. Mimeo.

Heyse T 'A propos d'un index bibliographique général du Congo belge et du Ruanda-Urandi' *Inst Colon Belge Bull* 1947 18 736-77. Contains 'Listes bibliographiques, 1933-47'.

— *Bibliographie du Congo belge et du Ruanda-Urundi, 1939-51* Brussels, Van Campehout, 1946-58, 17 vols.

— *Documentation générale sur le Congo et le Ruanda-Urundi* (1950-53) Brussels, Commission Belge de Bibliographie, 1954, 31p. (Bibliographia belgica, 4).

Ministère des Affaires Etrangères. Bibliothèque Africaine *La Bibliothèque Africaine: 85 ans d'activité bibliographique africaine* (By P Geeraerts) La Bibliothèque, 1972, 90p.

3c

CEDAF *Cahiers* 1971- . 10 a year.

Brussels, Association des Archivists et Bibliothécaires de Belgique *Archives, bibliothèques et musées de Belgique* 1923- . Contain articles about libraries in Equatorial Africa.

BURUNDI

1

Université Officielle de Bujumbura (UOB). Bibliothèque Centrale. 1961- . Formerly part of Belgian Congo and Ruanda-Burundi academic institutions.

Munumi H 'Bibliothèque Centrale de l'Université Officielle de Bujumbura' *SCAUL Newsletter* 1971 6 15-9.

Institut Murundi d'Information et de Documentation (IMIDOC), Bujumbura. 1964- . Information on the country.

Bibliothèque Publique, Bujumbura.

2a

Ministère de l'Education Nationale.

3a

Weinstein W *Historical dictionary of Burundi* Scarecrow, 1976, 378p. (African Historical Dictionaries, 8).

3b

Clément J *Essai de bibliographie du Ruanda-Burundi* Umumbura, Service des Affaires Indigènes, 1959, 201p.

Nyambariza D *Le Burundi, essai d'une bibliographie, 1959-1973* UOB, Centre de Recherches et de Documentation Pédagogiques, 1974, 110p. Mimeo. Classified by subjects.

Nahayo S 'Contribution à la bibliographie des ouvrages relatifs au Burundi' *Genève-Afrique* 1970- . Several issues.

UOB Bibliothèque Centrale *Bulletin d'acquisitions*.

3d

Institut Rundi des Statistiques *Bulletin*.

Banque de la République du Burundi *Bulletin*.

3e

Bulletin officiel du Burundi (BOB).

Bulletin administratif et juridique.

3f

Chrétien J-P 'La société du Burundi: des mythes aux réalités' *Rev Fr Etudes Polit Afr* 1979 (163/164) 94-118.

République du Burundi *Plan quinquennal de développement économique et social du Burundi* (1978-82) Bujumbura.

Staes J *Burundi, développement des services des archives nationales* Unesco, 1978, 30p. (FMR/BEP/PGI/78/104).

CAMEROON

1

Bibliothèque Nationale, Yaoundé. 1973- . See below.

Université Fédérale du Cameroun. 1962- . Bibliothèque Universitaire.

2a

Ministry of National Education.

Direction des Archives et de la Bibliothèque Nationale, 1952- . Library organized in 1973. Now the Bibliothèque Nationale.

Office National de la Recherche Scientifique et Technique (ONAREST). Founded in 1965 by the Ministère de l'Economie et du Plan. Organized into a number of specialized institutes. See its: Division de la Documentation et des Publications.

2b

Association des Bibliothécaires, Archivistes, Documentalistes et Muséographes du Cameroun (ABADCAM), Yaoundé. 1975- .

3a

LeVine V T and Nye R *Historical dictionary of Cameroon* Scarecrow, 1974.

Chateh P et al *Guide des bibliothèques et centres de documentation de Yaoundé* University Library, 1973.

3b

LeVine V T 'Introduction to the study of Cameroon: a bibliographic essay' *J Cam Affairs* 1972 1(2) 4-10).

Njikam M 'Quelques sources bibliographiques du Cameroun' in Pearson J D and Jones R *The bibliography of Africa*, 113-9. See under Africa, 3b.

Bibliographie nationale camerounaise 1976- . Bibliothèque Nationale? No details found.

Bibliographie des travaux publiés par l'ancien Institut Français d'Afrique Noire (IFAN), Centre Cameroun et par l'IRCAM IRCAM, 19p. Updated.

Bibliothèque Universitaire *Liste d'ouvrages reçus et catalogués.*

ONAREST Division de la Documentation *Catalogue du fonds documentaire.*

Bibliothèque Universitaire *Catalogue des mémoires soutenus à l'université de Yaoundé.*

Ecole Supérieure Internationale de Journalisme de Yaoundé *Liste des principaux articles de périodiques, des documents et des ouvrages enregistrés.* Weekly.

3c

ABADCAM Newsletter. 1975- . 6 a year.

3d

Service de la Statistique du Cameroun *Annuaire statistique du Cameroun* Yaoundé, 1938/45- .

3e

Journal officiel. 1960- . Previously *Journal officiel des Territoires du Cameroun*. 1916-59.

Legal deposit and organization of the archives and national library: Décret 66/DF/412.

3f

Mveng E *Histoire du Cameroun* Paris, Présence Africaine, 1963 535p, bibl.

Johnson W R *The Cameroon Federation: political integration of a fragmentary society* Princeton U P, 1970, 426p.

Vernon Jackson H O *Language, schools and government in Cameroon* Teachers College P, 1967, 31p, bibl.

Burnham P *Opportunity and constraint in a savanna society* Academic P, 1980.

'Cameroon' *FID News Bull* 1975 12 97.

Issock S P *Project de création des bibliothèques publiques au Cameroun* Lyons, ENSN, 1977, 33p. Thesis.

Chambellant S *Etude des termes de référence d'un système d'information scientifique et technologique au Cameroun* Report of a mission PNUD-Unesco, 1975 (not for general circulation).

CENTRAL AFRICAN REPUBLIC

For a time: Central African Empire.

1
Université Jean-Bedel Bokassa, Bangui. Bibliothèque Centrale, 1970- .
Archives Nationales, Bangui. 1969- .
Office de la Recherche Scientifique et Technique Outre-Mer (ORSTOM) Centre de Bangui. 1954- .

2a
Ministère de l'Education Nationale.
Mission Sociologique du Haut-Oubangui (MSHO), Bangassou. 1954- .

3a
Kalck P *Historical dictionary of the Central African Republic* Scarecrow, 1980, 152p. (African Historical Dictionaries, 27).

3b
Bibliography on the Central African Republic is included in *Bibliografia española*.

3c
MSHO *Recherches oubanguiennes*. Irregular.

3d
Direction de la Statistique Générale et des Etudes Economiques *Bulletin mensuel statistique*.

3e
Journal officiel 1958- . Formerly *Journal officiel de l'Oubangui-Chari.*

3f
Reitman E *République Centrafricaine: organisation des bibliothèques, 20 octobre 1966-12 janvier 1967* Unesco, 1967, 42p.

CHAD

1

Dépôt National d'Archives, N'Djamena.

Gut C *Création d'un service national d'archives: Tchad (Mission) décembre 1972-février 1973* Unesco, 1973, 54p. (2974/RMO.RD/DBA).

Université du Tchad. Bibliothèque Universitaire. 1902- .

Institut National des Sciences Humaines (INSH), N'Djamena. Bibliothèque 1961- . Under the Ministère du Plan et du Développement, Comité National de la Recherche Scientifique.

Office de la Recherche Scientifique et Technique Outre-Mer (ORSTOM), Centre de N'Djamena. 1958- . Service de Documentation.

2a

Ministère de l'Information. Direction de la Documentation. Legal deposit centre.

Ministère de l'Education Nationale, de la Culture, de la Jeunesse et des Sports.

3a

Annuaire du Tchad 1950/51- .

3b

Bibliographie du Tchad (Sciences Humaines), INTSH, 1968. (Etudes et Documents Tchadiens, série A4. Covers works published up to 31 December 1967. Updated by:

Moreau J and Stordeur D *Bibliographie du Tchad* 2nd ed rev, with a supplement INTSH, 1970. (Etudes et Documents Tchadiens, serie A5). Covers documents published up to 31 December 1969.

Bériel M-M *Complément à la bibliographie du Tchad (Sciences Humaines)* 1974, 103p. (Etudes et Documents Tchadiens, série AG). Covers documents published up to 31 December 1973.

Pantelidis V S *The Arab world libraries and librarianship 1960-1976: a bibliography* Mansell, 1979, 100p. Includes the Chad.

Depôt National d'Archives *Catalogue* in Etudes et Documents Tchadiens 1968 série B no 1.

3c

INSH (Formerly INTSH) *Etudes et documents tchadiens*. Série A prepared by the library; Série B prepared by the archives.

3d

Service de la Statistique *Bulletin mensuel statistique*.

3e

Journal oficiel 1959- .

3f

L'essor du Tchad Paris, PUF, 1969, bibl. pp. 373-84.

 Thompson V *Conflict in Chad* Hurst, 1981, ca 186p.

CONGO

1

Bibliothèque Nationale Populaire, Brazzaville. Formerly Bibliothèque Publique de Brazzaville.

Archives Nationales, Brazzaville.

Documentation Nationale. Being organized.

Université Marien-Ngouabi, Brazzaville. Bibliothèque Universitaire. Formerly Bibliothèque du Gouvernement Général de l'AEF, then of the Centre d'Enseignement Supérieur. 1959- .

2a

Ministère de la Culture et des Arts. Direction Générale des Services de Bibliothèques, d'Archives et de Documentation (DGSBAD), Brazzaville. 1971- . Under the Présidence du Conseil from 1971 to 1974.

Ministère de l'Information. Controls the legal deposit.

3b

Parent R A *Bibliography on the history of the Republic of Congo*. Reported in preparation in 1961. Not traced.

See also Accession lists from individual libraries.

3d

Service de la Statistique *Bulletin mensuel de la statistique de la République du Congo*. 1957- .

3e

Journal officiel de la République du Congo Imprimerie Nationale, 1958- .

Legal deposit Decree D 66/249, August 1966.

3f

Unesco Bull Lib 1952 6(11/12) E136.

— 1961 15(5) 246-7.

Clavel J-P *République populaire du Congo: plan de développement des bibliothèques, 10 septembre-10 novembre 1972* Unesco, 1973, 139p. (2958/RMO.RD/DBA).

Samba R A 'Les bibliothèques en République Populaire du Congo' *Unesco Bull Lib* 1971 25(4) 226-31 (French ed).

Oukounguila D *Lecteurs et bibliothèques à Brazzaville* ENSB thesis, 1976, 35p.

GABON

1

Archives Nationales, Libreville. 1969- .
Université Nationale du Gabon, Libreville. Bibliothèque centrale. 1972- .
— Institut Africain d'Informatique. Library. 1974- .
Ministère de l'Information. Centre d'Information, Libreville. 1960- .

3a

Gardinier D E *Historical dictionary of Gabon* Scarecrow, 1981, 254p. (African Historical Dictionaries, 30).

3b

Perrois F *Gabon: répertoire bibliographique des études de sciences humaines (1960-1970)* Libreville, ORSTOM, 1969, 2 vols.

3c

Institut Pédagogique National *Réalités gabonaises.*
— *Bulletin officiel de l'éducation nationale.*

3e

Journal officiel. 1959- .

3f

Pansin G *Réorganisation des archives nationales: Gabon (Mission) novembre-décembre 1972* Unesco, 1973, 33p.
ORSTOM *Activités de l'ORSTOM en République Gabonaise* July 1974. Includes a bibliography, 1949-1974.

RWANDA

1

Université Nationale du Rwanda (UNR). Bibliothèque, Butare. 1963- .

Brock J *Rapport de mission relatif à l'étude des modalités de création d'une bibliothèque universitaire au Rwanda* INRS, 1970, 32p.

Institut National de Recherche Scientifique (INRS), Butare. 1964- . Created in 1947 as Institut de Recherche Scientifique en Afrique Centrale, Centre d'Astrida (Butare).

Bibliothèque Publique, Kigali.

2a

Ministère de l'Education Nationale. Direction Générale de la Culture et des Beaux-Arts.

3a

Area handbook for Rwanda USAID, 1969.

3b

Clément J *Essai de bibliographie du Rwanda-Urundi* Usumbura Service des Affaires Indigènes, 1959, 201p.

Levesque A *Contribution à la bibliographie nationale du Rwanda, 1965-1970/ Contribution to the national bibliography of Rwanda, 1965-1970* G K Hall, 1979, 541p.

3d

Ministère du Plan, Kigali *Situation économique et conjoncturelle au 30 juin 1979.* Prepared by the Direction Générale de la Statistique et de la Documentation. (There is also a library).

3f

UNR *Trésors de la culture rwandaise* 1972.

— *Aspects de la culture rwandaise* 1972.

Erny P 'L'enseignement au Rwanda' *Tiers-Monde* 1974 15(59/60) 707-22.

Duchein M *Rapport sur la mission effectuée au Rwanza du 22 mars au 2 avril 1972 pour la création d'un service d'archives nationales au Rwanza* Conseil National des Archives, 1976.

ZAIRE

Formerly the Belgian Congo.

1

Bibliothèque Nationale, Kinshasa-Kalina. 1949- . Formerly Bibliothèque Centrale du Congo.

Archives du Zaïre, Kinshasa. 1949- .

Université Nationale du Zaïre (UNAZA). 1971- . Created by the amalgamation of three universities which now are the three campuses: Kinshasa, Kisangani and Lumumbasa. The libraries are scattered among the campuses, faculties, institutes, etc. They are centrally organized and developed through: Direction de la Recherche et des Publications du Rectorat de l'UNAZA.

2a

Direction de la Culture et des Arts. Division des Bibliothèques et des Archives Nationales.

2b

Association Zaïroise des Archivistes, Bibliothécaires et Documentalistes (AZABDO), Kinshasa. 1968-73 as: Association Congolaise des Archivistes, Bibliothécaires et Documentalistes.

2c

UNAZA. Lumumbashi Campus. Faculty of Philosophy, Letters and History.

Institut des Sciences et Techniques de l'Information (ISTI). Kinshasa, 1973- .

See also under 3f.

3a

Centre de Coordination des Recherches et de la Documentation en Sciences Sociales pour l'Afrique Sub-Saharienne (CERDAS) *Répertoire des institutions de recherche scientifique au Zaïre* 1975.

Direction de la Culture et des Arts (Then: Ministère de la Culture) *Liste des bibliothèques publiques*, 1971, 9p.

3b

Bibliographie nationale des publications congolaises ou relatives à RDC acquises par la Bibliothèque Nationale 1971- . Quarterly. From the *Listes d'acquisitions de la Bibliothèque Nationale*, 1970- . See also:

Répertoire alphabétique des collections d'ouvrages de la Bibliothèque Nationale 1969, 51p. And:

Répertoire du dépôt légal des publications éditées au Congo éd rev and augm. Direction des Archives et Bibliothèques, 1970, 22p.

Bustin E *A study guide for Congo-Kinshasa* Boston U, 1970, 167p. (African Studies Center, Publications series).

— *Congo-Kinshasa: guide bibliographique* Brussels, CEDAF, 1971, 2 vols, 63 and 72p. (Cahiers du CEDAF No 2 and No 4).

3c

ISTI *Cahiers Zaïrois de Communications Sociales* 1974- .
Centre d'Exécution des Programmes Sociaux et Economiques (CEPSE) *Problèmes Sociaux Zaïrois.*
AZABDO Mukanda: bulletin des archives, bibliothèques et documentation du Zaïre 1975- .

3d

Institut de Recherche Scientifique. Départment de Statistique et de Démographie. Centre de Documentation *Liste des acquisitions.*
Banque du Zaïre *Bulletin mensuel de statistiques.*

3e

Bulletin officiel du Congo Belge 1885-1960.
Moniteur Katangais 1960- .

3f

Bureau du Président *Profils du Zaïre* Kinshasa, 1972, 464p. English edition see:
President of the Republic of Zaire's Office *Profiles of Zaire* 197?, 494p.
Georis M et al *Evolution de l'enseignement en République Démocratique du Congo depuis l'indépendance* Brussels CEMUMBAC,1965, 166p.
Vrancx R L 'Congo, libraries in the Democratic Republic of' in *Encyclopedia* 5 (1971) 607-27, refs. Development and all aspects.
Perier G D 'Bibliothèques coloniales' *Arch Biblioth Belg* 1936 13(1) 39-53.
— 'Les bibliothèques du Congo belge' *Arch Biblioth Belg* 1932 9(5/6) 89-91.
Rees H 'Libraries and librarianship in Zaire' *Focus Int Comp Libp* 1974 5(3) 21-2.
Depasse C 'Les bibliothèques publiques au Congo' *Zaïre* (Brussels) 1948 277-302.
'Library resources' *Unesco Bull Lib* 1952 6(11/12) E135-6.
Kalala M *Les bibliothèques au Zaïre. Pour les bibliothèques universitaires: le cas de la bibliothèque facultaire des sciences sociales* ENSB Thesis, 1976, 50p.
Valetta J *République Populaire du Congo: la mise sur pied d'un service d'archives, avril-mai 1972* Unesco, 1972, 29p.
Kazenge K K 'La bibliothèque du CEPSE: ses origines — sa fréquentation' *Probl Soc Zaïrois* Jan-Dec 1975, Special issue, 27-31.
Ntumba M 'Library, documentation and publications section of the Makanda Kabobi Institute, Zaire' *Unesco Bull Lib* 1977 31 254.
Masens-Mukis D M D *Propositions pour un réseau national d'information scientifique et technique en République du Zaïre* Kinshasa, 1973.
Dewèze A *République du Zaïre, projet de système national d'information scientifique et technique* Unesco, 1976, 108p. (PP/1975-1976/2.131.7).
— 'Finalité et rentabilité de l'information scientifique et technique: formation des personnels' *Documentaliste* 1977 14 31-6. Excerpts from the Unesco report.

PORTUGUESE ASSOCIATED AFRICA

General and historical.

1
Instituto de Alta Cultura. Centro de Documentação Cientifica, Secção Ultramarina, Lisbon.
Junta de Investigações do Ultramar. Centro de Documentação Cientifica Ultramarina, Lisbon.

2a
Agência Geral das Colonias. Divisão de Publicações e Bibliotecas, Lisbon.

3a
Abshire D M and Samuels M A *Portuguese Africa: a handbook* Praeger, 1969, 466p.

3b
CDCU *Boletim bibliográfico* 1958.
Conover H F *A list of references on the Portuguese colonies in Africa* Library of Congress, 1942, 29p.
Moser G M *A tentative Portuguese-African bibliography: Portuguese literature on Africa and African literature in the Portuguese language* University Park, State U Libraries, 1970, 148p.

3d
Instituto Nacional de Estatística *Anuario estatístico Ultramar* Lisbon.

3e
Portuguese Africa: a guide to official publications Library of Congress, 217p.

3f
Newitt M *Portugal in Africa* London, Hurst, 1981.
Boyd H *The former Portuguese colonies: Angola, Mozambique, Guinea-Bissau, Cape Verde, Soa Tome and Principe* F Watts, 1981.

ANGOLA

1

Biblioteca Nacional de Angola, Luanda. 1971- .
Universidad de Angola, Biblioteca.

2a

Conseilho Nacional de Cultura, Luanda.

3a

Wheeler D L and Pélissier R *Angola* Pall Mall, 1971, 296p.
Martin P M *Historical dictionary of Angola* Scarecrow, 1980, 174p. (African Historical Dictionaries, 26).

3b

Instituto de Angola *Boletim bibliográfico.*
— *Boletim analitico.*
Universidad de Luanda *Informação bibliográfica.*
Instituto de Investigação Científica *Boletim bibliográfico.*
Biblioteca Nacional *Novas da Biblioteca Nacional.*
Greenwood M J *Angola: a bibliography* Cape Town U, 1967, 52p.

3c

Instituto de Angola *Boletim.*
— *Boletim informativo.*

3d

Direcção dos Serviços de Estatística *Anuario estatístico* 1943- .
— *Estatistica da educação.*

3e

Boletim oficial. 1845- .

3f

Carreira A *Angola: da escravatora ao trabalho livre* Lisbon, Arcádia, 1977.
Salvadorini V 'Biblioteche e archivi d'Angola' *Ass Afr Iral Bol* 1969 2(3/4) 16-30.

CAPE VERDE

3b

McCarthy J M *Guinea-Bissau and Cape Verde Islands: a comprehensive bibliography* Garland Pub, 1977.

3d

Secção de Estatística Geral *Anuario estatístico* Praia, 1933- .

3f

Descamps C and Barkey C 'L'Ile aux serpents [Cap Vert]' *Notes Afr* 1968 (120) 97-100, bibl.

GUINEA-BISSAU

1

Museu da Guiné, Bissau. 1947- . Biblioteca. Part of the Centro de Estudos da Guiné Portuguesa, Bissau, 1945- .

3b

McCarthy J M *Guinea-Bissau and Cape-Verde Islands: a comprehensive bibliography* Garland Pub, 1977.

3c

Centro de Estudos da Guiné Portuguesa *Boletim cultural* 1945- .

3d

Secção Tecnica de Estatística *Anuario*, Bissau 1946- .

3f

Rudebeck L *Guinea-Bissau* Uppsala, 1974.

Freire P *Pedagogy in progress: letters to Guinea-Bissau* London, W & R Publ Corp., 1978.

Rema H P 'O Centro de Estudos da Guiné Portuguesa lembra 25 anos de existência' *Bol Cult Guiné Port* 1971 26(101) 21-61.

MOZAMBIQUE

1

Biblioteca Nacional de Moçambique, Maputo (Lourenço Marques). 1961- .
Instituto de Investigação Científica Moçambique, Maputo. 1955- .
Sociedade de Estudos de Moçambique, Biblioteca. 1930- .
Ministry of Education. Biblioteca e Centro de Documentação, Maputo. 1977- .

3a

Anuario de Moçambique.

3b

Instituto de Investigação Científica *Boletim bibliográfico.*

3c

Sociedade de Estudos de Moçambique *Boletim.* 1931.

3d

Direcção dos Serviços de Economia e Estatística Geral *Annuario estatistico/ Annuaire statistique.* 1926/28- .

3f

Newitt M D D *Portuguese settlements on the Zambesi: exploration, land tenure and colonial rule in East Africa* Africana Pub Co, 1973, 434p.

SAO TOME E PRINCIPE

1

Museu de São Tomé e Principe.
Biblioteca Muncipal Dr Henrique da Silva, São Tomé.

3e

Boletim oficial.

SPANISH ASSOCIATED AFRICA

See also under Spain.

2b
Instituto des Estudios Africanos, Madrid.

3a
Anuario de Canarias, Africa Occidental, Guinea Española Las Palmas.

3f
Val M A 'El archivo y biblioteca de la Dirección General de Plazas y Provincias Africanas: posible base para un centro de documentación de Africa' *Rev Arch Bibliot Mus* (Madrid) 1958 65 123-8.

GUINEA ECUATORIAL

3e
Región Ecuatorial *Boletin oficial de la Región Ecuatorial* 1959-? .

3f
Baguena Corelía L *Guinea* Madrid, Instituto de Estudios Africanos, 1950.

SECTION 5

MIDDLE EAST AND NORTH AFRICA

THE MIDDLE EAST AND NORTHERN AFRICA

1

Collison R L and Moon B E *Directory of libraries and special collections on Asia and North Africa* Lockwood/Archon Books, 1970, 123p.

2a

Ljunggren F and Geddes C L *An international directory of institutes and societies interested in the Middle East* Amsterdam, Djambatan, 1962.

Arab League Educational, Cultural and Scientific Organisation (ALECSO). 1973- .

Association of Arab Universities, Giza. 1964- .

Arab States Fundamental Education Centre (ASFEC), Sirs al-Layyan. 1952- .

Islamic Library Information Centre, Karachi.

'Islamic Library Information Centre, Karachi' *Unesco Bull Lib* 1975 29 289-90.

League of Arab States. Documentation Centre, Tunis. 1981- . To coordinate the region's information resources.

National Research Centre, Documentation Service, Cairo. Deals with the region as a whole.

2c

Lohrer A and Jackson W V 'Education and training of librarians in Asia, the Near East and Latin America' *Lib Trends* 1959 8(3) 243-77, bibl.

Kent F L and Abu Haider F 'Professional training of librarians' *Unesco Bull Lib* 1960 14(3) 100-3, 123. Working paper at the Beirut seminar, 1959 (See under 3f).

Harby M K and Fahmy A 'Selection and training of research librarians and documentalists in Arab-speaking countries' *Working paper* at the Cairo regional seminar, 1962. (See under 3f).

Sharify N 'Education for library abroad: UAR, Iran, Iraq, Lebanon, and Syria' *Lib Trends* 1963 12(2) 227-59.

Kent F L 'The training of librarians and documentalists in Arab-speaking countries' *Unesco Bull Lib* 1967 21(6) 301-10.

3a

Thompson A ed *Vocabularium bibliothecarii* 2nd ed. Arabic edition issued in Cairo by the ARE National Commission for Unesco, 1965.

Clason W E *Elsevier's dictionary of library science, information and documentation (with Arabic translation by S Salem)* Amsterdam, 1976, 708p. Based on the translator's MA thesis, 1973.

The Middle-East and North Africa London, Europa (Yearbooks), 1948- . (27th ed, 1980/81 published 1980, 985p). History, facts and figures, bibliography.

Middle East Annual Review Saffron Walden, World of Information. 1980 edition published 1979, 430p.

Amer R C 'Middle East/North Africa area — report July 1976; Arab world' *Leads* 1976 18 8-9.

Historical and cultural dictionaries of Asia Scarecrow, 1972- . Series on individual countries.

Middle East News: a weekly research review Cairo, 1962- . Englsh and French editions. Includes statistics, texts of laws, etc.

Dagher J A *Répertoire des bibliothèques du Proche Orient et du Moyen Orient* Unesco, 1951, 182p.

Badr A *Directory of archives, libraries, documentation centres and bibliographical institutions in the Arab states* Cairo, Unesco Commission, 1965, 117p. Also in French and Arabic.

ALECSO *A guide to libraries in the Arab World* 1973.

— *A guide to documentation centres in the Arab world* 1973.

3b

Yenikomshian A comp *A bibliography of bibliographies of the Near Eastern countries* Amer U Beirut, Yafet Memorial Library, 1968, 16p.

Aman M M 'Bibliographical services in the Arab countries' *Coll Res Lib* 1970 31(4) 249-59.

Atiyeh G N et al 'Near East [national bibliographies]' *L of C Q J* 1969 26(3) 111-7.

Fodor M *The East: books in Western languages on Asian and Arabic countries* British Museum, 1965, 107p.

Pearson J D *Oriental and Asian bibliography: an introduction with some references to Africa* 1966; *Supplement* in *Progress in Library Science* 1967. (See details under Asia, 3b).

The 1969 bibliography of the Middle East Syrian Documentation Papers. By subject, country index.

Abdul-Rahman A J *Guide to Arabic reference books: an annotated bibliography of books in Arabic and books in Western languages dealing with the Arabs* Basrah, Modern P, 1970.

Kuwait National Library *Selected bibliography on Arab Islamic civilization*, Ca 1972. Foreign sources.

Unesco Regional Office for Education in the Arab Countries *Repertory of library holdings* Beirut, 1973, 3 vols. Arabic/English/French.

Birnbaum E *The Islamic Middle East: a short annotated bibliography for high school teachers and libraries* U of Toronto, Department of Islamic Studies, 1975, 45p.

Littlefield D W *The Islamic Near East and North Africa: an annotated guide to books in English for non specialists* Libraries Unlimited, 1976.

Bibliographical lists of books and references about the Arab world Cairo. Series on individual countries.

Library of Congress *Accessions Lists: Middle East* 1963- .

New books quarterly on Islam and the Muslim world London, Islamic Council of Europe, 1980- .

Quarterly index Islamicus: current books, articles and papers on Islamic studies Mansell, 1977- . Quarterly.

Selim D *United States doctoral dissertations on the Arab world, 1883-1974* 2nd ed Library of Congress.

Hopkins J F P ed *Arabic periodical literature* Heffer (for Cambridge U, Middle East Centre), 1966- .

Aman M M *Arab periodicals and serials: a subject bibliography* Garland Pub, 1979, 252p.

Dotan U *A bibliography of articles on the Middle East 1959-1967* Tel Aviv U, Shiloah Centre for Middle Eastern and African Studies, 1970, 227p.

Middle East Institute, Washington *Middle East Journal*, 1946- . Contains a bibliographical section for periodical literature.
Salem S 'The Arabic literature of library and information science' *J Info Sci* 1979 1(4) 231-4.
Al-Maktaba Harissa, St Paul Printing P, 1956- . For Iraq, Jordan, Lebanon and Syria.
Abd El-Hady F *Librarianship in the Arab world: a bibliography* Cairo, School Libraries Association, 1972, 180p. In Arabic only?.
Pantelidis V *The Arab world: libraries and librarianship, 1960-1976: a bibliography* Mansell, 1979, 100p.
See also some references in Africa and Asia under 3a, 3b.

3c

Ljunggren F and Hamdy M *Annotated guide to journals dealing with the Middle East and North Africa* American U in Cairo P, 1964, 107p.
Dewey R H *Check list of serial publications dealing with the Middle East* American U of Beirut, Library, 1968, 34p. Western languages.
Ahmed-Bioud A *3200 revues et journaux arabes de 1800 à 1965. Titres arabes et titres translittérés* Paris, Maison des Sciences de l'Homme, 1969, 252p.
ALECSO *Arab periodicals: general directory of periodicals issued in the Arab World*, Cairo, 1973, 99p.
Khouri Y *List of all Arabic periodicals in Yafet Library arranged alphabetically* The Library, 1967, 35p.
Auchterlonie J P C and Safadi Y H eds *Union catalogue of Arabic serials and newspapers in British libraries* Mansell, 1977, 146p.
ALECSO *Arabic Journal for Information*. 1977- . On librarianship, information, documentation.
The journals published in countries of the region deal with the region as a whole:
Alam al-Maktabat Cairo. 1958- .
Majala al-Jamaiyah Kuwait University Library. 1971- .
Risalat al-Maktabah Jordan Library Association. 1965- .

3d

ASFEC *Statistical sources of the Arab States: a comprehensive list* 1961, 29p.
Khurshid A et al, comp *Fact sheets on libraries in Islamic countries* U of Karashi, Department of Library Science, 1974.

3f

Miquel A *L'Islam et sa civilisation, VIIe-XXe siècles* Colin, 1968, 573p, bibl.
Reichmann F *The sources of Western literacy : the Middle Eastern civilization* Greenwood 1982, 296p. (Contributions in Librarianship and Information Science, 29.)
al-Attas M N S ed *Aims and objectives of Islamic education. Conference prooceedings* Hodder & Stoughton (for King Abdulaziz U, Jeddah), 1979, 169p.
Zahlan A B ed *The Arab brain drain: proceedings of a seminar organised by UN/ECWA, . . . Beirut 4-8 February 1980* Ithaca for UN, 1981, 309p.
Bloomfield B C *Middle East studies and libraries: a felicitation volume for Professor J D Pearson* Mansell, 1980, 231p.
Farsuni F 'Acquisition of Arabic books' *Risalat al-Maktabah* 1975 10(1) 5-18.
Calvin P 'Report on a book buying tour of the Middle East and North Africa' *Int Lib Rev* 1976 8(3) 271-81.
Unesco Meeting of experts on book development in the Arab countries (Cairo, May 1-6 1972) *Final report* Unesco, 1972, 28p.

Botros S 'Problems of book development in the Arab world with special reference to Egypt' *Lib Trends* 1978 26 567-73.

A number of meetings and conferences have taken place in the region on the theme of book development, exchanges of publications, etc. See for instance:

Meeting of experts on publication exchange between Arab countries, Damascus, June 1957. On book development Lebanon, 1961.

'Regional seminar on bibliography, documentation and exchange of publications in Arabic-speaking states, Cairo, 1962. Report' *Unesco Bull Lib* 1963 17(2) Suppl 137-45.

Vleeschauwer H J de 'History of the Western library' Vol 1, part 1: History of the libraries in antiquity, B: The library of the East' (Sumerian, Babylonian, Assyrian) *Mousaion* 1962 (70) 32p.

Weitemayer M 'Archive and library technique in ancient Mesopotamia' *Libri* 1956 6(3)217-38.

Johnson D R 'The library of Celsus, an Ephesian Phoenix' *Wilson Lib Bull* 1980 54(10) 651-3.

'Byzantine and Moslem libraries' in Johnson E D and Harris M H *History of libraries in the Western world* 3rd ed rev, 1976, 77-95. (See details under General, 3f).

Youssef E *Les bibliothèques publiques et semi publiques en Mésopotamie, en Syrie et en Egypte au Moyen Age* Beirut, Impr. Catholique, 1967, 449p.

Padovar S K 'Muslim libraries' in Thompson J W *The medieval library* 1957, 347-368. (See details under Europe, 3f).

Bashiruddin S 'Fate of sectarian libraries in medieval Islam' *Libri* 1967 17(3) 149-62.

Pinto O 'The libraries of the Arabs during the time of the Abbassids' *Pakistan Lib Rev* 1959 3(1/2) 44-72. Repr. from *Islamic culture* 1929 3.

Vilayat Hussein S 'Organisation and administration of Muslim libraries (from 786 to 1492 AD)' *Pakistan Lib Ass J* 1966 1(1) 8-11.

Winger F L 'Books and the early missionaries in the Near East' *J Lib Hist* 1971 6 21-33.

Buksh S K 'The Islamic libraries' *19th Century* 1902 52 125-39.

Sheniti M 'Unesco and library and related services in Arabic-speaking countries' *Unesco Bull Lib* 1966 20(5) 219-25.

'Regional seminar on library development in Arabic-speaking states, Beirut 1959. Report' *Unesco Bull Lib* 1960 14(3) 117-23. Includes education for librarianship. The whole issue is devoted to the region. Other special issues of periodicals devoted to the Middle East:

Library Journal 1955 80(2).

Leads (ALA International Relations Round Table) 1967 10(2).

Kent F L and Abu Haidar 'Library development in the Arab world' *Rev Int Doc* 1962 29(1) 13-7.

Chandler G *Libraries in the East: an internationnal and comparative study* Seminar P, 1971, 214p. Egypt, Iran, Lebanon are represented. See also:

Thompson A *J Libp* 1972 4(1) 64-8. Review of the book with tables.

Chandler G *Int Lib Rev* 1971 3 187-227. Summary of the book.

Harvey J F and Lambert B 'Librarianship in six Southwest Asian countries' *Int Lib Rev* 1971 3(1) 15-34. Afghanistan, Iran, Israel, Lebanon and Turkey are represented.

Arab League Seminar on library services: the Damascus seminar on library services, bibliography, documentation, Arabic manuscripts and national archives 1971.

Auda A al-Futoh *al-Nashat al-Iklimi fi majal al-Khadamat al-Maktaba al-Ara-*

biya, 1957-1971 Damascus, Ministry of Higher Education, 1972.

Unesco meeting of experts on the national planning of documentation and library services in Arab countries, Cairo, 11-17 February 1974: *Document* Unesco COM 73/CONF.611/3. *Final report*. COM 73/CONF.611/4. (See also *Unesco Bull Lib* 1974 28 182-7).

Lohrer A 'School libraries in Iran and the Near East' *ALA Bull* 1969 63(9) 1284-9, refs.

Unesco 'Seminar on the development of libraries in Arab universities' *Unesco Bull Lib* 1972 26(5) 288.

Seminar on university libraries: the Bagdad Seminar on the Development of Libraries in Arab Universities, March 1972 Council of the Association of Arab Universities.

Ansari M N 'National planning and academic libraries in Western Asia'. *Paper* at IFLA Conference (40th Meeting), Washington 1974, 13p.

Harvey J F 'West Asian special libraries and information centres' *Ann Lib Sci Doc* 1973 20(1/4) 26-38.

Akroush A 'Arab world and the need for special libraries' *Risalat al-Maktabah* 1974 9(4) 30-1.

Seminar on Documentation: meeting of experts on Documentation in the Arab World, Cairo September 1969.

Harvey J F ed Southwest Asian Documentation Centre Conference, Teheran, 1970. *Proceedings* IRANDOC, 1970, 192p.

FID/DC *Documentation in South West Asia and Unesco-UNISIST-Developing countries. Papers at the FID/DC Open Forum, Teheran, September 1973* Hungarian Central Technical Library and Documentation Centre (For FID), 1974, 73p. Iran, Turkey and Pakistan.

National and regional planning for scientific and technological information systems and services for development in the Arab countries, Tunis, April 1976. *Recommendations* Unesco (SC.76/CASTARAB/4). Recommendations to be presented to the Rabat workshop.

Improving information transfer: Workshop in Rabat, May 1976. *Final report* Unesco, 1976. Egypt, Morocco, Tunisia represented.

Madkour M A K 'Information processing and retrieval in Arab countries: traditional approaches and modern potentials' *Unesco J* 1980 2(2) 97-104.

Inayat F 'Computers and libraries in Arab countries' (In Arabic) *Risalat al-Maktabah* 1978 13(2) 26-34.

AFGHANISTAN

1

Kabul Public Library. Central body in the library system.

'Afghanistan first public library' *Unesco Bull Lib* 1958 12(1) 57-8.

'Kabul public library' *Unesco Bull Lib* 1958 12(6) 291.

Kabul Pohantoon (Kabul University) Library. Libraries centralized in 1964.

White N L 'The Kabul University Library' *Terminal report* Kabul, U of Wyoming Contract Team, 1966.

2a

Ministry of Education. Library Board.

Ministry of Information and Culture. Public Libraries.

National Archives Commission.

2b

Union of Afghanistan Librarians. 1971- .

2c

In-service training mostly.

3a

Afghanistan yearbook. Contains information on libraries.

3b

Wilber D N *Annotated bibliography of Afghanistan* 3rd ed New Haven, HRAF P, 1968, 252p.

Heravy M *Fehrest-e Matbu'e Afghanistan az sal 1330-1344 Panzdah sal* (1951-1965) Kabul, 1965, 77p.

Bibliographie der Afghanistan Literatur 1945-1967 Hamburg, Deutsches Orient-Institut, 1968-69, 2 vols.

3f

Wilber D N et al *Afghanistan: its people, its society, its culture* New Haven, HRAF P, 1962, 320p. (Survey of World Culture, 11).

Dupree L and Albert L *Afghanistan in the 1970s* Prager, 1975, 266p.

Griffiths J C *Afghanistan: key to a continent* A Deutsch, 1981, 225p.

Saber A A 'Historical survey and modern developments of libraries in Afghanistan' *Iranian Lib Ass Bull* 1975 8(3) 34p.

Sharify N 'Afghanistan, libraries in' in *Enclyclopedia* 1 (1968) 111-7.

Sohan Singh 'Libraries in Afghanistan' *Indian Lib Ass Bull* 1967 3(3/4) 171-3.

Harvey J 'Pakistan and Afghanistan librarianship' *Pakistan Lib Ass Bull* 1969 2 9-17.

Dumont-Faineux N 'Visite à quelques bibliothèques afghanes' *Ass Bibioth Fr Bull* 1970 (69) 249-55.

Parvani D M 'Razvite bibliotechnogo dela v Afganistane' *Biblioth i Bibliog za Rubezhom* 1977 (61) 58-62.

Eyre J J *Republic of Afghanistan: library development* (NATIS) Unesco, 1977, 58p. (Tech rep PP/1975-76/4.221.4).

IRAN

1

National Library of Iran, Tehran. Created in 1935 as Ketab Khaneh Omumi Máaref (Public Library of the Ministry of Education). There were plans to establish a much larger and more comprehensive library 'for the progress of research in the culture and civilization of Iran' (Decree 1973).

Kashan Z-S *National Library of Iran* Pahlavi U, School of Graduate Studies, 1977, 71p, refs.

Umpathy K S 'National Library' *Indian Libn* 1978 33(1) 15-8, refs.

Sharify N *The Pahlavi National Library of the future: a summary of its origin, its planning, its objectives and its services* Pahlavi National Library Board of Consultants (USA), 1976, 19p.

— 'The Pahlavi National Library of the future' in *Encyclopedia* 21 (1977) 247-55.

University of Teheran. Central Library and Documentation Centre. 1948- . Rehoused in 1970.

2a

Ministry for Cultural Affairs. Was planning to establish, as well as the new national library at the centre of a library complex within the NATIS concept, the:

Pahlavi Cultural, Scientific and Resource Centre due to open in 1980.

Ministry of Science and Higher Education, Institute of Planning and Research in Science and Education (IRPSE). Two bodies created within the Institute in 1968:

Iranian Documentation Centre (IRANDOC), specially concerned with periodical literature and processing.

Teheran Book Processing Centre (TEBROC), especially concerned with book processing.

Sinai A 'Iranian Documentation Centre (IRANDOC)' in *Encyclopedia* 13 (1975) 53-60.

Rahmani I *A review of the Iranian Documentation Centre's basic functions and activities* Pahlavai U, School of Graduate Studies, 1977, 95p.

Soltani P 'The Tehran Book Processing Centre (TEBROC) and its research function' *Int Cataloguing* Part I: 1975 4(1) 7-8; Part II: 1975 4(2) 4-6.

Ministry of Education for School libraries.

Ministry of Cultural Affairs 1967- for National Library and Public libraries.

Ministry of Science, Technology and Higher Education 1967- for University libraries.

Institute for the Intellectual Development of Children and Young Adults (INIDCYA). 1965- . To help produce reading material and promote school and children libraries, etc.

Iranian Culture Foundation 1964- .

Asian Cultural Documentation Centre for Unesco, Teheran. 1975- .

International Institute for Adult Literacy Methods, Teheran. 1970- .

Unesco Regional Office for Education in Asia *Study visit and seminar: work oriented adult literacy pilot project in Iran 27 October-9 November 1969. Final*

report Bangkok, The Office, 1970, 60p. Also in French. For the general literature on this Institute *see under* General: Developing Countries, 2a, 3a, 3b, 3f.

2b

Anjoman-e Ketab (Book Society of Iran), Teheran. 1955- .
Association of Chartered Archivists of Iran, Teheran.
Anjoman-e Ketabdaran-e Iran (Iran Library Association), Tehran. 1966.
Sinai A 'Iranian Library Association (ILA)' in *Enclyclopedia* 13 (1975) 60-3.
Shadman Z 'A short history of ILA' *ILA Bull* 1976 8(4) 485-507.

2c

'Amuzeshe ketabdari-ye jadid dar Iran' *ILA Bull* 1970 3 37-44.
Mangla P B 'Library education in Iran: a survey and some suggestions' *Unesco Bull Lib* 1972 26(5) 253-8.
Farzin F *Survey of the library education through free classes of Pahlavi University and Fars radio and television* Pahlavi U, School of Graduate Studies, 1976, 65p.
Pourhamzeh A *Current status of library education in Iran: a review of programs offered in Iranian academic institutions* Pahlavi U, School of Graduate Studies, 1977, 74p.
Dastouri N *A profile of librarians in Shiraz and five major cities in Fars Province* Pahlavi U, School of Graduate Studies, 1976, 62p.

3a

Afshar I *A dictionary for Iranian studies* Teheran, 1970.
Smith H H et al *Area handbook for Iran* Rev ed American U P, 1971, 626p.
Sepehri A *Rahnama-ye ketabkhane ha-ye Iran*, vols. IRANDOC, 1970- . (Directory of libraries).

3b

Haider S J 'Bibliographical development and its current status in Iran' *IFLA J* 1975 1(3) 190-7.
Afshar I *A bibliography of bibliographies on Iranian studies* Teheran U, 1963 (Special issue of *Iranica* Jan 1963, vol 1).
National Library *Ketab Shenassi Melli Iran* (National bibliography; Iranian publications) 1963- . Monthly and quarterly. Contains an annual list of periodicals published in Iran.
— *Bibliographie nationale de l'Iran. Cumulatif décennal.*
Book Society *Rahnama-ye Ketab* Ed. I Afshar. 1958- Monthly.
— *Decennial bibliography of Iranian publications 1958-1968* Ed I Afshar, 1970. (First cumulation).
TEBROC *Books processed by TEBROC* 1969- . Quarterly.
Bibliography des livres imprimés depuis le commencement de l'imprimerie en Iran jusqu'en 1345 [1966] 3 vols.
Abold-Hamd A and Pakravan N *Bibliographie française de civilisation irannienne* U of Teheran 1972-4, 3 vols.
Kazemi A *Iran-bibliographie: deutschsprachige Abhandlungen, Beiträge, Aufsätze, Bücher, Dissertationen* U of Teheran, 1970.
Nawabi Y M *Bibliography of Iran: a catalogue of books and articles on Iranian subjects mainly in European languages* Kajeh P, 1969-71, 2 vols.
Afshar I *Index Iranicus*. Index of Iranian periodical literature. Vol I: 1910-1958; Vol II: 1958-68? Published 1961- .

Bayanfar A *The bibliography of books and librarianship* U of Teheran, Department of Library Science, 1968.
Ta'avoni S *An annotated bibliography of library science* TEBROC, 1973.

3c

Ministry of Science and Higher Education *Directory of Iranian periodicals* 1969-70.
Directory of Iranian periodicals IRANDOC, 1971- .
Iranian Library Association *Bulletin*. 1966- .
University of Teheran Library *Ketabdari* (Librarianship). 1967- . Annual.
ILA *Akhbar-e Mahaneh*. Monthly.
ILA *Name-ye Anjoman-e Ketabdaran-e*. Quarterly.

3e

Legal deposit: Iran Press Law 1907. Modified by the Public Library Act 1965.
Harvey J F 'Iranian special library standards' *Ann Lib Sci Doc* 1974 21(1/2) 22-31.
— *Inspel* 1975 10(1/2) 3-18.
— 'Minimum activities for national library and bibliographic development' *Pakistan Lib Bull* 1974 6(3/4) 1-16.

3f

Bonine M E and Keddie N *Continuity and change in modern Iran* State U of New York P, 1981.
Bahnam J *Cultural policy of Iran* Unesco, 1973, 46p.
Filstrup J M 'Franklin Book of Programs/Tehran' *Int Lib Rev* 1976 8(4) 431-50.
Harvey J F 'Iranian vs. American serial selection policies' *Ann Lib Sci Doc* 1973 20(1/4) 81-91.
Afshar I 'Ketabdari va farhang melli' *Rahnama-ye Ketab* 1969 11/12 (12) 643-7. (Libraries and education).
International Symposium for Literacy, Persepolis, Iran. *Final report* 1975, 39p.
Haider S J 'Libraries in ancient and medieval Iran' *Pakistan Lib Bull* 1977 8(3/4) 26-40.
Aziz A 'The Imperial Library under Mughul emperors' *Lib Hist Rev* 1974 1(3) 22-50. 16th and 17th centuries.
Homayoun Farokh R *Ketab va ketabkhane ha-ye shahanshahi-ye Iran* Ministry of Culture and Arts, 1966-68, 2 vols. Imperial libraries and books in Iran; pre-20th century.
— *History of books and the Imperial libraries of Iran*, 1968.
Shenassa A *History of academic, religious, private and public libraries in Shiraz from the Constitutional Revolution to the Shah-and-People Revolution* Pahlavi U, School of Graduate Studies, 1977, 76p.
Pourhadi I V 'Iran's public and private libraries' *L of C Q J* 1968 25(3) 219-29.
Mehernoosh K and Umapathy K S 'Libraries and librarianship as reflected in the press' *Int Lib Rev* 1979 11 487-95.
Harvey J F 'Iranian library studies' *Int Lib Rev* 1973 5(1) 3-52.
Sinai A and Harvey J F 'The Iranian library scene' *Int Lib Rev* 1969 1(1) 107-17.
'Proposal for a national library plan in Iran' *Int Lib Rev* 1970 2(3) 253-61. Submitted by J F Harvey.
Ebrami H 'Iran, libraries in' in *Encyclopedia* 13 (1975) 15-53, bibl.
Umapathy K S 'Libraries and librarianship in Iran' *Int Lib Rev* 1978 10(2) 119-35, refs.
Harvey J F 'Librarians and libraries in a nation in revolution: letter from Iran' *Lib J* 1979 104(12) 1307-10.

— 'Iranian library update' *Lib J* 1979 104(19) 2288-9.

Homayuon Farokh R *Tarikhche-ye ketabkhane ha-ye Iran va ketabkhane ha-ye omumi* Organization of Teheran Municipal Libraries, 1965. Public libraries, with a brief history of libraries.

Haider S J 'Public libraries in Iran' *Unesco Bull Lib* 1974 28(6) 298-304.

Haqiqitalab D 'Bookmobile in Iran' *ILA Bull* 1974 7(3) 286-317.

Rahnamaie M *A survey of the adult and children's public libraries in Gilan Province* Pahlavi U, School of Graduate Studies, 1977, 48p, refs.

Mehrami M A *Adult public and children's libraries in Eastern Azarbaijan Province* Pahlavi U, School of Graduate Studies, 1977, 60p, refs.

Amir-Arjomand L 'Libraries for the children of Iran' *Wilson Lib Bull* 1967 41 1055-61.

Gaver M V 'Good news from Iran: a personal report' *Top of the News* 1971 27 256-71. On children's libraries.

Iman L 'Librarianship in libraries for children and young adults' *ILA Bull* 1976 8(4) 555-61.

Umapathy K S 'Iranian children and young adults: intellectual development furthered by libraries' *Unesco J* 1979 1(1) 51-5.

Mehdizadeh N *The present status of school libraries in Fars Province* Pahlavi U, School of Graduate Studies, 1977, 75p, refs.

— and Rogers A R 'School libraries in Fars Province, Iran' *Int Lib Rev* 1978 10(1) 77-91.

Shakuri A '[Prison libraries]' (In Persian) *ILA Bull* 1978 11(1).

Survey and evaluation of the university and college libraries of the country Ministry of Court, 1971, 358p.

Brewster B J 'Students' reference services: Pahlavi University experience, a case study' (In Persian) *ILA Bull* 1976 9(2) 28p.

Brewster B J 'A student reference service: the Pahlavi experiment' *Int Lib Rev* 1978 10(4) 411-26.

Sepehri A 'Academic libraries in Iran: a critical appraisal' *Unesco Bull Lib* 1978 33(2) 87-90.

Mangla P B 'Libraries in higher education in Iran: their development and proposals for the next five years' *Int Lib Rev* 1976 8(2) 173-200.

[Problems of Iranian university libraries], Meeting January 1976. *Proceedings* Teheran University Library.

Samimi M *Library use and academic research in Iran in the sciences, social sciences and humanities* Pahlavi U, School of Graduate Studies, 1976, 68p, refs.

Guinchat C *Centre de documentation sur le développement culturel Iran (Mission), 4 novembre-16 décembre 1973* Unesco, 1974, 48p.

Haider J S 'Scientific research and information facilities in Iran' *Spec Lib* 1976 67(2) 104-10.

Regional Documentation Centres Conference, held in Tehran April 29-May 1, 1974 at the Iranian Documentation Centre. CENTO Scientific Programme IRANDOC, 1974, 141p. Iran, Pakistan, Turkey.

IRAQ

1

Iraqi National Library, Baghdad. 1924- New building 1975.
University of Baghdad Central Library. 1960- .
National Documentation Centre. 1972- .
Helal A H *Iraq: Scientific Documentation Centre, February-April 1972* Unesco, 1972, 61p.
El-Sharifi T H 'Iraqi Scientific Documentation Centre' *Unesco Bull Lib* 1975 29(1) 37-9.

2a

Ministry of Information. Higher Committee of Libraries. 1970- . Representatives from the Ministry of Higher Education, Ministry of Interior, Governate of Baghdad.

2b

Iraqi Library Association. 1968- .

2c

Bonny H V 'Library training in Iraq' *Unesco Bull Lib* 1958 12(5/6) 123-6.
Srivastava A P *Iraq: education for library science and documentation, 28 January to 27 July 1968* Unesco, 1969, 30p.
— *Iraq: library training and special libraries, November 1969-May 1970* Unesco, 1970, 30p.
Al-Amin A 'Training of librarians in Iraq' *Rissalat al-Maktabat* 1977 12(3) ?p.

3b

Abd al-Rahmàn and Abd al-Jabbài *Bibliography of Iraq: a classified list of printed materials on the land, people, history, economy and culture published in Western languages* Al-Irshad P, 1977, 304p.
University Library *al-Nashrah al-Iraqiyah lil-matbuat* (Iraqi bulletin of publications) 1965- .
National Library *Deposition bulletin* 1971- . Now the national bibliography.
Hebrew University *Bibliografiyya al Iraq* Jerusalem, The University, 1969, 13, 19p.
Bulletin of the Documentation Centre. Abstracts and index of periodicals.

3e

Legal deposit Act no 71, 13 July 1963. Amended by Law no 37 of 1st of June 1970. See also Law no 189 of 1969 for libraries other than the National Library.

3f

El Basri A-G D *Aspects of Iraqi cultural policy* Unesco, 1980, 38p. (Studies and Documents on cultural policies).

Al-Nasri N A M *Library services in the Republic of Iraq* (In Arabic) Ministry of Education P, 1967.

Dietze J 'Bibliotheken im Irak -Eindrücke und Einsichten' *Zentr Biblioth* 1970 84(6) 336-42.

Al-Kindilchie A I 'Iraq, libraries in' in *Encyclopedia* 13 (1975) 63-7.

— 'Libraries in Iraq and Egypt: a comparative study' *Int Lib Rev* 1977 9(1) 113-23.

— 'Academic libraries in Iraq' *Int Lib Rev* 1973 5(4) 463-70.

Qazanchi F Y M 'Academic libraries in Iraq' *Unesco Bull Lib* 1971 25(2) 91-3.

Manzoor S 'Instruction in the use of academic library' *IASLIC Bull* 1980 24(1) 23-6, refs.

Francis S *Iraq: development of documentation and academic library services* Unesco, 1977, 51p. (FMR/BEP/PGI/77/314).

ISRAEL

1

Jewish National and University Library, Jerusalem. 1884- .

Hebrew University Library, Jerusalem. 1956- .

National Council for Research and Development. Centre for Scientific and Technological Information, Tel Aviv. 1961- .

2a

Ministry of Education and Culture. Library Section.

Guidance Centre for Public Libraries, Jerusalem. 1964- . Jointly sponsored by the Ministry of Education and Culture, the Library Association and the Hebrew University Graduate School of Librarianship. Central cataloguing, processing, exchanges, etc.

The Centre for Public Libraries in Israel — aims and activities The Centre, 1967, 11p.

Barkai M Z 'The Center for Public Libraries: twelve years of service to Israel libraries' *Yad-La-Koré* 1978 17(4) 187-93.

Goell Y 'Center for Public Libraries in Israel' in *Jewish Book Annual 1978/79 (5739)* Jewish Council of America 1978, 36, 67-78.

2b

Israel Library Association (ASI), Jerusalem, 1952- .

Israel Society of Special Libraries and Information Centres (ISLIC), Tel Aviv, 1966- .

2c

Carnovsky L *Report on a programme of library education in Israel* Unesco, 1956, 20p.

Wormann C D 'Education for librarianship abroad: Israel' *Lib Trends* 1963 12(2) 211-26.

The Graduate School Hebrew U, 1964, 12p.

Schur H 'Post-graduate science information course in Israel' *Unesco Bull Lib* 1970 24(5) 251-65.

Brass L J 'Library development and education for librarianship in Israel' *PNLA Q* 1971 35 25-32.

Vilentchuck L 'Training in librarianship and information science in Israel' *ISLIC Bull* 1971 (3) 43-51.

Hebrew University *Research report-Section Humanities: Social Sciences*. Annual. Includes research in librarianship.

3a

Shenaton ha-menshalah (Government yearbook) Tel Aviv, 1949- .

Israel Yearbook Israel Yearbook Publications.

Kutten *A Bibliography of guides and directories in Israel* 2nd ed Tel Aviv,

Technion Research and Development Foundation, 1970, 34p.
Centre of Scientific and Technological Information *Sidrat madrikhim li-mekorot infortsyah* (Guides to services of information) Series of directories, kept up to date.
Directory of special libraries in Israel. Directory No 1 in the above series. 3rd edition, 1969.
Jewish book annual Contains a section on Israel libraries.

3b

Jewish National and University Library *Kirjath Sepher* Quarterly. National bibliography.
Book Publishers Association *Qatalog ha-sefarim ha-kelali* (General catalogue of books), Tel Aviv. Annual. Now automated.
— *Hasefer be-Israel* 1959- . News on current publications.
Book and Printing Centre *Books from Israel: export catalogue* 1964- . Every two years. Annotated — all fields, mainly in foreign languages.
Library of Congress *Accessions list: Israel* Book Procurement Center, 1964-1973. Ceased when the Center closed down.
Alexander Y *Israel: selected, annotated and illustrated bibliography* Gilbertville, NY, V Buday, 1968, 116p. Sources in English.
State Archives *Israel Government Publications*, 1969- . Annual.
— *1948-1964*. Cumulation in 4 vols. 1972.

3c

Tronik R *Israeli periodicals and serials in English and other languages: a classified bibliography* Scarecrow, 1974, 193p.
Yad la-koré (Reader's aid), 1946-52, 1956- . Published by ILA, then by the Centre for Public Libraries.
ISLIC *Bulletin*, 1966- .
Centre of Scientific and Technological Information *Information bulletin for documentalists.*

3d

Even-Tov C *Pirsumim ha-kolelim nitunim statistyym 1965-1967* Jerusalem, 1969, 18, 269p. Publications containing statistics.
Ben-Nayem V and Shavit D 'Public libraries in Israel — a statistical survey' *Yad la-koré* 1979 18(1/2) 12-24.

3e

Yad la-koré 1968 9(4) 155-74. Draft of standards for public libraries.

3f

Lottman H R 'Publishing in Israel' *Publishers Weekly* 1979 215(12) 33-59.
Hay D and Silberner E 'Library history in Israel' *Lib Hist Rev* 1974 1(3) 64-76.
Sever S *Library and library development in Israel* U of Chicago, 1969. Thesis.
Rothschild J 'Israel, libraries and information centres in' in *Encyclopedia* 13 (1975) 111-21, bibl.
Frigiolini C 'Il sistema bibliotecario israeliano' *AIB Boll* 1976 16(2) 164-70.
Sever S 'Reading patterns and libraries in Israel' *J Lib Info Sci* 1975 1(1) 1-24.
The need for regional libraries in Israel: a survey Edmond James de Rothschild Memorial Group, 1963, 86p.
Golan K I 'The Ministry of Education and Culture and the public libraries' (In Hebrew) *Yad la-koré* 1964 7 124-8.

Deligdisch Y 'Public library development in Israel' *Lib Ass Rec* 1965 68(12) 434-9.

Sever S 'Some social aspects of public library development in Israel' *Lib Q* 1968 38(4) 388-405. Includes a bibliographical list.

Leef I 'Municipal libraries in Tel Aviv-Yaffo' (In Hebrew) *Yad la-koré* 1968 9(1/2) 50-7.

Ellingham 'A glimpse at public libraries in Israel' *Assist Libn* 1979 72(6) 82-5.

Stancia I and Naftali B-S 'C I Golan and public library research in Israel' *Yad la-koré* 1979 18(1/2) 5-11.

Kanner D and Nov M 'The non-municipal libraries of Jerusalem' *Yad la-koré* 1979 18(1/2) 46-68.

Sever S 'Arab library in Israel' *Lib Q* 1979 49 163-81.

— 'Public libraries and the acculturation of immigrants, 1948-1960' *Yad la-koré* 1979 18(1/2) 78-89, refs.

— 'Integration of immigrants and libraries in Israel' *Lib Res* 1979 1(1) 67-82, refs.

Nachman G 'Die öffentliche Bibliothek im Kibbuz' *Buch u Biblioth* 1978 30(4) 263-4.

Sterling-Cohen L 'Children's library service in Israel' *Top of the News* 1975 31(2) 160-6.

Kurzman C 'For the 'People of the Book': university libraries in Israel' *Wilson Lib Bull* 1977 51(10) 824-31.

Koren J 'Interlibrary lending among academic and research libraries in Israel' *Libri* 1975 25(2) 98-132, refs.

Sever S 'Special libraries in Israel' *Spec Lib* 1976 67(5/6) 265-70.

Palti S and Simon R C 'Audio-visual centre library, Technion-Israel Institute of Technology' *IATUL Proc* 1977 9 56-8.

Welt I B *Israel: library and information activities, June-August 1970* Unesco, 1971, 49p.

Kaula P N 'Library and information activity in Israel' *Herald Lib Sci* 1972 11 23-30.

Keren C 'Closing the gap: towards a national network in Israel' *ISLIC Bull* 1971 3(1) 19-22.

— and Hoffman E 'Planning a network for scientific and technical information service in Israel' *Info Stor Retrieval* 1973 9(12) 689-96.

— and Thomas P A 'The interrelationship between information systems and policy formation' *J Info Sci* 1979 1(2) 85-90.

JORDAN

1

University of Jordan Library, Amman. 1962- . Legal deposit library.

Ministry of Education. Educational Documentation Centre.

Al-Jam'iyat al-'Ilmiyat al Malakiyat, Al Maktabat wa Markas al Ma'lunat (Royal Scientific Society, Library and Information Centre). 1970- .

2a

Ministry of Culture and Youth. Mudeereyat al Maktabat wal Wathaeq (Directorate of Libraries and national documents). 1976- .

Ministry of Education. School Library Division.

2b

Jordan Library Association. 1963- . Has established its own library and documentation centre. (See under 2c). 1977- .

2c

Najdawi A 'The JLA eighth course in librarianship' *Rissalat al-Maktaba* 1975 10(2).

'Library and Information Science Centre' *Rissalat al-Maktaba* 1977 12(2). Plan approved by the Ministry of Education; the centre will provide courses in librarianship.

3a

Patai R *The Hashemite Kingdom of Jordan* New Haven, HRAF P, 1956, 605p.

Dahbour S and Shabeti F comps *The Directory of libraries in Jordan* JLA, 1976, 206p. English/Arabic.

3b

Al-Akhras M comp *Palestinian Jordanian bibliography 1900-1970* JLA, 1972.

— *Al-bibliographia al-Felatiniah al-Ardoneyah, 1970-1975* JLA, 1976, 283p.

— Current list of publications in *Rissalat al-Maktaba*, 1969- .

University of Jordan Library *Monthly list of accessions*. In English and Arabic. Serves as Jordan bibliography.

— *Abstracts* 1970- . Library science.

Patai R *Jordan, Lebanon and Syria: an annotated bibliography* HRAF P, 1957, 289p.

See also: under Syria, 3b.

3c

Jordan Library Association *Rissalat al-Maktaba* (Message of the library) 1965- . Quarterly.

3d

440 Al-Akhras M et al *Library finance: analytical study* JLA, 1976, 17p.

3f

Kalia D R *Report on a mission to some of the Arab States* ASFEC, 1957. Syria, Lebanon and Jordan.

Asali K J 'Jordan, libraries in' in *Encyclopedia* 13 (1975) 300-10.

Parker J S 'Proposals for library development in the Hashemite Kingdom of Jordan' *Rissalat al-Maktaba* 1975 10(4) 11-5.

Yasin B S '[How does Amman Municipal Public Library encourage its children to read?]' (In Arabic) *Rissalat al-Maktaba* 1976 11(2/3) ?p.

Abdel-Rahman H and Shbeitah F 'Jordan University Library (Field study)' *Rissalat al-Maktaba* 1974 9(4) ?p.

Said O H 'Status of special libraries in Jordan' *Rissalat al-Maktaba* 1978/9 14(4) ?p.

Qandil Y 'The Jordan Television Library (a report)' *Rissalat al-Maktaba* 1975 10(1) 21-2.

Grolier E de *Development of the National Documentation Centre. Hashemite Kingdom of Jordan (East Bank)* Unesco, 1977, 72p (ERIC report ED-167 150).

LEBANON

1

Bibliothèque National du Liban, Beirut. 1921- .
McEwan D 'The National Library of Lebanon' *Lib Ass Rec* 1958 60(7).
Sheniti M 'The National Library of Beirut' *Alam al-Maktabat* 1964 6(1).
American University of Beirut. University libraries. 1866- .
Office of Educational Documentation. Library. 1972- .
National Council for Scientific Research, Documentation Centre. 1973- .

2a

Ministère de l'Education Nationale.

2b

Association des Bibliothèques Libanaises, Beirut. 1960- .

2c

Beirut University College (Previously Beirut College for Women).
Franz E *Liban-Formation archivistique: création d'un centre de formation des archivistes, des bibliothécaires et des documentalistes, mars-avril 1974* Unesco, 1974, 32p.

3a

Patai R *The Republic of Lebanon* New Haven, HRAF P, 1956, 2 vols.

3b

Dagher J *Bibliographie du Liban* Beirut, 1945.
Bibliothèque Nationale *Bulletin bibliographique libanais des oeuvres intellectuelles et des imprimés du Liban* 1964-65. No more published.
— *Bibliographie nationale* 1971, 71p; 1972, 63p. Current?.
Mikdashi N *Thèses 1909-1970* American U, Yafet Memorial Library, 1971, 110p.
Khairallah S *Lebanon* Clio P, 1979, 154p. (World Bibliographical series).
See also: Syria, 3b.

3c

Association des Bibliothèques du Liban *Journal officiel.* Annual.

3e

Décrets législatifs de la réforme de 1959 Vol 2, décrets 128-162. Mainly on legal deposit amendment.

3f

Salibi K S *The modern history of Lebanon* London, 1965.
Murray G T *Lebanon: the new future* Beirut, Thomson-Rizk, 1974.

Kalia D R *Report on a mission to some of the Arab States* ASFEC, 1957. Syria, Lebanon, Jordan.

Lombard E J *Liban: évaluation et développement des bibliothèques* Unesco, 1965, 18p.

Villemin S *Liban: développement des bibliothèques, 15 novembre 1967-31 décembre 1968: report* Unesco 1969 (1612/BMS.RD/DBA). With an appendix on the libraries of the Lebanese University.

[Papers on the development of libraries] in *Leads* (ALA-Round Table) June 1967 and August 1972.

Kent F L 'Lebanon, libraries in' in *Encyclopedia* 14 (1975) 120-30.

Deliwannes D and Younan S *Les bibliothèques universitaires au Liban: situation et problèmes* Ecole Nationale Supérieure de Bibliothécaires (France), 1975, 30p. Thesis.

Khalaf N and Rubeiz J 'Economics of American University of Beirut library' *Libri* 1978 28(1) 58-82, refs.

Gilleo A 'Libraries and documentation in Beirut' *Orient* (Hamburg) 1968 (5) 159-64.

Messeke O *Esquisse d'un système national d'information au Liban* Beirut, Présidence du Conseil, 1975, 418p.

For the history of libraries in antiquity and Middle-Ages see under Syria and Middle East.

SYRIA

1

National Library al-Zahiriyah, Damascus. 1880- .
Clavel J-P 'La Bibliothèque Nationale de Damas' *IFLA J* 1975 1(3) 187-9. Competition for the building of the new library.
Damascus University Library Department. 1924- .
'Damascus University Library' *Unesco Bull Lib* 1967 21(6) 343-4.

2a

Ministry of Culture, Tourism and Guidance. Public libraries.
Arab Academy. National libraries.
Ministry of Higher Education. University libraries.
Ministry of Education. School libraries.
Institut Français d'Etudes Arabes, Damascus. 1928- .
Elisséeff N 'The library of the Institut Français at Damascus' *Unesco Bull Lib* 1965 10(10) 235.

2b

Syrian Library Association. 1972- .

2c

Sharify N 'Education for library abroad: UAR, Iran, Iraq, Lebanon and Syria' *Lib Trends* 1963 12(2) 227-59.

3a

Nyrop R F et al *Area handbook for Syria* 2nd ed American U P, 1974.

3b

Syrian national bibliography, 1971- .
Damascus University Library *Bulletin*. Contains lists of new accessions.
Ministry of Culture *Bulletin bibliographique de l'édition en Syrie en . . .* Annual.
UAR Ministry of Culture and National Guidance *A bibliographical list of works about Syria* Cairo, National Library P, 1965.
Patai R *Jordan, Lebanon and Syria: an annotated bibliography* HRAF P, 1957, 289p.
Al-Maktaba: a selective bibliography for Iraq, Jordan, Lebanon and Syria Harissa, St Paul Printing P, 1956- . Annotated. In Arabic with English translation.

3c

The 1970 directory of the press and periodicals in Syria Syrian Documentation Papers, 112p.

3d

Sharif A A *Sources of statistics in Syria* Damascus, Bureau des Documentations Syriennes et Arabes, 1964.

Central Bureau of Statistics *Annual statistics*, 1949- . General. The Bureau also publishes specialised surveys such as:

— *Studies in the relationship among the level of education, employment and emigration* 1973 with the assistance of Unesco.

3e

Ministry of Higher Education. Committee to follow up recommendations of the Damascus seminar October 1971. Began meeting in 1973.

3f

Petran T *Syria* Praeger, 1972.

Kalia D R *Report on a mission to some of the Arab States (Syria, Lebanon and Jordan)* ASFEC, 1957.

Burr V 'Bibliotheken in Ugarit' *Z Biblioth Bibliog* 1967 14(3).

Ministry of Culture *Takrer an al-Maktabat al-Mawgoda bel goter* 1972.

'4000 year old library discovered' *Lib News* (Ceylon Nat Lib Serv Board) 1977 5(2) 10-11. Also in *Unesco Courier* Feb 1977.

Estanbouli M N 'Syria, libraries in' in *Encyclopedia* 29 (1980) 394-453, refs.

First Conference of Library Science and Documentation Specialists, Damascus, October 1976. Summary in *BDT* 1978 32(2) 106-7.

Rifai A *Muzakara al-Maktabat Jameat Dimashq* Damascus U P, 1972.

TURKEY

1

Millî Kütüphane (National Library), Ankara. 1946- .

— Bibliyografya Enstitüsü (Bibliographical Institute). 1952- .

University of Ankara Library. Has a Department of Library Science.

University of Istanbul Library. Has a department of Library Science.

Türk Teknik Haherleşme Merkezi (Turkish Technical Information Centre) Istanbul. 1952- . Based on the Technical University.

Türkiye Bilimsel ve Teknik Arastirma Kurumu (TBTAK). Türkiye Bilimsel ve Teknik Dokümantasyon Merkezi (TURDOK), Ankara. 1966- . Scientific and Technical Documentation Centre, part of the Scientific and Technical Research Council.

Kismet B 'Turkish Scientific and Technical Documentation Centre' *Unesco Bull Lib* 1969 23(2) 88-90.

2a

Ministry of Education. General Directorate of Libraries.

2b

Türk Kütüphaneciler Dernegi (Association of Turkish Librarians) Ankara. 1949-

2c

Ludington F B 'Kütüphanecilik Bölümü (Department of Library Science) *Lib J* 1955 80(2) 122-3.

White C M 'The University of Ankara's Institute of Librarianship in 1960' *ALA Bull* 1960 54(9) 665-7.

Ersoy O and Yurdadog B U 'Education for librarianship abroad: Turkey' *Lib Trends* 1963 12(2) 205-10.

Çankaya L 'Education for librarianship in Turkey' *Unesco Bull Lib* 1974 28(6) 329-30.

3a

National Library *Turkiye kütüphaneleri rehkeri/Répertoire des bibliothèques de Turquie* The Library, 1957, 243p. Directory of libraries.

Ersoy O *Halk Kütüphanelerimiz Üzerine Bir Araştirma* (Survey of Turkish public libraries) Anadolu Matbaasi, 1966.

Rafokov A Kh 'Biblioteki Stambula' *Bibl Akad Nauk SSSR Trudy* 1962 6 303-15.

3b

Güçlü M *Turkey* Clio P, 1981, 331p. (World bibliographical series, 27).

Basbugoglu F et al *1928-1965 Yillari arasinda Turkiyede Basilmiş Biblyografyalarin Biblyografiasi* (Bibliography of Turkish bibliographies) Ankara, Unesco, 1966, 270p.

National Library *Türkiye Biblyografyasi* (National bibliography). 1928- . Quarterly.

Bakla L *Instanbul yayinlari biblyografyasi eserler ve makaleler* (University of Istanbul).

National Library *Türkiye makaleler biblyografyasi* (Bibliography of periodical articles) 1952- . Quarterly. Includes librarianship.

Churukian A P 'Current national bibliographies from the Near East as collection development tools' *Lib Resources Tech Services* 1979 23(2) 156-62. Studies mainly the Turkish bibliographies as aids to book acquisition for foreign countries.

Muzaffer Gökman comp *Türk kütüphaneciliginin biblyografyasi.* Turkish Library Association, 1964. Bibliography of Librarianship.

3c

National Library *Haberleri* (News bulletin).

Turkish Library Association *Bültini*, 1952- .

3d

Devlet Istatistik Enstitüsü *Milli Egitim Istatistikleri.* (Education statistics). Includes librarianship.

3e

Deposit law, 1934 law 2527.

3f

Kazamias A *Education and the quest for modernity in Turkey* Allen & Unwin, 1966.

Thompson L S 'Libraries in Turkey' *Lib Q* 1952 22(3) 270-82.

—*A program for library development in Turkey* Millî Egitim Basimevi, 1952, 11p.

Wolf Management *Books as tools for national growth and development. A case study of the use of books in Turkey* Chicago, 1965, 216p.

Ersoy O *Kütüphaneciligimizin Sorunlari* (Problems of librarianship) Turkish Library Association, 1966.

Rowhāni K [Libraries in Turkey] (In Persian) *Iranian Lib Ass Bull* 1977 10(1).

Zhukova L V 'Bibliotechnoe delo v Turetskoi Respublike' *Bibliot i Bibliog za Rubezhom* 1978 (70) 24-35, refs.

Kum I 'Utilfredsstillende utvikling en jort skisse av tyrkish bibliotekvesen' *Bog og Bibliot* 1979 46(4) 177-9. Critical comment of the present library system.

Cabin I *The analysis of the structure and functions of academic libraries in Turkey* London, U College, 1978. PhD Thesis.

Kurosman K 'Academic libraries in Turkey' *Int Lib Rev* 1980 12(2) 173-200, refs.

Bennett W W 'The Middle East Technical University library' *Unesco Bull Lib* 1964 18(6) 269-73.

Unesco *Middle East Technical University, Ankara, Turkey: report for the period 1960-1966* Paris, 1967.

Regional Documentation Centres Conference, held in Tehran April/May 1974 at the Iranian Documentation Centre CENTO Scientific Programme IRANDOC, 1974, 141p. Participants: Iran, Turkey and Pakistan. Includes general papers on UNISIST, etc.

ARABIAN PENINSULA AND GULF REGION

3a

Fiander W ed *Saudi Arabia and the Gulf States* rev ed London, Statistics and Market Intelligence Library, 1979, 48p.

3b

Bibliography of publications dealing with the Arabian Gulf States and the South Arabian Peninsula State U of Baghdad, Central Library, 1970.

SAUDI ARABIA

1

Al-Riyadh National Library. 1963- .
Al-Iman Muhammed bin Saud University Library, Riyadh.
King Abdul Aziz University Library, Jeddah.

2a

Ministry of Education.
Saudi Arabia Commission for Unesco.

2c

Courses in the Universities cited above.

3d

National Library *Muajam al Matbuat al Saudiah* (List of Saudi publications). The first volumes cover works published up to 1973. Current bibliography.
Macro E *Bibliography of the Arabian Peninsula* U of Miami P, 1958, 80p.
El-Manhal Special issue 1966 27(7), 276p. List of works by Saudi writers.
Sardar Z 'Saudi Arabia: indigenous sources of information' *Aslib Proc* 1979 31(5) 237-44.
Clements F A *Saudi Arabia* Clio, 1979, 197p. (World Bibliographical Series, 5).

3c

National Library *Bulletin*. 1963- . Quarterly.

3f

Lipsky G A et al *Saudi Arabia: its people, its society, its culture* New Haven, HRAF P, 1959.
Riley C L *Historical and cultural dictionary of Saudi Arabia* Scarecrow, 1972, 133p.
Fouad al-Farsy *Saudi Arabia: a case study in development* Kegan Paul Int Pub, 1981, 224p.
Tashkandy A S 'Saudi Arabia, libraries in' in *Encyclopedia* 26 (1979) 307-22, refs.
Khurshid Z 'Libraries and information centres in Saudi Arabia' *Int Lib Rev* 1979 11(4) 409-20, refs.
Celli J P 'Special libraries in the Kingdom of Saudi Arabia' *Spec Lib* 1980 71(8) 358-64.

YEMEN

Now two states: Yemen Democratic Republic (formerly Aden) and Yemen Arab Republic (or South Yemen).

1

Miswat Library, Aden.

3b

Macro E *Bibliography on Yemen and notes on Macha* U of Miami P, 1960, 63p.

Mondesir S L *A select bibliography of Yemen Arab Republic and People's Democratic Republic of Yemen* U of Durham, Centre for Middle Eastern and Islamic Studies, 1977, 59p. (The Centre, Occasional papers, 5).

3f

Sharify N 'Aden, libraries in' in *Encyclopedia* 1 (1968) 83.

GULF STATES

Including the United Arab Emirates and Oman.

3b

National Library, Kuwait *Source book on Arabian Gulf States: Arabian Gulf in general, Kuwait, Bahrain, Qatar and Oman* Kuwait, 1975.

Public Library of Qatar *A selected bibliography on Qatar and Arabian Gulf* 1972.

— *Arabian Gulf: a selected bibliography* 1974.

Kabeel S M *Selected bibliography on Kuwait and the Persian Gulf* Kuwait University, 1969, 104p. Foreign sources.

Selected bibliography on Kuwait and Arabian Gulf University Library, Kuwait, 1970. Arab sources.

3f

Yorke V *The Gulf in the 1980s* Royal Inst of Int Affairs, 1980, 80p.

Cottrell A J ed *The Persian Gulf States: a general survey* Johns Hopkins U P, 1980, 695p.

Osborne C *The Gulf States and Oman* Croom Helm, 1977.

United Arab Emirates: outline for a national documentation and information centre Unesco, 1975 (FMR/COM/DND/75/135).

BAHRAIN

1

Manama Public Library.

2a

Ministry of Education. Superintendent of Libraries.

3b

Public Library *Bahrain public libraries*. Bibliography.

— *Publications directory*.

3c

Public Library *Dunia al-Maktabat*. Newsletter.

3f

Aman M M *Plan for a documentation centre for the Ministry of Education* Unesco, 1977, 12p.

KUWAIT

1

Kuwait National and University Library. 1923- .
— National Heritage Centre. Prepares bibliographies concerning the Gulf Region.
Kuwait Central Library, Kuwait. 1923- .

2a

Ministry of Education. Libraries Department. Also has its own library, 1936- .

2b

Association of Friends of the Libraries.

2c

Stockham K A *The establishment of a two-years course in library and information studies: a report to the Ministry of Education in Kuwait* Kuwait, Ministry of Education, 1977, 19p.

3b

See under Gulf States.
National Library *Library Bulletin* Nos 1-17 (1966-71).
— *Quarterly accessions lists* Oct 1971- (1) - . Books and periodicals.

3c

Kuwait University Library *The University Library* Oct 1971- .

3d

Central Statistical Office *Statistical abstracts* 1964- .

3f

For general works see under: Gulf States.
Bqdr A 'Kuwait, libraries in' in *Encyclopedia* 14 (1975) 1-18.
'Library services in Arabic-speaking states: Kuwait' *Unesco Bull Lib* 1960 14(3) 124-5.
Zehery M H 'Libraries and librarianship in Kuwait' *Int Lib Rev* 1975 7(1) 3-13.
Yamani A-R 'Public libraries in Kuwait' *Rissalat al-Maktabat* 1974 9(4) ?p.
Parker J S *Development of school and public libraries network: report prepared for the Government of Kuwait by Unesco* Unesco, 1975, 85p.
Ghaheri H *Survey of the activities of the Department of Libraries and their relationship to the collections and services of high school libraries in Kuwait* Pahlavi U, School of Graduate Studies, 1976, 129p. Thesis.
'Kuwait University libraries' *Unesco Bull Lib* 1970 24(2) 79-82.
Zehery M H 'Special libraries in Kuwait' *Spec Lib* 1975 66(12) 595-602.
— *The role of information in the advancement of science and technology in Kuwait* (Kuwait National Symposium on Science and Technology for Development, 1978) Institute for Scientific Research.
Salem S 'The design of a microfilm information system for a petroleum well file' *Microdoc* 1979 8(2) 35-6, 38-40, 42, 44.

QATAR

1

Qatar Public Library, Doha. 1962- . Acts as the national library, with legal deposit privilege.

3b

Public Library *Bibliography of books and pamplets published in Qatar* 1970- . National bibliography.

Unwin P T H *Qatar* Clio P, 1982 c200p. (World Bibliographical Series, 36).

3f

Focus on Qatar: proceedings of a one-day conference held on 5 November 1980 Arab-British Chamber of Commerce, 1980, 36p.

AFRICAN REGION

EGYPT

1

Dar al-Kutub wal-Wathā'iq al-Qawmîyah (National House for Books and Archives). Previously: Dar al-Kutub al-Qawmîyak. Cairo, 1870- .

— National Bibliographical and Data Processing Centre.

University Library, Cairo.

National Information and Documentation Centre (NIDOC). 1954- .

2a

Ministry of Education. Cultural Administration.

Educational Documentation Centre. 1956- .

Arab States Fundamental Education Centre (ASFEC). Sirs al-Layyan, 1952- .

2b

Egyptian Association for Archives, Librarianship and Documentation 1946-70: Egyptian Association for Archives and Librarianship. Cairo.

School Library Association. 1968- . (Gamdyat Almaktabat Al-Madzasiya).

2c

Cairo University, Faculty of Arts, Department of Librarianship and Archives.

NIDOC: Courses for documentalists.

ASFEC: Courses for heads of cultural centres and popular libraries.

In-service training.

3a

NIDOC *Directory of Scientific and Technical Libraries in the UAR* The Centre, 1970, 242p.

3b

Alawady S M *Bibliographic controls and services in Egypt: a survey and study with emphasis on the role of the Egyptian National Library* Texas Women Institute, PhD Thesis, 1978, 157p.

National Library *Nashrat dar al-Kutub al-Misriyah* (Accessions lists) 1949-1955. Annual.

— *al-Nashrat al-Misriyah lil Matbuat* (Egyptian publications bulletin) 1956-1969. English and Arabic. Various cumulations.

— *Nashrat al-Ida' al-shariyah* (Monthly deposit bulletin). 1958- . Cumulated in the above.

— *Subject catalogue of Egypt*. Lists all publications, local or foreign about Egypt.

Al-Kitab al-Arabi fi'Aam (Arab book annual) 1960- . Sponsored by publishers.

National Centre of Bibliographical Services (National Library) *Al-Dalil al-Misri lil Kitab* 1972, 1161p. Directory of Egyptian books.

Majallat al-Ketāb al-Arabi (Arabic book journal) 1967- .

Nusayr A I *Al-Kutub al-Arabiyah allati nushirat fi UAR bin 'amay 1926-1940: disarah bibliographiyah* 1966, 457 leaves. Retrospective bibliography.

Graberg M L von 'Neueste deutsche Forschung zur Geschichte der Bibliotheken Alexandreia's (1955-1971); eine Bericht' *Libri* 1974 24(4) 277-301.

3c

'Alam al-Maktabah (Library world) 1958-70.
Al-Maktabah al-Arabiyah (Arab library journal) 1963-65. Irregular.
Shifat al-Maktabah School Library Association, 1969- .

3d

Central Agency for Mobilization and Statistics, Documentation Centre *Statistical yearbook* 1952-64.
— *Selection of the UAR general statistics 1951/52 to 1966/67* Cairo, 1967.
— *Nashrat al-Ihsa'at al-Thaqafiyah* (Bulletin of cultural statistics) 1970- . Annual.

3e

Legal deposit law: Article 48 of the Copyright Act 354 of 1954.

3f

Bilinski L 'Upo wszechnianie książki w Arabskiej Republice Egiptu' *Bibliotekarz* 1977 44(2) 47-52.
Grannis C R 'Ex-Franklin branch thrives in Cairo; Iran doubtful' *Publishers Weekly* 1980 (25 July) 218 82.
Husayn M A *Vom Papyrus zum Codex: der Beitrag Aegypteus zur Buchkultur* Ed Leipzig, 1970, 139p. Also in English: Hussein M A. 1972, 135p.
Nicholas C L *The library of Ramses the Great* Peacock P, 1964.
Lutz C E 'The oldest library motto: PSYCHE IATREION' (In Greek script) *Lib Q* 1978 48(1) 36-9, refs. Ramses II's library: 'The House of healing of the soul'.
Richardson E C *Some old Egyptian librarians* Scribner, 1911.
Sviridova I 'Giganty pozaproshlogo tysyacheletiya' *Bibliotekar* 1977 (4) 64-7. Pergamon and Alexandria libraries.
Muhadat M M 'The burning of the library of Alexandria' (In Arabic) *Rissalat al-Maktaba* 1978 13(2) 20-5.
Aman M M 'Libraries abroad: libraries in UAR' *J Lib Hist* 1969 4(2) 158-68.
— 'Egypt, libraries in' in *Encyclopedia* 7 (1972) 574-88, refs.
Al-Kindilchie A I 'Libraries in Iraq and Egypt: a comparative study' *Int Lib Rev* 1977 9(1) 113-23.
Awad Tewfik Awad 'School libraries in the Arab Republic of Egypt' *Unesco Bull Lib* 1972 26(4) 214-7.
Kazem M et al 'School library services: Egypt, Israel and Malta' *IFLA J* 1976 2(4) 266-70.
Aman M M 'Egyptian university libraries' *Int Lib Rev* 1970 2(2) 175-81.
— 'Egyptian university libraries' *Lib Hist Rev* 1975 2(1) 1-9.
Qasim H M 'A *al-Tawthiq al-ilmi was dawruh fi khidmat al-bahth fi UAR* Cairo, 1971, 6, 11, 507, 34 leaves. Scientific documentation.
Kasem H M A 'Administrative information services in the Arab Republic of Egypt' *Unesco Bull Lib* 1976 30 210-7.
'Georgia Tec to assist Egypt to create a comprehensive system of national information services' *Unesco Bull Lib* 1980 54 361.
Romerio G F *Arab Republic of Egypt: a telecommunication system for the National Information Centre* Unesco, 1977, 35p. Based on NIDOC, to serve the region.
Jeffreys A E *Arab Republic of Egypt: mechanisation of the National Library catalogues, October-November 1974* Unesco, 1975, 20p.

LIBYA

1

National Library, Benghazi. 1975- . A decision was made to build two national libraries — the second one at Tripoli, but this plan has been postponed.

Fannoush M O 'The National Library: why? and how?' *Risalat al-Maktabah* (Benghazi) 1975 2(3) 35-7.

University of El-Fateh. Main library, Tripoli. 1957- . (Previously: Tripoli University).

2a

Ministry of Education and National Guidance. Public libraries. In 1972 the Ministry of Information and Culture took over.

Ministry of State, Department of Culture. Cultural Centres. The Ministry of State used to fulfill some of the functions of a national library.

2c

Courses at University of El-Fateh, Faculty of Education, Department of Library Science. 1976- .

3a

Stanford Research Institute *Area handbook for Libya* USGPO, 1969.

3b

Ward P *A survey of Libyan bibliographical resources* 2nd ed Libyan Publishing House, 1965. Includes institutions as well as printed sources.

Schlüter H 'Non-arabic regional bibliographies pertaining to the Libyan Arab Republic' *Int Lib Rev* 1976 8 201-15.

— 'Nationale Bibliographie Libyens' *Z Biblioth Bibliog* 1975 22 47-9.

Ministry of State *National bibliography* 1972- . Yearly with two cumulative volumes:

Vol 1: Periodicals 1866-1971.

Vol 2: Printed material 1951-1971.

(The National Library is taking over the preparation of the national bibliography).

Schluter H *Index Libycus: bibliography of Libya, 1957-1969, with supplementary material 1915-1956* G K Hall, 1972, 305p.

Libya Series of bibliographical lists of books and references about the Arab world, Vol. 9.

Al-Barbar A M *Government and politics in Libya: 1969-1978, a bibliography* Vance Bibliographies, 1979, 139p.

3c

Ward P *Periodicals in Libya* Tripoli, 1963. Revised edition of the original list by Sayid Ali Misrati.

3d

Census and Statistical Department *Statistical abstract* 1958/62- . Five-yearly.

3f

Wright J *Libya : a modern history* Croom Helm, John Hopkins, 1981, 288p.

El-Fathaly O I and Palmer M *Political development and social change in Libya* Lexington Books, 1980. Period 1969- .

Gallal A M *Historial survey of libraries in Libya up to the present time*. Report to Unesco, August 1972. Published?

— 'Libraries in Libya' *Unesco Bull Lib* 1973 27(5) 257-61.

Savitz G S *The Libyan library development plan: a special report for the Ministry of Education and Guidance*, Tripoli 17 November 1970, 13p.

Parker J S *Libyan Arab Republic: development of documentation library and archive services. Report* Unesco, 1976, 128p.

Fannoush M O and Gallal A M 'Republic of Libya (Socialist People's Libyan Arab Jamahiriya), Libraries in' in *Encyclopedia* 25 (1978) 241-7, refs.

Fannoush M O 'Public libraries in the Libya Arab Republic: description, analysis of activities and a proposed plan for action' *Paper* presented at the Graduate School of Library and Information Sciences, U of Texas, Austin, 1972.

Sherief A 'University libraries in the Libyan Arab Republic' *Paper* presented at a conference on Bibliographic Preparation of Arabic Books, Riyadh, 1973.

Colvin P 'Organising a library in Libya' *Focus Int Comp Libp* 1978 9(2) 17-9. Library of the Department of Antiquities.

SUDAN

1

University of Khartoum Library. 1945- . Legal deposit.
Omdurman Central Library. 1951- . Deposit library.
National Research Council. National Documentation Centre. 1973- .

2a

Ministry of Information and Culture. Department of Culture.
Ministry of Youth, Sports and Social Affairs. Documentation and public libraries Section. Also runs a documentation centre.
National Research Council (1970-). National Committee for Information Services. 1979- . Created under the National Research Council Act to coordinate information services and further the national development plan.

2b

Sudan Library Association. First Conference in 1972.

3a

Voll J O *Historical dictionary of the Sudan* Scarecrow, 1978. (African Historical Dictionaries, 17).

3b

University of Khartoum Library *Accessions bulletin* 1963- . Legal deposit material and other acquisitions.
— *Classified catalogue of the Sudan collection in the University of Khartoum Library* The Library, 1970, 500p. Supplements:
Nasri A R *A bibliography of the Sudan, 1939-1958* OUP, 1962.
Keshkekian S *A bibliographical introduction to the Sudan Part I: Works in European languages* Khartoum U, 1958, 10p.
Ibrahim A and Nasri A R *A bibliography of the Sudan, 1959-1966* U of Khartoum Library, 1967.
Dagher J A *Al-Usal al-Arabiyah lil Disarat al-Sudaniyah* Beirut, The Author, 1968, 275p. Arabic sources, 1875-1967.
Sudan Vol 6 of the series: Bibliographical Lists of Books and References about the Arab World. See in: Middle East, 3b.

3c

Sudan Library Association *Journal*. 1975- . Supersedes: *Bulletin*.

3e

Deposit Law 1966. Amended 1971.

3f

Ministry of Information and Culture *Sudan today* U P of Africa, 1971, 234p.
 Bashir M O *Educational development in the Sudan* OUP, 1969, 287p.

Sudan: librarianship, documentation Budapest, FID/DC Secretariat, 1974, 59p. (FID/DC Occasional publications, 2).

Istasi C W 'Sudan, libraries in' in *Encyclopedia* 29 (1980) 228-41.

Sewell P H 'The development of library service in Sudan' *Unesco Bull Lib* 1961 15(2) 87-90.

— *Report and survey on library services in the Sudan* Unesco, 1963, 31p. (Unesco /PP/SUD/CUA/3).

Mamoun I E 'Past, present and possible future development of librarianship in the Sudan' Paper at the IFLA seminar for Developing Countries, 1971. Published in Chandler G ed *International librarianship*, Library Association, 1972, 27-32.

Parker J S *Democratic Republic of the Sudan: development of library and documentation services, 14 October 1971-5 January 1972* Unesco, 1972, 94p.

— 'Library development in the Sudan' *Unesco Bull Lib* 1973 27(2) 78-83.

— 'Library development in the Sudan' *Pakistan Lib Bull* 1975 7(2) 14-23.

King C 'Starting from scratch in Sudan's deep South' *Lib Ass Rec* 1978 80 237. On college and university libraries.

Nasri A R 'Research libraries in the Sudan with a note on general and subject bibliographies' in *Proceedings* of the 12th annual conference of the Philosophical Society of the Sudan The Society, 1964, 135-43.

Istasi C W *Planning guidelines for a national scientific and technical information system in the Sudan* U of Pittsburgh, 1976. (Thesis).

Sewell P H *Developing an information system for the Sudan* Unesco, 1979.

See also under: Africa.

NORTH AFRICA

2c

[Training and status of African librarians, archivists and documentalists] Conference, Dakar, 1977. *Papers and documents* U of Dakar, School of Librarianship. One paper concerns French-speaking Africa and the Maghreb. See Africa, 2c.

3a

Annuaire de l'Afrique du Nord Paris, CNRS for the Centre de Recherches et d'Etudes des Sociétés Méditerranéennes, 1962- . Includes a list of research centres concerned with North Africa.

3b

Aman M M 'Bibliographical activities of the Arab countries of North Africa' *Int Lib Rev* 1970 2(3) 263-73.

3c

SCOLMA 'Periodicals published in Africa. Part 2: Algeria, Morocco, Tunisia' *Lib Mater Afr* 1965 3(2), Suppl 26, 24, 29p.

3f

'Meeting of the directors of national libraries in countries of the Maghreb (22-27 November 1972)' *Unesco Bull Lib*1973 27(3) 188-9.

Squalli H 'Présentation du projet de création d'une banque maghrébine d'information industrielle' *Documentaliste* 1978 15(3) 27-31.

See also some references under: Africa, and French-speaking Africa.

ALGERIA

1

Bibliothèque Nationale, Algiers. 1960- .
Bouayed M *Bibliothèque Nationale d'Algérie* The Library, 1967.
Bibliothèque de l'Université, Algiers. 1887- .
'La bibliothèque universitaire d'Alger' *Bull Biblith Fr* 1962 7(11) 549-51.
Centre Culturel, Scientifique et Technique Français d'Alger, Section de Diffusion, Algiers. 1970- . Formerly: Centre Français de Documentation Technique. 1965-70.

2a

Ministère de l'Information et de la Culture.
Ministère de l'Education Nationale.

2c

Diploma for Libraries and Archives, Ministry of Information.

3a

Heggoy A A *Historical dictionary of Algeria* Scarecrow, 1980. (African Historical Dictionaries, 28).
Répertoire national des archives, bibliothèques et organismes de documentation Centre National de Documentation Economique et Sociale, 1977, 585p.

3b

Bibliothèque Nationale *Al-Bibliographiya al-Jaza'iriyah/Bibliographie de l'Algérie* 1963- . 2 a year.
Bouayed M and Khammar A *Dix ans de production intellectuelle en Algérie, 1962-1972; I: Les écrits de langue arabe* SNED, 1974. (National Library Publications; Series Bibliographies and catalogues).
Algeria. No 1 in the Series: Bibliographical lists of books and references about the Arab World. See under: Middle East 3b.
Lawless R I *Algeria* Clio P, 1980, 215p. (World Bibliographical Series, 19).
'Index cumulatif des périodiques: juillet 1962-juillet 1967' as *Bibliographie de l'Algérie* 1967 4(9).

3f

Lacheraf M *L'Algérie, nation et société* Maspéro, 1965.
Vatin J-C *L'Algérie politique, histoire et société* Paris, Fondation Nationale des Sciences Politiques, 1974.
Wood R F 'Berbrugger, forgotten founder of Algerian librarianship' *J Lib Hist* 1970 5 237-56.
Didi, E M *Les bibliothèques algériennes: passé, présent et avenir* ENSB, 1976, 50p. Librarianship thesis.
Gandon F 'La lecture publique en Algérie: l'exemple d'Oran' *Médiathèques Publ* 1978 (46) 39-44.
Tchuigoua J F 'Documentation and development: experience in Algeria' *Unesco Bull Lib* 1972 26(2) 73-9.

MOROCCO

1

Bibliothèque Générale et Archives du Maroc, Rabat. 1920- .

Secrétariat d'Etat au Plan. Centre National de Documentation (CND), Rabat. 1968- .

Centre Universitaire de la Recherche Scientifique, Rabat. 1961- .

2a

Secrétariat d'Etat aux Affaires Culturelles. Commission des Bibliothèques et de la Lecture Publique.

2c

Ecole des Sciences de l'Information, Rabat.

3a

CND *Répertoire des Centres de Documentation et des bibliothèques du Royaume* The Centre, 1972, 54p.

3b

Hariki G 'La bibliographie nationale marocaine' *Hesperis-Tamuda* 1966 7 97-100.

Hesperis 1931-1954 contained the national bibliography.

Bibliothèque Générale et Archives *Liste des publications déposées à la Bibliothèque Générale au titre du dépôt légal* 1939- . With variations in frequency, etc. Contains all forms of materials; published in Arabic and French.

— *Bibliographie national marocaine* 1963- Monthly.

Centre Universitaire de la Recherche Scientifique *Bulletin Signalétique* 1967- . Annual.

CND *Bibliographie des bibliographies*. Lists books and periodicals up to 1972, local and foreign, concerned with Morocco.

Al-Maghreb in the: Series of Bibliographical lists of Books and References about the Arab World. See under: Middle East 3b.

3c

Bibliothèque Générale *Al-Bibliografiyah al-wataniyah al-Maghribiyah*. Annual list of periodicals.

3f

Spencer W *Historical dictionary of Morocco* Scarecrow, 1980, 152p. (African Historical Dictionaries, 24).

Fasi M 'Les bibliothèques au Maroc et quelques uns de leurs manuscrits les plus rares' *Hesperis-Tamuda* 1961 2(1) 135-40.

Laredo R 'La lecture chez les lycéens marocains et européens' *Bull Biblioth Fr* 1970 15(4) 177-97.

TUNISIA

1

Bibliothèque Nationale de Tunisie, Tunis. 1956- .

Gärdemalm J and Falk C 'Nationalbilioteks i Tunis' *Biblioteksbladet* 1978 63(2) 41-2.

Centre de Documentation Nationale (CDN). 1957- .

Daly A 'Le Centre de Documentation Nationale: un pionnier de la documentation en Tunisie' *Documentaliste* 1980 17(1) 3-11.

2a

Ministère des Affaires Culturelles. Direction des Bibliothèques.

Institut Ali Bach Hamba.

2b

Association Tunisienne des Documentalistes, Bibliothécaires et Archivistes, Tunis. 1966- . Formerly: Association des Bibliothèques Tunisiennes.

2c

Ecole Nationale d'Administration, Tunis. 1969- .

Institut Ali Bach Hamba. Documentation.

3a

UTICA Annuaire économique de la Tunisie.

3b

Bibliothèque Nationale *Bibliographie nationale courante* 1969- . In two parts: Official publications and Non-official publications. Now 6 times a year.

— *Bibliographie nationale de la Tunisie. Publications non officelles* 1956-1968 1974, 330p.

— *Informations bibliographiques*. Publication resumed in 1966. Complement to the national bibliography. Miscellaneous topics.

Tunisia Vol 8 in the Series of Bibliographical Lists of Books and References about the Arab World. See under Middle East 3b.

Lawless R I *Tunisia* Clio P, 1982, c240p. (World Bibliographical Series).

3c

ATD *Liste des périodiques parus en Tunisie* 1974, 33p.

ATD *Bulletin* Tunis, 1966- . Monthly.

Institut Ali Bach Hamba *Cahiers* Tunis, 1969- .

3d

Institut National de la Statistique *Annuaire statistique de la Tunisie*.

Statistique des bibliothèques. Published in *Informations bibliographiques*: series V.

3e

Journal officiel de la République Tunisienne. Arabic and French editions.

Ministère des Affaires Culturelles *Bulletin officiel.*

3f

Stone R A and Simons J *Change in Tunisia: studies in the social sciences* State University of New York P, 1976.

Said R *Cultural policy in Tunisia* Unesco, 1970, 60p.

Chandler G *Tunisie: développement des bibliothèques* Unesco, 1964.

Ladjmi A *Ecrit, information et bibliothèques en Tunisie* ENSB, 1976, 48, 7p. Librarianship thesis.

Cooper D W 'Libraries in Tunisia' *Wilson Lib Bull* 1979 53(10) 694-9.

Schubarth-Engelschall K 'Bibliothekarische Eindrücke aus Tunesien' *Zentralbl Biblioth* 1977 91 17-21.

Masson A 'La lecture publique en Tunisie' *Bull Biblioth Fr* 1968 13(6) 103-7.

Pawlikowska E 'Biblioteki publiczne w Tunezji' *Bibliotekarz* 1971 38(4) 103-7.

Heggoy A A 'The national archives and research libraries of Tunis *Maghreb Digest* 5(3) 5-8.

Arntz H *Proposition pour l'organisation de la documentation en Tunisie (Mission) 4-17 décembre 1972* Unesco, 1973, 20p.

SECTION 6

ASIA AND THE PACIFIC

ASIA AND THE PACIFIC

1

Unesco *Information on national libraries in Asia and the Pacific Area* 1963, 54p. Also in French. Document prepared for the Unesco regional seminar on the development of national libraries, Manila, February 1964.

'Asia regional seminar on the development of national libraries in Asia and the Pacific Area, Manila, February 1964' *Unesco Bull Lib* 1964 18(4) 150-83. Final report and three papers.

— *Papers* available from Unesco (Unesco/LBA/*Sem* 11/1-17).

Collison R L and Moon B E *Directory of libraries and special collections on Asia and North Africa* Lockwood/Archon Books, 1970, 123p.

Pearson J D 'Orientalist libraries today' *Int Lib Rev* 1970 2(1) 3-18. Mostly in Great Britain with some references to the USA.

Benewick A J *Asian and African collections in British libraries — problems and prospects* P Peregrinus Ltd, 1974, 139p.

2a

Asian Research Service comp *International directory of centers for Asian studies* Hong Kong, Asian Research Service, 1973-74.

Conference of Asian Affairs *American institutions and organizations interested in Asia* 2nd ed, Taplinger, 1961.

Tokyo. East Asian Cultural Studies Centre *Research institutes for Asian studies in Japan* 1962, 110p.

— *Research institutes and researchers of Asian studies in the Republic of Korea* 1963, 94p. *Supplement*: 1964, 24p.

— *Research institutes and researchers of Asian studies in Thailand* 1964, 56p.

UN Economic Commission for Asia and the Far East (ECAFE), Bangkok.

Asian and Pacific Council (ASPAC).

Asian Foundation, San Francisco, 1954- .

Institut für Asienkunde, Hamburg, 1956- .

Honolulu. University of Hawaii. Center for Cultural and Technical Interchange between East and West (East-West Center).

Clearinghouse for Social Development in Asia, Bangkok, 1975- . Sponsored by Friedrich Ebert Stichtung (FES) and the National Research Council of Thailand.

Agriculture Information Bank for Asia (AIBA)

Viloria R V 'The Agricultural Information Bank for Asia: its development and activities' *Unesco Bull Lib* 1977 31(6) 340-3.

Asian Mass Communication Research and Information Centre (AMIC), Singapore, 1971- .

Lim L U Wen 'Asian Mass Communication Research and Information Centre (AMIC)' *Information* Dec 1974, 318-9.

Unesco Regional Office for Culture and Book Development in Asia, Karachi.

'Unesco Regional Office for Culture and Book Development in Asia, Karachi, Pakistan' *Unesco Bull Lib* 1977 31(4) 250-1. Review of programmes.

Asian Cultural Centre for Unesco, Tokyo.
Tokyo Book Development Centre. Holds conferences; gives training in book production, etc.
FID/CAO (Commission for Asia and Oceania). 1968- .

2b

International Union of Orientalists, Munich.
Michigan University. Association for Asian Studies. 1941- .
International Association of Orientalist Librarians. 1967- .
Asian Federation of Library Association, Tokyo, 1957- .

2c

Unesco. Japanese National Commission 'Training course in documentation techniques in Asia, 20 July-21 August 1970, Tokyo' *Final report.*
Tokyo Book Development Centre *The seventh training course on book production in Asia, September/November 1974, Tokyo: Report* The Centre, 1975, 103p.
IFLA Pre-conference seminar, Manila, 1980, on library education programmes in developing countries, with special reference to Asia condition. Documents not traced.
Library and information manpower development in the Asian region Bangalore, Unesco, Division of Libraries, 1977, 206p.

3a

Wajid M *Oriental dictionaries: a select bibliography* Karach, Book Promotion Bureau, 1967, 54p.
Historical and Cultural dictionaries of Asia. Series published by Scarecrow, 1972- . On individual countries.
The Far East and Australasia Europa Pub, 1969- . Includes a list of institutions interested in the Far East.
Asia and Pacific 1981- World of Information, 1980- .
Wint G *Asia: a handbook* Praeger, 1966, 856p.
US Army area handbooks American University. Foreign Area Studies Division. By regions and countries.
Area handbooks Nea Haven, Human Relations Area Files. By regions and countries. Also: bibliographies.
Unesco Regional Office for Education in Asia *Directory of educational research institutions in the Asian region* Bangkok, 1970, 402p.
Association for Asian Studies*Bibliography of Asian studies.*

3b

Pearson J D *Oriental and Asian bibliography, an introduction with some references to Africa* Crosby Lockwood/Shoestring, 1966, 261p.
— Supplement in *Progress in library science*, 1967.
Nunn G R *Asia: a selected and annotated guide to reference works* MIT, 1971, 223p.
Wijasuriya D E K 'ISBD applications to Asian national bibliographies *Unesco Bull Lib* 1977 31(4) 223-32.
Tokyo. Centre for East Asian Cultural Studies *A survey of Japanese bibliographies concerning Asian studies* 1963, 300p.
Bibliographies of bibliographies of East Asian studies in Japan 1964, 190p. Supplement to the above.

Fodor M *The East: books in western languages on Asia and Arabic countries* British Museum, 1965, 107p.
Birnbaum E *Books on Asia from the Near East to the Far East* Toronto U P, 1971, 341p.
Union catalogue of Asian publications Mansell, 4 vols.
— *Supplement* 1971, 1 vol. Works in British libraries acquired since 1965.
Library catalogue of the School of Oriental and African Studies (U of London) G K Hall, 1963, 26 vols.
— *Supplement* 1968, 16 vols.
University of Michigan. Association for Asian studies *Bibliography of Asian studies* 1956- . Annual; from 1956 to 1970 published in *Journal of Asian Studies*.
— *Cumulative bibliography of Asian studies 1941-1965* G K Hall, 1969, 4 vols: *Supplement 1966-1970*. Good coverage of librarianship and related subjects.
Library of Congress Quarterly Journal includes a section 'Orientalia' every year.
USA. Joint Publications Research Service *China and Asia* 1962- . Translations.
USSR Academy of Sciences *Novoya Sovetskaya i innostrannaya literatura po stranam Azii i Afriki* 1953- .
Bibliographia Asiatica Calcutta, K K Roy, 1970- .
Nunn G R *Asian libraries and librarianship: an annotated bibliography of selected books and periodicals and a draft syllabus* Scarecrow, 1973, 137p. The latter part points out some specific aspects of interest for comparative studies.

3c

Association for Asian Studies *Journal of Asian Studies*, 1941- (1941-56 as *Far Eastern quarterly*).
— *Asian Studies Newsletter*.
Royal Asiatic Society *Journal*.
Asia Foundation *Library Notes*.
Asia Society (New York) *Asia*, 1964- .
Hong Kong University *Journal of Oriental Studies*.
University of the Philippines. Institute of Asian Studies *Asian Studies*.
ASPAC *Quarterly of Cultural and Social Affairs*.
Clearinghouse for Social Development *Clearinghouse Journal*.
FID/CAO *Newsletter*, 1969- .
Unesco Regional Centre for Book Development in Asia *Newsletter*.
Asian Federation of Library Associations *Newsletter*.

3d

UN/ECAFE *Economic survey of Asia and the Far East* 1941- . Sometimes published as an issue of *Economic Bulletin for Asia and the Far East*.
Data Asia/Pacific: a statistical profile Hong Kong, Media Transasia, 1978- .

3f

Vente R E and Chen P S J eds *Culture and industrialization: an Asian dilemma. Conference papers* McGraw-Hill (for the Institut für Asienkunde), 1980, 295p.
Education in Asia and Oceania: a challenge for the 1980s Unesco, 1980, 60p. (Education 1 Studies and Documents, Ns 38).
Unesco Regional Office for Education in Asia and Oceania *Education in Asia and Oceania : 4th Regional Conference of Ministers of Education . . . Colombo, 27 July-1 August, 1978* Bangkok, Unesco Office, 1979, 357p. (Bull. Unesco Regional Office, 20).
Unesco *Books for the developing countries — Asia, Africa* 1962, 31p.
Book development in Asia: a report. Unesco Meeting of experts on book

production and distribution in Asia, Tokyo, May 1966 Unesco, 1967, 70p.

'Book development in Asia: Tokyo meeting' *Unesco Bull Lib* 1967 21(2) 105-6.

— *Final report* Unesco, 1966, 44p.

'Book development planning in Asia, a meeting in Singapore from 17 to 23 September 1968' *Unesco Bull Lib* 1969 23(2) 104-5.

Asian Cultural Centre for Unesco *Meeting on planning for book development in Asia, May 1976: report* Tokyo, The Centre, 1976, 71p. Tenth anniversary of the meetings; includes a review of the programmes and achievements.

Unesco *Promotion du livre in Asia* 1968, 74p.

Work-oriented functional literacy: reading and follow-up materials (Final report of the regional workshop for the specialists . . . of reading and follow-up materials, Bangkok, Nov/Dec 1968) 1969, 91p.

FALA *Asian libraries*. A compilation by the FALA Interim Committee for the delegates to the organizational conference in Tokyo November 1957 Manila, 1957.

Liebars H 'Asian and Pacific librarianship from a European angle' (Comments on the Manila Conference — see under 1) *LIBRI* 1964 14(2) 168-75.

Evans E J E 'Meeting of experts on national planning of library services in Asia' *Unesco Bull Lib* 1968 22(3) 114-8.

Expert meeting on national planning of library services in Asia, Colombo, 11-19 December 1967 *Main working document*, Unesco, 1969, 89p. (COM/CS/190/3).

— *Final report* Unesco, 1969, 30p. (COM/CS/190/6).

See also in *Int Lib Rev* 1969 1(1) 35-52.

Role of libraries in the process of modernisation. Asia-Pacific conference on libraries and national development *Report*, Korean Library Association, 1970, 118p. (Seoul conference, May 1969).

'Asia-Pacific conference on libraries and national development, Seoul, May 1969' *Lib in Int Dev* Nov/Dec 1969.

'Library resources and national development IFLA World-Wide seminar at Seoul 1976' *Unesco Bull Lib* 1977 31(1) 53 and *IFLA J* 1976 2(3), several papers. Mainly of Asian materials.

Kesavan B S 'Unesco's work in Asia vis-à-vis libraries, documentation and archives, 1946-1966' *Unesco Bull Lib* 1966 20(5) 226-40.

Chandler G *Libraries in the East: an international and comparative study* Seminar P, 1971, 214p. (For material related to this study see under: Middle East, 3f).

Tamkang College ed *Proceedings of the First Conference on Asian Library Cooperation* Taipei, The College, 1974.

International Conference of Directors of National Libraries on Resource Sharing in Asia and Oceania, Canberra, May 1979.

Anuar H 'Pattern of library service in Asia and the Pacific Islands' *Lib Trends* 1959 8(2) 130-62.

Kalia D R 'A new approach to library service in Asia' *Unesco Bull Lib* 1962 16(5) 239-43.

FID *Proceedings of the second congress and third general assembly of the FID/CAO, Seoul, September 1974* Korea Scientific and Technological Information Centre, 105p. Commission for Asia and Oceania of the FID.

SOUTHERN ASIA

South and Southeast Asia, in whole or parts.

2a

Colombo Plan for Cooperative Economic Development in South and South East Asia, Colombo, 1950- .

The Colombo Plan COI, Reference Division, 1964, 79p.

Gim W J 'Colombo Plan Staff College for Technician Education Library' *Singapore Lib* 1976 6 29-33. The library, open in 1974, is based in Singapore.

Asia Research Centre, Dehli, 1967- . Merger of Unesco Research Centre on Social and Economic Development in Southern Asia and Institute of Economic Growth.

University of Michigan. Center for South and Southeast Asian Studies.

2c

NATIS library and information science manpower development in the Asian region: report of a meeting of supervisors of library and documentation schools in the Asian region, Bangalore, November 1976 Indian Statistical Institute, 1977, 206p. The meeting involved representatives from the Southern region and was based on a paper (included in the above volume):

Neelameghan A *Library and information science personnel in Asia for the eighties*, and on country reports.

3d

Nunn G R *South and South East Asia: a bibliography of bibliographies* Honolulu, East West Center, 1966, 50 leaves. (Occasional papers, 4).

Hobbs C *Understanding the peoples of Southern Asia: a bibliographical essay* U of Illinois, Graduate School of Library Science, 1967, 58p. (Occasional papers, 81).

Library of Congress Orientalia Division *Southern Asia: accessions list*. 1952-1960. Replaced by lists for individual countries.

US Office of Education. Education Material Center *South and South East Asia: a bibliography* 1966, 11p.

Asia Research Centre *Union catalogue of Afghanistan, Burma, Malaysia, Nepal.*

3f

Sheel P 'Exchange of publications in South and South East Asia' *Ann Lib Sci* 1958 5(2) 52-4.

Rhodes D E *The spread of printing* (Eastern hemisphere: India, Pakistan, Ceylon, Burma and Thailand) Routledge and Kegan Paul, 1969.

Kamm A 'Children's literature. The South Asian scene' *Int Lib Rev* 1969 1(2) 183-96. (Unesco 5th Regional seminar, Tehran, 1964). South Asian countries, Thailand and Iran.

'Regional seminar on library development in South Asia, 1960. Summary report' *Unesco Bull Lib* 1961 15(2) 70-7.

Improving information transfer: workshop in Rabat, May 1976. Final report. Unesco, 1976. India and Malaysia took part.

SOUTH ASIA

Indo-Pak sub-continent.

2a

Unesco. Regional Centre for Reading Materials in South Asia, Karachi. 1958- .
'Regional Centre for Reading Materials in South Asia' *Unesco Bull Lib* 1977 31(4) 250-1.

2c

Saith S S 'Library training in South Asia, with particular reference to India' *Working paper*, Delhi Seminar, 1959.
Khurshid A 'Library education in South Asia' *Libri* 1970 20 59-76.
— *Standards for library education in Burma, Ceylon, India and Pakistan* U of Pittsburgh 1969. Thesis. See also:
— *Annals Lib Sci Doc* 1970 17(1/2) 23-34, refs.
— *Herald Lib Sci* 1970 9 335-6.
'Training needs in archival technology and management' *Pre-conference seminar* at the General Conference of the South and West Asia Branch of the International Council on Archives (SWARBICA) Colombo, January 1979.

3a

Inter University Board of India and Ceylon *Universities Handbook, India and Ceylon* New Delhi, 1964, 675p.

3b

Inter University Board of India and Ceylon *Research in progress Vol 2: Bibliographical Sciences* New Delhi, 1968,357p.
Patterson M L P 'Bibliographical controls for South Asian studies' *Lib Q* 1971 41(2) 83-105.
Hobbs C 'South Asia [national bibliographies] *L of C Q J* 1969 26(3) 117-20.
Wilson P *South Asia: a select bibliography on India, Pakistan, Ceylon* New York, American Institute of Pacific Relations, 1957.
Patterson M L P and Inden R B *South Asia, an introductory bibliography* U of Chicago P, 1962, 412p.
Harvard University Library *Southern Asia* Harvard U P, 1968, 543p (Widener Library shelflist, 19). Mainly on South Asia.
Catalog of the Ames Library of South Asia, University of Minnesota G K Hall, 1980- , 16 vols.
Pearson J D ed (for South Asia Library Group) *South Asian bibliography: a handbook and a guide* Harvester/Humanities P, 1979, 381p.
Library of Congress. Division of Orientalia *South Asia: accessions list.*
Unesco. Research Centre for the Social Implications of Industrialisation in Southern Asia *Southern Asia social science bibliography* Calcutta, 1952- . Annual.
472 *South Asian government bibliographies* Mansell, 1967- . 3 vols.

3c

Unesco. Regional Centre for Reading Materials in South Asia *Newsletter*, Karachi, 1959- .

3f

'Unesco project for the production of reading materials' *Unesco Bull Lib* 1958 12(5/6) 113-5. Includes the Rangoon seminar.

Sankaranarayanan N ed *Book distribution and promotion problems in South Asia* Unesco/Higginsbothams, 1963, 278p.

Ghazi M I *A librarian's musings: a study in brief of the problems of libraries and the library staff . . . of Indo-Pak sub-continent* Lahore, Ilmi Kitab Khana, 1963, 60p.

Gardner F M 'Public libraries in perspective: a candid commentary on a tour of South Asia' *Unesco Bull Lib* 1960 14(4) 145-52.

'Information services in selected Asian countries' *J Lib Info Sci* (India) 1977 2(1) 1-90. Bangladesh and Sri Lanka are included.

BANGLADESH

1

Central Library, Dacca, 1973- . Fulfils some of the functions of a national library. With the Directorate are trying to establish a national library.

Huq A M Abdul 'National library for Bangladesh' *Int Lib Rev* 1977 9(1) 95-112.

Dacca University Library, Dacca, 1921- . School of Librarianship.

Bangladesh National Scientific and Technical Documentation Centre (BANSDOC), 1956- . Developed from the Dacca Branch of PANSDOC.

Development of the Bangladesh National Scientific and Technical Documentation Centre (BANSDOC) Unesco, 1975.

2a

Directorate of Archives and Libraries.

National Book Centre of Bangladesh, Dacca, 1972- . Previously the regional office of Pakistan's National Book Centre. For its activities see *BDT* 1974 14(1) 33-4.

Bangladesh Library Council, Dacca, 1972- .

2b

Bangladesh Granthager Samity (Bangladesh Library Association) Previously East Pakistan Library Association 1956-72.

Rajshahi Library Association.

Khulna Library Association.

2c

Khorasan S S M A *Courses in library science in East Pakistan*. Dacca Univ., 1966. (Thesis).

Fazle Kabir A F M 'Library education in East Pakistan' *Eastern Libn* 1969 4(1) 1-9.

Hossain S 'Library education in Bangladesh: yesterday and today' *Unesco J* 1980 2(3) 180-3, refs.

Ahmad N 'Education for librarianship in Bangladesh' *Int Lib Rev* 1981 13(1) 103-15.

3b

Bangladesh Institute of Development Economics *Ten years of Bangladesh economic review articles and Bangladesh Institute of Development Economics publications* A Talukder comp and ed Dacca, The Institute, 1972, 65p. Index from *Pakistan development review*, 1961-70.

National bibliography of books, pamphlets, newspapers and periodicals published in Bangladesh in 1972- [published 1973-].

Shamsuddoulah A B M *Introducing Bangladesh through books: a select bibliography with introductions and annotations 1855-1976* Dacca, Great Eastern Books, 1976, 45p.

Ghos S and Biswas H comps *Bangladesh* Calcutta Univ. Bangladesh Sahayak Samity, 1972, 57p. Books and periodicals in English and Bengali.

3c

National Book Centre *BOI* (Book, a monthly journal); 1973- .

Eastern Librarian, 1961- Library Association of East Pakistan, then Bangladesh Library Association.

Bangladesh library science news bulletin 1975 (1) bimonthly. Dacca Univ., Dept. Lib. Sci.

3f

Thomas B and Lavan S *West Bengal and Bangladesh, perspectives from 1972* Michigan State University, Asian Studies Center, 1973, 327p.

Jones E A *Bangladesh, economics, social and political aspects of development* London, Commonwealth Human Ecology Council, (Annotated bibl. 2), 1974, 10p.

Islam N *Development planning in Bangladesh* London, C. Hurst, 1977.

Rahman M *Second thoughts on Bangladesh* London, News & Media Ltd., 1979.

'Franklin-USAID book aid planned for Bangladesh' *Publishers weekly* 18 Sept 1972 202 47.

Siddiqui A B 'Book crisis in Bangladesh' *East Libn* 1973 7(2 & 3) 63-79.

— 'Subscribing to foreign periodicals in Bangladesh' *Her Lib Sci* 1978 17(4) 275-280.

Alam A K Shamsul 'Libraries and library problems in Bangladesh' *Unesco Bull Lib* 1973 27(5) 262-4.

Syed M A *Public libraries in East Pakistan: yesterday and today* Dacca, Green Book House, 1968, 116p.

Siddiq Khan M 'The library situation in Bangladesh: yesterday today and tomorrow' *East Libn* 1973 7(1) 9-19.

Nazmutdinov I K 'Biblioteki Narodnoi Respubliki Bangladesh' *Bibliotek Bibliog za Rubezhom* 1974 (51) 27-35.

Abdul Huq A M 'International librarianship and library development in Bangladesh' *Focus Int Comp Libp* 1977 8(2) 15-17.

Abdul Huq A M 'Librarianship as a profession and the need for library planning in Bangladesh' *Her Lib Sci* 1978 17(2/3) 159-63.

Motahar Ali Khan 'Public libraries in East Pakistan' *East Libn* 1969 4(1) 51-8.

Parker J S *Bangladesh Public Library Survey: final report in three volumes*. Bath, Library Development Consultants, 1979.

Glaister G 'Literacy and libraries' *East Libn* 1973 7(1) 1-8.

Saiful Islam K M 'Libraries in the Education Commission Report' *Bang Lib Sci Newsbulletin* 1975 (4) 1-8.

Talukder A 'Bangladesh Institute of Development Studies (BIDS) and its socio-economic information services' *Unesco Bull Lib* 1978 32(3) 178-183.

Anwarul Islam A B M 'Need for national scientific information service in Bangladesh' *East Libn* 1973 7(2 & 3) 49-55.

Information systems: their interconnections and compatibility; proceedings of a Symposium on Information Systems; Connection and Compatibility organized by the International Atomic Energy Agency and co-sponsored by FAO and Unesco, held in Varna, Bulgaria, 30 Sept.-3 Oct. 1974. Vienna, Inter. Atomic Energy Agency, 1975. 470p. Bangladesh took part.

For the pre-1972 period see also the references including East Pakistan, under: Pakistan.

See also: Korea, Republic of 3f (last entry).

INDIA

1

National Library of India, Calcutta, 1948- . Previously: Calcutta Public Library, 1836- , Imperial Library, 1903- .

- Central Reference Library, 1958- Section in charge of the National Bibliography.

Kesavan B S *India's National Library* Calcutta, 1961.

— 'The concept of the National Library as a network institution and as a national documentation base' *Timeless Fellowship* 1978/9 12 1-15, refs. Platinum Jubilee of the National Library, 1978.

University of Delhi Department of Library Science, Library.

Council of Scientific and Industrial Research, Indian National Scientific Documentation Centre (INSDOC), New Delhi, 1952- .

Kesavan B S 'Indian National Scientific Documentation Centre (INSDOC)' in *Encyclopedia* 11 (1974) 43-9.

2a

Federal Ministry of Education. Library Division, and state ministries.

Indian Bureau of Bibliography.

Documentation Research and Training Centre (DRTC), Bangalore, 1962- .

Neelameghan A 'Documentation Research and Training Centre (Bangalore)' in *Encyclopedia* 7 (1974) 269-90.

2b

Federation of Indian Library Associations (FILA), 1975- Previously National Council of Indian Library Associations (NACILA).

'Federation of Indian Library Associations' *Her Lib Sci* 1975 14(2/3) 181-3.

Indian Association of Academic Librarians, 1978- . Feature on this association in *Her Lib Sci* 1978 17 228-9.

Indian Association of Special Libraries and Information Centres (IASLIC), Calcutta, 1955- .

Raghavendra Rau B V 'Indian Association of Special Libraries and Information Centres (IASLIC)' in *Encyclopedia* 11 (1974) 431-3.

Institute of Librarians (IOL) Calcutta, 1974- Concerned in training and innovation.

Indian Library Association. 1933- . Public libraries.

Kaula P N 'Library Associations in India' *Unesco Bull Lib* 1970 24(6) 319-25.

2c

Hintz C W *Education for librarianship in India* U of Illinois Graduate School of Library Science, 1964, 32p. (Occasional papers, 73).

Sharma C D 'Library science education in United States, Canada, Great Britain and India: patterns, equivalences and illusions' *Her Lib Sci* 1971 10(3) 222-33.

Neelameghan A 'India, education for librarians and documentalists in' *Encyclopedia* 11 (1974) 312-49.

Mangla P B and Vashishth C P 'Library and information science education in India' *J Lib Inf Sci* (India) 1976 1(2) 127-60.
Mangla P B 'Library science faculty' *Indian Libn* 1976 31(2) 80-4.
Umapathy K S 'Education for librarianship in India' *Int Lib Rev* 1977 9(3) 289-301.
Davinson D E 'Accreditation of library science education' *Her Lib Sci* 1978 17 154-9.
Dharam S A 'Education for library system' *Her Lib Sci* 1978 17(4) 287-93.
[Indo-US seminar on information science education and user education] *Lib Sci Slant Doc* 1978 15(2) 67-98.
Library Science with a Slant to Documentation 1978 (Sept) 15(3) 99-157 Special issue on education in librarianship and information science in India. Papers of 2nd US/Indian Seminar 1977.
Deshpande K S 'Training of librarians at the undergraduate level' *Timeless Fellowship* 1978/79 12 47-56. Seminar on 'Education for librarianship at the undergraduate level, Hyderabad'.
Subhaiah R 'New innovations in the library and information science education in India based on job requirements' *Indian Libn* 1979 34(1) 31-8, refs.
Pathan A M 'Education for medical librarianship in India' *Int Lib Rev* 1978 10(2) 187-203, refs.
Sharma L P 'Training of documentalists in India' *Ind Lib Movement* 1974 1(4) 147-50.
Patil R C and Karisiddappa C R 'In-service training in library science course: a successful experiment' *Timeless Fellowship* 1974-75 (9) 65-75, refs.
Seetarama S 'Library and information science research in India: an analytical study based on the input to ISORID' *Develop'ts in Lib Sci* 1976 13(3/4) 121-37.
Setty Umapathy K 'Research in library science in Indian universities' *Indian Libn* 1976 30(4) 171-6.
Bhagi N K *Research in library education, occupation and career* Ambala City, International Movement, 1979, 36p.
Chitala T B 'A review of library profession in India' *Her Lib Sci* 1971 10(1) 42-54. From 1910 onward.
Kaula P N 'Government of India libraries and salary scales of librarians: memorandum to the Central Pay Commission' *Her Lib Sci* 1970 9 205-24.
Mittal R L 'Dimensions of library personnel in India' *Ind Lib Movement* 1974 1(3) 103-22.
Kaul R N 'Service condition of libraries and librarians in India: working paper of the First All India Library Convention' *Her Lib Sci* 1975 14(1) 65-9.
Kumar K 'Academic content of librarianship' *Indian Lib Ass Bull* 1979 15(1/2) 1-10.
Rajan T N 'Manpower development for information work' *Ann Lib Sci Doc* 1976 23(1) 149-55.

3a

Bhattacharya S *A dictionary of Indian history* New York, Brazillier, 1967, 888p.
Trade Indian directory New Delhi, Trade Builders, 1942- . Educational and scientific organizations as well as commercial.
India: a reference annual Delhi, Ministry of Information and Broadcasting, 1953- .
Ministry of Information and Broadcasting *India, 1977-78* The Ministry, 1978.
INSDOC *The directory of scientific research institutions in India* New Delhi, 1969, 1120p.

Khosla R K *Men of library science and libraries in India* New Delhi, Premier Publications, 1967.

IASLIC *Directory of special and research libraries in India* Calcutta, 1962, 282p.

Delhi Library Association *Directory of libraries and who's who in library profession in Delhi* 1964, 91p.

Rajagopalan T S and Ramaswani K *Libraries serving the CSIR complex* INSDOC, 1970.

3b

Mahar J M *India, a critical bibliography* U of Arizona P, 1964, 119p.

Patil H S and Binarani *History and culture (select bibliographies)* Indian Council for Cultural Relations, 1970, 217p.

Sampath P and Samulski P 'Bibliographical services in India' *Dok Fachbiblioth Werksbüch* 1971 19(4) 149-62.

The national bibliography of Indian literature, 1901-1953 Seliitya Akademi, 1962-4 vols.

National Library *Indian national bibliography* 1958- with annual cumulation. All languages of India and English.

Govi K M 'The genesis and growth of India's national bibliography' *Libri* 1977 27(2) 165-74.

Visiwanathan C G 'What ails the Indian National Bibliography' *LA Rec* 1979 81(7) 333.

Singh S and Sadhu S N *Indian books in print 1955-1967: a select bibliography of English books published in India* Indian Bureau of Bibliographies, 1969, 116p.

— *Indian books in print, 1972: a bibliography of Indian books published up to December 1971, in English language* 2nd ed Indian Bureau of Bibliographies, 1972, 2 vols. (Contents and authors).

Reference catalogue of Indian books in print for 1977 N Delhi, Today & Tomorrow Printers & Publishers, 1977, 1633p.

Library of Congress *Accessions list: India* American Libraries Book Procurement Center, 1962- . Monthly. Includes commercial and official publications, monographs and serials, by language: annual author index.

Indian books: a yearly bibliography of Indian books published or reprinted in the English language Delhi, Research Co, 1969- . Annual.

BEPI: a bibliography of English publications in India DKF Trust, n.d.

Roy R P Mohan 'Indian reference materials' *Indian Libn* 1978 33(1) 19-24. General — not on librarianship.

Guha B 'Indian current awareness services' *Unesco Bull Lib* 1969 22 74.

Guide to Indian periodical literature (Social science and humanities) 1964- . Gurgaon, Prabhu Book Service. Cumulative author and subject index. See section: Librarians, librarianship, libraries and library science.

Index India (Index of periodical literature) Rajasthan U Lib 1967- . Material in English on India.

Education in India: keyword in context index and bibliography U of Michigan, School of education, 1966, 220p.

Kaula P N *Indian library literature: a bibliography of publications* Delhi Lib Assoc, 1956, 22p.

Prasher R G *Indian library literature: an annotated bibliography* Today and Tomorrow, 1971, 504p. (1955-).

Umapathy K S *American books for library science programs in developing countries (with special reference to India)* Titpur, Sudarshana Prakashana, 1972, 123p.

Sharma O P 'Literature of the history of library movement in India' *Her Lib Sci* 1968 7(1) 8-16.
IASLIC *Indian library science abstracts* 1967- .
Vohra H H and Kalra V *Bibliography of work flow in libraries* INSDOC, 1966, 29p.

3c

Gidwani N N and Navalani K *Indian periodicals — an annotated guide* Jaipur, The Authors, 1969, 191p.
— *Indian periodicals — an annotated guide* 2nd ed Sarswati Pub, 1974. (Includes a list of the Indian indexing and abstracting periodicals).
Gandhi H N D comp *Indian periodicals in print*, 1973, vol 1 Vidya Mandal, 1973- .
Annals of library science and documentation INSDOC, 1954- .
Herald of library science Hindu U, 1962- .
IASLIC bulletin, 1955- .
Institute of Librarians *Indian journal of library science* 1 1975- .
Indian librarian, 1945- . Jullundur. Quarterly.
Indian Library Association bulletin, 1955- .
Indian library movement 1(1) March 1974- . Ambala, Cantt. Quarterly.
Journal of library and information science 1(1) June 1976- . 2 p.a. U of Delhi, Dept of Library Science.
Library herald Delhi Library Association, 1958- .
Library science with a slant to documentation Documentation Research and Training Centre, 1964- .

3d

India. Central Statistical Organization *Statistical abstract of the Indian Union* 1949- . Government of India, Manager of Publications, 1950- .
— *Monthly abstract of statistics.* Ministry of Education.
Kalia D R *Survey of public library services in India conducted by the Planning Commission's Working Group on libraries, 1965* India Library Association, 1965, 66p.

3e

Srivastava S N 'Library legislation in India' *Indian Libn* 1967 22(3) 148-52.
Sadhur S N and Saraf B N *Library legislation in India: a historical and comparative study* New Delhi, Sagar Publications, 1967, 285p.
Krishnamurti C S 'Library legislation in India' *Lib Her* 1970 11 102-11.
Srivastava S N 'Library legislation in India' *Int Lib Rev* 1972 4(3) 329-39.
Taneja R D 'Indian standards for documentation' *Encyclopedia* 11(1974) 439-47.
Gopinath M A 'Standards for use in the planning of library and documentation systems: comparative data from India, UK, USA and Canada' *Lib Sci Slant Doc* 1974 11(3-4) 407-13.

3f

Seminar on book publishing, Delhi 1969. *Report* Federation of Publishers & Booksellers Association in India, 1969, 182p.
Kapoor A L 'Acquisition of foreign periodicals in India: some problems' *Indian Lib Ass Bull* 1979 15(3/4) 67-76.
Razvi M H 'Regional language as medium of instruction and its impact on libraries' *Her Lib Sci* 1974 13(1) 33-38.
Mookherjee S K *Librarianship — its philosophy and history* Asia Publishing House, 1966.

Mittal R L 'Mahatma Gandhi's philosophy of library service' *Libri* 1969 19 121-5.

Datta B K *Libraries and librarianship of ancient and medieval India* Delhi, Atma Ram & Sons, 1970, 248p.

— 'Early monastic and other institutional libraries in India' *Lib Hist Rev* 1974 1(2) 18-42.

Barua P 'The libraries of the Mughal rulers' *Lib Her* 1972-73 14(3 & 4) 89-96.

Aziz A 'The Imperial library under Mughul emperors' *Lib Hist Rev* 1974 1(3) 22-50.

Dasgupta K 'How learned were the Mughals: reflections on Muslim libraries in India' *J Lib Hist* 1975 10(3) 241-54.

Kabir A M F 'English libraries in eighteenth century Bengal' *J Lib Hist* 1979 14(4) 436-56, refs.

Ohdedar A K *The growth of the library in modern India: 1498-1836* Calcutta, World Press Private Ltd, 1966, 268p.

Jogesh M *History of libraries and librarianship in modern India since 1850* Atma Ram & Sons, 1979, 188p, bibl.

Sen N B *Development of libraries in New India* New Book Society of India, 1965, 355p.

— *Progress of libraries in Free India* New Book Society of India, 1967, 247p.

Mookherjee S K *Development of libraries and library science in India* Calcutta, World Press Private, 1969, 534p.

Kaula P *Library science today: Ranganathan Festschrift* Asia Publishing House, 2 vols.

Ranganathan S R 'A librarian looks back' *Her Lib Sci* Series of articles in 1969-71 vols 8-10.

Kurshid A 'Growth of libraries in India' *Int Lib Rev* 1972 4(1) 21-65.

Venkatappaiah V ed *March of library science: Kaula Festschrift. Papers presented in honour of Pr. P. N. Kaula* Vikes Publishing House, 1979, 626p.

Goyal S P *Indian librarianship (essays in honour of S R Bhatia)* Delhi, Scientific Book Store, 1972, 207p.

Gujrati B S *Library organisation and its development in India* 2nd rev ed New Delhi, Hemkunt P, 1971, 315p.

Singh M 'Library improvement: some human factors' *Indian Libn* 1972 26 164-81.

'India, libraries and information centers in' in *Encyclopedia* 11(1974) 350-430. 7 papers on various aspects of librarianship and categories of libraries.

Kumar P S G 'Significance of 1974 in Indian librarianship' *Her Lib Sci* 1974 13(2) 123-5.

Kaula P N 'Indian librarianship number' *Her Lib Sci* 1977 16(2/3) 107-223. Whole issue.

Rat'kova E V 'Bibliotechnoe delo v Indii' *Bibliot i Bibliog za Rubezhom* 1978 (70) 36-51, 32 refs.

Bhattacharjee K K *Modern trends in librarianship in India* Calcutta, World Press, 1979, 203p.

For current problems see: *All India Library Conferences.*

Recent vols on a theme see for instance: 1980 *Library services for a developing society* ed Guha B Indian Lib Ass, 1980, 49p.

Documentation Research & Training Centre, annual seminar 11, 1974: *Planning of library and documentation systems* Bangalore, DRTC, 1974, 406p.

British Council Library, Madras *Librarianship and information science in 2001* (Seminar, Silver Jubilee of B.C. Library, Oct 1975) The Library, 1975, 163p.

Seminar on Library Cooperation, Bangalore Nov 1974 Karnataka Lib Ass, 1974, 31p.

Mittal R L 'Need of library cooperation in India' *Indian Lib Movement* 1978 5(1) 1-6.

Indian Library Association *Bulletin* 1978 14(1/4) 1-93. Issue devoted to cooperation amongst libraries.

Verma R S 'Types of libraries in India' *Her Lib Sci* 1975 14(2-3) 175-81.

Sharma O P *Forces behind the Indian public library movement 1858-1892* PhD Thesis, Chicago U, 1970, 335p.

Nagar M L *Public library movement in Baroda 1901-1949* Columbia, Miss, International Library Center, 1969, 371p.

Khan H A 'Public library development: policies, problems, and performance' *Timeless Fellowship* 1975-76 10 20-33.

Rao K N and T R 'Rise and growth of the public library movement in India' *Her Lib Sci* 1977 16 131-64.

Nayar N A 'Production and distribution of reading materials for neo-literates in India' *Indian Libn* 1970 25 5-19.

Sahai S N 'Reading trends of library users in Bihar' *Unesco Bull Lib* 1971 25(3) 151-7.

Sinha A K 'National adult education programme and public library' *Her Lib Sci* 1978 17(4) 293.

Unesco *Public libraries for Asia, the Delhi seminar* Paris, Unesco, 1956.

Ranganathan S R and Neelameghan A eds *Seminar on public library system* S Ranganathan Endowment for Library Science, 1972, 253 53p.

Mehta J C 'Rural libraries in India' *Unesco Bull Lib* 1972 26(1) 25-9.

'Books are for use: proceedings of the 22nd All-India Library Conference, Delhi 1976' *Indian Lib Ass Bull* 1975 11(3 & 4) 1-87. (Published 1977); 1976 12(2) 57-115.

Int Lib Rev 1974 6(1) 1-107. INTAMEL Meeting 1973 in India.

Trehan G L *Administration and organisation of school libraries in India* Sterling Publ, 1965, 291p.

Gupta K B 'School libraries today — their problems' *IASLIC Bull* 1968 13(2) 174-7.

Tewari B N 'Modern youth and their reading' *Indian Lib Movement* 1977 4(1) 3-18.

Shah A A 'The role of the library in the education of the deaf: an Indian case-study' *Unesco J* 1979 1(4) 249-51.

Sharma O P 'History of the development of the university library in India: an appraisal' *Indian Libn* 1964 19 128-43.

Sybrahmanyan M *History and development of university libraries in India* London, FLA Thesis, 1967.

Mangla P B 'University libraries in India' *Int Lib Rev* 1974 6(4) 453-70.

Sahai S 'Development of university libraries in India since independence' *Indian Lib Ass Bull* 1976 12(1) 37-42.

Henschke E 'Development aid for a university library of the Third World' *Int Lib Rev* 1978 10(1) 29-42. West Germany's programmes compared to UK, USA & USSR's; aid to Institute of Technology Madras.

Seminar of university librarians in India, Jaipur 1966 *Proceedings* U of Rajasthan, 1967, 4 vols.

Trehan G L *Administration and organisation of college libraries in India* Sterling Publ. 1969, 252p. Comparison with UK & USA.

Kumar G et al 'College libraries in India: a survey report' *J Lib Info Sci* (India) 1979 4(1) 1-23.

Rajchopra H 'Reading habits of the members of the Punjab University Library, Chandigarh' *Indian Libn* 1976 31(2) 87-92.

Setty Umapathy K 'Teachers College libraries in the state of Kamataka India' *Ann Lib Sci Doc* 1975 22(3) 108-19.

Final report of the ICAR institutes and agricultural university libraries New Delhi, Indian Council of Agricultural Research, 1969, 182p.

Saha J *Special libraries and information services in India and the United States* Scarecrow, 1969, 216p.

Kesavan B S 'Organization of national documentation and information services in India' *Lib Trends* 1968/69 17 231-44.

Lázár P *India: a national information system for science and technology, March-April 1972* Unesco, 1972, 53p.

Impact of information services on national development, Bangalore COSTED, 1978, 60p. mimeo.

Kumar P S G 'India and its information activities' *Indian Libn* 1978 33(3) 116-21. Participation in UNISIST programmes.

Singh S N 'Assessing information needs and uses: a state of the art report' *Her Lib Sci* 1979 18(1/2) 38-45, refs.

Parthasarathy S 'National Information System for Science and Technology (NISSAT)' *Ann Lib Sci Doc* 1975 22(4) 179-84.

Rajagopalan T S 'Towards evolution of a national information system for science and technology in India' *Ann Lib Sci Doc* 1976 23(2) 169-72.

Champawat C S 'Information storage and documentation services in libraries' *Her Lib Sci* 1979 18(1/2) 60-8.

Dasgupta K 'Indian libraries: documentation and automation in library services' *Int Forum Inf Doc* 1979 4(2) 33-8.

- Also in *Int Lib Rev* 1979 11(4) 463-86.

Raizada A S 'Development of computer-based information services in India' *Ann Lib Sci Doc* 1976 23(1) 141-8.

NEPAL

(With Bhutan and Sikkim)

1

National Library, Katmandu, 1956- .
Tribhuvan University Library, Kirtipur, 1959- .
CEDA Documentation Centre, 1971- . Based on Tribhuvan University.
British Council Library, Katmandu, 1959- .
American Library, Katmandu.

2a

Ministry of Education. Directorate of Archives and Libraries.
Educational Materia Centre, Sanu Themi.

2b

Nepal Library Association.
Mahottery Zila Pustakalaya Sangh. Regional Library Association.

3a

Area handbook for Nepal (with Sikkim and Bhutan) American U, 1964. Includes a bibliography.

Hedrick B C *Historical and cultural dictionary of Nepal* Scarecrow, 1972 (Historical and Cultural Dictionaries of Asia series, 2).

3b

Library of Congress, Delhi Book Procurement Center *Accessions list: Nepal* 1966- . Quarterly.

Wood H B *Nepal bibliography* Eugene, Oregon, American-Nepal Education Foundation, 1959, 108p. Includes periodical articles.

Husain A *Bibliography of Nepal: historical and political* Katmandu, Ministry of Information, 1966.

Fischer M W *A selected bibliography of source materials for Nepal* U of California, Institute for International Relations, 1966, 54p. First published in 1956.

Boulnois L and Millot H *Bibliographie du Népal. Vol. 1: Sciences humaines, références en langues européennes* Paris, CNRS, 1969, 289p (Cahiers népalais, 1).

Schappert L G *Sikkim 1800-1968: an annotated bibliography* Honolulu, East-West Center Library, 1968, 69p. (Occasional papers, 10).

3f

Karan P P and Jenkins W M *The Himalayan Kingdoms: Bhutan, Sikkim and Nepal* Van Nostrand, 1963.

Singh N *Bhutan, a kingdom in the Himalayas: a study of the land, its people and their government* New Delhi, Thompson P, 1972, 202p.

Aris M *Bhutan: the early history of a Himalayan kingdom* Aris & Phillips, 1979, 344p.

Rose L E and Scholz J T *Nepal: profile of a Himalayan Kingdom* Westview P, 1980.

Bhooshan B S *The development experience of Nepal* Delhi, Concept Pub'g, 1979.

'Modern library activities in Nepal' *Unesco Bull Lib* 1961 15(3) 163-4.

Mishra S 'Library movement in Nepal' *Unesco Bull Lib* 1974 28(1) 58-60.

— 'Libraries in Nepal' *Her Lib Sci* 1973 12(4) 331-4.

Mishra N and Mishra S 'Nepal, libraries in' in *Encyclopedia* 19 (1976) 229-39.

'Three day seminar on management of campus libraries — July 1974' *Unesco Bull Lib* 1975 29(2) 109.

Foster B 'Special libraries in Katmandu' *Spec Lib* 1979 70(8) 333-40. American Library, British Council, Nepal/Soviet Friendship Library, and other libraries.

Gyawall B M and Stanford G L *Information resources on Nepal* Documentation Centre, 1973, 84p. Also includes foreign libraries with a research interest in Nepal.

PAKISTAN

1

National Library of Pakistan, Islamabad.

Liaquat Memorial Library, Karachi, 1951- . Both are legal deposit libraries.

University of Karachi, Department of Library Science Library.

Pakistan National Scientific Documentation Centre (PANSDOC), Karachi, 1957- (with a regional centre in Dacca, 1963- , now developed as the Bangladesh centre).

Pakistan Scientific and Technological Information Centre (PASTIC), Karachi, 1976?- Extension of PANSDOC. Responsible for the scientific information system.

PANSDOC *Project for the establishment of the Pakistan Scientific and Technological Information Centre (PASTIC): expansion of PANSDOC; feasibility report* Karachi, 1972.

2a

Ministry of Education, Directorate of Archives and Libraries.

Library Promotion Bureau. National Book Centre, Karachi, 1962- .

2b

Society for the Promotion and Improvement of Libraries (SPIL), Karachi, 1960- .

Pakistan Library Association (PLA), 1957- .

Pakistan Association of Special Libraries (PASLIB), Karachi, 1968- .

Haider S J 'Library Associations in Pakistan' *Unesco Bull Lib* 1969 23(3) 148-50, 165.

2c

Axford H W 'Library education at the university of the Punjab: American influence' *J Educ Libp* 1966 6(4) 280-9.

'First graduate library school in Pakistan' *Unesco Bull Lib* 1968 22(3) 160-1.

[Library education in Pakistan] *J Pakistan Lib Ass* 1968 2(April) special issue.

Anwar M 'Graduate study in library science in Pakistan: a statistical analysis' *East Libn* 1970 4(4) 247-58.

'Pakistan: library education in Pakistan' *Int Lib Rev* 1972 3(1) 83-8.

Anwar M 'Library education in Pakistan: a statistical appraisal' *Federal Lib* 1972 (April) 30-6.

Khan S A *Pakistani muhtamim-e-kutub khanoon ki talimi aur paisha-warana iarbiyat ka tangidi-o-iajziyati mutalia*. [in Urdu]. U of Karachi, Thesis in Library Science, 1973.

'Pakistan, library education in' *Encyclopedia* 21 (1977) 282-99.

Qureshi N 'The education and training of librarians and information scientists in Pakistan' *Libri* 1979 29(1) 79-89, refs.

Khurshid A 'Library education and training in Pakistan; as seen through NATIS' *Pak Lib Bull* 1980 11 (1/2) 13-24.

Haider J 'Status of library research in Pakistan' *Libri* 1978 28(4) 326-37.

3a

Pakistan yearbook National Publishing House, 1969- .

Supersedes:

Twenty years of Pakistan, 1947-67.

West Pakistan yearbook, 1957- . Lahore, Directorate of Publications, Information Department.

Usmani M A and Sabzwari G A *Pakistan book trade directory* Library Promotion Bureau, 1966, 204p.

National Book Centre *Libraries in Pakistan: a guide* 1968, 36p.

Pakistan library directory 1970 Dacca, Great Eastern Books, 1970, 156p.

Sabzwari G A and Usmani M W *Who's who in librarianship in Pakistan* Karachi, Library Promotion Board, 1969, 273p.

3b

Usmani M A *Bibliographical services throughout Pakistan* Karachi, Dr Mahmud Husain Library, 1978 74p. Rev ed of *Status of bibliography in Pakistan* 1968.

Bibliography of bibliographies published in Pakistan PBWG, 1961, 6p.

Pakistan Bibliographical Working Group, comp. *The Pakistan national bibliography 1947 to 1961* National Book Centre, 1972. Part 1: General works of Islam 001 to 297 (AD581-877).

Directorate of Archives and Libraries *Pakistan national bibliography* 1962- Government of Pakistan Publications, 1965- .

Retrospective bibliography of Pakistan National Book Centre, 1969- . 10 vols; in progress.

Books from Pakistan, 1958-1968- National Book Centre, 1969- .

Satyaprakash ed *Pakistan: a bibliography 1962-1974* Indian Documentation Service, 1975, 338p.

Library of Congress accessions list: Pakistan American Libraries Book Procurement Center, Karachi, 1962- .

Accessions list. Pakistan: annual supplement. Cumulative list of serials American Libraries Book Procurement Center for Library of Congress.

PANSDOC *List of Pansdoc bibliographies* 1970.

Khurshid A and Irshad A *Librarianship in Pakistan: fifteen years' work* (1947-62) Karachi U, Department of Library Science, 1965, 65p.

Kurshid Z *Librarianship in Pakistan: 10 years' work (1963-1972)* U Karachi, Department of Library Science, 1974, 214p. Suppl.

Zia M I H comp *Bibliography of theses submitted to the Department of Library Science, 1967-1972* U Karachi, Department of Library Science, 1973, 59p. (Library science publications, 6).

Fatima N *Bibliography of theses submitted to the Department of Library Science, University of Karachi 1973-75* The Department, 1976, 34p.

3c

Pakistan Library Association Quarterly Journal 1960/61- . (1968 vol 2).

Library Promotion Bureau *Pakistan Library Bulletin* 1966- .

Pakistan Library Review 1958-64. New Series, 1968- . Karachi U, Library Science Alumni Association.

3d

Pakistan Central Statistical Office *Pakistan statistical yearbook*, 1952- . Sometime: *Pakistan statistical annual*.

3e

Gazette of Pakistan.

Curle A *Educational problems of developing societies with case studies of Ghana, Pakistan and Nigeria.* Praeger, 1973, 200p.

3f

Brown E et al *Book production, importation and distribution in Pakistan. A study of needs with recommendations within the context of social and economic development* Wolff Management for AID, 1966, 120p.

Faruqui J A *Reading habits in Pakistan* National Book Centre of Pakistan, 1974, 131p.

Harvey J F 'Pakistan and Afghanistan librarianship' *Pak Lib Bull* 1969 2 9-17.

Khurshid A 'Pakistan, libraries in' *Encyclopedia* 21 (1977) 255-81.

Pakistan Library Association *Pakistan librarianship 1972-73. Being the proceedings of the 9th Annual Conference of the Pakistan Library Association Saida Sharif, August 4-5 1973* The Association, 1973, 113p.

Hasain M *Of libraries and librarians* U of Karachi, 1974, 90p.

Siddiqui A H *Library resources in Pakistan* Lahore, Student Services, 1976.

Islam M 'Library resources and the national development' *Pak Lib Bull* 1978 9(1/2) 17-28, refs.

Role of the library in the development of the community: a seminar SPIL, 1965, 142p.

Karachi Public Library: a scheme SPIL, 1967, 68p. (SPIL publications, 5).

Aslam M 'Rural libraries in Pakistan' *Unesco Bull Lib* 1975 29(3) 156-8.

Wajid M *Library services to children in Pakistan* Karachi U, Department of Library Science, 1964.

Anwar M A 'Secondary school libraries in Pakistan' *Int Lib Rev* 1971 3(3) 349-52.

Usmani M A 'College library resources in Karachi' *Pak Lib Bull* 1975 7(3 & 4) 25-40, refs.

— 'Book bank scheme of Karachi University' *Pak Lib Bull* 1974 7(2) 1-8.

Jalaluddin Haider S 'University libraries in Pakistan' *Coll Res Lib* 1975 36(5) 379-383.

Harvey J F 'West Asian special libraries and information centres' *Ann Lib Sci Doc* 1973 20(1-4) 26-38.

Aslam M 'Survey of special libraries in Lahore' *Pak Lib Bull* 1974 6(3 & 4) 29-35.

Akhtar A H 'Special libraries' *Pak Lib Bull* 1975 7(3 & 4) 7-13.

Siddiqui A H 'Special libraries' *Pak Lib Bull* 1977 8(1-2) 27-36.

Haider S J 'Science-technology libraries in Pakistan' *Spec Lib* 1974 65(10-11) 472-78.

Fazle Kabir A F M 'Research resources and information dissemination' *East Libn* 1971 6(1/2) 1-7, refs.

Integrated rural information system. A preliminary report on the organization of libraries and information networks in Pakistan Chicago Public Library, [197?].

FID/DC *Documentation in South West Asia and Unesco-UNISIST-Developing countries — Papers at the FID/DC Open Forum, Tehran, September 1973* Budapest, OMKDK (for FID), 1974, 73p.

Regional Documentation Centres Conference, held in Tehran April 29/May 1st 1974 at the Iranian Documentation Centre CENTO Scientific Programme IRANDOC, 1974, 141p.

Mohajir A R 'Development of a national scientific information system with reference to Pakistan' *Pak Lib Bull* 1978 9(1/2) 29-46.

SRI LANKA

1

National Library, Colombo, 1979- .

Goonetileke H A I 'The meaning and purpose of a national library for Sri Lanka' *Libri* 1979 29(1) 350-2.

University of Ceylon, Peradeniya Campus, Library, 1921- Librarianship.

Colombo Public Library, 1925- .

Corea I 'The Colombo Public Library' *Ceylon Lib Rev* 1968 3(1) 11-8.

— *Libraries and people: Colombo Public Library 1925-1975, a commemorative volume* Municipal Council of Colombo, 1975, 282p.

Sri Lanka Scientific and Technological Information Centre (SLSTIC).

2a

Ceylon National Library Services Board (CNLSB), 1970- Legal deposit right.

Lydersen A 'Litt lost og fast om Sri Lankas Bibliotekvesen' *Bog og Bibliot* 1977 44(3) 186-7.

National Bibliographical Information Centre, Colombo.

National Science Council of Sri Lanka; Participate in the UNISIST system.

2b

Sri Lanka Library Association, Colombo, 1960- as the Ceylon Library Association.

Book Development Council, Colombo, 1972- .

2c

Redmond D A 'Library training in Ceylon' *Unesco Bull Lib* 1958 12(10) 230-1.

Kruse P and Mahalingam V 'Education for librarianship in Ceylon' *J Educ Libp* 1966 6(4) 295-9.

Mahalingam V 'Education for librarianship' *Ceylon Lib Ass J* 1962 1(1) 41-3.

Lankage J 'Library education in Ceylon' *Ceylon Lib Rev* 1971 4(1) 69-74.

Also in *Her Lib Sci* 1971 10(2) 116-21.

3a

Department of Census and Statistics *Ceylon yearbook* Colombo, 1948- .

Ferguson's Ceylon directory Observer Press, 1858- .

3b

Blok S C 'Current national bibliography of Ceylon *Ceylon Lib Ass J* 1962 1(2) 32-4.

National bibliography 1964-73 published by the Department of National Archives; 1973- published by the National Library Services Board.

Government Archivist in *Gazette of the Republic of Sri Lanka:* quarterly statement of books printed in Sri Lanka, 1885- .

Office of the Registrar of Books and Newspapers *Catalogue of books* (Legal deposit) 1960-64.

Ware E W *Bibliography of Ceylon* U of Miami P, 1962, 181p.
Goonetileke H A I *A bibliography of Ceylon: a systematic guide to the literature of the land, people, history and culture published in Western languages from the 16th century to the present day* Inter Documentation Co, 1970, 2 vols (Biblioteca Asiatica, 5). Based on an FLA thesis, 1966.
— Vol. 3 1976, 507p. (Suppl. to vols 1-2).
National Museum Library *Ceylon periodicals index* 1969- bimonthly. In 1974 becomes: *Sri Lanka periodicals index*.

3c

National Museum Library *Ceylon periodicals directory*, 1971- .
Ceylon National Library Services Board *Library News* 1973 1(1)- . Quarterly.
Sri Lanka Library Association *Sri Lanka Library Review* Previously: *Ceylon Library Association Journal* 1962- , then *Ceylon Library Review* 1966- .
Ceylon Education Department *The School Library* 1960- .

3d

Dept of Census and Statistics *Statistical abstract of Ceylon* 1949- Govt. Publications Bureau, 1949- .

3e

Gazette of the Republic of Sri Lanka.

3f

De Silva K M *A history of Sri Lanka* London, Hurst, 1981.
Education in Ceylon (From the 6th Century B.C. to the present day): a centenary volume Government Press, 1969. Cultural activities.
Bandara H H *Cultural policy in Sri Lanka* Unesco, 1972, 70p.
Wickremaratne K D L 'Palm leaf manuscripts of Ceylon' *Ceylon today* 1969 16(1) 16-21.
Diehl K S 'The Dutch press in Ceylon, 1734-96' *Lib Q* 1972 42(3) 329-42.
Bandara S B 'Provision of periodicals in the libraries of Sri Lanka' *Int Lib Rev* 1975 7(1) 17-28.
Piyadasa T G *Origin and history of libraries in Ceylon* U of London Diploma in Library Science, 1964.
Thambiah R S 'Ceylon, libraries in' *Encyclopedia* 4 (1970) 412-22, refs.
Khurdish A 'Libraries on the island of Ceylon' *Libri* 1973 23(2) 142-54.
Silva M 'Trends in librarianship and documentation in Sri Lanka' *Unesco Bull Lib* 1975 29(2) 80-6.
Amarasinghe N *The development of library service in Sri Lanka* ERIC, 1977, 7p. (ERIC report ED-176 758).
— 'Development of library services in Sri Lanka' *Her Lib Sci* 1978 17 163-8.
Blok S C 'Public library service: the formative years' *Ceylon Lib Rev* 1967 2(1) 1-6.
'Encouragement of reading in Ceylon' *Unesco Bull Lib* 1961 5(2) 105.
Hulugalle H A J 'Books for the people' *Ceylon Lib Ass J* 1962 1(2) 3-8.
Kamaldeen S M 'Changing patterns of readership at the Public Library, Colombo' *Ceylon Lib Rev* 1967 2(1) 14-8.
Ottover A 'En undertrykt minoritets bibliotek' *Bibliotek 70* 1978 (3) 84-7. (Tamil minority group).
Evans E J A 'School libraries in Ceylon' *Unesco Bull Lib* 1969 23(6) 287-92, 299.
De Souza V 'The impact of swabasha medium arts entrants in the University libraries in Colombo and at Peradeniya' *Ceylon Lib Rev* 1971 4(1) 1-10.

Jayawardene A P 'The Red Triangle Library of Colombo YMCA' *Ceylon Lib Rev* 1969 July 39-43.

Navaratne J 'The library of the National Council of Sri Lanka' *Libradoc* 1979 4(4) 9-10. Cooperative Movement.

Kruse P 'Tea brings books to Ceylon' *Spec Lib* 1965 56(2) 112-6.

Samarasinghe L E *Ceylon National Scientific and Technical Documentation Centre, Report* Unesco, 1969.

Nethsinghe C L M 'Special libraries in Ceylon with special reference to the CISIR Library' *Ceylon Lib Rev* 1971 4(1) 38-51.

Goonetileke H A E *Scientific and technical documentation in Sri Lanka* Singapore, Asian Mass Communication Research and Information Centre, 1973.

Schwarz S *Sri Lanka: development of scientific and technological information services*. Unesco, 1979, 65p. (Restricted UNDP/SRL/77/004 Technical Report).

Kamaldeen K M 'Public library buildings in Sri Lanka. Some general observations' *Lib News* 1977 5(3) 6-10.

EASTERN ASIA

Pacific region of Asia: South East Asia and North East Asia.

2a

Centre for East Asian Cultural Studies, Tokyo, 1961- .
University of Michigan. Association for Asian Studies. Committee on East Asian Libraries.
East Asian Librarians Group of Australia.

3b

Besterman T ed *A world bibliography of oriental bibliographies.* Rev and updated ed by J D Pearson Rowman & Littlefield, 1975.
Centre for East Asian Cultural Studies *Survey of bibliographies in Western languages concerning East and South East Asian studies* Bunko, 1966, 227p.

3c

East Asian Librarians Group of Australia *Newsletter*, 1978- .

3f

Fairbank J K et al *East Asia: tradition and transformation* Houghton, 1973, 969p.
Proceedings of the Second Asian Conference on Publications Publishers Association of the Republic of China, 1978, 164p.
Bevis D 'Libraries and people — worldwide' *J Educ Libp* 1970 10(3) 159-65, refs. Japan, Taiwan, Korea, Philippines, Singapore, Hong Kong, Thailand.
Bixler P 'Libraries in the Far East: an inquiry into the state of the library art in Burma, Taiwan, Communist China, Korea, Indonesia and East Pakistan' *Lib J* 1962 87(20) 4123-53.
Bixler P 'Educational overseamanship: a librarian in Asia' *Teachers Coll Rec* 1963 65 230-42.
Kaser D 'Books and libraries in the Far East' *Wilson Lib Bull* 1969 43(10) 974-9. Burma, Malaysia, Indochina, Philippines, Korea and Taiwan.
— et al *Library development in eight Asian countries* Scarecrow, 1969, 243p.
Proceedings of the First Conference on Asian library cooperation Taipei, Tamkang College, 1974, 647p. Hong Kong, Korea, Philippines, Singapore, Thailand (and USA).
Ching-Chih C '[Public libraries]: contemporary libraries in the Far East' in *Encyclopedia* 24 (1978) 358-90, refs. Indochinese region not included.
LARC *A survey of automated activities in the libraries of the Far East,* 1972.

NORTH EAST ASIA

China and related areas, Japan, Korea

2a

Washington State University. Far Eastern and Russian Institute.

East Asia Cultural Studies Centre, Tokyo, 1961- .

Yonsei University. Institute of Far Eastern Studies, Seoul, 1955- .

2c

Stevens R D and Suzuki Y 'Education for East Asia librarianship' *Austr Lib J* 1970 19 363-71.

3a

Fodor's guide to Japan and East Asia New York, D McKay.

3b

Readings in Oriental bibliograhy and classification Korean Library Association, 1966.

Kimpei Goto *Bibliography of bibliographies of East Asian studies in Japan* East Asia Cultural Studies Centre, 1964, 190p. (Bibliographies, 3).

Nunn G R *East Asia: a bibliography of bibliographies* Honolulu, East West Center, 1967, 92p.

'Oriental literature and bibliography' in *Encyclopedia* 21 (1977) 35-240. China, Japan and Korea treated individually. Extensive bibliographies of sources: general, subject. Includes published catalogues of large collections on Asian studies, and sections on libraries.

China, Japan, Korea Harvard U P, 1968, 494p. (Widener shelflist, 14).

Gillin D G et al *East Asia: a bibliography for undergraduate libraries* Williamsport, Bro-dart, 1970, 130p.

Ma J T *East Asia: a survey of holdings at the Hoover Institution on War, Revolution and Peace* Stanford U P, 1971, 24p.

University of Chicago Catalogs of the Far Eastern library G K Hall, 1974, 18 vols.

See also *Index Sinicus* in: People's Republic of China, 3b.

3f

Tsuneishi W M 'Acquisition of library materials from China, Japan and Korea' *Lib Resources & Tech Services* 1963 (7) 28-33.

CHINA, People's Republic of

With the historical section on pre-1949 China

1

Pei-ching Tu shu kuan (Peking National Library), 1912- . Founded on the Imperial collections of Southern Sung, Ming and Ching dynasties.

Chiu A K 'National Libraries in China' *Lib Q* 1933 3 146-69.

Winkleman J H *The Imperial Library in Southern Sung China, 1126-1279* American Philosophical Society, 1974, 175p.

See also shorter versions:

— *Lib Q* 1969 39(4) 299-317.

— *NTU Lib Sci Circular* (Taiwan), 1968 (8), 3p.

On the modern National Library see:

Goldberg B 'Peking Bibliotek' *Bibliotek* 1975 (4) 108-111.

Lodén T 'Pekings Bibliotek' *Tidsk Dok* 1976 32(6) 101-4.

Symons B 'The National Library of Peking: an Australian librarian's view' *Aust Lib J* 1978 27(6) 88-90.

Eide E 'Nasjonalbiblioteket i Peking' *Bog og Bibliot* 1978 45(1) 24-5.

Ying W 'China's house of words keeps growing' *East Asian Librarians' Group of Australia. Newsletter* 1979 (3) 6-8.

Bottomley G 'The Peking Library' *APLA Bull* 1979 42(4) 1,3.

Academy of Sciences. Central Library, Peking, 1951- . With subsidiary libraries in various parts of the country.

'The library system of the Chinese Academy of Sciences' *T'u shu kuan* 3 Sep 1964 35-9.

2a

Ministry of Culture.

Ministry of Education.

State Council. Science and Technology Commission. Coordinating Library Committee, 1957- .

University of Michigan. Center for Chinese Studies, 1961- .

US Association of Research Libraries. Center for Chinese Research Materials, Washington.

2b

Library Association, Peiping, 1925-49. Reorganized in Taiwan.

Papers on the occasion of the 10th anniversary of the Library Association of China Peiping, The Association, 1935, 132p.

Tsien T-H 'China, Library Association of' in *Encyclopedia* 4 (1970) 656-7.

Zhongguo Tushuguan Xuehui/Society of Library Science (CSLS), Peking 1979- . See *Lib of Congress Bull* 1979 38 369.

Zhongguo Kexue Jishu Qingbao Xuehui/Chinese Science and Technology Information Society, Peking. 1978- .

2c

Hsü Chia-Lin et al 'Library cadres training over the past fifteen years' Hong Kong US Consulate *Selections from China mainland magazines* 20 Apr 1965 (465) 3-12. (Translations from *T'u shu kuan* 20 Sep 1964).

3a

Greater encyclopedia of China The Publishing House of the Greater Encyclopedia . . ., 1980- , 62 vols.

Jen-min shou-ts'e (People's handbook), Peking, Ta-kung pao, 1950- .

Communist China, 1955- Hong Kong Union Research Institute, 1956- .

Shin chungoku nenkan, 1962- Tokyo, Taishukan shoten, 1962- .

Wu Yuan-li ed *China: a handbook* Praeger, 1973.

China: a general survey China Books, 1979.

Watkins R J *Directory of selected scientific institutions in mainland China* Hoover Institution, 1970, 469p. In Chinese with transliterations.

Yang Chia-lo *Book yearbook* Nan-ching, 1933, 2 vols. Bibliography, libraries, laws of libraries and publications, etc.

Lu Chien-ching *Encyclopedia of library science* Rev ed, 1958, 898p.

Directory of Chinese libraries China National Publications Import and Export Co, 1982, ca 500p. (World Books Reference Guides, 3). Bilingual.

Chinese American Librarians Association (USA) *Directory of Chinese American librarians* Chinese Culture Service Inc, 1977, 36p.

3b

Liang Tsu-han *Chung-kuo li tai shu mu tsung lu* (A catalogue of Chinese bibliographies), Taipei, 1953.

Ichiko C *A list of bibliographies and catalogues on modern China* (In Chinese) Tokyo, Bunko nai Kindai Chugoku Kenkyu Inkai, 1960, 44p. Covers 1945- ; section on library science.

Hucker C O *China, a critical bibliography* U of Arizona P, 1962, 125p. History and culture; books and periodicals in subject order.

Berton P and Wu E *Contemporary China: a research guide* Hoover Institution, 1967, 695p. Includes Taiwan, 1945-1963.

Ma J T [Section on bibliographic sources for the study of mainland China] in Wu Yuan-li *China: a handbook* (See above under 3a).

Wolff E 'Recent bibliographical sources on mainland China' *J Lib Info Sci* (USA/Taiwan) 1978 4(2) 91-105. Continuation of the above.

Wong W S 'Chinese literature and bibliography in fields of study' in *Encyclopedia* 21 (1977) 36-131. Extensive and annotated listing.

Yu P K *Bibliographic control in the People's Republic of China*, 1949-1972 Paper, IFLA Congress, Grenoble, 1973, 31p. (See: General, 2b).

— *Ibid* in *Ch'ien Mu hsien sheng pa shih sui chi nien lun wen chi* (Festschrift to Dr Ch'ien Mu's 80th birthday) Hong Kong, New Asia Research Institute, 1974, 1-42.

Wu K T and Wang C 'China [national bibliographies]' *L of C Q J* 1969 26(3) 92-6.

Hsia Tao-tai and Haun K 'Ch'üan-kuo hsin shu mu' (Chinese national bibliography) Association for Asian Studies, Committee on East Asian Libraries *Newsletter* 1973 (40) 27-32.

Ch'üan-kuo hsin shu-mu (National bibliography) 1950- Ministry of Culture, Bureau of Publications, 1951- . Cumulations.

Cordier H *Bibliotheca sinica: dictionnaire bibliographique des ouvrages relatifs à l'empire chinois* 2nd ed Paris, Librairie Orientale et Américaine, 1904-1908; Supplément 1922-1924.

Author index to the Bibliotheca sinica of Henri Cordier Columbia U, East Asiatic Library — Reprinted: Burt Franklin, 1968.

Yuang Ting-li *China in Western literature: a continuation of Cordier's Bibliotheca sinica* New Haven, Far Eastern Pub. 1958, 802p. Section 11 of the appendix covers library science.

Lust J *Index sinicus: catalogue of articles relating to China . . . 1920-1955* Heffer, 1964, 663p. Another continuation of Cordier's work. In subject order with subdivisions for : China, Mongolia, Sinkiang and Hong Kong.

Skachkov P E *Bibliografiia kitaiia* Moscow, Izdatelstvo Vostochnoi Literaturi, 1960, 690p. Russian sources.

Yuan T'ung-li *Russian works on China, 1918-1960* Yale U, Far Eastern Pub, 1961, 162p. Taiwan included.

Tanis N E et al *China in books: a basic bibliography in Western language* JAI P, 1979, 328p.

Quah R *Library resources in Singapore on contemporary mainland China* Singapore, Institute of South East Asian Studies, 1971.

Skinner W G et al *Modern Chinese society: an analytical bibliography* Stanford U P, 1973, 3 vols. 31,000 items on 72 subjects in Chinese, Japanese and Western languages.

Education in communist China: a selective list of books, pamphlets and periodical articles on the state of education in mainland China, 1953-1963 US Department of State, Bureau of Intelligence and Research, 1964, 110p.

Seybolt P J *Revolutionary education in China: documents and commentary* Int Arts and Sciences P, 1973, 408p.

Fraser S E and Hsu Kuang-liang *Chinese education and society, a bibliographic guide: the cultural revolution and its aftermath* Int Arts and Sciences P, 1972, 204p.

Shih N S *Critical bibliographical essay about the history of printing in China during the Ming dynasty (1368-1644)* Long Island U, Research paper, 1970, 100p.

Doctoral dissertations on China U of Washington P.

Chinese periodicals: a guide to indexes of periodicals relating to China Yale U Library, East Asian collection, 1965, 101p.

Tu shu yueh pao (Book readers monthly) 1955-58.

Tu shu (Book readers), 1958- .

Li Chung-li *T'u shu kuan hsueh shu-chi lien-ho mu-lu* (Union list of library literature) Peking, Chung-hua shu-chu, 1958, 77p. Period 1910-1957.

Nanking Library *Tu shu kuan lun-wen so-yin* (Index to library literature) Vol. 1: 1900-1949; Vol. 2: Oct 1949-1957.

3c

Nunn G R *Chinese periodicals, international holdings, 1949-1960* Ann Arbor, 1961, 85p.

Hervouet Y *Catalogue des périodiques chinois dans les bibliothèques d'Europe* Mouton, 1958, 102p.

Chinese periodicals in British libraries, handlist 1- Trustees of the British Musuem, 1965- .

Pei-ching Tu shu kuan *T'u shu kuan kung tso* (Library work), 1955-60. For school and rural libraries.

— *T'u shu kuan hsueh t'ung hsun* (Library science bulletin) 1955-60. Both superseded by:

— *T'u shu kuan* (The library), 1961-1965?

Tu shu guan xue tong xuen (Library science bulletin) 1979- . CSLS.

Library and Information Service 1980- . Chinese Science and Technology Information Association.

3d

State Statistical Bureau *Ten great years: statistics of the economic and cultural achievement of the People's Republic of China* Peking, Foreign Languages P, 1960, 223p.

Chen N R *Chinese economic statistics: a handbook for mainland China* Aldine, 1967, 539p. A supplement to *Ten great years*.

3e

Hsia Tao-tai *Guide to selected legal sources of mainland China, a listing of laws and regulations, and periodical legal literature . . .* Library of Congress, 1967, 357p. From Chinese sources.

Hsia Tao-tai and Haun K 'Communist Chinese legislation on publishing and libraries' *L of C Q J* 1970 27 20-37.

3f

Meskill J *An introduction to Chinese civilisation* Heath, 1973, 689p.

Thomson J *Illustrations of China and its people* U Pub of America, 1980, 320p. Reprint of 1873-4 edition with new text.

Clubb O E *Twentieth Century China* 2nd ed Columbia U P, 1972.

Bastid M *Quelques aspects de la réforme de l'enseignement en Chine au début du 20e siècle, d'après les écrits de Zhang Jian* Mouton, 1971, 321p.

Roy K K 'Earliest forms of libraries in China' *Lib Hist Rev* 1974 1(2) 43-83.

Shen Wong W 'The development of archives and libraries in China: an historical account' *Libri* 1976 26(2) 40-55.

Kau Lai-bing *The organization and treatment of libraries in the Ming and Ch'ing dynasties* Hong Kong U, 1968, 2 vols. English summary, 49p. PhD thesis.

Taam Chenk-woon *The development of Chinese libraries under the Ch'ing dynasty, 1644-1911* Shanghai, Commercial P, 1935, 107p.

Nelson D M and Nelson R B ''The red chamber' [1888-1927]: Li Ta-chao and sources of radicalism in modern Chinese librarianship' *J Lib Hist* 1979 14(2) 121-8, refs.

Pélissier R *Les bibliothèques en Chine pendant la première moitié du 20e siècle* Mouton, 1971, 366p.

Huang G W 'Miss Mary Elizabeth Wood: pioneer of the library movement in China' *Lib Hist Rev* 1974 1(4) 42-5, refs.

Lo Y-C *Library development in China, 1905-1949* London, LA, 1979, 274p, refs.

Kirkes S 'Mao as a library user and worker: how early experiences in traditional Chinese libraries contributed to Mao's revolutionary ideas' *Amer Lib* 1976 7(10) 628-31.

For shorter texts relating to the pre-1949 period see:

Lib J 1916 41 384-9.

Lib J 1918 43 764-5.

Lib J 1919 44 423-9.

ALA Bull 1926 20(2) 35-48.

Lib Q 1937 7 401-32.

Modern period

Chesneaux J *China: the People's Republic, 1949-1976* Pantheon Books 1979, 255p. (Translation from the French: *La Chine*).

496 Oksenberg M *China's developmental experience* Discussion papers at meetings of

the National Academy of Political Sciences, Oct 1972 NAPS, 1973, 227p. (Proceedings, Vol. 31, No.1).
Barnett A D *Uncertain passage: China's transition to the post Mao era* Brooking Inst P, 1974.
Garside R *Coming alive: China after Mao* A Deutsch, 1981, 458p.
Hu C T *Aspects of Chinese education* Teachers College P, 1969, 101p.
Sidel R and Sidel V W 'Education in the People's Republic of China' Columbia U *Teachers College Record* 1975 76 605-16.
Price R F *Education in modern China* 2nd ed Routledge and K P, 1979, 344p. (1st ed Praeger, 1970, 308p).
Nunn G R *Publishing in mainland China* MIT P, 1966, 83p.
Wang S W 'Impressions of Chinese libraries and the Chinese book market' *Austr Acad Res Lib* 1974 5 19-24.
Goldberg B 'Libraries and mass communication in the People's Republic of China' *Scand Pub Lib Q* 1975 8(2) 62-71.
Also in *Library Literature* 7, 1977, 32-46. No illustrations.
Wang J Ju-Lie *A study of the criteria for book selection in communist China's public libraries, 1949-1964* San Jose State College, MA thesis, 1966; also Hong Kong, Union P, 1968.
Wu K T 'China, libraries in the People's Republic of' in *Encyclopedia* 4 (1970) 627-46.
Fang J R 'People's Republic of China, libraries in' in *Encyclopedia* 22 (1977) 5-34.
Huan N Lai-shen *Library development in communist China, 1949-1962* Chicago U, School of Library Science, 1964, 114p. MA thesis.
Ma J T 'Libraries in the People's Republic of China since 1949' *Wilson Lib Bull* 1971 45 970-5.
Brewer J G 'Libraries in China: a comparative view' *Lib Ass Rec* 1968 70(5) 124-7.
Fang J R 'Contemporary development in librarianship in the People's Republic of China' *Int Lib Rev* 1981 13(2) 211-9.
Fang J R 'Chinese libraries carry out Chairman Mao's dictum 'Serve the people'' *Wilson Lib Bull* 1975 49(10) 744-9.
Barclay J 'China: libraries serve the people' *Austr Lib J* 1978 27 54-63.
Barclay J 'The Four Modernisations embrace libraries in the People's Republic of China' *Austr Lib J* 1979 28(7) 102-10.
Castagna E 'A visit to two Chinese libraries' *Wilson Lib Bull* 1978 52(10) 789-92. Peking University Library and Shanghai public library.
Goldberg B 'Kvinden baerer den halve himmel' *Bibliotek* 1975 (6) 146-8.
Richnell D T and Nelson H 'Libraries in the People's Republic of China: a report of a visit, June 1976' *J Libp* 1977 9(1) 1-16.
Poarch M E 'A librarian visits mainland China' *Top of the News* 1980 36(3) 293-5.
Ta li kai chin kung-hui t'u shu kuan kung tso Workers Pub'g Co, 1956, 72p. Unions libraries.
Hinrup H J 'De socialistiske tanker styrkes ved konfrontation med revisionistik og kapitalistisk tankegang' *Bibliotek* 1975 70 (21) 524-6. Academic libraries.
Wood F 'Peking University Library' *Focus Int Comp Libp* 1976 7(3) 27-8.
Takao Fukudome 'China Medical Board and medical libraries in the Far East' *Med Lib Ass Bull* 1968 56(2) 150-6.
Lo K 'Rationed like rice: information services in the People's Republic of China' *PNLA Q* 1977 42 4-8.
Chunrong N 'Chinese scientific and technical information: present status and future prospects' *Unesco J* 1980 2(2) 74-7.
Broadbent K P *Dissemination of scientific information in the People's Republic of China* Ottawa, International Development Research Centre, 1980, 60p.

Tell B 'Bibliotek, dokumentation och datorer i Kina' *Tidskr Dok* 1979 35(2) 34-7.
Use of computers.
Ding Z 'Towards a wider library resource sharing' *Int Lib Rev* 1980 12 3-6.

CHINA, Republic of (Taiwan)

1

National Central Library (NCL), Taipei. Transferred from Nankin in 1949, opened in 1954. Has a bibliographical centre.

Chung yang t'u shu kuan [History of the National Central Library] Taipei, 1964, 7p.

National Taiwan University (NTU) Library.

National Science Council: Science and Technology Information Centre.

Shen Tseng-chee 'The Science and Technology Information Center, National Science Council, Republic of China' *J Lib Info Sci* (USA/Taiwan) 1975 1(2) 94-105.

2a

Ministry of Education.

2b

Library Association of China (LAC), Taipei, 1953- .

NTU. Library Science Society.

2c

Lai Yung-hsiang 'The present status of education for librarianship in Taiwan' *NTU Lib Sci Circular* 1966 (4) 15p.

Ozolins K L 'The role of library science education in the development of public libraries in Taiwan' *NTU Lib Sci Circular* 1966 (2) 19p.

Li Tze-chung 'Library science education in the Republic of China: an appraisal' *J Educ Libp* 1973 14(1) 16-31.

Chou T et al 'Library education in the Republic of China today' *J Lib Info Sci* (USA/Taiwan) 1976 2(1) 45-73.

Berminghausen D K 'Research in librarianship' *NTU Lib Sci Circular* 1966 (1) 16p.

Seng H B H 'Research in librarianship in the Republic of China' *Res Libp* 1971 3(17) 133-6.

3a

Yearbook of the Republic of China China Pub Co, 1951- .

NCL *Directory of cultural organizations of the Republic of China* 1st ed, 1963; 4th ed 1972. In three parts: 3rd part Libraries.

['Libraries in Taiwan, 1968 survey'] (In Chinese) *LAC Bull* 1968 20(8) 1-38.

NCL *Chuan-kuo t'u-shu-kuan chien-chieh* (Guide to libraries of the Republic of China) The Library, 1975.

Wu G *Survey of special libraries in Taiwan* Kent State U, Research paper, 1970, 39p.

LAC *T'u-shu-kuan hsüeh* (Library science) 1974, 566p. Manual of librarianship for Taiwan.

3b

Li Tze-chung 'The current state of bibliographical services in Taiwan' *ASPAC Q Cult Soc Affairs* 1971 2(4) 95-105.

NCL *Kuo-li chung yang t'u shu kuan sung chiao kuan shu mu* 1967- .

NCL *Chung-hua-min-kuo ch'u-pan t'u-shu mu-lu* 1970- m. Deposit list.

NCL *Chung hua min kuo ch'u pan t'u shu mu lu hui pien* 1964, 2 vols. Cumulative vols for 1949-1963.

NCL *Chung-hua-min-kuo ch'u-pan t'u-shu mu-lu shu-chi* (Supplement) 1970, 1177p.

NCL *Chung-hua-min-kuo ch'u-pan t'u-shu mu-lu hui-pien san-chi* (3rd compilation), 1975, 2114p.

Government Information Office *Chung hua min kuo t'u shu tsung mu lu* 1974. (Books in print record).

Hung Jui-k'un ed *Chung hua min kuo ch'üan kuo t'u shu tsung mu lu* Hong's Book-Publishing House, 1976; Previous edition: 1969. (Same format as above).

Cheng H-H 'Selected list of reference books published in the Republic of China, 1977-78' *J Lib Info Sci* (USA/Taiwan) 1979 5(1) 111-26. (136 references, classified and annotated).

NTU *Chung wen ch'i kan lun wen fen lei so yin*, 1960- (Classified index to periodicals).

NCL *Chung-hua-min-kuo chi-kan lun-wen so-yin* 1 1970- m. (Index to Chinese periodicals).

Cheng W and Tu J-c *T'u-shu kuan hsüeh lun-chu tsu-liao tsung-mu* Taichung, Wen-cheng chü pan she, 1969, 190p. (Bibliography of library science).

3c

NCL *Chung hua min kuo ch'u pan ch'i kan chih nan* 1970 (Directory).

Jeng H-s 'Periodical publications in the Republic of China, 1950-71' *NCL Newsletter* 1973 5(2) 1-5.

NCL *Kuan kan* 1957- .

NCL *Newsletter* 1969- (In English).

NTU *Library science circulars.*

NTU Dept of Library Science *T'u shu kuan hsüeh kan* 1967- .

Chung-kuo t'u-shu-kuan hsüeh-hui hui-wu tung-hsin 1975- (LAC Newsletter).

Chung-kuo t'u-shu-kuan hsüeh-hui hui-pao 1953- (LAC Bulletin).

Journal of Library and Information Science 1 1975- 2 a year. Published by The National Taiwan Normal University, Dept of Social Education and the Mid-West Chinese American Librarians Association.

3d

Directorate General of Budget, Accounts and Statistics *Statistical abstract of the Republic of China* 1955- . (In Chinese).

Department of Education *Taiwan education statistics* Taichung, 1949- . (Now bilingual).

3e

LAC *Library standards* 1965, var. p. Comprehensive.

3f

Kaser D E *Book pirating in Taiwan* U of Pennsylvania P, 1969, 154p.

— *Library development in eight Asian countries* Scarecrow, 1969. 'Republic of China', 72-86.

Chiang Fu-tsung 'Modern Chinese library under Sino-American cooperation' *Chinese Culture* 1960 3 140-54.

Wu P 'Libraries in Taiwan: continuation of new patterns' *Lib J* 1962 87(23) 4129-32.

Pao I T P 'China, Libraries in' in *Encyclopedia* 4 (1970) 647-55.

Li, Tze-chung 'Taiwan, library services and development in the Republic of China' in *Encyclopedia* 30 (1980) 1-70, bibl.

Taipei City Library *Taipei City Library: today and its future* The Library, 1974.

Wang C [A survey of College and university libraries in Taiwan] (In Chinese) *J Lib Info Sci* (USA/Taiwan) 1976 2(1) 74-104.

Ferguson A W 'Taiwan college and university libraries: problems and prospects' *Int Lib Rev* 1978 10(4) 397-405.

Scientific and technical information needs and resources in the Republic of China Washington, National Academy of Sciences, 1974.

Eyre J J 'The impact of automation on libraries: a review' *J Lib Info Sci* (USA/Taiwan) 1979 5(1) 1-15.

For the pre-1949 period and for general sources see People's Republic of China (under 3b in particular).

HONG KONG

1

City Hall Library, 1962- Public Library with deposit privilege, and headquarters of the public library services.

University of Hong Kong Library, 1911- .

2a

Department of Education.

2b

Hong Kong Library Association (HKLA), 1958- .

O'Hara R 'Hong Kong Library Association' in *Encyclopedia* 10 (1973) 494-8.

2c

Gleave B M 'Education for librarianship: a review of the courses organised by the department of extra-mural studies' *J Educ* (HKU) 1963 70-4.

Quinn M et al 'Report of the Hong Kong Library Association sub-committee on professional training for librarians in Hong Kong' *HKLA J* 1975 (3) 17-22.

3a

Hong Kong Yearbook Government Printer [Latest: 1981, published 1980, 307p].

Kan Lai-Bing *Libraries in Hong Kong: a directory* 2nd ed HKLA, 1973?.

See also Southeast Asia, Section 3a.

3b

A catalogue of books printed in Hong Kong Government Printer. Published as supplements to the *Hong Kong Government Gazette*.

Berkowitz M I and Poon E K K *Hong Kong studies: a bibliography* Hong Kong, Chinese U, Dept of Extra Mural Studies, 1969, 137p.

Poon P W T 'An annotated bibliography of libraries and librarianship in Hong Kong' *Int Lib Rev* 1975 7(4) 479-86.

3c

HKLA *Bulletin* 1963-65. Mimeo, for members only.

— *Newsletter* 1965-68. Mimeo, for members only.

— *Journal* 1969- .

Department of Education *Adult Education Bulletin*. On adult education and leisure libraries.

3e

Hong Kong Government Gazette.

The Laws of Hong Kong.

3f

Lin Tzong-Bian et al *Hong Kong: economical, social and political studies in development* M E Sharpe, 1979, 410p.

Kan L-B 'Present-day publishing in Hong Kong' *Lib Resour Tech Serv* 1978 22(1) 47-60.

Rydings H A 'Hong Kong, Libraries in' in *Encyclopedia* 10 (1973) 478-93.

Chow T 'Library facilities available to the public in Hong Kong' *Int Lib Rev* 1974 6(1) 83-90.

Yeong Shuk-Chun A and Kan L-B 'Recent development in librarianship in Hong Kong' *HKLA J* 1975 (3) 1-6 refs.

O'Halloran J V 'Libraries in and around Hong Kong' *Catholic Lib Wld* 1966 37 289-91.

Cave M and Harley J 'The public libraries in Hong Kong' *Lib Ass Rec* 1963 65(10) 370-3.

Deakyne W 'Serving the pearl of the Orient' *Wilson Lib Bull* 1971 45(10) 966-9.

Kan L-B 'Provision of library services by Hong Kong schools' *Int Lib Rev* 1976 8(4) 461-75.

Chow T-A 'Report on library provision for children and young people' *HKLA J* 1977 (4) 14-22.

Scott D 'The Morrison Library: an early 19th century collection in the library of the University of Hong Kong' Royal Asiatic Society *Journal of the Hong Kong Branch* 1960 1 50-67.

Rydings H A 'University of Hong Kong libraries: from a quarter to half a million volumes, 1963 to 1976' *HKLA J* 1977 (4) 23-4.

JAPAN

1

Kokuritsu Kokkai Toshokan (National Diet Library), Tokyo. 1948- . Former Imperial Library, 1872- . Library of the Parliament with deposit privilege and bibliographical functions.

Hatch L 'The National Diet Library, the National Library of the Philippines and the Singapore National Library' *J Lib Hist* 1972 7(4) 329-59.

The National Diet Library: organization, functions and activities The Library, 1974, 60p. Supersedes earlier similar publications.

Suzuki H 'Japan National Diet Library' in *Encyclopedia* 13 (1975) 249-62.

Kaula P N 'National library function of the National Diet Library' *Her Lib Sci* 1976 15(1) 26-31.

Keio University Library School Library, Mita, 1951- .

Nihon Kagaku Gijutsu Zyoho Senta (Japan Information Centre for Science and Technology — JICST), Tokyo, 1957- .

Tanabe K 'Japan Information Centre of Science and Technology' in *Encyclopedia* 13 (1975) 205-21.

2a

Ministry of Education, Science and Culture. Its Information Section has a collection of professional material. 1952- .

Japan Reading Institute, Tokyo.

Sidorova A 'Institut Chteniya v Tokyo' *Bibliotekar* 1977 (3) 68-70.

2b

Nippon Toshokan Kyōkai (Japan Library Association), Tokyo. Created in 1892 as: Nippon Bunko Kyōkai. In 1908 became: Nippon Toshokan Kyokai.

JLA *Nippon Toshokan Kyōkai 80-nenshi nenpyo* The Association, 1971, 72p. Chronology of the JLA.

[Japan Library Association] (In Japanese) *Tosh Zasshi* 1974 68(11) 457-71. Special section.

Nakamura H 'Japan Library Association (JLA)' in *Encyclopedia* 13 (1975) 238-47.

Toshokan Gakkai (Society of Library Science), Tokyo.

Special Libraries Association, Tokyo, 1952- .

Japan Medical Library Association.

Japan Association of Agricultural Librarians and Documentalists (JAALD) (Nippon Nogaku Toshokan Kyogikai), Tokyo, 1965- .

Japan Society for Documentation (Nippon Dokumenteishon Kyōkai), Tokyo, 1950- .

2c

Gitler R L 'Education for librarianship abroad: Japan' *Lib Trends* 1963 12(2) 273-94.

'Draft on improvement of library science education' (In Japanese) *Tosh Zasshi* 1973 67(2) 69-72.

Nakamura Y [Approaches to education and training problems of information specialists for NIST] (In Japanese) *Lib Info Sci* 1974 (12) 177-82.
Staveley R 'Impressions of library and information studies in Japan: 1973' *Lib Info Sci* 1974 (12) 11-4.
SLIS Curriculum Committee [A comprehensive review of the curriculum of the School of Library and Information Science at Keio University] (In Japanese) *Lib Info Sci* 1974 (12) 275-97.
Sawamoto T 'Revisions of curricula and new PhD programme at the School of Library and Information Science, Keio University: a progress report' *Lib Info Sci* 1975 (13) 247-60.
Havelka F 'Výchova informačnich pracovníku v Japansku' *Tech Knihovna* 1976 20(2) 42-50.
Hase T et al [Symposium: making of librarians] *Tosh-Kai* 1977 28(6) 223-51.
[Opinions of members of the Japan Library Association] (In Japanese) *Tosh Zasshi* 1975 69(3) 126-35.
[Highlights of the 1974 Annual National Meeting of Librarians] (In Japanese) *Tosh Zasshi* 1975 69(2) 48-73.
Tazawa Y 'Female library staffs — an opinion from the opposite sex' *Libns for Soc Change* 1974 (5) 9-12.
Koto K et al [Woman librarianship, cases of private college and university libraries in Japan 1977] (In Japanese) *Lib Info Sci* 1978 (16) 253-80, refs.

3a

Uemura C *Toshokangaku shoshigaku jiten/Dictionary of librarianship and bibliographical terms* Tokyo, Yurindo, 1967, 726p. Japanese into: English, French, German and Russian.
Tsuneta Yano Memorial Society *Nippon: a chartered survey of Japan* 1957- Kokusei-sha, 1957- . Japanese edition: *Nihon Kokusei-Zue* 1927- .
Science Council of Japan *Zenkoku gaku kyokai soran* (Directory of learned societies) Okurasho Insatsukyoku, 1966, 337p.
Araki K comp *Verzeichnis Japanischer Informations- und Dokumentationsstellen / Directory of institutions relating to information and documentation in Japan* Institut für Dokumentationswesen (IDW), 1977, 24p.
Toshokan shokuin meibo JLA, 1960, 190p. (Directory of librarians).
Special Libraries Association *Directory of special libraries* 4th ed? The Association, 1976.
Takayama M 'A statistical analysis of special libraries in Japan' (In Japanese) *Lib Info Sci* 1977 (15) 139-64. From data in the above directory.

3b

Suzuki Y and Suzuki M T 'Current bibliographic services in East Asia: Japan' *J Lib Info Sci* 1978 4(2) 106-23.
Ministry of Education *Nihon ni Okeru Niji-kankôbutsu no Genjô*, 1961.
Nihon no Sankō Tosho Henshú Iinkai Nihon no Sankō Tosho, 1962, 353p.
Guide to Japanese reference books ALA, 1966, 303p. Translation of the above.
Kaneko H 'Japanese literature and bibliography' in *Encyclopedia* 21 (1977) 131-76.
Kuroda A Y et al 'Japan [national bibliographies]' *L of C Q J* 1969 26(3) 98-104.
Oda Y 'Japan National Bibliograhpy' in *Encyclopedia* 13 (1975) 247-9.
National Diet Library *Zen Nihon shuppambutsu sōmokuroku* 1948- Monthly, 1948-1955, and annual cumulations of the weekly record:
— *Nōhon Shūho* 1955- .

— *Kokuritsu Kokkai Toshokan zōsho mokuroku* (Cumulations) 1948-58 Published 1960-68, 6 vols., 1959-68 Published 1970- .

Kokusho sokuroku (General catalogue of Japanese books), Iwanami Pub. 1963-72, 8 vols. Early books to mid 19th century.

The period 1870 to 1920s is covered by commercial catalogues, then:

Shuppan nenkan (Publication yearbook) 1926-28, 3 vols.; 1929-40, 12 vols.; 1930-41, 12 vols.

Shoseki nenkan, 1942.

Nihon shuppan nenkan 1943-48, 3 vols.

Shuppan nenkan, 1948- Annual. All published by Shuppan Nyūsu Sha who also publishes the current record *Shuppan nyūsu* (Publication news).

Ministry of Finance, Commission for Dissemination of Government Publications *Seifu kankōbutsu geppō* (Monthly report of Government publications), 1957- . Classified by issuing bodies.

National Diet Library *Kuni no kankōbutsu* (Government publications) 1948-1970 published in 1971; 1971-1974 published as a *Supplement* 1975.

Kuroki T *An introduction to Japanese government publications — with an annotated bibliography* Pergamon, 1981, 204p. Translation of *Seifu kankobutsu gaisetsu.*

National Diet Library *Zasshi kiji sakuin* (Index of periodicals) 1948- .

Passin H *Japanese education: a bibliography of materials in the English language* Teachers College P, 1970, 135p.

Jajiki S *Classified annotated bibliography of Japanese books in the field of library science published between 1965 and 1970* Kent State U, Research paper, 1970, 23p.

Jones A 'Bibliography on library literature in Japan' *Lib Q* 1971 41(1) 54-60, 20 refs.

Toshokagaku bunku mokuroku Nihon Shiritsu Daigaku Kyokai, 1971, 257p. Bibliography of librarianship.

3c

Nihon zasshi soran (Directory of Japanese periodicals) Shuppan Nyusu Sha, 1967, etc. Latest edition noted: 1975. Classified.

The main periodicals in librarianship are:

National Diet Library *Kokuritsu Kokkai Toshokan Nenpo* (Report), 1948- .

— *Kokuritsu Kokkai Toshokan geppō* (Newsletter).

— *Biblos* 1950- .

Library Association *Toshokan Zasshi*, 1907- .

— *Gendi no Toshokan*, 1963- .

Society of Library Science *Toshokan Gakkai Nenpo*, 1954- .

Special Library Association *Senmon Toshokan Kyogakai Kaiho*, 1960- .

Mita Toshokan Gakkai *Library and Information Science*, 1963- .

Toshokan-kai (Library world) Toshokan Kenkyūkai, 1947- .

Japan Documentation Society *Dokumenteishon Kenkyu*, 1950- .

3d

Statistical Bureau *Nihon tokei nenkan* 1949- . In Japanese and English.

National Diet Library *Statistical abstract of Japan.*

Japan Library Association *Nippon no Toshokan* 1963- . Published annually.

[Library network in Japan — holdings and expenditure] *Outlook on Res Lib* 1980 2(1) 2-6.

Takayama M 'Statistical analysis of special libraries in Japan' *Lib Info Sci* 1977 (15) 139-64.

3e

National Diet Library *Index to the Japanese laws and regulations* Annual.

Nomura Y 'General revision of the copyright laws in Japan' *Rev Int Droit d'Auteur* 1968 57 27-131.

Library Association *Toshokan kankei hoki kijunshu* JLA, 1962, 121p.

Urata T *Toshokan ho seiritsushi shiryo* Toshokan Kyokai, 1968, 473p. Sources on the history of library law.

[School library act] (In Japanese) *Tosh Zasshi* 1969 63(10) 517-36.

See also below: Welsh T F.

3f

National Commission for Unesco *Japan, its land, people and culture* Rev ed, Ministry of Finance Printing Bureau, 1964, 883p.

Reischauer E O *Japan: tradition and transformation* Houghton Mifflin, 1978, 347p.

Beasley W G *The modern history of Japan* 3rd ed Weidenfeld, 1981, 358p.

Shikaumi N *Cultural policy in Japan* Unesco, 1970, 55p.

L'information au Japon (Presse, radio, télévision) Documentation Française, 1969, 94p.

Hashimoto M *Nihon Shuppan hambaishi* Kodan Sha, 1964, 774p. History of publishing in Japan.

Sasaki S *The publishing world in Japan: chronicle of its past and present situation* Japan Book Pub Association, 1967, 106p.

Welsh T F *Toshokan: libraries in Japanese society* ALA/Bingley 1976, 306p. Includes a chronology of librarianship 1868-1968, and the text of some key laws.

Nakamura H 'Japan, libraries and information centers in' in *Encyclopedia* 13 (1975) 222-38.

Siggins J A *American influence on modern Japanese library development, 1860-1948* U of Chicago P, 1969, 117p.

Kitahara K [The early development of reference work in Japanese libraries, 1868-1920] (In Japanese) *Lib Info Sci* 1970 (8) 17-49 199, refs.

Tung L W 'Library development in Japan' *Lib Q* 1956 26(2) 79-104; 26(3) 196-223.

[Development of libraries and library science during the decade 1965-1974] (In Japanese) *Tosh Zasshi* 1976 28(2/3) 41-150. Special section.

Mamiya F *Toshokan to waga shōgai* Fujikai, 1969-71, 2 vols.

Stevens R D and Stevens H C 'Japanese libraries from a Hawaiian angle' *Hawaii Lib Ass J* 1971 28 17-23.

Thirion G 'Visite aux bibliothèques japonaises' *Bull Bibliot Fr* 1975 20(11) 519-23.

Powers L 'From Chicago to Tokyo: reflections on Japanese librarianship' *J Lib Info Sci* (USA/Taiwan) 1976 2(3) 147-75, refs.

Humphreys K W 'Order of priority of national library services' *Lib Info Sci* 1974 (12) 35-6.

Suzuki H 'National plan for library/information services and the National Diet Library' *Lib Info Sci* 1976 (14) 1-14.

Tamura S [The development of public libraries in post-war Japan] (In Japanese) *Lib Info Sci* 1979, (17) 153-81.

Nagai N 'Problems of the public libraries in metropolitan Tokyo' *Lib Trends* 1965 14(1) 68-74.

Yoneda T 'Public libraries in Japan' *East Libn* 1970 4(3) 197-206.

Nippon Toshokan Kyokai *Minna ni Hon o : toshokan hakusho 1972* NTK, 1972, 56p. Books for all; review of the library situation.
Matsuoka K 'Home libraries in Japan' *Top News* 1970 26 169-74.
[The leisure society and libraries] (In Japanese) *Tosh Zasshi* 1975 69(1) 6-25. Special section.
Downs L D 'Services for children provided by public libraries in Japan' *Top News* 1970 26 169-74.
Tsutsui Y 'School libraries in Japan, past and present' *Libri* 1972 22(2) 114-9.
Nagakura M 'Comparative study of school library administration and management systems: England, The United States and Japan' *Lib Info Sci* 1971 (9) 245-60.
Zenkoku Kokuritsu Daigaku Toshokan-cho Kaigi *Daigaku toshokan no gyōmu bunseki* Nihon Toshokan Kyōkai, 1968, 209p. Conference of Heads of national university libraries; analysis of university library administration.
University and research libraries in Japan and the United States Proceedings of the Japan-USA conference on library and information science in higher education, Tokyo, 1969 ALA, 1972, 299p.
Humphreys K W 'University libraries in Japan: a report' *Lib Info Sci* 1974 (12) 15-30.
Suzuki H [A commentary to Humphreys' report] *Lib Info Sci* 1974 (12) 31-4.
Tanabe H 'University libraries in Japan: present state and problems' *Int Lib Rev* 1973 5(2) 209-23.
Shibata M [The progress and problems of university libraries] *Tosh Zasshi* 1977 29(2) 57-67.
Bradman E 'Japanese medical libraries' *Med Lib Ass Bull* 1963 51(1) 16-25.
Tanigushi M 'Japanese medical libraries' *Spec Lib* 1963 54(10) 623-9.
[Doctors and libraries] (In Japanese) *Igaku Tosh* 1969 16(4) 279-315. Special section.
'Symposium: interchange and cooperation among special libraries' *Spec Lib Ass Bull* (Japan) 1975 (61) 6-19.
Nihon Dokumenteishon Kyōkai *Science information in Japan* The Association, 1967, 192p. Revised edition of 1959 and 1962 publications.
Kabayashi Y 'Development of a comprehensive network for scientific and technical information in Japan' *Lib Trends* 1969 17(3) 258-66.
'Scientific and technological information activities in Japan' *National Diet Library Newsletter* 1975 42 1-12.
[On the final report of NIST] (In Japanese) *Dok Kenkyu* 1975 25(2) 51-74. National Information System for Science and Technology.
Takayama M [Changing features of library services in industry] (In Japanese) *Lib Info Sci* 1976 (14) 339-53.
'Japanese research library system' *Outlook on Res Lib* 1978 1(2) 5-8. 1973 report on the 'Basic measures necessary today for the promotion of science' by the Science Council of Japan.
Sakurai N 'Computer applications in the libraries of Japan' *Network* 1974 1(7) 15-6, 18.
Hosono K [The effect on the mechanized library system caused by changes in computers] (In Japanese) *Lib Info Sci* 1975 (13) 99-107.
'Mechanisation projects at the National Institute of Japanese Literature, Tokyo, 1972-1977' *Program* 1978 12(3) 125-38.
Inose H ed *Scientific information systems in Japan* North Holland, 1981, 257p.

KOREA, Republic of

1

Kungnip Chungang Tosŏgwan (Central National Library — CNL), Seoul, 1923-. Among its departments are:
- An International Book Exchange Centre and
- A Korean Library Science Research Institute (Hangug Doseogwanhak Yunkuhoe), 1969-.

A general catalogue of the Central National Library, Korea, 1971-72 CNL, 1973, 29p. Korean and English parallel texts. History, activities, statistics 1923-45, 1945-70 of the library.

Kukhoe Tosŏgwan (National Assembly Library), Seoul, 1951-. Shares the legal deposit privilege and some of the bibliographical responsibilities of the CNL.

National Assembly Library *Gug-hoe doseogwan an-nae* (Guide to the National Assembly Library) The Library, 1971.

Seoul National University Library, 1926-.

Korea Scientific and Technological Information Centre (KORSTIC) Seoul, 1962-.

KORSTIC *KORSTIC yoram* 1971, 14p. Korean and English text; short survey of functions and activities of KORSTIC.

2a

Ministry of Culture and Information

Yong-shin Academy. Research Institute of Korean Studies.

Korean Library Science Research Institute (Part of the CNL).

Maŭl Mungo Ponbu (Microlibraries Headquarters), Seoul.

2b

Hangug Tosŏgwan Hyŏphoe (Korean Library Association — KLA) 1955-. Previously: 1947 — Choson Tosŏgwan Hyŏphoe.

KLA *Korean Library Association* 1971, 10p. Short introduction.

Korean Library Science Society (KLSS), Seoul. 1970-.

Korean Micro-library Association, Seoul. 1960-.

2c

Burgess R 'Korea: a case study in American assistance' *J Educ Libp* 1961 1(4) 183-90.

Kang Chu-Chin 'Future needs for trained library workers in the Republic of Korea' in Bonn G *Library education and training in developing countries* East West Center P, 1966. 120-30.

3a

Korea annual 1964 — Hapdong News Agency. Korean edition as *Hapdong yon'gam*.

A handbook of Korea Ministry of Culture and Information, 1978, 825p.

National Assembly Library *Kungnae haksul mit yon'gu tanch'e p'yonllam* (Research institutes), 1966-7, 2 vols.

Tae segye paekkwa sajŏn Seoul, T'aegŭk Ch'ulp'ansa, 1972-73, 16 vols Encyclopaedia.

Glossary of library terms KLA, 1966.

KLA *Konggong tosŏgwan ŭi sisŏl* (Public library handbook) 1966, 216p.

KLA *Hakkyo tosŏgwan ŭi sisŏl* (School library handbook) 1965, 166p.

KLA *Han'guk ŭi taehak tosŏgwan silt'ae punsŏk* (College and university library handbook) 1967, 107p. These three works are comprehensive surveys of the libraries: facilities, laws, standards, etc.

KLA *Hanguk tosŏgwan illam* (Summaries of libraries) 1969-.

KLA *Jeon-gug do-seo-gwan siltae jo-sa* (Survey of Korean libraries) 1971. Part I: Academic and public libraries; Part II: School and special libraries.

Maŭl Mungo Ponbu *Maŭl mungo yoram* (Directory of microlibraries), 1967-68, Seoul, 1968, 372p.

3b

Kang T H 'Oriental literature and bibliography' in *Encyclopedia* 21 (1977) 176-240: Section on Korea, including libraries.

An Chun-gun *Hangug Sojihak* (History of Korean bibliography). Dongmungwan, 1967.

Central National Library *Hanguk somok* 1945-62 CNL 1964, 722p. Retrospective records. The periods 1897-1910, and 1910-1945 have also been recorded.

CNL *Chulpanmul Chong Mogros* (Current national bibliography) 1963/64 - Annual.

Dae-han Chulpan Munhwa Hyeobhoe *Hangguk Chulpan Yungam* (Books in print). Annual.

Jonghab Doseo Mogrog Korea Publishing Co-operatives. Annual.

National Assembly Library *Jeongbu ganhaengmul mogrog: daehag ganhaegmul pohom* (Government publications, including university publications), 1966-75, 8 vols. Cumulations of annual vols.

Pusan National University Library *Hagsul nonmun saeginlub* 1971 (Index of theses).

National Assembly Library *Guknae ganhaengmul gisa saekin* 1960- (Title varies) Index of periodicals in Korean.

Ministry of Culture and Information *Guk nae jeong-gi haeng mul illam pio* 1968- . Annual. Index of Korean periodicals.

Keun-su Kim comp *Hanguk jabji gaegwan mit hobyeol mogchajib* Research Institute of Korean Studies, 1973. Review of periodicals and contents lists.

Kang Sang-un *Hanguk kwangye oeguk nomun kisa ch'ong mongnok* Tamgu dang, 1967, 192p. Articles on Korea in Western languages, 1800-1964, mainly modern: 1945- .

Ko Hu-sŏk *Han'guk tosŏgwan kwan'gye munhon mongnok, 1921 ўon-1961 yŏn* Ihwa Yoja Taehakkyo Ch'ulp'anbu, 1965, 208p. Bibliography of library literature, in two parts: 1921-45; 1945-61.

3c

Ministry of Information *Chonggi kan-haengmul siltae illam, 4294* (Directory of periodicals and newspapers, 1961) 1962, 1053p.

CNL *Tosŏgwan* (The Library), 1946- . Previously *Kungnip Tosŏgwan po.*

National Assembly Library *Kukhoe Tosogwan po* 1964- . Monthly. Includes a 'Korean periodicals index'.

KLA *To hyop Wol-bo* 1969- . Monthly (KLA Bulletin).

Maul Mungo *Monthly bulletin* 1968- .
KLSS *Tosogwan Hak* 1970- . Annual.

3d

Economic Planning Board *Korea statistical yearbook* 1952- . In Korean and English.
KLA *Han'guk tosogwan t'onggye* 1970- . (Statistics of libraries).

3e

Daehan min-gug beobryeong saeg-in, 1948-1971, 1972, 1948-1973. National Assembly Library, 1972-73, 3 vols. Index of laws and regulations. Annual with cumulations.

3f

Korea: its people and culture Hakwon-sa, 1970. Issued periodically.
McGinn N F et al *Education and development in Korea* Harvard U P, 1980, 285p. (Harvard East Asian monographs, 90).
Study for the improvement of the Asia Foundation Book Program in Korea Central Education Research Institute, 1965, 107p.
Barnett S A et al *Developmental book activities and needs in Korea* USAID, 1966, 164p.
Books and national development: seminar report, April 1968 Korean Publishers Association, 1969.
Unesco activities in Korea 1954-1964 National Commission for Unesco, 1964, 226p.
Rin Paik *Han-guk do'seo-gwan-sa yeon-gu* (History of Korean libraries) KLA, 1969 (Korean Library Science Series, 3).
Rust J E *Problems in Korean library development* U of Pittsburgh Library, 1964, 33p.
'Republic of Korea' in Kaser D et al *Library development in eight Asian countries* Scarecrow, 1969, 7-30.
KLA *The role of libraries in the process of modernisation* (Report of a conference, May 1969), 1969, 118p.
Koh G S L 'Korea, libraries in' in *Encyclopedia* 13 (1975) 455-96.
Ishikawa T [Review of Korean libraries] (In Japanese) *Dok Kenkyu* 1975 25(11) 493-7.
Ye-kwon Kang 'The new community movement and country library services' *KLA Bull* Nov 1973 14 11-15.
'Public libraries' *KLA Bull* 1974 15(6) Whole issue.
Kaser D C 'Korean micro-libraries and private reading rooms' *Lib J* 1966 91(22) 6035-8.
Kim C H 'Reading public of the mini-libraries in rural Korea' *Libri* 1978 28(3) 215-27.
— 'The mini-library movement in rural Korea: a successful experiment with a rural public library alternative' *Int Lib Rev* 1979 11(14) 421-40, refs.
Hower M L 'School libraries in Korea' *Hoosier Sch Lib* 1961 17-9.
Lewis R 'Book reading among college students in Pusan, Korea' *Coll Res Lib* 1969 30(6) 518-24.
KORSTIC *Documentation activities in Korea* 1971, 64p.
'Information services in selected Asian countries' *J Lib Info Sci* (India) 1977 2(1) 1-90. Bangladesh, South Korea, Sri Lanka.

KOREA, People's Democratic Republic of

1

State Central Library, Pyongyang.

Academy of Sciences Library, Pyongyang.

Science and Technology Information Centre.

Akos T 'A Koreai népi demokratikus köztársag tudományos és muszaki tajekoztatasi kospontja és tevékenysége' *Tudom és Muszaki Tajékoz* 1968 15(2) 119-21.

3a

Choson chungang yon'gam (Korean official yearbook) Choson chungang t'ongshisa, 1949- English edition, 1959- .

Paekkwa sajŏn Ch'ulp'ansa, 1974- , Vol 1- . Encyclopedia.

3b

Choson toso (Korean books) Kukse sedom. Irregular and incomplete.

Fraser S E et al *North Korean education and society: a select and partially annotated bibliography pertaining to the Democratic People's Republic of Korea* U of London, Institute of Education, Peabody International Centre, 1972, 149p.

See also Republic of Korea: 3b Ko Hu-sok, and early vols of *Hanguk somok*.

3d

State Planning Commission, Central Statistical Board *Statistical returns of national economy of the DPR Korea, 1946-60* Foreign Languages Publ House, 1961, 189p.

3f

La République Populaire de Corée, 1948-1968 Editions en Langues Etrangères, 1968.

Nahm A C *North Korea: her past, reality and impression* Kalamazoo, Western Michigan U, Center for Korean Studies, 1978.

MONGOLIA

1

Gosudarstevnnaja Publicnaja Biblioteka MNR, Ulan Bator, 1921- .

2b

Royal Central Asian Society, London.

3a

Mongolia London, Diplomatist Pub, 1976, 26p.

3b

National Library *Bibliografia Mongol'skikh knig,* 1967- .

Krueger J R 'The translations on Mongolia series of the US Joint Publications Research Service' *Mongolia Soc Bull* 1965 (4) 51-7.

Washington U. Far Eastern and Russian Institute *Bibliography of the Mongolian People's Republic* Human Relations Files, 1956, 101p.

Chang Hsing-t'ang *Meng-ku ts'an kao shu mu* (Reference catalogue on Mongolia), Taipei, 1958, 278p. Some of the bibliographies published in the People's Republic of China include Mongolia.

Rupen R 'Mongols of the twentieth century' Mouton, 1964, Vol. 2: bibliography of books and articles, mainly in English and Russian. Vol. 1 is a historical survey of the country.

3e

No legal deposit law.

3f

Brown W A and Onon V *History of the Mongolian People's Republic* Harvard U P, 1976.

Jagshid S and Hyer P *Mongolia's culture and society* West View, 1980, 450p.

Shuger T S 'Bookprinting in the MPR' *Mongolia today* 1966 8(5) 18-9.

Bayanzul M 'Bibliotechnoe delo v Mongol'skoi narodnoi Respublike za 45 let' *Bibliot i Bibliog za Rubezhom* 1968 26 3-14.

Polikarpov F 'Svidel'stvo bratskogo sotrudnichestva' *Bibliotekar* 1976 (5) 62-3. Cooperation with USSR.

Tserenkhand D 'Neot'emlemyi element kultury' *Bibliotekar* 1976 (5) 61. Libraries as a cultural element.

See also some references in: China, 3b and Eastern Europe, 3f.

SOUTH EAST ASIA

1

Anuar H *The planning of national libraries in Southeast Asia* Paper at the 40th IFLA Conference, Washington, 1974. Reprinted in:

Foskett D J ed *Reader in comparative librarianship*, 1976, 173-84. (See under: General and International 2c Research).

National Library of Singapore. Has a collection on South East Asia.

2a

Singapore Institute of Southeast Asia studies, 1968- .

Joo T S 'The Institute of Southeast Asia Studies and its library of research resources' *Singapore Lib* 1974 (4) 1-6.

Australian National University. Southeast Asian Studies Department, Canberra.

Australian Asian University Cooperation Scheme (AAUCS) to assist Malaysia, Singapore and Indonesia.

Borchardt D H 'Australian aid to university libraries in Indonesia, Malaysia and Singapore' *Int Lib Rev* 1975 7(2) 279-82.

Kyoto University. Center for Southeast Asian Studies. (Publishes monographs on various subjects).

2b

Association of South East Asian Nations (ASEAN), Bangkok, 1967- . Economic and cultural cooperation.

- South East Asian University Library Network (SAULNET). Proposal in 1977. Would be the forerunner of a broader scheme: South East Asian Library Network (SEANET).

Association of South East Asia (ASA), 1961- .

USA. Association for Asian Studies. Committee on Research Materials on South East Asia (CORMOSEA).

Association of South East Asian Institutions of Higher Learning (ASAIHL), Bangkok.

Conference of South East Asian Librarians (CONSAL), 1970- To promote exchanges and cooperation.

'Conference of South East Asian Librarians (CONSAL)' *Unesco Bull Lib* 1971 25(1) 52-3. Conferences every two years, 1970- (6th Congress in Singapore, 1982).

2c

Dayrit M G and Hidalgo N P eds *Education and training for librarianship in South East Asia: papers and proceedings of the Second Conference of Southeastern Librarians, held at the University of the Philippines, Quezon City, December 1973* U of the Philippines Library, 1975, 301p. (CONSAL II).

3a

Dobby E H G *South East Asia* London U P.

ASAIHL *Handbook of South East Asian Institutions of higher learning* Bangkok, 1965- . Annual; includes Hong Kong.

3b

Nunn G R 'Bibliographical controls for Southeast Asia studies' *Lib Q* 1971 41(4) 292-310.

Anuar H et al, eds *Conference on Universal Bibliographical Control (UBC) in Southeast Asia: papers and proceedings* Singapore Library Association, 1975, 208p.

Lee H-W 'Co-operative regional bibliographic projects in South East Asia' *Unesco Bull Lib* 1977 31(6) 344-51, 370. On microforms, mass communication, specialized information.

Bixler P H 'Southeast Asia: problems in complexity' *Choice* 1972 9(9) 1087-99. Bibliographical essay on sources for South East Asia. Followed by:

— 'Area studies' *Choice* 1972 9(10) 1247-67; 1973 9(11) 1411-26; 9(12) 1561-8; 10(1) 41-8; 10(5) 245-54.

Hobbs C 'Guidelines for augmenting a library's collection of South-East Asian materials' *Int Lib Rev* 1970 2(2) 193-9. Includes also lists of publishers and suppliers.

Johnson D C *A guide to reference materials on Southeast Asia* Yale U P, 1970, 160p. (Yale Southeast Asia studies, 6).

Singapore National Library *South East Asian countries: a reading list* Singapore U, 1967.

Anuar H 'South east Asian research material — Singapore' *Int Lib Rev* 1971 3(4) 389-94.

Library of Congress *Southeast Asia subject catalog at the Library of Congress* G K Hall, 1970, 4 vols.

— *Accessions list: Southeast Asia* 1975- .

Cornell University Library *Southeast Asia accessions list*, 1959- .

Stucki C W *American doctoral dissertations on Asia* . . . Cornell U, Southeast Asian Program, 1968, 304p. (Data paper, 71). Covers 1933-1966. Revision of earlier editions.

Johnson D C *Index to Southeast Asian journals 1960-1974: a guide to articles, book reviews and composite works* G K Hall, 1977.

Hart D V 'South East Asia and education: a bibliographical introduction' *Silliman J* 1963 10(3) 241-71.

3c

Yale University Library. Southeast Asia collection *Checklist of Southeast Asia serials* G K Hall 1969, 320p.

Nunn G R *South-East Asian periodicals* Mansell Info Pub'g, 1977. Singapore. Institute of South East Asian Studies *Newsletter*.

Unesco. Regional Office for Education *Bulletin*, Bangkok, 1966- .

Southeast Asia Library Group *Newsletter*, 1964- .

3f

Swearer D K *Southeast Asia* West Haven, Pendulum P, 1973, 128p, bibl.

Kho L T 'Southeast Asia: area report' *Leads* 1978 20 7-8.

Jones S and Cleverley P *Contrasts in South East Asia* Longman, 1981, 49p.

Evers H D ed *Sociology of South-East Asia: readings in social change and development* Oxford in Asia University Readings, 1980, 350p.

Book publishing in Asia. Report on the Regional Seminar on Book Publishing, March 1969 in Singapore NTS Chopra, 1970, 60p.

Hobbs C *Southeast Asia field trip for the Library of Congress, 1970-1971* Cornell U, Southeast Asian Program, 1972, 95p.

'Southeast Asia research materials — shortened from the papers delivered to the Conference on South East Asian Research Materials' *Int Lib Rev* 1971 3 365-97. Jakarta Conference, April 1969.

Wolf Management Services 'Recommendations regarding a regional book and library effort to be sponsored by the SEAMES' *Report* submitted to AID, 1967, 19p.

Symposium on Southeast Asian Library Resources held at the Australian National University Library 23-24 February 1973: papers and proceedings Australian National University Library, 1974, 87p.

ASAIHL *Seminar on library science in Southeast Asia, Bangkok, December 1964* 1965, 106p.

Lim Pui Huen P et al, eds *Proceedings of the First Conference of Southeast Asian Librarians held at the University of Singapore August 1970* Chopmen Enterprises, 1972, 201p. (CONSAL I).

Pringgoadisurjo L and Sjahrial K eds *Integrated planning of library and documentation services in Southeast Asia within the framework of NATIS* (conjointly with 3rd conference of SARBICA), Jakarta December 1975 Proceedings National Scientific Documentation Centre for Indonesian Library Association, 1977, 189p. (CONSAL III).

Gim Wee Joo 'CONSAL IV — a personal impression' *Singapore Lib* 1978 8 31-5. Conference in Bangkok, June 1978 on Southeast Asia library cooperation.

[Southeast Asian papers presented at the International Conference of National Libraries on resource sharing in Asia and Oceania, Canberra, 1979] *Int Lib Rev* 1980 12(2) 137-71. Whole issue.

Wijasuriya D E K et al *The barefoot librarian: library development in Southeast Asia with special reference to Malaysia* Bingley, 1975, 120p.

McDonald P 'The planning and development of school library services' *New Zeal Lib* 1976 39(6) 206-10.

Anuar H 'Children's information services in South East Asia' *School Libn* 1979 27(1) 11-6.

Dhir S C and Anand S K 'Enquête sur les bibliothèques des écoles de médecine en Asie du Sud Est' *Bull Unesco* 1972 26(6) 343-51. English version: *Unesco Bull Lib* 1972 26(6) 315-22.

Urata T ed *Medical and health libraries in South East Asia. Selected papers from the last four SEAMIC workshop on health documentation* Tokyo, South East Asian Medical Information Center, 1977, 222p.

Dhir S C and Anand S K 'A profile of health sciences libraries in Southeast Asia' *Bull Med Lib Ass* 1979 66(3) 290-5.

Valls J *Improving access to information services in South East Asia* Unesco, 1977, 11p. Workshop in Indonesia.

'Workshop on modern techniques in cultural information services: Bangkok' *Herald Lib Sci* 1978 17 241-4.

Valls J 'Some information projects in South East Asia based on UNISIST's recommendations' *Baca* 1976 3(5/6) 141-8. Role of Thailand's Asian Institute of Technology.

[UNISIST — First UNISIST meeting on Regional Information policy and planning in South East Asia, Bali, July 1977] Published?.

BURMA

1

National Library, Rangoon, 1952- .

Carter E J 'The development of national libraries in Pakistan and Burma' *Unesco Bull Lib* 1955 9(4) 65-8.

University of Rangoon Library, 1929- .

National Archives, 1973- .

Sarpay Beikman Board, (1947- Formerly Burma Translation Society) Library, 1956- Concerned with the promotion of Burmese Culture.

2a

Ministry of Education.

2b

Burma Library Association, Rangoon, 1958- .

'Burma Library Association' *Unesco Bull Lib* 1959 13(11/12) 278.

3a

Burma Yearbook and Directory, 1957:58- Rangoon, Student P, 1957- .

Burmese Encyclopedia Sarpay Beikmen Board, nd, 15 vols.

Maring J M and Maring E G *Historical and cultural dictionary of Burma* Scarecrow, 1973, 290p, bibl.

3b

Book Depot *Catalogue of books of the Revolutionary Government of the Union of Burma Book Depot*. (Previously: *Catalogue of publications in stock at the Book Depot, 1919-)*.

Bernot D *Bibliographie birmane, années 1950-1960* Paris, CNRS, 1968, 230p.

Whitbread K *Catalogue of Burmese printed books in the India Office* London, HMSO, 1969, 231p.

Trager F N et al *Burma: a selected and annotated bibliography* HRAF, 1973, 356p.

Ton S J *Bibliography of library resources in Singapore on Burma* Singapore, Institute of Southeast Asia Studies, 1972.

3d

Central Statistic and Economic Department *Quarterly bulletin of statistics* 1951- .

— *Statistical yearbook*.

3e

Burma Gazette. Quarterly. Includes a list of works deposited.

3f

Quigley E P *Some observations on libraries, manuscripts and books of Burma from the third century AD to 1886, with special reference to the Royal Library of the last kings of Burma* London, Probsthain, 1956, 34p.

Gelfand M A *Nation-wide library service for Burma*. Working paper at the First General Meeting of the Burma Library Association, 1959.
Bixler P H 'Libraries in the Far East: Burma — ambivalence and inner conflict' *Lib J* 1962 87(20) 4124-8.
— 'Burma, libraries in' in *Encyclopedia* 3 (1970) 494-508.
Khurshid A 'Library development in Burma' *J Lib Hist* 1970 5 323-40.
Eaton A J 'Repaving the road to Burma: librarian's visit ends moratorium' *Wilson Lib Bull* 1975 49(10) 741-3.
Nunn G R 'Libraries in Burma' *Int Lib Rev* 1975 7(4) 475-8.
Hill M W 'Some reflections on the library scene in Burma today' *Int Lib Rev* 1976 8(2) 151-63.
Miller G 'Notes on libraries in Burma' *Int Lib Rev* 1978 10(3) 279-82.
Birkelund P *Report on the development of Burmese university and research libraries* Unesco, 1969, 21p. (1186/BMS.RD/DBA).
Htar K T 'Medical libraries in Burma' *Unesco Bull Lib* 1974 28(6) 321-4.
See also Eastern Asia: 3f Bixler P; South Asia: 2c Khurshid A and 3f Gardner F M.

THAILAND

1

Hō Samud Hāeng Chāt (National Library) Bangkok, 1903- . Originally Vajirana-na Library.

'New building of the National Library of Thailand' *Unesco Bull Lib* 1966 20(6) 325.

Chavalit M *Prawat Hō Samud Hāeng Chāt* (History of the National Library) Phranakhōn Siwaphon, 1966, 91p.

Chulalongkorn University Library, Bangkok. Department of Library Science.

Sun Borikan Eksan Kap Haeng Prathet Thai (Thai National Documentation Centre), Bangkok, 1961- . Started as a division of the Office of the National Research Council. In 1964 became active under the Applied Scientific Corporation of Thailand.

Chitrakorn N *History of the Thai National Documentation Centre and its future development plans* Kent State U, 1971, 42p. (Research paper).

2a

Ministry of Education.

Unesco Regional Office. Based on Bangkok.

2b

Thai Library Association, Bangkok, 1954- .

Ambhanwong S 'Thai Library Association' *Unesco Bull Lib* 1971 25(4) 217-20.

2c

Ambhanwong S 'Education for librarianship in Thailand' *J Educ Libp* 1966 6(4) 289-95.

Thai Library Association Library education and training in Thailand Paper given at the Conference of South Asian Librarians, Singapore, 1970 (See under Southeast Asia).

Ambhanwong S 'Present scene in library education in universities in Thailand' *Int Lib Rev* 1975 7(3) 368-80, refs.

3a

Thailand official yearbook, 1964- Government House Printing Office.

Thailand yearbook, 1964/65 — Temple Pub Services, 1964- .

Thailand at a glance Information Service of Thailand.

Smith H E *Historical and cultural dictionary of Thailand* Scarecrow, 1976, 213p, bibl.

Unesco Regional Office *A directory of libraries in Bangkok* The Office, 1970, 64p.

3b

Ambhan Wong S 'Bibliographical control in Thailand' *Int Lib Rev* 1972 4(2) 157-68.

National Library *Bannaphiphop* (World of books) 1955- Monthly list of works deposited in the library. Cumulations:
— *Thai national bibliography*, 1962-67, 1968-73, then annual cumulations.
Chulalongkorn U Library *Bibliography of materials about Thailand in Western languages* The Library, 1960, 325p.
Thrombley W G and Siffin W J *Thailand: politics, economy and socio-cultural setting. A selective guide to literature* Indiana U P for International Affairs Center, 1972, 148p.
Ministry of Education. Teacher Training Department *Datchani nittayasan Thai* (Index to articles in Thai periodicals), 1957- .
Development Document Centre Library *Index to Thai periodical literature, 1960-1970*. Also publishes monthly records of indexes.
Ambhanwong S 'Research in librarianship in Thailand: a bibliographical survey' *Int Lib Rev* 1970 2(3) 247-52.
Minaikit N *An annotated bibliography of librarianship in Thailand* Chulalongkorn U, Department of Library Science, 1967, 47p. (Library Science papers, 7).

3c

National Library *Periodicals and newspapers printed in Thailand between 1935-1971: a bibliography* The Library, 1972. In Thai.
Development Document Centre Library *MIDA Bulletin*. Monthly. Lists current periodicals indexes.
Thai Library Association *Thai Library Bulletin*.
— *Newsletter*.

3d

National Office of Statistics *Statistical yearbook* 1915/16- .
Ministry of Education *Educational statistics*.

3e

Thai Library Association *Bibliography of Thai government publications*, 1962- .

3f

Chavalit M *Survey report on reading materials in Thailand* Ministry of Education, 1966, 30p.
Barnett S A et al *Developmental book activities and needs in Thailand* USAID, 1967, 160p.
Gelfand M A *The National Library and library development and training in Thailand: a draft report* Unesco, 1962, 65p.
Spain F Lander *Some notes on library science development in Thailand, 1951-1965* Chulalongkorn U, 1965, 28p. (Library Science Papers, 10).
— 'Library development in Thailand 1951-1965' *Unesco Bull Lib* 1966 20(3) 117-25.
Suthilak A *Libraries and librarianship in Thailand* Chulalongkorn U, Department of Library Science, 1967, 51p. (Library Science Papers, 5).
Kaser D 'Kingdom of Thailand' in *Library development in eight Asian countries*, Scarecrow, 1969, 135-71.
Pomgsatit S *Report about libraries in Thailand*. Paper at the Conference of Southeast Asian Librarians, Singapore, 1970. (See under Southeast Asia 3f).
Chavalit M 'Thailand, libraries in' in *Encyclopedia* 30 (1980) 401-10, refs.
Nybroe J 'Folkebiblioteket i Phuket' *Bogens Verden* 1974 56(8) 270-1.

Rufsvold M and Lowell M H 'Developing libraries for higher education in Thailand: a co-operative project' *ALA Bull* 1960 54(10) 833-43.

Lee Hwa-Wai 'Fragmentation of academic library resources in Thai university libraries' *Int Lib Rev* 1971 3(2) 155-67.

Gorton T 'Development of academic libraries and librarianship in Thailand 1950-76' *J Libp* 1979 11 50-66.

Prabhavi-Vadhana C 'Documentation in Thailand' *Unesco Bull Lib* 1967 21(4) 207-9.

— Amended version in *Amer Doc* 1967 48(4) 249-50.

Lee Hwa-Wai 'Library mechanization at the Asian Institute of Technology (Bangkok)' *Int Lib Rev* 1971 3(3) 257-70.

Valls J *Thailand: pilot project on the mechanization of documentation services in Asia (23 July-22 November 1974)* Unesco, 1975, 30p. (3116/RMO/RD/DBA).

Massil S W *Thailand: possibility of establishing a computerised catalogue of Thai material at the National Library of Thailand, Bangkok* Unesco, 1976, 14p.

Marshall K E *Scientific library and information services in Thailand* 1977. Paper at the 68th Meeting of the Special Libraries Association, New York, June 1977.

INDOCHINA

Relevant only to the historical part of the sources.

1

National Library, Hanoi, 1882- . Was the main library for the region under French influence.

UN-ECAFE Mekong Documentation Centre, Bangkok.

3b

Library of Congress. Reference Department *Indochina: a bibliography of the land and people* 1950, 367p. (Reprint: Greenwood, 1969).

Boudet P and Bourgeois R *Bibliographie de l'Indochine française* . . . Hanoi, Imprimerie d'Extrême Orient, 1929-1967, 4 vols.

Auvade R *Bibliographie critique des oeuvres parues sur l'Indochine française* Maisonneuve-Larose, 1965, 156p.

3d

Indochine Française. Service de la Statistique Générale *Annuaire statistique de l'Indochine* 1913-1948 Hanoi, 1927-48.

3f

Van Kuyk R H J *Rapport d'une mission pour la réorganisation de la documentation éducative et des bibliothèques: Laos, Viet-Nam, République Khmère, 23 avril-10 mai 1973* Bangkok, Bureau Régional de l'Unesco pour l'Education en Asie, 1973.

KAMPUCHEA

1

Bibliothèque Nationale, Phnom-Penh. Now: Bibliothèque Centrale, 1972- responsible for collecting and maintaining materials on all subjects.

Centre Culturel de l'Alliance Française, Phnom-Penh.

University of Phnom-Penh, Library, 1960- .

3b

Dik Keam *Catalogue des auteurs khmers et étrangers* Association des Ecrivains Kmers, 1966, 24p.

Bibliothèque Nationale *Liste des journaux, des bulletins, des revues et des livres en dépôt légal aux archives nationales* Typescript of the catalogue.

Fischer M L *Cambodia: an annotated bibliography of its history, geography, politics and economy since 1954* MIT, Center for International Studies, 1967.

UN-ECAFE Mekong Documentation Centre *Cambodia: a select bibliography* Bangkok, 1967, 101p.

3d

Ministère du Plan *Statistical yearbook of Cambodia, 1937-1957* 1958, 214p.

— *Annuaire statistique du Cambodge, 1958-1961* 1962, 184p.

Institut National de la Statistique et des Recherches Economiques *Annuaire statistique*, 1963- .

— *Bulletin de Statistique*.

3f

Ministère de l'Information *Les progrès du Cambodge, 1954-1964* 1964, 13p.

Ponchaud F *Cambodge: année zéro* Julliard, 1977.

— *Cambodia: year zero* Penguin, 1978.

Desroches J G *Cambodge: service des bibliobus scolaires et situation actuelle des bibliothèques, 1er octobre au 20 novembre 1968* Unesco, 1969, 20p. (1070/BMS.RD/COM).

LAOS

1

Bibliothèque Nationale, Vientiane, 1957- .
Présidence du Conseil. Centre National de Documentation, Vientiane.

2a

Ministère de l'Education Nationale.
Laotian National Commission for Unesco.

2b

Association des Bibliothécaires Laotiens. Now: Association Laotienne des Bibliothèques, 1972- .

3a

Hickey G C *Area handbook on Laos* New Haven, HRAF, 1955, 308p.
Berval R de *Kingdom of Laos* Saigon, France-Asie, 1959, 506p, bibl.

3b

Bibliothèque Nationale *Bibliographie nationale du Laos* 1968- . Annual. Works published in Laos, and works about Laos.
Thao Kene *Bibliographie du Laos* Ministère de l'Education Nationale 1958, 68p.
Mackinstry J *Bibliography of Laos and ethnically related areas* U of California, Berkeley, 1962, 89p.
Lafont P B *Bibliographie du Laos* Ecole Française d'Extrême-Orient 1964, 270p. (Publications, 50).

3d

Ministère du Plan et de la Coopération. Service National de la Statistique *Bulletin de statistique* 1951- . Title varies.

3e

Centre National de Documentation *Journal Officiel.* Monthly.

3f

LeBar F M and Suddard A *Laos: its people, its society, its culture* New Haven, HRAF, 1960, 294p.
Projections à long terme de l'éducation au Laos: rapport de la mission consultative régionale de l'Unesco pour la planification de l'éducation en Asie Bangkok, Bureau Régional de l'Unesco 1965.
Chartrand G *Laos: développement des bibliothèques, 8 octobre-14 décembre 1966* Unesco, 1967, 26p.
Marcus R 'Laos and library development' *Coll Res Lib* 1967 28(6) 398-402.
Barnett S A et al *Developmental book activities and needs in Laos* USAID, 1967, 95p.
Kaser D et al *Library development in eight Asian countries* Scarecrow, 1969, 243p.
524 Includes Laos.

VIETNAM

Between 1954 and 1976 Vietnam was divided into two: the Republic of Vietnam (South Vietnam) and the Democratic Republic of Vietnam (North Vietnam). Most of the information on the period 1954-75 applies to North or to South Vietnam only. When not obvious, this will be indicated in the entry. It must be remembered that most activities recorded under South Vietnam have now ceased.

1

Thu Viên Quôc Gia (National Library), Hanoi, 1919- . Deposit library since 1922 for all Indochina, as long as the region was a French colony. In 1976 its functions were confirmed by a new decree; they include bibliographical activities, training, coordination and technical guidance.

Nazmutdinov I 'V bibliotekakh DRV' *Bibliotekar* 1975 (9) 72-4.

'National Library No. 2 Ho Chi Minh City' (Former National Library of the Republic of Vietnam, in Saigon), 159- . Now integrated in the public library system of the country without any 'national' activities.

'La Bibliothèque Nationale de la République du Vietnam' *Soc Et Indochin Bull* 1972 47 506-9.

University of Hanoi Library. The University has a department of library science, 1973- .

Hanoi People's Library 1950?- .

2a

Ministry of Culture.

Library Council.

2b

Hoi Thú-viên Viêt-nam (Library Association), Saigon, 1959- ?

3a

Vietnam Library Association *Niên-giam thú-viên* (Directory of libraries) Saigon, 1970, 62p.

3b

National Library (Hanoi) *Thú muc quôc gia Viêt Nam* (National bibliography) 1957- Monthly and annually.

— *Muc-lu xuat ban pham* (Catalogue of published works), 1954- .

Keyes J G *A bibliography of North Vietnamese publications in Cornell University Library* Dept of Asian Studies, 1962, 116p.

— *A bibliography of Western language publications concerning North Vietnam in the Cornell University Library* 1966, 280p.

Direction des Archives et Bibliothèque Nationales (Saigon) *Sach moi* (New acquisitions), 1962-64.

— *Thu Muc* (Catalogue of books) 1965-? Annual.

— *Thu tich quoc-gia Viet-nam* (National bibliography) 1965-? .

Tran Thi Kimsa *Bibliography on Vietnam, 1954-1964* Saigon, 1965, 255p.

- *Muc-luc phan-tich tap-chi Viet-ngu 1954-1964* (Guide to periodical literature), Saigon, 1965, 318p. Both issued by the National Institute of Administration.

Bibliographies with a comprehensive coverage for the whole of Vietnam:

National Commission for Unesco *Thu muc chu-giai ve van hoa Viet-nam* Saigon, 1966, 226p. By subject, with a list of books in French on Vietnam 1945-1954.

UN-ECAFE Makong Documentation Centre *Vietnam, a reading list,* Bangkok, 1966, 119p. Classified order.

Chen J H M *Vietnam: a comprehensive bibliography* Scarecrow, 1973, 314p.

3c

Direction des Archives et Bibliothèque Nationales *An pham dinh ky quoc noi, 1968* (Comprehensive list of periodicals) Saigon, 1969, 182p.

Vietnam Library Association *Công tacthu Viên* (Bulletin for librarians). Period of publication not confirmed.

National Library *Library service* 1976?- Quarterly.

3d

Institut National de la Statistique *Annuaire statistique du Vietnam* 1949-? .

3e

See below Miller G.

3f

Hall R H *Textbook development program: Vietnam 1964-66* Saigon, USAID, 1965, 75p.

Barnett S A et al *Developmental book activities and needs in the Republic of Vietnam* USAID, 1966, 131p.

Education projects in South Vietnam Saigon, USAID, 1966, 26p.

Kaser D 'Republic of Vietnam' in *Library development in eight Asian countries* Scarecrow, 1969, 89-113.

Hayman J H 'Libraries in Vietnam' *Unesco Bull Lib* 1959 13(10) 231-2 234.

Gardner R K 'Library aid to Vietnam' *Lib J* 1959 84(20) 3517-21.

Boaz M 'The American library specialist in an underdeveloped country' *J Educ Libp* 1967 8(2) 106-14.

The libraries of Vietnam: seminar at Dalat Saigon, 1965, 10p. Mimeo.

Miller G 'All for reconstruction: library service in a reunified Vietnam' *Int Lib Rev* 1978 10(2) 109-18.

'The public libraries — 20 years' activities' *Vietnam Courier* February 1977 (57) 20-2. (North Vietnam).

'Medical libraries USA move to aid North Vietnam' *Lib J* 1973 98 1430.

Van F 'Teknicheskie biblioteki Sotsialisticheskoi Respubliki V'etnam' *Bibliot i Bibliog za Rubezhom* 1976 (59) 16-20.

Sutter J O *Scientific and information services of the Republic of Vietnam* Honolulu, Pacific Science Information Center, 1961, 236p.

Aubrac R 'Les structures et les problèmes de l'information scientifique, technique, économique et sociale dans la République Socialiste du Viet-Nam' *Documentaliste* 1978 15(5/6) 27-9.

MALAYSIA, SINGAPORE, BRUNEI

Historical and general.

1

University of Singapore Library. Singapore-Malaysia collection.

2a

Australian Asian University Co-operation Scheme (AAUCS). To assist Malaysia and Singapore (and Indonesia) in the development of their library services.

2b

Library Association of Malaya and Singapore 1958-65. Replaced the Malaya Library Group.

Malaysian Library Association and Singapore Library Association, Joint Standing Committee on Library Cooperation and Bibliographical Services (JSCLCBS). Coordinates common activities of the two associations: conferences, publications, etc.

3a

Straits Times Directory of Singapore and Malaya (1949-1964), Singapore Straits Times. In 1965 became:

Straits Times Directory of Malaysia. Includes Brunei.

Sutter J O *Scientific facilities and information services of the Federation of Malaya and the State of Singapore* Honolulu, Pacific Science Information Center, 1961, 43p.

Keeth K H *A Directory of Libraries in Malaysia* U of Malaya Library, 1965, 163p.

3b

Lim B 'Malaya, a background bibliography' *R Asiatic Soc* (*Malayan Branch*) *J* 1962 35(2/3) 1-199.

Cheeseman H R *Bibliography of Malaya, being a classified list of books wholly or partly relating to the Federation of Malaya and Singapore* Longmans, 1959, 234p.

Singapore University Library *Catalogue of the Singapore-Malaysia collection* Boston, G K Hall, 1968, 757p.

— *Supplement 1968-1972* Singapore U P, 1974.

Library of Congress Bureau in Jakarta *Accession list: Indonesia* Since 1970 5(9/10) includes acquisitions from Malaysia and Singapore.

Singapore City University of Malaya, Reference Department *Education in Malaysia, a bibliography* 1964, 35p.

JSCLCBS *Index to current Malaysia, Singapore and Brunei periodicals* 1967-1968. After these two issues replaced by two separate indexes.

Pelzer K J *West Malaysia and Singapore: a selected bibliography* New Haven, HRAF, 1971, 394p.

Hazra K and Cheng E L S *Malaysian serials, a checklist of current official serials of the Malaysian governments* U of Singapore, 1965, 18p.

3c

Roff W R *Bibliography of Malay and Arabic periodicals published in the Straits Settlements and Peninsular Malay States 1876-1941: with an annotated union list of holdings in Malaya, Singapore and the United Kingdom* OUP, 1972, 74p.

Harris L J *Guide to current Malaysian serials* Kuala Lumpur U of Malaya Library, 1967. English language periodicals.

Malayan Library Group Newsletter Singapore, The Group, 1955-59 1-3(3). The last issue as: *Library Association of Malaya and Singapore Newsletter.*

Malayan Library Journal and Madjallah Perpustakaan Singapura 1961-64.

Perpustakaan Malaysia 1965.

Continued by separate periodicals for Malaysia and for Singapore.

3d

Malayan statistics, digest of economic and social statistics (State of Singapore and Federation of Malaya) Singapore, 1954-61.

Starner F L 'Malaysia and the North Borneo Territories' *Asian Survey* 1963 3 519-34.

3f

Byrd C K *Early printing in the Straits Settlements 1806-1858* Singapore National Library, 1970, 53p.

Tee Lim Huck 'Books and libraries in Malaya before the coming of the West' *Lib Ass Rec* 1964 66 241-7.

— *Libraries in West Malaysia and Singapore: a short history* U of Malaya Library, 1970, 161p, bibl.

Kaser D et al 'Federation of Malaysia and Republic of Singapore' in Kaser D et al *Library development in eight Asian countries* Scarecrow, 1969, 215-43.

Harrod L M 'Libraries in the Federation of Malaya and Singapore' *Lib World* 1962/63 64 241-4, 262-8.

— 'Libraries in Malaya and Singapore' *Malayan Lib J* 1964 2 140-51.

Waller J M 'One linear foot: a partial measurement of professional achievement in Singapore and Malaysia' *Austr Lib J* 1972 21(5) 110-6.

Wisè M B 'Opening school library doors in Malaysia and Singapore' *ALA Bull* 1969 63 1586-95.

Borchardt D H 'Australian aid to the university libraries in Indonesia, Malaysia and Singapore' *Int Lib Rev* 1975 7(2) 279-82.

Regular conferences are held jointly by the Malaysian Library Association and the Singapore Library Association. The papers are published as monographs or in their journals. See some of the themes of these conferences:

- Public libraries in national development, 1967.
- Planning for the 70s, 1968.
- Scientific and technical information needs for Malaysia and Singapore, 1971.
- National and academic libraries, 1974.
- UBC in South East Asia, 1975.
- The need to know — developing public library services for the community, 1977.

MALAYSIA

1

Perpustakaan Negara Malaysia, Kuala Lumpur, 1971- . Created as division of the National Archives and Library.

Penyata tahunan Arkiv dan Perpustakaan Negara Malaysia/Annual report of the National Archives and Library of Malaysia, 1971 Arkiv Negara Malaysia, 1973, 114p. First annual report.

Anuar H and Wijasuriya D E K 'Malaysia, National Library of' in *Encyclopedia* 17 (1976) 67-71.

University of Malaysia, Library, Kuala Lumpur. Its deposit privilege now has been transferred to the National Library.

Wijasuriya D E K 'The University of Malaya Library: a developmental appraisal. *Libri* 1973 23(2) 129-41.

Institiut Penyelidikan Sains dan Perusahaan Negara (NISIR), 1970- . National Institute for Scientific and Industrial Research.

2a

National Library Services.

2b

Persatuan Perpustakaan Malaysia (Library Association of Malaysia), 1955- .

Anuar H and Wijasuriya D E K 'Malaysian Library Association' *Encyclopedia* 17 (1976) 71-5.

2c

Nadarajah R 'Education for librarianship in Malaysia: with special reference to law librarianship' *Int J Law Lib* 1975 3(2) 134-51.

Wijasuriya D E K 'Library and information science education and training in Malaysia' *Lib News* (Sri Lanka) 1977 5(1) 6-9.

3a

Malaysia official yearbook 1961- . Government Printer.

New Straits Times and Directory of Malaysia (1979 latest noted) Int Pub Services.

Keeth K H *A directory of libraries in Malaysia* U of Malaya Lib, 1965, 163p.

Soosai J S *A survey of special libraries and scientific information facilities in Malaysia* n.p., 1970, misc pags.

3b

Wijasuriya D E K 'Current national bibliography in Malaysia and Universal Bibliographic Control' *Majallah Perpustakaan Malaysia* 1974/75 (3) 31-52. Paper at 40th FLA Meeting Nov '74.

Tee L H 'UAP and Malaysia' *Unesco J* 1979 1(1) 92-5.

National Library. Bibliographical Division *Bibliografi negara Malaysia* (Malaysia national bibliography) 1967-[1969] quarterly and annual cumulation.

Tee L H *Malaysia* ABC Clio, 1980 (World Bibliographical Series, 12).
Tee L H and Wijasuriya D E K *Index Malaysia: 1878-1963* Royal Asiatic Society, Malayan Branch, 1970.
Wijasuriya D E K and Tee L H *Index Malaysiana: Suppl 1* Royal Asiatic Soc, Malaysian Branch, 1974.
Perpustakaan Negara Malaysia *Index Majalah Malaysia*, 1973- (Malaysia periodicals index) 1974- .
Tee Lim Tuck and Sarachandran V V *Mass communication in Malaysia* Asia Mass Communication Research and Information Centre (AMIC), 1975. A bibliography.

3c
Library Association of Malaysia *Majallah Perpustakaan Malaysia* 1973- .

3d
Department of Statistics *Bulletin of statistics*.
— *List of publications*.

3e
Government Printing Office *Government Gazette* (Includes a list of new publications).
Index to federal law, as at 12th July, 1973 Law Library, Attorney General Chambers, 1973.
Wijasuriya D E K 'Laws, policies and libraries: the Malaysian experience' *Paper* at 2nd Conference of Southeast Asian Librarians, Manila, December 1973.

3f
Gullick J M *Malaysia* E Benn, 1969.
Grenfell N *Switch on, switch off: mass media audiences in Malaysia* OUP, 1979, 260p.
Perpustakaan 1(2)/2(1) 1967. Proceedings of conferences on book production and distribution. See in particular a paper on a national library for Malaysia.
Lim Hucktee E 'Libraries in Malaysia before the coming of the West' *Lib Hist Rev* 1974 1(1) 1-8.
Huck E L 'Libraries and librarianship in Malaysia 1817-1961' *Lib Hist Rev* 1975 2(1) 43-81, 73 refs.
Anuar H and Wijasuriya D E K 'Malaysia, libraries in' *Encyclopedia* 17 (1976) 56-67, refs.
Lan L-S 'The economics of inter-library communication in Peninsular Malaysia' *Majallah Perpustakaan Malaysia* 1974-75 (3) 53-82.
Tell B *Malaya: pilot project on the development of a library network* Unesco, GPI, 1976, 30p. (First of a series of reports on the project).
Wijasuriya D E K *The barefoot librarian. Library development in Southeast Asia with special reference to Malaysia*. Bingley, 1975, 120p.
Anuar H *Blueprint for public library development in Malaysia* Malaysia Library Association, 1968.
Wijasuriya D E K 'Public library development in Malaysia: a brief statement of existing conditions together with a research proposal' *Int Lib Rev* 1974 6(1) 91-102.
Martin D 'Public library development in Malaysia' *J Lib Hist* 1974 9 159-70.
Leong A 'Library services in Sabah' *Majallah Perpustakaan Malaysia* 1977 5 40-55.
530 Kader Z A 'Educational policy and its importance to the growth of public libraries

and librarianship in West Malaysia and the Philippines' *Majallah Perpustakaan Malaysia* 1977 5 17-39.

Van Niel E S 'Children and the Penang library' *Hawaii Lib Ass J* 1971 28 17-20.

Lim Huck Tee and Tang Wan Fing 'Survey on the sources of information in science, technology and commerce in the State of Penang, Malaysia' *Int Lib Rev* 1973 5(1) 229-45.

SINGAPORE

1

National Library, 1958- . Previously Raffles Library, 1923-58. National and public library with a special collection of Southeast Asian material.

National Library *Guide to the National Library* Government Printing Office, 1970, 11p.

Taylor A P 'National Library of Singapore today' *Perpustakaan* 1965 1(1) 19-28.

Hatch L 'The National Diet Library, the National Library of the Philippines and the Singapore National Library' *J Lib Hist* 1972 7(4) 329-59.

Anuar H 'The National Library of Singapore' *East Libn* 1973 7(1) 21-4.

University of Singapore Library, 1949- .

Wang Hsiu Chin *The University of Singapore Library: its resources, services and problems* The Library, 1964, 10p.

Industrial Technical Information Service (ITIS), 1973- as a section of the Singapore Institute of Standards (SISIR).

2a

Department of Culture.

Institute of South East Asian Studies, 1958- .

National Book Development Council of Singapore, 1969- .

2b

Persatuan Perpustakaan Singapura (Library Association of Singapore). 1965- .

2c

Koh T N 'Library conditions and library training in Singapore' *Libri* 1970 20 263-77.

Wicks Y-L 'Staff training in the National Library' *Singapore Lib* 1975 5 41-5.

3a

Singapore yearbook 1965- . Government Printing Office.

Singapore 1980 Ministry of Culture. Information Division, 283p.

Lim L U Wen et al, comps *Directory of libraries in Singapore* 2nd ed Persatuan Perpustakaan Singapura, 1975, 166p.

3b

Anuar H 'Bibliographical services and control' *Paper* in CONSAL I. (See South East Asia, 3f).

National Library *Singapore national bibliography 1967-* . Annual. 1969- .

— *Books about Singapore* Government Printing Office. Biennial.

[List of publications received on legal deposit] quarterly in *Singapore Government Gazette*.

Singapore books in print 1977/78 National Book Development Council.

Quah R 'Reference books about Singapore: a select annotated list' *Singapore Lib* 1972 2 23-32.

National Library *Singapore periodicals index 1969-70* Previously in JSCLCBS *Index to current Malaysia, Singapore and Brunei periodicals* 1967-68.

Singh R 'The Singapore library scene 1955-1975: an introductory bibliography' *South East Asia Library Group Newsletter* 1978 15 2-31.

3c

Library Association of Singapore *Singapore Library Journal* 1961-1964. For sequence see in: South East Asia, 3c.

— *Singapore Libraries* 1971- . Supersedes: *Perpustakaan* 1966-70.

National Book Development Council of Singapore *Singapore Book World* 1970- . Annual.

3d

National Statistical Commission. Library *List of principal Singapore statistical publications* The Library, 1974.

Department of Statistics *Yearbook of statistics*.

3e

Singapore *Laws, statutes, etc* Rev ed of *Acts*, Law Revision Commission, 1970-71 8 vols. See in particular Vol 8 Chap 311, Vol 7 Chap 224.

'Recommended minimum standards for secondary school libraries (State Committee on Libraries, sub-committee on Standards)' *Singapore Lib* 1972 2 67-73, 6 refs.

3f

Byrd C K *Books in Singapore: a survey of publishing, printing, bookselling and library activity in the Republic of Singapore* Chopmen Enterprises for the National Book Development Council, 1970, 161p.

Library Association of Singapore 'Annual General Meeting 1977' *Singapore Lib* 1977 7 47-71, tables.

Gim W J 'Singapore libraries: a decade of development 1965-74' *Singapore Lib* 1975 5 16-23.

Anuar H 'Singapore, libraries in' *Encyclopedia* 27 (1979) 410-32.

Daily J E 'City-States and the future of the library and information sciences' *Penn Lib Ass Bull* 1971 26 309-14.

Chan, Thye Seng 'Libraries and library development in Singapore' Paper in CONSAL I. (See in: South East Asia, 3f).

Lan Q S *Resource sharing in Singapore libraries* ERIC, 1977, 17p. (ERIC report ED-176 763).

— 'Resource sharing in Singapore libraries' *Singapore Lib* 1978 8 57-61.

Seng C T 'Mobile library service in Singapore' *Unesco Bull Lib* 1976 30(4) 218-23.

Anuar H 'The public library as a community service: the Singapore example' in IFLA Worldwide Seminar, Seoul 1976 *Proceedings* Korean L A 1976, 333-41.

Report on survey of adult and young people's programmes organized by the National Library and its branches National Library, 1978, 51p.

Singh R 'Programming for adults and young people — report of a survey on adult and young people's programmes organised by the National Library and its branches' *Singapore Lib* 1978 8 11-5, refs.

Anuar H 'Public libraries and children' *Perpustakaan* 1967 2 209-15.

Klass E and Perumbulavil V 'Public library services to children in Singapore' *Singapore Book World* 1979 10 3-5, 7-8.

Koh D 'School libraries in Singapore' *ALA Bull* 1969 63(12) 1596-9.

Eu M and Anuar H 'School libraries in Singapore' *Singapore Lib* 1971 1 31-42.

Mosbergen R W 'Present trends in school library development' *Singapore Lib* 1978 8 28-30.
Koh L 'Library services to students at the Southeast Asia Union College' *Singapore Lib* 1978 8 22-3.
'Special libraries in Singapore' *Singapore Lib* 1972 2 94-8.
Gim, Wee Joo 'Special libraries in Singapore' *Singapore Lib* 1978 8 16-21.
Leong A 'Special libraries in Singapore' *Spec Lib* 1979 70(3) 140-6.

INDONESIA

1

Perpustakaan Museum Pusat (National Museum Library), Jakarta, 1778- as a private research institution and since 1962 a governmental institution. Designated to be the nucleus of national library.

Tairas J N B *Toward a national library for Indonesia* New Zealand National Library Service, 1960, 30p.

Hardjo-Prakoso M *Pentingnya perpustakaan nasional bagi Indonesia* Jakarta, 1973.

Poon P W T 'A proposed national library system in Indonesia' *Austr Acad Res Lib* 1975 6(1) 20-30.

Natadjumena B 'An Indonesian national library' *Austr Acad Res Lib* 1977 8(3) 127-30.

Universitas Indonesia, 1950- ; Fakultas Sastra, Library.

Madjelis Ilmu Pengetahuan Indonesia (MIPI) — Pusat Dokumentasi Ilmiah Nasional (PDIN), 1956- . In 1971 designated as the national documentation centre, with the task of creating a coordinated network of information services for the sciences.

Stephens H L *Indonesia National Scientific Documentation Centre* The Centre, 1972, 6p.

2a

Departemen Pendidikan dan Kebudayaan (Ministry of Education and Culture): Pusat Pembinaan Perpustakaan (Library Development Centre), 1975- . (-1967 as: Biro Perpustakaan dan Pembinaan Buku; 1967-1975 as: Lembaga Perpustakaan). For the promotion of public and school libraries, and with coordination functions, of its division:

- Bidang Bibliografi dan Deposit (Previously: 1953-74 Kantor Bibliografi Nasional Indonesia), in the field of bibliographical control.

Ministry of Education and Culture — Directorate of Higher Education. For university libraries.

Ministry of Information. Runs a number of 'reading rooms': Taman Bacaan.

Yayasan Idayu, 1954. Private foundation created by the publishing firm Gunung Agung, with a library collection.

2b

Ikatan Penerbit Indonesia (IKAPIT) Publishers Association.

Asosiasi Perpustakaan Arsip dan Dokumentasi Indonesia (APADI), 1954- . Inactive since 1963; replaced in 1973 by: Ikatan Pustakawan Indonesia (IPI), 1973- .

Dammerboer I 'Indonesia library associations — from PAPSI to IPI' *Austr Lib J* 1975 24(8) 355-8.

Himpunan Pustakawan Khusus Indonesia (Association of Special Librarians), 1969- . Sponsored by PDIN.

2c

Vreede-De Stuers C 'The first library school in Indonesia' *Unesco Bull Lib* 1953 7(5) 496.

Trimo S 'The education and training of Indonesian librarians: problems and prospects' Paper at First Conference of South-east Asian Librarians, Singapore, 1970, 29p. (See under: South East Asia. 3f).

Williamson W L 'Education for librarianship in Indonesia' *J Educ Libp* 1971 12 Summer 27-32.

Partaningrat W 'Indonesian library and documentation course, Indonesia National Scientific Documentation Centre, Djakarta 3 May-23 July 1971' *Unesco Bull Lib* 1972 26(1) 52-3.

Ward P 'The democratization of library education in Indonesia' *Majalah IPI* 1974 1(1) 17-9.

Zultanawar 'Kebutuhan tenaga kerja dan latihan bagi perpustakaan khusus' *Baca* 1977 4(4/6) 124-34.

3a

Area handbook for Indonesia USGPO, 1970.

National Scientific Documentation Centre *Istilah perpustakaan an dokumentasi Inggeris-Indonesia/List of library and documentation terms English-Indonesian* The Centre, 1970, 40p.

Sutter J O *Scientific facilities and information services of the Republic of Indonesia* Honolulu, for Pacific Science Information Center, 1961, 136p.

National Scientific Documentation Centre *Directory of special libraries in Indonesia* Rev ed 1970, 144p (first published 1967, 67p.)

3b

Tairas J N B and Kertosedono S 'National bibliographic control in Indonesia' *Int Cat'g* 1977 6 47-8.

Berita bulanan dari Kantor Bibliografi Nasional, 1953-1962, 10 vols. Continued by:

Bidang Bibliografi dan Deposit (Previously Kantor Bibliografi Nasional) *Bibliografi nasional Indonesia 1963-* . Quarterly. New series 1971- .

-- *Kumulasi 1945-1963* Balai Pustaka, 1965, 2 vols. *Kumulasi 1964-65*, supplement. 1964-1972 in progress.

Yayasan Idayu *Berita bibliografi*. 1955- . Trade list, in Dewey order.

Library of Congress (Jakarta Book Procurement Center) *Accessions list: Indonesia 1964-* . From 1970 5(9/10) covers Southeast Asia as a whole.

National Library of Australia *Indonesian acquisitions list* Nov 1971 no 1- . Irregular.

Galis K W *Biblographie van Nederlands-Nieuw Guinea* 3rd rev and enlarged ed The Hague, 1962, 275p.

Cayrac F 'L'Indonésie 1958-1967: état des travaux' *Rev Fr Sci Polit* 1967 17(5) 959-92.

Kennedy R *Bibliography of Indonesian peoples and cultures* rev ed by T W Maretski and H T Fischer New Haven, HRAF, 1962, 207p.

PDIN *Index majalah Ilmiah* (Index of Indonesian learned periodicals) 1960- .

— *Indonesian abstracts*, 1959- . These cover the whole field of knowledge.

Perpustakaan Chusus (Handbook for special libraries): chap. 'Referens dan penelusuram' 1970.

PDIN *Bibliografi pernabitan pemerintah Indonesia, 1950-69* 1971, 419p. (Government publications).

3c

Council for Science *Berita MIPI* Includes news of activities of special libraries in particular.

IPADI *Perpustakaan (Arsip Dokumentasi)* published for a short time by the Library Association 1954-1961. Now replaced by:

Indonesian Library Association (IPI) *Majalah Ikatan Pustakawan Indonesia* 1974- . Quarterly.

Association of Indonesian Special Libraries *Madjalah Himpunan Pustakawan Chusus Indonesia* 1970- . Quarterly.

PDIN *BACA/READ*: brief communication for information workers and information users in science and technology 1974- . Bimonthly.

3d

Biro Pusat Statistik *Statistical pocketbook of Indonesia* 1941, 1947 then annual 1957- .

Nugroho *Indonesia, facts and figures* Terbitan Pertjohaan, 1967, 608p.

3e

Kantor Bibliografi Nasional *Perpustakaan di Indonesia dari Zaman ke Zaman* 1966, 135p. History of library development through laws and decrees. Includes accounts of individual libraries.

3f

Caldwell M and Utrecht E *Indonesia, an alternative history* Sydney, Alternative Pub Co. 1979.

Legge J D *Indonesia* 3rd ed Prentice Hall of Australia, 1980, 214p.

Educational innovation in Indonesia Unesco, 1975, 50p. (Experiments and innovations in Educ: Asian series no 13).

Isa Z *Printing and publishing in Indonesia 1602-1970* Indiana U. 1972, 217p. Ph.D. Thesis.

Barnett S A et al *Developmental book activities and needs in Indonesia* USAID, 1967, 218p.

Pearce D *Indonesia — book development* Unesco, 1974.

Indonesian Publications Seminar held at the National Library of Australia, 16th July 1974 Canberra, The Library, 1975, 126p.

Dunningha, A G W and Pringgoadisurjo L 'National book resources' *Berita MIPI* 1963 7 128-32.

Stewart L J 'Indonesia: librarianship for a new order' *Lib J* 1968 93(20) 4255-7.

Kaser D 'Republic of Indonesia' in *Library development in eight Asian countries* Scarecrow, 1969, 172-214 (See under: Eastern Asia 3f).

Scott D 'The persistence of Indonesian libraries' *Wilson Lib Bull* 1971 45(10) 976-82.

Miller G 'Development of libraries and librarianship in Indonesia' *Austral Lib J* 1972 21(4) 99-109.

Williamson W L 'Revival of Indonesian librarianship' *Int Lib Rev* 1972 4(3) 409-15.

Hardjo-Prakoso M 'Indonesia, libraries in' in *Encyclopedia* 11 (1974) 477-83.

Ward P 'Indonesian libraries today' *Unesco Bull Lib* 1975 29(4) 182-7.

Hardjo-Praksos M 'Government policies affecting the development and growth of libraries in Indonesia' Paper at 2nd Conference of Southeast Asian Librarians, Manila, December 1973.

Rompas J P *Organization and development of library and information service in a developing country: the Indonesian case* Loughborough U of Technology, 1978, 159p, refs.

Djoko D 'The public library situation in Indonesia' *Int Lib Rev* 1974 6 79-81.

Rahim A R *Kearah pembentukan* Perpustakaan Umum Makassar, 1974, 34p.

Ward P *Indonesia. Evaluation of provincial library services* Unesco, 1975.

Hockey S W *Indonesia: development of public library services* Unesco, 1976, 8p.

Ward P 'Focus on young public library services: bookmobiles and youth librarianship in Indonesia' *Focus Int & Comp Libp* 1974 5(4) 27.

Williamson W L *University library development in Indonesia: a report to the Ministry of Education and Culture, Republic of Indonesia* 1970, 19p. (PIP/T 497-186-3-00218).

Borchardt D H 'Australian aid to university libraries in Indonesia, Malaysia and Singapore' *Int Lib Rev* 1975 7(2) 279-82.

Pusat Dokumentasi Ilmiah Nasional *Improvement of library and documentation facilities in the field of science and technology in Indonesia by the National Scientific Documentation Centre* 1971, 12p.

'Scientific documentation and information network for Indonesia: workshop held at Bandung from 22 to 24 July 1971' *Unesco Bull Lib* 1972 26(2) 109-10.

'Indonesia network of scientific documentation and information' *Unesco Bull Lib* 1972 26(5) 290-1.

Harrison B *Report on the development of national documentation and information services in Indonesia* ERIC, 1972, 41p.

Myatt A *Scientific and technical information services: Indonesian (Mission) July 1973* Unesco, 1973, 128p.

Nasution A S *Program pemerintak bagi perkembanagan perpustakaan di Indonesia* Jakarta, 1974.

Pringgoadisurjo L 'Indonesia: main problems in developing library and information services in science and technology' *Baca* 1976 3(2) 35-39. (Paper at 1st UNISIST meeting April 1976).

Zultanawar 'Information services for R & D in Indonesia' *Baca* 1977 4(1) 1-5.

Indonesia: the development of scientific and technical information service Loughborough U, 1977, 153p. (Thesis).

Hernandono 'Indonesia: development of a scientific information network' *Unesco Bull Lib* 1978 32(5) 338-41.

Pringgoadisurjo L 'Major issues related to the problems of access to information in Indonesia' *Baca* 1979 6(1) 1-3.

1

National Library, Manila, 1901- . Deposit and bibliographical functions. Setting up an advisory body on bibliographical matters: Philippines Advisory Council on Bibliographical Services (PACBS) and converting the Bibliography Division into a Bibliographical Centre. This move related to the plans to participate in UBC, 1975?- .

National Library. Development Plan Committee *The National Library service and development plan* The Committee, 1967, 98p.

Hatch L 'The National Diet Library, the National Library of the Philippines and the Singapore National Library' *J Lib Hist* 1972 7(4) 329-59.

National Library *Your National Library* 1975.

University of the Philippines Library, Quezon City, 1922- . (Institute of Library Science).

National Institute of Science and Technology, Division of Documentation, Manila, 1902- .

2a

Department of Education.

2b

Philippine Library Association (PLA) 1923- .

Saniel I 'Forty nine years of the Philippine Library Association' *J Lib Hist* 1972 7 301-12.

Roño J A 'Philippine Library Association' *PLA Bull* 1973 8(3/4) 13-5.

Association of Special Libraries of the Philippines (ASLP), 1954. In 1974 became a chapter of the Philippine Library Association.

Collantes A L 'ASLP: Association of Special Libraries of the Philippines' *Unesco Bull Lib* 1961 15(1) 25-37.

Philippine Association for the Advancement of Science Information Communication (PAASIC), 1966- .

2c

Marvin J C *Institute of Library Science, University of the Philippines; final report* ALA, 1965, 14p mimeo.

Cervantes Asubar V *A study of the librarian-training program and library services at the University of San Carlos* U of San Carlos, 1963, 197p. (Thesis).

Damasco C 'Library education in the Philippines' *J Educ Libp* 1966 6(4) 310-7.

Edralin J S 'Advanced formal training and in-service training of librarians in the Philippines' *J Phil Libp* 1969 2(1/2) 111-23.

Mercado F C *Education for librarianship in the Philippines* U of Hawaii, Graduate School of Library Studies, 1971, 98p.

Picache U G 'Library schools and the education of the librarian' *PLA Bull* 1974/75 9/10 17-21, refs.

— 'Education for librarianship in the Philippines (Ceylon Library Services Board) *Library News* 1977 5(2) 12-8.
Rasmussen R 'Education for librarianship in the Philippines' *Libri* 1977 27(4) 273-81.
Cristobal Cruz A 'The Filipinization of Philippine libraries and politicalization of Filipino librarians' *J Phil Libp* 1969 2(1/2) 124-9 refs.
'The Filipino librarian in search of identity: papers at the 1st annual Convention of the Integrated Philippine Library Association, University of the Philippines at Los Baños (Laguna) May 1975' *PLA Bull* 1974/75 9/10 1-62.

3a

Office of Public Information *Republic of the Philippines official directory* Manila, 1949- .
Maring E G and Maring J M *Historical and cultural dictionary of the Philippines* Scarecrow, 1973, 240p.
Philippines mass media directory 1971 Philippines Press Institute, 1971, 326p.
Dayrit M C et al, comp *Directory of libraries in the Philippines* U of the Philippines Library, 1973, 131p.
Sanches C *The libraries of the Philippines* PLA, 1973.
PLA/ALSP *Directory of special library resources and research facilities in the Philippines*, 1975. Previously published *ASLP Bull* 1968 14(3/4) 31-81. (3rd ed.).

3b

Bernado G A *Bibliography of Philippine bibliographies 1593-1961* Ateneo de Manila U P, 1968, 192p.
Houston C O *Philippine bibliography. An annotated preliminary bibliography of Philippine bibliographies since 1900* U of Manila, 1960, 60p. Supplement up to 1965 as:
Saito S *The Philippines, a review of bibliographies* East West Center Library, 1966, 80p.
National Library *Catalog of copyright entries, 1964-1968* The Library, 1972- , ? vols.
National Library. Bibliography Division *Philippine national bibliography* 1974- .
University of the Philippines Library *Philippine bibliography* 1968-1969, 1970-1972. Published 1973.
University of the Philippines Library *Union catalog of Philippine materials* The Library, 1970-, vols. (Vol. 1 A-O).
- *Philippine union catalog*, 1974- Quarterly.
College of Public Administration, IDRS *Index to Philippine periodicals*, 1955- .
Mercado F C 'A bibliography on Philippine libraries and librarianship' *PLA Bull* 1965 New Series 1(1).

3c

PLA Bulletin, N.S. 1965- .
ASLP Bulletin 1954, 1956- . Quarterly.
U of the Philippines, Institute of Library Science *Journal of Philippine Librarianship* 1968- Quarterly.

3d

Bureau of Census and Statistics *Yearbook of Philippine statistics* 1958- . Published at intervals.

3e

Official gazette, Manila, GPO. Monthly.

Espinas L A *Public library legislation: a compilation of laws and orders pertaining to public libraries* Bureau of Public Libraries (Dept of Education), 1964, 168p mimeo.

New Copyright Law (Presidential Decree No. 49 of 14 November 1972).

3f

'Publishing problems in the Philippines' *Comment* 1965 (22) 123-35.

Albert L N et al *Developmental book activities and needs in the Philippines* USAID, 1966, 134p.

Arcedo L B *Library development of the Philippines from 1900 up to the present* UC London, School of Library . . . Studies, 1970. (Thesis).

Augustra R *Professor Gabriel A Bernardo: librarian and bibliographer* U of the Philippines, 1974, 103p. (Thesis, MLS).

'Libraries in infrastructure development: papers of the 1973 Golden Jubilee Convention of the PLA, Manila, October 1973'. *PLA Bull* 1973 8(3/4) 1-132.

Buenviaje R O 'Government policies affecting the development and growth of libraries in the Philippines' *Paper* at 2nd Conference of Southeast Librarians, Manila, December 1973.

Kader Z A 'Educational policy and its importance to the growth of public libraries and librarianship in West Malaysia and the Philippines' *Majallah Perpust Malaysia* 1977 5 17-39. (Colonial period).

Sanchez C *Philippine school libraries, their organization and management* MCS Enterprises, 1971, 172p.

Siega G D 'Looking backward: the first fifty five years of the Silliman University Library' *Silliman J* 1965 12 262-78.

Valesco S I 'Philippine heritage from American librarianship' *ASPL Bull* 1965 11(1) 10-20.

Bichteler J 'Special libraries in the Philippines' *Spec Lib* 1977 68(1) 28-34.

Wise D A 'An assessment of map collections in the Philippines' *Geog Map Div Bull* 1980 (119) 33-7.

Feliciano M S 'Law libraries and legal documentation in the Philippines' *Int J Law Lib* 1976 4(3) 176-87.

Lorch W T 'The Scientific and Documentation Center of the Philippines' *Unesco Bull Lib* 1961 15(1) 25-37.

Raizada A S *Philippines. Development of information infrastructures. Initiation of information activities at the National Library* Unesco, 1977, 27p.

Amores I D 'Planning for a scientific and technical information system in the Philippines' *Int Forum Info Doc* 1979 4(4) 20-2.

PACIFIC REGION

1

South Pacific Commission/Commission du Pacifique Sud. Library and Information Service, Noumea, 1949- .

University of the South Pacific. Main library at Suva (Fiji), with libraries in other groups of islands.

Peasgood A N 'The library of the University of the South Pacific' *New Zeal Lib* 1971 35(6) 246-51.

Alexander Turnbull Library, Wellington.

Nelson Memorial Library, Apia.

2a

South Pacific Commission, 1947- . Effective 1948- . Includes the South Pacific countries and France, UK and USA. Its role is to coordinate the development of the region, cultural as well as economic.

Foundation of the People of the South Pacific, New York, 1945- . To stimulate development.

2b

Société des Océanistes, Paris. For the study of Pacific cultures.

Standing Conference of Pacific Librarians (SCOPAL). Chairman at Lae. 1979- .

2c

Peacock D J 'Training island librarians' *South Pac Bull* 1965 15(1) 41-3.

Turner B H 'Library assistants' training course' *South Pac Bull* 1967 17 20.

Goulding S ed *Basic librarianship. Essential notes for students in the Islands* Noumea, South Pacific Commission, 1968.

Jackson M M 'Library education and training in Oceania' *Int Lib Rev* 1979 11 301-9. American Samoa, Guam, Fiji, Papua New Guinea.

3a

Tudor J *Pacific islands yearbook and who's who* Sydney, Pacific Publications, 1962- .

The Far East and Australia 12th ed Europa, 1980, 1365p.

Kennedy T F *A descriptive atlas of the Pacific Islands* Praeger, 1969, 64p.

Luster A D C et al 'A directory of libraries and information sources in Hawaii and the Pacific islands' *HLA J* 1970 27(2) 4-96.

— *A directory of libraries and information sources in Hawaii and the Pacific islands* rev ed, HLA, 1977, 110p.

3b

Baker L R *National and regional bibliography in the Pacific — a developmental appraisal* Papua New Guinea U of Technology, n.d., 30p, refs.

Meetings on national and regional bibliography in the South Pacific, Suva, 1978. *Proceedings* (Organised by the International Development Research Centre — IDRC). Second meeting in Papua New Guinea, 1979.

Leeson I *A bibliography of bibliographies of the South Pacific* OUP, 1954, 61p.
Conover H F *Islands of the Pacific: a select list of references* Library of Congress, 1943, 181p (Repr 1945). Supplement, 1945, 68p.
Taylor C R *A Pacific bibliography* 2nd ed Clarendon P, 1965.
'Bibliographie de l'Océanie' Section in Société des Océanistes, *Journal.*
University of the South Pacific Library *Pacific collection accession list*, Suva, 1975- .
Dam E *Bibliography of periodical articles relating to the South Pacific* University of the South Pacific Library, Vol. 1, 1974 (Published 1976).

3c

Journal de la Société des Océanistes, Paris.
New Zealand Libraries, Wellington.
South Pacific Bulletin/Bulletin du Pacifique Sud Noumea, South Pacific Commission, 1951- .

3d

Data Asia/Pacific: a statistical profile Hong Kong, Media Transasia, 1978,- Annual.

3e

'South Pacific government serials: a selected list' *U Auckland Bibliog Bull* 1967 (4).

3f

Crocombe R G *The new South Pacific* Australian National U P, 1973.
King F F ed *Oceania and beyond: essays on the Pacific since 1945* Greenwood P, 1976.
Gunson W N ed *The changing Pacific: essays in honour of H E Maude* Melbourne, OUP, 1978, 351p.
Langness L et al *Melanesia: readings on a culture area* Chandler Pub Co, 1971, 382p.
Brookfield H C *Melanesia: a geographical interpretation of an island world* Methuen, 1974, 464p. Economic conditions.
Chowning M A *An introduction to the peoples and cultures of Melanesia* 2nd ed Menlo Park, Cummings Pub Co, 1977, 124p.
Howard A *Polynesia: readings on a culture area* Chandler Pub Co, 1971, 336p.
Unesco *Meeting of experts on the study of Oceanic cultures, Suva, 13-17 September 1970* Australian National Advisory Committee for Unesco, 1971.
Roberts B 'Des ouvrages imprimés pour les insulaires' *Bull Pac Sud* 1960 10(3) 21.
— *Report on the Literature Production Training Centre, Honiara* SPC, 1963.
Education in Asia and Oceania: a challenge for the 1980s Unesco, 1980, 60p. (Educational Studies and Documents, N.S., 38).
Adam R S *A short study of reading problems in the Pacific Islands* Fiji, Department of Education, 1953.
Bonny H V *Library services in the South Pacific. A report made to the SPC by a Unesco expert on a tour in 1962* Noumea, SPC, 1962.
Jackson M M *A report on the libraries of the Pacific Islands* ERIC, 1979. (Document ED-156 185).
— 'Library and information services in the Pacific Islands' *Int Lib Rev* 1981 13(1) 25-41.
Conference on library cooperation in Micronesia, Guam, October 1979 *Conference report* Saipan, 1979.

Borchardt D H and Horacek, J I *Librarianship in Australia, New Zealand and Oceania: a brief survey* Pergamon P, 1975, 80p.

SPC *La bibliothèque du village* Document technique (3), 1950.

Peacock D J 'The Pacific Islands Central School library' *South Pac Bull* 1963 13(4) 53-4.

McDonald P 'The planning and development of school library services' *New Zeal Lib* 1976 39(6) 206-10.

Bird B K 'Medical library services in the South Pacific' *New Zeal Lib* 1976 39(2) 68-74.

FID *Proceedings of the second Congress and third General Assembly of the FID Commission for Asia and Oceania (FID/CAO), Seoul, September 1974*, Korea Scientific and Technological Information Centre, 105p.

'Networking: towards a blueprint for South Pacific Basin Library and Information Cooperation' Symposium at the University of Hawaii Graduate School of Library Studies, June 1978.

US ASSOCIATED PACIFIC

HAWAII

1

University of Hawaii. Center for Cultural and Technical Interchange between East and West, Honolulu. 1960- . Known as East-West Center. Bibliographical and information centre with a librarianship collection.

2a

Hawaii being one of the American states the libraries are under the authority of the US Office of Education and the State Department of Public Instruction.

2b

Hawaii Library Association (HLA), Honolulu, 1922- .

Harris I W Hawaii Library Association, (HLA) in *Encyclopedia,* 10 (1973) 377-81.

Dabagh J 'A history of the Hawaii Library Association, 1921-1974' *HLA J* 1974 31(1) 11-3.

Hawaii Association of School Librarians (HASL), 1960- (Previously a section of the HLA).

2c

University of Hawaii. Graduate School of Library Science.

Stevens R D 'Hawaii, University of Hawaii Graduate School of Library Science' in *Encyclopedia*, 10 (1973) 381-5.

3a

See under United States of America and Pacific Region.

Some issues of the *HLA Journal* are devoted to records of libraries: 'Directory of one hundred Hawaiian libraries' 1968 25(1).

'Directory of libraries and information sources in Hawaii and the Pacific Islands' 1970 27(2). Later published in book form:

Luster A D C *A Directory of libraries and information sources in Hawaii and Pacific Islands* Rev ed, HLA, 1977, 110p.

3b

Hori J 'Survey of indexes to Hawaiiana' *HLA J* 1971 28(2) 10-6.

Current Hawaiiana 1944- . First published by the HLA, Hawaiiana Section; now issued by the University of Hawaii Library.

East-West Center *Annotated bibliography series.*

Kittelson D 'Bibliography of Hawaii library history' *J Lib Hist* 1970 5 41-55.

3c

Hawaii Library Association Journal, Honolulu, 1944- .

Hawaii Library Association Newsletter, Honolulu, 1958- .

3e

Analysis of service and development of performance measurements for State of Hawaii libraries, 5 parts, Honolulu, Survey and Marketing Services Inc, 1977 91p. (ERIC Report ED-160 047-051).

3f

Tabrah R *Hawaii, a bicentennial history* Norton/American Association for State and Local History, 1980, 233p.

Hunt J R 'Concept of total library service' *Calif Lib News* 1970 65 Suppl 361-6.

Paters K A 'Kanai interlibrary cooperation conference' *HLA J* 1971 28 29-30.

Nakamura H S 'Hawaii reaches out: services to the disadvantaged' *HLA J* 1971 28 3-8.

Kittelson D 'University of Hawaii library, 1907-1920' *HLA J* 1971 28 3-9.

West S 'Hawii, University of Hawaii libraries' in *Encyclopedia,* 10 (1973) 385-90.

AMERICAN SAMOA

3f

Lommen J 'Library service in American Samoa' *HLA J* 1965 21 24-5.

Lunnon B S 'O le fale tusi o Amerika Samoa' *Florida Lib* 1969 20 204-7. Revised version as:

Lunnon B S 'Library in American Samoa' *HLA J* 1970 27 14-7.

Jackson M M 'A community library in American Samoa' *Unesco Bull Lib* 1964 18(3) 144-5.

PACIFIC ISLAND TRUST TERRITORY (USA)

Main islands: Palau, Ponape, Truk, Yap. Marshall Islands and Palau now have their internal constitution.

3f

Jackson M M *The Trust Territory and a Pacific Basin Consortium: a point of view* ERIC Document Reproduction Service, 1979, 8p. (ERIC Report ED-167 101).

Colletta N J *American schools for the native of Ponape: a study of education and culuture change in Micronesia* Univ of Hawaii P (for East-West Center), 1980, 181p.

American Samoa Library Conference 21 to 23 March 1978 *Final Report* Pago Pago, Office of Library Services, 1978.

Peacock D J 'Bookmobile programme in the US Trust Territory of the Pacific Islands' *South Pacific Bull* 1969 19(4) 50-1.

AUSTRALIA

1

National Library of Australia, Canberra, 1961- Designated as the National Information Transfer Centre for Unesco's ISORID project.

'Australia, National Library of' in *Encyclopedia* 2 (1969) 113-8.

[National Library of Australia] *Int Lib Rev* 1975 7(2) 129-269. Special section on the library.

Stone R T 'The National Library of Australia' *J Lib Info Sci* 1975 1(2) 70-81. The Library in the library service.

Freeman C 'Data bases currently available from the National Library of Australia' *Austr Acad Res Lib* 1976 7(3) 147-55.

State libraries in every capital with legal deposit privilege.

Australian Centre for Research in Library and Information Science (ACRILIS).

'ACRILIS — an Australian Centre for Research in Library and Information Science' *Res in Libp* 1975 (30) 210-11.

2a

Australian Advisory Council on Bibliographical Services (AACOBS), Canberra, 1956- .

AACOBS *Library Services for Australia: the work of AACOBS, 1956-70* National Library, 1971, 30p.

Bryan H 'AACOBS: its purpose, performance and present perils' *Austr Lib J* 1979 28(8) 117-24.

Borchardt D H 'Australian Advisory Council on Bibliographical Services (AACOBS): a partial history by a partial observer' *Austr Acad Res Lib* 1979 10(1) 1-14.

2b

Committee of Australian University Librarians (CAUL), 1928- .

Fielding D 'CAUL and AACOBS' *Austr Acad Res Lib* 1979 10(1) 15-28.

Library Association of Australia, Sydney, 1937- .

'Australia, Library Association of' in *Encyclopedia*' 2 (1969) 109-13.

2c

White J P 'Education for librarianship: Australia' *Lib Trends* 1963 12(2) 295-305.

[Library education in Australia] *Austr Lib J* 1971 20(3). Whole issue.

Kosa G A 'The proliferation of courses in library science and an estimate of student output 1975-1980' *Austr Acad Res Lib* 1975 6(4) 175-182.

Howes B R *Acceptability of qualifications in librarianship by employers of professional librarians*. Report of a survey made from January to March 1976 for the Centre for Research in Library and Information Science, Wagga Wagga, 1976.

— 'Qualifications in librarianship in Australia: their acceptance by the profession' *Res Libp* 1976 6(32) 41-65.

Radford N A 'Education for librarianship: the changing role' *Austr Lib J* 1978 27(7) 102-6.
Maguire C 'The development of educational programmes in information science: opportunities and problems' *LASIE* 1978 8(4) 23-30, refs.
— 'Problems of research in librarianship' *Austr Lib J* 1975 24(7) 290-7, refs.
Kosa G A 'Research in library science: what needs to be done and who should do it?' *Austr Lib J* 1975 24(8) 348-54.
'Sources of funding for Australian research in librarianship' *Austr Lib J* 1976 25(1) 28-32.
Metcalfe J 'The profession of librarianship in Australia' *New Zeal Lib* 1960 23(2) 36-43.
McMahon A *Personality of the librarian, prevalent social values and attitudes towards the profession* Library Boards of South Australia, 1967, 127p.
Brian R F 'Unionism in university libraries' *Austr Acad Res Lib* 1974 5(4) 163-8.
Creelman M 'The librarian in the community' *Austr Lib J* 1975 24(2) 60-5.
LAA *School library personnel: types of staff and their educational requirements* Draft document, 1979.

3a

Official yearbook of the Commonwealth of Australia Canberra, Bureau of Census and Statistics.
Learmonth A T A and Learmonth A M *Encyclopedia of Australia* Warne, 1968, 147p.
Davis M 'What, where and who in the Australian library world' *Austr Lib J* 1976 25(14) 340-6. Review of existing directories.
Directory of state and public library service in Queensland Library Board of Queensland, 1980, 28p. (Then annually).
LAA *Directory of special libraries in Australia* 3rd ed, 1972.
Finlay R J M 'Law library directories and guides in Australia' *Int J Law Lib* 1977 5(2) 149-64.
Rauchle N M and Alonso P A G eds *Directory of map collections in Australia State Library of Victoria*, 1974, 20p.

3b

AACOBS *Australian bibliography and bibliographical services* National Library, 1960, 219p.
Borchardt D H *Australian bibliography. A guide to printed sources of information* Pergamon, 1976, 106p.
— *Twelve essays on Australian subject bibliography* National Library of Australia, 1980, 121p.
Rothwell R 'The outlook for bibliographic tape services' *LASIE* 1976 7(1) 22-4.
Ferguson J comp *Bibliography of Australia, 1784-1900* Sydney, Angus & Robertson, 1941-69, 7 Vols. Reprinted, 1975- .
National Library *Retrospective Australian national bibliography, 1901-1950.*
National Library *Australian national bibliography (ANB)* 1961- .
Australian books in print Melbourne, D W Thorpe.
Annual catalogue of Australian publications. In classified order, includes librarianship.
Reid-Smith E R 'ACRILIS abstracts of Australian theses and dissertations of interest to librarians: part 1, University of Melbourne 1936-1955' *Res Libp* 1976 (31) 5-19.
Downs R B *Australian and New Zealand library resources* Mansell, 1979, 164p. A survey and bibliography.

3c

National Library *Current Australian serials*. Recurrent publication.
Library Association of Australia *Australian Library Journal* 1951- .
- University and Colleges Libraries section *Australian Academic and Research Libraries* 1970- . Previously, 1960-70, Section's *Newsletter.*
- Public Libraries section *Australian Public Libraries Issues* 1971- .
- Special Libraries section *Australian Special Libraries News* 1967- .

Australian School Librarian Melbourne.
Children's Libraries Newsletter. In 1977 became *Orana.*

3d

Australia in facts and figures:
Census and Statistics Commonwealth Bureau *Quarterly summary of Australian statistics.*
[Australian and New Zealand university library statistics] Annual feature in *Austr Acad Res Lib*, Suppl.
IFLA. Libraries in Hospitals sub-section *Organization, description of work and statistics of library services in hospitals, institutions and for the handicapped in Australia* [and other countries] IFLA, 1977, 116p.

3e

Fischer G 'Australian university library laws and administrative responsibility' *Austr Acad Res Lib* 1971 2(1) 1-15.
Secondary Schools Libraries Committee *Standards for secondary school libraries* Australian Government Publication Service, 1971, 54p.
Schools Commission *Guidelines for library services in primary schools* 1973?.
Lahore J 'Photocopying in Australian libraries: developments in copyright law' *Int J Law Lib* 1976 4(1) 32-7.
Dutton G and Harris M *Australia's censorship crisis* Melbourne, Sun Books, 1970, 224p.

3f

The Far East and Australasia Europa Yearbooks, 1969- .
Page R *Australian bookselling* Deutsch, 1970.
Brenac P and Stevens A *The reading and buying of books in Australia* Prepared for the Australian Council Literature Board. Sydney, Arts Information Program, 1978, 116p.
Bryan H and McGreal R M *Pattern of library services in Australia; a statement for the Australian Advisory Council on Bibliographical Services* National Library, 1972, 37p.
Biskup P and Goodman D M *Australian libraries* 3rd ed Bingley, 1982, 221p (1st ed 1966).
The Libraries Board of South Australia in its series of *Occasional papers in librarianship* has reprinted a number of early works of historical interest. See for instance:
- *Australian libraries: a survey of conditions and suggestions for their improvement* 1935 (Paper 6, 1967).
- *Library Association of Australasia. Conference proceedings, 1896.* (Paper 7, 1969).
- *Conference proceedings 1898.* (Paper 8, 1969).
- *Transactions and proceedings of the Library Association of Australasia at its second general meeting, 1900.* 2 vols. (Paper 9, 1969).

- Holgate C W *An account of the chief libraries of Australia and Tasmania* 1886; (Paper 11, 1971).

Metcalfe J 'Libraries in Australia: a revolution comes of age' *Lib Rev* 1958 (125) 312-7.

Rayward W B ed *The variety of librarianship: essays in honour of John Wallace Metcalfe* LAA, 1976, 242p. Essays on all aspects of Australian librarianship; progress and problems.

For current information on the prevalent conditions it is useful to consult the LAA *Proceedings of the Biennial Conferences*, published in substantial volumes. See for instance the latest recorded to date:

Baskin J ed *Alternative futures: proceedings of the 20th Biennial Conference*, Canberra, 1979; LAA, 1979, 458p.

Lodewycks K A 'State libraries in Australia: some impressions based on their annual reports' *Austr Acad Res Lib* 1976 7(4) 231-4. National, Government, academic, special libraries.

Bryan H 'Australian library and information services' *Int Lib Rev* 1975 7(2) 121-7. Mainly the National Library and AACOBS.

'Seminar on systems approach to library management, August 1976' *LASIE* 1976 7(2) 2-34; 7(3) 3-42. 9 papers.

Borchardt D H 'Australian aid to university libraries in Indonesia, Malaysia and Singapore' *Int Lib Rev* 1975 7(2) 279-82. Australian Asian University Cooperation Scheme (AACS).

Development of resource sharing networks National Library, 1979, 208p. International Conference of Directors of National Libraries on Resource Sharing in Asia and Oceania.

National Library of Australia *Development of resource sharing in the framework of UNISIST, NATIS and ALBIS. Interim report and surveys* The Library, 1975, 686p. (ALBIS: Australia Library Based Information Systems).

'Resource sharing' *Austr Lib J* 1976 25(13) 306-12, 320-30.

Development of resource sharing networks: library services for the handicapped National Library, 1979, 165p. (Networks study, 9).

McColvin L R *Public libraries of Australia: present conditions and future possibilities. . .* ACER, 1947.

Sharr F A 'Commonwealth aid for public libraries' *Austr Lib J* 1969 18 107-16.

Whatley A *Report on a study visit to Australian public libraries in July-September 1977* British Library, 1978, 141p.

Browne M 'Librarians, social workers — and community information: the territorial stake-out' *Austr Lib J* 1976 25(16) 383-7.

Lundin R and Marsh D *An educational growing point: a review of studies, surveys and reports relating to school libraries in Australia, 1935-1976* Brisbane, Kelvin Grove College of Advanced Education, Dept of School Librarianship, 1978, 50p.

Brown C 'Libraries in education' *Q Rev Austr Educ* 1970 3(3) 1-69, refs.

Jarrett L 'The school library in the modern educational process' *Austr Lib J* 1970 18(8) 282-6.

Balson M 'Educational trends affecting school librarians' *Austr School Libn* 1976 13(2) 37-42.

McGrath L H ed *Planning and development of school library services:* proceedings of the Unesco Regional Seminar on School Libraries, Perth, 1976 Australian National Commission for Unesco, 1976, 209p.

McArthur J T 'Whatever happened to the pilot libraries?' *Austr School Libn* 1978 15(1) 5-8, refs. Refers to a follow-up scheme on the Schools Commission's *Guidelines. . .* (See under 3e).

[School libraries] *Austr Lib J* 1977 26(13) and (14). Whole issues.
Dwyer A C *South Australian toy libraries: a survey, 1976* South Australia Institute of Technology, 1976, 174p.
Garlick M 'Library service to migrant children in Australia' *Wilson Lib Bull* 1979 54(2) 104-6.
Edwards C A 'In support of school community libraries'. Parts 1 and 2 *Austr School Libn* 1977 14(1) 5-8; 1977 14(2) 43, 46-50.
Dwyer J G *Co-operation or compromise: school/community libraries in Australia.* A report of the Schools Commission, 1978, 81p.
Lodewycks K A 'Australia — notes on the problems and progress of university libraries' *Melbourne Studies in Education 1961-62*, Melbourne U P, 1964, 114-28.
Fielding F D O *Australian university library administration* Australia & New Zealand Book Co, 1971, 2 vols.
Bryan H 'Australian university library development — a revolution in our time' *New Zeal Lib* 1974 37(4) 190-203.
— 'Growth patterns of British and Australian university libraries' *Austr Acad Res Lib* 1976 7(2) 100-5.
Steele C ed *Steady-state, zero-growth and the academic library* Bingley/Linnet Books, 1978, 148p. Seven papers on the Atkinson report, some on Australia.
Bryan H 'Australian academic libraries: the incomplete revolution' *Coll Res Lib* 1980 41(1) 17-26, refs.
Trezise M 'Gramophone record libraries in Australia' *Austr Lib J* 1968 17(11) 377-82.
Bentley P 'Music libraries and librarianship: Australia' *Austr Spec Lib News* 1974 7(5) 119-22.
Murdoch J 'Australia Music Centre and Library' *Austr Spec Lib News* 1976 9(4) 116-9.
O'Shea R 'Law libraries in Australia' *Austr Spec Lib News* 1974 7(5) 112-4.
Darvall B 'Law libraries in Australia and Canada: a note on two recent surveys' *Austr Acad Res Lib* 1976 7(4) 245-8.
Ballie J 'Medical libraries in Australia' *Austr Spec Lib News* 1974 7(5) 118-9.
Andrews R R 'The role of libraries in medical education for the future' *Austr Spec Lib News* 1976 9(2) 41-5.
Harrison A 'The problem of Australian university medical libraries' *Austr Acad Res Lib* 1979 10(4) 225-9.
Schilter E 'Wissenschaftliche Bibliotheken in Australien' *Biblos* 1975 24(1) 20-7.
Fussler H H and Bryan H *Reflections on the future of research libraries: two essays* Monash U, Graduate School of Librarianship, 1978, 36p.
Slight O E 'The plight of Australia's research libraries and information services in a time of multidimensional change' *Austr Acad Res Lib* 1976 7(3) 133-46.
Science and Technology Information Services Enquiry Committee *The STISEC Report,* May 1973 [to the Council of the National Library of Australia]. Vol. 1: *Scientific and technological services in Australia* National Library, 1973, 40p.
Chandler G 'Planning national information systems: Australia with some reference to New Zealand and Papua New Guinea' *Unesco Bull Lib* 1977 31(2) 98-106, 115.
Huey R M and Howard P 'Stored information, libraries and the future' *Austr Spec Lib News* 1975 8(4) 116-38.
Dobrovits A 'Some thought on MARC' *Austr Lib J* 1975 24(1) 20-6.
Schmidmaier D 'Co-operative computer based systems in Australia' *Austr Spec Lib News* 1979 12(1) 16-9.

NEW ZEALAND

1

National Library of New Zealand, Wellington, 1966- . Established by the 1965 National Library Act, combines three existing libraries:

National Library Centre created in 1945 as a division of the:

National Library Service, National Lending Library.

Alexander Turnbull Library created in 1920 as State Reference Library, with collections on New Zealand, the Pacific region and English literature.

General Assembly Library created in 1845 as the Library of Parliament, with reference service to Parliament and collection of official publications.

Alley G T 'National Library in the social process' *New Zeal Lib* 1967 30(5) 141-56.

New Zealand Department of Scientific and Industrial Research. Information Service.

2a

New Zealand Library Resources Committee, restructured in 1974 with broader functions. Advises the Minister of Education on all matters on library resources.

McEldowney W J 'The New Zealand Library Resources Committee' *Austr Acad Res Lib* 1976 7(4) 240-4.

2b

New Zealand Library Association (NZLA), Wellington, 1910- .

McEldowney W J *The New Zealand Library Association 1910-1960,* 1962.

— 'The New Zealand Library Association 1960-1970' *New Zeal Lib* 1970 33(5) 144-74.

2c

McEldowney W J 'Education for librarianship abroad: New Zealand' *Lib Trends* 1963 12(2) 306-21.

'The future of library education in New Zealand' *New Zeal Lib* 1966 161-76.

Working Party on Education for Librarianship *Education for librarianship. Report to the Minister of Education* Government Printer, 1969, 69p.

Morgan P 'The diploma course of the New Zealand Library School 1974' *New Zeal Lib* 1975 38(6) 300-3.

Wylie D M 'Library education in the year 2001' *New Zeal Lib* 1976 39(3) 82-4.

— 'A new era in library education' *New Zeal Lib* 1978 41(2) 52-4. Planning of two new schools: Victoria University and Wellington Teachers College.

Delahunty J P 'Professional associations: their changing role' *New Zeal Lib* 1971 34(4) 132-7. Librarians' salaries.

'Women in professional library work' *New Zeal Lib* 1969 32(1) 4-31.

Gully J S ed 'Librarians' salaries and conditions of work' *New Zeal Lib* 1976 39(4) 132-65. Set of papers.

'Guidelines for conditions of employment and appointments for staff in New Zealand libraries' *COMLA Newsletter* 1979 (25) 38-40.

3a

Department of Statistics *New Zealand Official Yearbook* Government Printer, 1892- Includes a bibliography.

Orsman H W ed *Heinemann New Zealand dictionary* Heinemann Educ., 1979.

Olsson A L *Who's who in New Zealand libraries* NZLA, 1967, 77p.

Special libraries and collections, a New Zealand directory 2nd ed, 1968, 52p.

3b

Grover R *New Zealand* Clio P, 1980, 254p. (World Bibliographical series, 18).

Broadbent A M 'Bibliographical work in progress 1977' *New Zeal Lib* 1977 40(3/4) 91-9.

NZLA *Bibliography of New Zealand bibliographies* The Association, 1967, 58p.

Bagnall A G ed *New Zealand national bibliography to the year 1960* Government Printer, 1969-75, 5 vols.

Bagnall A G 'Reflections on some unfinished business: the retrospective national bibliography, 1946-1976' *New Zeal Lib* 1977 40(2) 40-6.

Alexander Turnbull Library *New Zealand national bibliography* 1966- monthly with annual cumulation. Supersedes *Current national bibliography* and *Copyright publications.*

New Zealand books in print New Zealand Book Publishers Association.

National Library *Index to New Zealand periodicals* 1950- First issued with the *National bibliography* now published separately.

Szentirmay P 'Automation and computer based services in New Zealand: a bibliography' in *New Zealand Library Association 45th Conference* 1978 68-7.

Downs R B *Australian and New Zealand library resources*, Mansell, 1979, 164p. A survey and bibliography.

3c

NZLA *New Zealand Libraries* 1938- . 1933-37 as *NZLA Bulletin.*

— *Library life* 1978- . 1956-77 as *NZLA Newsletter.*

3d

Department of Statistics *Census of libraries.* Published every five years.

'Australian and New Zealand university library statistics' Annual feature in *Austr Acad Res Lib* Supplement to no. 3.

3e

New Zealand Statutes.

Public Library Committee *Standards for public library services in New Zealand* NZLA, 1966, 49p.

Standards for teachers' college libraries NZLA 1967.

3f

Munn R and Barr J *New Zealand libraries, a survey of conditions and suggestions for their improvement* NZLA, 1934, 71p.

Osborn A D *New Zealand library resources; report of a survey made for the New Zealand Library Association under the auspices of the Carnegie Corporation of New York* NZLA, 1960, 70p.

MacLean H de S C 'New Zealand, libraries in' in *Encyclopedia* 19 (1976) 420-45.

Traue J E 'Parliamentary report of the Royal Commission on State Services' *New Zeal Lib* 1963 26(5) 146-9. See also *New Zeal Lib* 1961 24(8) 169-73.

Wylie D M 'At the crossroads: New Zealand libraries 1972' *Austr Lib J* 1972 21(3) 93-8.

NZLA *Annual conference of the New Zealand Library Association: report of proceedings*. . . Published in monograph form by the Association.

McSweeney D B 'Library services for the changing rural community' *New Zeal Lib* 1964 27(2) 33-7.

O'Neill T B 'The cost and value of state aid to public libraries' *New Zeal Lib* 1971 34(3) 96-100.

Gadd B 'Making the library multicultural' *New Zeal Lib* 1976 39(3) 118-22. First of a series on minority groups.

Murphy S 'Maoritanga at Paraparaum public library' *New Zeal Lib* 1979 42(2) 46-6.

Roe E *Teachers, librarians and children: a study of libraries in education* Reed/Crosby Lockwood/Archon Books, 1965.

Fenwick S I *Library services for children in New Zealand schools and public libraries: a report to the New Zealand Library Association.* New Zealand Council for Educational Research and NZLA, 1975, 48p.

Ridling C and Hills H 'Working with non European children' *New Zeal Lib* 1968 31(1) 33-43.

[Library services in hospitals] *New Zeal Lib* 1975 38(4) 178-217. Special issue.

Green W 'Hospital library services and music' *New Zeal Lib* 1975 38(4) 209-17.

Freed D W 'Music in libraries' *New Zeal Lib* 1974 37(4) 177-81.

Griffin L 'New Zealand map collections' *Spec Lib* 1980 71(1) 30-6.

Durey P 'University library services to undergraduates' *Int Lib Rev* 1973 5(3) 321-7.

Durey P 'Academic libraries in New Zealand' *Coll Res Lib* 1980 41(4) 313-27, refs.

'Problems of research in New Zealand' *New Zeal Lib* 1968 31(2) 168-88.

National Library, Trustees *A scientific and technical Information service for New Zealand: recommendations*. . . National Library, 1972.

PAPUA NEW GUINEA

1

National Library, Boroko 1978- Headquarters of the Library Service.

Chandler G 'The Papua New Guinea National Library' *Int Lib Rev* 1979 11(3) 313-9.

2a

Department of Education — Library Service Division.

National Library Service (NLS) 1975- Coordinating role in establishing a national collection through legal deposit and publishing the national bibliography, previously published by the University of Papua New Guinea.

Baker L R 'An end and a beginning? The National Library Service at Papua New Guinea' *Austr Acad Res Lib* 1979 10(1) 45-50, refs.

Library Council of Papua New Guinea, 1975- .

2b

Papua New Guinea Library Association (PNGLA) Previously Library Association of Australia — Papua New Guinea Branch, Boroko.

School Library Association of Papua New Guinea (SLAPNG) 1970- (as School Libraries Association of Australia to 1973).

2c

Gordon T 'Education for librarianship' *Toktok Bilong Haus Buk* 1975 (14) 3-8.

Dean J *Professional and sub-professional education in librarianship: the future requirements of Papua New Guinea* Perth, Western Australia Institute of Technology, Department of Library Studies, 1976.

Holdsworth H 'Training — library education and training' *COMLA Newsletter* 1979 (23/24) 11-14.

3a

Ryan P *Encyclopedia of Papua New Guinea* Melbourne U P 1972 3 vols.

PNGLA *Directory of libraries* 1974.

PNGLA *Directory of special libraries 1975.*

3b

University of Papua New Guinea Library:

New Guinea bibliography 1967- .

New Guinea periodical index 1968- (Periodicals published in the country and abroad about New Guinea).

Possin H comp *Education in Papua New Guinea, a bibliography* PNG U of Technology, 1970.

Department of Education Research Branch *Bibliography of education in Papua New Guinea* The Branch 1971.

Wooden D comp *Bibliography of education in Papua New Guinea* 1974- Department of Education Research Branch.

Baker L R *Librarianship in Papua New Guinea: a checklist 1961-1977* PNG U of Technology, 1977, 7p.

3c

PNGLA *Toktok bilong haus buk 1* 1972- .

3f

Ford E ed *Papua New Guinea resource atlas* Jacaranda P, 1974.

Linklater W 'Libraries and librarians in Papua and New Guinea' in *Library Association of Australian Conference proceedings 1971* LAA, 1972, 82-98.

Bailey P et al, eds *Libraries in an independent Papua New Guinea* PNGLA and LAA PNG Branch, 1974.

Holdsworth H *The development of library services in Papua New Guinea: report on a consultant visit to Papua New Guinea in September 1975* Commonwealth Foundation, 1976, 80p.

Avafia K E 'Library development in Papua New Guinea' *Libri* 1975 *25*(4) 271-97.

Baker L R 'Papua New Guinea, Libraries in' in *Encyclopedia* 21 (1977) 371-96, bibl.

'Librarianship in PNG — where is it going?' *Toktok bilong haus buk* 1978 (25/26) 3-15.

Membrey R A 'The Papua New Guinea public library service' *Austr Pub Lib Issues* 1975 3(1) 3-7.

Howe L J 'Library profile no 28: Bulolo Public Library' *Toktok bilong haus buk* 1978 (25/26) 28-9.

Thompson R P 'Library training and reader education in Papua New Guinea' in *Library Association of Australia Conference proceedings 1973* 165-78.

Roe M 'Educational materials centre at the University of Papua New Guinea, a summary' in *Library Association of Australia Conference proceedings 1969* LAA, 1971, 603-5.

Baker L R *Development of university libraries in Papua New Guinea* Scarecrow, 1981, 399p.

Gardner J and Obi M 'Special libraries as information centres' *Toktok bilong haus buk* 1974 *10* 9-15.

Gardner J *Special libraries in Papua New Guinea* PNGLA, 1974.

Westwood M 'Profiles of the specials — International Training Institute Library' *Austr Spec Lib News* 1978 *11*(4) 131-3. (1945-).

Gardner J 'National report: Papua New Guinea — Law and law libraries in Papua New Guinea' *Int J Law Libs* 1974 *2*(3) 128-32.

Chandler G 'Planning national information systems: Australia with some reference to New Zealand and Papua New Guinea' *Unesco Lib Bull* 1977 31(2) 98-106, 115

Baker L R *Design of a national information network for Papua New Guinea* Lae, U of Technology. Mimeo.

NEW ZEALAND ASSOCIATED ISLANDS

COOK ISLANDS

2b
Cook Islands Library and Museum Society, Avarua (on Rarotonga).

3b
Coppell W G *A bibliography of the Cook Islands* Australia U P, 1970.

3f
Hynes B 'Library services in the Cook Islands' *New Zeal Lib* 1965 28(7) 153-8.

WESTERN SAMOA

1
Nelson Memorial Public Library, Apia, 1956- .

3f
Turner B 'Library services in Western Samoa' *New Zeal Lib* 1965 28(7) 158-63.
Te'o M T 'Library conditions in Western Samoa' *Libri* 1968 18(3/4) 216-22.
Mainly about the Nelson Memorial Library.
Thornhill M A 'Six weeks in Samoa' *Lib World* 1968 69(814) 243-6.

General, with Kiribati and Tuvalu (formerly Gilbert and Ellice Islands).

1

National Library and Archives of Kiribati, Bairiki (Tarawa). 1979- . Previously Gilbert Islands National Archives.

University of the South Pacific — Kiribati Extension, Bairiki Centre, Library 1973- .

3a

Coates A *Western Pacific Islands* HMSO, 1971.

Gilbert and Ellice Islands Colony *Annual report.* Until independence.

3b

Kunz E F *New bibliography of Pacific languages. An annotated bibliography of the languages of the Gilbert Islands, Ellice Islands and Nauru* Public Library of New South Wales, 1959.

Snow P A *A bibliography of Fiji, Tonga and Rotuna* Australian National U P/Miami U P, 1969, 418p.

3f

Whincup T *Nareau's nation: a portrait of the Gilbert Islands* Stacey International, 1979, 227p.

Gilbert and Ellice Islands Colony *Development plan 1970-72* Tarawa, 1970.

Kittermaster A M *Report on information and broadcasting services in the Gilbert and Ellice Islands* UK Ministry of Overseas Development, 1970.

Bonny H V *Report on library services dealing with Gilbert and Ellice Islands Colony* Available in the Western Pacific Archives, Suva.

Stenderup V 'Libraries and librarianship in the South Pacific' *Unesco Bull Lib* 1976 30(2) 93-100. Gilbert and Ellice, Nauru, Solomons, Vanuatu.

FIJI

1

University of the South Pacific Library, Suva. National Library for Fiji.

Peasgood A N 'Library of the University of the South Pacific' *New Zeal Lib* 1971 35(6) 246-51.

Fiji Library Service, Lautoka. Formerly the Western Regional Library. 1964- .

2a

Ministry of Urban Development, Housing and Social Welfare. Library Service of Fiji. 1970- .

2b

Fiji Library Association, Suva.

2c

Library Service *Certificate course in librarianship* 1973.

3a

Colonial Office *Fiji, Annual report.* Up to 1970.

Fiji annual report Suva, Government Printer, Includes a section on libraries.

3b

University of the South Pacific Library *Pacific collection accession list* 1975- .

Publications bulletin Fiji Government Printer.

Fiji Library Service *Fiji national bibliography* December 1979- . Twice a year. The first issue covers 1970-1978.

3c

Fiji Library Association *Newsletter* 1974- . Now *Journal* 1979- .

3f

Holdsworth H 'Bookselling with special reference to Fiji' *Fiji Lib Ass J* 1979 (1) 40-62.

Library Advisory Committee *Library resources in Fiji: a report* 1965.

Coman T E 'Libraries in Fiji' *Calif Libn* 1968 29(1) 46-50.

— 'Fiji, libraries in' in *Encyclopedia* 8 (1972) 397-404.

Krishnamurti D 'Library service in the Fiji Islands' *Unesco Bull Lib* 1959 13(7) 158-60.

Roberts D B *Report on the library service in Fiji* Noumea, SPC, 1960.

'Fiji, new library service' *Unesco Bull Lib* 1965 19(4) 221.

Pearce R 'Starting from scratch: some problems in launching Fiji's public library service' *New Zeal Lib* 1966 29(4) 61-9.

Ramachandran R 'Nation-wide public library services for Fiji — birth and development' *Libri* 1974 24(3) 229-39.

Library service of Fiji *Communication media and secondary school students in Lautoka* Western Regional Library, 1966.

University of the South Pacific *First development plan* 1970.

SOLOMON ISLANDS

1

National Library, 1974- Housed in the Honiara Public Library. Headquarters of the Solomon Islands National Library Service.

3a

British Solomon Islands, Protectorate *Report for the year. . .* Honiara. Until independence, 1978.

3b

Stenderup V *Research material on British Solomon Islands Protectorate: a selected reading list,* [1976?].

3c

Solomon Islands Research Register Honiara, 1972, No.1- .

3f

Kittermaster A M *Report on information and broadcasting services in Solomon Islands* London, Ministry of Overseas Development, 1970.

Green R 'The British Solomon Islands and the Samoans. A culture historian's view of needs and prospects for preservation and conservation of cultural material' in Unesco *Meeting of experts on the study of Oceanic cultures* (See Pacific 3f) 199-209.

Edridge S 'Library work in the Solomon Islands' *New Zeal Lib* 1978 41(2) 46-50.

— 'Solomon Islands, libraries in' in *Encyclopedia* 28 (1980) 110-5.

Allison W A 'A travelling library for the Solomons' *Unesco Bull Lib* 1960 14(1) 20-1.

Hockey S W 'What is the use of teaching our children to read if they never see any books? — Development of library services in the Solomon Islands: an interim report' *COMLA Newsletter* 1978 (21) 64-6.

VANUATU

Formerly the Condominium of the New Hebrides. Until July 1980.

1

Vola Cultural Centre Library. 1956- .

3a

New Hebrides Condominium Advisory Council *Biennial report* Vila.

3b

Robequin C *Madagascar et les bases dispersées de l'Union française* Paris, PUF, 1958.

O'Reilly P *Bibliographie méthodique, analytique et critique des Nouvelles Hébrides* Paris, Musée de l'Homme, 1957, 302p.

FRENCH ASSOCIATED ISLANDS

1

South Pacific Commission Library, Noumea, 1949- .

2b

Institut Français d'Océanie, Noumea.
Société d'Etudes Océaniennes, Papeete.

3b

O'Reilly P *Bibliographie méthodique, analytique et critique de la Nouvelle Calédonie* Paris, Musée de l'Homme, 1958, 306p. (Société des Océanistes publications, 4).

— *Bibliographie des Iles Wallis et Futuna* Paris, Musée de l'Homme, 1964, 68p. (Société des Océanistes publications, 13).

— and Reitman E *Bibliographie de Tahiti et de la Polynésie française* Paris, Musée de l'Homme, 1967. 1046p. (Société des Océanistes publications, 14).

3f

Levy R I *Tahitians; mind and experience in the Society Islands* U of Chicago P, 1973.

Thompson V and Thompson R A *The French Pacific Islands: French Polynesia and New Caledonia* California U P , 1971, 539p, bibl.

'Le bibliobus de la Nouvelle Calédonie' *Bull Pac Sud* 1960 10(3) 10.

Frouin M 'The 'bibliobus' and education in New Caledonia' *South Pac Bull* 1963 13(4) 41-2.

INDEX

Abbreviations: Periodicals names have been abbreviated in accordance with general sources such as *LISA* and *Library literature* (see pp 21-22). A recurrent source has been cited as *Encyclopedia*. This is the *Encyclopedia of library and information science* (Eds Kent, A et al) to be found on p 14.

Acronyms: International conventions have standardized the form of acronyms related to international and local bodies and institutions. These have been used here and have been given with the full name of the body in the relevant sections (see in particular 2a and 2b). Some general sources of acronyms are cited on p 13.

Topics: There is no index of topics. Their arrangement follows a set pattern, which is detailed in the introductory section, under 'Organization of sources' (p ix).

In all cases the user is advised to consult the 'General and International Section' pp 3-46 under the relevant heading, in order to trace the main secondary sources useful in any aspect of a search.

Geographical index: The following index is a complement to the introduction to the 'Geographical organization' (p x).

KEY

Listed below are the headings used in the text and their contents. The user should expect a few variations on points of details caused by the nature of the material found.

1 Libraries and information centres with national or similar status and scope of functions within the network of libraries. Other libraries able to supply information on bibliography, librarianship or documentation have been included as necessary.

2a Official or semi-official bodies with organizing functions in the fields of bibliography, librarianship or documentation. These may include regional or international bodies with a supportive role.

2b Professional organizations whose aim is to promote librarianship and related fields exclusively or as part of their overall purpose.

2c Professional activities: Professional education and research; Professional issues, seen through the literature.

3a Reference sources: dictionaries, encyclopaedias, directories and yearbooks, guides and surveys (but for these see also under 3d or 3f). Not included: the yearbooks of library associations or similar bodies, which can be easily traced.

3b Bibliographical services, bibliographies; abstracts and other recurrent sources; special bibliographies.

3c Librarianship periodicals and serials.

3d Statistical sources: publishing bodies, printed sources; surveys (see also under 3a or 3f).

3e Legislation, including copyright, censorship, lending rights; standards for libraries.

3f Further readings, in the following sequence:

- — General background of the region or country: history, culture, education.
- — Librarianship: History, philosophy, sociology, trends.
  Organization, management, cooperation, assistance.
- — Public libraries: Structure and functions, services.
  Provision to special groups: minority groups, hospitals, prisons, etc.
- — School and children's libraries.
- — Academic and research libraries, special libraries.
- — Documentation, information.
- — Automation, networks, etc.
- — Architecture and design (only if it has a specific interest).

KEY

Listed below are the headings used in the text and their contents. The user should expect a few variations on points of details caused by the nature of the material found.

1 Libraries and information centres with national or similar status and scope of functions within the network of libraries. Other libraries able to supply information on bibliography, librarianship or documentation have been included as necessary.

2a Official or semi-official bodies with organizing functions in the fields of bibliography, librarianship or documentation. These may include regional or international bodies with a supportive role.

2b Professional organizations whose aim is to promote librarianship and related fields exclusively or as part of their overall purpose.

2c Professional activities: Professional education and research; Professional issues, seen through the literature.

3a Reference sources: dictionaries, encyclopaedias, directories and yearbooks, guides and surveys (but for these see also under 3d or 3f). Not included: the yearbooks of library associations or similar bodies, which can be easily traced.

3b Bibliographical services, bibliographies; abstracts and other recurrent sources; special bibliographies.

3c Librarianship periodicals and serials.

3d Statistical sources: publishing bodies, printed sources; surveys (see also under 3a or 3f).

3e Legislation, including copyright, censorship, lending rights; standards for libraries.

3f Further readings, in the following sequence:

- — General background of the region or country: history, culture, education.
- — Librarianship: History, philosophy, sociology, trends.
  Organization, management, cooperation, assistance.
- — Public libraries: Structure and functions, services.
  Provision to special groups: minority groups, hospitals, prisons, etc.
- — School and children's libraries.
- — Academic and research libraries, special libraries.
- — Documentation, information.
- — Automation, networks, etc.
- — Architecture and design (only if it has a specific interest).